# Collins
# COBUILD
# English
# Grammar

William Collins' dream of knowledge for all began with the publication of his first book in 1819. A self-educated mill worker, he not only enriched millions of lives, but also founded a flourishing publishing house. Today, staying true to this spirit, Collins books are packed with inspiration, innovation, and practical expertise. They place you at the centre of a world of possibility and give you exactly what you need to explore it.

Language is the key to this exploration, and at the heart of Collins Dictionaries is language as it is really used. New words, phrases, and meanings spring up every day, and all of them are captured and analysed by the Collins Word Web. Constantly updated, and with over 2.5 billion entries, this living language resource is unique to our dictionaries.

Words are tools for life. And a Collins Dictionary makes them work for you.

**Collins. Do more.**

# Collins
# COBUILD
# English
# Grammar

**HarperCollins Publishers**
Westerhill Road
Bishopbriggs
Glasgow
G64 2QT
Great Britain

Second Edition 2005

Latest Reprint 2007

© HarperCollins Publishers 1992, 2002,
2005

ISBN-13  978-0-00-718387-6
ISBN-10  0-00-718387-9

Collins®, Cobuild® and Bank of
English® are registered trademarks of
HarperCollins Publishers Limited

www.collins.co.uk

A catalogue record for this book is
available from the British Library

This edition typeset by Davidsons,
Glasgow

Printed in United States by
Courier-Stoughton

**Acknowledgements**
We would like to thank those authors
and publishers who kindly gave
permission for copyright material to be
used in the Collins Word Web. We
would also like to thank Times
Newspapers Ltd for providing valuable
data.

Entered words that we have reason to
believe constitute trademarks have
been designated as such. However,
neither the presence nor absence of
such designation should be regarded as
affecting the legal status of any
trademark.

# Contents

## Second Edition

### Founding Editor-in-Chief
John Sinclair

**Publishing Director**
Lorna Knight

**Editorial Director**
Michela Clari

**Managing Editor**
Maree Airlie

**Project Manager**
Alison Macaulay

**Lexicographer**
Laura Wedgeworth

**Editorial Assistance**
Sue Ogden

---

### First Edition

### Editor-in-Chief
John Sinclair

### Managing Editor
Gwyneth Fox

**Editors**
Stephen Bullon
Ramesh Krishnamurthy
Elizabeth Manning
John Todd

**Assistant Editors**
Mona Baker
Jane Bradbury
Richard Fay
Deborah Yuill

**Senior researcher**
Rosamund Moon

**Computer Officer**
Tim Lane

**Clerical Staff**
Sue Smith
Jane Winn

**Consultants**
Gottfried Graustein
M.A.K. Halliday

**For HarperCollins Publishers**
Annette Capel, Lorna Heaslip, Douglas Williamson

---

We would also like to thank the following people for their contributions to the first edition of the text:
Patrick Hanks, Dominic Bree, Jane Cullen, Clare Ramsey, Ron Hardie,
David Brazil, Helen Liebeck, Christina Rammell, Michael Hoey, Charles Owen,
Richard Francis, Agnes Molnar, Iria Garcia, Ramiro Restrepo,
Christopher Royal-Dawson, Bob Walker, John Curtin, Henri Béjoint, John Hall,
Sue Inkster, Anne Pradeilles, Georgina Pearce, Herman Wekker, Marcel Lemmens,
Nicholas Brownlees, Tony Buckby, Anthony Harvey, Georgina Pert, Roger Hunt,
Andy Kennedy, Christopher Pratt, Toñi Sanchez, Mary Snell-Hornby, Katy Shaw,
Tom Stableford, Adriana Bolívar

# Introduction

This grammar is for anyone who is interested in the English language and how it works. Many people will come to this book because they are learning English and trying to master the structure of the language. As soon as they have enough practical English to master the text, they will find this grammar helpful to them, although it has been written primarily for students of advanced level.

The information the book contains, however, will also engage the attention of a different sort of student—those who make a study of English because they are simply interested in language and languages. They include teachers, examiners, syllabus planners and materials writers. The grammar has several unique features which will give them very useful information.

The information in this book is taken from a long and careful study of present-day English. Many millions of words from speech and writing have been gathered together in a computer and analyzed, partly by the computer and partly by a team of expert compilers. It is the first grammar of its kind, and it is different in many respects from other kinds of grammar.

This grammar attempts to make accurate statements about English, as seen in the Bank of English corpus, part of the Collins Word Web. The main patterns of English are picked out and described, and the typical words and phrases found in each pattern are listed.

This is what a grammar ought to do, but only in recent years has it been possible. For a long time there has been a credibility gap between a grammar and the language that it is supposed to describe. Many of the rules seem too abstract to apply to actual examples. There is no room to show how the strong structural patterns can be varied and developed to allow users great freedom of expression.

## A Grammar of Functions

People who study and use a language are mainly interested in how they can do things with the language—how they can make meanings, get attention to their problems and interests, influence their friends and colleagues and create a rich social life for themselves. They are only interested in the grammatical structure of the language as a means to getting things done.

A grammar which puts together the patterns of the language and the things you can do with them is called a functional grammar.

This is a functional grammar: each chapter is built around a major function of language, such as 'concept building', 'making up messages', and 'reporting what someone said'. Each of these functions is regularly expressed in English by one particular structure. For example, concept building is usually expressed by structures built around a noun, called noun groups; messages are very often expressed in clauses; and reports typically involve a pair of clauses, with one of them containing a reporting verb such as 'say', and the other one beginning with 'that' or having quote marks (" ") round it.

This grammar is based on these important correspondences between structure and function, which are set out in the Cobuild Grammar Chart on the following pages. The skeleton of English grammar is seen in this chart.

However, there are many minor features of English that cannot appear on a simple summary chart. The grammar of a language is flexible, and with the passage of time there are changes in meaning and use of grammatical forms.

For example, although it is true to say that the noun group is the structure we choose for the things we want to talk about, it is not the only one. Sometimes we want to talk about an event or an idea that is not easy to express in a noun group. Instead we can use a clause as the subject of another clause.

*All I want* is a holiday.

We can also use a clause as the object or complement of another clause.

That's *what we've always longed for*.

By extending the basic grammar occasionally, speakers of English can express themselves more easily and spontaneously.

The same kind of extension works in the other direction also: noun groups are not only used as subjects, objects and complements. They can function as adjuncts of time, for example, among a range of minor uses.

He phoned back with the information *the very next day*.

But there is a major area of English grammar based on prepositions (see Chapter 6), which allows noun groups to be used in all sorts of subsidiary functions in the clause.

I went *to a village school.*
This has been my home *for ten years* now.
*With a click*, the door opened.

So it can be seen that the structural patterns can have more than one function, and that different structures can have similar functions. This may sound confusing, and it can be confusing if the grammar is not carefully organized around the major structures and functions.

This grammar follows up each major statement (often called 'rule' in other grammars) with a detailed description of the usages surrounding that statement—including 'exceptions'. Other ways of achieving the same sort of effect are then presented, with cross-references to the main structural patterns involved. Later in the chapter, the various extensions of use of a structure are set out, with cross-references to places where those functions are thoroughly treated.

These extensions and additions to the functions of a structure are not just random. Usually they can be presented as ways of widening the scope of the original function. For example, the basic, central function of reporting verbs (Chapter 7) is to introduce what someone has said.

*He said* he would be back soon.

It can easily be extended to include what someone has written:

*His mother wrote* that he had finally arrived home.

Then it can be widened to include thoughts and feelings; these do not need to be expressed in words, but the report structure is very convenient.

*The boys thought* he was dead.

From this we can see the reporting clause as a more general way of introducing another clause. The reporting clause becomes a kind of preface, commenting on the other clause, which contains the main message.

*It is true* that some children are late talkers.

The subject of the reporting clause is the pronoun 'it', which refers forward to the that-clause. The verb is now a link verb (Chapter 3) and not a special reporting verb.

## A Grammar of Examples

All the examples are taken from texts, usually with no editing at all. It is now generally accepted that it is extremely difficult to invent examples which sound realistic, and which have all the features of natural examples. I am convinced that it is essential for a learner of English to learn from actual examples, examples that can be trusted because they have been used in real communication.

From a Cobuild perspective, no argument is needed. At Cobuild there are file stores bulging with examples, and we do not need to invent any. By examining these real examples closely, we are gradually finding out some of the ways they differ from made-up examples. Until we know a lot more about naturalness in language we do not think it is safe to use invented examples.

There is a special note developing this point, which can be found immediately after this Introduction.

## A Grammar of Classes

The actual words and phrases that are regularly used in each structure are printed in the grammar in a series of lists. Instead of just a few illustrative examples, this grammar gives information about the grammar of a large number of words. The student can get a good idea of how large or small a grammatical class is, how many words a certain rule applies to. The teacher has the raw material for making up exercises that suit a particular group of students, and can point to general features of a grammatical class.

These lists are worth detailed investigation by student and teacher, because the lists provide the main link between the abstractions of grammar and the realities of the texts which learners of English are likely to encounter in the 'real world'.

In grammar lists of this kind are called 'classes'; a class is the grouping together of words and phrases which all behave in the same way. Hence this grammar is very much a grammar of classes because it features so many lists of words and phrases.

The job of preparing the lists was one of the most interesting and challenging problems in the preparation of this book. The computer does the first stage, and produces a list by searching out all words that fit a pattern it is given. For example, it might be asked to pick all the words that end in '-ing' and do not have a corresponding form without the '-ing'. The first list it produces includes words such as 'overweening' and 'pettifogging', which are not very common, and which in our view can be left to a later stage of language learning. Also found are 'blithering' and 'whopping', which have a special function and are treated in a separate paragraph 2.41. A few words fit the pattern well but are only found in very restricted combinations, or collocations. 'Piping' goes with 'voice', and 'gangling' goes with 'youth' or 'boy'. Since grammar mostly deals with generalities, we feel that it could be misleading to print them in lists which are intended to encourage composition.

At present the computer has difficulties in detecting similarities and differences of meaning. But in the Cobuild database notes on meaning are made by the compilers, and the computer can also report back on this information. So, for example, it will know that in the case of 'fetching', there is a verb to 'fetch', but it does not have the same meaning. In most cases we omit a word like 'fetching' from our lists, to avoid confusion; otherwise the grammar would be full of special notes. If we put it in, we give an appropriate warning.

When we were preparing the first edition of this book, I worked with a large number of English teachers in Europe, South East Asia and South America, to find out their reactions to our lists, and to have their suggestions for revising them and editing them. The clear message was that the lists, to be teachable, should be orderly and comprehensible. Problem cases, on the whole, should be omitted rather than explained in a grammar at this level; on the other hand words which an experienced teacher would expect to find in a list should be there, or there should be an explanation.

The results of all this careful editing can be found in the lists at, for example, 2.77, 2.78, and 2.79.

Wherever we can see a good reason, we put the words and phrases in a list in a meaningful arrangement. This approach was suggested in the teachers' workshops, and on that basis, for example, we put verbs with a prefix (2.79) in a different list from other verbs (2.78) which behave in the same way.

Another good example of this can be found at 1.21, where in a single list we put in separate groups animals, fish, words ending in '-craft', foreign words ending in '-s', and a miscellaneous list. These all share the same feature, namely that they can be either singular or plural nouns without any change of form—moose, salmon, aircraft, corps, crossroads. From a purely grammatical point of view they could all go in a single alphabetical list; however from a teaching and learning point of view it is helpful to have them further classified.

## A Grammar of Meanings

Many English words have several meanings and uses. This is particularly true of the common words which make up most of our everyday language. Because of this it is difficult to make statements about the grammatical behaviour of a word, as this can vary according to its meaning. For example, in one meaning a verb may be transitive, and in another meaning intransitive.

An instance of this is 'manage', which in its meaning of 'be responsible for controlling an organization, business, or system' is transitive, and in its meaning of 'be able to continue with a reasonable way of life, even though you do not have much money' is intransitive, usually followed by an adverbial phrase.

> Drouet returned to Ecuador to manage a travel agency.
> I don't know if I can manage much longer.

Each meaning of a word may well have its own grammar, and it is unlikely that the statements about a word will cover all its meanings. However, the grammar would be very long and cumbersome if each statement had to indicate which meaning was being referred to. Throughout this grammar, therefore, the examples and the lists have been chosen so that the relevant meaning is the one that should first come to mind.

Many users will need a little time to adjust to this; we have lived so long with the assumption that grammar is independent of lexical meaning that it will be surprising to many people to see that grammar and lexis are very closely related. Where the choice of one word in a structure is very closely connected with the choice of another, this is pointed out. For example, the preposition 'aboard' is almost always used with a singular count noun referring to a form of transport such as 'ship', 'plane', 'train', or 'bus'.

> . . . two weeks aboard the royal yacht Britannia.

Another example is a verb referring to physical senses such as 'see', 'feel', 'hear', and 'smell'. When such a verb is used to refer to the present time, it is typically preceded by the modal 'can' or 'can't' rather than being in the simple present tense:

> I can see George's face as clearly as if he were here with me.
> When we come down, I can smell the aroma from the frying trout.

However, some of the verbs can be used with other, non-physical meanings, and in the other meanings the simple present tense is much used.

> *I see you had a good trip.*
> *Many people feel that he should resign immediately.*

This grammar is a halfway house between grammars which ignore the meaning of words, and dictionaries which give some grammatical information. We have left out reference to uncommon meanings, and we only occasionally draw attention to distinctions of meaning that entail a different grammar.

If you think about it, it is obvious that different meanings of a word are likely to occur in different structures. The meaning of a word includes the relations it makes with other words; so a verb such as 'see' in its physical meaning is likely to go along with a noun that means what was seen, or perhaps an adverb such as 'well' which gives an evaluation of the power of seeing. When 'see' is used to mean something like 'understand', it will naturally be followed by a 'that'-clause. On the rare occasions when it has a noun group as object, the noun will be something like 'problem', 'point', or 'position'—nouns describing messages.

## A Grammar for Access

When using a grammar, it is often difficult to find the information that you want. This is often the biggest single problem for users of grammars, and a good reason why grammars are often unpopular with students. This grammar makes a special effort to support the user, and there are several interlocking systems of access.

The well-known grammatical terms are all used here—subject and object, present and past tense, and so on. New terms are kept to a minimum and are only used where there is no obvious alternative. A glossary of terms is provided and they are also, of course, all listed in the index.

There is a contents list and chart at the beginning of the book and a more detailed contents list at the beginning of each chapter. Using this or the index, the student will be able to find the section or paragraph where a function is associated with a structure. By reading around a little, the student will find a few alternatives, or will learn more about the exact meaning of the structure.

Throughout the book there is an extra column at the side which shows the topic of almost every paragraph, and there are frequent additional headings for each section of a chapter. At the top of each page is another heading to guide the user.

Each paragraph is written to be read separately from every other, so that a small piece of information can be found and understood without the user having to read a whole section. But if a user does want to read straight through a section or chapter, it will be found both readable and interesting.

## A Grammar for Production

The main purpose of this grammar is to help students to choose structures which accurately express the meanings they want to create. Hence the book is largely organized around the functions or meanings.

In particular, we set out many 'productive features' to guide the student towards confidence in personal expression. In some areas of grammar the rules are very flexible. Rather than giving a definite class, we feel it is better to give guidance so that the user can make individual choices, with no serious risk of error. By describing the language in this way, we give plenty of scope for creativity and innovation, a feature which is not commonly found in grammars. There are many productive features in current English. Some are well-known, for example the fact that almost any noun in English can modify almost any other noun. For example, the noun 'steam' can be used in, among others, the following combinations: 'steam bath', 'steam boiler', 'steam coal', 'steam engine', 'steam iron', 'steam power', 'steam radio', 'steam train', 'steam yacht', and even 'a flat-bed steam table'.

Just the act of putting two nouns together at random shows how a speaker of the language immediately searches for a meaningful interpretation.

*trick finger*

There is no accepted meaning of 'trick finger'. It could be a medical problem, or a skill similar to juggling. But it is grammatically acceptable, and invites us to imagine a meaning for it.

A productive feature invites and encourages us to use our imagination. The list of words and phrases that will fit a structure is often impossible to define completely. There may be a number of words in regular use, but in addition to that many other possibilities, offering the user a safe place to experiment.

Other places in the grammar allow very little variation, and the learner must simply keep to the rules in these cases. Many grammar books concentrate on these restrictive rules, and make grammar appear to be a dangerous area where the main job is to avoid mistakes. 'You do this, and you don't do that.' In this grammar we concentrate on positive statements, and relate function to structure. 'If you want to do this, then you say that.'

Although there are many potential productive features, in this grammar we have only introduced the main and most obvious ones. If we find that this approach is popular with teachers and learners, it may be possible gradually to shift the whole perspective away from grammar as a list of arbitrary problems, and towards grammar as a means of free expression.

We have tried to produce a grammar of real English—the English that people speak and write. It contains detailed information about English, collected from the large corpus we have built up, and it is new both in what it says and in the relationship between its statements and the evidence on which they are based. It is designed above all to be really useful to student and teacher.

# Note on Examples

One of the really unusual features of this grammar is that all the examples are chosen from the *Bank of English* corpus, part of Collins Word Web. The Bank of English currently stands at around 524 million words, and is the largest corpus of its kind in the world. I believe this to be a sound basis for a grammar, and I think that it is very important for learners and other users to examine and study only real instances of a language. This is particularly important when they are using the examples as models for their own usage.

Some great grammars of English—for example Otto Jespersen's A Modern English Grammar—support each statement with citations from published books, just as the major dictionaries of English do. This provides hard evidence for the statements, and gives important information in the surrounding context.

There is no justification for inventing examples. To illustrate a simple subject-verb clause, something like 'Birds sing' is not good enough. With the *Bank of English*, it is not difficult to find examples even of a fairly rare event like this structure. 'Trains stopped' is a genuine example, and so is 'Frey agreed'. Even in a two-word structure it can be seen that the real examples have a communicative value that the invented one lacks. However, the job of searching shows us how rare such a structure is, and makes us wonder if it should be prominent in a grammar.

It is sad that many teachers seem doomed to work with invented material. However, I would like to make a distinction between the formal presentation of an instance of a language, and the quick, informal examples that teachers have to produce from their own resources many times a day, without warning. The latter are not intended as reliable models to follow, but as explanations of a specific point. The teacher will, and must, rely on personal competence, just as a teacher of any other subject will call on memory rather than look everything up.

There is a big difference between this and putting into print as an example of usage a stretch of English that is not known to have been used. The mind plays tricks, and, specially, is unreliable when one is thinking about very short utterances, without a clear context to support them. Perhaps the biggest single improvement for language teaching is the ability of the computer to find and organize real examples.

Our experience in the classroom with real examples is that learners have a lot less difficulty with them than is often supposed. These examples, after all, are the kind of material that the learner will have to understand eventually; learners appreciate and know instinctively how to cope with the loose ends of natural examples; they know they can trust them and learn directly from them.

The independence of real examples is their strength. They are carefully selected instances of good usage. A set of real examples may show, collectively, aspects of the language that are not obvious individually.

> *The moment work stops, disorder is liable to break out.*
> *If he gets promoted, all hell will break out.*
> *This caused an epidemic to break out among them.*
> *This final destructive fever had to break out somewhere.*

Note that it is bad things that break out, not good ones. Any such points emerging from a set of constructed examples could not, of course, be trusted.

People who work with languages should be open to what they can learn from this exciting source of information. There is no doubt at all that new language teaching materials will rely more and more on the evidence from large text stores, and that in a few years teachers will look back and wonder how they coped with the lifeless examples they used to work with. This book, along with the Cobuild Dictionaries, and the Cobuild English Usage, gives the user an opportunity to work with real language.

John Sinclair
Founding Editor-in-Chief
Emeritus Professor of Modern English Language, University of Birmingham
President, the Tuscan Word Centre

# Guide to the Use of the Grammar

The Collins Cobuild English Grammar is designed to be used both for quick reference and for study in depth. For example, the use of the word 'before' with specific tenses is dealt with in Chapter 5, and the differences in meaning between 'may' and 'might' are dealt with in Chapter 6. The book can also be used more broadly, to find out, for example, a great deal about the behaviour of adjectives (Chapter 2) or the transitivity of clauses (Chapter 3).

In order for you to use it as efficiently and effectively as possible, we have included a number of different ways to help you find the information you are looking for.

## Organization of the main text

The main text of the Grammar is divided into ten Chapters. The first two Chapters deal with the noun group, Chapters 3, 4, and 5 with the verb group, Chapter 6 with adverbs and prepositions, Chapter 7 with reporting, Chapter 8 with joining clauses and sentences, and Chapters 9 and 10 with continuous text. The Cobuild Grammar Chart on pages xxiv–xxv shows the main subdivisions of the text, and the different word classes dealt with in each Chapter.

Each Chapter consists of a series of main topics and each topic is divided into sections. The section headings are repeated at the top of the appropriate right hand pages, so that it is easy to find the sections. Each individual paragraph in the Chapter is numbered, so that Chapter 1 runs from 1.1 to 1.236, Chapter 2 from 2.1 to 2.320 and so on.

This numbering system makes it easy for the user to refer to different but related points. There are cross-references throughout the text, either pointing to the main place where a topic is dealt with or to another paragraph where more information is given.

Most paragraphs also have a heading in a column on the left of the main text, saying in three or four words what the paragraph deals with, especially which grammatical structure is being explained. Those paragraphs that do not have a Left Column heading either summarize information which is about to be given in more detail, as is usually the case immediately after a section heading, or they continue the subject matter of the last Left Column heading. For example, in Chapter 1 paragraph 1.119 has a Left Column heading which says 'mass nouns'. Paragraphs 1.120 and 1.121 do not have a Left Column heading because they are still explaining mass nouns.

Some Left Column headings do not show specifically what the paragraph deals with, but indicate information of a rather different kind. The headings are 'Warning', 'Usage Note', and 'Productive Feature'.

'Warning' highlights points where we know that people often have problems with a particular grammatical feature of English, because it is different from what you would expect, for example because it is a feature where English is different from many other languages.

'Usage Note' gives information about the use of individual words or small groups of words. This information is important but cannot be generalized into a grammatical rule. The Usage Notes will therefore help you to distinguish those features which are relevant for the understanding of particular words from those features which are relevant to large numbers of words.

'Productive Feature' indicates that the rule that has been mentioned can be applied quite freely in English to a very large number of words. For example, it is nearly always possible to make the present participle of a verb into an adjective used in front of a noun. This is therefore labelled 'Productive Feature' in the Left Column. By taking note of these features, you can use the rules that have been presented in a creative and original manner, giving you greater freedom of expression in English. Productive Features are explained in greater detail in the Introduction.

Most of the grammatical statements that are made are followed by examples showing the structure in use. These examples are all taken from the Cobuild collections of texts, and show how the structures have been used naturally in speech or writing. The examples therefore give important information about the typical use of a structure, the words it is frequently used with, and the contexts in which it is likely to occur. More information about the examples and how they can be used will be found in the Note on Examples on page x.

Wherever appropriate, grammatical statements in this book are followed by lists of the words which typically exemplify that grammatical point. For example, in Chapter 3 we say that many verbs can be either transitive or intransitive with the same meaning. This statement is followed by a list of verbs that are frequently used in this way.

The lists should help to increase awareness of the use of English, going beyond the actual examples given to other words which behave in similar ways. They show whether the point being made is relevant to a small number or a large number of words. If the word class is small, then all members of it are given. If it is large, then the most frequently used members are given.

These lists can be used to help you increase your vocabulary and to check that you are using newly-learned English words correctly. There is also a book of Cobuild Grammar Exercises, in which the lists are used as the basis of many exercises, for those students who want more practice in a particular area of grammar.

# Additional contents

In addition to the main text, there are various other sections which are included to help you to get the most out of this Grammar. These additional sections are described below.

### Introduction

The Introduction sets out the principles from which the grammar has been developed. It explains the close relationship which exists between function and structure, which is the basis of this Grammar, and it explains the type of functional approach that is taken.

### Cobuild Grammar Chart

The Cobuild Grammar Chart sets out in schematic form the contents of the grammar. It shows the progression from word to group to clause to sentence, and shows where the different word classes are focused on. It also shows the main discourse or text topic in each chapter. For example, Chapter 4 focuses on 'mood', 'negation' and 'modality' at clause level, as these are expressed through the verb group. The individual words that are dealt with are the modal verbs and negative words such as 'not' and 'never'. The whole Chapter shows different ways of expressing attitudes to what is being said, and so this is the main discourse topic of the Chapter.

**Glossary of Grammatical Terms**

The Glossary explains the meaning of grammatical terms. It features the terms that are systematically used in this grammar, and also includes terms that are used in other grammars, with a cross-reference to the term used in this book, where appropriate. For example, this grammar talks about 'noun groups', whereas some other grammars call them 'noun phrases' or 'nominal groups'. All three of these terms are mentioned in the Glossary, with the explanation being given at 'noun group'.

**Contents pages**

There is a complete list of contents on page iii. This gives the titles of the Chapters, enabling you to get an overview of the way the Grammar is organized. Then, at the beginning of every Chapter, there is a detailed contents page giving all the headings dealt with in that particular Chapter.

**The Reference Section**

This section at the back of the book provides an easy-to-use reference guide in which morphological information is gathered together, showing how the following groups of words are formed:

plurals of nouns
the comparative and superlative of adjectives
'-ly' adverbs formed from adjectives
the comparative and superlative of adverbs
tenses
passives
principal parts of irregular verbs

The Reference Section also includes other topics. For example, it starts with a pronunciation guide, to remind you of the sounds of English. There are also lists of numbers, and an explanation of how numbers are expressed aloud.

**Index**

The Index is a comprehensive list of everything dealt with in the Grammar. It covers primarily the grammatical and functional topics dealt with in the Grammar, and the way those topics are broken down into their major parts. It also includes individual words where they are used as examples of a particular class, and grammatical terms, both those used in this book and those commonly used in other books.

# Glossary of grammatical terms

*Note*: entries in **bold** are Cobuild Grammar terms.

**abstract noun** a noun used to describe a quality, idea, or experience rather than something physical or concrete; EG *joy, size, language*. Compare with **concrete noun**.

**active voice** verb groups such as 'gives', and 'has made', where the subject is the person or thing doing the action or responsible for the action. Compare **passive voice**.

adjectival clause another name for **relative clause**.

**adjective** a word used to tell you more about a thing, such as its appearance, colour, size, or other qualities; EG *...a pretty blue dress*.

**adjunct** a word or combination of words added to a clause to give more information about time, place, or manner. See also **sentence adjunct** and **linking adjunct**.

**adverb** a word that gives more information about when, how, where, or in what circumstances something happens. EG *quickly, now*. There are several different kinds of adverb; adverbs of degree, manner, place, time, duration, and frequency. There are also **focusing adverbs**.

**adverbial group** a group of words which does the same job as an adverb, thus giving more information about when, how, where, or in what circumstances something happens; EG *in the street, again and again*.

**adverb of degree** an adverb indicating the amount or extent of a feeling or quality; EG *extremely*.

**adverb of duration** an adverb which indicates how long something lasts; EG *briefly*.

**adverb of frequency** an adverb indicating how often something happens; EG *often*.

**adverb of manner** an adverb indicating the way in which something happens or is done; EG *carefully*.

**adverb of place** an adverb which gives more information about position or direction; EG *Move closer*.

**adverb of time** an adverb which gives more information about when something happens; EG *I saw her yesterday*.

**adverb particle** an adverb used as part of a phrasal verb; EG *hide out, sit up, turn round*.

affirmative another name for **positive**.

affix a letter or group of letters that is added to the beginning or end of a word to make a different word; EG *anti-communist, harmless*. See also suffix and prefix.

**agent** the person who performs an action.

**agreement** another name for **concord**.

**apostrophe s** an ending ('s) added to a noun to mark possession; EG *...Harriet's*

daughter... the professor's husband... **the Managing Director's** secretary.

**apposition** the placing of a noun group after a headword in order to identify it or give more information about it; EG *...my daughter Emily*.

article see **definite article**, **indefinite article**.

aspect the use of verb forms to show whether an action is continuing, repeated, or finished.

**attributive** used to describe adjectives that are normally only used in front of a noun; EG *classical, outdoor, woollen*.

**auxiliary verb** one of the verbs 'be', 'have', and 'do' when they are used with a main verb to form tenses, negatives, questions, and so on. Also called auxiliary. **Modals** are also auxiliary verbs.

**bare infinitive** the infinitive of a verb without 'to'; EG *Let me think*.

**base form** the form of a verb which has no letters added to the end and is not a past form; EG *walk, go, have, be*. The base form is the form you look up in a dictionary.

**broad negative adverb** one of a small group of words including 'barely' and 'seldom' which are used to make a statement almost negative; EG *I barely knew her*.

**cardinal number** a number used for counting; EG *one, seven, nineteen*.

case the use of different forms of nouns or pronouns in order to show whether they are the subject or object of a clause, or whether they are possessive; EG *I/me, Jim/Jim's*.

**classifying adjective** an adjective used to identify something as being of a particular type; EG *Indian, wooden, mental*. They do not have comparatives or superlatives. Compare with **qualitative adjective**.

**clause** a group of words containing a verb. See also **main clause** and **subordinate clause**.

**clause of manner** a subordinate clause which describes the way in which something is done, usually introduced with 'as' or 'like'; EG *She talks like her mother used to*.

**cleft sentence** a sentence in which emphasis is given to either the subject or the object by using a structure beginning with 'it', 'what', or 'all'; EG *It's a hammer we need... What we need is a hammer*.

**collective noun** a noun that refers to a group of people or things; EG *committee, team*.

**colour adjective** an adjective referring to a colour; EG *red, blue, scarlet*.

**common noun** a noun used to refer to a person, thing, or substance; EG *sailor, computer, glass*. Compare with **proper noun**.

**comparative** an adjective or adverb with '-er' on the end or 'more' in front of it; EG *friendlier, more important, more carefully.*

**complement** a noun group or adjective which comes after a link verb such as 'be', and gives more information about the subject or object of the clause; EG *She is a teacher... She is tired... They made her chairperson.*

**complex sentence** a sentence consisting of a main clause and a subordinate clause; EG *She wasn't thinking because she was tired.*

**compound** a combination of two or more words functioning as a unit. For example, 'self-centred' and 'free-style' are compound adjectives, 'bus stop' and 'state of affairs' are compound nouns, and 'dry-clean' and 'roller-skate' are compound verbs.

**compound sentence** a sentence consisting of two or more main clauses linked by a coordinating conjunction; EG *They picked her up and took her into the house.*

**concessive clause** a subordinate clause, usually introduced by 'although' or 'while', which contrasts with a main clause; EG *Although I like her, I find her hard to talk to.*

**concord** the relationship between a subject and its verb, or between a number or determiner and its noun; EG *I look/she looks... one bell/three bells.* Also called **agreement**.

**concrete noun** a noun which refers to something we can touch or see; EG *table, dress, flower.* Compare with **abstract noun**.

**conditional clause** a subordinate clause usually starting with 'if'. The event described in the main clause depends on the condition described in the subordinate clause; EG *If it rains, we'll go to the cinema... They would be rich if they had taken my advice.*

**conjunction** a word linking together two clauses, groups, or words. There are two kinds of conjunction - coordinating conjunctions, which link parts of a sentence of the same grammatical type (and, but, or), and subordinating conjunctions, which begin subordinate clauses (although, when).

**continuous tense** a tense which contains a form of the verb 'be' and a present participle; EG *She was laughing... They had been playing badminton.* Also called progressive tense.

**contraction** a shortened form in which an auxiliary verb and 'not', or a subject and an auxiliary verb, are joined together and function as one word; EG *aren't, she's.*

**coordinating conjunction** a word such as 'and', 'but', or 'or' which joins together two clauses, groups, or words of the same grammatical type.

**coordination** the linking of groups of words of the same grammatical type, or the linking of clauses of equal importance.

**copula** a name sometimes used to refer to the verb 'be'. In this grammar, the term **link verb** is used.

**count noun** a noun which can be singular or

plural. EG *dog/dogs, lemon/lemons, foot/feet.* Also called countable noun.

**declarative mood** a clause in the declarative mood has the subject followed by the verb. Most statements are made in the declarative mood. Also called indicative mood.

defective verb a verb which does not have all the inflected forms that regular verbs have; for example, all modals are defective verbs.

**defining non-finite clause** a participle clause which is placed after a noun group to identify the person or thing you are talking about; EG *The girl wearing the red hat.*

**defining relative clause** a relative clause which identifies the person or thing that is being talked about. EG *I wrote down everything that she said.*

**definite article** the determiner 'the'.

**delexical verb** a verb which has very little meaning in itself and is used with an object that carries the main meaning of the structure. 'Give', 'have', and 'take' are commonly used as delexical verbs; EG *She gave a small cry... I've had a bath.*

**demonstrative** one of the words 'this', 'that', 'these', and 'those' used in front of a noun; EG *...this woman... that tree.* They are also used as pronouns; EG *That looks nice... This is fun.*

dependent clause another name for subordinate clause.

**determiner** one of a group of words including 'the', 'a', 'some', and 'my' which are used at the beginning of a noun group.

**direct object** a noun group referring to a person or thing affected by an action, in a sentence with an active verb; EG *She wrote her name... I shut the windows.*

direct speech speech reported in the words actually spoken by someone, without any changes in tense, person, and so on.

disjunct another name for **sentence adjunct**.

**ditransitive verb** a verb such as 'give', 'take', or 'sell' which can have both an indirect and a direct object; EG *She gave me a kiss.*

dynamic verb a verb such as 'run', 'give' or 'slice' which describes an action. Compare with stative verb.

'-ed' form another name for **past participle**.

**ellipsis** the leaving out of words when they are obvious from the context.

**emphasizing adjective** an adjective such as 'complete', 'utter' or 'total' which stresses how strongly you feel about something; EG *I feel a complete fool.*

**ergative verb** a verb which can be either transitive or intransitive in the same meaning. To use the verb intransitively, you use the object of the transitive verb as the subject of the intransitive verb; EG *He had boiled a kettle... The kettle had boiled.*

**exclamation** a word or sentence spoken suddenly and loudly in order to express surprise, anger, and so on; EG *Oh God!*

**finite** a finite verb is inflected according to person, tense, or mood rather than being an infinitive or a participle.

**first person** see person.

**focusing adverb** a sentence adjunct which indicates the most relevant thing involved; EG *only, mainly, especially.*

**fronting** a structure with a topic at the beginning of a clause which is not the subject of the clause; EG *Lovely hair she had.*

**gender** a grammatical term referring to the difference between masculine and feminine words such as 'he' and 'she'.

**genitive** the possessive form of a noun; EG *man's, men's.*

**gerund** another name for '-ing' noun.

**gradable** a gradable adjective can be used with a word such as 'very' to say that the person or thing referred to has more or less of a quality; EG *very boring, less helpful.*

**group noun** another name for **collective noun.**

**head** another name for **headword.**

**headword** the main word of a noun group; EG *...a soft downy **cushion** with tassles.*

**idiom** a group of two or more words with a meaning that cannot be understood by taking the meaning of each individual word; EG *to kick the bucket, to run wild.*

**if-clause** a conditional clause; or a clause used to report a 'yes/no'-question.

**imperative** a clause in the imperative mood has the base form of the verb without a subject. EG *Come here... Take two tablets every four hours... Enjoy yourself.*

**impersonal 'it'** 'it' is an impersonal subject when it is used to introduce a fact, or when it is used in a cleft structure; EG *It's raining... It was you who asked.*

**indefinite article** the determiners 'a' and 'an'.

**indefinite place adverb** a group of adverbs including 'anywhere' and 'somewhere' used to indicate position or location in a general or vague way.

**indefinite pronoun** a group of pronouns including 'someone' and 'anything' used to refer to a person or thing in a general way.

**indicative mood** another name for declarative mood.

**indirect object** a second object used with a transitive verb to indicate who or what benefits from an action, or gets something as a result of it; EG *She gave me a rose.*

**indirect question** another name for **reported question.**

**indirect speech** another name for **reported speech.**

**infinitive** the base form of a verb. It is often used with 'to' in front of it; EG *(to) take, (to) see, (to) bring.*

**inflection** the variation in the form of a word to show differences in tense, number, case, and degree.

**'-ing' adjective** an adjective which has the same form as the present participle of a verb; EG *...a smiling face... ...a winning streak.*

**'-ing' form** see present participle.

**'-ing' noun** a noun which has the same form

as the present participle of a verb; EG *Swimming is good for you.*

**intensifier** a submodifier which is used to reinforce an adjective and make it more emphatic; EG *very, exceptionally.*

**interjection** another name for **exclamation.**

**interrogative adverb** one of the adverbs 'how', 'when', 'where', and 'why' when they are used to ask questions.

**interrogative mood** a clause in the interrogative mood has part or all of the verb group in front of the subject. Most questions are asked in the interrogative mood.

**interrogative pronoun** one of the pronouns 'who', 'whose', 'whom', 'what', and 'which' when they are used to ask questions.

**intransitive verb** a verb which is used to talk about an action or event that only involves the subject and so does not have an object; EG *She arrived... I was yawning.*

**inversion** changing the word order in a sentence, especially changing the order of the subject and the verb.

**irregular** not following the normal rules for inflection. An irregular verb has a past form and/or past participle which is formed in a different way from the regular '-ed' ending.

**lexical verb** another name for **main verb.**

**linking adjunct** a sentence adjunct used to introduce a comment or reinforce what is said; EG *moreover, besides.*

**link verb** a verb which links the subject and complement of a clause; EG *be, become, seem, appear.* Also sometimes called copula.

**main clause** a clause which is not dependent on, or is not part of, another clause.

**main verb** all verbs which are not auxiliaries. Also called lexical verb.

**mass noun** (in this grammar), a noun which is usually an uncount noun, but which can be used as a count noun when it refers to quantities or types of something; EG *...two sugars... ...cough medicines.*

**modal** an auxiliary verb which is used with a main verb to indicate a particular attitude, such as possibility, obligation, prediction, or deduction; EG *can, could, may, might.* Also called modal auxiliary or modal verb.

**modifier** a word or group of words which come in front of a noun; EG *...a beautiful sunny day... ...a psychology conference.*

**mood** there are three main moods in English: the declarative mood, the interrogative mood, and the imperative mood. There is also a less common mood, the subjunctive mood. See the individual entries for declarative mood, interrogative mood, imperative, and subjunctive.

**negative sentence** a sentence which uses a word like 'not', 'never', or 'no-one' to indicate the absence or opposite of something, or to say that something is not the case; EG *I don't know you... I'll never forget.* The opposite is positive sentence.

**negative word** a word such as 'never' and 'not' which expresses a negative meaning.

**nominal group** another name for **noun group**.

**non-defining relative clause** a relative clause which gives more information about someone or something, but which is not needed to identify them; EG *That's Mary, who was at university with me.* Compare with **defining relative clause**.

**non-finite** the non-finite forms of a verb are the infinitive and participle forms; EG *to take, taking, taken.*

**noun** a word which refers to people, things, and abstract ideas such as feelings and qualities; EG *woman, Harry, guilt.*

**noun group** a group of words which acts as the subject, complement, or object of a clause, or as the object of a preposition. Also called nominal group or noun phrase.

**noun modifier** a noun used in front of another noun, as if it were an adjective; EG *...a car door... ...a steel works.*

**number** the way in which differences between singular and plural are shown; EG *flower/ flowers, that/those.* See also **cardinal number** and **ordinal number**.

**object** a noun group which refers to a person or thing, other than the subject, which is involved in or affected by the action of a verb. See also **direct object** and **indirect object**. Prepositions are also followed by objects.

**object complement** a word which is used to describe the object of a clause and which occurs with verbs such as 'make' and 'find'; EG *It made me tired... I found her asleep.*

**ordinal number** a number that is used to indicate where something comes in an order or sequence; EG *first, fifth, tenth, hundredth.*

**participial adjective** another name for **'-ing' adjective**.

**participle** a verb form used for making different tenses. See **past participle** and **present participle** for more details.

**partitive** a word which gives information about the amount of a particular thing; EG *pint, loaf, portion.*

**partitive structure** a structure in which quantifiers and partitives are linked to a noun group with 'of'; EG *many of them, a bottle of milk.*

**passive voice** verb forms such as 'was given', 'were taken', 'had been made', where the subject is the person or thing that is affected by the action. Compare with **active voice**.

**past form** the form of a verb, often ending in '-ed', which is used for the simple past tense.

**past participle** a verb form such as 'seen', 'broken', and 'given' which is used to form perfect tenses and passives, or in some cases an adjective. Also called the '-ed' form, especially when an adjective.

**past tense** a tense used to describe actions or events which took place in the past. See **tense** for more details.

**perfect tense** a tense formed with 'have' and a past participle; EG *I have met him... We had won.*

**performative verb** a verb which states explicitly what action the speaker is performing when he or she uses it; EG *apologize, resign, christen.*

**person** a term used to refer to the three classes of people who are involved in something that is said. They are the first person (the person speaking or writing), the second person (the person being addressed), and the third person (the people or things that are being talked about).

**personal pronoun** a group of pronouns such as 'I', 'you', and 'me', used to refer back to the people or things you are talking about.

**phase** a structure in which you use two verbs in a clause in order to talk about two processes or events that are closely linked. EG *She helped to clean the house... They remember buying the tickets.*

**phrasal verb** a combination of a verb and an adverb and/or a preposition, which have a single meaning; EG *back down, hand over, look forward to.*

**plural** the form used to refer to more than one person or thing; EG *dogs, women.*

**plural noun** a noun which is only used in the plural form; EG *trousers, scissors, vermin.*

**positive sentence** a sentence which does not contain a negative word.

**possessive** a structure used to show possession; EG *your, Jerry's, mine.*

**possessive determiner** a determiner such as 'my', 'your', and 'their'. They are also called possessive adjectives.

**possessive pronoun** one of the words 'mine', 'yours', 'hers', 'his', 'ours', and 'theirs'.

**postdeterminer** a small group of adjectives used after a determiner and in front of other adjectives; EG *certain, remaining.*

**predeterminer** a word which comes in front of a determiner; EG *...all the boys... ...double the trouble... ...such a mess.*

**predicate** what is said about the subject of a clause.

**predicative** used to describe adjectives that are normally only used after a link verb such as 'be'; EG *alive, asleep, sure.* Compare **attributive**.

**prefix** a letter or group of letters added to the beginning of a word in order to make a new word; EG *semi-* in *semi-circular.* Compare with suffix and affix.

**premodifier** another name for **modifier.**

**preposition** a word such as 'by', 'with' or 'from', which is always followed by a noun group or an '-ing' form.

**prepositional phrase** a structure consisting of a preposition and its object; EG *on the table, by the sea.*

**present participle** a verb form ending in '-ing' which is used to form verb tenses, and as an adjective. Also called the '-ing'-form.

**present tense** a tense used to describe

xxi

events taking place in the present or situations which exist in the present.

**productive feature** a grammatical point which can be applied to an open class of words. See the Introduction for more details.

progressive tense another name for **continuous tense.**

**pronoun** a word used instead of a noun, when you do not want to name someone or something directly; EG *it, you, none.*

**proper noun** a noun which refers to a particular person, place, or institution; EG *Nigel, Edinburgh, Christmas.* Compare with **common noun.**

**purpose clause** a subordinate clause, usually introduced by 'in order to', or 'so that'; EG *I came here in order to ask you out to dinner.*

**qualifier** any word or group of words which comes after a headword and is part of the noun group; EG *...a book with a blue cover... the shop on the corner.*

**qualitative adjective** an adjective which is used to indicate a quality, and which is gradable; EG *funny, intelligent, small.* Compare with **classifying adjective.**

**quantifier** a phrase ending in 'of' which allows you to refer to a quantity of something without being precise about the exact amount; EG *some of, a lot of, a little bit of.*

**question** a structure which typically has the verb in front of the subject and which is used to ask someone about something; EG *Have you any money?* Also called interrogative.

**question tag** a structure consisting of an auxiliary verb followed by a pronoun, which is used at the end of a **tag question.**

**quote structure** a structure which reports the exact words used by a speaker without any changes. EG *She said 'I'll be late'.* Compare with **report structure.**

**reason clause** a subordinate clause, usually introduced by 'because', 'since', or 'as'; EG *Since you're here, we'll start.*

**reciprocal pronoun** the pronoun 'each other' and 'one another', used to show that two people do or feel the same thing; EG *They loved each other.*

**reciprocal verb** a verb which describes an action which involves two people doing the same thing to each other; EG *They met in the street... He met her yesterday.*

**reflexive pronoun** a pronoun ending in '-self', such as 'myself' or 'themselves', which is used as the object of a verb when the person affected by an action is the same as the person doing it.

**reflexive verb** a verb which is typically used with a reflexive pronoun; EG *shave yourself; pride yourself on.*

**relative clause** a subordinate clause which gives more information about someone or something mentioned in the main clause. See also **defining relative clause** and **non-defining relative clause.**

**relative pronoun** a 'wh'-word such as 'who' or 'which', used to introduce a relative clause; EG *...the girl who was carrying the bag.*

**reported clause** the part of a report structure which describes what someone has said; EG *She said that I couldn't see her.*

**reported question** a question which is reported using a report structure rather than the exact words used by the speaker. Also called indirect question.

**reported speech** speech which is reported using a report structure rather than the exact words used by the speaker. Also called indirect speech.

**reporting clause** a clause which contains a reporting verb, which is used to introduce what someone has said; EG *They asked if I could come.*

**reporting verb** a verb which describes what people say or think; EG *suggest, say, wonder.*

**report structure** a structure which reports what someone has said by using a reported clause rather than repeating their exact words; EG *She told me she'd be late.* Compare with **quote structure.**

**result clause** a subordinate clause introduced by 'so that' which gives the result of something; EG *The house was severely damaged, so that it is now uninhabitable.*

**rhetorical question** a question which you use in order to make a comment rather than to obtain information; EG *Oh, isn't it silly?*

**second person** see person.

**semi-modal** the verbs 'dare', 'need', and 'used to' which behave rather like modals.

**sentence** a group of words which express a statement, question, or command. A sentence usually has a verb and a subject, and may be a simple sentence, consisting of one clause, or a complex sentence, consisting of two or more clauses. A sentence in writing has a capital letter at the beginning and a full-stop, question mark, or exclamation mark at the end.

**sentence adjunct** an adjunct which applies to the whole clause, rather than to part of it; EG *We possibly have to wait and see.* See also linking adjunct.

**'s' form** the base form of a verb with 's' on the end, used in the simple present tense.

**simple tense** a tense formed without using an auxiliary verb; EG *I waited... She sang.*

**singular** the form used to refer to or talk about one person or thing; EG *dog, woman.* Compare with **plural.**

**singular noun** a noun typically used in the singular form; EG *sun, business, jumble.*

split infinitive the placing of a word between 'to' and the base form of a verb; EG *...to boldly go where no man has gone before.*

stative verb a verb which describes a state; EG *be, live, know.* Compare with **dynamic verb.**

strong verb another name for **irregular verb.**

**subject** the noun group in a clause that refers to the person or thing who does the action expressed by the verb; EG *We were going shopping.*

**subjunctive** a verb form which is used in some languages to express attitudes such as wishing, hoping, and doubting. The subjunctive mood is not very common in English, and is used mainly in conditional clauses such as 'If I were you...'.

**submodifier** an adverb which is used in front of an adjective or another adverb in order to strengthen or weaken its meaning; EG ...*very interesting*... ...*quite quickly.*

**subordinate clause** a clause which begins with a subordinating conjunction such as 'because' or 'while' and which must be used with a main clause.

**substitution** the special use of pronouns and other words to replace part or all of a clause; EG *'Are you going to the party?'*—'I hope **so.**

**suffix** a letter or group of letters added to the end of a word in order to make a different word, tense, case, and so on; EG *slowly,* *Heidi's.* Compare with affix and prefix.

**superlative** an adjective or adverb with '-est' on the end or 'most' in front of it; EG *thinnest, quickest, most wisely.*

**tag question** a statement to which a question tag (an auxiliary verb and a pronoun) has been added; EG *She's quiet, isn't she?*

**tense** the verb form which shows whether you are referring to the past, present, or future.

**future** the use of 'will' or 'shall' with the base form of the verb to refer to future events; EG *She **will come** tomorrow.*

**future continuous** the use of 'will be' or 'shall be' and a present participle to refer to future events; EG *She **will be going** soon.*

**future perfect** the use of 'will have' or 'shall have' and a past participle to refer to future events; EG *I **shall have finished** tomorrow.*

**future perfect continuous** the use of 'will' or 'shall' with 'have been' and a present participle to refer to future events; EG *I **will have been walking** for three hours by then.*

**past** the use of the past form to refer to past events; EG *They **waited**.*

**past continuous** the use of 'was' or 'were' with a present participle, usually to refer to past events. EG *They **were worrying** about it yesterday.*

**past perfect** the use of 'had' with a past participle to refer to past events; EG *She had finished.*

**past perfect continuous** the use of 'had been' with a present participle to refer to past events; EG *He **had been waiting** for hours.*

**present** the use of the base form and the 's' form, usually to refer to present events; EG *I like bananas... My sister **hates** them.*

**present continuous** the use of the simple present of 'be' with a present participle to refer to present events; EG *Things **are** improving.*

**present perfect** the use of the simple present of 'have' with a past participle to refer to past events which exist in the present; EG *She has loved him for ten years.*

**present perfect continuous** the use of 'have been' and 'has been' with a present participle to refer to past events which exist in the present; EG *We **have been sitting** here for hours.*

**'that'-clause** a clause starting with 'that' which is used mainly when reporting what someone has said; EG *She said **that she'd wash up for me.** 'That'* can be omitted when the clause is used after a reporting verb.

**third person** see person.

**time clause** a subordinate clause which indicates the time of an event; EG *I'll phone you **when I get back.***

**title** a word used before a person's name to show their position or status; EG *Mrs, Lord, Queen.*

**'to'-infinitive** the base form of a verb preceded by 'to'; EG *to go, to have, to jump.*

**transitive verb** a verb used to talk about an action or event that involves more than one person or thing, and so is followed by an object; EG *She's **wasting her money.***

**uncount noun** a noun which refers to a general kind of thing rather than to an individual item, and so has only one form; EG *money, furniture, intelligence.* Also called uncountable noun.

**verb** a word used with a subject to say what someone or something does, or what happens to them; EG *sing, spill, die.*

**verbal noun** another name for '-ing' noun.

**verb group** a main verb, or a main verb preceded by one or more auxiliaries, which combines with a subject to say what someone does, or what happens to them; EG *I'll show them... She's been sick.*

**vocative** a word used when speaking to someone, just as if it were their name; EG *darling, madam.*

**'wh'-clause** a clause starting with a 'wh'-word.

**'whether'-clause** a clause used to report a 'yes/no'-question; EG *I asked her **whether she'd seen him.***

**'wh'-question** a question which expects an answer giving a particular person, place, thing, amount, and so on, rather than just 'yes' or 'no'.

**'wh'-word** one of a group of words starting with 'wh-', such as 'what', 'when' or 'who', which are used in 'wh'-questions. 'How' is also called a 'wh'-word because it behaves like the other 'wh'-words.

**'yes/no'-question** a question which can be answered simply with either 'yes' or 'no'; EG *Would you like some more tea?*

# Cobuild Grammar Chart

| | concepts | | propositions | |
|---|---|---|---|---|
| | **1**<br>Concept Identification | **2**<br>Concept Building | **3**<br>Message Building | **4**<br>Author and Message |
| **discourse** | nominalization | | expression of attitudes | |
| **sentence** | | | | |
| **clause** | subjects objects | comparison | simple clauses transitivity complement-ation verbless clauses | mood negation modality |
| **group** | noun group | noun group | verb group | verb group |
| **word** | nouns pronouns determiners | adjectives numbers quantifiers partitives | verbs | modal verbs negative words |
| **morpheme** | noun inflections | adjective inflections | verb inflections | |

*Note*: the tinted areas of the chart feature the main concerns of each Chapter, as well as illustrating the overall progression through the Grammar.

| circumstances | | development | | text | |
|---|---|---|---|---|---|
| **5**<br>Timing | **6**<br>Manner and Place | **7**<br>Reporting | **8**<br>Expansion | **9**<br>Cohesion | **10**<br>Tactics |
| narrative | | expression of complicated meanings | | evaluation<br>language about language | |
| simple sentence | simple sentence | compound sentence: report structures | compound sentence: combination of clauses | complex sentence | tags<br>clefts<br>conventions<br>theme and focus |
| tense aspect time | location clauses | direct speech report clauses other *that* clauses | clauses types | ellipsis | passivization<br>*it/there* clauses |
| adjuncts of time | other adjuncts | | | | |
| adverbs of time, frequency, duration | adverbs of place, manner prepositions place names | reporting verbs *that,* *wh*-words | conjunctions | linkers sentence adverbs | focussing adverbs vocatives |
| | adverb inflections | | | | |

# Contents of Chapter 1

# 1 Referring to people and things

## Introduction to the noun group

**1.1** At its simplest, we use language to talk about people and things. We do this by using words in a variety of ways, for example to make statements, to ask questions, and to give orders. The words we choose are arranged into groups, either around a noun or around a verb. They are called **noun groups** and **verb groups.**

**Noun groups** tell us which people or things are being talked about. **Verb groups** tell us what is being said about them, for example what they are doing.

Chapters 1 and 2 of this grammar deal with noun groups. For information about verb groups, see Chapter 3.

**position in clause**

**1.2** A noun group can be the **subject, object,** or **complement** of a **clause,** or the object of a **preposition.**

*Babies cry when they are hungry.*
*I couldn't feel anger against him.*
*They were teachers.*
*Let us work together in peace.*

**common nouns and proper nouns**

**1.3** You can use a noun group to refer to someone or something by naming them. You do this by using a general name, called a **noun** or **common noun,** or by using a specific name, called a **proper noun.** Proper nouns are mainly used for people, places, and events.

*Mary likes strawberries.*
*I went to Glasgow University and then I went down to London to work for a psychiatrist.*
*We flew to Geneva with British Airways.*

See paragraphs 1.53 to 1.59 for more information about **proper nouns.**

**determiners with common nouns**

**1.4** If you use a common noun, you are saying that the person or thing you are talking about can be put in a set with others that are similar in some way.

If you just want to say that the person or thing is in that set, you use a **general determiner** with the common noun.

*I met a girl who was a student there.*
*Have you got any comment to make about that?*
*There are some diseases that are clearly inherited.*

If you want to show which member of a set you are talking about, you use a **specific determiner** with a common noun.

*I put my arm round her shoulders.*
*...the destruction of their city.*
*She came in to see me this morning.*

See paragraphs 1.161 to 1.236 for more information about **determiners,** and paragraphs 1.14 to 1.93 for more information about **nouns.**

**personal and demonstrative pronouns**

**1.5** You may decide not to name the person or thing and to use a **pronoun** rather than a proper noun or common noun.

You usually do this because the person or thing has already been named,

2

so you refer to them by using a **personal pronoun** or a **demonstrative pronoun.**

*Max will believe us, won't <u>he</u>?*
*'Could <u>I</u> speak to Sue, please?'—'<u>I</u>'m sorry, <u>she</u> doesn't work here now.'*
*Some people have servants to cook for <u>them</u>.*
*<u>This</u> led to widespread criticism.*

See paragraphs 1.96 to 1.109 for more information about **personal pronouns,** and paragraphs 1.123 to 1.126 for more information about **demonstrative pronouns.**

**indefinite pronouns**

**1.6** You may decide not to name the person or thing at all, for example because you do not want to, you think it is not important, you do not know, or you want to be vague or mysterious while telling a story. In such cases you use an **indefinite pronoun,** which does not refer to any particular person or thing.

*I had to say <u>something</u>.*
*In this country <u>nobody</u> trusts <u>anyone</u>.*
*A moment later, his heart seemed to stop as he sensed the sudden movement of <u>someone</u> rushing into the hut.*

See paragraphs 1.127 to 1.140 for more information about **indefinite pronouns.**

**noun group choice**

**1.7** In the relation between language and the world, these different types of noun group show a range of choices between a very clear identification of someone or something, and a very clear decision not to identify. The range can be set out as follows, resulting from the choices that have just been explained.

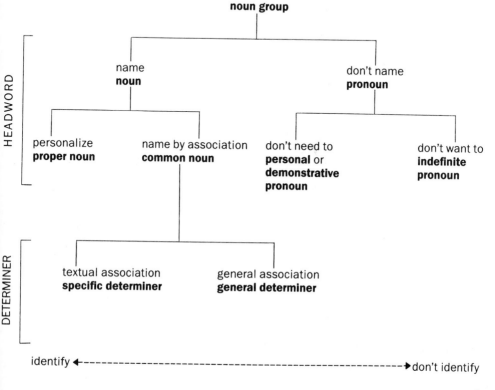

**modifiers and qualifiers**

**1.8** If you want to give more information about the person or thing you are talking about, rather than just giving their general or specific name, you can use **modifiers** and **qualifiers**.

Anything which you put in front of a noun is called a modifier. Anything which you put after a noun is called a qualifier.

**modifiers**

**1.9** Most **adjectives** are used as modifiers. Nouns are also often used as modifiers.

...a _big_ city.
..._blue_ ink.
He opened the _car_ door.
...the _oil_ industry.

See paragraphs 2.2 to 2.173 for more information about **adjectives,** and paragraphs 2.174 to 2.179 for more information about **noun modifiers.**

**qualifiers**

**1.10** The use of **qualifiers** allows us great freedom in expanding the noun group. Qualifiers can be prepositional phrases, relative clauses, adverbs of place or time, or 'to'-infinitives.

...a girl _in a dark grey dress._
...the man _who employed me._
...the room _upstairs._
...the desire _to kill._

Adjectives and participles are also sometimes used as qualifiers, usually in combination with other words.

...the Minister _responsible for national security._
...the three cards _lying on the table._

See paragraphs 2.289 to 2.320 for more information about **qualifiers.**

**1.11** In particular, prepositional phrases beginning with 'of' are very common, because they can express many different kinds of relationship between the two noun groups.

...strong feelings _of jealousy._
...a picture _of a house._
...the rebuilding _of the old hospital._
...the daughter _of the village cobbler._
...problems _of varying complexity._
...the arrival _of the police._

For more information about the use of 'of' in the noun group see paragraphs 2.294 to 2.300.

**coordination**

**1.12** If you want to refer separately to more than one person or thing, or you want to describe them in more than one way, you can link noun groups, modifiers, or qualifiers using the **conjunctions** 'and', 'or', or 'but'. Sometimes you can use a comma instead of 'and', or just put one word next to another.

...a table _and_ chair.
...his obligations with regard to Amanda, _Robert and_ Matthew.
...some fruit _or_ cheese afterwards.
...her long _black_ skirt.

See paragraphs 8.159 to 8.189 for more information about the use of conjunctions to link noun groups and words within noun groups.

**numbers and quantifiers**

**1.13** If you want to say how many things you are talking about, or how much of something there is, you use **numbers** and **quantifiers**.

*Last year I worked <u>seven</u> days a week <u>fourteen</u> hours a day.*
*She drinks <u>lots of</u> coffee.*

**Numbers** are dealt with in paragraphs 2.225 to 2.256, and **quantifiers** are dealt with in 2.193 to 2.210.

# Identifying people and things: nouns

**1.14** A noun is used to identify a person or thing. In this chapter we describe six main types of noun. They are classified according to whether they have a plural form, whether they need a determiner in front of them, and whether they occur with a singular verb or a plural verb when they are the subject of the verb.

The six types are:

| classification | example | comments | paragraph |
|---|---|---|---|
| count nouns | *a bird* *birds* | have plural need determiner | 1.16 to 1.23 |
| uncount nouns | *happiness* *equipment* | no plural usually no determiner | 1.24 to 1.34 |
| singular nouns | *the moon* *a day* | no plural need determiner | 1.35 to 1.41 |
| plural nouns | *clothes* *scissors* | no singular | 1.42 to 1.47 |
| collective nouns | *the public* *the staff* | either singular or plural verb | 1.48 to 1.52 |
| proper nouns | *Mary, London* *The United Nations* | start with capital letter | 1.53 to 1.59 |

Many nouns have a number of different meanings, and so can be, for example, a count noun for one meaning, an uncount noun for another, and a singular noun for another.

There are a few other groups of nouns with special features. These are dealt with in paragraphs 1.60 to 1.93.

**capital letters**

**1.15** Most nouns do not begin with a capital letter, unless they are used to start a sentence. However, the following types of nouns are always spelled with a capital letter:

● **proper nouns** or names

*...my sister <u>Elizabeth.</u>*
*I love reading <u>Shakespeare.</u>*
*I'll be in the office on <u>Monday.</u>*

*I thought he'd gone to London.*

For more information on proper nouns, see paragraphs 1.53 to 1.59. Proper nouns that are time expressions are dealt with in Chapter 5, and those that are place names in Chapter 6.

● nouns which identify people of a particular nationality, or languages

*Can you think of some typical problems that confront Germans learning English?*

● nouns which are the name of a particular product

*He drives a Porsche.*
*Put a bit of Sellotape across it.*

## Things which can be counted: count nouns

**1.16** Many nouns have two forms, the **singular** form, which is used to refer to one person or thing, and the **plural** form, which is used to refer to more than one person or thing.

These nouns refer to people or things which can be counted. You can put numbers in front of them.

*...book...books.*
*...day...days.*
*...three brothers.*
*...ten minutes.*

These nouns make up the largest group of nouns in English. They are called **count nouns** or **countable nouns.**

**noun-verb agreement**    **1.17** When you use the singular form of a count noun as the subject of a verb, you use a singular verb. When you use the plural form of a count noun as the subject, you use a plural verb.

*A dog likes to eat far more meat than a human being.*
*Bigger dogs cost more.*

**use of determiners**    **1.18** Count nouns have a determiner in front of them when they are used in the singular.

*He got into the car and started the motor.*
*They left the house to go for a walk after tea.*

When you use the plural form of a count noun to refer to something in general, you do not use a determiner.

*They all live in big houses.*
*Most classrooms have computers.*

However, if you are specifying a particular instance of something, you need to use a determiner.

*The houses in our street are all identical.*
*Our computers can give you all the relevant details.*

**list of count nouns** 1.19 Here is a list of some common count nouns:

| | | | | |
|---|---|---|---|---|
| accident | cat | father | lake | river |
| account | chair | field | library | road |
| actor | chapter | film | line | room |
| address | chest | finger | list | scheme |
| adult | child | foot | machine | school |
| animal | cigarette | friend | magazine | ship |
| answer | city | game | man | shirt |
| apartment | class | garden | meal | shock |
| article | club | gate | meeting | shop |
| artist | coat | girl | member | sister |
| baby | college | group | message | smile |
| bag | computer | gun | method | son |
| ball | corner | hall | minute | spot |
| bank | country | hand | mistake | star |
| battle | crowd | handle | model | station |
| beach | cup | hat | month | stream |
| bed | daughter | head | motor | street |
| bell | day | heart | mouth | student |
| bill | desk | hill | nation | table |
| bird | doctor | horse | neck | task |
| boat | dog | hospital | newspaper | teacher |
| book | door | hotel | office | tent |
| bottle | dream | hour | page | thought |
| box | dress | house | park | tour |
| boy | driver | husband | party | town |
| bridge | ear | idea | path | valley |
| brother | edge | island | picture | village |
| bus | effect | issue | plan | walk |
| bush | egg | job | plane | wall |
| camp | election | journey | plant | week |
| captain | engine | judge | problem | window |
| car | eye | key | product | woman |
| card | face | king | programme | year |
| case | factory | kitchen | project | |
| castle | farm | lady | ring | |

Note that many of these nouns have some meanings in which they are uncount nouns, but they are count nouns in their commonest meanings.

**singular and plural forms** 1.20 For most count nouns the plural form has '-s' at the end, which distinguishes it from the singular form.

...bed...*beds.*
...car...*cars.*

Some count nouns have other differences between the singular and plural forms.

...bus...*buses.*
...lady...*ladies.*
...calf...*calves.*
...man...*men.*
...mouse...*mice.*

For full information about the plural forms of count nouns, see the Reference Section.

**same form for singular and plural**

**1.21** Some count nouns have the same form for both singular and plural.

*...a sheep.*
*...nine sheep.*

Many of these nouns refer to animals or fish, others are more varied in meaning:

| | | | | |
|---|---|---|---|---|
| bison | cod | whitebait | fruit | ~ |
| deer | fish | ~ | gallows | bourgeois |
| greenfly | goldfish | aircraft | grapefruit | chassis |
| grouse | halibut | hovercraft | insignia | corps |
| moose | mullet | spacecraft | mews | patois |
| reindeer | salmon | ~ | offspring | précis |
| sheep | shellfish | crossroads | series | rendezvous |
| ~ | trout | dice | species | |

**singular form with plural meaning**

**1.22** The names of many animals and birds have two forms, one singular and one plural. However, when you are referring to them in the context of hunting or when you are saying that there are large numbers of them, it is quite common to use the form without '-s', even though you are referring to several animals or birds.

*We went up north to hunt deer.*

Note that the plural form of the verb is used when several animals or birds are the subject of the sentence, even if you use the form without '-s'.

*Zebra are a more difficult prey.*

Similarly, when you are referring to a large number of trees or plants growing together, you can use the singular form of their name. When you are referring to a small number or to individual trees or plants, you usually use the form with '-s'.

*...the rows of willow and cypress which lined the creek.*
*...the poplars and willows along the Peshawar Road.*

**PRODUCTIVE FEATURE**

**1.23** Although some names of animals, birds, trees, and plants are commonly used in the singular form with plural meaning, in fact all such names can be used in this way. This is a productive feature of English. Productive features are explained in the Introduction.

## Things not usually counted: uncount nouns

**1.24** Some nouns refer to general things such as qualities, substances, processes, and topics rather than to individual items or events. These nouns have only one form, are not used with numbers, and are not usually used with the determiners 'the', 'a', or 'an'.

*...a boy or girl with intelligence.*
*Make sure everyone has enough food and drink.*
*...new techniques in industry and agriculture.*
*I talked with people about religion, death, marriage, money, and happiness.*

These nouns are called **uncount nouns** or **uncountable nouns**.

**noun-verb agreement**

**1.25** When you use an uncount noun as the subject of a verb, you use a singular form of the verb.

*Love makes you do strange things.*

*They believed that <u>poverty</u> was a threat to world peace.*
*<u>Electricity is</u> potentially dangerous.*

**list of uncount nouns**

1.26 Here is a list of some common uncount nouns:

| | | | |
|---|---|---|---|
| absence | evil | loneliness | security |
| access | existence | love | silence |
| age | experience | luck | sleep |
| agriculture | failure | magic | strength |
| anger | faith | marriage | snow |
| atmosphere | fashion | mercy | spite |
| beauty | fear | music | status |
| behaviour | finance | nature | stuff |
| cancer | fire | paper | teaching |
| capacity | flesh | patience | technology |
| childhood | food | peace | time |
| china | freedom | philosophy | trade |
| comfort | fun | pleasure | training |
| concern | ground | policy | transport |
| confidence | growth | poverty | travel |
| courage | happiness | power | trust |
| death | health | pride | truth |
| democracy | help | protection | violence |
| depression | history | purity | waste |
| design | ice | rain | water |
| duty | independence | reality | wealth |
| earth | industry | relief | weather |
| education | insurance | religion | welfare |
| electricity | intelligence | respect | wind |
| energy | joy | safety | work |
| environment | justice | salt | worth |
| equipment | labour | sand | youth |

**WARNING**

1.27 There are some words which are uncount nouns in English, but which refer to things that are considered countable in other languages.

Here is a list of the most common uncount nouns of this type:

| | | | | |
|---|---|---|---|---|
| advice | hair | knowledge | money | research |
| baggage | homework | luggage | news | spaghetti |
| furniture | information | machinery | progress | traffic |

**quantifying**

1.28 Although uncount nouns refer to things which cannot be counted and are not used with numbers, you often want to refer to an amount of something which is expressed by an uncount noun.

Sometimes, you can do this by putting a **general determiner** such as 'all', 'enough', 'little', or 'some' in front of the noun.

*Do you have <u>enough</u> money?*
*There's <u>some</u> chocolate cake over there.*

For more information on general determiners which can be used with uncount nouns, see paragraph 1.210.

You can also put a **quantifier** in front of the noun. For example, when you refer to water you can say 'drops of water', 'a cup of water', 'four gallons of water', and so on.

The use of quantifiers with uncount nouns is explained in paragraphs 2.193 to 2.210.

**mass nouns**  **1.29** When you are sure that your reader or hearer will understand that a quantity of something is being referred to, you do not need to use a quantifier.

For example, in a restaurant you can ask for 'three cups of coffee', but you can also ask for 'three coffees' because the person you are talking to will know that you mean 'three cups of coffee'. In this way, the uncount noun 'coffee' has become countable.

Nouns used in this way are called **mass nouns**.

**1.30** Mass nouns are often used to refer to quantities of a particular kind of food or drink.

*We spent two hours talking over coffee and biscuits in her study.*
*We stopped for a coffee at a small café.*

**1.31** Similarly, some uncount nouns can be mass nouns when they refer to types of something. For example, 'cheese' is usually an uncount noun but you can talk about 'a large range of cheeses'.

*...plentiful cheap beer.*
*...profits from low-alcohol beers.*

*We were not allowed to buy wine or spirits at lunch time.*
*I like wines and liqueurs.*

Mass nouns referring to different types of a substance are mainly used in technical contexts. For example 'steel' is nearly always an uncount noun, but in contexts where it is important to distinguish between different kinds of steel it can be a mass noun.

*...imports of European steel.*
*...the use of small amounts of nitrogen in making certain steels.*

**list of**  **1.32** The following is a list of frequently used mass nouns:
**mass nouns**

| | | | | |
|---|---|---|---|---|
| adhesive | deodorant | jam | paint | steel |
| beer | detergent | jelly | perfume | sugar |
| brandy | disinfectant | juice | pesticide | tea |
| cake | dye | lager | plastic | vodka |
| cheese | fabric | liqueur | poison | whisky |
| claret | fertilizer | lotion | preservative | wine |
| cloth | fuel | meat | ribbon | wood |
| coal | fur | medicine | salad | wool |
| coffee | gin | metal | sauce | yarn |
| cognac | glue | milk | sherry | yoghurt |
| coke | ink | oil | soap | |
| cotton | insecticide | ointment | soil | |
| curry | iron | ore | soup | |

**nouns that**  **1.33** There are also some other nouns that can be uncount nouns when
**are**  they refer to a thing in general, and count nouns when they refer to a
**uncount**  particular instance of it.
**and count**

Some nouns are commonly both uncount nouns and count nouns. For example, 'victory' refers to the idea of winning in general but 'a victory' refers to a particular occasion when someone wins.

*He worked long and hard and finally led his team to victory.*
*...his victory in the Australian Grand Prix.*

*Many parents were alarmed to find themselves in open conflict with the church.*

*Hundreds of people have died in ethnic <u>conflicts</u>.*

Some uncount nouns are rarely or never count nouns; that is, they do not occur in a plural form, or with a number.

*...a collection of fine <u>furniture</u>.*
*We found Alan weeping with <u>relief</u> and <u>joy</u>.*
*He saved <u>money</u> by refusing to have a <u>telephone</u>.*

**uncount**
**nouns**
**ending in '-s'**

**1.34** Some nouns which end in '-s' and look as if they are plural are in fact uncount nouns. This means that when they are the subject of a verb, the verb is in the singular.

These nouns refer mainly to subjects of study, activities, games, and diseases.

*<u>Physics is</u> fun.*
*<u>Politics plays</u> a large part in village life.*
*<u>Economics is</u> the oldest of the social sciences.*
*<u>Darts is</u> a very competitive sport.*
*<u>Measles is</u> in most cases a relatively harmless disease.*

Here are three lists of uncount nouns ending in '-s'.

These nouns refer to subjects of study and activities:

| | | | |
|---|---|---|---|
| acoustics | classics | logistics | politics |
| aerobics | economics | mathematics | statistics |
| aerodynamics | electronics | mechanics | thermodynamics |
| aeronautics | genetics | obstetrics | |
| athletics | linguistics | physics | |

Note that some of these nouns are occasionally used as plural nouns, especially when you are talking about a particular person's work or activities.

*His <u>politics are</u> clearly right-wing.*

These nouns refer to games:

| | | | |
|---|---|---|---|
| billiards | cards | draughts | tiddlywinks |
| bowls | darts | skittles | |

These nouns refer to diseases:

| | | |
|---|---|---|
| diabetes | mumps | rickets |
| measles | rabies | shingles |

# When there is only one of something: singular nouns

**1.35** There are certain things in the world that are unique. There are other things which you almost always want to talk about one at a time. This means that there are some nouns, or more often some meanings of nouns, for which only a singular form is used.

When a noun is used with such a meaning, it is called a **singular noun**. Singular nouns are always used with a determiner, because they behave like the singular form of a count noun.

**noun-verb agreement**

**1.36** When you use a singular noun as the subject of a verb, you use a singular form of the verb.

*The sun was shining.*
*The atmosphere is very relaxed.*

**things that are unique**

**1.37** Some singular nouns refer to one specific thing and therefore are used with 'the'. Some of these nouns, in fact, refer to something of which there is only one in the world.

*There were huge cracks in the ground.*
*The moon had not yet reached my window.*
*Burning tanks threw great spirals of smoke into the air.*
*He's always thinking about the past and worrying about the future.*

**using the context**

**1.38** Other singular nouns can be used to refer to one thing only when it is obvious from the context what you are referring to. For example, if you are in Leeds and say 'I work at the university', you will almost certainly mean Leeds University.

However, in the following examples we cannot be sure exactly who or what the singular noun refers to, because we do not have enough context.

*In many countries the market is small numerically.*
*Their company looks good only because the competition looks bad.*
*You've all missed the point.*

Unless we are told which goods or products are being talked about, we cannot be sure which group of potential buyers 'the market' refers to. Similarly we do not know exactly which company or group of companies 'the competition' refers to. In the last example, the speaker or writer is presumably going to tell us what he or she thinks 'the point' is.

**used with delexical verbs**

**1.39** There are some activities which you do not usually do more than once at a time. The nouns that refer to them are usually the object of a verb, and are used with the determiner 'a'.

In this structure the verb has very little meaning and the noun carries most of the meaning of the whole structure. The verbs in such structures are called **delexical verbs**. For more information about these, see paragraphs 3.33 to 3.46.

*I went and had a wash.*
*Bruno gave it a try.*

Some singular nouns are used so regularly with a particular verb that they have become fixed phrases and are idiomatic.

*I'd like very much for you to have a voice in the decision.*
*Isn't it time we made a move?*

**singular noun structures**

**1.40** There are two special kinds of structure in which a singular noun is used.

A singular noun is sometimes used with the determiner 'a' as the **complement** of a clause. See paragraphs 3.127 to 3.182 for more information about complements.

*Decision-making is an art.*
*The quickest way was by using the car. It was a risk but he decided it had to be taken.*
*They were beginning to find Griffiths' visits rather a strain.*

A singular noun is sometimes used with the determiner 'the', followed by a prepositional phrase beginning with 'of'.

*Comedy is the art of making people laugh.*
*Old diesel locomotives will be replaced by newer ones to reduce the risk of breakdown.*
*He collapsed under the strain of a heavy workload.*

This group includes nouns used metaphorically; see paragraph 1.65 for more details.

Some singular nouns are always used to refer to one particular quality or thing, but are rarely used alone; that is, they need to be specified in some way by the use of supporting material. They can be used with a number of different determiners.

*There was a note of satisfaction in his voice.*
*Bessie covered the last fifty yards at a tremendous pace.*
*Simon allowed his pace to slacken.*
*She was simply incapable of behaving in a rational and considered manner.*
*...their manner of rearing their young.*

Nouns which are rarely used alone without supporting material are discussed in detail in paragraphs 1.60 to 1.66.

**USAGE NOTE**  1.41 Some nouns are used in the singular with a particular meaning only in an idiomatic phrase. They have the appearance of singular nouns, but they are not used as freely as singular nouns.

*What happens down there is none of my business.*
*It's a pity I can't get to him.*

# Referring to more than one thing: plural nouns

1.42 There are some things which are thought of as being plural rather than singular, so some nouns have only a plural form. For example, you can buy 'goods', but not 'a good'. These nouns are called **plural nouns.**

Other nouns have only a plural form when they are used with a particular meaning. For example, an official meeting between American and Russian leaders is usually referred to as 'talks' rather than as 'a talk'. In these meanings, these nouns are also called **plural nouns.**

*Union leaders met the company for wage talks on October 9.*
*It is inadvisable to sell goods on a sale or return basis.*
*Take care of your clothes.*
*The weather conditions were the same.*
*All proceeds are going to charity.*
*Employees can have meals on the premises.*

Note that some plural nouns do not end in '-s': for example 'clergy', 'police', 'poultry', and 'vermin'.

**noun-verb agreement**  1.43 When you use a plural noun as the subject of a verb, you use a plural form of the verb.

*Expenses for attending meetings are sometimes claimed.*
*The foundations were shaking.*
*Refreshments were on sale in the café.*
*Attempts were made where resources were available.*

**use with modifiers and qualifiers**  1.44 You do not usually use numbers in front of these nouns. You can, however, use some **general determiners** such as 'some' or 'many'. For more information about the general determiners which can be used with plural nouns, see the section beginning at paragraph 1.208.

Some plural nouns usually have a specific determiner in front of them, because they are specific; some never have a determiner at all, because they are very general; and some are rarely used alone without a modifier or qualifier, because they need supporting material.

The lists in the following two paragraphs contain some common plural nouns which are frequently used in one of these ways. Many of them have other meanings in which they are count nouns.

**with or without determiners**

**1.45** Some plural nouns are most commonly used with 'the'.

*Things are much worse when the rains come.*
*The authorities are concerned that the cocaine may be part of an international drug racket.*
*The coach tour of Gran Canaria was a wonderfully relaxing way to see the sights.*

Here is a list of plural nouns that are most commonly used with 'the':

| | | | |
|---|---|---|---|
| authorities | heavens | pictures | sights |
| foundations | mains | races | waters |
| fruits | odds | rains | wilds |

Some plural nouns are most commonly used with a possessive determiner such as 'my' or 'his'.

*It offended her feelings.*
*My travels up the Dalmation coast began in Dubrovnik.*
*This only added to his troubles.*

Here is a list of plural nouns that are most commonly used with a possessive determiner:

| | | | |
|---|---|---|---|
| activities | likes | terms | wants |
| attentions | movements | travels | |
| feelings | reactions | troubles | |

Some plural nouns are most commonly used without a determiner.

*There were one or two cases where people returned goods.*
*There is only one applicant, which simplifies matters.*
*They treated us like vermin.*

Here is a list of plural nouns that are most commonly used without a determiner:

| | | | |
|---|---|---|---|
| airs | expenses | matters | solids |
| appearances | figures | refreshments | talks |
| events | goods | riches | vermin |

Some plural nouns can be used both with or without determiners.

*The house was raided by police.*
*We called the police.*

*A luxury hotel was to be used as headquarters.*
*The city has been his headquarters for five years.*

*We didn't want it to dampen spirits which were required to remain positive.*

*Jessica has been keeping up the spirits of her family and friends.*

Here is a list of plural nouns that can be used with or without a determiner:

| | | | | |
|---|---|---|---|---|
| arms | greens | morals | proceeds | thanks |
| basics | grounds | papers | rates | tracks |
| brains | handcuffs | particulars | resources | troops |
| clergy | headquarters | people | specifics | values |
| costs | interests | police | spirits | |
| directions | looks | poultry | supplies | |
| essentials | means | premises | talks | |

**other modifiers and qualifiers**

**1.46** Some plural nouns are rarely used alone without a modifier or qualifier, because they need supporting material.

*He doesn't tolerate bad manners.*
*...the hidden pressures of direct government funding.*
*Our country's coastal defences need improving.*

Here is a list of plural nouns that are rarely used alone without a modifier or qualifier:

| | | | | |
|---|---|---|---|---|
| affairs | effects | matters | sands | works |
| clothes | forces | pressures | services | writings |
| conditions | hopes | proportions | thoughts | |
| defences | lines | quarters | wastes | |
| demands | manners | relations | ways | |
| details | materials | remains | words | |

**typical meanings: clothes and tools**

**1.47** Two special groups of nouns are usually plural: nouns referring to clothes and some other things that people wear, and nouns referring to tools and some other things that people use.

This is because some clothes and tools, such as 'trousers' and 'scissors', are made up of two similar parts.

*She wore brown trousers and a green sweater.*
*He took off his glasses.*
*...using the pliers from the toolbox.*

When you want to refer to these items in general, or to an unspecified number of them, you use the plural form with no determiner.

*Never poke scissors into a light bulb socket.*
*The man was watching the train through binoculars.*

Here is a list of some plural nouns which refer to clothes and other things that people wear:

| | | | |
|---|---|---|---|
| bermudas | flares | overalls | sunglasses |
| braces | galoshes | panties | tights |
| briefs | glasses | pants | trousers |
| cords | jeans | pyjamas | trunks |
| corduroys | jodhpurs | shorts | underpants |
| culottes | knickerbockers | slacks | |
| dungarees | knickers | specs | |
| flannels | leggings | spectacles | |

Here is a list of plural nouns which refer to tools and other things that people use:

| | | | | |
|---|---|---|---|---|
| binoculars | dividers | pincers | scissors | tongs |
| clippers | field-glasses | pliers | secateurs | tweezers |
| compasses | nutcrackers | scales | shears | |

When you want to refer to a single piece of clothing or a single tool, you can use 'some' or 'a pair of' in front of the noun. You can refer to more than one item by using a number or a quantifier with 'pairs of'.

*I got some scissors out of the kitchen drawer.*
*I was sent out to buy a pair of scissors.*

*He was wearing a pair of old grey trousers.*
*Liza has three pairs of jeans.*

You can also use 'a pair of' when you are talking about things such as gloves, shoes, and socks which typically occur in twos.

*...a pair of new gloves.*

A possessive determiner such as 'my' can be used instead of 'a'.

*...his favourite pair of shoes.*

When you use 'a pair of' with a noun in the plural form, the verb is singular if it is in the same clause. If the verb is in a following relative clause, it is usually plural.

*It is likely that a new pair of shoes brings more happiness to a child than a new car brings to a grown-up.*
*I always wear a pair of long pants underneath, or a pair of pyjamas is just as good.*

*He put on a pair of brown shoes, which were waiting there for him.*
*He wore a pair of earphones, which were plugged into a tape-recorder.*

You use a plural pronoun after 'a pair of'.

*She went to the wardrobe, chose a pair of shoes, put them on and leaned back in the chair.*
*He brought out a pair of dark glasses and handed them to Walker.*

## Referring to groups: collective nouns

**1.48** There are a number of nouns in English which refer to a group of people or things. These nouns are called **collective nouns**. They have only one form, but many collective nouns have other meanings in which they are count nouns with two forms.

**singular or**
**plural verb**

**1.49** When you use a collective noun, you can use either a singular verb or a plural verb after it.

You choose a singular verb if you think of the group as a single unit, and a plural verb if you think of the group as a number of individuals.

*Our little group is complete again.*
*A second group are those parents who feel that they were too harsh.*

*Our family isn't poor any more.*
*My family are perfectly normal.*

*The enemy was moving slowly to the east.*
*The enemy were visibly cracking.*

*His arguments were confined to books which the public was unlikely to read.*
*The public were deceived by the newspapers.*

The names of many organizations are collective nouns, and can be used with a singular or a plural verb.

*The BBC is sending him to Tuscany for the summer.*
*The BBC are planning to use the new satellite next month.*

*England was leading 18-0 at half-time.*
*England are seeking alternatives for their B team.*

If you want to refer back to a collective noun, you choose a singular pronoun or determiner if the previous verb is singular, and a plural pronoun or determiner if the previous verb is plural.

*The government has said it would wish to do this only if there was no alternative.*
*The government have made up their minds that they're going to win.*

**USAGE NOTE** **1.50** Note that the words 'bacteria', 'data', and 'media' are now often used as collective nouns, that is with either a singular or a plural verb and no change in form. Some careful speakers think they should only be used with a plural verb because they have the rare singular forms 'bacterium', 'datum', and 'medium' and are therefore count nouns.

*Medieval Arabic data show that the length of the day has been increasing more slowly than expected.*
*Our latest data shows more firms are hoping to expand in the near future.*

**WARNING** **1.51** Although you can use a plural verb after a collective noun, these nouns do not behave like the plural forms of count nouns. For example, you cannot use numbers in front of them. You cannot say 'Three enemy were killed'. You have to say 'Three of the enemy were killed'.

**list of collective nouns** **1.52** Here is a list of common collective nouns:

| | | | | |
|---|---|---|---|---|
| aristocracy | committee | enemy | herd | press |
| army | community | family | jury | proletariat |
| audience | company | flock | media | public |
| bacteria | council | gang | navy | staff |
| brood | crew | government | nobility | team |
| cast | data | group | opposition | |

Some collective nouns are also **partitives.** For example, you talk about 'a flock of sheep' and 'a herd of cattle'. See paragraph 2.215 for more information about these.

# Referring to people and things by name: proper nouns

**1.53** When you refer to a particular person, you can use their name. Names are usually called **proper nouns.**

People's names are spelled with a capital letter, and do not have a determiner in front of them.

17

*...Michael Hall.*
*...Jenny.*
*...Smith.*

Ways of using people's names when you are speaking to them directly are explained in paragraphs 10.115 to 10.117.

**1.54** Sometimes a person's name can be used to refer to something they create. You can refer to a painting, sculpture, or book by a particular person by using the person's name like a count noun. You still spell it with a capital letter.

*In those days you could buy a Picasso for £300.*
*I was looking at their Picassos and Matisses.*
*I'm reading an Agatha Christie at the moment.*

You can refer to music composed or performed by a particular person by using the person's name like an uncount noun.

*I remembered it while we were listening to the Mozart.*
*...instead of playing Chopin and Stravinsky all the time.*

**relationship nouns** **1.55** Nouns that refer to relationships between the people in a family, such as 'mother', 'dad', 'aunt', 'grandpa', and 'son', can also be used like names to address people or refer to them. They are then spelled with a capital letter.

*I'm sure Mum will be pleased.*

**titles** **1.56** Words which show someone's social status or job are called **titles**. They are spelled with a capital letter.

You use a title in front of a person's name, usually their surname or their full name, when you are talking about them in a fairly formal way or are showing respect to them.

*...Doctor Barker.*
*...Lord Curzon.*
*...Captain Jack Langtry.*
*...Mrs Ford.*

Here is a list of the most common titles which are used before names:

| | | | |
|---|---|---|---|
| Admiral | Dame | Lord | Princess |
| Archbishop | Doctor | Major | Private |
| Baron | Emperor | Miss | Professor |
| Baroness | Father | Mr | Queen |
| Bishop | General | Mrs | Saint |
| Brother | Governor | Ms | Sergeant |
| Captain | Inspector | Nurse | Sir |
| Cardinal | Justice | Police Constable | Sister |
| Colonel | King | Pope | |
| Constable | Lady | President | |
| Corporal | Lieutenant | Prince | |

A few titles, such as 'King', 'Queen', 'Prince', 'Princess', 'Sir', and 'Lady', can be followed just by the person's first name.

*...Queen Elizabeth.*
*...Prince Charles' eldest son.*
*Sir Michael has made it very clear indeed.*

Ways of using titles when you are speaking to people directly are explained in paragraphs 10.117 and 10.118.

**titles used without names**

**1.57** Determiners, other modifiers, and qualifiers are sometimes used with titles, and the person's name is omitted.

...Her Majesty the Queen and the Duke of Edinburgh.
...the Archbishop of Canterbury.
...the President of the United States.
...the Bishop of Birmingham.

**titles used as count nouns**

**1.58** Most words which are titles can also be count nouns, usually without a capital letter.

...lawyers, scholars, poets, presidents and so on.
...a foreign prince.
Maybe he'll be a Prime Minister one day.

**other proper nouns**

**1.59** The names of organizations, institutions, ships, magazines, books, plays, paintings, and other unique things are also proper nouns and are spelled with capital letters.

...British Rail
...Birmingham University.

They are sometimes used with 'the' or another determiner.

...the United Nations ...the Labour Party ...the University of Birmingham
...the Queen Mary ...the Guardian ...the Wall Street Journal.

The determiner is not spelled with a capital letter, except in the names of books, plays, and paintings.

...The Grapes of Wrath
...A Midsummer Night's Dream.

Some time expressions are proper nouns, and are dealt with in Chapter 5.

# Nouns which are rarely used alone

**1.60** There are some nouns which are rarely used alone, because they need supporting material. They cannot be used without a modifier or qualifier, because the meaning of the noun would not be clear. Some of these nouns have many meanings, others have very little meaning on their own.

For example, you cannot usually refer to someone as 'the head' without saying which organization they are head of. Similarly, you cannot say that there was 'a note' in someone's voice without describing it as, for example, 'a triumphant note' or 'a note of triumph'.

These nouns can be used on their own only if it is obvious from the context what is meant. For example, if you have just mentioned a mountain and you say 'the top', it is clear that you mean the top of that mountain.

| | |
|---|---|
| **used with modifiers** | **1.61** If a **modifier** is added to one of these nouns, the modifier is usually an adjective or another noun. |

> ...her wide experience of <u>political affairs.</u>
> I had detected an <u>apologetic note</u> in the agent's voice.
> He did not have <u>British citizenship.</u>
> Check the <u>water level.</u>

For more information on modifiers, see Chapter 2.

| | |
|---|---|
| **used with qualifiers** | **1.62** If the noun is followed by a **qualifier,** the qualifier is usually a prepositional phrase beginning with 'of'. |

> ...at the <u>top of the hill.</u>
> There he saw for himself the <u>extent of the danger.</u>
> Ever since the <u>rise of industrialism,</u> education has been geared towards producing workers.
> ...this high <u>level of interest.</u>

For more information on qualifiers, see paragraphs 2.289 to 2.320.

| | |
|---|---|
| **always used with modifiers** | **1.63** Some nouns are always used with a modifier. For example, it is pointless to say that someone is 'an eater' because all people eat, but you may want to say that he or she is 'a meat eater' or 'a messy eater'. |

Similarly, if you use 'range' to refer to a particular set of values, you have to specify which set you mean by referring to a particular 'price range' or 'age range'. If you use 'wear' to mean 'clothing', you have to say what sort of clothing, for example 'sports wear' or 'evening wear'.

> Tim was a <u>slow eater.</u>
> ...the other end of <u>the age range.</u>
> The company has plans to expand <u>its casual wear.</u>

| | |
|---|---|
| **always used with possessives** | **1.64** Some nouns are almost always used with a possessive, that is a **possessive determiner, 's,** or a prepositional phrase beginning with 'of', because you have to indicate who or what the thing you are talking about relates to or belongs to. |

> The company has grown rapidly since <u>its formation</u> ten years ago.
> Advance warning of <u>the approach of enemies</u> must have been of the greatest importance.
> ...the portrait of a man in <u>his prime.</u>

| | |
|---|---|
| **metaphorical uses** | **1.65** Nouns which are being used metaphorically often have a modifier or qualifier to indicate what is really being referred to. |

> ...the <u>maze of politics.</u>
> He has been prepared to sacrifice this company on <u>the altar of his own political ambitions.</u>
> He has worked out a scheme for <u>an economic lifeline</u> by purchasing land.
> Lloyd's of London is <u>the heart of the world's insurance industry.</u>
> ...those on the lower rungs of <u>the professional ladder.</u>

| | |
|---|---|
| **list of nouns rarely used alone** | **1.66** Many nouns have some meanings which require supporting material and other meanings which do not. For example, most nouns can be used metaphorically. However, there are some nouns which very typically need |

supporting material in most or all of their meanings. Here is a list of these nouns:

| | | | |
|---|---|---|---|
| affair | edge | limit | stage |
| approach | edition | line | status |
| area | element | matter | structure |
| back | end | movement | stuff |
| band | enterprise | nature | style |
| base | epidemic | note | system |
| bottom | experience | period | texture |
| boundary | extent | point | theory |
| branch | feeling | position | thought |
| case | field | power | time |
| centre | formation | prime | tone |
| circumstances | fringe | range | top |
| citizenship | ground | rate | transfer |
| class | growth | regime | type |
| condition | head | relic | version |
| crisis | height | repertoire | view |
| culture | impression | rise | wave |
| depth | inception | role | way |
| development | kind | scale | wear |
| discovery | length | side | wing |
| eater | level | sort | world |

# Sharing the same quality: adjectives as headwords

**1.67** When you want to talk about groups of people who share the same characteristic or quality, you often choose an adjective rather than a noun as a headword.

You do this by using the appropriate adjective preceded by 'the'. For example, instead of saying 'poor people', you say 'the poor'.

*...the help that's given to the blind.*
*No effort is made to cater for the needs of the elderly.*
*...the task of rescuing the injured.*
*...men and women who would join the sad ranks of the unemployed.*
*Working with the young is stimulating and full of surprises.*
*...providing care for the sick, the aged, the workless and the poor.*

Note that you never add '-s' to the headword, even though it always refers to more than one person.

**PRODUCTIVE**
**FEATURE**

**1.68** Although some adjectives are commonly used in this way, in fact it is possible to use almost any adjective in this way. This is a productive feature of English. Productive features are explained in the Introduction.

**noun-verb**
**agreement**

**1.69** When the adjective being used as headword is the subject of a verb, you use a plural form of the verb.

*The rich have benefited much more than the poor.*

**being**
**more**
**specific**

**1.70** In order to refer to a more specific group of people, you can put a **submodifier** or another adjective in front of the headword. For more information about submodifiers, see paragraphs 2.145 to 2.173.

*In this anecdote, Ray shows his affection for <u>the very old</u> and <u>the very young</u>.*
*...<u>the highly educated</u>.*
*...<u>the urban poor</u>.*

If you mention two groups, you can sometimes omit 'the'.

*...a study that compared the diets of <u>rich and poor</u> in several nations.*
*...to help break down the barriers between <u>young and old</u>.*

With a few words such as 'unemployed' and 'dead', you can say how many people you are referring to by putting a number in front of them.

*We estimate there are about <u>three hundred dead</u>.*

**qualities**　**1.71** When you want to refer to the quality of something rather than to the thing itself, you can use the appropriate adjective with 'the'.

*Don't you think that you're wanting <u>the impossible</u>?*
*He is still exploring the limits of <u>the possible</u>.*
*...a mix of <u>the traditional</u> and <u>the modern</u>.*

**colours**　**1.72** All colour adjectives can also be used as headwords.

*...patches of <u>blue</u>.*
*...brilliant paintings in <u>reds</u> and <u>greens</u> and <u>blues</u>.*

Clothing of a particular colour can be referred to simply by using the colour adjective.

*The men wore <u>grey</u>.*
*...the fat lady in <u>black</u>.*

**USAGE NOTE**　**1.73** Nationality adjectives which end in '-ch', '-sh', '-se', or '-ss' can be used in a similar way, unless there is a separate noun for the people. For example, French people are referred to as 'the French' but Polish people are referred to as 'the Poles'.

*For many years <u>the Japanese</u> have dominated the market for Chinese porcelain.*
*Britons are the biggest consumers of chocolate after <u>the Swiss</u> and <u>the Irish</u>.*

# Nouns referring to males or females

**1.74** English nouns are not masculine, feminine, or neuter in the way that nouns in some other languages are. For example, most names of jobs, such as 'teacher', 'doctor', and 'writer', are used for both men and women.

But some nouns refer only to males and others only to females.

For example, some nouns indicating people's family relationships, such as 'father', 'brother', and 'son', and some nouns indicating people's jobs, such as 'waiter' and 'policeman', can only be used to refer to males.

In the same way 'mother', 'sister', 'daughter', 'waitress', 'actress', and 'sportswoman' can only be used to refer to females.

**'-ess' and**　**1.75** Words that refer to women often end in '-ess', for example 'actress',
**'-woman'**　'waitress', and 'hostess'. Another ending is '-woman', as in 'policewoman' and 'needlewoman'.

*...his wife Susannah, a former <u>air stewardess</u>.*
*A <u>policewoman</u> dragged me out of the crowd.*
*...Margaret Downes, who is this year's <u>chairwoman</u> of the examination committee.*

**'-man' and '-person'**

**1.76** Words ending in '-man' are either used to refer only to men or to both men and women. For example, a 'postman' is a man, but a 'spokesman' can be a man or a woman.

Some people now use words ending in '-person', such as 'chairperson' and 'spokesperson', instead of words ending in '-man', in order to avoid appearing to refer specifically to a man.

**USAGE NOTE**

**1.77** Most names of animals are used to refer to both male and female animals, for example 'cat', 'elephant', 'horse', 'monkey', and 'sheep'.

In some cases there are different words that refer specifically to male animals or female animals, for example a male horse is a 'stallion' and a female horse is a 'mare'.

In other cases the general name for the animal is also the specific word for males or females: 'dog' also refers more specifically to male dogs, 'duck' also refers more specifically to female ducks.

Many of these specific words are rarely used, or used mainly by people who have a special interest in animals, such as farmers or vets.

Here is a list of some common specific words for male and female animals:

| | | | | |
|---|---|---|---|---|
| stallion | ~ | vixen | ram | tiger |
| mare | dog | ~ | ewe | tigress |
| ~ | bitch | gander | ~ | ~ |
| bull | ~ | goose | buck | boar |
| cow | drake | ~ | hind | sow |
| ~ | duck | lion | stag | |
| cock | ~ | lioness | doe | |
| hen | fox | ~ | ~ | |

# Referring to activities and processes: '-ing' nouns

**1.78** You often want to refer to an action, activity, or process in a general way. When you do, you can use a noun which has the same form as the **present participle** of a verb.

These nouns are called different things in different grammars: **gerunds, verbal nouns,** or **'-ing' forms.** In this grammar we call them **'-ing' nouns.**

It is sometimes difficult to distinguish an **'-ing' noun** from a **present participle,** and it is usually not necessary to do so. However, there are times when it is clearly a noun, for example when it is the subject of a verb, the object of a verb, or the object of a preposition.

*<u>Swimming</u> is a great sport.*
*They were at school when the emphasis was on <u>teaching</u> rather than <u>learning</u>.*
*He told how hard the days of <u>walking</u> had been, how his muscles had ached.*
*The <u>closing</u> of so many mills left thousands unemployed.*
*Some people have never actually done any <u>computing</u>.*

The spelling of '-ing' forms is explained in the Reference Section. The use of '-ing' adjectives is explained in paragraphs 2.67 to 2.80.

**uncount nouns**

1.79 Because '-ing' nouns refer to activities in a general way, they are usually **uncount nouns**; that is, they have only one form, cannot be used with numbers, and do not usually have a determiner in front of them.

For more information on **uncount nouns,** see paragraphs 1.24 to 1.34.

1.80 You often use an '-ing' noun because it is the only noun form available for certain verbs, such as 'eat', 'hear', 'go', 'come', and 'bless'. Whereas other verbs have related nouns that are not '-ing' nouns: for example 'see' and 'sight', 'arrive' and 'arrival', 'depart' and 'departure'.

*Eating, unlike fighting, is a pursuit in which both sexes freely indulge.*
*...loss of hearing in one ear.*
*Only 6 per cent of children receive any further training when they leave school.*

**used with adjectives**

1.81 If you want to describe the action expressed by the noun, you can use one or more adjectives or nouns in front of it.

*He served a jail sentence for reckless driving.*
*The police need better training in dealing with the mentally ill.*
*He called for a national campaign against under-age drinking.*

1.82 A small number of '-ing' nouns, most of which refer to sporting or leisure activities, are much more common than their related verbs. In some cases there is at the moment no verb, although it is always possible to invent one. For example, you are more likely to say 'We went caravanning round France' than 'We caravanned round France'.

Here is a list of the commonest of these nouns:

| | | | |
|---|---|---|---|
| angling | caravanning | paragliding | surfing |
| blackberrying | electioneering | shoplifting | weightlifting |
| boating | hang-gliding | sightseeing | window-shopping |
| bowling | heliskiing | skateboarding | windsurfing |
| canoeing | mountaineering | snorkelling | yachting |

Although these words are not always associated with a verb, most of them can be used as present participles.

*He fell fully-clothed into the lake while boating with a girl-friend.*
*I spent the afternoon window-shopping with Grandma.*

**count nouns**

1.83 Some '-ing' nouns which are related to verbs are **count nouns**. They generally refer to the result of an action or process, or to an individual instance of it. Sometimes their meaning is not closely related to that of the verb.

Here is a list of the commonest of these nouns:

| | | | | |
|---|---|---|---|---|
| beginning | feeling | meeting | setting | turning |
| being | finding | offering | showing | warning |
| building | hearing | painting | sitting | |
| drawing | meaning | saying | suffering | |

For more information on count nouns, see paragraphs 1.16 to 1.23.

# Specifying more exactly: compound nouns

1.84 A single noun is often not sufficient to refer clearly and unambiguously to a person or thing. When this is the case, a **compound**

**noun** can be used. A compound noun is a fixed expression which is made up of more than one word and which functions in the clause as a noun.

*Some people write out a new <u>address book</u> every January.*
*How would one actually choose a small <u>personal computer</u>?*
*Where did you hide the <u>can opener</u>?*
*...a private <u>swimming pool</u>.*

Once it is clear what you are referring to, it is sometimes possible to use just the second word of a two-word compound noun. For example, after mentioning 'a swimming pool', you can just refer to 'the pool'.

Most compound nouns consist of two words, but some consist of three or more words.

*...a vase of <u>lily of the valley</u>.*

**use of hyphens**

**1.85** Some compound nouns are written with hyphens instead of spaces between the words.

*I'm looking forward to a <u>lie-in</u> tomorrow.*
*He's very good at <u>problem-solving</u>.*
*Judy's <u>brother-in-law</u> lived with his family.*

Some are written with either a hyphen or a space between the words. For example, both 'air-conditioner' and 'air conditioner' are widely used.

A few compound nouns which consist of more than two words are written partly with hyphens and partly with spaces, for example 'back-seat driver' and 'bring-and-buy sale'.

*...children from <u>one-parent families</u>.*
*Another route is by active participation in a <u>Parent-Teacher Association</u>.*

**lists of compound nouns**

**1.86** Compound nouns may be countable, uncountable, singular, or plural.

Here is a list of some common countable compound nouns:

| | |
|---|---|
| address book | credit card |
| air conditioner | dining room |
| air raid | drawing pin |
| alarm clock | driving licence |
| assembly line | estate agent |
| baby-sitter | fairy tale |
| back-seat driver | film star |
| bank account | fire engine |
| bird of prey | fork-lift truck |
| book token | frying pan |
| blood donor | guided missile |
| bride-to-be | health centre |
| bring-and-buy sale | heart attack |
| brother-in-law | high school |
| burglar alarm | human being |
| bus stop | letter-box |
| can opener | lily of the valley |
| car park | looker-on |
| come-on | musical instrument |
| compact disc | nervous breakdown |
| comrade in arms | news bulletin |
| contact lens | old hand |
| cover-up | one-parent family |

| | |
|---|---|
| package holiday | swimming pool |
| Parent-Teacher Association | T-shirt |
| parking meter | tea bag |
| passer-by | telephone number |
| pen-friend | traveller's cheque |
| personal computer | tea-table |
| polar bear | washing machine |
| police station | X-ray |
| post office | youth hostel |
| runner-up | zebra crossing |
| sleeping bag | |
| summing-up | |

**1.87** Here is a list of some common uncountable compound nouns:

| | | |
|---|---|---|
| air conditioning | further education | show business |
| air-traffic control | general knowledge | show jumping |
| barbed wire | hay fever | sign language |
| birth control | heart failure | social security |
| blood pressure | higher education | social work |
| bubble bath | hire purchase | soda water |
| capital punishment | income tax | stainless steel |
| central heating | junk food | table tennis |
| chewing gum | law and order | talcum powder |
| common sense | lost property | toilet paper |
| cotton wool | mail order | turn-over |
| data processing | make-up | tracing paper |
| do-it-yourself | mineral water | unemployment benefit |
| dry-cleaning | nail varnish | value added tax |
| family planning | natural history | washing powder |
| fancy dress | old age | washing-up liquid |
| fast-food | pocket money | water-skiing |
| first aid | remote control | writing paper |
| food poisoning | science fiction | |

**1.88** Here is a list of some common singular compound nouns:

| | | |
|---|---|---|
| age of consent | general public | public sector |
| arms race | generation gap | rank and file |
| brain drain | greenhouse effect | solar system |
| colour bar | human race | sound barrier |
| cost of living | labour force | space age |
| death penalty | labour market | welfare state |
| diplomatic corps | long jump | women's movement |
| dress circle | mother-tongue | |
| drying-up | open air | |
| fire brigade | private sector | |

**1.89** Here is a list of some common plural compound nouns:

| | | |
|---|---|---|
| armed forces | industrial relations | social services |
| baked beans | inverted commas | social studies |
| civil rights | licensing laws | swimming trunks |
| current affairs | luxury goods | vocal cords |
| French fries | modern languages | winter sports |
| grass roots | natural resources | yellow pages |
| high heels | race relations | |
| human rights | road works | |

**composition of compound nouns**

**1.90** Most compound nouns consist of two nouns, or an adjective and a noun.

*I listened with anticipation to the radio news bulletin.*
*...a big dining room.*
*She came in and sat down at the tea-table.*
*Red wine is best enjoyed with red meat.*
*Old age is sickness only if one makes it so.*

However, a few compound nouns are related to **phrasal verbs**. These are often written with a hyphen.

*The President was directly involved in the Watergate cover-up.*
*The registry office is famous for its turn-over of fashionable weddings.*

For more information about phrasal verbs, see paragraphs 3.84 to 3.117.

**USAGE NOTE**

**1.91** In some cases, the meaning of a compound noun is not obvious from the words it consists of.

For example, someone's 'mother-tongue' is not the tongue of their mother but the language they learn as a child, and an 'old hand' is not a hand which is old but a person who is experienced at doing a particular job.

In other cases, the compound noun consists of words which do not occur on their own, for example 'hanky-panky', 'hodge-podge', and 'argy-bargy'. These nouns are usually used in informal conversation rather than formal writing.

*The rest of your question I find rhetorical hocus-pocus.*
*She is invariably up to some sort of jiggery-pokery.*

**plural forms**

**1.92** The plural forms of compound nouns vary according to the type of words that they consist of. If the final word of a compound noun is a count noun, the plural form of the count noun is used when the compound noun is plural.

*Air raids were taking place every night.*
*...health centres, banks, post offices, and police stations.*
*Shrill voices would be heard through letter-boxes.*
*...the refusal of dockers to use fork-lift trucks.*

For full information about the plural forms of count nouns, see the Reference Section.

Compound nouns that are directly related to phrasal verbs usually have a plural form ending in '-s'.

*Nobody seems disturbed about cover-ups when they are essential to the conduct of a war.*
*Naturally, I think people who drive smarter, faster cars than mine are a bunch of low-grade show-offs.*

A few compound nouns are less directly related to phrasal verbs, and consist of a count noun and an adverb. In these cases, the plural form of the count noun is used before the adverb when the compound noun is plural.

For example, the plural of 'looker-on' is 'lookers-on', and the plural of 'summing-up' is 'summings-up'.

*Passers-by helped the victim, who was unconscious.*

Compound nouns which consist of two nouns linked by the prepositions 'of' or 'in', or a noun followed by 'to-be', have a plural form in which the first noun in the compound is plural.

*I like birds of prey and hawks particularly.*
*She was treated with contempt by her sisters-in-law.*
*Most mothers-to-be in their forties opt for this test.*

Some compound nouns have been borrowed from other languages, mainly French and Latin, and therefore do not have normal English plural forms.

*...aided by agents provocateurs sent into our midst.*
*...while the nouveaux riches of younger states built themselves palatial mansions.*

**1.93** Compound nouns are fixed expressions. However, nouns can always be used in front of other nouns in order to refer to something in a more specific way. For the use of nouns as **modifiers,** see paragraphs 2.174 to 2.179.

# Referring to people and things without naming them: pronouns

**1.94** When we use language, both in speech and writing, we constantly refer to things we have already mentioned or are about to mention.

We can do this by repeating the noun group, but unless there is a special reason to do so we are more likely to use a **pronoun** instead.

Pronouns make statements less repetitive while showing how the subjects and objects of a clause or a series of clauses are connected.

*John took the book and opened it.*
*Deborah recognized the knife as hers.*
*Shilton was pleased with himself.*
*This is a very busy place.*

However, if you have mentioned two or more different things, you usually have to repeat the noun group to make it clear which thing you are now talking about.

*Leaflets and scraps of papers were scattered all over the floor. I started to pick up the leaflets.*
*I could see a lorry and a car. The lorry stopped.*

For other ways of talking about things that have already been mentioned, see **cohesion** in paragraphs 9.2 to 9.40.

**types of pronoun**

**1.95** There are several different types of pronoun:

- **personal pronouns.** See paragraphs 1.96 to 1.109.
- **possessive pronouns.** See paragraphs 1.110 to 1.114.
- **reflexive pronouns.** See paragraphs 1.115 to 1.122.
- **demonstrative pronouns.** See paragraphs 1.123 to 1.126.
- **indefinite pronouns.** See paragraphs 1.127 to 1.140.
- **reciprocal pronouns.** See paragraphs 1.141 to 1.144.
- **relative pronouns.** See paragraphs 1.145 to 1.149.
- **interrogative pronouns.** See paragraphs 1.150 to 1.152.

There are a few other words which can be used as pronouns. For more information about these, see paragraphs 1.153 to 1.160.

# Referring to people and things: personal pronouns

**1.96** You use **personal pronouns** to refer to yourself, the people you are talking to, or the people or things you are talking about.

There are two sets of personal pronouns: subject pronouns and object pronouns.

**subject pronouns**

**1.97** Subject pronouns are used to refer to the subject of a clause.

Here is a table of subject pronouns:

|            | singular          | plural |
|------------|-------------------|--------|
| 1st person | I                 | we     |
| 2nd person | you               |        |
| 3rd person | he<br>she<br>it   | they   |

**'I'**

**1.98** You refer to yourself by using the pronoun 'I'. 'I' is always written with a capital letter.

*I don't know what to do.*
*I think I made the wrong decision.*
*May I ask why Stephen's here?*

**'you'**

**1.99** You refer to the person or people you are talking to as 'you'. Note that the same word is used for the singular and the plural.

*You may have to wait a bit.*
*Would you come and have a drink?*
*How did you get on?*

'You' is also used, especially in spoken English, to refer to people in general, rather than to the person you are talking or writing to.

*You can't predict what these things are going to do.*
*You get some old people who are very difficult.*

Note that 'you' is also an **object pronoun**. For more information on this, see paragraphs 1.104 to 1.106.

**'he' and 'she'**

**1.100** You refer to a man or a boy as 'he', and to a woman or a girl as 'she'.

*My father is fat—he weighs over fifteen stone.*
*Billy Knight was a boxer, wasn't he?*
*Mary came in. She was a good-looking woman.*
*'Is Sue there?'—'I'm sorry, she doesn't work here now.'*

**'it'**

**1.101** You use 'it' to refer to anything which is not male or female; for example, an object, place, or organization, or something abstract.

*I've seen Toy Story before. It's a good film for kids.*
*'Have you been to London?' 'Yes, it was very crowded.'*
*How much would the company be worth if it were sold?*
*It is not an idea that has much public support.*

'It' is often used to refer to an animal when its gender is not known or not considered to be important. Some people also refer to babies in this way.

*They punched the crocodile until it let go of her.*
*If the shark is still around it will not escape.*
*How Winifred loved the baby! And how Stephanie hated it!*

You also use 'it' in general statements, for example to refer to a situation, the time, the date, or the weather.

*It is very quiet here.*
*It is half past three.*
*It is January 19th.*
*It is rainy and cold.*

For more information on the use of 'it' in general statements, see paragraphs 10.31 to 10.45.

Note that 'it' is also an **object pronoun**. For more information on this, see paragraphs 1.104 to 1.107.

**'we'**   **1.102** You use 'we' to refer to a group of people which includes yourself. The group can be:

● you and the person or people you are talking to.

*Where shall we meet, Sally?*

● you and the person or people you are talking to and one or more others not there at the time.

*We aren't exactly gossips, you and I and Watson.*

● you and one or more other people, but not including the person or people you are talking to.

*I do the washing; he does the cooking; we share the washing-up.*

● any group which you feel yourself to be part of, such as a school, your local community, or even mankind as a whole.

*We are in fact a multicultural society.*
*We all need money.*

**'they'**   **1.103** You use 'they' to refer to a group of things, or to a group of people not including yourself or the person or people you are talking to.

*All the girls think he's great, don't they?*
*Newspapers reach me on the day after they are published.*
*Winters here vary as they do elsewhere.*

'They' is also often used to refer to people in general.

*Isn't that what they call love?*

'They' can also refer to a group of people whose identity does not need to be stated. For example, in the sentence 'They've given John another pay rise' it is clear that 'they' refers to John's employers.

*'Don't worry', I said to Mother, 'they are moving you from this ward soon.'*

**object pronouns**   **1.104** Object pronouns refer to the same sets of people or things as the corresponding subject pronouns.

Here is a table of object pronouns:

|  | singular | plural |
|---|---|---|
| 1st person | me | us |
| 2nd person | you ||
| 3rd person | him<br>her<br>it | them |

**position
in clause**

**1.105** Object pronouns are used as the object of a clause.

*The nurse washed me with cold water.*
*He likes you —he said so.*
*The man went up to the cat and started stroking it.*

They can be the indirect object of a clause.

*Send us a card so we'll know where you are.*
*A man gave him a car.*
*You have to offer them some kind of incentive.*

They can also be the object of a preposition.

*She must have felt intimidated by me.*
*Madeleine, I want to talk to you immediately.*
*We were all sitting in a café with him.*

**1.106** Object pronouns can also be used after **link verbs**. For example, you can say 'It was me', 'It's her'. However, in formal or written English, people sometimes use a subject pronoun after a link verb. For example, 'It was I', 'It is she'.

For more information on link verbs, see paragraphs 3.127 to 3.182.

**USAGE NOTE**

**1.107** Although 'it' is used as both a subject pronoun and an object pronoun to refer to something that is not male or female, 'she' and 'her' are often used to refer to ships, cars, and countries.

*When the repairs had been done she was a fine and beautiful ship.*
*...Britain and her allies.*

**USAGE NOTE**

**1.108** Sometimes, you may not want to specify whether a person you are talking about is male or female.

One way of doing this is to use 'they' or 'them'. This use is very common after **indefinite pronouns** such as 'someone' or 'anyone'. These are explained in paragraphs 1.127 to 1.140. Note that the plural form of the verb is always used after 'they', even when it refers to only one person.

*If anyone wants to be a child minder, they must attend a course.*
*If I think someone may take an overdose, I will spend hours talking to them.*

Another way is to use 'he or she' instead of 'they', and 'him or her' instead of 'them'. This is often used in formal or written English.

*'Would a young person be able to get a job in Europe?' 'That would depend on which country he or she wanted to go to'.*
*The student should feel that the essay belongs to him or her.*

Some people consider it wrong to use 'they' and 'them' to refer to one person. It is, however, clumsy to repeat 'he or she' and 'him or her'. When you want to make a general statement you can avoid this problem by using a plural noun instead of a singular noun.

For example, instead of saying 'As soon as a child goes to school he or she is taught to read', you could say 'As soon as children go to school they are taught to read'.

Some people use 'he' and 'him' in general statements or after indefinite pronouns, but many people object to this use because it suggests that the person being referred to is male.

**'one' as a
personal
pronoun**

**1.109** 'One' is sometimes used as a singular personal pronoun, but this use is considered formal. The same form is used as both the subject pronoun and the object pronoun.

'One' is used to make statements about people in general which also apply to yourself.

*One has to think of the practical side of things.*
*Going round Italy, one is struck by the number of opera houses there are.*
*This scene makes one realize how deeply this community has been afflicted.*

Other uses of 'one' as a pronoun are explained in paragraphs 1.157 to 1.160.

# Mentioning possession: possessive pronouns

**1.110** When you are talking about people or things, you often want to say in what way they are connected with each other. There are several different ways in which you can do this, but you most often do it by using a **possessive pronoun** to indicate that something belongs to someone or is associated with them.

**1.111** Here is a table showing possessive pronouns:

|  | singular | plural |
|---|---|---|
| 1st person | mine | ours |
| 2nd person | yours | |
| 3rd person | his<br>hers | theirs |

Note that 'its' cannot be used as a possessive pronoun.

**typical use**     **1.112** You use possessive pronouns when you are talking about the same type of thing that has just been mentioned but want to indicate that it belongs to someone else.

For example, in the sentence 'Jane showed them her passport, then Richard showed them his', 'his' refers to a passport and indicates that it belongs to Richard.

Possessive pronouns are often used to contrast two things of the same type which belong to or are associated with different people. For example, 'Sarah's house is much bigger than ours'.

*Her parents were in Malaya, and so were mine.*
*He grinned at her and laid his hand on hers.*
*Is that coffee yours or mine?*
*My marks were higher than his.*
*Fred gambled his profits away while Julia spent hers all on dresses.*
*...the difference between his ideas and ours.*
*It was his fault, not theirs.*

**used with 'of'**     **1.113** Possessive pronouns can be used in prepositional phrases beginning with 'of' to qualify a noun group. This structure suggests that you are talking about one of a group of things.

For example, if you say 'a friend of mine' you are talking about one of a number of friends whereas if you say 'my friend' you are talking about one friend in particular.

*He was an old friend of mine.*
*A student of yours has just been to see me.*

*David Lodge? I've just read a novel of his.*
*It was hinted to him by some friends of hers.*
*The room was not a favourite of theirs.*

**1.114** For other ways of indicating that something belongs to someone or is associated with them, see paragraphs 2.180 to 2.192.

# Referring back to the subject: reflexive pronouns

**1.115** When you want to show that the object or indirect object of a verb is the same person or thing as the subject of the verb, you use a **reflexive pronoun**.

Some verbs are very frequently used with reflexive pronouns. For information about these, see paragraphs 3.27 to 3.32.

Here is a table of reflexive pronouns:

|  | singular | plural |
|---|---|---|
| 1st person | myself | ourselves |
| 2nd person | yourself | yourselves |
| 3rd person | himself<br>herself<br>itself | themselves |

**WARNING**

**1.116** Unlike personal pronouns and possessive pronouns, there are two forms of the reflexive pronoun used for the second person. You use 'yourself' when you are talking to one person. You use 'yourselves' when you are talking to more than one person, or referring to a group which includes the person you are talking to.

**used as object**

**1.117** You can use a reflexive pronoun to make it clear that the object of a verb is the same person or thing as the subject of the verb, or to emphasize this.

For example, 'John killed himself' means that John did the killing, and he was also the person who was killed.

*He forced himself to lie absolutely still.*
*She stretched herself out flat on the sofa.*
*I'm sure history repeats itself.*
*All of us shook hands and introduced ourselves.*
*The men formed themselves into a line facing the boys.*
*...the questions you had to ask yourselves.*

You can also use reflexive pronouns to indicate or emphasize that the indirect object of a verb is the same person or thing as the subject of the verb. For example, in the sentence 'Ann poured herself a drink', Ann did the pouring and she was also the person who the drink was for.

*Here's the money, you can go and buy yourself a watch.*

**WARNING**

**1.118** Reflexive pronouns are not usually used with actions that people normally do to themselves, such as washing, dressing, or shaving. So you do not usually say 'He shaves himself every morning'.

You can, however, sometimes use reflexive pronouns with these actions for emphasis, or to indicate a surprising event, such as a child or invalid doing something that they were not previously able to do.

**used as objects of prepositions**

**1.119** If the subject of a clause and the object of a preposition refer to the same person and the clause does not have a direct object, you use a reflexive pronoun after the preposition.

*I was thoroughly ashamed of myself.*
*Barbara stared at herself in the mirror.*
*We think of ourselves as members of the local community.*
*They can't cook for themselves.*

However, if the clause does have a direct object, you usually use a personal pronoun after the preposition.

*I will take it home with me.*
*They put the book between them on the kitchen table.*
*I shivered and drew the rug around me.*
*Mrs Bixby went out, slamming the door behind her.*

Note that if the clause has a direct object and it is not obvious that the subject of the clause and the object of the preposition refer to the same person, you use a reflexive pronoun. For example, 'The Managing Director gave the biggest pay rise to himself'.

**used for emphasis or contrast**

**1.120** Especially in speech, people sometimes use reflexive pronouns rather than personal pronouns as the object of a preposition, in order to emphasize them.

*...people like myself who are politically active.*
*...the following conversation between myself and a fifteen-year-old girl.*
*The circle spread to include himself and Ferdinand.*
*People like yourself still find new things to say about Shakespeare.*
*There is always someone worse off than yourself.*
*With the exception of a few Algerians and ourselves everyone spoke Spanish.*

**1.121** You can use reflexive pronouns in addition to nouns or personal pronouns. You usually do this in order to make it clear or to emphasize who or what you are referring to.

*I myself sometimes say things I don't mean.*
*Sally herself came back.*

You can also use a reflexive pronoun to compare or contrast one person or thing with another.

*His friend looked as miserable as he felt himself.*
*It is not Liverpool I miss, but England itself.*

The reflexive pronoun can follow the noun or pronoun that it relates to.

*Sally herself came back.*
*It is hot in London; but I myself can work better when it's hot.*
*The town itself was so small that it didn't have a priest.*
*The lane ran right up to the wood itself.*

It can also be placed at the end of the clause.

*I am not a particularly punctual person myself.*
*You'll probably understand better when you are a grandparent yourself.*
*It is rare for Governments to take the initiative themselves.*

**1.122** You can use a reflexive pronoun to emphasize that someone did something without any help or interference from anyone else. In this use, the reflexive pronoun is normally placed at the end of the clause.

*She had printed the card herself.*
*I'll take it down to the police station myself.*
*Did you make these yourself?*

# Referring to a particular person or thing: demonstrative pronouns

**1.123** When 'this', 'that', 'these', and 'those' are used as pronouns, they are called **demonstrative pronouns**. They can be used as the subject or the object of a clause, or the object of a preposition.

Demonstrative pronouns are rarely used as the indirect object of a clause, because the indirect object is usually a person and demonstrative pronouns normally refer to things.

**'this' and 'that'**

**1.124** 'This' and 'that' are usually used as pronouns only when they refer to things. You use them instead of a singular count noun or an uncount noun.

*This is a list of the rules.*
*This is the most important part of the job.*
*The biggest problem was the accent. That was difficult for me.*
*That looks interesting.*

**1.125** 'This' and 'that' can be used as pronouns to refer to a person when you are identifying someone or asking who they are.

*Who's this?*
*He paused at a photograph which stood on the dressing table. 'Is this your wife?'*
*Was that Patrick on the phone?*

When you are introducing people, you can say 'This is Mary' or 'This is Mr and Mrs Baker'. Note that you use 'this' even when you are introducing more than one person.

**'these' and 'those'**

**1.126** 'These' and 'those' can be used as pronouns instead of a plural count noun. They are most often used to refer to things, although they can be used to refer to people.

*'I brought you these.' Adam held out a bag of grapes.*
*Vitamin tablets usually contain vitamins A, C, and D. These are available from any child health clinic.*
*These are no ordinary students.*
*It may be impossible for them to pay essential bills, such as those for heating.*
*Those are easy questions to answer.*
*There are a great number of people who are seeking employment, and a great number of those are married women.*

'This', 'that', 'these', and 'those' can also be **specific determiners**. For more information, see paragraphs 1.182 to 1.191. See also **cohesion** in Chapter 9.

# Referring to people and things in a general way: indefinite pronouns

**1.127** When you want to refer to people or things but you do not know exactly who or what they are, or their identity is not important, you can use an **indefinite pronoun**. An indefinite pronoun indicates only whether you are talking about people or about things, rather than referring to a specific person or thing.

*I was there for over an hour before anybody came.*
*Jack was waiting for something.*

Here is a list of indefinite pronouns:

| | | | |
|---|---|---|---|
| anybody | everybody | nobody | somebody |
| anyone | everyone | no one | someone |
| anything | everything | nothing | something |

Note that all indefinite pronouns are written as one word except 'no one' which can also be spelled with a hyphen: 'no-one'.

**used only with singular verbs**

**1.128** You always use singular verbs with indefinite pronouns.

*Is anyone here?*
*Everybody recognizes the importance of education.*
*Everything was ready.*
*Nothing is certain in this world.*

**referring to things**

**1.129** You use the indefinite pronouns ending in '-thing' to refer to objects, ideas, situations, or activities.

*Can I do anything?*
*Jane said nothing for a moment.*

**referring to people**

**1.130** You use the indefinite pronouns ending in '-one' and '-body' to refer to people.

*It had to be someone like Dan.*
*Why does everybody believe in the law of gravity?*

**used with personal pronouns**

**1.131** Although you use singular verbs with indefinite pronouns, if you want to use a pronoun to refer back to an indefinite pronoun, you use the plural pronouns 'they', 'them', 'their', or 'themselves'.

*Ask anyone. They'll tell you.*
*There's no way of telling somebody why they've failed.*
*Everyone put their pens down.*
*No one liked being young then as they do now.*
*Everybody's enjoying themselves.*

See paragraph 1.108 for more information about 'they' used to refer to one person.

**USAGE NOTE**

**1.132** In more formal English, some people prefer to use 'he', 'him' or 'himself' to refer back to an indefinite pronoun, but many people object to this use because it suggests that the person being referred to is male.

*Somebody shouted and other voices joined him.*
*Everybody has his dream.*
*Everybody determines his own rates.*

For other ways of using pronouns when you do not want to specify whether the person you are talking about is male or female, see paragraph 1.108.

**'s**

**1.133** You can add 's (apostrophe s) to an indefinite pronoun to refer to things that belong to or are associated with people.

*She was given a room in someone's studio.*
*That was nobody's business.*

*I would defend anyone's rights.*
*Everything has been arranged to everybody's satisfaction.*

**WARNING**

**1.134** You do not usually add 's to indefinite pronouns referring to things. So, for example, you would be more likely to say 'the value of something' than 'something's value'.

**qualifiers**

**1.135** When you want to give more information about the person or thing referred to by an indefinite pronoun, you can do so by using a **qualifier**, for example a prepositional phrase or a relative clause.

*Anyone over the age of 18 can apply.*
*He would much rather have somebody who had a background in the humanities.*

For more information about qualifiers, see paragraphs 2.289 to 2.320.

**use of adjectives**

**1.136** You can also use adjectives to add information. Note that adjectives are placed after the indefinite pronoun rather than in front of it, and that you do not use a determiner. You do not say 'an important someone', you say 'someone important'.

*What was needed was someone practical.*
*They are doing everything possible to take care of you.*
*There is nothing wrong with being popular.*

**used with 'else'**

**1.137** If you have already mentioned a person or thing and you want to refer to a different person or thing, or an additional one, you can use 'else' after an indefinite pronoun.

*Somebody else will have to go out there.*
*She couldn't think of anything else.*
*Everyone knows what everyone else is doing.*
*He held his job because nobody else wanted it.*

Note that if you want to indicate association or possession with an indefinite pronoun and 'else', you add the 's to 'else'.

*Problems always became someone else's fault.*
*No one has control over anyone else's career.*

**structures used with 'some-' and 'every-'**

**1.138** Like all noun groups, indefinite pronouns are used as the subject, object, or indirect object of clauses. They can also be used as the objects of prepositions. The indefinite pronouns beginning with 'some-' and 'every-' are most often used in affirmative clauses.

*Everything went according to plan.*
*I remember somebody putting a pillow under my head.*
*'Now you'll see something,' he said.*
*I gave everyone a generous helping.*
*I want to introduce you to someone who is helping me.*
*Have you seen Frank? Is everything all right?*

They are sometimes used as the subject of a negative clause.

*He could tell that something wasn't right.*
*Everyone hadn't arrived yet.*

Note that the indefinite pronouns beginning with 'some-' cannot be used as the object of a negative clause, unless they are followed by a qualifier, usually a prepositional phrase or a relative clause.

*He wasn't someone I admired as a writer.*
*I wouldn't forget something that I finished reading only half an hour ago.*

**structures used with 'any-'** 1.139 Indefinite pronouns beginning with 'any-' can be used as the object or indirect object of a question or a negative clause.

*Don't worry – I won't tell anyone.*
*You still haven't told me anything.*
*Take a good look and tell me if you see anything different.*
*I haven't given anyone their presents yet.*

They are often used as the subject of both negative and affirmative questions. Note that they are not used as the subject of a negative statement. That is, you do not say 'Anybody can't come in'.

*Does anybody agree with me?*
*Won't anyone help me?*
*If anything unusual happens, could you call me on this number?*

Note that when you are making an affirmative statement, 'anyone' and 'anybody' are used to refer to people in general and not to only one person.

*Anybody who wants to can come in and buy a car from me.*

**structures used with 'no-'** 1.140 Indefinite pronouns beginning with 'no-' are always used with the affirmative form of a verb, and they make the clause negative. For more information on negative statements, see paragraphs 4.43 to 4.94.

*Nobody said a word.*
*There was nothing you could do, nothing at all.*
*She was to see no one, to speak to nobody, not even her own children.*

Note that they are sometimes used in questions. When this is the case, the answer to the question is usually expected to be 'no'.

*'Is there nothing I can do?' 'Not a thing'.*
*'Is there nobody else?' 'Not that I know of'.*

# Showing that two people do the same thing: reciprocal pronouns

1.141 The **reciprocal pronouns** 'each other' and 'one another' are used to indicate that people do the same thing, feel the same way, or have the same relationship.

For example, if your brother hates your sister and your sister hates your brother, you can say 'My brother and sister hate each other' or 'They hate one another'.

Reciprocal pronouns are not used as the subject of a clause. You can use them as the object or indirect object of a verb.

*We help each other a lot.*
*You and I understand each other.*
*We support one another through good times and bad.*
*They sent each other gifts from time to time.*

You can also use them as the object of a preposition.

*Terry and Mark were jealous of each other.*
*...two lights moving towards one another.*
*They didn't dare to look at one another.*

Some verbs are very commonly used with reciprocal pronouns. For more information about these, see paragraphs 3.69 to 3.73.

**1.142** Note that there is very little difference between 'each other' and 'one another'. They can both be used to refer to two or more people or things, although some people prefer the use of 'each other' when there are only two people or things, and 'one another' when there are more than two.

**'each'**
**as subject**

**1.143** In formal written English, you can also use 'each' as the subject of a clause and 'the other' as the object of a clause or preposition. So a more formal way of saying 'They looked at each other' is 'Each looked at the other'. Note that 'each' is always followed by a singular verb.

*Each accuses the other of dirty tricks.*
*Each appears to be unwilling to learn from the experience of the others.*

'Each' can also be a determiner. For more information about this, see paragraph 1.228.

**'s**

**1.144** You can add 's (apostrophe s) to 'each other', 'one another', and 'the other' to form possessives.

*I hope that you all enjoy each other's company.*
*Apes spend a great deal of time grooming one another's fur.*
*The male shelducks fight fiercely, each trying to seize the other's long neck in its beak.*

## Joining clauses together: relative pronouns

**1.145** When a sentence consists of a main clause followed by a **relative clause** introduced by 'who', 'whom', 'which', or 'that', these words are known as **relative pronouns**.

Relative pronouns do two things at the same time. Like other pronouns, they refer to somebody or something that has already been mentioned. At the same time they are **conjunctions**, because they join clauses together.

For more information about conjunctions, see Chapter 8.
For more information about relative clauses, see paragraphs 8.83 to 8.116.

**'who' and**
**'whom'**

**1.146** 'Who' and 'whom' always refer to people.

'Who' can be the subject of a relative clause.

*...mathematicians who are concerned with very difficult problems.*
*...a man who I met recently.*

In the past, 'whom' was normally used as the object of a relative clause. Nowadays, 'who' is more often used, although some careful speakers of English think that it is more correct to use 'whom'.

*Who's that man over there who looks like President Bush?*
*He's the man who I saw last night.*
*...two girls whom I met in Edinburgh.*

'Who' is sometimes used as the object of a preposition when the object is separated from the preposition. Some careful speakers think that it is more correct to use 'whom'.

*That's the man who I gave it to.*
*...those whom we cannot talk to.*

'Whom' is almost always used when the object comes immediately after the preposition.

*...Lord Scarman, a man for whom I have immense respect.*

'which'     **1.147** 'Which' always refers to things. It can be used as the subject or object of a relative clause, or as the object of a preposition.

*...a region which was threatened by growing poverty.*
*...two horses which he owned.*
*...the house in which I was born.*

Note that 'which' cannot be used as the indirect object of a clause.

'that'      **1.148** 'That' can refer to either people or things. It can be used as the subject or the object of a relative clause or the object of a preposition.

*...the games that politicians play.*
*He's the boy that sang the solo last night.*
*It was the first bed that she had ever slept in.*

'That' cannot be used as the indirect object of a clause.

'whose'     **1.149** 'Whose' shows who or what something belongs to or is connected with. Note that it cannot be used by itself, but must come in front of a noun.

'Whose' is often included with relative pronouns, although it is in fact a kind of possessive determiner. For more information on determiners, see paragraphs 1.161 to 1.235.

*...the thousands whose lives have been damaged.*
*There was a chap there whose name I've forgotten.*
*...predictions whose accuracy will have to be confirmed.*
*...sharks, whose brains are minute.*

## Asking questions: interrogative pronouns

**1.150** One way of asking questions is by using an **interrogative pronoun.**

The interrogative pronouns are 'who', 'whose', 'whom', 'what', and 'which'. They can be used as the subject or object of a clause, or as the object of a preposition. 'Whose' and 'which' can also be determiners. Other words, such as 'where', 'when', 'why', and 'how', can also be used to ask questions.

Interrogative pronouns are not used as the indirect object of a clause.

*Who was at the door?*
*'There's a car outside.' 'Whose is it?'*
*Whom will this cottage appeal to?*
*What are you doing?*
*Which is best, gas or electric?*

For more information about structures in which interrogative pronouns are used, see paragraphs 4.10 to 4.30.

**1.151** Interrogative pronouns refer to the information you are asking for.

'Who', 'whose', and 'whom' are used when you think that the answer to the question will be a person.

*'He lost his wife.' 'Who? Terry?'*
*He looked at the cat. 'Whose is it? Have you ever seen it before?'*

*'To whom, if I may ask, are you engaged to be married?' 'To Daniel Orton.'*

'Which' and 'what' are used when you think that the answer to the question will be something other than a person.

*'Is there really a difference? Which do you prefer?'*
*'What did he want?' 'Maurice's address.'*

**reported**
**questions**

**1.152** Interrogative pronouns are also used to introduce reported questions.

*I asked her who she had been talking to.*
*He wondered what Daintry would do now.*

For more information about reported questions, see paragraphs 7.29 to 7.35.

# Other pronouns

**1.153** Many other words can be pronouns, provided that it is clear what is being talked about, because it is then unnecessary to repeat the headword.

For example, most **general determiners** can also be pronouns. For more information about general determiners, see paragraphs 1.208 to 1.235.

Here is a list of general determiners which are also pronouns:

| | | | | |
|---|---|---|---|---|
| all | each | fewer | more | several |
| another | either | less | most | some |
| any | enough | little | much | |
| both | few | many | neither | |

Like all noun groups, they can be used as the subject, direct object, or indirect object of a clause, or the object of a preposition.

*Both were offered jobs immediately.*
*Children? I don't think she has any.*
*I saw one girl whispering to another.*

**1.154** Although 'a', 'an', 'every', and 'no' are general determiners, they cannot stand alone as pronouns.

To refer back to a noun group which includes the determiner 'a' or 'an', you can use the pronoun 'one'. Similarly, you use 'each' to refer back to a noun group which includes 'every', and 'none' to refer back to a noun group which includes 'no'.

Note that 'another' and 'others' are pronouns, but 'other' cannot be a pronoun.

**'all', 'both',**
**and 'each'**
**for emphasis**

**1.155** 'All', 'both', and 'each' can be used in addition to nouns or personal pronouns for emphasis, in a similar way to the use of **reflexive pronouns** described in paragraphs 1.120 to 1.122.

*The brothers all agreed that something more was needed.*
*He loved them both.*
*Ford and Duncan each had their chances.*

They can also come after main verbs, an auxiliary verb, a modal, or 'be', rather than directly after the noun or pronoun.

*They were both still working at their universities.*
*The letters have all been signed.*
*The older children can all do the same things together.*

'Each' can also come at the end of the clause.

*Three others were fined £200 each.*

**numbers**   **1.156  Cardinal numbers** can also be pronouns. For example, the answer to the question 'How many children do you have?' is usually 'Three' rather than 'Three children'.

*'How many people are there?'—'Forty five.'*
*Of the other women, two are dancers.*
*They bought eight companies and sold off five.*

For more information on cardinal numbers, see paragraphs 2.230 to 2.248.

**other**   **1.157**  The number 'one' is a special case. Like other cardinal numbers, it
**pronouns**   can be used to refer to one of a group of things.

'One' is also used to refer back to a noun group with the determiner 'a'.

*Could I have a bigger one, please?*

It can also be used for emphasis after another determiner.

*There are systems of communication right through the animal world; each one is distinctive.*

'One' can be used as a **personal pronoun.** This use is explained in paragraph 1.109.

**1.158**  Note that 'the one' and 'the ones' can be used to refer to a noun alone, rather than to the whole of the noun group. They are nearly always used with a modifier such as an adjective, or a qualifier such as a prepositional phrase.

*'Which poem?' 'The one they were talking about yesterday.'*
*There are three bedrooms. Mine is the one at the back.*
*He gave the best seats to the ones who arrived first.*

**1.159**  You use 'the other', 'the others', 'others', or 'another' to refer to different members of a group of things or people.

*Some writers are greater than others.*
*One runner was way ahead of all the others.*

**1.160**  If you want to say something about a member of a group of people or things you can use 'one'. You can then refer to the rest of the group as 'the others'.

*The bells are carefully installed so that disconnecting one will have no effect on the others.*
*They had three little daughters, one a baby, the others twins of twelve.*

You can use 'the one' and 'the other' to refer to each of a pair of things.

*The same factors push wages and prices up together, the one reinforcing the other.*

If you do not wish to specify exactly which of a group you are talking about, you can refer to 'one or other' of them.

*It may be that one or other of them had fears for their health.*

# Identifying what you are talking about: determiners

**1.161**  In English, there are two main ways in which you can use a **noun group.** You can use it to refer to someone or something, knowing that the person you are speaking to understands which person or thing you are talking about. This can be called the **specific** way of referring to someone or something.

*The man began to run towards the boy.*
*Young people don't like these operas.*
*Thank you very much for your comments.*
*...a visit to the Houses of Parliament.*

Alternatively, you can use a noun group to refer to someone or something of a particular type, without saying which person or thing you mean. This can be called the **general** way of referring to someone or something.

*There was a man in the lift.*
*I wish I'd bought an umbrella.*
*Any doctor would say she didn't know what she was doing.*

In order to distinguish between these two ways of using a noun group, you use a special class of words called **determiners**. There are two types of determiner, **specific determiners** and **general determiners**. You put them at the beginning of a noun group.

# The specific way: using 'the'

**1.162** 'The' is the commonest specific determiner; it is sometimes called the **definite article**.

'This', 'that', 'these', and 'those' are often called **demonstratives** or **demonstrative adjectives**. For more information on these, see paragraphs 1.182 to 1.191.

'My', 'your', 'his', 'her', 'its', 'our' and 'their' are **possessive determiners**. They are also sometimes called **possessive adjectives** or just **possessives**. For more information about these, see paragraphs 1.192 to 1.207.

Here is the list of specific determiners:

| the | that | ~ | his | our |
|-----|------|-----|-----|-------|
| ~ | these | my | her | their |
| this | those | your | its | |

Note that in English you cannot use more than one specific determiner before a noun.

**1.163** Because 'the' is the commonest specific determiner, you can put 'the' in front of any common noun.

*She dropped the can into the grass.*
*The girls were not in the house.*

In these examples, the use of 'the can' means that a can has already been mentioned; 'the grass' is probably definite because it has already been stated that 'she' is outside, and the presence of grass may also have been stated or is presumed; 'the girls', like 'the can', must have been mentioned before, and 'the house' means the one where the girls were staying at the time.

**pronouncing 'the'** **1.164** 'The' always has the same spelling, but it has three different pronunciations:

- /ðə/ when the following word begins with a consonant sound.

43

...*the dictionary...the first act...the big box.*

● /ðɪ/ when the following word begins with a vowel sound.

...*the exhibition...the effect...the impression.*

● /ði:/ when it is emphasized.

*You don't mean the Ernest Hemingway?*

See paragraph 1.179 for more information about emphatic uses of 'the'.

**'the' with
a noun**

**1.165** You can use a noun group consisting just of 'the' and a noun when you are referring to a specific person or thing, or to a specific group of people or things, and you know that the person you are talking or writing to will understand which person, thing, or group you are referring to.

*The expedition sailed out into the Pacific.*
...*the most obnoxious boy in the school.*
*He stopped the car in front of the bakery.*

**nouns
referring to
one thing
only**

**1.166** Some nouns are normally used with 'the' because they refer to only one person, thing, or group. Some of these are specific names or **proper nouns,** for example titles such as 'the Pope', unique things such as 'the Bastille', and place names such as 'the Atlantic'.

...*a concert attended by the Queen.*
*We went on camel rides to the Pyramids.*

See paragraphs 1.53 to 1.59 for more information about proper nouns.

Some are **singular nouns,** that is they refer to something of which there is only one in the world, such as 'the ground', or 'the moon'.

*The sun began to turn crimson.*
*In April and May the wind blows steadily.*

See paragraphs 1.35 to 1.41 for more information about singular nouns.

**specific
places and
organizations**

**1.167** Other nouns are used to refer to just one person, thing, or group in a particular place or organization, so that if you are talking about that place or organization or talking to someone in it, you can use just 'the' and the noun.

For example, if there is only one station in a town, the people who live in the town will talk about 'the station'. Similarly, people living in Britain talk to each other about 'the economy', meaning 'the British economy', and people working for the same organization might talk about 'the boss', 'the union', or 'the canteen' without needing to specify the organization.

*Mrs Robertson heard that the church had been bombed.*
*There's a wind coming off the river.*
*We've had to get rid of the director.*
*The mayor is a forty-eight-year-old former labourer.*
*What is the President doing about all this?*

**generalizing**

**1.168** Another group of nouns which can be used with just 'the' are nouns which are normally **count nouns** but which are used in the singular to refer to something more general.

For example, you can use 'the theatre' or 'the stage' to refer to all entertainment performed in theatres. Similarly, 'the screen' refers to films in general, and 'the law' refers to the system of laws in a country.

*For him, the stage was just a way of earning a living.*

*He was as dashing in real life as he was on the screen.*
*They do not hesitate to break the law.*

Some nouns which normally refer to an individual thing or person can be used in the singular with 'the' to refer generally to a system or service in a particular place. For example, you can use 'the bus' to refer to a bus service and 'the phone' to refer to a telephone system.

*How long does it take on the train?*
*We rang for the ambulance.*

Nouns referring to musical instruments can be used in the singular with 'the' when you are talking about someone's ability to play a particular kind of instrument.

*'You play the oboe, I see,' said Simon.*
*Geoff plays the piano for hours.*

**formal**
**generalizations** **1.169** Nouns referring to living things can be used in the singular with 'the' when you are making a statement about every member of a species. For example, if you say 'The swift has long, narrow wings', you mean that all swifts have long, narrow wings.

*The primrose can grow abundantly on chalk banks.*
*Australia is the home of the kangaroo.*

Similarly, a noun referring to a part of the human body can be used with 'the' to refer to that part of anyone's body.

*These arteries supply the heart with blood.*
*...the arteries supplying the kidneys.*

'The' is sometimes used with other nouns in the singular to make a statement about all the members of a group.

*Too often these writings dwell on how to protect the therapist rather than on how to cure the patient.*

These uses are fairly formal. They are not common in ordinary speech. Usually, if you want to make a statement about all the things of a particular kind, you use the plural form of a noun without a determiner. See paragraph 1.212 for more information about this.

**USAGE NOTE** **1.170** Many common time expressions consist of just 'the' and a noun.

*We wasted a lot of money in the past.*
*The train leaves Cardiff at four in the afternoon.*
*...the changes which are taking place at the moment.*

See Chapter 5 for more information about time expressions.

**referring**
**back** **1.171** In each of the preceding paragraphs showing uses of 'the' and a noun, it is possible to understand who or what is being referred to because the noun group is commonly accepted as referring to one particular person, thing, or group.

However, you can use 'the' with any noun, if it is obvious who or what you are referring to from what has already been said or written. For example, if you have already mentioned that you have seen a mouse, you can say afterwards 'We tried to catch the mouse'.

**1.172** You can also use 'the' and a noun when you are referring to someone or something closely connected with something you have just mentioned.

For example, you do not usually say 'We tried to get into the room, but the

45

door of the room was locked'. You say 'We tried to get into the room, but the door was locked', because it is obvious which door you are referring to.

*She stopped and lit a match. The wind almost blew out <u>the flame.</u>*

**'the' with longer noun groups**

**1.173** Although there are many situations where you use just 'the' and a noun, there are other occasions when you need to add something else to the noun in order to make it clear which person, thing, or group you are referring to.

**adding modifiers**

**1.174** Sometimes you can indicate who or what you are referring to by putting a **modifier** between 'the' and the noun. The commonest type of modifiers are **adjectives.**

*This is <u>the main bedroom.</u>*
*'Somebody ought to have done it long ago,' remarked <u>the fat man.</u>*

Sometimes you need to use more than one adjective.

*After the crossroads look out for <u>the large white building.</u>*

For more information about modifiers, see Chapter 2. For more information about adjectives, see paragraphs 2.2 to 2.173.

**modifiers: specifying or expanding**

**1.175** When you use a modifier between 'the' and a noun, you do not always do it in order to make clear who or what is being referred to. There are two other reasons why you might use a modifier.

Firstly, if you have already referred to someone or something using a modifier, you sometimes continue to use the modifier when referring to them again. For example, if you first refer to a car as 'a yellow car', you may continue to refer to it as 'the yellow car', even though no other cars are involved in what you are saying or writing.

Secondly, you might want to add further information about someone or something that you have already mentioned. For example, if you first refer to someone as 'a woman' in a sentence such as 'A woman came into the room', you might later want to refer to her as 'the unfortunate woman' or 'the smiling woman'.

This is a very common use in written English, especially in stories, but it is not often used in conversation.

*<u>The astonished waiter</u> was now watching from the other end of the room.*
*<u>The poor woman</u> had witnessed terrible violence.*
*The loss of pressure caused <u>the speeding car</u> to go into a skid.*

**adding qualifiers**

**1.176** Another way of indicating who or what you are referring to is by adding a **qualifier** after 'the' and a noun, for example a prepositional phrase, a relative clause, a 'to'-infinitive, an adverb of place or time, or a phrase introduced by a participle.

So you might refer to particular people at a party by using noun groups such as 'the girl in the yellow dress', 'the woman who spilled her drink', or 'the man smoking a cigar'.

*<u>The cars in the driveways</u> were all Ferraris and Porsches.*
*<u>The book that I recommend</u> now costs over three pounds.*
*<u>The thing to aim for</u> is an office of your own.*
*Who made the bed in <u>the room upstairs?</u>*
*It depends on <u>the person being interviewed.</u>*

For more information about qualifiers, see paragraphs 2.289 to 2.320.

| 'the' with uncount nouns | **1.177** You do not normally use 'the' with **uncount nouns** because they refer to something in a general way. However, 'the' is required if the uncount noun is followed by a qualifier which relates it to a particular person, thing, or group. |
|---|---|

For example, you cannot say 'I am interested in education of young children'. You have to say 'I am interested in the education of young children'.

*Babies need the comfort of their mother's arms.*
*Even the honesty of Inspector Butler was in doubt.*
*I've no idea about the geography of Scotland.*

For more information about uncount nouns, see paragraphs 1.24 to 1.34.

| superlatives | **1.178** 'The' is also used with **superlative adjectives.** |
|---|---|

*I'm not the best cook in the world.*
*They went to the most expensive restaurant in town.*

See paragraphs 2.117 to 2.127 for more information about superlative adjectives.

| emphasizing 'the' | **1.179** 'The' is often used in front of a noun to indicate that someone or something is the best of its kind. |
|---|---|

*New Zealand is now the place to visit.*

You can also use 'the' in front of a person's name to indicate that you are referring to the most famous person with that name.

*You actually met the George Harrison?*

When you use 'the' in either of these ways, you emphasize it and pronounce it /ði:/.

| 'the' with general determiners | **1.180** 'The' can be used in front of some **general determiners**, usually to give an indication of amount or quantity. The general determiners function as headwords in the noun group and can be modified or qualified. |
|---|---|

The general determiners which can be headwords are:

| | | | |
|---|---|---|---|
| few | little | many | other |

*...pleasures known only to the few.*
*...a coup under the leadership of the select few.*
*He was one of the few who knew where to find me.*
*We have done the little that is in our power.*

You use 'the' with 'other' to refer to the second of two things, when you have just mentioned one of them.

*The men sat at one end of the table and the women at the other.*

For more information about general determiners, see paragraphs 1.213 to 1.235.

| 'the' with numbers | **1.181** 'The' can also be used with the 'one' and 'ones', which then function as headwords and are usually modified or qualified. |
|---|---|

*I'm going to have the green one.*
*The shop was different from the ones I remembered.*
*...a pair of those old glasses, the ones with those funny square lenses.*

'The' can also be used with other **numbers.**

*It is a mistake to confuse the two.*
*Why is she so different from the other two?*

See paragraphs 2.225 to 2.256 for more information about numbers.

# The specific way: using 'this', 'that', 'these', and 'those'

**1.182** You use the specific determiners 'this', 'that', 'these', and 'those' to refer to people or things in a definite way.

You use 'this' and 'these' to talk about people and things that are close to you in place or time. When you talk about people or things that are more distant in place or time, you use 'that' and 'those'.

You put 'this' and 'that' in front of singular nouns, uncount nouns, and the singular pronoun 'one'. You put 'these' and 'those' in front of plural nouns and the plural pronoun 'ones'.

'This', 'that', 'these', and 'those' are often called **demonstratives** or **demonstrative adjectives.**

**'this' and 'these'** **1.183** 'This' and 'these' are used to talk about people or things that are very obvious in the situation that you are in. You use 'this' and 'these' to distinguish these people or things from others of the same kind. For example, if you are inside a house, you can refer to it as 'this house'. If you are holding some keys in your hand, you can refer to them as 'these keys'. If you are at a party, you can refer to it as 'this party'.

*I have lived in this house my entire life.*
*I am going to walk up these steps towards you.*
*I'll come as soon as these men have finished their work.*
*I like this university.*
*Good evening. In this programme we are going to look at the way in which British music has developed in recent years.*

When it is clear who or what you are referring to, you can use 'this' and 'these' as **pronouns.** This use is explained in paragraphs 1.123 to 1.126.

**1.184** 'This' and 'these' are also used in many expressions which refer to current periods of time, for example 'this month', 'this week', and 'these days'. This use is explained in Chapter 5.

**'that' and 'those'** **1.185** You use 'that' and 'those' when you are talking about things or people that you can see but that are not close to you.

*How much is it for that big box?*
*Can I have one of those brochures?*
*Can you move those books off there?*

**1.186** When it is clear who or what you are referring to, you can use 'that' and 'those' as **pronouns.** This use is explained in paragraphs 1.123 to 1.126.

*Could you just hold that?*
*Please don't take those.*

**USAGE NOTE** **1.187** You can indicate that you are referring to the same person or thing you have just mentioned by using 'this', 'that', 'these', or 'those' in front of a noun. For example, if you have just mentioned a girl, you can refer to her as 'this girl' or 'that girl' the second time you mention her. Normally, you use a **pronoun** to refer to someone or something you have just mentioned, but sometimes you cannot do this because it might not be clear who or what the pronoun refers to.

*Students and staff suggest books for the library, and normally we're quite happy to get those books.*
*Their house is in a valley. The people in that valley speak about the people in the next valley as 'foreigners'.*
*They had a lot of diamonds, and they asked her if she could possibly get these diamonds to Britain.*

The use of demonstratives to refer again to something which has already been mentioned is fully explained in paragraphs 9.7 to 9.10.

**1.188** In informal English, you can also use 'that' and 'those' in front of a noun to refer to people or things that are already known to the person you are speaking or writing to.

*That idiot Antonio has gone and locked our cabin door.*
*Have they found those missing children yet?*
*Do you remember that funny little attic apartment?*

**1.189** You can use 'that' in front of a noun when you are referring to something that has just happened or to something that you have just been involved with.

*I knew that meeting would be difficult.*

'That' is often used as a **pronoun** to refer to something that has just happened. This use is explained in paragraphs 1.123 to 1.126.

**using 'those' instead of 'the'** **1.190** In more formal English, 'those' can be used instead of 'the' in front of a plural noun when the plural noun is followed by a **relative clause**. In this use, the relative clause specifies exactly which group of people or things are being referred to.

*...those workers who are employed in large enterprises.*
*The parents are not afraid to be firm about those matters that seem important to them.*

**informal use of 'this' and 'these'** **1.191** In informal spoken English, people sometimes use 'this' and 'these' in front of nouns even when they are mentioning someone or something for the first time.

*And then this woman came up to me and she said, 'I believe you have a goddaughter called Celia Ravenscroft.'*
*At school we had to wear these awful white cotton hats.*

# The specific way: using possessive determiners

**1.192** You often want to indicate that a thing belongs to someone or that it is connected in some way with someone.

One way of doing this is to use a word like 'my', 'your', and 'their', which tells you who something belongs to. These words are a type of determiner called **possessive determiners**.

*Are your children bilingual?*
*I remember his name now.*
*They would be welcome to use our library.*
*I'd been waiting a long time to park my car.*

| table of possessive determiners | **1.193** There are seven possessive determiners in English, and each one is associated with a particular **personal pronoun:** |

|            | singular        | plural |
|------------|-----------------|--------|
| 1st person | my              | our    |
| 2nd person | your            |        |
| 3rd person | his<br>her<br>its | their |

Personal pronouns are explained in paragraphs 1.96 to 1.109.

**WARNING** **1.194** You do not spell the possessive 'its' with an apostrophe. 'It's' is short for 'it is'.

**position** **1.195** Possessive determiners, like other determiners, come after a **predeterminer,** if there is one, and before any numbers, or adjectives.

...all *his* letters.
...*their* next message.
...*my* little finger.
...*our* two lifeboats.

See paragraph 1.236 for more information about predeterminers.

**WARNING** **1.196** In English, you do not use more than one specific determiner before a noun. Therefore, possessive determiners must be used on their own. You cannot say 'I took off the my shoes'. You have to choose whether to say 'I took off my shoes', or 'I took off the shoes'.

**agreement with noun** **1.197** You choose which possessive determiner to use according to the identity of the person or thing that owns something. For example, if you want to identify something as belonging or relating to a particular woman, you always use 'her'. The following noun does not affect the choice.

*I* took off *my* shoes.
*Her* husband remained standing. He had *his* hands in his pockets.
*She* had to give up *her* job.
The *group* held *its* first meeting last week.
The *creature* lifted *its* head.
...the two dark *men,* glasses in *their* hands, waiting silently.
...the car *companies* and *their* workers.

**use of 'own'** **1.198** When you want to draw attention to the fact that something belongs or relates to a particular person or thing, you can use the word 'own' after the possessive determiner.

*I helped him to some more whisky but left my own glass untouched.*
*Residents are allowed to bring their own furniture with them if they wish to do so.*
*Make your own decisions.*
*I heard it with my own ears.*
*She felt in charge of her own affairs.*

If you use a number in this structure, you put the number after 'own'.

...*their own three children.*
...the *Doctor's own two rooms.*

**uses of possessives** **1.199** You use possessive determiners in front of nouns which refer to objects and things which can be owned. For example, 'our house' refers to the house which belongs to us.

You can also use possessive determiners in front of many other types of noun. This is because, in spite of their name, possessive determiners do not always indicate that what follows them is actually possessed (or owned) by someone. They can just mean that it is connected or associated with them in some way.

*They then turned their attention to other things.*
*...the vitality of our music and our culture.*
*In summer, hay fever interfered with all her activities.*
*It's his brother who has the workshop.*

**1.200** You can use a possessive determiner in front of a noun which refers to an action in order to indicate who or what is doing the action.

*...not long after our arrival.*
*...his criticism of the Government.*
*...their fight for survival.*
*I'm waiting for your explanation.*
*Most of their claims were worthy.*

In the last example, 'their claims' refers to the claims which they have made.

**1.201** You can also use a possessive determiner to indicate who or what is affected by an action.

*My appointment as the first woman chairman symbolizes change.*
*...the redistribution of wealth, rather than its creation.*
*They expressed their horror at her dismissal.*

In the last example, 'her dismissal' probably refers to the fact that she was dismissed by someone or by some company.

In the first of the following examples, 'his supporters' means the people who support him.

*...Birch and his supporters.*
*She returned the ring to its owner.*
*...a campaign against his critics.*

**USAGE NOTE**    **1.202** Sometimes in English the determiner 'the' is used where there is an obvious possessive meaning. In these cases the possession is already made clear by a preceding noun or pronoun. The following paragraphs explain the situations in which you use 'the' rather than a possessive determiner.

**1.203** When you refer to a specific part of someone's body, you normally use a possessive determiner.

*She has something on her feet and a bag in her hand.*
*Nancy suddenly took my arm.*
*The children wore nothing on their feet.*
*She thanked him shyly and patted his arm.*
*I opened the cupboard and they fell on my head.*
*He shook his head.*

However, when you are describing an action which someone does to a part of someone else's body, you often use the definite article, especially when the body part is the object of a preposition and when the object of the verb is a pronoun. For example, if you say 'She hit me on the head', 'head' is the object of the preposition 'on' and 'me' is the object of the verb 'hit'.

*...so I encouraged him and I <u>patted him on the head.</u>*
*She <u>hit him</u> smartly and swiftly <u>on the head.</u>*
*He <u>took her by the arm</u> and began drawing her firmly but gently away.*

You use the definite article because the 'owner' of the body part has already been identified, and you do not need to repeat this information.

Similarly, if the object of the verb is a **reflexive pronoun** such as 'myself', 'yourself', and so on, you use the definite article. This is because the reflexive pronoun already refers to you or to the person who is doing the action, so you do not need to repeat this information by using a possessive determiner.

*I accidentally <u>hit myself on the head</u> with the brush handle.*
*We can <u>pat ourselves on the back</u> for bringing up our children.*

Uses of reflexive pronouns are explained in paragraphs 1.115 to 1.122.

**1.204** If you want to describe something that you do to yourself or that someone else does to themselves, you normally use a possessive determiner.

*She was brushing <u>her hair.</u>*
*'I'm going to <u>brush my teeth,</u>' he said.*
*She <u>gritted her teeth</u> and carried on.*
*He walked into the kitchen and <u>shook his head.</u>*

**WARNING**

**1.205** You usually use possessive determiners when you refer to things that are alive, such as a person, a group of people, or an animal. You do not usually use them to refer to things that are not alive. It is, for example, more usual to say 'the door' or 'the door of the room' than 'its door'.

**other possessives**

**1.206** There are other ways of indicating that something is owned by or connected with someone or something else. For example, you can use '**s** (apostrophe s) or a prepositional phrase beginning with 'of'.

*<u>Mary's daughter</u> is called Elizabeth.*
*Very often the person appointed has <u>no knowledge of that company's end product.</u>*
*...<u>the house of a rich banker</u> in Paris.*
*In <u>the opinion of the team,</u> what would they consider to be absolutely necessary?*

For more information about the use of 's and 'of', see paragraphs 2.180 to 2.192.

**used in titles**

**1.207** Possessive determiners are also sometimes used in titles such as 'Your Majesty' and 'His Excellency'. This use is explained in paragraph 1.57.

## The general way

**1.208** General determiners are used in noun groups when you are talking about people or things in a general or indefinite way, without identifying them.

Here is a list of general determiners:

| | | | | |
|---|---|---|---|---|
| a | both | few | much | some |
| all | each | little | neither | |
| an | either | many | no | |
| another | enough | more | other | |
| any | every | most | several | |

'A', and 'an' are the commonest general determiners; they are sometimes called the **indefinite article**. For more information about 'a' and 'an', see paragraphs 1.213 to 1.220.

For more information about the other general determiners, see paragraphs 1.221 to 1.235.

**with count nouns**

**1.209** 'A' and 'an' are used with singular count nouns, and indicate that you are talking about just one of something that is countable.

'Another' is used with singular count nouns and 'other' with plural count nouns, but only after one or more of the same type of person or thing has been mentioned.

'Any' can be used with singular and plural count nouns to talk about one or more people or things. 'Enough', 'few', 'many', 'more', 'most', 'several', and 'some' are used with plural count nouns to indicate that a number of people or things are being referred to. Each of these determiners indicates a different set or group within the total number. For more information about their meanings, see the section beginning at paragraph 1.221.

'All', 'both', 'each', 'either', and 'every' indicate that you are talking about the total number of people or things involved. 'Both' and 'either' specify that only two people or things are involved. 'Both' is used with a plural noun, and 'either' with a singular noun. 'All', 'each', and 'every' usually indicate that there are more than two. 'All' is used with plural nouns, and 'each' and 'every' with a singular noun.

'No' and 'neither' also refer to the total number of things involved, but in negative statements. 'No' is used with singular or plural nouns, and 'neither' only with singular nouns. 'No' and 'neither' are not dealt with in detail here, as they are fully treated in the section on **negation** in Chapter 4.

For more information about count nouns, see paragraphs 1.16 to 1.23.

**with uncount nouns**

**1.210** For nouns which are usually regarded as uncountable, 'any', 'enough', 'little', 'more', 'most', 'much', and 'some' are used to indicate a quantity of something. 'No' and 'all' indicate the total quantity of it.

For more information about uncount nouns, see paragraphs 1.24 to 1.34.

**WARNING**

**1.211** 'A', 'an', 'another', 'both', 'each', 'either', 'every', 'few', 'many', 'neither', 'other', and 'several' are not usually used with uncount nouns.

**using nouns without determiners**

**1.212** When you are referring to things or people in an indefinite way, you can sometimes use a noun without a determiner.

...raising _money_ from _industry, government,_ and _trusts._
_Permission_ should be asked before _visitors_ are invited.

**Uncount nouns** are usually used without a determiner.

_Health_ and _education_ are matters that most voters feel strongly about.
_Wealth,_ like _power,_ tends to corrupt.

**Plural nouns** are used without a determiner when you are referring to all the people or things of a particular kind.

_Dogs_ need a regular balanced diet, not just meat.
Are there any jobs that _men_ can do that _women_ can't?

Plural nouns can also be used without a determiner to refer to an unspecified number of things.

*Teachers should read stories to children.*
*Cats and dogs get fleas.*

For more information about plural nouns, see paragraphs 1.42 to 1.47.

# The general way: using 'a' and 'an'

**1.213** 'A' and 'an' are the commonest **general determiners**. They are used to talk about things or people in an indefinite way. You put 'a' or 'an' in front of the singular form of a **count noun**.

*He's bought the children a puppy.*
*He was eating an apple.*
*An old lady was calling to him.*

**choosing**
**'a' or 'an'**

**1.214** You use 'a' when the following word begins with a consonant sound.

*...a piece...a good teacher...a language class.*

This includes some words that begin with a vowel in their written form, because the first sound is a 'y' sound, /j/.

*...a university...a European language.*

You use 'an' when the following word begins with a vowel sound.

*...an example...an art exhibition...an early train.*

This includes some words that begin with the letter 'h' in their written form, because the 'h' is not pronounced.

*...an honest politician...quarter of an hour.*

'A' is usually pronounced /ə/. 'An' is usually pronounced /ən/.

**mentioning**
**things for**
**the first time**

**1.215** You usually use 'a' or 'an' when you are mentioning someone or something for the first time.

*She picked up a book.*
*After weeks of looking, we eventually bought a house.*
*A colleague and I got some money to do research on rats.*

**adding**
**modifiers**
**and**
**qualifiers**

**1.216** You can use a noun group consisting of just 'a' or 'an' and a noun.

*I got a postcard from Susan.*
*The FBI is conducting an investigation.*

At other times, you may want to add **modifiers** or **qualifiers** to the noun group to give more information about the person or thing you are referring to.

*I met a Swedish girl on the train from Copenhagen.*
*I've been reading an interesting article in The Economist.*
*We had to write a story about our parents' childhood.*
*I chose a picture that reminded me of my own country.*

For more information about modifiers and qualifiers, see Chapter 2.

**complements**
**of link verbs**

**1.217** You can also use 'a' or 'an' in a noun group after a **link verb**, as the **complement** of a clause, to give more information about someone or something.

*She is a model and an artist.*
*His father was an alcoholic.*
*Noise was considered a nuisance.*

Sometimes the new information is given by a modifier or a qualifier, rather than by the noun itself.

*His brother was a sensitive child.*
*I met the vicar. He was a worried man.*

For more information about link verbs and complements, see Chapter 3.

**'a' and 'an' with uncount nouns**

**1.218** Although you do not normally use determiners with uncount nouns, you can use 'a' or 'an' with an uncount noun when it is modified or qualified.

*A general education is perhaps more important than an exact knowledge of some particular theory.*
*She had an eagerness for life.*
*Everything went on with a friendliness that was uncommon in such circles.*

**using individuals to generalize**

**1.219** You can use 'a' or 'an' with a noun when you are using one individual person or thing to make a general statement about all people or things of that type. For example, if you say 'A gun must be kept in a safe place', you are talking about an individual gun in order to make a general statement about all guns.

*A computer can only do what you program it to do.*
*A dog likes to eat far more meat than a human being.*
*An unmarried mother was looked down on.*

This is not the usual way of referring to groups. Normally, if you want to make a statement about all the people or things of a particular kind, you use the plural form of a noun without a determiner. See paragraph 1.212 for more information about this.

**nouns referring to one thing only**

**1.220** 'A' and 'an' are sometimes used with **singular nouns** such as 'sun', 'moon', and 'sky' which refer to just one thing. You normally use 'the' with these nouns, but you use 'a' or 'an' when you are drawing attention to some special feature by adding a modifier or qualifier to the noun. This use is particularly common in literature.

*We drove under a gloomy sky.*
*A weak sun shines on the promenade.*

For more information on singular nouns, see paragraphs 1.35 to 1.41.

# The general way: other determiners

**'some'**

**1.221** 'Some' is usually used to indicate that there is a quantity of something or that there are a number of things or people, without being precise. It is therefore used with uncount nouns and plural count nouns.

'Some' is usually used in affirmative statements.

*There is some evidence that the system works.*
*There's some chocolate cake over there.*
*I had some good ideas.*
*Some people expect rapid economic development.*

'Some' can be used in questions, when we expect the answer to be 'yes'.

*Could you give me some examples?*
*Would you like some coffee?*

'Some' is also used to mean quite a large amount or number. For example, in 'I did not meet her again for some years', 'some' means almost the same as 'several' or 'many'.

*You will be unable to restart the car for some time.*
*It took some years for Dan to realize the truth.*

**1.222** You can also use 'some' in front of numbers, in slightly more literary English, to show that you are not being totally accurate.

*I was some fifteen miles by sea from the nearest village.*
*...an animal weighing some five tons.*

**1.223** When you want to emphasize that you do not know the identity of a person or thing, or you think their identity is not important, you can use 'some' with a singular count noun, instead of 'a' or 'an'.

*Most staff members will spend a few weeks in some developing country.*
*Supposing you had some eccentric who came and offered you a thousand pounds.*

**'any'** **1.224** 'Any' is used before plural nouns and uncount nouns when you are referring to a quantity of something which may or may not exist.

*The patients know their rights like any other consumers.*
*Check if you're in any doubt.*
*You can stop at any time you like.*

'Any' is also used in questions asking whether something exists or not. It is also used in negative statements to say that something does not exist.

*Do you have any advice on that?*
*Do you have any vacancies for bar staff?*
*It hasn't made any difference.*
*Nobody in her house knows any English.*
*I rang up to see if there were any tickets left.*

Questions and negative statements are explained further in Chapter 4.

Note that you can use 'any' with singular count nouns to talk about someone or something of a particular type, when you do not want to mention a specific person or thing.

*Any big tin container will do.*
*Cars can be rented at almost any US airport.*

'Any' can also be used as a **pronoun.** See paragraphs 1.94 to 1.160 for more information about pronouns. It is also used in **'if'-clauses.** For more information about these, see Chapter 8.

**'another'** **1.225** 'Another' is used with singular count nouns to talk about an
**and 'other'** additional person or thing of the same type as you have already mentioned.

*Could I have another cup of coffee?*
*He opened another shop last month.*

It can also be used before numbers to talk about more than one additional thing.

*The woman lived for another ten days.*
*Five officials were sacked and another four arrested.*

'Other' is used with plural nouns, or occasionally with uncount nouns.

*Other people must have thought like this.*
*They are either asleep or entirely absorbed in play or other activity.*

**selecting from a group**

**1.226** 'Enough' is used to say that there is as much of something as is needed, or as many things as are needed. You can therefore use 'enough' in front of uncount nouns or plural nouns.

*There's enough space for the children to run around.*
*They weren't getting enough guests.*

When you want to emphasize that there are only a small number of things of a particular kind, you use 'few' with a plural count noun.

*There are few drugs that act sufficiently swiftly to be of effect.*
*There were few doctors available.*

'Many' indicates that there are a large number of things, without being very precise.

*He spoke many different languages.*

It can also be used in negative statements about quantity.

*There aren't many gardeners like him left.*

'Most' indicates nearly all of a group or amount.

*Most people recover but the disease can be fatal.*
*Most farmers are still using the old methods.*

'Several' usually indicates an imprecise number that is not very large, but is more than two.

*Several projects had to be postponed.*
*I had seen her several times before.*
*There were several reasons for this.*

**'all', 'both', and 'either'**

**1.227** 'All' includes every person or thing of a particular kind.

*You cannot say that all prisoners should be treated the same.*

'Both' is used to say something about two people or things of the same kind. The two people or things have usually been mentioned or are obvious from the context. 'Both' is sometimes used to emphasize that two people or things are involved, rather than just one.

*There were excellent performances from both actresses.*
*Denis held his cocoa in both hands.*

'Either' is also used to talk about two things, but usually indicates that only one of the two is involved. When it is part of the subject of a clause, the verb is in the singular.

*No argument could move either old gentleman from this decision.*

Note that 'either' can mean both of two things, especially when it is used with 'end' and 'side'.

*They stood on either side of the bed.*

**'each' and 'every'**

**1.228** You use 'each' and 'every' when you are talking about all the members of a group of people or things. You use 'each' when you are thinking about the members as individuals, and 'every' when you are making a general statement about all of them. 'Each' and 'every' are followed by a singular count noun.

*Each seat was covered with a white lace cover.*
*They would rush out to meet each visitor.*
*. This new wealth can be seen in every village.*
*Every child would have milk every day.*
*Each applicant has five choices.*
*I agree with every word Peter says.*

You can modify 'every' but not 'each'. You can say things such as 'Almost every chair is broken' or 'Not every chair is broken' but you cannot say 'Almost each chair is broken' or 'Not each chair is broken'. This is because 'each' is slightly more precise and definite than 'every'.

Note that 'each' can be used when talking about two people or things, but 'every' is only used for numbers larger than two.

**'little' and 'much'** 1.229 If you want to emphasize that there is only a small amount of something, you use 'little'. You use 'much' to emphasize a large amount. 'Little' and 'much' are used with uncount nouns.

*There was little applause.*
*We've made little progress.*
*We have very little information.*
*Do you watch much television?*

'Much' is also used in negative statements as well as in affirmative statements, but 'very much' is only used in negative statements. For example, 'I don't have very much sugar' means 'I have only a small quantity of sugar'.

*He did not speak much English.*
*I haven't given very much attention to this problem.*

**'certain', 'numerous', 'various'** 1.230 Some other words can be general determiners, such as 'certain', 'numerous', and 'various'.

'Certain' is used to refer to some members of a group, without specifying which ones.

*We have certain ideas about what topics are suitable.*

'Numerous', like 'many', indicates a large number in an imprecise way.

*I have received numerous requests for information.*
*...a privilege from which numerous auxiliary benefits flowed.*

'Various' is used to emphasize that you are referring to several different things or people.

*We looked at schools in various European countries.*

**'more', 'few', 'less'** 1.231 There are three comparatives that are determiners. 'More' is used in front of plural and uncount nouns, usually with 'than', to refer to a quantity or amount of something that is greater than another quantity or amount.

*He does more hours than I do.*
*His visit might do more harm than good.*

But 'more' is also often used to refer to an additional quantity of something rather than in comparisons.

*More teachers need to be recruited.*
*We need more information.*

'Less' is used to refer to an amount of something that is smaller than another amount. 'Fewer' is used to refer to a group of things that is smaller than another group. 'Less' is usually used before uncount nouns and 'fewer' before plural nouns, but in informal English 'less' is also used before plural nouns.

*The poor have less access to education.*
*...machinery which uses less energy.*
*As a result, he found less time than he would have hoped for his hobbies.*
*There are fewer trees here.*

For more information about **comparison**, see paragraphs 2.108 to 2.144.

**other expressions**

**1.232** Some other expressions also behave like general determiners: 'a few', 'a little', 'a good many', 'a great many'. These have a slightly different meaning from the single word determiners 'few', 'little', and 'many'.

If you are mentioning a small number of things, but without any emphasis, you can use 'a few' with plural count nouns.

*They went to London for a few days.*
*A few years ago we set up a factory.*
*I usually do a few jobs for him in the house.*

Similarly, if you are just mentioning a small amount of something without any emphasis, you can use 'a little' with uncount nouns.

*He spread a little honey on a slice of bread.*
*I have to spend a little time in Oxford.*
*Charles is having a little trouble.*

However, 'a good many' and 'a great many' are more emphatic forms of 'many'.

*I haven't seen her for a good many years.*
*He wrote a great many novels.*

**modifying determiners**

**1.233** Some general determiners can be modified by 'very', 'too', and 'far', or sometimes by another general determiner.

You can modify 'more' with numbers or with other general determiners.

*Downstairs there are four more rooms.*
*There had been no more accidents.*
*You will never have to do any more work.*

You can use 'too many' or 'too much' to say that a quantity is more than is wanted or needed, and 'too few' or 'too little' if it is not enough.

*There were too many competitors.*
*They gave too much power to the Treasury.*
*There's too little literature involved.*

You can use 'very' before 'few', 'little', 'many', and 'much'. You can also say 'a very little' or 'a very great many'.

*Very many women have made their mark on industry.*
*Very few cars had reversing lights.*
*I had very little money left.*

**using 'one'**

**1.234** You use 'one' as a determiner when you have been talking or writing about a group of people or things and you want to say something about a particular member of the group. 'One' is used instead of 'a' or 'an' and is slightly more emphatic.

*We had one case which dragged on for a couple of years.*
*'They criticise me all the time,' wrote one divorced woman.*

*I know <u>one</u> household where that happened, actually.*

The use of 'one' as a **number** is explained in paragraphs 2.230 to 2.232.

**1.235** Many determiners are also **pronouns,** that is they can be used without a following noun. For more information about these, see paragraphs 1.153 to 1.160.

**predeterminers**  **1.236** Normally, a determiner is the first word in a noun group. However, there is a class of words called **predeterminers** which can come in front of a determiner.

Here is a list of predeterminers:

| | | | |
|---|---|---|---|
| all | half | twice | rather |
| both | many | ~ | such |
| double | quarter | quite | what |

The first group are used to indicate amounts or quantities. 'All' can also be used to refer to every part of something. When used with this meaning it is used with an uncount noun.

*<u>All</u> the boys started to giggle.*
*He will give you <u>all</u> the information.*
*<u>All</u> these people knew each other.*
*I shall miss <u>all</u> my friends.*
*I invited <u>both</u> the boys.*
*<u>Both</u> these parties shared one basic belief.*
*She paid <u>double</u> the sum they asked for.*
*I see advertisements for jobs with <u>twice</u> the pay I'm getting now.*

In the second group, 'quite' and 'rather' can be used either to emphasize or to reduce the effect of what is being said. In speech, the meaning is made clear by your tone of voice. In writing, it is sometimes difficult to know which meaning is intended without reading more of the text.

*It takes <u>quite</u> a long time to get a divorce.*
*It was <u>quite</u> a shock.*
*Seaford is <u>rather</u> a pleasant town.*
*It was <u>rather</u> a disaster.*

'Such' and 'what' are used for emphasis.

*He has <u>such</u> a beautiful voice.*
*<u>What</u> a mess!*

# Contents of Chapter 2

# 2 Giving information about people and things

## Introduction

**2.1** In the previous chapter the use of nouns, pronouns, and determiners to name and identify people and things was explained. This chapter explains ways of giving more information about the people and things that have already been named or identified.

One way of giving more information within a noun group about people or things is by the use of an **adjective**, such as 'small', 'political', or 'blue'. Adjectives can be used as modifiers of a noun or as complements of a link verb. They are explained in paragraphs 2.2 to 2.173.

Sometimes nouns can also be used to modify the headword. This is explained in paragraphs 2.174 to 2.179.

**Possessives** such as 'grandmother's' are used to indicate the relationship between people and things and the headword. They can also be used to modify a noun or as complements of a link verb. They are explained in paragraphs 2.180 to 2.192.

There are other groups of words which are used before a noun group to give more information about people and things. They are linked to the noun group by 'of' in a **partitive structure**. These words include **quantifiers,** such as 'many of' and 'some of', and other **partitives** such as 'a piece of' and 'a bottle of'. Quantifiers are used to indicate the amount of people or things you are talking about. They are explained in paragraphs 2.193 to 2.210. Other partitives are used to indicate a particular amount of people or things. They are explained in paragraphs 2.211 to 2.224.

**Numbers** and **fractions** are also used to indicate the amount of people or things you are talking about. Numbers are explained in paragraphs 2.225 to 2.256 and fractions are explained in paragraphs 2.257 to 2.266.

The other way of giving more information within a noun group about people or things is by using a **qualifier** after headwords to expand their meaning. Qualifiers are explained in paragraphs 2.289 to 2.320.

## Describing things: adjectives

**2.2** When you want to give more information about something than you can give by using a noun alone, you can use an **adjective** to identify it or describe it in more detail.

...a new idea.
...new ideas.
...new creative ideas.
Ideas are important.
...to suggest that new ideas are useful.

**main points about adjectives**

**2.3** The most important things to notice about an English adjective are

- what structure it is in (e.g. before a noun or after a link verb)
- what type of adjective it is (e.g. qualitative or classifying).

**WARNING**

**2.4** The form of an adjective does not change: you use the same form for singular and plural and for subject and object.

*We were looking for a good place to camp.*
*The next good place was forty-five miles further on.*
*Good places to fish were hard to find.*
*We found hardly any good places.*

**structure**

**2.5** Adjectives are nearly always used in connection with a noun or pronoun to give information about the person, thing, or group referred to. When this information is not the main purpose of a statement, adjectives are placed in front of a noun, as in 'hot coffee'. Adjectives which are used in a noun group are said to be used **attributively.**

The use of adjectives in a noun group is explained in paragraphs 2.19 to 2.20.

**2.6** Sometimes, however, the main purpose of a statement is to give the information expressed by an adjective. When this happens, adjectives are placed after a **link verb** such as 'be' or 'become', as in 'I am cold' and 'He became ill'. Adjectives which are used after a link verb are said to be used **predicatively.** They are called the **complement** of the link verb. The subject can be any noun group, including pronouns.

The use of adjectives as complements of a link verb is explained in paragraphs 3.127 to 3.138.

**types of adjective**

**2.7** There is a large group of adjectives which identify qualities which someone or something has. This group includes words such as 'happy' and 'intelligent'. These are called **qualitative adjectives.**

Qualitative adjectives are explained in paragraphs 2.24 to 2.28.

**2.8** There is another large group of adjectives which identify someone or something as a member of a class. This group includes words such as 'financial' and 'intellectual'. These are called **classifying adjectives.**

Classifying adjectives are explained in paragraphs 2.29 to 2.32.

Some adjectives can be both qualitative and classifying. These are explained in paragraph 2.33.

**2.9** There is a small group of adjectives which identify the colour of something. This group includes words like 'blue' and 'green'. They are called **colour adjectives.**

Colour adjectives are explained in paragraphs 2.34 to 2.39.

**2.10** Another small group of adjectives are used to emphasize your feelings about the person or thing you are talking about. These adjectives are called **emphasizing adjectives,** and they include adjectives such as 'complete', 'absolute', and 'utter'.

Emphasizing adjectives are explained in paragraphs 2.40 to 2.43.

**2.11** There is a small group of adjectives which are used in a very similar way to **determiners** (see paragraphs 1.161 to 1.236) to make the reference more precise.

These are called **postdeterminers** because their place in a noun group is immediately after the determiner, if there is one, and before any other adjectives.

Postdeterminers are explained in paragraph 2.44.

**structural restrictions**

**2.12** Most adjectives can be used in attributive and predicative structures. However, there are some which can be used only in one or the other. This is explained in paragraphs 2.45 to 2.57.

**2.13** There are a small number of adjectives that can be used after the noun rather than attributively or predicatively. They are explained in paragraphs 2.62 to 2.66.

**order of adjectives**

**2.14** When two or more adjectives are used in a structure, they usually occur in a particular order. This is explained in paragraphs 2.58 to 2.61.

**'-ing' and '-ed' adjectives**

**2.15** There are a large number of English adjectives ending in '-ing', many of which are related to the **present participle** of a verb. In this grammar they are called '**-ing' adjectives.**

There are also a large number of English adjectives ending in '-ed', many of which are related to the **past participle** of a verb. In this grammar they are called '**-ed' adjectives.**

'-ing' adjectives are explained in paragraphs 2.67 to 2.80. '-ed' adjectives are explained in paragraphs 2.81 to 2.97.

**compound adjectives**

**2.16 Compound adjectives** are made up of two or more words, usually written with hyphens between them.

Compound adjectives are explained in paragraphs 2.98 to 2.107.

**comparing things**

**2.17** When you want to indicate the amount of a quality that something or someone has, you can use **comparative** and **superlative** adjectives. There are also some other ways of comparing things.

Comparatives are explained in paragraphs 2.108 to 2.116, and superlatives are explained in paragraphs 2.117 to 2.127. Other ways of comparing things are explained in paragraphs 2.128 to 2.144.

**submodifiers**

**2.18** You can also indicate the amount of a quality that something or someone has by using a **submodifier** with an adjective. You can also use some submodifiers with some comparatives and superlatives.

Submodifiers are explained in paragraphs 2.145 to 2.173.

# Information focusing: adjective structures

**2.19** Adjectives are used in two main structures. One of them involves adjectives modifying a noun group. If you say 'Julia was carrying a battered old suitcase', your main purpose is to say that Julia was carrying a suitcase. The adjectives 'battered' and 'old' give more information about what kind of suitcase it was.

*He had a beautiful smile.*
*...a technical term.*
*...a pretty little star-shaped flower bed.*

**attributive position**

**2.20** Most adjectives can be used to modify nouns. This is called the **attributive** position.

**2.21** The other main structure involves adjectives being used as

**complements** after **link verbs**. Placing an adjective after a link verb has the effect of focusing attention on the adjective. If you say 'The suitcase she was carrying was old and battered', your main purpose is to describe the suitcase, so the focus is on the adjectives 'old' and 'battered'.

*The roads are <u>busy</u>.*
*The house was <u>quiet</u>.*
*He became <u>angry</u>.*
*I feel <u>cold</u>.*
*Nobody seemed <u>amused</u>.*

The use of adjectives as complements of link verbs is explained in paragraphs 3.133 to 3.138.

**predicative position**    **2.22** Most adjectives can be used as complements after link verbs. This is called the **predicative** position.

**attributive and predicative positions**    **2.23** In the following examples, the first example in each pair shows an adjective being used attributively, while the second example shows it being used predicatively.

*There was no <u>clear</u> evidence.*
*'That's very <u>clear</u>,' I said.*

*It had been a <u>pleasant</u> evening.*
*It's not a big stream, but it's very <u>pleasant</u>.*

*She bought a loaf of <u>white</u> bread.*
*The walls were <u>white</u>.*

# Identifying qualities: qualitative adjectives

**2.24** There are two main types of adjective, **qualitative** and **classifying**. Adjectives that identify a quality that someone or something has, such as 'sad', 'pretty', 'small', 'happy', 'healthy', 'wealthy', and 'wise', are called **qualitative adjectives.**

*...a <u>sad</u> story.*
*...a <u>pretty</u> girl.*
*...a <u>small</u> child.*
*...a <u>happy</u> mother with a <u>healthy</u> baby.*
*...<u>wealthy</u> bankers.*
*I think it would be <u>wise</u> to give up.*

**gradability**    **2.25** Qualitative adjectives are **gradable**, which means that the person or thing referred to can have more or less of the quality mentioned.

**2.26** The usual way in which you can indicate the amount of a quality that something or someone has is by using **submodifiers** such as 'very' and 'rather' in front of qualitative adjectives. This is explained in paragraphs 2.145 to 2.161.

**2.27** The other way in which you can indicate the amount of a quality that something or someone has is by using a **comparative**, such as 'bigger', and 'more interesting', or a **superlative**, such as 'the biggest', and 'the

most interesting'. Comparatives and superlatives are explained in
paragraphs 2.108 to 2.127.

**2.28** Here is a list of qualitative adjectives:

| | | | |
|---|---|---|---|
| active | effective | lovely | silly |
| angry | efficient | low | simple |
| anxious | expensive | lucky | slow |
| appropriate | fair | narrow | small |
| attractive | familiar | nervous | soft |
| bad | famous | new | special |
| beautiful | fast | nice | steady |
| big | fat | obvious | strange |
| brief | fine | odd | strong |
| bright | firm | old | stupid |
| broad | flat | pale | successful |
| busy | frank | patient | suitable |
| calm | free | plain | sure |
| careful | fresh | pleasant | surprised |
| cheap | friendly | poor | sweet |
| clean | frightened | popular | tall |
| clear | funny | powerful | terrible |
| close | good | pretty | thick |
| cold | great | proud | thin |
| comfortable | happy | quick | tight |
| common | hard | quiet | tiny |
| complex | heavy | rare | tired |
| cool | high | reasonable | typical |
| curious | hot | rich | understanding |
| dangerous | important | rough | useful |
| dark | interesting | sad | violent |
| dear | kind | safe | warm |
| deep | large | sensible | weak |
| determined | late | serious | wet |
| different | light | sharp | wide |
| difficult | likely | shocked | wild |
| dirty | long | short | worried |
| dry | loose | sick | young |
| easy | loud | significant | |

# Identifying the class that something belongs to: classifying adjectives

**2.29** The other main type of adjective consists of adjectives that you use
to identify the particular class that something belongs to. For example, if
you say 'financial help', you are using the adjective 'financial' to classify
the noun 'help'. There are many different kinds of help, 'financial help' is
one of them. Adjectives which are used in this way are called **classifying
adjectives**.

...*financial* help.
...*abdominal* pains.
...a *medieval* manuscript.
...my *daily* shower.
...an *equal* partnership.
...a *sufficient* amount of milk.

Note that **noun modifiers** (see paragraphs 2.174 to 2.179) are used in a similar way to classifying adjectives. For example, 'financial matters' and 'money matters' are similar in both structure and meaning.

**2.30** Here is a list of classifying adjectives:

| | | | | |
|---|---|---|---|---|
| absolute | double | industrial | official | rural |
| active | due | inevitable | open | scientific |
| actual | east | intellectual | original | separate |
| agricultural | eastern | internal | personal | sexual |
| alternative | economic | international | physical | single |
| annual | educational | legal | political | social |
| apparent | electric | local | positive | solid |
| available | empty | magic | possible | south |
| basic | external | male | potential | southern |
| central | female | medical | private | standard |
| chemical | financial | mental | professional | straight |
| civil | foreign | military | proper | sufficient |
| commercial | free | modern | public | theoretical |
| communist | full | moral | raw | traditional |
| conservative | general | national | ready | urban |
| cultural | golden | natural | real | west |
| daily | historical | negative | religious | western |
| democratic | human | north | revolutionary | wooden |
| direct | ideal | northern | right | wrong |
| domestic | independent | nuclear | royal | |

**2.31** Adjectives such as 'British', 'American', and 'Australian', which indicate nationality or origin, are also classifying adjectives. They start with a capital letter because they are related to names of countries.

...*American* citizens.

Some classifying adjectives are formed from people's names, for example 'Victorian' and 'Shakespearian'. They also start with a capital letter.

...*Victorian* houses.

**2.32** Because they place something in a class, classifying adjectives are not **gradable** in the way that qualitative adjectives are. Things are either in a particular class or not in it. Therefore, classifying adjectives do not have comparatives and superlatives and are not normally used with submodifiers such as 'very' and 'rather'.

However, when you want to indicate that you feel strongly about what you are saying, you can use a submodifier such as 'absolutely' with a classifying adjective. This is explained in paragraphs 2.152 to 2.153.

**adjectives which are of both types** **2.33** Some adjectives can be either **qualitative** or **classifying** depending on the meaning that you want to convey. For example, in 'an emotional person', 'emotional' is a qualitative adjective meaning 'feeling or expressing strong emotions'; it has a comparative and superlative and it can be used with submodifiers. Thus, a person can be 'very emotional', 'rather emotional', or 'more emotional' than someone else. However, in 'the emotional needs of children', 'emotional' is a classifying adjective meaning 'relating to a person's emotions', and so it cannot be submodified.

Here is a list of adjectives frequently used both as qualitative adjectives and as classifying adjectives:

| | | | | |
|---|---|---|---|---|
| academic | effective | modern | regular | scientific |
| conscious | emotional | moral | religious | secret |
| dry | extreme | objective | revolutionary | similar |
| educational | late | ordinary | rural | |

# Identifying colours: colour adjectives

**2.34** When you want to say what colour something is, you use a **colour adjective.**

...her *blue* eyes.
...a *red* ribbon.

Here is a list of the main colour adjectives:

| | | | | |
|---|---|---|---|---|
| black | cream | orange | red | white |
| blue | green | pink | scarlet | yellow |
| brown | grey | purple | violet | |

**submodifying colour adjectives**

**2.35** If you want to specify a colour more precisely, you can use a submodifier, such as 'light', 'pale', 'dark', 'deep', or 'bright', in front of a colour adjective.

...*light brown* hair.
...a *pale green* suit.
...a *dark blue* dress.
...*deep red* dye.
...her *bright blue* eyes.

These combinations are sometimes hyphenated.

...a *light-blue* suit.
...the plant's tiny *pale-pink* flowers.

Note that submodifiers such as 'light' and 'dark' are not used to submodify the colours 'black' or 'white', because you cannot have different shades of black and white.

**approximate colours**

**2.36** If you want to talk about a colour which does not have a definite name you can

● use a colour adjective with '-ish' added to the end

...*greenish* glass.
...permed *yellowish* hair.

● combine two colour adjectives, often with '-ish' or '-y' on the end of the first one

...*greenish-white* flowers.
...a *greeny blue* line.
...the *blue-green* waves.

**PRODUCTIVE FEATURE**

**2.37** You can mix colours in these ways to produce whatever new colour you are trying to describe. This is a **productive feature** of English. Productive features are explained in the Introduction.

| | |
|---|---|
| **comparison of colour adjectives** | **2.38** Colour adjectives such as 'blue' and 'green' occasionally have comparatives and superlatives ending in '-er' and '-est'.<br><br>*His face was <u>redder</u> than usual.*<br>*...the <u>bluest</u> sky I have ever seen.*<br><br>**Comparatives** and **superlatives** are explained in paragraphs 2.108 to 2.127. |
| **colour nouns** | **2.39** The colours can also be headwords, and the main colours can also be plural headwords.<br><br>*The snow shadows had turned to a deep <u>blue</u>.*<br>*They blended in so well with the khaki and <u>reds</u> of the landscape.*<br>*...brilliantly coloured in <u>reds, yellows, blacks,</u> and <u>purples</u>.* |

## Showing strong feelings: emphasizing adjectives

**2.40** You can emphasize your feelings about something that you mention by putting an adjective such as 'complete', 'absolute', and 'utter' in front of a noun.

*He made me feel like a <u>complete</u> idiot.*
*Some of it was <u>absolute</u> rubbish.*
*...<u>utter</u> despair.*
*...<u>pure</u> bliss.*

You generally use an adjective of this kind only when the noun indicates your opinion about something.

Because they are used to show strong feelings, these adjectives are called **emphasizing adjectives.**

Here is a list of emphasizing adjectives:

| | | | |
|---|---|---|---|
| absolute | outright | pure | true |
| complete | perfect | real | utter |
| entire | positive | total | |

| | |
|---|---|
| **emphasizing disapproval** | **2.41** A small group of adjectives ending in '-ing' are used in very informal spoken English for emphasis, usually to indicate disapproval or contempt.<br><br>*Everybody in the whole <u>stinking</u> town was loaded with money.*<br>*Shut that <u>blinking</u> door!* |

Here is a list of adjectives used informally for emphasis:

| | | | | |
|---|---|---|---|---|
| blinking | blundering | freezing | scalding | thundering |
| blithering | crashing | piddling | stinking | whopping |
| blooming | flaming | raving | thumping | |

| | |
|---|---|
| **WARNING** | **2.42** Many of these adjectives are usually used with one particular noun or adjective after them: 'blithering idiot', 'blundering idiot', 'crashing bore', 'raving lunatic', 'thundering nuisance', 'freezing cold', 'scalding hot', 'piddling little', 'thumping great', 'whopping great'.<br><br>*He'll either die or become a <u>raving</u> lunatic.* |

*I've got a stinking cold.*
*...piddling little cars like yours.*

**2.43** The word 'very', which is normally a **submodifier**, is sometimes used to emphasize a noun, in expressions like 'the very top' and 'the very end'.

*...at the very end of the shop.*
*...the very bottom of the hill.*
*These molecules could have formed in the seas of the earth at the very beginning of its history.*

## Making the reference more precise: postdeterminers

**2.44** There is a small group of adjectives which are used in a very similar way to **determiners** (see paragraphs 1.161 to 1.236) to make the reference more precise. These are called **postdeterminers**, because their place in a noun group is immediately after the determiner, if there is one, and before any other adjectives.

*...the following brief description.*
*...certain basic human qualities.*
*...improvements in the last few years.*
*...further technological advance.*
*He wore his usual old white coat.*
*...the only sensible thing to do.*

You often need to make it clear precisely what you are referring to. For example, if you say 'Turn left at the tall building' someone might ask which tall building you mean. If you say 'Turn left at the next tall building', there can be no doubt which one you mean. The postdeterminer 'next' picks it out precisely.

Here is a list of adjectives which are postdeterminers:

| | | | | |
|---|---|---|---|---|
| additional | first | next | past | same |
| certain | following | only | present | specific |
| chief | further | opposite | previous | usual |
| entire | last | other | principal | |
| existing | main | particular | remaining | |

Some of these adjectives can also be ordinary classifying adjectives.

*He had children from a previous marriage.*
*There are two main reasons for this.*

Here is a list of postdeterminers which can also be classifying adjectives:

| | | | |
|---|---|---|---|
| additional | further | particular | principal |
| chief | main | past | remaining |
| existing | other | previous | specific |

Adjectives which are used to indicate the position of something are also used for precise reference.

*...the middle button of her black leather coat.*
*...the top 100 British companies.*

Here is a list of adjectives sometimes used to indicate the position of something as well as for precise reference:

| | | | |
|---|---|---|---|
| left | lower | middle | back |
| right | top | end | |
| upper | bottom | front | |

Postdeterminers can also be used with numbers. This is explained in paragraph 2.236.

# Special classes of adjectives

**2.45** Most adjectives can be used both attributively and predicatively but there are some which can only be used in one position or the other.

There are a few adjectives which are always or almost always used in front of a noun and are never or rarely used as the complement of a link verb. These adjectives are called **attributive adjectives.**

Examples are 'atomic' and 'outdoor'. You can talk about 'an atomic explosion', but you do not say, 'The explosion was atomic'. You can talk about 'outdoor pursuits', but you do not say 'Their pursuits are outdoor'.

**attributive adjectives**

**2.46** A few **qualitative adjectives** (see paragraphs 2.24 to 2.28) are only used attributively. Here is a list of qualitative adjectives always used attributively:

| | | | |
|---|---|---|---|
| adoring | commanding | knotty | scant |
| belated | fateful | paltry | searing |
| chequered | flagrant | punishing | thankless |
| choked | fleeting | ramshackle | unenviable |

Most adjectives which can only be used attributively are **classifying adjectives** (see paragraphs 2.29 to 2.32). Here is a list of classifying adjectives used attributively:

| | | | |
|---|---|---|---|
| atomic | federal | neighbouring | smokeless |
| bridal | forensic | north | south |
| cardiac | indoor | northern | southern |
| countless | institutional | occasional | subterranean |
| cubic | introductory | orchestral | supplementary |
| digital | investigative | outdoor | underlying |
| east | judicial | phonetic | west |
| eastern | lone | preconceived | western |
| eventual | maximum | remedial | woollen |
| existing | nationwide | reproductive | |

**2.47** There are no **colour adjectives** (see paragraphs 2.34 to 2.39) which are restricted to the attributive position.

**Emphasizing adjectives** (see paragraphs 2.40 to 2.43) are usually used attributively.

**predicative adjectives**

**2.48** Some adjectives are normally used only as the complement of a link verb and not in front of a noun. These adjectives are called **predicative adjectives.**

For example, you can say 'She felt glad', but you do not normally talk about 'a glad woman'.

Here is a list of adjectives usually used predicatively:

| | | | | |
|---|---|---|---|---|
| afraid | asleep | glad | safe | unlikely |
| alive | aware | ill | sorry | well |
| alone | content | likely | sure | |
| apart | due | ready | unable | |

Note that they do not have to be followed by a prepositional phrase.

**2.49** Because their meaning would otherwise be unclear or incomplete, some adjectives are usually followed by a prepositional phrase. For example, you cannot simply say that someone is 'accustomed'. You have to say that they are 'accustomed to' something.

The following usage note explains which prepositions you use after a particular adjective.

**USAGE NOTE**   **2.50** There are a few adjectives which are followed by the preposition 'to' when they are used predicatively.

*She's allergic to cats.*
*Older people are particularly susceptible to heart problems.*

Here is a list of adjectives which are usually or always used predicatively and are followed by 'to':

| | | | |
|---|---|---|---|
| accustomed | close | prone | resistant |
| adjacent | conducive | proportional | similar |
| allergic | devoted | proportionate | subject |
| attributable | impervious | reconciled | subservient |
| attuned | injurious | related | susceptible |
| averse | integral | resigned | unaccustomed |

**2.51** There are a few adjectives which are followed by the preposition 'of' when they are used predicatively.

*He was aware of the danger that faced him.*
*They seemed capable of winning their first game of the season.*
*He was devoid of any talent whatsoever.*
*His mind seemed to have become incapable of any thought.*

Here is a list of adjectives which are usually or always used predicatively and are followed by 'of':

| | | | |
|---|---|---|---|
| aware | desirous | heedless | mindful |
| bereft | devoid | illustrative | reminiscent |
| capable | fond | incapable | representative |
| characteristic | full | indicative | |

**2.52** There are a few adjectives which are followed by the preposition 'with' when they are used predicatively.

*His surprise became tinged with just the smallest suspicion of disbelief.*
*The plastic has to be compatible with the body tissues that make contact with it.*
*This way of life is fraught with danger.*

Here is a list of adjectives which are usually or always used predicatively and are followed by 'with':

| | | | |
|---|---|---|---|
| compatible | conversant | fraught | tinged |
| consonant | filled | riddled | |

**2.53** Some adjectives are followed by other prepositions when they are used predicatively.

*These ideas are <u>rooted in</u> self-deception.*
*Didn't you say the raid was <u>contingent on</u> the weather?*
*Darwin concluded that people were <u>descended from</u> apes.*

Here is a list of adjectives which are usually or always used predicatively and are followed by the preposition indicated:

| | | | |
|---|---|---|---|
| contingent on | inherent in | rooted in | swathed in |
| descended from | lacking in | steeped in | unhampered by |

In some cases, there is a choice between two prepositions.

*Many of their courses are <u>connected with</u> industry.*
*Such names were arbitrarily given and were not <u>connected to</u> any particular event.*

Here is a list of adjectives which are usually or always used predicatively and which can be followed by the prepositions indicated:

| | | | |
|---|---|---|---|
| answerable for | dependent on | incumbent on | parallel to |
| answerable to | dependent upon | incumbent upon | parallel with |
| burdened by | immune from | insensible of | reliant on |
| burdened with | immune to | insensible to | reliant upon |
| connected to | inclined to | intent on | stricken by |
| connected with | inclined towards | intent upon | stricken with |

**2.54** 'Different' is most commonly followed by 'from'. It is also sometimes followed by 'to' or 'than', but some people think this is incorrect.

*Students today are <u>different from</u> the students ten years ago.*

**adjectives followed by 'to'-infinitive clauses**

**2.55** To complete the meaning of some adjectives which are used predicatively, you need to follow with a clause beginning with a **'to'-infinitive**. For example, you cannot just say 'He is unable'. You have to add a clause beginning with 'to'-infinitive such as 'to do': 'He is unable to do it'. **'To'-infinitive clauses** are explained in the Reference Section.

*They were <u>unable to help her</u>.*
*I am <u>willing to try</u>.*
*She is <u>bound to notice there's something wrong</u>.*
*I'm <u>inclined to agree with the minister</u>.*

Here is a list of adjectives always or nearly always followed by 'to'-infinitive clauses:

| | | | | |
|---|---|---|---|---|
| able | due | inclined | loath | unwilling |
| bound | fated | liable | prepared | willing |
| doomed | fit | likely | unable | |

**2.56** You can also use a clause beginning with a 'to'-infinitive after many other adjectives to give more information about something.

*I was afraid to go home.*
*I was happy to see them again.*
*He was powerless to prevent it.*
*I was almost ashamed to tell her.*
*The path was easy to follow.*

Note that the subject of the main clause is also the subject of the 'to'-infinitive clause.

**adjectives followed by 'that'-clauses**

**2.57** When adjectives which refer to someone's beliefs or feelings are used predicatively, they are often followed by a **'that'-clause** (see paragraphs 7.85 to 7.87). The subject of the 'that'-clause is not always the same as the subject of the main clause, and so you need to specify it.

*She was sure that he meant it.*
*He was frightened that something terrible might be said.*
*I'm aware that I reached a rather large audience through the book.*

Note that the word 'that' is not always used in a 'that'-clause.

*They were sure she had been born in the city.*

Here is a list of common adjectives often followed by a 'that'-clause:

| | | | | |
|---|---|---|---|---|
| afraid | certain | happy | sorry | upset |
| angry | confident | pleased | sure | worried |
| anxious | frightened | proud | surprised | |
| aware | glad | sad | unaware | |

Note that all of these adjectives except 'angry', 'aware', 'unaware', 'upset', and 'worried' can also be followed by a 'to'-infinitive clause.

*I was afraid that she might not be able to bear the strain.*
*Don't be afraid to ask questions.*

*She was surprised that I knew about it.*
*The twins were very surprised to see Ralph.*

## Position of adjectives in noun groups

**2.58** When you use more than one adjective in a noun group, the usual order for the adjectives is: qualitative adjectives, followed by colour adjectives, followed by classifying adjectives.

...*a little white wooden house.*
...*pretty black lacy dresses.*
...*a large circular pool of water.*
...*a beautiful pink suit.*
...*rapid technological advance.*
...*a nice red apple.*
...*the black triangular fin.*

This order is nearly always followed in English. Occasionally however, when you want to focus on a particular characteristic of the person or thing you are describing, you can vary this order, especially when one of the adjectives refers to colour or size.

...*a square black hole.*

Note that you sometimes put a comma or 'and' between adjectives. This is explained in paragraphs 8.168 to 8.174 and paragraph 8.189.

*...the long, low caravan.*
*It was a long and tedious business.*

**2.59 Comparatives** (see paragraphs 2.108 to 2.116) and **superlatives** (see paragraphs 2.117 to 2.127) normally come in front of all other adjectives in a noun group.

*...better parental control.*
*...the highest monthly figures on record.*

**position of noun modifiers and adjectives**

**2.60** When a noun group contains both an adjective and a noun modifier (see paragraphs 2.174 to 2.179) the adjective is placed in front of the noun modifier.

*...the booming European car industry.*
*...the world's biggest and most prestigious book fair.*

**two or more adjectives as complement**

**2.61** When you use two adjectives as the complement of a link verb, you use a conjunction, usually 'and', to link them. If you use more than two adjectives as a complement, you usually put a conjunction between the last two adjectives and commas between the others. This is fully explained in paragraphs 8.168 to 8.174 and paragraph 8.189.

*The room was large and square.*
*We felt hot, tired, and thirsty.*

Note that you put the adjectives in the order that you think is the most important.

**adjectives after nouns**

**2.62** There are a few adjectives which are usually or always used after a noun. Here is a list indicating the different groups of adjectives used after a noun:

| designate | ~ | old | concerned | ~ |
|-----------|------|-------|-------------|-----------|
| elect | broad | tall | involved | affected |
| galore | deep | thick | present | available |
| incarnate | high | wide | proper | required |
| manqué | long | ~ | responsible | suggested |

**USAGE NOTE**

**2.63** The adjectives 'designate', 'elect', 'galore', 'incarnate', and 'manqué' are only used immediately after a noun.

*She was now president elect.*
*There are empty houses galore.*

**2.64** The adjectives 'broad', 'deep', 'high', 'long', 'old', 'tall', 'thick', and 'wide' are used immediately after measurement nouns when giving the size, duration, or age of a thing or person. This use is fully explained in paragraph 2.270.

*...six feet tall.*
*...three metres wide.*
*...twenty five years old.*

**2.65** The adjectives 'concerned', 'involved', 'present', 'responsible', and 'proper' have different meanings depending on whether you put them in front of a noun or immediately after one. For example, 'the concerned mother' describes a mother who is anxious, but 'the mother concerned' simply refers to a mother who has just been mentioned.

*...the approval of interested and concerned parents.*
*The idea needs to come from the individuals concerned.*

*All this became a very involved process.*
*He knew all of the people involved.*

*...the present international situation.*
*Of the 18 people present, I know only one.*

*...parents trying to act in a responsible manner.*
*...the person responsible for his death.*

*...a proper training in how to teach.*
*...the first round proper of the FA Cup.*

**2.66** The adjectives 'affected', 'available', 'required', and 'suggested' can be used in front of a noun or after a noun without any change in meaning.

*Newspapers were the only available source of information.*
*...the number of teachers available.*

*...the required changes.*
*You're way below the standard required.*

*...the cost of the suggested improvements.*
*The proposals suggested are derived from successful experiments.*

*Aside from the affected child, the doctor checks every other member of the household.*
*...the proportion of the population affected.*

## Special forms: '-ing' adjectives

**2.67** There are a large number of adjectives ending in '-ing'. Most of them are related in form to the **present participles** of verbs. In this grammar they are called '**-ing' adjectives.**

*He was an amiable, amusing fellow.*
*He had been up all night attending a dying man.*

Adjectives which end in '-ing' are sometimes called **participial adjectives.**

The present participle is explained in the Reference Section.

**describing**   **2.68** One group of '-ing' adjectives describe the effect that something has
**an effect**   on your feelings and ideas, or on the feelings and ideas of people in
general.

*...an alarming increase in racial hostility.*
*A surprising number of men stay bachelors.*
*...a charming house on the outskirts of the town.*
*...a warm welcoming smile.*

**2.69** These adjectives are normally **qualitative adjectives.** This means that they can be used with a submodifier, and have comparatives and superlatives.

*...a very convincing example.*
*There is nothing very surprising in this.*
*...a very exciting idea.*
*...a really pleasing evening at the theatre.*
*When Bernard moans he's much more convincing.*
*...one of the most boring books I've ever read.*

**2.70** They can be used in attributive or predicative position.

*They can still show amazing loyalty to their parents.*
*It's amazing what they can do.*

*...the most terrifying tale ever written.*
*The present situation is terrifying.*

**2.71** These '-ing' adjectives have a related transitive verb which you use to describe the way someone is affected by something. For example, if you speak of 'an alarming increase', you mean that the increase alarms you. If you speak of 'a surprising number', you mean that the number surprises you.

Here is a list of '-ing' adjectives that describe an effect and which have a similar meaning to the usual meaning of the related verb:

| | | | | |
|---|---|---|---|---|
| alarming | compelling | embarrassing | intimidating | shocking |
| amazing | confusing | enchanting | intriguing | sickening |
| amusing | convincing | encouraging | menacing | startling |
| annoying | demeaning | entertaining | misleading | surprising |
| appalling | depressing | exciting | mocking | tempting |
| astonishing | devastating | frightening | overwhelming | terrifying |
| astounding | disappointing | harassing | pleasing | threatening |
| bewildering | disgusting | humiliating | refreshing | thrilling |
| boring | distracting | infuriating | relaxing | tiring |
| challenging | distressing | inspiring | rewarding | welcoming |
| charming | disturbing | interesting | satisfying | worrying |

Transitive verbs are explained in paragraphs 3.15 to 3.26.

**describing a process or state**

**2.72** The other main group of '-ing' adjectives are used to describe a process or state that continues over a period of time.

*...her growing band of supporters.*
*Oil and gas drillers are doing a booming business.*
*...a life of increasing labour and decreasing leisure.*

**2.73** These adjectives are **classifying adjectives,** so they are not used with ordinary submodifiers such as 'very' and 'rather'. However, adjectives used to identify a process can be submodified by adverbs which describe the speed with which the process happens.

*...a fast diminishing degree of personal freedom.*
*...rapidly rising productivity.*

**2.74** These '-ing' adjectives have related intransitive verbs.

Here is a list of '-ing' adjectives which describe a continuing process or state and which have a similar meaning to the usual meaning of the related verb:

| | | | | |
|---|---|---|---|---|
| ageing | bursting | dying | prevailing | resounding |
| ailing | decreasing | existing | recurring | rising |
| bleeding | diminishing | increasing | reigning | ruling |
| booming | dwindling | living | remaining | |

Intransitive verbs are explained in paragraphs 3.9 to 3.14.

**2.75** These '-ing' adjectives are only used attributively, so when '-ing' forms of intransitive verbs appear after the verb 'be' they are actually part of a continuous tense.

PRODUCTIVE
FEATURE

**2.76** The '-ing' form of most intransitive English verbs can be used attributively as adjectives to indicate what someone or something is doing.

...a _walking_ figure.
...FIFA, world football's _ruling_ body.
...bands performing in front of _screaming_ crowds.
...two years of _falling_ employment.
...a tremendous noise of _crashing_ glass.

The use of the '-ing' form of verbs as adjectives is a **productive feature** of English. Productive features are explained in the Introduction.

**form and
meaning**

**2.77** Most of the '-ing' adjectives talked about so far are related to verbs. Sometimes however, '-ing' adjectives are not related to verbs at all. For example, there is no verb 'to neighbour'.

_Whole families came from neighbouring villages._

Here is a list of '-ing' adjectives which are not related to verbs:

| | | |
|---|---|---|
| appetizing | enterprising | neighbouring |
| balding | excruciating | scathing |
| cunning | impending | unwitting |

**2.78** Sometimes, an '-ing' adjective is related to an uncommon use of a verb, or appears to be related to a verb but is not related exactly to any current use. For example, the verb 'haunt' is most commonly used in connection with ghosts, but the adjective 'haunting' is more often used of things such as songs and memories. A haunting tune is a tune you cannot forget.

Here is a list of qualitative '-ing' adjectives which are not related to a common transitive use of a verb:

| | | | | |
|---|---|---|---|---|
| becoming | engaging | penetrating | ravishing | trying |
| bracing | fetching | piercing | retiring | |
| cutting | halting | pressing | revolting | |
| dashing | haunting | promising | searching | |
| disarming | moving | rambling | taxing | |

Here is a list of classifying '-ing' adjectives which are not related to a common intransitive use of a verb:

| | | | |
|---|---|---|---|
| acting | floating | going | missing |
| driving | gathering | leading | running |

**2.79** Some adjectives are derived from a verb and a prefix. For example, 'outgoing' is derived from the verb 'go' and the prefix 'out-'. There is no verb 'to outgo'.

_Wouldn't that cause a delay in outgoing mail?_

Here is a list of '-ing' adjectives derived from a verb and a prefix:

| | | |
|---|---|---|
| forthcoming | ongoing | overbearing |
| incoming | outgoing | uplifting |
| oncoming | outstanding | upstanding |

**2.80** A small group of '-ing' adjectives are used in informal spoken

English for emphasis, usually to express disapproval. This use is explained in paragraphs 2.41 to 2.42.

Some **compound adjectives** (see paragraphs 2.98 to 2.107) end in '-ing'.

# Special forms: '-ed' adjectives

**2.81** A large number of English adjectives end in '-ed'. Many of them have the same form as the **past participle** of a verb. Others are formed by adding '-ed' to a noun. Others are not closely related to any other words.

...a disappointed man.
...a bearded man.
...sophisticated electronic devices.

**2.82** Adjectives with the same form as irregular past participles (see the Reference Section) which do not end in '-ed' are also included here as '-ed' adjectives.

Was it a broken bone, a torn ligament, or what?

The past participles of some **phrasal verbs** (see paragraphs 3.84 to 3.117) can also be used as adjectives. When they are used attributively, the two parts of the phrasal verb are usually written with a hyphen between them.

...the built-up urban mass of the city.

**2.83** Most '-ed' adjectives are related to a transitive verb and have a passive meaning. They indicate that something has happened or is happening to the thing being described. For example, 'a frightened person' is a person who has been frightened by something. 'A known criminal' is a criminal who is known by the police.

We have a long list of satisfied customers.
We cannot refuse to teach children the required subjects.

**qualitative '-ed' adjectives**

**2.84** '-ed' adjectives that refer to a person's mental or emotional reaction to something are generally qualitative.

He was a worried old man.
...a bored old woman.
...an interested student.

These adjectives can be submodified by words such as 'very' and 'extremely', just like other qualitative adjectives (see paragraphs 2.145 to 2.161).

**form and meaning**

**2.85** Like other adjectives referring to feelings, these adjectives are often used to describe the expression, voice, or manner of the person affected, instead of referring directly to that person.

...her big blue frightened eyes.
She could hear his agitated voice.
Barry gave him a worried look.

**2.86** Here is a list of qualitative '-ed' adjectives which have a similar meaning to the most common meaning of the related verb:

| | | | | |
|---|---|---|---|---|
| agitated | confused | disgusted | inhibited | shocked |
| alarmed | contented | disillusioned | interested | surprised |
| amused | delighted | distressed | pleased | tired |
| appalled | depressed | embarrassed | preoccupied | troubled |
| astonished | deprived | excited | puzzled | worried |
| bored | disappointed | frightened | satisfied | |

Here is a list of qualitative '-ed' adjectives which do not have a similar meaning to the usual meaning of the related verb:

| | | | |
|---|---|---|---|
| animated | determined | guarded | mixed |
| attached | disposed | hurt | strained |
| concerned | disturbed | inclined | |

**classifying '-ed' adjectives**

**2.87** Many other '-ed' adjectives are used for classifying, and so are not gradable. For example, 'a furnished apartment' is one type of apartment, contrasting with 'an apartment without furniture.'

...a _furnished_ apartment.
...a _painted_ wooden bowl.
...the _closed_ bedroom door.

Most adjectives which refer to physical distinctions are classifying adjectives.

**2.88** Here is a list of classifying '-ed' adjectives which have a similar meaning to the most common meaning of the related verb:

| | | | | |
|---|---|---|---|---|
| abandoned | closed | established | integrated | reduced |
| armed | concentrated | fixed | known | required |
| blocked | condemned | furnished | licensed | torn |
| boiled | cooked | haunted | loaded | trained |
| broken | divided | hidden | paid | united |
| canned | drawn | improved | painted | wasted |
| classified | dried | infected | processed | |

Here is list of '-ed' classifying adjectives which have a different meaning from the most common meaning of the related verb:

| | | |
|---|---|---|
| advanced | noted | spotted |
| marked | pointed | veiled |

**modifying '-ed' adjectives**

**2.89** Classifying '-ed' adjectives cannot normally be submodified with ordinary submodifiers such as 'quite' and 'very'. However, an **adverb of manner,** (see paragraphs 6.36 to 6.44) or an **adverb of degree,** (see paragraphs 6.45 to 6.52) is often used before an '-ed' adjective.

For example, 'a pleasantly furnished room' is a room which has been furnished with pleasant furniture.

...pleasantly _furnished_ rooms.
...a well-_known_ novelist.

**2.90** Some '-ed' adjectives do not make sense on their own, and an adverb is necessary to complete the sense. We do not usually talk about 'dressed people' because people usually wear clothes, but we can say that they are 'well dressed' or 'smartly dressed' for example. The '-ed' adjectives in the following examples nearly always have an adverb in front of them.

...a *cautiously worded* statement.
...*impeccably dressed* men.
...*strongly motivated* students.
It was a *richly deserved* honour.
...*superbly cut* clothes.
...the existence of a *highly developed* national press.
...a *well organized* campaign.
...a tall, *powerfully built* man.
...*perfectly formed* people.

Note that combinations like this are sometimes hyphenated, making them **compound adjectives.**

...a *well-equipped* army.

**'-ed' adjectives with an active meaning**

**2.91** A few '-ed' adjectives are related to the past participle of intransitive verbs and have an active meaning, not a passive meaning. For example, 'a fallen tree' is a tree which has fallen.

...a *capsized* ship.
She is the daughter of a *retired* army officer.
...an *escaped* prisoner.

Here is a list of '-ed' adjectives with an active meaning:

| | | | |
|---|---|---|---|
| accumulated | escaped | fallen | swollen |
| dated | faded | retired | wilted |

**'-ed' adjectives after link verbs**

**2.92** Most '-ed' adjectives can be used both in front of a noun and as the complement of a link verb.

The *worried* authorities decided to play safe.
My husband was *worried.*

A small number of '-ed' adjectives are normally only used as the complement of a link verb. Often, they are followed by a prepositional phrase, a 'to'-infinitive clause, or a 'that'-clause.

I was *thrilled* by the exhibition.
The Brazilians are *pleased* with the results.
...food *destined* for areas of south Sudan.
He was always *prepared* to account for his actions.

Here is a list of '-ed' adjectives often used as the complement of a link verb, with or without a phrase or clause after them:

| | | | |
|---|---|---|---|
| convinced | intimidated | pleased | thrilled |
| delighted | intrigued | prepared | tired |
| interested | involved | scared | touched |

Here is a list of '-ed' adjectives normally used as the complement of a link verb with a phrase or clause after them:

| | | | |
|---|---|---|---|
| agreed | dressed | lost | shut |
| destined | finished | prepared | stuck |

**PRODUCTIVE FEATURE**

**2.93** The past participle of almost any transitive verb can be used as an adjective, though some are more commonly used than others. This is a productive feature of English. Productive features are explained in the Introduction.

...she said, with a _forced_ smile.
There was one _paid_ tutor and three volunteer tutors.
The _recovered_ animals will be released.
...the final _corrected_ version.

**PRODUCTIVE FEATURE**

**2.94** Some '-ed' adjectives are formed from nouns. For example, if a living thing has wings, you can describe it as 'winged'. If someone has skills, you can describe them as 'skilled'. This is a productive feature of English. Productive features are explained in the Introduction.

..._winged_ angels.
...a _skilled_ engineer.
She was dressed in black and carried a black _beaded_ purse.
..._armoured_ cars.
...the education of _gifted_ children.

**'-ed' adjectives formed from nouns**

**2.95** Here is a list of '-ed' adjectives formed from nouns:

| | | | | |
|---|---|---|---|---|
| armoured | detailed | gloved | principled | striped |
| barbed | flowered | hooded | salaried | turbaned |
| beaded | freckled | mannered | skilled | walled |
| bearded | gifted | pointed | spotted | winged |

'-ed' adjectives formed from nouns are commonly used as the second part of **compound adjectives** (see paragraph 2.98 to 2.107) such as 'grey-haired' and 'open-minded', because we often want to describe the feature that someone or something has.

**'-ed' adjectives unrelated to verbs or nouns**

**2.96** There are also a number of '-ed' adjectives in regular use which are not related to verbs or nouns in the ways described above. For example, there are no words 'parch' or 'belove'. There is a noun 'concert', but the adjective 'concerted' does not mean 'having a concert'.

He climbed up the dry _parched_ grass to the terrace steps.
...a complex and _antiquated_ system of taxation.
...attempts to mount a _concerted_ campaign.
...the purchase of expensive _sophisticated_ equipment.

**2.97** Here is a list of '-ed' adjectives not related to verbs or nouns:

| | | | | |
|---|---|---|---|---|
| antiquated | beloved | crazed | indebted | sophisticated |
| ashamed | bloated | deceased | parched | tinned |
| assorted | concerted | doomed | rugged | |

# Compound adjectives

**2.98 Compound adjectives** are made up of two or more words, usually written with hyphens between them. They may be qualitative, classifying, or colour adjectives.

*I was in a light-hearted mood.*
*She was dressed in a bottle-green party dress.*
*...the built-up urban mass of the city.*
*...an air-conditioned restaurant.*
*...a good-looking girl.*
*...one-way traffic.*
*...a part-time job.*

**PRODUCTIVE FEATURE**

**2.99** The forming of compound adjectives is a productive feature of English. Productive features are explained in the Introduction.

**formation patterns**

**2.100** These are the most common and least restricted patterns for forming compound adjectives:

● adjective or number plus noun plus '-ed', e.g. 'grey-haired' and 'one-sided'
● adjective or adverb plus past participle, e.g. 'low-paid' and 'well-behaved'
● adjective, adverb, or noun plus present participle, e.g. 'good-looking', 'long-lasting' and 'man-eating'.

**2.101** These are less common and more restricted patterns for forming compound adjectives:

● noun plus past participle, e.g. 'tongue-tied' and 'wind-blown'
● noun plus adjective, e.g. 'accident-prone', 'trouble-free'
● adjective plus noun, e.g. 'deep-sea', 'present-day'
● past participle plus adverb, e.g. 'run-down', 'cast-off'
● number plus singular count noun, e.g. 'five-page' and 'four-door'.

Note that compound adjectives formed according to the last of these patterns are always used attributively.

**compound qualitative adjectives**

**2.102** Here is a list of compound qualitative adjectives:

| | | | |
|---|---|---|---|
| absent-minded | light-hearted | second-class | tongue-tied |
| accident-prone | long-lasting | second-rate | top-heavy |
| big-headed | long-standing | shop-soiled | trouble-free |
| clear-cut | long-suffering | short-handed | two-edged |
| close-fitting | low-cut | short-lived | two-faced |
| cold-blooded | low-paid | short-sighted | warm-hearted |
| easy-going | low-slung | short-tempered | well-balanced |
| far-fetched | mouth-watering | slow-witted | well-behaved |
| far-reaching | muddle-headed | smooth-talking | well-dressed |
| good-looking | narrow-minded | soft-hearted | well-known |
| good-tempered | nice-looking | starry-eyed | well-off |
| hard-up | off-hand | strong-minded | wind-blown |
| hard-wearing | off-putting | stuck-up | worldly-wise |
| ill-advised | old-fashioned | sun-tanned | wrong-headed |
| kind-hearted | one-sided | swollen-headed | |
| labour saving | open-minded | tender-hearted | |
| laid-back | run-down | thick-skinned | |

**compound classifying adjectives**

**2.103** Here is a list of compound classifying adjectives:

| | | |
|---|---|---|
| air-conditioned | full-blown | off-peak |
| all-out | full-face | one-way |
| all-powerful | full-grown | open-ended |
| audio-visual | full-length | open-mouthed |
| blue-blooded | full-scale | panic-stricken |
| bow-legged | gilt-edged | part-time |
| brand-new | grey-haired | present-day |
| breast-fed | half-price | purpose-built |
| broken-down | half-yearly | ready-made |
| broken-hearted | hand-picked | record-breaking |
| built-up | high-heeled | red-brick |
| bullet-proof | home-made | remote-controlled |
| burnt-out | ice-cold | right-angled |
| cast-off | interest-free | right-handed |
| clean-shaven | knee-deep | second-class |
| cross-Channel | last-minute | second-hand |
| cross-country | late-night | see-through |
| cut-price | lead-free | silver-plated |
| deep-sea | left-handed | single-handed |
| deep-seated | life-size | so-called |
| double-barrelled | long-distance | so-so |
| double-breasted | long-lost | south-east |
| drip-dry | long-range | south-west |
| drive-in | loose-leaf | strong-arm |
| duty-bound | made-up | tax-free |
| duty-free | man-eating | tone-deaf |
| empty-handed | mass-produced | top-secret |
| face-saving | middle-aged | unheard-of |
| far-flung | never-ending | wide-awake |
| first-class | north-east | world-famous |
| free-range | north-west | worn-out |
| free-standing | nuclear-free | year-long |
| freeze-dried | odds-on | |
| front-page | off-guard | |

**compound colour adjectives**

**2.104** Here is a list of compound colour adjectives:

| | | | |
|---|---|---|---|
| blood-red | flesh-coloured | nut-brown | shocking-pink |
| blue-black | ice-blue | off-white | sky-blue |
| bottle-green | iron-grey | pea-green | snow-white |
| dove-grey | jet-black | pearl-grey | |
| electric-blue | lime-green | royal-blue | |

**long compound adjectives**

**2.105** A few compound adjectives are made up of more than two words. Compounds of three or more words are often written with hyphens when they are used in front of nouns and without hyphens when they are used as the complement of a link verb.

...the day-to-day chores of life.
...a down-to-earth approach.
...a free-and-easy relationship.
...life-and-death decisions.
...a trip to an out-of-the-way resort.
Their act is out of date.

**2.106** Some compound adjectives seem rather odd because they contain

words that are never used as single words on their own, for example
'namby-pamby', 'higgledy-piggledy', and 'topsy-turvy'. Words like these are
usually informal.

*...all that arty-crafty spiritualism.*
*...his la-di-da family.*

**foreign compound adjectives**

**2.107** Some compound adjectives are borrowed from foreign languages,
especially from French and Latin.

*...the arguments once used to defend laissez-faire economics.*
*...their present per capita fuel consumption.*
*In the commercial theatre, almost every production is ad hoc.*

Here is a list of compound adjectives borrowed from other languages:

| | | |
|---|---|---|
| à la mode | compos mentis | hors de combat |
| a posteriori | cordon bleu | infra dig |
| a priori | de facto | laissez-faire |
| ad hoc | de jure | non compos mentis |
| ad lib | de luxe | per capita |
| au fait | de rigueur | prima facie |
| avant-garde | de trop | pro rata |
| bona fide | ex gratia | sub judice |

# Comparing things: comparatives

**2.108** You can describe something by saying that it has more of a quality
than something else. You do this by using **comparative adjectives.** Only
qualitative adjectives usually have comparatives, but a few colour
adjectives also have them. Comparatives normally consist of the usual
form of the adjective with either '-er' added to the end, as in 'harder' and
'smaller', or 'more' placed in front, as in 'more interesting' and 'more
flexible'.

Note that 'good' and 'bad' have the irregular comparative forms 'better'
and 'worse'.

The patterns for forming regular and irregular comparatives are explained
in the Reference Section.

**as modifiers**

**2.109** Comparatives can be used as **modifiers** in front of a noun.

*The family moved to a smaller home.*
*He dreams of a better, more exciting life.*
*A harder mattress often helps with back injuries.*

Note that comparatives can also be used as modifiers in front of 'one'.

*An understanding of this reality provokes a better one.*

**as complements**

**2.110** Comparatives can also be used as **complements** after a link verb.

*The ball soaked up water and became heavier.*
*His breath became quieter.*
*We need to be more flexible.*

The use of adjectives as the complements of link verbs is explained in
paragraphs 3.133 to 3.138.

**qualifiers after comparatives**

**2.111** Comparatives are often followed by 'than' when you want to specify
what the other thing involved in the comparison is. You say exactly what
you are comparing by using one of a number of structures after 'than'.

These structures can be

• noun groups

*Charlie was more honest than his predecessor.*
*...an area bigger than Great Britain.*

Note that when 'than' is followed by a pronoun on its own, the pronoun must be an object pronoun such as 'me', 'him', or 'her'.

*My brother is younger than me.*
*Lamin was shorter than her.*

• adjuncts

*The changes will be even more striking in the case of teaching than in medicine.*
*The odds of surviving childhood in New York City are worse than in some Third World countries.*

• clauses

*I would have done a better job than he did.*
*I was a better writer than he was.*
*He's taller than I am.*

Note that when a comparative is not followed by a 'than' phrase, the other thing in the comparison should be obvious. For example, if someone says 'Could I have a bigger one, please?' they are likely to be holding the item which they think is too small.

*A mattress would be better.*

**position of comparatives**

**2.112** If you choose a qualifying phrase or clause beginning with 'than' when you are using a comparative as a modifier, you usually put the qualifier after the whole noun group, not directly after the comparative.

*The world is a more dangerous place than it was.*
*Willy owned a larger collection of books than anyone else I have ever met.*

A comparative can also come immediately after a noun, but only when it is followed by 'than' and a noun group.

*We've got a rat bigger than a cat living in our roof.*
*...packs of cards larger than he was used to.*

**'more' and 'more than'**

**2.113** 'More' is sometimes used in front of a whole noun group to indicate that something has more of the qualities of one thing than another, or is one thing rather than being another.

*Music is more a way of life than an interest.*
*This is more a war movie than a western.*

Note that 'more than' is used before adjectives as an emphatic adverb of degree.

*Their life may be horribly dull, but they are more than satisfied.*
*You would be more than welcome.*

**comparatives as headwords**

**2.114** Comparative adjectives are sometimes used as headwords in fairly formal English. When you use a comparative adjective as a headword, you put 'the' in front of it, and follow it with 'of' and a noun group which refers to the two things being compared.

*...the shorter of the two lines.*
*Dorothea was the more beautiful of the two.*
*There are two windmills, the larger of which stands a hundred feet high.*

If it is clear what you are talking about, you can omit 'of' and the following noun group.

*Notice to quit must cover the rental period or four weeks, whichever is the longer.*

**'less'** **2.115** The form which is used to indicate that something does not have as much of a quality as something else is 'less' followed by an adjective.

*The answer had been less truthful than his own.*

You can also use 'less' and an adjective to say that something does not have as much of a quality as it had before.

*As the days went by, Sita became less anxious.*

Note that 'less than' is used before adjectives like an emphatic negative.

*It would have been less than fair.*

**contrasted comparatives** **2.116** You can indicate that one amount of a quality or thing is linked to another amount by using two contrasted comparatives preceded by 'the'.

*The smaller it is, the cheaper it is to post.*
*The more militant we became, the less confident she became.*
*The larger the organization, the less scope there is for decision.*

## Comparing things: superlatives

**2.117** Another way of describing something is to say that it has more of a quality than anything else of its kind. You do this by using a **superlative adjective**. Only qualitative adjectives usually have superlatives, but a few colour adjectives also have them. Superlatives normally consist of either '-est' added to the end of an adjective and 'the' placed in front of it, as in 'the hardest' and 'the smallest', or of 'the most' placed in front of the adjective, as in 'the most interesting' and 'the most flexible'.

Note that 'good' and 'bad' have the irregular superlative forms 'the best' and 'the worst'.

The patterns for forming regular and irregular superlatives of adjectives are explained in the Reference Section.

Note that superlative adjectives are nearly always preceded by 'the', because you are talking about something definite. Occasionally, when superlatives are used as **complements**, 'the' is omitted (see paragraph 2.122).

**WARNING** **2.118** Adjectives with 'most' in front of them are not always superlatives. 'Most' is also used as a **submodifier**, with the meaning 'very'.

*This book was most interesting.*
*My grandfather was a most extraordinary man.*

Submodifiers are explained in paragraphs 2.145 to 2.161.

**used as modifiers** **2.119** Superlatives can be used as **modifiers** in front of a noun.

*He was the cleverest man I ever knew.*
*It was the most exciting summer of their lives.*
*She came out of the thickest part of the crowd.*
*Now we come to the most important thing.*

...*the oldest* rock paintings in North America.
...*the most eminent* scientists in Britain.

Note that superlatives can also be used as modifiers in front of 'one'.

*No one ever used the smallest one.*

**used as**
**complements**

**2.120** Superlatives can also be used as **complements** after a **link verb.**

*He was the youngest.*
*The sergeant was the tallest.*

The use of adjectives as the complements of link verbs is explained in paragraphs 3.133 to 3.138.

**qualifying**
**structures**

**2.121** You can use a superlative on its own if it is clear what is being compared. For example, if you say 'The sergeant was the tallest', you are referring to a group of soldiers which has already been identified.

If you need to refer to the point of the comparison, you use a qualifying phrase or clause which consists of

● a prepositional phrase normally beginning with 'in' or 'of'

*Henry was the biggest of them.*
*The third requirement is the most important of all.*
*These cakes are probably the best in the world.*

Note that if the superlative is a modifier in front of a noun, the prepositional phrase comes after the noun.

...*the best hotel for families.*
*I'm in the worst business in the world.*

● a relative clause

*The best I'm likely to get.*
*The visiting room was the worst I had seen.*

Note that if the superlative is a modifier in front of a noun, the relative clause comes after the noun.

... *the most dangerous man in the country.*
*He and Nell had the most expensive dinner of their lives.*
*That's the most convincing answer that you've given me.*

**USAGE NOTE**

**2.122** You usually put 'the' in front of the superlative, but you can occasionally omit it, especially in informal speech or writing.

*Wool and cotton blankets are generally cheapest.*
*It can be used by whoever is closest.*

However, you cannot omit 'the' when the superlative is followed by 'of' or another structure indicating what group of things you are comparing. So, for example, you can say 'Amanda was the youngest of our group' or 'Amanda was the youngest' or 'Amanda was youngest', but you cannot say 'Amanda was youngest of our group'.

You can sometimes use the possessive form of a noun or a possessive determiner instead of 'the' in front of a superlative. Often the possessive form of a noun is used instead of a prepositional phrase. For example, you can say 'Britain's oldest man' instead of 'the oldest man in Britain'.

...*the world's most popular cheese.*
...*my newest assistant.*

The possessive form of nouns is explained in paragraphs 2.180 to 2.192, and possessive determiners are explained in paragraphs 1.192 to 1.207.

**used with other adjectives**

**2.123** A superlative is sometimes accompanied by another adjective ending in '-able' or '-ible'. This second adjective can be placed either between the superlative and the noun group or after the noun group.

*...the narrowest imaginable range of interests.*
*...the most beautiful scenery imaginable.*

*...the longest possible gap.*
*I say that in the nicest way possible.*

**superlatives as headwords**

**2.124** Superlative adjectives are sometimes used as headwords in fairly formal English. When you use a superlative adjective as a headword, you put 'the' in front of it, and follow it with 'of' and a noun group which refers to the things being compared. When superlative adjectives are used as headwords they can refer to one thing or to more than one.

*They are often too poor to buy or rent even the cheapest of houses.*
*He made several important discoveries. The most interesting of these came from an examination of an old manuscript.*

If it is clear what you are talking about, you can omit 'of' and the following noun group.

*There are three types of ant-eater. The smallest lives entirely in trees.*

**USAGE NOTE**

**2.125** In informal speech, people often use a superlative rather than a comparative when they are talking about two things. For example, someone might say 'The train is quickest' rather than 'The train is quicker' when comparing a train service with a bus service. However, some people think that it is better to use superlatives only when comparing more than two things.

**used with ordinal numbers**

**2.126 Ordinal numbers** are used with superlatives to indicate that something has more of a quality than nearly all other things of their kind. For example, if you say that a mountain is 'the second highest mountain', you mean that it is higher than any other mountain except the highest one.

*Cancer is the second biggest cause of death in Britain.*
*...the second most important man in her life, her hairdresser.*
*It is Japan's third largest city.*

Ordinal numbers are explained in paragraphs 2.249 to 2.256.

**'the least'**

**2.127** When you want to indicate that something has less of a quality than anything else, you use 'the least' followed by an adjective.

*This is the least popular branch of medicine.*

Similarly, when you are talking about a group of things which have less of a quality than other things of their kind, you use 'the least'.

*...the least savage men in the country.*

## Other ways of comparing things: saying that things are similar

**2.128** Another way of describing things is by saying that something is similar in some way to something else.

**indicating things with the same quality**

**2.129** If you want to say that a thing or person has as much of a quality as something or someone else, you can use a structure based on the word 'as' in front of a qualitative adjective. Usually this adjective is then followed by a qualifying phrase or clause which also begins with 'as'.

The qualifying phrase can be

- a prepositional phrase beginning with the preposition 'as'

You're just *as bad as your sister.*
...huge ponds *as big as tennis courts.*
Takings were *as high as ever.*

- a clause introduced by the conjunction 'as'

Conversation was not *as slow as I feared it would be.*
The village gardens aren't *as good as they used to be.*

**2.130** When this comparative structure is followed by a prepositional phrase consisting of 'as' and a pronoun on its own, the pronoun must be an appropriate object pronoun such as 'me', 'him', or 'her'. However, when the comparative structure is followed by a clause consisting of the conjuction 'as' and a pronoun which is the subject of a clause, then that pronoun must be an appropriate subject pronoun such as 'I', 'he' or 'she'.

Jane was not as clever as *him.*
They aren't as clever as *they appear to be.*

**2.131** If it is clear what you are comparing something or someone to, you can omit the qualifying phrase or clause.

Frozen peas are just *as good.*

**2.132** You can also use the 'as...as...' structure to say that something has much more or less of a quality than something else. You do this by putting an expression such as 'twice', 'three times', 'ten times', or 'half' in front of the first 'as'. For example, if one building is ten metres high and another building is twenty metres high, you can say that the second building is 'twice as high as' the first building or that the first building is 'half as high as' the second one.

The grass was *twice as tall as in the rest of the field.*
Water is *eight hundred times as dense as air.*

This structure is often used in the same way to refer to qualities that cannot be measured. For example, if you want to say that something is much more useful than something else, you can say that the first thing is 'a hundred times as useful as' the second one.

Without this rearing our children would be *ten times as hard as it is.*

**USAGE NOTE** **2.133** When the 'as...as...' structure is preceded by 'not', it has the same meaning as 'less...than'. For example, 'I am not as tall as George' means the same as 'I am less tall than George'. Some people use 'not so...as...' instead of 'not as...as...'.

The film is *not as good as the book.*
The young otter is *not so handsome as the old.*

**2.134** Submodifiers such as 'just', 'quite', 'nearly' and 'almost' can be used in front of this comparative structure, modifying the comparison with their usual meanings.

Sunburn can be *just as severe as a heat burn.*

The use of submodifiers in comparison is explained in paragraphs 2.162 to 2.173.

**2.135** When you are using the 'as...as...' structure you can sometimes put a noun group after the adjective and before the qualifying phrase or clause. This noun group must begin with 'a' or 'an'. For example, instead of saying 'This knife is as good as that one', you can say 'This is as good a knife as that one'.

*I'm as good a cook as she is.*
*This was not as bad a result as they expected.*

Sometimes, instead of using 'not' before this structure, you can use 'not such' followed by 'a' or 'an', an adjective, a noun, and 'as'.

*Water is not such a good conductor as metal.*

**2.136** Instead of using this 'as...as...' structure you can use expressions such as 'the height of' and 'the size of' to indicate that something is as big as something else, or bigger or smaller.

*The tumour was the size of a golf ball.*
*It is roughly the length of a man's arm.*

'like'  **2.137** If something has similar qualities or features to something else, instead of using the 'as...as...' comparative structure you can say that the first thing is 'like' the second one. You do this by using prepositional phrases beginning with 'like' after **link verbs.**

*He looked like an actor.*
*That sounds like an exaggeration.*
*The whole thing is like a bad dream.*

The meaning of this structure is close to the meaning of an ordinary complement structure (see paragraphs 3.139 to 3.148). Compare the last example with 'the whole thing is a bad dream'. This is a more definite statement, where 'a bad dream' is the complement of the link verb.

Here is a list of the link verbs used with 'like':

| | | | |
|---|---|---|---|
| be | look | smell | taste |
| feel | seem | sound | |

When you want to say that one thing resembles another, you can use a prepositional phrase beginning with 'like' after these link verbs.

*It was like a dream.*
*Sometimes I feel like a prisoner here.*
*He looked like a nice man.*
*The houses seemed like mansions.*
*You smell like a tramp!*
*It sounded like a fine idea.*

**2.138** 'Like' has the comparative 'more like' and 'less like', and the superlative 'most like' and 'least like'.

*It made her seem less like another of Theodore's possessions.*
*Of all his children, she was the one most like me.*

USAGE NOTE  **2.139** You can use some submodifiers in front of 'like'.

*He looks just like a baby.*
*She looked like a queen, just exactly like a queen*

This is explained in paragraph 2.170.

**'same as'**   **2.140** If you want to say that one thing is exactly like something else, you can say that it is 'the same as' the other thing.

*The rich are the same as the rest of us.*

'The same as' can be followed by a noun group, a pronoun, an adjunct, or a clause.

*24 Spring Terrace was the same as all its neighbours.*
*Her colouring was the same as mine.*
*The furnishings are not exactly the same as when Morris lived there.*

If two or more things are exactly like each other, you can say that they are 'the same'.

*Come and look! They're exactly the same.*
*They both taste the same.*

You can use 'the same' when you are comparing people or things with other people or things that you have just mentioned.

*It looks like a calculator and weighs about the same.*
*The message was the same.*
*The end result is the same.*

Note that you use 'the opposite', 'the converse', and 'the reverse' in a similar way.

*The kind of religious thoughts I had were just the opposite.*
*Older men are attractive to women but the reverse is not true.*

**USAGE NOTE**   **2.141** You can use some submodifiers in front of 'the same as' and 'the same'.

*They are virtually the same as other single cells.*
*You two look exactly the same.*

Here is a list of submodifiers used with 'the same as' and 'the same':

| | | |
|---|---|---|
| exactly | more or less | nearly |
| just | much | virtually |

Submodifiers are explained in paragraphs 2.145 to 2.173.

**2.142** You can put a noun such as 'size', 'length', or 'colour' after 'the same'. For example, if you want to say that one street is as long as another one, you can say that the first street is 'the same length as' the second one, or that the two streets are 'the same length'.

*Its brain was about the same size as that of a gorilla.*
*They were almost the same height.*

**adjectives meaning 'the same'**   **2.143** The adjectives 'alike', 'comparable', 'equivalent', 'identical', and 'similar' can also be used to say that two or more things are like each other. You can put the preposition 'to' after all of them except 'alike' in order to mention the second of the things being compared.

*They all looked alike.*
*The houses were all identical.*
*Flemish is similar to Afrikaans.*

**submodifiers used in comparisons**   **2.144** When you want to suggest that you are comparing different amounts of a quality, you can use submodifiers such as 'comparatively', 'relatively', and 'equally'.

*Psychology's a comparatively new subject.*
*The costs remained relatively low.*
*Her technique was less dramatic than Ann's, but equally effective.*
*He was extra polite to his superiors.*

# Indicating different amounts of a quality: submodifiers

**2.145** When you want to indicate something more about the quality which an adjective describes, you can use a **submodifier** such as 'very' and 'rather' with it. You do this in order to indicate the amount of the quality, or to intensify it. Many submodifiers are **adverbs of degree** (see paragraphs 6.45 to 6.52).

**submodifying adjectives**
**2.146** Because qualitative adjectives are **gradable**, allowing you to say how much or how little of the quality is relevant, you are more likely to use submodifiers with them than with other types of adjective.

*...an extremely narrow road.*
*...a highly successful company.*
*...in a slightly different way.*
*I was extraordinarily happy.*
*...helping them in a strongly supportive way.*
*...a very pretty girl.*
*She seems very pleasant.*
*...a rather clumsy person.*
*His hair was rather long.*

**2.147** Although qualitative adjectives are the most frequently submodified, you can use submodifiers with classifying adjectives (see paragraphs 2.151 to 2.153) and with colour adjectives (see paragraph 2.35). Note that most '-ed' adjectives can be submodified by words such as 'very' and 'extremely', just like other qualitative adjectives.

*...a very frightened little girl.*
*...an extremely disappointed young man.*

**intensifying qualitative adjectives**
**2.148** You can use many submodifiers with qualitative adjectives in order to intensify their meaning.

*...extremely high temperatures.*
*Geoffrey was a deeply religious man.*
*France is heavily dependent on foreign trade.*

Here is a list of submodifiers used to intensify the meaning of adjectives:

| | | | |
|---|---|---|---|
| amazingly | exceedingly | incredibly | suspiciously |
| awfully | extraordinarily | infinitely | terribly |
| bitterly | extremely | notably | unbelievably |
| critically | fantastically | particularly | very |
| dangerously | greatly | radically | violently |
| deeply | heavily | really | vitally |
| delightfully | highly | remarkably | wildly |
| disturbingly | hopelessly | seriously | wonderfully |
| dreadfully | horribly | strikingly | |
| eminently | hugely | supremely | |
| especially | impossibly | surprisingly | |

Note that 'very' can be used to submodify superlative adjectives when you want to be very emphatic. This is explained in paragraphs 2.172 to 2.173.

Note also that adjectives with 'most' in front of them are not always superlatives. 'Most' is also used as a submodifier with the meaning 'very'.

*This book was most interesting.*
*My grandfather was a most extraordinary man.*

**2.149** Many of these submodifiers not only intensify the meaning of the adjective but also allow you to express your opinion about what you are saying. For example, if you say that something is 'surprisingly large', you are expressing surprise at how large it is as well as intensifying the meaning of 'large'.

*He has amazingly long eyelashes.*
*...a delightfully refreshing taste.*
*...a shockingly brutal scene.*
*...a horribly uncomfortable chair.*
*...incredibly boring documents.*

However, you use a few of these submodifiers with no other purpose than to intensify the meaning of the adjective.

*They're awfully brave.*
*The other girls were dreadfully dull companions.*

Here is a list of submodifiers only used to intensify adjectives:

| | | | |
|---|---|---|---|
| awfully | extremely | really | very |
| dreadfully | greatly | so | |
| especially | highly | terribly | |

Note that 'awfully', 'dreadfully', and 'terribly' are used in informal language and 'highly' is used in very formal language.

Note also that 'so' is normally only used after a link verb.

*I am so sorry.*

**reducing qualitative adjectives**

**2.150** Some submodifiers are used to reduce the effect of qualitative adjectives.

*The story was mildly amusing.*
*It's a fairly common feeling.*
*...moderately rich people.*
*...his rather large stomach.*
*My last question is somewhat personal.*

Here is a list of submodifiers used to reduce the effect of an adjective:

| | | | |
|---|---|---|---|
| faintly | moderately | rather | somewhat |
| fairly | pretty | reasonably | |
| mildly | quite | slightly | |

Note that 'quite' and 'rather', as well as being used as submodifiers to reduce the effect of an adjective, are also **predeterminers** (see paragraph 1.236).

Note also that 'quite' is normally only used with adjectives which are used after a link verb.

*She was quite tall.*

**indicating extent** 2.151 Some submodifiers are used to indicate the extent of the quality which you are describing.

Here is a list of submodifiers used to indicate the extent of a quality:

| | | | |
|---|---|---|---|
| almost | nearly | absolutely | quite |
| exclusively | partly | altogether | simply |
| fully | predominantly | completely | totally |
| largely | primarily | entirely | utterly |
| mainly | roughly | perfectly | |
| mostly | ~ | purely | |

**USAGE NOTE** 2.152 The first group in the list above are used almost always just to indicate the extent of a quality. They are most commonly used with classifying adjectives.

*It was an almost automatic reflex.*
*...a shop with an exclusively female clientele.*
*...the largely rural south east.*
*The wolf is now nearly extinct.*
*The reasons for this were partly economic and practical, and partly political and social.*

'Almost' and 'nearly' are also used with qualitative adjectives.

*The club was almost empty.*
*It was nearly dark.*

Note that 'roughly' can be used when you want to say that something is nearly or approximately like something else.

*West Germany, Japan and Sweden are at roughly similar levels of economic development.*

Note also that 'half' can sometimes be used in this way. For example, you can describe someone as 'half American' if just one of their parents was American.

2.153 The second group in the list above are used not only to indicate the extent of a quality but also to emphasize the adjective. They can be used with classifying adjectives as well as qualitative adjectives.

*You're absolutely right.*
*This policy has been completely unsuccessful.*
*Everyone appeared to be completely unaware of the fact.*
*The discussion was purely theoretical.*
*It really is quite astonishing.*
*...a totally new situation.*
*We lived totally separate lives.*
*...utterly trivial matters.*

Note that 'absolutely' is frequently used with qualitative adjectives which express enthusiasm or lack of enthusiasm. When you use 'absolutely' in this way you are emphasizing how strongly you feel about what you are saying.

*...an absolutely absurd sermon.*
*I think it's absolutely wonderful.*

*The enquiry is absolutely crucial.*

Here is a list of qualitative adjectives often emphasized by 'absolutely':

| | | | | |
|---|---|---|---|---|
| absurd | crucial | furious | perfect | wonderful |
| awful | enormous | huge | splendid | |
| brilliant | essential | impossible | terrible | |
| certain | excellent | massive | vital | |

Note also that 'completely' and 'utterly' can also be used in this way.

*It is completely impossible to imagine such a world.*
*He began to feel utterly miserable.*

**indicating sufficiency**

**2.154** You can use submodifiers such as 'adequately', 'sufficiently', and 'acceptably' when you want to indicate that someone or something has a sufficient amount of the quality you are describing.

*The roof is adequately insulated.*
*We found a bank of snow sufficiently deep to dig a cave.*

**USAGE NOTE**

**2.155** You can also indicate that you think something is sufficient by using 'enough'. 'Enough' always comes after the adjective, and never before it.

*I was not a good enough rider.*
*It seemed that Henry had not been careful enough.*

'Enough' can be followed by a prepositional phrase beginning with 'for' to indicate a person involved, or by a 'to-'infinitive clause to indicate a related action.

*A girl in the factory wasn't good enough for him.*
*If you find that the white wine is not cold enough for you, ask for some ice to be put in it.*
*The children are old enough to travel to school on their own.*
*None of the richly growing crops was ripe enough to eat.*

Note that when 'enough' is used after an adjective, you can use 'just' in front of the adjective to indicate that someone or something has a sufficient amount of the quality described by the adjective, but no more than that.

*Some of these creatures are just large enough to see with the naked eye.*

**2.156** 'Enough' can also be a determiner (see paragraphs 1.208 to 1.232).

*He hasn't had enough exercise.*

When 'enough' is a determiner, it can have a submodifier in front of it.

*There was just enough space for a bed.*
*I have almost enough tokens for one book.*

**indicating insufficiency**

**2.157** If you want to indicate that you think something you are describing is insufficient, you can use submodifiers such as 'inadequately', 'insufficiently', and 'unacceptably'.

*...people growing up in insufficiently supportive families.*
*Their publications were inadequately researched.*

**indicating excess**

**2.158** If you want to indicate that you think someone or something has an excessive amount of a quality, you normally use the submodifier 'too' in front of a qualitative adjective which is used predicatively.

*My feet are too big.*
*It was too hot.*
*Dad thought I was too idealistic.*

'Too' can be followed by a prepositional phrase beginning with 'for' to indicate a person involved or by a 'to-'infinitive clause to indicate a related action.

*The shoes were too big for him.*
*He was too old for that sort of thing.*
*She was too weak to lift me.*
*He was too proud to apologise.*

Note that you do not usually use 'too' with an adjective in front of a noun, although you do use 'too' in front of the determiners 'many', 'much', and 'few'.

*You ask too many questions, Sam.*
*There is too much chance of error.*
*Too few people nowadays are interested in Literature.*

**WARNING**   **2.159** 'Too' cannot be used instead of 'very'. Rather than saying 'I am too happy to meet you', you must say 'I am very happy to meet you.'

**2.160** Other words that indicate too much of a quality are 'excessively', 'overly', and the prefix 'over-'. These can be used, like 'too', with predicative adjectives, but they can also be used with attributive adjectives.

*...excessively high accident rates.*
*...an intellectual but over-cautious man.*
*They were overly eager.*

**PRODUCTIVE**   **2.161** As well as adverbs of degree, you can use some other types of
**FEATURE**   adverb such as adverbs of time in front of adjectives to modify their meaning. This is a productive feature of English. Productive features are explained in the Introduction.

*...the once elegant palace.*
*...a permanently muddy road.*
*...internationally famous golfers.*
*...naturally blonde hair.*
*...coolly elegant furniture.*
*...purposely expensive gadgets.*

Adverbs are explained in Chapter 6.

# Indicating the degree of difference: submodifiers in comparison

**2.162** When you are using comparative adjectives, you may want to say that something has much more or much less of a quality than something else. You can do this by adding a **submodifier**.

*It is a much better school than yours.*
*These creatures are much less mobile.*
*There are far worse dangers.*
*Some children are a lot more difficult than others.*

You can also use a submodifier to say that something has much more or much less of a quality than it had before.

*He had become much more mature.*
*That's much less important than it was.*

**2.163** Some submodifiers can only be used when comparative adjectives are being used as complements.

*You look a lot better.*
*It would be a good deal easier if you came to my place.*
*The journey back was a great deal more unpleasant than the outward one had been.*

Here is a list of submodifiers used in front of comparative adjectives:

| a good deal | a great deal | a lot | heaps | lots |
|---|---|---|---|---|

Note that 'lots' and 'heaps' are only used in informal spoken English.

**2.164** However, other submodifiers can be used with comparative adjectives which are being used as either modifiers or complements.

*They are faced with a much harder problem than the rest of us.*
*The risk from smoking is much greater if you have a weak heart.*
*Computers can be applied to a far wider range of tasks.*
*The delay was far longer than they claimed.*

Here is a list of submodifiers used with adjectives that are used both attributively and predicatively:

| considerably | infinitely | vastly |
|---|---|---|
| far | much | very much |

**2.165** If you want to say that something has more of a quality than something else which already has a lot of it, you can use 'even' or 'still' before a comparative adjective, or 'still' after it.

*She's even lazier than me!*
*She was even more possessive than Rosamund.*
*I had a still more recent report.*
*The text is actually worse still.*

Similarly, you can use 'even' or 'still' to say that something has less of a quality than something else which has little of this quality.

*This did not happen before the war, and is now even less likely.*

You can also use 'even' or 'still' when comparing the amount of a quality that something has at one time with the amount that it has at another.

*The flight was even faster coming back.*
*They will become richer still.*

In formal or literary English, 'yet' is sometimes used as a submodifier in the same way as 'still'.

*He would have been yet more alarmed had she withdrawn.*
*The planes grow mightier yet.*

**2.166** You can indicate that something has an increasing or decreasing amount of a quality by repeating comparative adjectives. For example, you can say that something is getting 'bigger and bigger', 'more and more difficult', or 'less and less common'.

*He's getting fatter and fatter.*
*...defences that were proving more and more effective.*

'Increasingly' can be used instead of 'more and more' and 'decreasingly' instead of 'less and less'.

*I was becoming increasingly depressed.*
*It was the first of a number of increasingly frank talks.*

**2.167** If you want to say that something has a little more or a little less of a quality than something else, you can use 'rather', 'slightly', 'a bit', 'a little bit', or 'a little' with comparative adjectives.

*It's a rather more complicated story than that.*
*She's only a little bit taller than her sister.*

You can also use these constructions to say that something has a little more or a little less of a quality than it had before.

*We must be rather more visible to people in the community.*
*...the little things that made life slightly less intolerable.*

**2.168** If you want to say emphatically that something has no more of a quality than something else or than it had before, you can use 'no' in front of comparative adjectives.

*Some species of dinosaur were no bigger than a chicken.*

'Any' is used for emphasis in front of comparatives in negative clauses, questions, and conditional clauses. For example, 'He wasn't any taller than Jane' means the same as 'He was no taller than Jane'.

*I was ten and didn't look any older.*
*If it will make you any happier, I'll shave off my beard.*
*Is that any clearer?*

Note that you can only use 'no' and 'any' like this when comparatives are being used as **complements**. You cannot use 'no' and 'any' with comparatives when they are being used in front of a noun group. For example, you cannot say 'It was a no better meal' or 'Is that an any faster train?'

**2.169** When you use the comparative structure 'as ... as ...' (see paragraphs 2.129 to 2.135), submodifiers such as 'just', 'quite', 'nearly', and 'almost' can be used in front of it, modifying the comparison with their usual meanings.

*Mary was just as pale as he was.*
*There is nothing quite as lonely as illness.*
*...a huge bird which was nearly as big as a man.*
*The land seemed almost as dark as the water.*

'Nearly' can also be used as a submodifier when the 'as ... as ...' structure is preceded by 'not' with the meaning 'less......than'. You put it after the 'not'. For example, 'I am not nearly as tall as George' means the same as 'I am much less tall than George'.

*This is not nearly as complicated as it sounds.*

**2.170** When you use 'like' to describe someone or something by comparing them with someone or something else (see paragraphs 2.137 to 2.139), you can use a submodifier in front of it.

*...animals that looked a little like donkeys.*

*It's a plane exactly like his.*

Here is a list of submodifiers used with 'like':

| a bit | exactly | quite | somewhat |
|-------|---------|-------|----------|
| a little | just | rather | very |

**2.171** When you use 'the same as' and 'the same' to describe someone or something by saying they are identical to someone or something else, you can use a number of submodifiers in front of them, including 'just', 'exactly', 'much', 'nearly', 'virtually', and 'more or less'. These modify the meaning with their usual meanings.

*I'm just the same as everyone else.*
*The situation was much the same in Germany.*
*The moral code would seem to be more or less the same throughout the world.*

**2.172** When you are using superlative adjectives, you may wish to say that something has much more or much less of a quality than anything else of its kind. As with comparatives, you can do this by using **submodifiers.**

The submodifiers 'much', 'quite', 'easily', 'by far', and 'very' can be used with the superlative adjectives.

'Much', 'quite', and 'easily' are placed in front of 'the' and the superlative.

*Music may have been much the most respectable of his tastes.*
*...the most frightening time of my life, and quite the most dishonest.*
*This is easily the best film of the year.*

'By far' can be placed either in front of 'the' and the superlative or after the superlative.

*They are by far the most dangerous creatures on the island.*
*The Union was the largest by far.*

**2.173** 'Very' can only be used with superlatives formed by adding '-est' or with irregular superlatives such as 'the best' and 'the worst'. 'Very' is placed between 'the' and the superlative.

*...the very earliest computers.*
*It was of the very highest quality.*

'Very' can also be used to submodify superlative adjectives when you want to be very emphatic. It is placed after a determiner such as 'the' or 'that' and in front of a superlative adjective or one such as 'first' or 'last'.

*...in the very smallest countries.*
*...one of the very finest breeds of dogs.*
*...on the very first day of the war.*
*He had come at the very last moment.*
*That very next afternoon he was working in his room.*
*He spent weeks in that very same basement.*

# Modifying using nouns: noun modifiers

**2.174** Nouns can be used as modifiers in front of other nouns when you want to give more specific information about someone or something.

Sometimes, when nouns are used like this they become fixed expressions which are called **compound nouns** (see paragraphs 1.84 to 1.93).

When the nouns used in front of other nouns are not in fixed expressions, they are called **noun modifiers**.

...the _car_ door.
..._tennis_ lessons.
...a _football_ player.
..._cat_ food.
...the _music_ industry.
...a _surprise_ announcement.

**singular**
**and plural**
**forms**

**2.175** You normally use the singular form of a **count noun** (see paragraphs 1.16 to 1.23) as a noun modifier, even when you are referring to more than one thing. For example, you refer to a shop that sells books as 'a book shop', not 'a books shop', even though it sells a large number of books, not just one.

Many **plural nouns** lose their '-s' endings when used in front of other nouns.

...my _trouser_ pocket.
..._pyjama_ trousers.
..._paratroop_ attacks.

Here is a list of common plural nouns which lose their '-s' and '-es' endings when they are used as modifiers:

| | | | |
|---|---|---|---|
| knickers | pyjamas | spectacles | trousers |
| paratroops | scissors | troops | |

However, some plural nouns keep the same form when used in front of other nouns.

...._arms_ control.
...the _arms_ race.
..._clothes_ pegs.

Here is a list of common plural nouns which remain the same when they are used as modifiers:

| | | |
|---|---|---|
| arms | clothes | jeans |
| binoculars | glasses | sunglasses |

Plural nouns are explained in paragraphs 1.42 to 1.47.

**using more**
**than**
**one noun**
**modifier**

**2.176** If you want to be even more specific, you can use more than one noun modifier. For example, a 'car insurance certificate' is a certificate which indicates that a car has been insured, and a 'state pension scheme' is a scheme that is run by the state and concerns workers' pensions.

...a _Careers Information_ Officer.
..._car body repair_ kits.
...a _family dinner_ party.
...a _school medical_ officer.

**used with**
**adjectives**

**2.177** If you want to give more information about a noun that has a noun modifier in front of it, you can put **adjectives** in front of the noun modifier.

...a _long car_ journey.
...a _new scarlet_ silk handkerchief.

*...complex business deals.*
*...this beautiful morning sunlight.*
*...the French film industry.*

When an adjective comes in front of two nouns, it is usually obvious whether it is modifying the two nouns combined or only the noun modifier.

For example, in 'an electric can opener', the adjective 'electric' is modifying the combination 'can opener'; whereas in 'electric shock treatment', 'electric' is modifying the noun 'shock' and then both the adjective and the noun modifier are modifying the noun 'treatment'.

Adjectives are explained in paragraphs 2.2 to 2.107.

**use of proper nouns**

**2.178 Proper nouns** can also be used as noun modifiers. For example, if you want to show that something is connected with a place, organization, or institution, you put the name of the place, organization, or institution in front of all other noun modifiers. You also put them in front of classifying adjectives.

*...Brighton Technical College.*
*...the Cambridge House Literacy Scheme.*

Proper nouns are explained in paragraphs 1.53 to 1.59.

**PRODUCTIVE FEATURE**

**2.179** The use of noun modifiers in English is very common indeed. In fact, when the context makes it clear what you mean, you can use almost any noun to modify any other noun. You can use noun modifiers to indicate a wide range of relationships between the two nouns.

For example, you can say what something is made of, as in 'cotton socks'. You can also say what is made in a particular place, as in 'a glass factory'. You can say what someone does, as in 'a football player', or you can say where something is, as in 'my bedroom curtains'.

You can say when something happens, as in 'the morning mist' and 'her wartime activities'. You can also describe the nature or size of something, as in 'a surprise attack' and 'a pocket chess-set'.

The use of noun modifiers is a **productive feature** of English. Productive features are explained in the Introduction.

# Indicating possession or association: possessive structures

**2.180** One way of specifying something is by saying who or what it belongs to or is associated with. So that, for example, you can talk about 'Elizabeth's book', or 'the teacher's role'.

This section deals with ways of expressing possession within a noun group, typically by using a structure based on **apostrophe s ('s)**. When apostrophe s ('s) is added to a noun or name it is called the **possessive form**; some grammars call it the **genitive**.

**possessive form**

**2.181** You usually show that something belongs to or is associated with someone by adding 's to the name of the person, and by placing this possessive form in front of the thing that belongs to them, or is associated with them. For example, if John owns a motorbike, you can refer to it as 'John's motorbike'.

*Sylvia put her hand on <u>John's</u> arm.*
*...the main features of <u>Mr Brown's</u> economic policy.*

When you use a noun rather than a name to refer to the person, the noun group containing the possessive form also contains a determiner in the usual way.

*...<u>his grandmother's</u> house.*
*<u>Your mother's</u> best handbag.*

Note that the determiner applies to the possessive form and not to the noun which is being modified by the possessive.

**spelling and pronunciation**  **2.182** The spelling and pronunciation patterns used to form possessives change according to the spelling and pronunciation of the name or noun. These are explained in the Reference Section.

**other uses of 's**  **2.183** The use of apostrophe s ('s) is not just restricted to nouns and names or to indicating possession or association. For example, it can be used in a qualifying phrase beginning with the preposition 'of', and it can be used like a possessive pronoun. Some nouns with 's added can also be used as modifiers in front of a noun. These other uses of the possessive form are explained in paragraphs 2.188 to 2.192.

Note that in addition to being the possessive form, the pattern 's can also be added to words as a contraction of 'is' or 'has'. This is explained in the Reference Section.

**other ways of indicating possession**  **2.184** It is also sometimes possible to indicate possession by using either a prepositional phrase beginning with 'of', or by using a structure with a noun modifier in it.

Prepositional phrases beginning with 'of' are explained in paragraphs 2.294 to 2.300. Noun modifiers are explained in paragraphs 2.174 to 2.179.

# Indicating close connection: apostrophe s ('s)

**2.185** Apostrophe s ('s) is most often added to a noun referring to a person or an animal.

*I wore a pair of my <u>sister's</u> boots.*
*Philip watched his <u>friend's</u> reaction.*
*Billy patted the <u>dog's</u> head.*

It can also be used to show that something belongs to or is associated with a group of people or an institution.

*She runs the foreign exchange desk for the <u>bank's</u> corporate clients.*
*They also prepare the <u>university's</u> budget.*
*...the <u>paper's</u> political editor, Mr Fred Emery.*
*There was a raid on the <u>Democratic Party's</u> headquarters.*
*What is your <u>government's</u> policy?*

**2.186** Apostrophe s ('s) is sometimes added to a noun referring to an object when specifying a part of it or a quality or feature that it has.

*I like the <u>car's</u> design.*

*You can predict a <u>computer's</u> behaviour because it follows rules.*

Apostrophe s ('s) is used after nouns and names referring to places to specify something in that place.

*He is the administrative head of the <u>country's</u> biggest city.*
*The <u>city's</u> population is in decline.*
*...<u>Britain's</u> most famous company.*

**2.187** If you want to emphasize that something belongs or relates to a particular person and nobody else, you use 'own'. 'Own' can be used after the possessive form of a name or noun, as well as after a possessive determiner.

*Professor <u>Wilson's own</u> answer may be unacceptable.*
*We must depend on <u>David's own</u> assessment.*

If you are specifying a number of things, you put the number after 'own'.

*...the Doctor's <u>own two</u> rooms.*

## Other structures with apostrophe s ('s)

**2.188** When you are talking about two things of the same type which belong to different people you can use the possessive form of a name or noun like a possessive pronoun so that you can omit repeating the thing itself. In the first example below, 'David's' is used instead of 'David's hand'.

*Her appearance is very different to <u>her brother's.</u>*
*My room is next to <u>Karen's.</u>*
*It is your responsibility rather than your <u>parents'.</u>*

The possessive form can also be used on its own to refer to someone's home or place of work.

*He's round at <u>David's.</u>*
*She stopped off at the <u>butcher's</u> for a piece of steak.*
*She hasn't been back to the <u>doctor's</u> since.*

Possessive pronouns are explained in paragraphs 1.110 to 1.114.

**used in qualifying phrases**   **2.189** The possessive form can be used in a prepositional phrase beginning with 'of' which qualifies a noun group. You use this structure when you are talking about one of a number of things that belong to someone or are associated with them, rather than about something unique.

*Julia, a friend <u>of Jenny's,</u> was there too.*
*That word was a favourite <u>of your father's.</u>*

**USAGE NOTE**   **2.190** Possessive forms can also be used to refer to things of a particular type which are usually associated with someone.

*...a woman dressed in a <u>man's</u> raincoat.*
*...a <u>policeman's</u> uniform.*
*...<u>women's</u> magazines.*
*...the <u>men's</u> lavatory.*

**2.191** The possessive form can sometimes be used with nouns which refer to an action in order to indicate who or what is performing the action.

*...the <u>banking service's</u> rapid growth.*

*...Madeleine's arrival at Fairwater House School.*

Note that prepositional phrases beginning with 'of' are used more commonly to do this, and that they are more formal than this use of possessive forms. The use of prepositional phrases beginning with 'of' to indicate who or what is performing an action is explained in paragraph 2.299.

**2.192** Sometimes you can add apostrophe s ('s) to a noun referring to the thing affected by the performer of an action and put it in front of the noun referring to that performer. For example, you can talk about 'the scheme's supporters'.

*...Christ's followers.*
*...the car's owner.*

Sometimes an apostrophe s ('s) structure can be used to indicate the thing affected by an action.

*...Sven Goran Eriksson's appointment as England manager.*

Note again that 'of' structures are more commonly used to do this.

# Talking about quantities and amounts

**2.193** This section deals with ways of referring to quantities and amounts of things. You often refer to quantities by using a number, but sometimes in everyday situations you can do this by using a word or a phrase such as 'several' and 'a bottle' and link it with 'of' to the following noun group in a **partitive structure**. When words like 'several' are used like this, they are called **quantifiers**. Quantifiers are explained in paragraphs 2.194 to 2.210. When phrases such as 'a bottle' are used like this, they are called **partitives**. Partitives are explained in paragraphs 2.211 to 2.224.

When you want to be very precise about the quantity or amount of something, you can use **numbers** (see paragraphs 2.225 to 2.256) or **fractions** (see paragraphs 2.257 to 2.266).

Numbers, fractions, and quantifiers are also used in expressions of measurement to indicate the size, weight, length, and so on, of something. Ways of talking about measurements are explained in paragraphs 2.267 to 2.274. Approximate measurements are explained in paragraphs 2.281 to 2.288. Numbers are also used to say how old someone or something is. This is explained in paragraphs 2.275 to 2.280.

## Talking about amounts of things: quantifiers

**2.194** When you want to refer to a quantity of things or to an amount of something in everyday language, you use a **quantifier**.

*I am sure both of you agree with me.*
*...a house with lots of windows.*
*Most of the population have fled.*
*I make a lot of mistakes.*
*In Tunis there are a number of art galleries.*
*I never found the rest of my relatives.*

Note that all quantifiers consist of two or more words, because 'of' is needed in every case. 'Of' is printed in the lists below as a reminder.

**2.195** Here is the list of quantifiers:

| | | | |
|---|---|---|---|
| all of | more of | an amount of | a majority of |
| another of | most of | a bit of | the majority of |
| any of | much of | a little bit of | a minority of |
| both of | neither of | a couple of | ~ |
| certain of | none of | a good deal of | the remainder of |
| each of | numbers of | a great deal of | the rest of |
| either of | one of | a few of | the whole of |
| enough of | part of | a little of | ~ |
| few of | plenty of | a lot of | heaps of |
| fewer of | quantities of | a good many of | loads of |
| less of | several of | a great many of | masses of |
| little of | some of | a number of | tons of |
| lots of | various of | a quantity of | |
| many of | ~ | ~ | |

Note that the quantifiers in the last group in this list are used in informal speech only.

**only with specific determiners**   **2.196** Some of these quantifiers can be linked by 'of' only to noun groups that begin with a specific determiner such as 'the', 'these', or 'my'. A pronoun such as 'us', 'them', or 'these' can also be used after 'of'.

*Nearly all of the increase has been caused by inflation.*
*Part of the farm lay close to the river bank.*
*Only a few of the attackers were armed.*

Here is a list of quantifiers usually or always used with noun groups beginning with specific determiners:

| | | | |
|---|---|---|---|
| all of | few of | neither of | a few of |
| another of | fewer of | none of | a little of |
| any of | less of | one of | a good many of |
| both of | little of | part of | a great many of |
| certain of | many of | several of | ~ |
| each of | more of | some of | the remainder of |
| either of | most of | various of | the rest of |
| enough of | much of | ~ | the whole of |

All other quantifiers can be used with noun groups beginning with either specific or general determiners.

**with place names**   **2.197** Some of these quantifiers can also be used with place names.

*The whole of America will be shocked by what happened.*
*...involving a large part of Africa and a large part of South America.*

Here is a list of quantifiers used with place names:

| | | | | |
|---|---|---|---|---|
| all of | much of | ~ | a great deal of | the whole of |
| less of | none of | a bit of | a lot of | |
| more of | part of | a little bit of | ~ | |
| most of | some of | a good deal of | the rest of | |

**verb agreement**   **2.198** When you use a quantifier as the subject of a verb, the verb is singular or plural depending on whether the quantifier refers to one thing or to more than one thing.

*Some of the information has already been analysed.*
*Some of my best friends are policemen.*

**with plural nouns**

**2.199** Many quantifiers can only be used in front of plural noun groups.

*I am sure both of you agree with me.*
*Start by looking through their papers for either of the two documents mentioned below.*
*Few of these organizations survive for long.*
*Several of his best books are about space flight.*
*I would like to ask you a couple of questions.*
*The report contained large numbers of inaccuracies.*

Here is a list of quantifiers only used with plural noun groups:

| | | | |
|---|---|---|---|
| another of | few of | one of | a few of |
| both of | fewer of | several of | a good many of |
| certain of | many of | various of | a great many of |
| each of | neither of | ~ | a number of |
| either of | numbers of | a couple of | |

For more information about 'each of' see paragraphs 2.203 to 2.204, about 'fewer of' see paragraph 2.206, and about 'a number of' see paragraphs 2.208 to 2.209.

Note that 'neither of' is used in a similar way to 'either of' when you are talking about two things in negative clauses. This is explained in paragraph 4.75.

**with uncount nouns and singular nouns**

**2.200** A few quantifiers are only used with uncount nouns and singular noun groups.

*Much of the day was taken up with classes.*
*This is a bit of a change.*
*There was a good deal of smoke.*
*If you use rich milk, pour off a little of the cream.*
*I spent the whole of last year working there.*

Here is a list of quantifiers only used with uncount nouns and singular noun groups:

| | | | |
|---|---|---|---|
| less of | part of | a little bit of | a little of |
| little of | ~ | a good deal of | ~ |
| much of | a bit of | a great deal of | the whole of |

For more information about 'less of' see paragraph 2.206.

**with plural nouns and uncount nouns**

**2.201** A very few quantifiers can be used only with plural noun groups and uncount nouns.

*...the seizure of vast quantities of illegal weapons.*
*Very large quantities of aid were needed.*
*They had loads of things to say about each other.*
*We had loads of room.*
*...plenty of the men.*
*Make sure you give plenty of notice.*

Here is a list of quantifiers only used with plural noun groups and uncount nouns:

| | | | |
|---|---|---|---|
| plenty of | ~ | loads of | tons of |
| quantities of | heaps of | masses of | |

Note that when the second group of quantifiers in this list are used with an uncount noun as the subject of a verb, the verb is singular, even though the quantifier looks plural.

*Masses and masses of food was left over.*

**with all types of noun**   **2.202** Some quantifiers can be used with plural noun groups, with singular noun groups, or with uncount nouns.

*...some of the most distinguished men of our time.*
*We did some of the journey by night.*
*Some of the gossip was surprisingly accurate.*

Here is a list of quantifiers used with plural noun groups, singular noun groups, or uncount nouns:

| | | | |
|---|---|---|---|
| all of | more of | ~ | ~ |
| any of | most of | an amount of | the remainder of |
| enough of | none of | a lot of | the rest of |
| lots of | some of | a quantity of | |

Note that 'an amount of' is nearly always used with an adjective such as 'small': 'a small amount of'. This is explained in paragraph 2.209.

Note also that when 'lots of' is used with an uncount noun as the subject of a verb, the verb is singular, even though the quantifier looks plural.

*He thought that lots of lovely money was the source of happiness.*

'Any of' is explained more fully in paragraph 2.205.

**USAGE NOTE**   **2.203** When you want to refer to each member of a particular group, you can use 'each of' and a plural noun group.

*Each of the drawings is slightly different.*
*We feel quite differently about each of our children.*
*Work out how much you can afford to pay each of them.*

Note that 'each one' and 'every one' can be used before 'of' instead of 'each', for emphasis.

*This view of poverty influences each one of us.*
*Every one of them is given a financial target.*

**WARNING**   **2.204** When the quantifier 'each of' is used with a plural noun group, the verb after the noun group is always singular.

**USAGE NOTE**   **2.205** 'Any of' can refer to one or several people or things, or to part of something. Note that if it is the subject of a verb, when it refers to several things, the verb is plural, and when it refers to a part of something, the verb is singular.

*She has those coats. She might have been wearing any of them.*
*Hardly any of these find their way into consumer products.*
*Has any of this been helpful?*
*It was more expensive than any of the other magazines we were normally able to afford.*

**2.206** There are three comparative quantifiers, which can be used before noun groups. 'Less of' is usually used with singular noun groups and uncount noun groups, 'fewer of' is usually used with plural noun groups, and 'more of' is used with all three types of noun group.

*I enjoy cooking far more now, because I do less of it.*

*Fewer of these children will become bored.*
*He was far more of an existentialist.*

Note that 'more of' is sometimes used in front of a noun group to intensify it.

*He could hardly have felt more of a fool than he did at that moment.*
*She was more of a flirt than ever.*
*America is much more of a classless society.*

Note also that 'less of' is sometimes used instead of 'fewer of', but many people think that this is not correct.

**omitting 'of'** **2.207** When the context makes it clear, or when you think that the person you are talking to will understand what you mean, you can sometimes reduce the structure to the quantifier only. For example, if you are talking about applications for a job and there were twenty candidates, you can say 'Some were very good' rather than 'Some of them were very good'.

*A few crossed over the bridge.*
*Some parts can be separated from the whole.*
*I have four bins. I keep one in the kitchen and the rest in the dustbin area.*
*Most of the books had been packed into an enormous trunk and the remainder piled on top of it.*

**USAGE NOTE** **2.208** You can add adjectives to 'a number of' and 'a quantity of' to indicate how large or small an amount or number of things is.

*There are a large number of students.*
*We had a limited number of people to choose from.*
*The novel provides an enormous quantity of information.*
*...a tiny quantity of acid.*

'An amount of' is always used with adjectives, and is usually used with uncount nouns.

*Pour a small amount of the sauce over the chicken.*
*He has a large amount of responsibility.*
*It only involves a small amount of time.*
*There has to be a certain amount of sacrifice.*
*They have done a vast amount of hard work.*

The plural forms of 'quantity', 'number', and 'amount' are used, especially when referring to separate amounts.

*...groups which employ large numbers of low-paid workers.*
*Enormous amounts of money are spent on advertising.*

**submodifying** **2.209** When a quantifier contains an adjective, you can put 'very' in front
**quantifiers** of the adjective.

*...a very great deal of work.*
*...a very large amount of money.*

**2.210** Some quantifiers can be submodified using 'quite'.

*I've wasted quite enough of my life here.*
*Quite a few of the employees are beginning to realise the truth.*
*Most of them have had quite a lot of experience.*
*...quite a large amount of industry.*

Here is a list of quantifiers which can be submodified by 'quite':

| | | | |
|---|---|---|---|
| enough | a lot of | a small amount of | a large number of |
| a few | a large amount of | a number of | |

# Talking about amounts of things: partitives

**2.211** When you want to talk about a particular quantity of something, you can use a **partitive** structure which consists of a particular partitive linked by 'of' to another noun. The partitives are all count nouns.

*Who owns this bit of land?*
*...portions of mashed potato.*

If the partitive is singular, then the verb used with it is usually singular. If it is plural, the verb is also plural.

*A piece of paper is lifeless.*
*Two pieces of metal were being rubbed together.*

Note that all partitives consist of two or more words, because 'of' is needed in every case. 'Of' is printed in the lists below as a reminder.

**partitives with uncount nouns**
**2.212** When the noun after the partitive is an uncount noun, you can use count nouns such as 'bit', 'drop', 'lump', or 'piece' as the partitive.

*Here's a bit of paper.*
*...a drop of blood.*
*Drops of sweat dripped from his forehead.*
*...a tiny piece of material.*
*...a pinch of salt.*
*...specks of dust.*

These partitives can be used without 'of' when it is obvious what you are talking about.

*He sat down in the kitchen before a plate of cold ham, but he had only eaten one piece when the phone rang.*

**2.213** Here is a list of partitives used with uncount nouns:

| | | | | |
|---|---|---|---|---|
| amount of | grain of | mountain of | scrap of | touch of |
| bit of | heap of | piece of | sheet of | trace of |
| blob of | knob of | pile of | shred of | |
| clump of | lump of | pinch of | slice of | |
| dash of | mass of | pool of | speck of | |
| drop of | morsel of | portion of | spot of | |

Some of these partitives are also used with plural nouns which refer to things which together form a mass.

*...a huge heap of stones.*
*...a pile of newspapers.*

Here is a list of partitives used with both uncount and plural nouns:

| | | | |
|---|---|---|---|
| amount of | heap of | mountain of | portion of |
| clump of | mass of | pile of | |

**PRODUCTIVE FEATURE**
**2.214** Many nouns which indicate the shape of an amount of something can also be partitives with uncount or plural nouns.

*...a ball of wool.*

*...columns of smoke.*
*...a ring of excited faces.*

Here is a list of partitives indicating the shape of an amount of something:

| | | | |
|---|---|---|---|
| ball of | shaft of | strip of | wall of |
| column of | square of | thread of | |
| ring of | stick of | tuft of | |

Many nouns which indicate both shape and movement can also be used as partitives.

*It blew a jet of water into the air.*
*...a constant stream of children passing through the door.*

Here is a list of partitives indicating both shape and movement:

| | | | |
|---|---|---|---|
| dribble of | gust of | spurt of | torrent of |
| gush of | jet of | stream of | |

This use of partitives to indicate shape, and shape and movement, is a productive feature of English because you can use any noun indicating shape in this way. For example you can talk about 'a triangle of snooker balls'. Productive features are explained in the Introduction.

**PRODUCTIVE FEATURE**  **2.215** There are many nouns which refer to groups that can be used as partitives. They are linked by 'of' to plural nouns which indicate what the group consists of.

*It was evaluated by an independent team of inspectors.*
*A group of journalists gathered at the airport to watch us take off.*
*...a bunch of flowers.*

Here is a list of partitives referring to groups:

| | | | |
|---|---|---|---|
| audience of | company of | gang of | team of |
| bunch of | family of | group of | troupe of |
| clump of | flock of | herd of | |

This use of partitives referring to groups is a productive feature of English because you can use any noun referring to a group of people or things in this way. For example, you can talk about 'an army of volunteers'. Productive features are explained in the Introduction.

**measurement nouns**  **2.216** Nouns referring to measurements are often used in partitive structures to refer to an amount of something which is a particular length, area, volume, or weight. Uncount nouns are used after 'of' in structures referring to length, and both uncount and plural nouns are used in structures referring to weight.

*...ten yards of velvet.*
*Thousands of square miles of land have been contaminated.*
*I drink a pint of milk a day.*
*...three pounds of strawberries.*
*...10 ounces of cheese.*

Nouns referring to measurements are explained in paragraphs 2.267 to 2.274.

**referring to contents and containers**  **2.217** You can use partitives when you want to refer to the contents of a container as well as to the container itself. For example, you can refer to a carton filled with milk as 'a carton of milk'.

*I went to buy a bag of chips.*
*The waiter appeared with a bottle of red wine.*
*...a packet of cigarettes.*
*...a pot of honey.*
*...tubes of glue.*

You can also use partitives to refer to the contents only.

*They drank another bottle of champagne.*
*She ate a whole box of chocolates.*

Here is a list of partitives referring to containers:

| | | | | |
|---|---|---|---|---|
| bag of | bucket of | glass of | pot of | tub of |
| barrel of | can of | jar of | sack of | tube of |
| basin of | carton of | jug of | spoon of | tumbler of |
| basket of | case of | mug of | tablespoon of | |
| bottle of | cask of | pack of | tank of | |
| bowl of | crate of | packet of | teaspoon of | |
| box of | cup of | plate of | tin of | |

**ending in '-ful'**

**2.218** You can add '-ful' to these partitives referring to containers.

*He brought me a bagful of sweets.*
*Pour a bucketful of cold water on the ash.*
*...a cupful of boiled water.*
*...a tankful of petrol.*

Here is a list of partitives referring to containers which can very commonly be used with '-ful':

| | | | |
|---|---|---|---|
| bag | bucket | spoon | teaspoon |
| basket | cup | tablespoon | |
| box | plate | tank | |

When people want to make a noun ending in '-ful' plural, they usually add an '-s' to the end of the word, as in 'bucketfuls'. However some people put the '-s' in front of '-ful', as in 'bucketsful'.

*She ladled three spoonfuls of sugar into my tea.*
*They were collecting basketfuls of apples.*
*...two teaspoonfuls of powder.*
*...2 teaspoonsful of milk.*

**PRODUCTIVE FEATURE**

**2.219** You can also add '-ful' to other partitives.

*Eleanor was holding an armful of red roses.*
*I went outside to throw a handful of bread to the birds.*
*He took another mouthful of whisky.*
*...a houseful of children.*

This is a **productive feature** of English. Productive features are explained in the Introduction.

**USAGE NOTE**

**2.220** You can sometimes use a mass noun instead of a partitive structure. For example, 'two teas' means the same as 'two cups of tea', and 'two sugars' means 'two spoonfuls of sugar'.

*We drank a couple of beers.*
*I asked for two coffees with milk.*

**Mass nouns** are explained in paragraphs 1.29 to 1.32.

**referring to parts and fractions**

**2.221** You can use a partitive when you want to talk about a part or a fraction of a particular thing.

*I spent a large part of my life in broadcasting.*
*The system is breaking down in many parts of Africa.*
*An appreciable portion of the university budget goes into the Community Services area.*
*…a mass movement involving all segments of society.*

Here is a list of partitives referring to a part of something:

| | | | |
|---|---|---|---|
| part of | portion of | section of | segment of |

**referring to individual items**

**2.222** You can use a partitive with an uncount noun referring to things of a certain type when you want to refer to one particular thing of that type.

*…an article of clothing.*
*I bought a few bits of furniture.*
*Any item of information can be accessed.*

Here is a list of partitives referring to one thing of a particular type:

| | | | |
|---|---|---|---|
| article of | bit of | item of | piece of |

Here is a list of uncount nouns referring to things of a certain type that are often used with the partitives listed above:

| | | | | |
|---|---|---|---|---|
| advice | clothing | homework | luggage | research |
| apparatus | equipment | information | machinery | |
| baggage | furniture | knowledge | news | |

**'pair of'**

**2.223** Some plural nouns refer to things which are normally thought to consist of two parts, such as trousers or scissors. Some others refer to things which are made in twos, such as shoes or socks. When you want to talk about one of these two-part items, or two-item sets, you can use the partitive 'pair' linked to these plural nouns by 'of'.

*…a pair of jeans.*
*…a pair of tights.*
*…a dozen pairs of sunglasses.*
*I bought a pair of tennis shoes.*
*I smashed three pairs of skis.*

These plural nouns are explained in paragraphs 1.42 to 1.47.

**PRODUCTIVE FEATURE**

**2.224** Whenever you want to talk about a limited amount of something, to indicate the area that something occupies, or to specify a particular feature that it has, you can use a noun group which indicates the amount or the nature of the thing linked by 'of' to a noun group which indicates what the thing is. For example, if you say 'a forest of pines', you are talking about a large area of trees. Similarly, you can talk about 'a border of roses'. This structure can be extended very widely, so that you can talk about 'a city of dreaming spires', for example. This is one of the most **productive features** of English. Productive features are explained in the Introduction.

# Referring to an exact number of things : numbers

**cardinal numbers**

**2.225** When you want to refer to an exact number of things, you use numbers such as 'two', 'thirty', and '777' which are called **cardinal numbers,** or sometimes **cardinals.**

*I'm going to ask you thirty questions.*
*...two hundred and sixty copies of the record.*

The cardinal numbers are listed in the Reference Section and their use is explained in paragraphs 2.230 to 2.248.

**ordinal numbers**

**2.226** When you want to identify or describe something by indicating where it comes in a series or sequence, you use an **ordinal number,** or an **ordinal,** such as 'first', 'second', 'fourteenth', or 'twenty-seventh'.

*She received a video camera for her fourteenth birthday.*
*I repeated my story for the third time that day.*

The ordinal numbers are listed in the Reference Section and their use is explained in paragraphs 2.249 to 2.256.

**fractions**

**2.227** When you want to indicate how large a part of something is compared to the whole of it, you use a **fraction** such as 'a third' and 'three-quarters'.

*A third of the American forces were involved.*
*The bottle had been about three-quarters full when he'd started.*

Fractions are explained in paragraphs 2.257 to 2.266.

**measuring things**

**2.228** When you want to refer to a size, distance, area, volume, weight, speed, or temperature, you can do so by using a number or quantifier in front of a **measurement noun** such as 'feet' and 'miles'.

*He was about six feet tall.*
*It's four miles to the city centre from here.*

Measurement nouns are explained in paragraphs 2.267 to 2.274.

If you do not know the exact number, size, or quantity of something, you can give an approximate amount or measurement using one of a group of special words and expressions. These are explained in paragraphs 2.281 to 2.288.

**age**

**2.229** When you want to say how old someone or something is, you have a choice of ways in which to do it. These are explained in paragraphs 2.275 to 2.288.

## Referring to the number of things: cardinal numbers

**2.230** If you want to refer to some or all of the things in a group, you can indicate how many things you are referring to by using a **cardinal number.**

The cardinal numbers are listed in the Reference Section.

*By Christmas, we had ten cows.*

When you use a determiner and a number in front of a noun, you put the determiner in front of the number.

*...the three young men.*
*...my two daughters.*
*Watch the eyes of any two people engrossed in conversation.*
*All three candidates are coming to Blackpool later this week.*

When you put a number and an adjective in front of a noun, you usually put the number in front of the adjective.

*...two small children.*
*...fifteen hundred local residents.*
*...three beautiful young girls.*

**'one'**  **2.231** 'One' is used as a number in front of a noun to emphasize that there is only one thing, to show that you are being precise, or to contrast one thing with another. 'One' is followed by a singular noun.

*That is the one big reservation I've got.*
*He balanced himself on one foot.*
*There was only one gate into the palace.*
*This treaty was signed one year after the Suez Crisis.*
*It was negative in one respect but positive in another.*

'One' can also be used, like other numbers, as a quantifier.

*One of my students sold me her ticket.*

*...one of the few great novels of the century.*
*It's one of the best films I've ever seen.*

'One' also has special uses as a determiner and a pronoun. These are explained in paragraph 1.234 and paragraphs 1.157 to 1.160.

**2.232** When a large number begins with the figure '1', the '1' can be said or written as 'a' or 'one'. 'One' is more formal.

*...a million dollars.*
*...a hundred and fifty miles.*
*Over one million pounds has been raised.*

**talking about**  **2.233** The number 0 is not used in ordinary English to indicate that the
**negative**  number of things you are talking about is zero. Instead the negative
**amounts**  determiner 'no' or the negative pronoun 'none' is used, or 'any' is used with a negative. These are explained in paragraphs 4.45 and 4.65 to 4.67.

**numbers and**  **2.234** When you use any number except 'one' in front of a noun, you use a
**agreement**  plural noun.

*There were ten people there, all men.*
*...a hundred years.*
*...a hundred and one things.*

**2.235** When you use a number and a plural noun to talk about two or more things, you usually use a plural verb. You use a singular verb with 'one'.

*Seven guerrillas were wounded.*
*There is one clue.*

However, when you are talking about an amount of money or time, or a distance, speed, or weight, you usually use a number, a plural noun, and a singular verb.

*Three hundred pounds is a lot of money.*
*Ten years is a long time.*
*Twenty six miles is a long way to run.*
*90 miles an hour is much too fast.*
*Ninety pounds is all she weighs.*

Ways of measuring things are explained in paragraphs 2.267 to 2.274.

**numbers with ordinals and post-determiners**

**2.236** You can use cardinal numbers with both ordinals (see paragraphs 2.249 to 2.256) and postdeterminers (see paragraph 2.44). When you use a cardinal number with a determiner followed by an ordinal number or a postdeterminer, the cardinal number usually comes after the determiner and the ordinal or postdeterminer.

*The first two years have been very successful.*
*...throughout the first four months of this year.*
*...the last two volumes of the encyclopedia.*
*...in the previous three years of his reign.*

Note that some postdeterminers can be used like ordinary classifying adjectives (see paragraph 2.44). When they are used like this, the cardinal number comes before them.

*He has written two previous novels.*
*...two further examples.*

**numbers as pronouns**

**2.237** When either the context makes it clear, or you think that your listener already knows something, you can use the cardinal number without a noun.

*These two are quite different.*

When cardinal numbers are used like this, you can put ordinal numbers, postdeterminers, or superlative adjectives in between the determiner and the cardinal number.

*I want to tell you about the programmes. The first four are devoted to universities.*
*The other six are masterpieces.*
*The best thirty have the potential to be successful journalists.*

**expressing large numbers**

**2.238** When you use 'dozen', 'hundred', 'thousand', 'million', or 'billion' to indicate exact numbers, you put 'a' or another number in front of them.

*...a hundred dollars.*
*...six hundred and ten miles.*
*...a thousand billion pounds.*
*...two dozen diapers.*

**WARNING** **2.239** When you use 'dozen', 'hundred', 'thousand', 'million', or 'billion' they remain singular even when the number in front of them is greater than one.

**2.240** You can use 'dozen', 'hundred', 'thousand', 'million', or 'billion' without 'of' in a less precise way by putting 'several', 'a few', and 'a couple of' in front of them.

*...several hundred people.*
*A few thousand cars have gone.*
*...life a couple of hundred years ago.*

**approximate quantities**

**2.241** When you want to emphasize how large a number is without stating it precisely, you can use 'dozens', 'hundreds', 'thousands', 'millions', and 'billions' in the same way as cardinals followed by 'of'.

*That's going to take hundreds of years.*
*...hundreds of dollars.*
*We travelled thousands of miles across Europe.*
*...languages spoken by millions of people.*
*We have dozens of friends in the community.*

You can put 'many' in front of these plural forms.

*I have travelled many hundreds of miles with them.*

**USAGE NOTE**     **2.242** People often use the plural forms when they are exaggerating.

*I was meeting thousands of people.*
*Do you have to fill in hundreds of forms before you go?*

You can also emphasize or exaggerate a large number by using these words in qualifying prepositional phrases beginning with 'by'.

*...a book which sells by the million.*
*...people who give injections by the dozen.*
*Videos of the royal wedding sold by the hundred thousand.*

**numbers as labels**     **2.243** Cardinal numbers can be used to label or identify things.

*Room 777 of the Stanley Hotel.*
*Number 11 Downing Street.*

**numbers as quantifiers**     **2.244** You can also use cardinal numbers as quantifiers linked by 'of' to a noun group referring to a group. You do this when you want to emphasize that you are talking about a part or all of a group.

*I saw four of these programmes.*
*Three of the questions today have been about democracy.*
*I use plastic kitchen bins. I have four of them.*
*All eight of my great-grandparents lived in the city.*
*All four of us wanted to get away from the Earl's Court area.*
*The clerk looked at the six of them and said, 'All of you?'*
*I find it less worrying than the two of you are suggesting.*

Quantifiers are explained in paragraphs 2.194 to 2.210.

**number quantifiers as pronouns**     **2.245** Cardinal numbers can be used to quantify something without the 'of' and the noun group, when it is clear what you are referring to.

*...a group of painters, nine or ten in all.*
*Of the other wives, two are dancers and one is a singer.*
*...the taller student of the two.*
*...breakfast for two.*

**numbers as qualifiers**     **2.246** Cardinal numbers can also be used after pronouns as qualifiers.

*In the fall we two are going to England.*
*You four, come with me.*

**numbers in compound adjectives**     **2.247** Cardinal numbers can be used as part of a **compound adjective**, (see paragraphs 2.98 to 2.107). The cardinal number is used in front of a noun to form a compound adjective which is usually hyphenated

*He took out a five-dollar bill.*
*I wrote a five-page summary of the situation.*

Note that the noun remains singular even when the number is two or more, and that compound adjectives which are formed like this cannot be used as complements. For example, you cannot say 'My essay is five-hundred-word'. Instead you would probably say 'My essay is five hundred words long'.

**numbers with time expressions** 2.248 Cardinal numbers are sometimes used with general time words such as 'month' and 'week'. You do this when you want to describe something by saying how long it lasts. If the thing is referred to with an uncount noun, you use the **possessive form** (see paragraphs 2.180 to 2.192) of the general time word.

*She's already had at least nine months' experience.*
*On Friday she had been given two weeks' notice.*

Sometimes the apostrophe is omitted.

*They wanted three weeks holiday and three weeks pay.*

The determiner 'a' is usually used when you are talking about a single period of time, although 'one' can be used instead when you want to be more formal.

*She's on a year's leave from Hunter College.*
*She was only given one week's notice.*

Cardinal numbers can also be used with general time words as modifiers of adjectives.

*She was four months pregnant.*
*The rains are two months late.*
*His rent was three weeks overdue.*

## Referring to things in a sequence: ordinal numbers

2.249 If you want to identify or describe something by indicating where it comes in a series or sequence, you use an **ordinal number.**

*Quietly they took their seats in the first three rows.*
*Flora's flat is on the fourth floor of this five-storey block.*
*They stopped at the first of the trees.*

Note that you can also use 'following', 'last', 'next', 'preceding', 'previous', and 'subsequent' like ordinal numbers to indicate where something comes in a series or sequence.

*The following morning he checked out of the hotel.*
*...the last rungs of the fire-escape.*
*...at the next general election.*
*The preceding text has been professionally transcribed.*
*I mentioned this in a previous programme.*
*...the subsequent career patterns of those taking degrees.*

'Following', 'subsequent', 'previous', and 'preceding' are only used to indicate the position of something in a sequence in time or in a piece of writing. 'Next' and 'last' are used more generally, for example to refer to things in rows or lists.

The ordinal numbers are listed in the Reference Section.

**as modifiers** 2.250 Ordinals are often used in front of nouns. They are not usually used as complements after link verbs like 'be'. They are usually preceded by a determiner.

*...the first day of autumn.*

*He took the lift to the sixteenth floor.*
*...on her twenty-first birthday.*
*...his father's second marriage.*

In some idiomatic phrases ordinals are used without determiners.

*The picture seems at first glance chaotic.*
*I might. On second thoughts, no.*
*First children usually get a lot of attention.*

**written forms**　**2.251** Ordinals can be written in abbreviated form, for example in dates or headings or in very informal writing. You write the last two letters of the ordinal after the number expressed in figures. For example, 'first' can be written as '1st', 'twenty-second' as '22nd', 'hundred and third' as '103rd', and 'fourteenth' as '14th'.

*...on August 2nd.*
*...the 1st Division of the Sovereign's Escort.*
*...the 11th Cavalry.*

**ordinals**　**2.252** You can specify which group the thing referred to by an ordinal
**with 'of'**　belongs to by using the preposition 'of' after the ordinal.

*It is the third of a series of eight programmes.*
*Tony was the second of four sons.*

When ordinals are used like this, they usually refer to one person or thing. However, when they are used with a 'to'-infinitive clause or another qualifying phrase or clause after them, they can refer to one person or thing or to more than one. 'First' is used like this more than the other ordinals.

*I was the first to recover.*
*They had to be the first to go.*
*The proposals—the first for 22 years—amount to a new charter for the mentally ill.*
*The withdrawals were the first that the army agreed to.*

**as pronouns**　**2.253** You can use an ordinal to refer to a member of a group that you have already mentioned or to something of the kind already mentioned, and you can omit the noun which identifies the thing.

*In August 1932 two of the group's members were expelled from the party and a third was suspended.*
*The third child tries to outdo the first and second.*
*A second pheasant flew up. Then a third and a fourth.*

**2.254** The adjectives 'next' and 'last' can be used, like ordinals, by themselves when the context makes the meaning clear.

*You missed one meal. The next is on the table in half an hour.*
*Smithy removed the last of the screws.*

**ordinals**　**2.255** The ordinal 'first' is also used as an adverb to indicate that
**used**　something is done before other things. Other ordinals are also sometimes
**as adverbs**　used to indicate the order in which things are done, especially in informal English. People also use ordinals as adverbs when they are giving a list of points, reasons, or items. This is explained fully in paragraph 10.79.

**other uses
of ordinals**

**2.256** The use of ordinals in expressing fractions is explained in paragraphs 2.258 and 2.260. The use of ordinals to express dates, as in 'the seventeenth of June', is explained in paragraph 5.87.

Ordinal numbers can be used in front of cardinal numbers. This is explained in paragraphs 2.236 to 2.237.

# Referring to an exact part of something: fractions

**2.257** When you want to indicate how large a part of something is compared to the whole of it, you use a **fraction,** such as 'a third', followed by 'of' and a noun group referring to the whole thing. Fractions can also be written in figures (see paragraph 2.265).

**singular
fractions**

**2.258** When you express a fraction in words, the way you do so depends on whether the fraction is singular or plural. If it is singular, you write or say an **ordinal number** or the special fraction terms 'half' or 'quarter', with either the number 'one' or a determiner such as 'a' in front of them. The fraction is linked to a noun group by 'of'.

This state produces a third of the nation's oil.
...a quarter of an inch.
You can take a fifth of your money out on demand.
A tenth of our budget goes on fuel.
Forests cover one third of the country.
...one thousandth of a degree.
... one quarter of the total population.

An adjective can also be placed after the determiner and before the fraction.

...the first half of the twentieth century.
I read the first half of the book.
...the southern half of England.
...in the first quarter of 2004.

**USAGE NOTE**

**2.259** If you are using 'half' in front of a pronoun, you still use 'of' after the 'half'.

Nearly half of it comes from the Middle East.
More than half of them have gone home.
Half of us have lost our jobs.

Note that when the fraction 'a half' is used with 'of' as a quantifier you usually write or say it as 'half' without a determiner. 'A half' and 'one half' are rarely used.

They lost half of their pay.
Half of the people went to private schools.
I had crossed more than half of America.

**plural
fractions**

**2.260** If the fraction is plural, you put a **cardinal number** in front of a plural form of the **ordinal number** or special fraction word 'quarter'.

...the poorer two thirds of the world.
The journey is going to take three quarters of an hour.

*...four fifths of the money.*
*Nine tenths of them live on the land.*
*...3 millionths of a centimetre.*

When 'half' is used with whole numbers or amounts, it is used with the determiner 'a'.

*...one and a half acres of land.*
*...four and a half centuries.*

**agreement with verb**   **2.261** When you talk about fractions of a single thing, you use a singular form of a verb afterwards.

*Half of our work is to design programmes.*
*Two thirds of the planet's surface is covered with water.*
*Two fifths of the forest was removed.*

However, when you talk about fractions of a number of things, you use a plural form of a verb afterwards.

*Two thirds of Chad's exports were cotton.*
*A quarter of the students were seen individually.*
*More than half of these photographs are of her.*

**fractions as pronouns**   **2.262** When it is clear to your listener or reader who or what you are referring to, either because of the context or because you and your listener or reader know what is meant, you can use fractions as pronouns without the quantifying 'of' and noun group after them.

*Of the people who work here, half are French and half are English.*
*Two thirds were sterilized.*
*One sixth are disappointed with the service.*

**numbers followed by fractions**   **2.263** Besides their use as quantifiers linked by 'of' to a noun group, fractions can also be used after a whole number or amount plus 'and', with a noun placed after the fraction. The noun must be plural even if the number is 'one'.

*You've got to sit there for one and a half hours.*
*...five and a quarter days.*
*...more than four and a half centuries ago*

If you are using 'a' instead of 'one', the 'and' and the fraction come after the noun.

*...a mile and a half below the surface.*
*...a mile and a quarter of motorway.*

**'half' as predeterminer**   **2.264** Besides being used with 'of' as a quantifier, 'half' can also be used as a **predeterminer,** (see paragraph 1.236), directly in front of a determiner.

*I met half the girls at the conference.*
*The farmers sold off half their land.*
*...half a pound of coffee.*
*...half a bottle of milk.*

Note that 'half' is always used with 'of' before a pronoun (see paragraph 2.259).

**fractions expressed in figures**   **2.265** You can write a fraction in figures, for example $\frac{1}{2}$, $\frac{1}{4}$, $\frac{3}{4}$ and $\frac{2}{3}$. These correspond to 'a half', 'a quarter', 'three quarters' and 'two thirds' respectively.

**expressing**
**percentages**

**2.266** Fractions are often given in a special form as a number of hundredths. This type of fraction is called a **percentage.** For example, 'three hundredths', expressed as a percentage, is 'three per cent'. It can also be written as 'three percent' or '3%'. 'A half' can be expressed as 'fifty per cent', 'fifty percent', or '50%'.

*90 percent of most food is water.*
*About 20 per cent of student accountants are women.*
*Before 1960 45% of British trade was with the Commonwealth.*

You can use percentages on their own as noun groups when it is clear what they refer to.

*Ninety per cent were self employed.*
*...interest at 10% per annum.*

# Talking about measurements

**2.267** You can refer to a size, distance, area, volume, weight, speed, or temperature by using a number or quantifier in front of a **measurement noun.** Measurement nouns are countable.

*They grow to twenty feet.*
*...blocks of stone weighing up to a hundred tons.*
*Reduce the temperature by a few degrees.*
*Average annual temperatures exceed 20° centigrade.*

Other ways of expressing distance are explained in paragraphs 6.71 to 6.72. Measurement nouns referring to size, area, volume, and weight are often used in **partitive structures** (see paragraphs 2.211 to 2.224) such as 'a pint of milk' and 'a pound of onions'. They can also be used as **qualifiers** beginning with 'of' (see paragraph 2.300).

**imperial**
**and metric**
**measurements**

**2.268** There are two systems of measurement used in Britain—the **imperial system** and the **metric system.** Each system has its own measurement nouns.

Here is a list of the imperial units of measurement indicating size, distance, area, volume, and weight:

| | | | |
|---|---|---|---|
| inch | ~ | quart | pound |
| foot | acre | gallon | stone |
| yard | ~ | ~ | hundredweight |
| mile | pint | ounce | ton |

Note that the plural of 'foot' is 'feet', but 'foot' can also be used with numbers. Similarly 'stone' is often used instead of 'stones'.

Here is a list of the metric units of measurement indicating size, distance, area, volume, and weight:

| | | | | |
|---|---|---|---|---|
| millimetre | kilometre | ~ | litre | gram |
| centimetre | ~ | millilitre | ~ | kilogram |
| metre | hectare | centilitre | milligram | tonne |

**as**
**complements**

**2.269** Measurement nouns are often used as the **complements** of link verbs such as 'be', 'measure' and 'weigh'.

*The fish was about eight feet long.*

It _measures_ approximately 26 inches wide x 25 inches long.
...a square area _measuring_ 900 metres on each side.
It _weighs_ fifty or more kilos.

The use of adjectives as the complements of link verbs is explained in paragraphs 3.133 to 3.138.

**adjectives after measurements**

**2.270** When measurement nouns that give the size of something are used as complements, they can often be followed by an adjective which makes it clear exactly what the measurement refers to.

He was about _six feet tall_.
The spears were about _six foot long_.
...a room _2 metres wide_.
The water was _fifteen feet deep_.
...a layer of stone _four metres thick_.

Here is a list of the adjectives that follow measurement nouns indicating size:

| broad | high | tall | wide |
|-------|------|------|------|
| deep | long | thick | |

Note that you do not say 'two pounds heavy' but 'two pounds in weight' instead.

**prepositional phrases after measurements**

**2.271** Similarly, some measurement nouns can be followed by prepositional phrases beginning with 'in'.

...a block of ice one cubic foot _in size_.
I put on nearly a stone _in weight_.
They are thirty centimetres _in length_.
...deposits measuring up to a kilometre _in thickness_.
It was close on ten feet _in height_.

Here is a list of prepositional phrases used after measurements:

| in area | in height | in thickness | in width |
|---------|-----------|--------------|----------|
| in depth | in length | in volume | |
| in distance | in size | in weight | |

**measurement nouns used as modifiers**

**2.272** Measurement nouns can also be used as modifiers in front of a noun when you want to describe things in terms of their measurements.

...a _5 foot 9 inch_ bed.
..._70 foot high_ mounds of dust.
..._12 x 12 inch_ tiles.
...a _five-pound_ bag of lentils.

Note that the measurement noun is singular.

**USAGE NOTE**

**2.273** If you want to describe fully the size of an object or area, you can give its dimensions; that is, you give measurements of its length and width, or length, width, and depth. When you give the dimensions of an object, you separate the figures using 'and', 'by', or the multiplication sign 'x'.

...planks of wood about _three inches thick and two feet wide_.
The island measures about _25 miles by 12 miles_.
Lake Nyasa is _450 miles long by about 50 miles wide_.
The box measures approximately _26 inches wide x 25 inches deep x 16 inches high_.

If you are talking about a square object or area, you give the length of each side followed by the word 'square'.

*Each family has only one room eight or ten feet square.*
*The site measures roughly 35 feet square.*

'Square' is used in front of units of length when expressing area. 'Cubic' is used in front of units of length when expressing volume.

*...a farm covering 300 square miles.*
*The brain of the first ape-men had been about the same size as that of a gorilla, around 500 cubic centimetres.*

You express temperature in degrees, using either degrees centigrade, or degrees Fahrenheit. Note that in everyday language the metric term centigrade is used to indicate temperature, whereas in scientific language the term 'Celsius' is used which refers to exactly the same scale of measurement.

**2.274** You talk about the speed of something by saying how far it can travel in a particular unit of time. To do this, you use a noun such as 'mile' or 'kilometre', followed by 'per', 'a', or 'an', and a time noun.

*The car could do only forty-five miles per hour.*
*Wind speeds at the airport were 160 kilometres per hour.*
*Warships move at about 500 miles per day.*

# Talking about age

**2.275** When you want to say how old someone is, you have a choice of ways in which to do it. You can be exact or approximate. Similarly, when you want to say how old something is, you can use different ways, some exact, and some approximate.

**indicating exact age**

**2.276** When you want to talk about a person's exact age, you can do so by using

- 'be' followed by a number, and sometimes 'years old' after the number

*I was nineteen, and he was twenty-one.*
*I'm only 63.*
*She is twenty-five years old.*
*I am forty years old.*

- 'of' (and less commonly 'aged') and a number after a noun

*...a child of six.*
*...two little boys aged about nine and eleven.*

- a compound adjective, usually hyphenated, consisting of a number, followed by a singular noun referring to a period of time, followed by 'old'

*...a twenty-two-year-old student.*
*...a five-month-old baby.*
*...a quaint 350-year-old cottage.*
*...a violation of a six-year-old agreement.*

- a compound noun consisting of a number followed by '-year-old'

*The servant was a pale little fourteen-year-old who looked hardly more than ten.*

*All the six-year-olds are taught by one teacher.*
*...Melvin Kalkhoven, a tall, thin thirty-five-year-old.*

**indicating approximate age**

**2.277** When you want to talk about a person's age in an approximate way, you can do so by using

● 'in', followed by a possessive determiner, followed by a plural noun referring to a particular range of years such as 'twenties' and 'teens'

*He was in his sixties.*
*I didn't mature till I was in my forties.*
*...the groups who are now in their thirties.*
*...when I was in my teens.*

Note that you can use 'early', 'mid-', 'middle', or 'late' to indicate approximately where someone's age comes in a particular range of years.

*He was then in his late seventies.*
*She was in her mid-twenties.*
*Jane is only in her early forties.*

● 'over' or 'under' followed by a number

*She was well over fifty.*
*She was only a little over forty years old.*
*There weren't enough people who were under 25.*

Note that you can also use 'above' or 'below' followed by 'the age of' and a number.

*55 per cent of them were below the age of twenty-one.*

● a compound noun indicating a group of people whose age is more or less than a particular number, which consists of 'over' or 'under' followed by the plural form of the particular number

*The over-sixties do not want to be turned out of their homes.*
*Schooling for under-fives should be expanded.*

**2.278** You can put several of the above structures after a noun to indicate the age of a person or thing.

*...a woman in her early thirties.*
*...help for elderly ladies over 65.*
*She had four children under the age of five.*

**2.279** If you want to indicate that someone's age is similar to someone else's age, you can use structures such as 'of his age' and 'of her parents' age' after a noun. The 'of' is often dropped.

*Most girls of Helen's age are interested in boys.*
*It's easy to make friends because you're with people of your own age.*
*She will have a tough time when she plays with children her own age.*

**indicating the age of a thing**

**2.280** If you want to say what the age of a thing is, you can use

● 'be' followed by a number followed by 'years old'

*It's at least a thousand million years old.*
*The house was about thirty years old.*

Note that you can also use this pattern after a noun.

*...rocks 200 million years old.*

● a compound adjective indicating the century when something existed or was made, which consists of an ordinal number and 'century'

...a *sixth-century* church.
...life in *fifth-century* Athens.

# Approximate amounts and measurements

**2.281** If you do not know the exact number, size, or quantity of something, you can give an approximate amount or measurement using one of a group of special words and expressions. Some of these words and expressions are put in front of a quantity and some are put after it.

Here is a list of some of the words and expressions used to give approximate amounts and measurements:

| | | | |
|---|---|---|---|
| about | at most | nearly | or under |
| almost | at the maximum | no more than | over |
| a maximum of | at the most | odd | roughly |
| a minimum of | less than | or less | some |
| approximately | maximum | or more | something like |
| around | minimum | or so | under |
| at least | more than | or thereabouts | up to |

**expressing minimum amounts** **2.282** Some of these indicate that a number is a minimum figure and that the actual figure is or may be larger.

Here is a list of expressions which indicate a minimum number:

| | | | |
|---|---|---|---|
| a minimum of | minimum | or more | plus |
| at least | more than | over | |

**USAGE NOTE** **2.283** You put 'a minimum of', 'more than', and 'over' in front of a number.

He needed *a minimum of* 26 Democratic votes.
...a school with *more than* 1300 pupils.
The British have been on the island for *over* a thousand years.

You put 'or more' and 'plus' after a number or amount, and 'minimum' after an amount.

...a choice of three *or more* possibilities.
This is the worst disaster I can remember in my 25 years *plus* as a police officer.
He does an hour's homework per night *minimum*.

You put 'at least' in front of a number or after a number or amount.

She had *at least* a dozen brandies.
I must have slept twelve hours *at least*!

**expressing maximum amounts** **2.284** Some of these expressions are used to indicate that a number is a maximum figure and that the actual figure is or may be smaller.

Here is a list of expressions which indicate a maximum number:

| | | | |
|---|---|---|---|
| almost | at the most | no more than | up to |
| a maximum of | less than | or less | |
| at most | maximum | or under | |
| at the maximum | nearly | under | |

**USAGE NOTE**  **2.285**  You put 'almost', 'a maximum of', 'less than', 'nearly', 'no more than', 'under', and 'up to' in front of a number.

*The company now supplies almost 100 of Paris's restaurants.*
*These loans must be repaid over a maximum of three years.*
*...a puppy less than seven weeks old.*
*She had nearly fifty dollars.*
*We managed to finish the entire job in under three months.*
*Their bodies might be up to a metre wide.*

You put 'at the maximum', 'at most', 'at the most', 'maximum', 'or less', and 'or under' after a number.

*Classes are of eight at the maximum.*
*The images take thirty-six hours maximum.*
*The area would yield only 200 pounds of rice or less.*
*...12 hours a week or under.*

**expressing**   **2.286**  Some of these expressions are used to indicate that a number is
**approximate**   approximate and that the actual figure could be larger or smaller.
**amounts**
Here is a list of the expressions indicating that a number is approximate:

| | | |
|---|---|---|
| about | odd | roughly |
| approximately | or so | some |
| around | or thereabouts | something like |

**USAGE NOTE**  **2.287**  You put 'about', 'approximately', 'around', 'roughly', 'some', and 'something like' in front of a number.

*About 85 students were there.*
*Every year we have approximately 40 pupils who take mathematics.*
*It would cost around 35 million pounds.*
*A loft conversion costs roughly £12,000.*
*They have to pay America some $683,000 this year.*
*Harrington has cheated us out of something like thirty thousand quid over the past two years.*

You put 'odd' and 'or so' after a number or amount, and 'or thereabouts' after an amount.

*...a hundred odd acres.*
*For half a minute or so, neither of them spoke.*
*Get the temperature to 30°C or thereabouts.*

**2.288**  You can indicate a range of numbers using 'between' and 'and', or 'from' and 'to', or just 'to'.

*Most of the farms around here are between four and five hundred years old.*
*My hospital groups contain from ten to twenty patients.*
*...peasants owning two to five acres of land.*

Note the use of 'anything' before 'between' and 'from', to emphasize how great the range is.

*An average rate of anything between 25 and 60 per cent is usual.*
*It is a job that takes anything from two to five weeks.*

# Expanding the noun group : qualifiers

**2.289** This section deals with structures which can be used to **qualify** headwords; that is, structures which can be used after headwords to add further information about the person or thing referred to. These are called **qualifiers** or **qualifying structures** The headword is usually a noun but can be an indefinite pronoun or 'those'.

**qualifying structures**

**2.290** Qualifiers can consist of one or more words. The qualifiers which are dealt with in this section are

● prepositional phrases

...*a girl* with red hair.
...*the man* in the dark glasses.

The use of prepositional phrases as qualifiers is explained in paragraphs 2.292 to 2.307.

● adjectives followed by phrases or clauses

...*machinery* capable of clearing rubble off the main roads.
...*the type of comments* likely to provoke criticism.
...*a concept* inconceivable a hundred years earlier.

The use of adjectives followed by phrases or clauses as qualifiers is explained in paragraphs 2.308 to 2.309.

● non-finite clauses

...*a simple device* to test lung function.
...*two of the problems* mentioned above.
*He gestured towards the three cards* lying on the table.

The use of non-finite clauses as qualifiers is explained in paragraphs 2.310 to 2.318.

● noun groups giving further information about other noun groups. This is explained in paragraphs 2.319 to 2.320.

**2.291** Some other structures can also be used as qualifiers. These are explained fully in other sections. They include

● one word qualifiers such as 'galore' and 'concerned' which are explained in paragraphs 2.62 to 2.66.

● relative clauses

*Shortly after the shooting, the man* who had done it *was arrested.*
*Where's* that cake your mother made?

Relative clauses are explained in paragraphs 8.83 to 8.116.

● place adverbs and time adverbs

...*down in the dungeon* beneath.
...*a reflection of life* today in England.

Adverbs of time are explained in paragraphs 5.7 to 5.83 and adverbs of place are explained in paragraphs 6.82 to 6.100.

## Nouns with prepositional phrases

**2.292** In general, any prepositional phrase which describes or classifies something can be used directly after a noun or pronoun to qualify it.

*...the man in charge.*
*...a film about four men on holiday.*
*She reached into the room behind her.*

**2.293** In particular, there are several kinds of prepositional phrase which are usually only used as qualifiers. Of these, prepositional phrases beginning with 'of' are the most numerous. Others include certain uses of 'with', 'in' and 'by'.

**'of'** **2.294** Many nouns referring to things and actions can be expanded by using prepositional phrases beginning with 'of' as qualifiers after them. This allows the noun to be expanded with a wide range of meanings. You can use 'of' with nouns referring to feelings such as 'love' and 'fear' to indicate what the feeling relates to; for example, 'fear of flying' and 'love of animals'. Further meanings are described in the following paragraphs.

**WARNING** **2.295** **Personal pronouns** are not usually put after 'of'. For example, you cannot say 'Joyce was the daughter of him' or 'the pages of it'. **Possessive determiners** are used instead to indicate possession. These are explained in paragraphs 1.192 to 1.207.

**2.296** Prepositional phrases beginning with 'of' can be used to indicate what something consists of.

*...a letter of confirmation.*
*...strong feelings of jealousy.*

They can also be used to indicate what the subject matter of something is.

*...a picture of a house.*
*...Gretchen's account of her interview with Nichols.*
*...the idea of death.*

**2.297** Prepositional phrases beginning with 'of' can be used to say that something belongs to or is associated with someone or something.

*COBUILD is a trademark of William Collins Sons & Co. Ltd.*
*No.28 was the town house of Sir Winston Churchill.*
*James is the son of a Methodist minister.*
*The acting ability of the pupils is admirable.*
*...the beauty of the Welsh landscape.*
*Four boys sat on the floor of the living room.*
*Ellen aimlessly turned the pages of her magazine.*

Note that apostrophe s ('s) structures are much more frequently used to say that something belongs to someone or something. **Apostrophe s** ('s) is explained in paragraphs 2.180 to 2.192.

**2.298** Prepositional phrases beginning with 'of' can be used to say that someone or something has a particular quality.

*...a woman of energy and ambition.*
*...problems of varying complexity.*
*...a flower of monstrous proportions.*
*A household of this size inevitably has problems.*

'Of' can also be used in front of a number to indicate someone's age.

*...a woman of twenty-two.*
*...a child of six.*

Other ways of indicating age are explained in paragraphs 2.275 to 2.280.

**2.299** Prepositional phrases beginning with 'of' can be used with nouns referring to an action to indicate who or what is performing the action.

*...the arrival of the police.*
*...the growth of modern industry.*

They can also be used to show who or what someone does something to. For example, if you are talking about people who support a scheme, you can call them 'the supporters of the scheme'.

*...supporters of the hunger strike.*
*...critics of the Trade Union Movement.*
*...the creator of the universe.*
*...a student of English.*
*...the cause of the tragedy.*

'Of' structures are also used to indicate the thing affected by an action.

*...the destruction of their city.*
*...the dismissal of hundreds of workers.*

**2.300** Prepositional phrases beginning with 'of' and containing measurement are used to indicate how great an area, speed, distance, or temperature is.

*There were fires burning over a total area of about 600 square miles.*
*It can barely maintain a speed of 25 kilometres an hour.*
*...an average annual temperature of 20°.*

Ways of measuring things are explained in paragraphs 2.267 to 2.274.

**'with'** **2.301** Prepositional phrases beginning with 'with' can be used to say that someone or something has a particular characteristic, feature, or possession.

*...a girl with red hair.*
*...a girl with a foreign accent.*
*...a big car with reclining seats.*
*...a man with a violent temper.*
*...the man with the gun.*
*...those with large families.*

They can also be used to indicate what something has on or in it.

*...a sheet of paper with writing on it.*
*...a round box with some buttons in it.*
*...a white, plain envelope with her name printed on it.*
*...fragments of wrapping paper with bits of sticky tape still adhering to them.*

**'in'** **2.302** Prepositional phrases beginning with 'in' can be used to indicate what someone is wearing.

*...a grey-haired man in a raincoat.*
*...the man in the dark glasses.*
*...little groups of people in black.*

**'by'** **2.303** Prepositional phrases beginning with 'by' can be used after a noun referring to an action to indicate who or what is performing it.

*...his appointment by the King.*
*...the compression of air by the piston.*

**with** **2.304** Some nouns, especially abstract nouns, need to be followed by a
**prepositional** prepositional phrase to show what they relate to. There is often little or no
**phrases** choice about which preposition to use after a particular noun.

*He has an allergy to peanuts.*
*...his authority over them.*
*...the solution to our energy problem.*
*...the bond between mother and child.*

**2.305** Here is a list of nouns which usually or often have 'to' after them:

| | | | | |
|---|---|---|---|---|
| access | answer | disloyalty | recourse | susceptibility |
| addiction | antidote | exception | reference | testimony |
| adherence | approach | fidelity | relevance | threat |
| affront | attachment | immune | reply | vulnerability |
| allegiance | aversion | incitement | resistance | witness |
| allergy | contribution | introduction | return | |
| allusion | damage | preface | sequel | |
| alternative | devotion | prelude | solution | |

Here is a list of nouns which usually or often have 'for' after them:

| | | | | |
|---|---|---|---|---|
| admiration | cure | disrespect | recipe | search |
| appetite | demand | hunger | regard | substitute |
| aptitude | desire | love | remedy | sympathy |
| bid | disdain | need | respect | synonym |
| craving | dislike | provision | responsibility | taste |
| credit | disregard | quest | room | thirst |

Here is a list of nouns which usually or often have 'on' after them:

| | | | | |
|---|---|---|---|---|
| assault | comment | curb | hold | restriction |
| attack | concentration | dependence | insistence | stance |
| ban | constraint | effect | reflection | tax |
| claim | crackdown | embargo | reliance | |

Here is a list of nouns which usually or often have 'with' after them:

| | | | |
|---|---|---|---|
| affinity | correspondence | familiarity | link |
| collision | date | identification | parity |
| collusion | dealings | intersection | quarrel |
| connection | dissatisfaction | intimacy | relationship |
| contrast | encounter | involvement | sympathy |

Here is a list of nouns which are usually followed by one of two prepositions. The list indicates the choice of prepositions available:

| | | | |
|---|---|---|---|
| agreement about | battle against | debate about | transition from |
| agreement on | battle for | debate on | transition to |
| argument against | case against | decision about | |
| argument for | case for | decision on | |

Here is a list of other nouns usually followed by a preposition.

| | | | |
|---|---|---|---|
| complex about | safeguard against | excerpt from | awareness of |
| crime against | anger at | freedom from | authority over |
| grudge against | bond between | quotation from | control over |
| insurance against | departure from | foray into | |
| reaction against | escape from | relapse into | |

As you can see from the lists and examples given above, it is often the case that words with a similar meaning are typically followed by the same preposition. For example, 'appetite', 'craving', 'desire', 'hunger', and 'thirst' are all followed by 'for'.

**USAGE NOTE**  **2.306** Some nouns are related to verbs which are always or often followed by a particular preposition. These nouns are followed by the same preposition as their related verbs, and they are used to indicate the thing that is affected by the action. For example, 'to' is used after both the verb 'refer' and the related noun 'reference'.

We have already *referred to* this phenomenon.
...reverent *references to* the importance of home.

They swim about busily *searching for* food.
...the *search for* food.

I want to *escape from* here.
...an *escape from* reality.

**2.307** Some nouns referring to a feeling or state are related to an adjective which is usually followed by a preposition. These nouns are followed by the same preposition as their related adjectives. For example, 'of' is used after the adjective 'aware' and the related noun 'awareness'.

She was quite *aware of* her current situation.
...the public's increasing *awareness of* the problems.

He was *angry at* Sally Gardner for accusing him.
...her *anger at* the kids.

I am, of course, *familiar with* your work.
...*familiarity with* western ideas.

It is clean and *free from* pollutants and infections.
...*freedom from* oppression.

## Nouns with adjectives

**2.308** When adjectives are used in qualifying clauses after nouns or pronouns they can be followed by

- prepositional phrases

...machinery *capable of clearing rubble off the main roads.*
...a warning to people *eager for a quick cure.*
...those *responsible for the project.*
...the vicious poverty cycle *so common in single-parent families.*

- 'to'-infinitive clauses

...remarks *likely to cause offence.*
It has been directed against those *least able to retaliate.*

- adjuncts of time or place

...a concept *inconceivable a hundred years earlier.*
For the facilities *available here,* I must ask for a fee.
...the stars *visible in the night sky.*

Note that you can use adjectives as qualifiers when they are preceded by adjuncts of time or measurement.

...those *still alive.*

*...a small hill <u>about 400 feet high</u>.*

Note also that a few adjectives, such as 'present' and 'responsible', can be used on their own after a noun or pronoun. The use of these adjectives is explained in paragraphs 2.62 to 2.66.

**other**
**qualifying**
**structures**

**2.309** There are some other structures, especially those which indicate comparison, degree, or result, which often involve a qualifier. In particular, some kinds of submodifiers of adjectives often have a qualifier to complete their meaning.

*Peter came in, <u>more excited than anyone had seen him before</u>.*
*Ralph was too <u>angry to think clearly</u>.*
*...steel cylinders <u>strong enough to survive a nuclear catastrophe</u>.*
*...a grand piano <u>as big as two coffins</u>.*
*She was <u>so ill that she couldn't eat</u>.*
*Technology has made <u>such spectacular advances that it is difficult to keep up</u>.*

The use of comparative adjectives plus 'than' after noun groups is explained in paragraphs 2.111 to 2.113. Other ways of comparing things are explained in paragraphs 2.128 to 2.144. The use of 'so...that' and 'such...that' is explained in paragraphs 8.58 to 8.63.

# Nouns with non-finite clauses

**2.310** There are three types of non-finite clauses which can be used as qualifiers. These are 'to'-infinitive clauses (see paragraphs 2.311 to 2.316), past participle clauses (see paragraph 2.317), and present participle clauses (see paragraph 2.318).

**with**
**'to'-infinitive**
**clauses**

**2.311** A 'to'-infinitive clause is often put after nouns in order to show what the thing referred to is intended to do.

*The government of Mexico set up a programme <u>to develop new varieties of wheat</u>.*
*...a simple device <u>to test lung function</u>.*
*They need people <u>to work in the factories</u>.*

**2.312** You can refer to something or someone that should or can have something done to them by using a clause containing a 'to'-infinitive after a noun or indefinite pronoun.

*I make notes in the back of my diary of things <u>to be mended or replaced</u>.*
*...when I've had something <u>to eat</u>.*

You can also use a clause consisting of a 'to'-infinitive followed by a preposition.

*There wasn't even a chair <u>to sit on</u>.*
*There would always be a sofa <u>to sleep on</u>.*
*He remembered he had nothing <u>to write with</u>.*

**2.313** You can also use a 'to'-infinitive clause when you want to say that you are talking about, for example, the first, oldest, or only person who did something.

*...the first woman <u>to be elected to the council</u>.*
*...the next person <u>to speak</u>.*
*...the oldest person <u>to be chosen</u>.*

**2.314** A clause containing a 'to -infinitive is used after some abstract nouns to show what action they relate to.

*...people who didn't have the opportunity to go to university.*
*...trying to think of a way to stop him.*

**USAGE NOTE**  **2.315** Many of these nouns are related to verbs or adjectives which are also often followed by 'to'-infinitive clauses. For example, a 'to'-infinitive clause is used after both the verb 'need' and the noun 'need', and after both the adjective 'able' and the related noun 'ability'.

*I need to borrow five thousand dollars.*
*...the need to preserve secrecy about their intentions.*

*I may be able to help you.*
*...the ability to read.*

*It failed to grow.*
*...our failure to adapt ourselves to modern life.*

**2.316** Here is a list of nouns which usually or often have a 'to'-infinitive clause after them:

| | | | | |
|---|---|---|---|---|
| ability | compulsion | inability | reason | way |
| attempt | desire | need | refusal | willingness |
| bid | disinclination | opportunity | unwillingness | |
| chance | failure | readiness | urge | |

**with past participle clauses**  **2.317** A past participle clause can be used directly after a noun to show that something has been produced or affected by an action.

*...a girl called Patricia.*
*...dresses made of paper.*
*...two of the problems mentioned above.*
*...the machine already mentioned.*
*...a minister appointed by the Prime Minister.*
*...a story written by a nine-year-old girl.*
*...instruments designed to extend the range of our senses.*

**with present participle clauses**  **2.318** A present participle clause can be used directly after a noun to indicate that something is doing something.

*He gestured towards the three cards lying on the table.*
*...a wicker shopping-basket containing groceries.*
*...those still working.*
*...the scream of a man dying in torment.*

**apposition**  **2.319** When you want to give further information about someone or something by using a noun group which describes them or identifies them you can put this noun group after the headword. This is often called **apposition.** The use of noun groups in apposition is closely associated with defining and non-defining relative clauses, which are explained in paragraphs 8.83 to 8.111.

**2.320** If you put this noun group after the main noun group, a comma is almost always put after the main noun group because the second noun group is separate from it, not part of it.

*...the bald eagle, the symbol of America.*
*...Orville Wright, the first man to fly.*
*...David Beckham, a first-class football player.*
*...Steve Race, the musician and broadcaster.*
*Her mother, a Canadian, died when she was six.*

*...a book by a distinguished Scotsman, <u>Ramsey Weir.</u>*

If you put this noun group before the main noun group, you can sometimes choose whether to use a comma to separate the two noun groups or not.

*...the American writer Alvin Toffler.*
*...Joan's husband, Jim Inglis.*
*...my husband George.*

# Contents of Chapter 3

# 3 Making a message

3.1 When you make a statement, you use a **clause**. A clause which is used to make a statement contains a **noun group,** which refers to the person or thing that you are talking about, and a **verb group,** which indicates what sort of action, process, or state you are talking about.

The noun group, which usually comes in front of the verb group, is called the **subject** of the verb or the clause. For example, in the clause 'Ellen laughed', 'Ellen' is the subject. The formation of noun groups is explained in Chapters 1 and 2.

A verb group used in a statement is **finite.** The elements of a finite verb group and their form depend on what tense you want to use and whether one person or thing is performing the action, or more than one. The formation of verb groups is explained in the Reference Section. Quite often in statements the verb group is a single word, and it is quite common to talk about the 'verb' of a clause.

When you say something, you can be talking about an action that involves one or more participants. Indicating participants in a clause is called **transitivity.** See paragraphs 3.2 to 3.126. You can also be describing someone or something, or saying that they are a particular thing. Describing and identifying things is called **complementation.** See paragraphs 3.127 to 3.182. A third kind of statement involves talking about two actions that are closely linked. This is called **phase.** See paragraphs 3.183 to 3.213.

Although this chapter mainly describes finite clauses, the information that it gives about transitivity and complementation also applies to **non-finite clauses,** that is, clauses whose verb is an infinitive or a participle. Non-finite verb groups can be followed by objects, adjuncts, and complements, just as finite verb groups can.

This chapter deals mainly with the use of verbs in **active** clauses, where the subject is the performer of an action rather than the person or thing affected by an action. The use of verbs in **passive** clauses, where the subject is the person or thing affected, is explained in paragraphs 10.8 to 10.24.

## Indicating how many participants are involved: transitivity

3.2 In this grammar, transitivity is explained in relation to the clause as a whole. Many grammars deal with transitivity in terms of the way in which a verb selects objects. However, the verb, while usually central in clause structure, is not necessarily chosen first. This grammar explains subject, verb, and object relations by describing how statements are created.

**intransitive verbs** 3.3 If an action or event involves only one person or thing, you mention only the performer of the action (the subject) and the action (the verb).

*The girl screamed.*

*I waited.*
*An awful thing has happened.*

Clauses of this kind are called **intransitive clauses**. Verbs which occur in intransitive clauses are called **intransitive verbs**.

However, you can then mention another person or thing which is involved using a **prepositional phrase.**

*She walked across the street.*

Intransitive verbs are explained in paragraphs 3.9 to 3.14.

**transitive verbs**
**3.4** If the action or event involves another person or thing which the action affects, relates to, or produces, you put a noun group referring to them after the verb group. This is called the **object** of the verb or clause. If it is necessary to distinguish it from other objects, it is called the **direct object.**

*He closed the door.*
*I hate sport.*
*Some of the women noticed me.*

Clauses which have a direct object are called **transitive clauses,** and verbs which occur in transitive clauses are called **transitive verbs**. Transitive verbs are explained in paragraphs 3.15 to 3.26.

**Reflexive verbs** and **delexical verbs** are special kinds of transitive verbs. They are explained in paragraphs 3.27 to 3.32 and 3.33 to 3.46.

**intransitive or transitive verbs**
**3.5** The majority of verbs in English give you the option of presenting an event either as involving the subject only or as involving the subject and someone or something else as a direct object.

*She paints pictures by holding the brush in her teeth.*
*Yarkov paints vivid portraits of friends and acquaintances.*

*Gus asked me whether I'd like to have dinner with him. I accepted.*
*I accepted the invitation.*

This means that most verbs can be used in transitive clauses as well as intransitive clauses. Verbs which can be used in either type of clause are explained in paragraphs 3.47 to 3.55.

With some verbs, the thing affected by the action can be put as the object of the verb or as the object of a preposition after the verb. These verbs are explained in paragraphs 3.56 to 3.59.

**Ergative verbs** are a special kind of verb which can be used in intransitive or transitive clauses. They are explained in paragraphs 3.60 to 3.68.

**reciprocal verbs**
**3.6** There are two kinds of **reciprocal verbs,** which refer to actions which involve people doing the same thing to each other. One kind is used in intransitive or transitive clauses; the other kind is used in intransitive clauses, with or without a prepositional phrase mentioning one of the participants.

*We met at Hargreaves' place.*
*I had met him in Zermatt.*

*We argued over this question for a long time.*
*I argued with this man for half an hour.*

Reciprocal verbs are explained in paragraphs 3.69 to 3.73.

**ditransitive verbs**
**3.7** A small number of transitive verbs also allow you to mention a person who benefits from an action or receives something as a result. The clause then has both a direct object and an **indirect object.**

*Hand me my bag.*

*His uncle had given him books on India.*
*She sends you her love.*
*She passed him his cup.*

Verbs which can take an indirect object as well as a direct object are called **ditransitive verbs**. They are explained in paragraphs 3.74 to 3.83.

**phrasal verbs, compound verbs**

**3.8** Some verbs have two or three parts. These are **phrasal verbs** and **compound verbs**. Phrasal verbs are explained in paragraphs 3.84 to 3.117, and compound verbs are explained in paragraphs 3.118 to 3.126.

# Talking about events which involve only the subject: intransitive verbs

**3.9** When you are talking about an action or event which does not involve anyone or anything other than the subject, you use an **intransitive verb**.

*Her whole body ached.*
*Such people still exist.*
*My condition deteriorated.*

Many intransitive verbs describe physical behaviour or the making of sounds.

*Bob coughed.*
*Vicki wept bitterly.*
*The gate squeaked.*

**3.10** Here is a list of verbs which are normally used in intransitive clauses and which usually or often have no adjunct after them:

| | | | | |
|---|---|---|---|---|
| ache | disappear | fluctuate | rise | squeal |
| advance | disintegrate | gleam | roar | stink |
| arise | doze | growl | scream | subside |
| arrive | droop | happen | shine | sulk |
| bleed | economize | hesitate | shiver | surrender |
| blush | elapse | howl | sigh | swim |
| cease | ensue | itch | sleep | throb |
| collapse | erupt | kneel | slip | tingle |
| cough | evaporate | laugh | smile | vanish |
| crackle | exist | moan | snarl | vary |
| cry | expire | occur | sneeze | vibrate |
| decay | faint | pause | snore | wait |
| depart | fall | persist | snort | waver |
| deteriorate | falter | prosper | sob | weep |
| die | fidget | quiver | sparkle | wilt |
| digress | flinch | recede | speak | work |
| dine | flourish | relent | squeak | yawn |

A few of these verbs are used transitively in idioms or with very specific objects, but they are intransitive in all their common meanings.

**intransitive verbs followed by prepositional phrases**

**3.11** Many intransitive verbs always or typically have an adjunct after them. With some, the adjunct must be a prepositional phrase beginning with a particular preposition. This use of a preposition allows something affected by the action to be mentioned, as the object of the preposition.

*Everything you see here belongs to me.*
*Landlords often resorted to violence.*
*I sympathized with them.*
*I'm relying on Bill.*
*He strives for excellence in all things.*

**3.12** Here is a list of verbs which always or typically have a particular preposition after them when they are used with a particular meaning:

| | | |
|---|---|---|
| rave about | stem from | adhere to |
| ~ | suffer from | allude to |
| insure against | ~ | amount to |
| plot against | believe in | appeal to |
| react against | consist in | aspire to |
| ~ | culminate in | assent to |
| hint at | dabble in | attend to |
| ~ | indulge in | belong to |
| alternate between | invest in | bow to |
| differentiate between | result in | cling to |
| oscillate between | wallow in | defer to |
| ~ | ~ | dictate to |
| appeal for | lapse into | lead to |
| atone for | ~ | listen to |
| care for | complain of | object to |
| clamour for | conceive of | refer to |
| hope for | consist of | relate to |
| long for | despair of | resort to |
| opt for | learn of | revert to |
| pay for | smack of | stoop to |
| qualify for | think of | ~ |
| strive for | tire of | alternate with |
| yearn for | ~ | associate with |
| ~ | bet on | consort with |
| detract from | feed on | contend with |
| emanate from | insist on | flirt with |
| emerge from | spy on | grapple with |
| radiate from | trample on | sympathize with |
| shrink from | ~ | teem with |

Here is a list of verbs which can have either of two prepositions after them:

| | | |
|---|---|---|
| abound in | end in | lust after |
| abound with | end with | lust for |
| cater for | engage in | prevail on |
| cater to | engage on | prevail upon |
| conform to | enthuse about | profit by |
| conform with | enthuse over | profit from |
| contribute to | gravitate to | rely on |
| contribute towards | gravitate towards | rely upon |
| depend on | hunger after | revolve around |
| depend upon | hunger for | revolve round |
| dote on | improve on | spring from |
| dote upon | improve upon | spring out of |
| embark on | liaise between | |
| embark upon | liaise with | |

Note that some intransitive verbs can be used in the passive when they are followed by a preposition. See paragraph 10.23.

**intransitive verbs followed by adjuncts**

**3.13** With other verbs, the adjunct after them can be a variety of prepositional phrases, or an adverb. The adjunct is often an **adjunct of place**. See Chapter 6 for information on these adjuncts.

Verbs of movement are usually or often followed by adjuncts of direction.

*He went back to his own room.*
*I travelled south.*

Here is a list of verbs of movement:

| | | | |
|---|---|---|---|
| come | flow | hurtle | spring |
| crawl | gallop | plunge | stroll |
| creep | glide | run | travel |
| drift | go | soar | walk |

'Look', 'gaze', and 'stare' are also followed by adjuncts of direction.

Verbs of position are usually followed by adjuncts of position.

*Donald was lying on the bed.*
*She lives in Lausanne.*
*I used to live here.*

Here is a list of verbs of position:

| | | | |
|---|---|---|---|
| be | lie | sit | stay |
| belong | live | be situated | |
| hang | remain | stand | |

Verbs such as 'extend' or 'stretch' are followed by adjuncts indicating extent.

*...an area stretching from London to Cambridge.*

There are a few verbs which are always followed by adjuncts of other sorts.

*It behaves rather like a squirrel.*
*My brother agreed to act as a go-between.*

*I hoped that the absorption of poison hadn't progressed too far.*

Here is a list of verbs which are always followed by adjuncts of other sorts:

| | | | |
|---|---|---|---|
| act | behave | campaign | progress |

**verbs which are occasionally transitive**

**3.14** There are a small number of verbs which are usually intransitive but which can be transitive when used with one particular object. The object is usually directly related to the verb. For example, 'smile' is usually used intransitively, but you can use it transitively with the noun 'smile'. For example, 'He smiled a patient smile' is a literary alternative to saying 'He smiled patiently'. The focus is on the type of smile rather than on the act of smiling.

*Steve smiled his thin, cruel smile.*
*He appears to have lived the life of any other rich gentleman.*
*Alice laughed a scornful laugh.*
*I once dreamed a very nice dream about you.*

Here is a list of verbs which can only be used transitively when the object is directly related to the verb:

| | | | |
|---|---|---|---|
| dance (a dance) | dream (a dream) | live (a life) | smile (a smile) |
| die (a death) | laugh (a laugh) | sigh (a sigh) | |

A more common way of focusing on the noun group is to use a **delexical verb** such as 'give', 'take', or 'have', as in 'Mary gave him a really lovely smile'. See paragraphs 3.33 to 3.46 for more information about the use of delexical verbs.

# Involving someone or something other than the subject: transitive verbs

**3.15** Many verbs describe events that must, in addition to the subject, involve someone or something else. Some of these verbs can only be used in transitive clauses.

*The extra profit justifies the investment.*
*He had committed a disgraceful action.*
*They are employing more staff.*

This means that they are followed by a direct object.

*She had friends.*
*Children seek independence.*
*The trial raised a number of questions.*

**different types of object**

**3.16** Many verbs which are only used in transitive clauses can take a large range of objects. For example, there are many things you can 'want': money, a rest, success, and so on.

*She wanted some help.*
*I put my hand on the door.*
*She described her background.*
*I still support the government.*
*He had always liked Mr Phillips.*
*Japan has a population of about a hundred million.*

Some transitive verbs have a restricted range of objects, because of their meaning. For example, the object of the verb 'kill' must be something that is alive. The object of the verb 'waste' must be something you can use, such as time, money, or food.

*They killed huge elephants with tiny poisoned darts.*
*Why waste money on them?*

**3.17** Here is a list of verbs which are transitive:

| | | | | |
|---|---|---|---|---|
| achieve | cut | get | maintain | rent |
| address | damage | give | make | report |
| admire | defy | grant | mean | respect |
| affect | demand | guard | mention | reveal |
| afford | describe | handle | name | risk |
| avoid | design | hate | need | see |
| bear | desire | have | own | seek |
| believe | destroy | hear | plant | sell |
| blame | discover | heat | please | shock |
| build | discuss | hire | prefer | specify |
| buy | display | hit | prevent | spot |
| calm | do | include | process | support |
| carry | dread | influence | produce | take |
| catch | enjoy | introduce | pronounce | tease |
| claim | equal | issue | protect | test |
| commit | exchange | justify | provide | threaten |
| complete | expect | keep | raise | trust |
| concern | experience | kill | reach | upset |
| consider | express | know | receive | use |
| control | favour | lack | recommend | value |
| convince | fear | like | record | want |
| correct | fill | list | release | waste |
| cover | find | love | remember | wear |
| create | free | lower | remove | welcome |

Note that 'do' and 'have' are also very often used as **auxiliaries**. See the Reference Section for this use.

'Have got' and 'has got' are often used instead of the present tense of 'have' when talking about possession. The forms of 'have' behave like auxiliaries when used like this before 'got'. 'Had got' is sometimes used when referring to the past, but 'had' is often used instead.

*I've got an umbrella.*
*She's got a degree.*
*He'd got over fifty horses.*

'Measure' and 'weigh' are sometimes considered to be transitive verbs when used to state measurements and weights. This use is explained in paragraph 2.269. 'Cost' is used to state the cost of something, as in 'An adult ticket costs 90p'.

**human objects**

**3.18** When you are talking about something that affects a person rather than a thing, it is normal in English to say who that person is. Therefore, verbs such as 'anger', 'thank', and 'warn', which involve affecting people, usually occur in transitive clauses.

*I tried to comfort her.*
*Her sudden death had surprised everybody.*
*Blue suits you.*
*Money did not interest him very much.*
*Lebel briefed Caron on the events of the afternoon.*

**3.19** Here is a list of verbs which usually have a human object:

| | | | |
|---|---|---|---|
| anger | contact | suit | thank |
| brief | frighten | surprise | trouble |
| comfort | interest | tease | warn |

**transitive verbs which need an adjunct**

**3.20** With some transitive verbs, you have to give additional information about what is going on by using an **adjunct** after the object of the verb.

Some verbs typically have a prepositional phrase beginning with a particular preposition after their object.

*The judge based his decision on constitutional rights.*
*He had subjected me to the pressure of financial ruin.*
*My parents still view me as a little boy.*

Here is a list of verbs which always or usually have a particular preposition after their object:

| | | | |
|---|---|---|---|
| regard as | deprive of | condemn to | subordinate to |
| view as | remind of | confine to | ~ |
| ~ | rid of | consign to | acquaint with |
| mistake for | rob of | dedicate to | associate with |
| swap for | ~ | entitle to | confront with |
| ~ | accustom to | liken to | engrave with |
| dissociate from | ascribe to | owe to | pelt with |
| prevent from | attribute to | return to | ply with |
| ~ | compare to | subject to | trust with |

With the following verbs, there is a choice of preposition:

| | | | |
|---|---|---|---|
| divide by | ~ | ~ | present to |
| divide into | base on | entrust to | present with |
| ~ | base upon | entrust with | supply to |
| incorporate in | lavish on | equate to | supply with |
| incorporate into | lavish upon | equate with | |

**3.21** Other verbs are typically followed by an adjunct, but not one containing a particular preposition. The adjunct is often an **adjunct of place**.

*He placed the baby on the woman's lap.*
*I positioned my chair outside the room.*
*He never puts anything away.*
*He treated his labourers with kindness.*

Here is a list of verbs which usually have an adjunct of some kind after their object:

| | | | | |
|---|---|---|---|---|
| bring | escort | lead | rip | store |
| chuck | fling | place | send | throw |
| convey | hoist | point | set | thrust |
| cram | jab | position | shove | tie |
| direct | jot | prop | smear | treat |
| drag | lay | put | stick | |

**Adjuncts** are explained in Chapter 6.

**transitive**
**verbs**
**of position**
**and**
**movement**

**3.22** Note that some verbs of movement and position are transitive, not intransitive; they are followed by noun groups referring to places rather than by adverbs or prepositional phrases. This is because the verbs themselves indicate that you are talking about movement or position of a particular kind. For example, 'enter' implies movement 'into' a place and 'occupy' implies position 'in' a place.

*He approached the house nervously.*
*It was dark by the time they reached their house.*
*A small ornamental pool occupied the centre of the room.*
*Everyone had left the room.*

Here is a list of transitive verbs of movement:

| | | |
|---|---|---|
| approach | leave | reach |
| enter | near | round |

Here is a list of transitive verbs of position:

| | | |
|---|---|---|
| cover | fill | occupy |
| crowd | inhabit | throng |

Some verbs of movement can be followed either by a noun group or by a prepositional phrase. See paragraph 3.59.

**USAGE NOTE**

**3.23** Note that even verbs which are almost always followed by a direct object can occasionally be used intransitively. This is possible in very restricted contexts. For example, if you are contrasting two actions, it is not necessary to say what else is involved.

*Money markets are the places where people with money buy and sell.*
*Some people build while others destroy.*
*We gave, they took.*

If you use a list of different verbs for emphasis, you do not need to name the object.

*They set out to be rude; to defy, threaten, or tease.*

If you repeat a verb in order to contrast it with a similar action, or to emphasize it, the object can be omitted.

*She had ceased to love as she had once loved.*

**3.24** Verbs which describe feelings and attitudes can sometimes be used without an object, particularly in the '**to**'-**infinitive** form. This is because the object is assumed to be people in general. For example, 'please' usually requires an object, but you can say 'He likes to please', meaning he likes to please people.

*He likes to shock.*
*She was anxious to please.*
*He must be convinced if he is to convince.*
*I have a tendency to tease.*

**reporting**
**verbs**
**3.25** There is a large group of verbs, such as 'say', 'suggest', and 'think', which are used to report what people say or think. They are called **reporting verbs**. They are followed by a 'that'-clause which is called the **reported clause**.

*She said that she would come.*

The reported clause is often thought of as being an object, and so these verbs are usually said to be transitive verbs. In this grammar, reporting verbs are explained in Chapter 7.

Reporting verbs such as 'advise' and 'persuade', which have an object which refers to the person being addressed, are explained in paragraphs 7.71 and 7.72.

Some reporting verbs can take as their object a noun such as 'question' or 'story' which refers to something that is said or written. These verbs are listed in paragraph 7.78. Some take an object which refers to an event or fact, and is therefore closely related to a 'that'-clause. These are listed in paragraph 7.79.

Verbs such as 'believe' and 'know' which can be used as report verbs but which are ordinary transitive verbs when used with another common meaning are included in the lists of transitive verbs given above.

**3.26** Most transitive verbs can be used in the passive. See paragraphs 10.8 to 10.21.

# Verbs where the object refers back to the subject: reflexive verbs

**PRODUCTIVE**
**FEATURE**
**3.27** If an action usually involves two different people but you want to talk about a case where the same person is involved twice, you can use a **reflexive pronoun** as the object of a clause. For example, it is usual to blame someone else if something goes wrong, but you can say 'I blame myself for what happened' if you are the only person involved in the blaming.

Although a few verbs are typically used with reflexive pronouns, you can actually use a reflexive pronoun as the object of any transitive verb, when the meaning allows you to do so.

*I blame myself for not paying attention.*
*She freed herself from my embrace.*
*After the meeting, he introduced himself to me.*
*Why not buy a book and teach yourself?*

*Don't deceive yourself.*
*We Americans must ask ourselves several questions.*
*Every country has the right to defend itself.*

This is a **productive feature** of English. Productive features are explained in the Introduction.

**Reflexive pronouns** are explained in paragraphs 1.115 to 1.122.

**true reflexive verbs**

**3.28** Note that the verbs 'busy', 'content', and 'pride' are true reflexive verbs: they must be used with a reflexive pronoun.

*He had busied himself in the laboratory.*
*Many scholars contented themselves with writing textbooks.*
*He prides himself on his tidiness.*

**3.29** Another small group of verbs can only take an object which refers to a person when the object is a reflexive pronoun. For example, you can 'express an opinion' and you can 'express yourself', meaning that you can put ideas into words, but you cannot 'express a person'.

*Professor Baxendale expressed himself very forcibly.*
*She enjoyed herself enormously.*
*He applied himself to learning how Parliament worked.*

Here is a list of verbs which take a reflexive pronoun as their object when you refer to a person:

| | | | |
|---|---|---|---|
| apply | distance | excel | express |
| compose | enjoy | exert | strain |

**reflexive pronouns used for emphasis**

**3.30** Some verbs which normally do not have objects, because they involve only the performer of the action, can have a reflexive pronoun as their object if you want to emphasize that the subject is doing something that affects himself or herself. You can therefore say 'Bill washed himself' rather than 'Bill washed'.

*I always wash five times a day.*
*Children were encouraged to wash themselves.*

*I stood in the kitchen while he shaved.*
*He prefers to shave himself before breakfast.*

*Ashton had behaved abominably.*
*He is old enough to behave himself like a gentleman.*

*The Eskimoes are adapting to change.*
*You've got to be willing to adapt yourself.*

Here is a list of verbs which have senses in which you can use a reflexive pronoun for emphasis:

| | | | |
|---|---|---|---|
| acclimatize | dress | readjust | wash |
| adapt | hide | shave | |
| behave | move | undress | |

**WARNING**

**3.31** Note that reflexive pronouns are not used as much in English as in some other languages when talking about actions that you do to yourself. As mentioned above, you would usually say 'I washed' rather than 'I washed myself' in English. Sometimes a noun group with a possessive is used instead. For example, you would say 'I combed my hair' rather than 'I combed myself'.

**3.32** Note that reflexive verbs are not used in the passive.

# Verbs with little meaning: delexical verbs

**3.33** There are a number of very common verbs which are used with nouns as their object to indicate simply that someone performs an action, not that someone affects or creates something. These verbs have very little meaning when they are used in this way.

For example, 'had' in 'She had a shower' has very little meaning in itself. Most of the meaning of the sentence is carried by the noun 'shower'.

*We were having a joke.*
*Roger gave a grin of sheer delight.*
*He took a step towards Jack.*

**verbs which are often delexical**

**3.34** In this section we focus on the very common verbs which are used in this transitive structure. They are called **delexical verbs**, and the structure which consists of a delexical verb followed by a noun group is called a **delexical structure**.

Here is a list of verbs which are used as delexical verbs. The first four are very commonly used in this way.

| | | |
|------|------|------|
| give | take | hold |
| have | ~ | keep |
| make | do | set |

Note that 'have got' is not used instead of 'have' in delexical structures.

Delexical structures are very common in current English. Although the total number of delexical verbs is small, they include some of the very commonest words in the language. Delexical structures contribute to the impression of fluency in English given by a foreign user.

**3.35** In many cases, there is a verb which has a similar meaning to the meaning of the delexical structure. For example, the verb 'look' means almost the same as 'have a look'. When the word is a verb, as in 'I looked round the room', you are focusing on the action of looking. When you use the word as a noun in a delexical structure, you are naming an event, something which is complete. This structure often seems to be preferred to a structure in which the verb has greater prominence. Note that the verb which corresponds to the delexical structure is often intransitive.

*She made a signal.*
*She signalled for a taxi.*

*A couple were having a drink at a table by the window.*
*A few students were drinking at the bar.*

*She gave an amused laugh.*
*They both laughed.*

*He gave a vague reply.*
*They replied to his letter.*

There are also some verbs which are transitive.

*Fans tried to get a glimpse of the singer.*
*I glimpsed a bright flash of gold on the left.*

*He gave a little sniff.*
*She sniffed the air.*

*Comis took a photograph of her.*
*They photographed the pigeons in Trafalgar Square.*

**with singular noun** 3.36 The noun which is the object of the delexical verb is often in the singular and is usually preceded by the indefinite article.

*She made a remark about the weather.*
*She gave a cry when I came in.*
*I might take a stroll.*

There are some count nouns which are almost always used in the singular after a delexical verb. Here is a list of these nouns:

| | | |
|---|---|---|
| cry | grumble | smell |
| feel | need | taste |
| grouse | read | try |

Note that these words are more commonly used as verbs in the language as a whole.

**with plural noun** 3.37 You can also use a delexical verb followed by a plural noun.

*She took little ladylike sips of the cold drink.*
*He took photographs of Vita in her summer house.*
*The newspaper had made disparaging remarks about his wife.*

**with uncount noun** 3.38 It is also occasionally possible to follow a delexical verb with an uncount noun.

*We have made progress in both science and art.*
*Cal took charge of this side of their education.*

**indicating a brief event** 3.39 One difference in meaning between using a delexical structure and a verb with a similar meaning is that the delexical structure can give the impression that the event you are describing is brief. For example, 'She gave a scream' suggests that there was only one quick scream, whereas 'She screamed' does not suggest that the event was brief.

*Mr. Sutton gave a shout of triumph.*
*Zoe gave a sigh of relief.*
*He gave a laugh.*

**using adjectives** 3.40 Another reason for choosing a delexical structure is that you can add further details about the event by using adjectives in front of the noun, rather than by using adverbs. It is more common, for example, to say 'He gave a quick furtive glance round the room' than to say 'He glanced quickly and furtively round the room', which is felt to be rather clumsy and unnatural.

*He gave a long lecture about Roosevelt.*
*She had a good cry.*
*He was forced to make a humiliating apology.*
*These legends hold a romantic fascination for many Japanese.*

**nouns with no equivalent verb** 3.41 There are some nouns used in delexical structures which do not correspond in form to a verb which has a similar meaning to the delexical structure. Sometimes there is such a verb, but the form is slightly different.

*Work experience allows students to make more effective career decisions.*
*I decided I wouldn't resign after all.*

*He made the shortest speech I've ever heard.*
*Iain spoke candidly about the crash.*

In other cases, there is no corresponding verb with a similar meaning at all and so there is no other structure that can be used.

*He had been out all day taking pictures of the fighting.*
*That is a very foolish attitude to take.*
*She made a number of relevant points.*
*Try not to make so much noise.*

**nouns used with 'have'**

**3.42** In most cases, only one delexical verb is used with any particular noun.

The following examples show nouns which are used after 'have'.

*They have a desperate need to communicate.*
*The Americans had a nonchalant belief in their technological superiority.*
*She had had a good cry.*
*Let's not have a quarrel.*
*We could have a talk.*

Here is a list of nouns which are used after 'have':

| belief | dance | grumble | respect |
|--------|-------|---------|---------|
| chat | fall | need | sleep |
| cry | grouse | quarrel | talk |

**nouns used with 'take'**

**3.43** The following examples show nouns which are used after 'take'.

*He takes no interest in his children.*
*...kids taking turns to use a playground slide.*
*He was taking no chances.*
*She was prepared to take great risks.*
*Mr Korwin takes a protectionist attitude towards women who, he claims, look for someone to take care of them.*
*Davis took the lead in blaming the pilots.*
*The Government fought against suggestions that it should take full blame for the affair.*

Here is a list of nouns which are used after 'take'. The first set of nouns are count nouns; the second set of nouns are uncount nouns or always either singular or plural:

| attitude | picture | charge | power |
|----------|---------|--------|-------|
| chance | risk | consequences | responsibility |
| decision | turn | form | shape |
| interest | ~ | lead | time |
| photo | blame | offence | trouble |
| photograph | care | office | |

**nouns used with 'give'**

**3.44** Many nouns can be used after 'give'.

Some of these nouns refer to verbal or facial actions. Using 'give' with one of these nouns often suggests that the action is involuntary or that it is not necessarily directed at other people. For example, 'She gave a scream' suggests that she could not help screaming.

*The young cashier gave a patient sigh.*
*Roger gave a grin of sheer delight.*
*He gave a shrill gasp of shock.*
*Both of them gave an involuntary little giggle.*

*He gave a rare chuckle.*

Here is a list of nouns which refer to verbal or facial actions:

| | | | | |
|---|---|---|---|---|
| chuckle | grin | scream | smile | yell |
| cry | groan | shout | sniff | |
| gasp | laugh | shriek | snigger | |
| giggle | scowl | sigh | whistle | |

Another group of nouns are often preceded by an indirect object because they describe activities which involve someone else, apart from the subject.

*They gave us a wonderfully warm welcome.*
*Elaine gave him a hug.*
*He gave her hand a squeeze.*
*He gave him a good kick.*
*She gave him a long kiss.*

Here is a list of nouns which can be preceded by an indirect object:

| | | | | |
|---|---|---|---|---|
| clue | hug | look | ring | squeeze |
| glance | kick | punch | shove | welcome |
| hint | kiss | push | slap | |

A third group of nouns refer to speech actions.

*The Oxford poetry professor is required to give a lecture every term.*
*Lord Young will be giving a first-hand account of the economic difficulties the Russians are struggling to overcome.*
*Sir Stephen Brown has given warning that conflict over the plans could lead to a constitutional crisis.*

Here is a list of nouns which refer to speech actions:

| | | | | |
|---|---|---|---|---|
| account | example | lecture | report | talk |
| advice | information | news | speech | thought |
| answer | interview | reason | summary | warning |

**nouns used with 'make'**

3.45 Many nouns can be used after 'make'.

The delexical structures using a lot of these nouns are closely related to **reporting structures**, which are explained in Chapter 7. There is usually a related verb which can be used followed by a reported clause.

*She made a remark about the weather.*
*Allen remarked that at times he thought he was back in America.*

*Now and then she makes a comment on something.*
*He commented that he was only doing his job.*

*I haven't made a full confession, sir.*
*Fox confessed that he had stolen the money.*

*The cricketers made a public protest against apartheid.*
*She protested that his comments were sexist.*

*I made a secret signal to him.*
*The Bank of England signalled that there would be no change in interest rates.*

You *made the right decision.*
One candidate resigned, *deciding* that banking was not for her.

Here is a list of nouns which are used after 'make' and have a related reporting verb:

| | | | |
|---|---|---|---|
| arrangement | confession | protest | suggestion |
| claim | decision | remark | |
| comment | promise | signal | |

Other nouns used with 'make' express speech actions other than reports, or describe change, results, effort, and so on.

I'll *make some enquiries for you.*
They agreed *to make a few minor changes.*
They *made an emotional appeal* for their daughter's safe return.

He *made an attempt to calm down.*
He has *made a significant contribution* to the success of the business.

Here is a list of other nouns which are used after 'make':

| | | | |
|---|---|---|---|
| appeal | contribution | noise | sound |
| attempt | effort | point | speech |
| change | enquiry | progress | start |
| charge | impression | recovery | success |

Note that, unlike the other nouns in this list, 'progress' is uncountable.

**nouns used with 'have' and 'take'**
3.46 There are a number of nouns which can be used after either 'have' or 'take'. 'Have' is more common with these nouns in British English, whereas 'take' is more common in American English.

One group of these nouns refer to physical activities.

I'd rather *have a swim.*
*Have a drink.*
She decided *to take a stroll* along the beach.
I *took a bath,* my second that day.

Here is a list of nouns which refer to physical activities:

| | | | |
|---|---|---|---|
| bath | holiday | rest | stroll |
| break | jog | run | swim |
| drink | paddle | shower | walk |

Another group refer to actions which involve using our senses.

She should let a doctor *have a look* at you.
Even Lally *had a little sip* of wine.
A Harvard scientist was once allowed in to *have a peep.*
Meadows *took a bite* of meat.

Here is a list of nouns which refer to such actions:

| | | | |
|---|---|---|---|
| bite | look | sip | sniff |
| feel | peep | smell | taste |

# Verbs which can be used in both intransitive and transitive clauses

**3.47** There are several reasons why you can use verbs in intransitive as well as transitive clauses.

**different meanings**

**3.48** One important reason for using verbs in intransitive as well as transitive clauses is that many verbs have more than one common meaning. For example, the verb 'run' is intransitive when it is used in the sense 'to move quickly'. But 'run' is transitive when it is used in the sense 'to manage or operate'.

*She runs in order to keep fit.*
*She runs a hotel.*

*She reflected for a moment and then decided to back out.*
*The figures reflected the company's attempts to increase its profile.*

*I can manage perfectly well on my own.*
*I can no longer manage my life.*

*She moved rather gracefully.*
*The whole incident had moved her profoundly.*

**3.49** Here is a list of verbs which can be used in intransitive as well as transitive clauses, depending on which meaning you are using:

| | | | | |
|---|---|---|---|---|
| add | drive | leak | propose | study |
| aim | escape | lose | reflect | tend |
| beat | exercise | manage | run | touch |
| blow | fit | meet | shoot | turn |
| call | fly | miss | show | win |
| change | follow | move | sink | |
| cheat | hang | pass | spread | |
| count | head | play | stand | |
| draw | hold | point | stretch | |
| dress | hurt | press | strike | |

**verbs which do not always need an object**

**3.50** Many verbs in English can be used with or without an object, with the same basic meaning. The object is not needed when it is obvious what type of thing you are talking about.

For example, you could say either 'She eats food slowly' or 'She eats slowly'. It is obvious in this context that what she eats is food, and so you only mention food if you want to emphasize the fact (which is unlikely), or if you want to say what kind of food she eats.

With verbs like these, you normally use an object only when you want to be specific or when you want to contrast what happened on one specific occasion with what happens normally. For example, you would say 'I've been studying history', as opposed to 'I've been studying', only if you want or need to mention the subject specifically, or if you normally study something else.

*...a healthy person who eats sensibly.*
*Twice a week he eats an apple for lunch.*

*Father never smoked or drank.*
*He drank a good deal of coffee.*

*He had won—and she had helped.*
*She could help him to escape.*

*I cooked for about eight directors.*
*She had never cooked dinner for anyone.*

*I washed and ironed for them.*
*She ironed my shirt.*

*Rudolph waved and went into the house.*
*She smiled and waved her hand.*

*She sat and typed.*
*She typed a letter to the paper in question.*

You need to give the object when it is different from the one that people would normally associate with the verb. For example, 'to wave' is usually interpreted as meaning 'to wave your hand', so if something else is being waved, you have to mention it.

*He waved a piece of paper in his left hand.*
*Charlie washed Susan's feet.*
*Many growers save their own seeds.*

You also mention the object when you want to say something specific about it.

*He washed his summer clothes and put them away.*
*Bond waved a cheerful hand.*
*I could save quite a lot of money.*

**3.51** Here is a list of verbs which can be used without an object when it is obvious what sort of thing is involved:

| | | | | |
|---|---|---|---|---|
| borrow | drive | learn | read | steal |
| change | dust | lend | ride | study |
| clean | eat | marry | save | type |
| cook | film | paint | sing | wash |
| draw | help | park | smoke | wave |
| drink | iron | point | spend | write |

**object already mentioned** **3.52** There is another group of verbs which are usually transitive but which can be used intransitively with the same meaning. These are verbs where the object is obvious because it has already been mentioned. For example, if you have already mentioned the place where something happened, you can say 'I left', without naming the place again.

*At last she thanked them and left.*
*He turned away and walked quickly up the passage. I locked the door and followed.*
*I was in the middle of a quiet meal when the tanks attacked.*
*She did not look round when he entered.*
*The sentry fired at the doctor and fortunately missed.*
*Only two or three hundred men belonged to the Union before the war, now thousands joined.*

**3.53** Here is a list of verbs which can be used without an object when the object has already been mentioned:

| | | | | |
|---|---|---|---|---|
| accept | check | guess | notice | ring |
| aim | choose | improve | observe | rule |
| answer | consider | join | offer | search |
| approach | direct | judge | order | serve |
| ask | dry | know | pass | share |
| attack | enter | lead | phone | sign |
| begin | explain | leave | play | strike |
| bite | fit | lose | produce | telephone |
| blow | follow | mind | pull | understand |
| board | forget | miss | push | watch |
| call | gain | move | remember | win |

**3.54** If you think that the object may not be obvious from what has been said or if you particularly want to draw attention to it, you mention it.

*All I know is that Michael and I never left the house.*
*Miss Lindley followed Rose into the shop.*
*They were unaware they had attacked a British warship.*
*A man entered the shop and demanded money.*
*She threw the first dart and missed the board altogether.*
*I had joined an athletic club in Chicago.*

**speaker's decisions on transitivity**

**3.55** There are not many verbs which are always transitive or always intransitive. The decision about whether or not to mention an object is left to the users. If they think that the people reading or listening to them will have no difficulty in working out what person or thing is affected by the action, then they can leave out the object. If they think that this will not be clear, they will use an object in order to prevent misunderstanding. The main reasons for omitting the object are that it is obvious from the meaning of the verb itself, or that it is obvious from what has already been said.

# Verbs which can take an object or a prepositional phrase

**3.56** There is a small group of verbs which can be followed by either an object or a prepositional phrase. The verb 'fight' is one of these verbs, so that, for example, you can say 'He fought the enemy' or 'He fought against the enemy'.

*The Polish Army fought the Germans for nearly five weeks.*
*He was fighting against history.*

*The New Zealand rugby team played South Africa's Springboks.*
*In his youth, Thomas had played against Glamorgan.*

**3.57** There is usually little difference in meaning between using the verb on its own and following it with a preposition. For example, there is very little difference in meaning between 'brush' and 'brush against', 'gnaw' and 'gnaw at', and 'hiss' and 'hiss at' in the following examples.

*Her arm brushed my cheek.*
*Something brushed against the back of the shelter.*

*Rabbits often gnaw the woodwork of their cages.*

*Insects had been gnawing at the wood.*
*They hissed the Mayor at the ceremony.*
*Frederica hissed at him.*

**3.58** Here is a list of verbs which can be used with a direct object or a prepositional phrase, with little difference in meaning:

| | | |
|---|---|---|
| boo (at) | gnaw (at) | play (against) |
| brush (against) | hiss (at) | rule (over) |
| check (on) | infiltrate (into) | sip (at) |
| distinguish (between) | jeer (at) | sniff (at) |
| enter (for) | juggle (with) | tug (at) |
| fight (against) | mock (at) | twiddle (with) |
| fight (with) | mourn (for) | |
| gain (in) | nibble (at) | |

**verbs of movement** **3.59** Many of the verbs which can take an object or a prepositional phrase are verbs such as 'wander' and 'cross' which describe physical movement. The preposition is one which indicates place, and so allows you to emphasize the physical position of the subject in relation to the object.

*He wandered the halls of the Art Institute.*
*He wandered through the streets of New York.*

*I crossed the Mississippi.*
*The car had crossed over the river to Long Island.*

*We climbed the mountain.*
*I climbed up the tree.*

Here is a list of verbs which describe movement, and the prepositions that can follow them:

| | | | |
|---|---|---|---|
| chase (after) | jump (over) | roam (through) | wander (through) |
| climb (up) | leap (over) | skirt (round) | |
| cross (over) | roam (over) | walk (through) | |

# Changing your focus by changing the subject: ergative verbs

**3.60** Some verbs allow you to describe an action from the point of view of the performer of the action or from the point of view of something which is affected by the action. This means that the same verb can be used transitively, followed by the object, or intransitively, without the original performer being mentioned.

In the first example below, 'the door' is the object of the verb 'opened', but in the second example 'the door' is the subject of 'opened' and there is no mention of who opened the door.

*I opened the door and peered into the room.*
*Suddenly the door opened.*

*An explosion shook the rooms.*
*The whole room shook.*

Note that the object of the transitive verb, which is the subject of the intransitive verb, usually refers to a thing, not a person.

Verbs which can have the same thing as their object, when transitive, or their subject, when intransitive, are called **ergative verbs**. For many students of English, the ergative verb is a new idea, and may take a little time to learn. However, it is an important type of verb, as the common examples below make clear. There are several hundred ergative verbs in regular use in current English.

**changes**   **3.61** Many ergative verbs describe events which involve a change from one state to another.

*He was slowing his pace.*
*She was aware that the aircraft's taxiing pace had slowed.*

*I shattered the glass.*
*Wine bottles had shattered all over the pavement.*

*They have closed the town's only pub.*
*The street markets have closed.*

*The firm has changed its name.*
*Over the next few months their work pattern changed.*

*The driver stopped the car.*
*A big car stopped.*

**3.62** Here is a list of ergative verbs which describe events which involve a change of some kind:

| | | | | |
|---|---|---|---|---|
| age | continue | empty | rot | stop |
| begin | crack | end | shatter | stretch |
| bend | darken | fade | shrink | tear |
| bleach | decrease | finish | shut | thicken |
| break | diminish | grow | slow | widen |
| burn | disperse | improve | split | worsen |
| burst | double | increase | spread | |
| change | drown | open | start | |
| close | dry | quicken | stick | |

**food,**   **3.63** There are many other ergative verbs which relate specifically to
**movement,**   certain areas of meaning. For example, there are a number which relate to
**vehicles**   food and cooking, others which describe physical movement, and others which involve a vehicle as the object of the transitive verb or the subject of the intransitive verb.

*I've boiled an egg.*
*The porridge is boiling.*

*I'm cooking spaghetti.*
*The rice is cooking.*

*The birds turned their heads sharply at the sound.*
*Vorster's head turned.*

*She rested her head on his shoulder.*
*Her head rested on the edge of the table.*

*She had crashed the car twice.*
*Pollock's car crashed into a clump of trees.*

**3.64** Here is a list of verbs relating to food, physical movement, and vehicles:

| | | | | |
|---|---|---|---|---|
| bake | simmer | rock | ~ | run |
| boil | thicken | shake | back | sail |
| cook | ~ | spin | crash | |
| defrost | balance | stand | drive | |
| fry | drop | steady | fly | |
| melt | move | swing | park | |
| roast | rest | turn | reverse | |

**restrictions on ergative subjects**

**3.65** Note that some verbs are used ergatively with one or two nouns only. For example, you can say 'He fired a gun' or 'The gun fired'. You can also say 'He fired a bullet', but you would not normally say 'The bullet fired'.

I rang the bell.
The bell rang.

A car was sounding its horn.
A horn sounded in the night.

He had caught his sleeve on a splinter of wood.
The hat caught on a bolt and tore.

**3.66** Here is a list of verbs which can be used ergatively with the noun, or kind of noun, that is given:

| | |
|---|---|
| catch (an article of clothing) | ring (a bell, the alarm) |
| fire (a gun, rifle, pistol) | show (an emotion such as fear, anger) |
| play (music) | sound (a horn, the alarm) |

**ergative verbs which need adjuncts**

**3.67** There are a small number of ergative verbs which usually have an adverb or other adjunct when they are used intransitively. This is because you choose this structure when you want to emphasize how something behaves when affected in some way, and so the person who does the action is not important.

I like the new Range Rover. It handles beautifully.
Wool washes well if you treat it carefully.

Here is a list of ergative verbs which usually have an adjunct when they are used intransitively:

| | | | |
|---|---|---|---|
| clean | handle | polish | stain |
| freeze | mark | sell | wash |

**comparison of passive voice and ergative use**

**3.68** Note that ergative verbs perform a similar function to the **passive** because they allow you to avoid mentioning who or what does the action. For example, you could say 'Jane froze a lot of peas from the garden'. If you were not interested in who froze them but in what she froze, you could say 'A lot of peas were frozen', using the passive voice. If you were interested in how they froze, you could say 'The peas from the garden froze really well', making use of the fact that the verb is ergative.

For information about the **passive**, see 10.8 to 10.24.

# Verbs which involve people doing the same thing to each other: reciprocal verbs

**3.69** Some verbs can describe processes which involve two people or two groups of people doing the same thing to each other. For example, 'John and Mary argued' means that John argued with Mary and Mary argued with John.

*The pair of you have argued about that for years.*
*He came out and we hugged.*
*They competed furiously.*

These verbs are called **reciprocal verbs.**

**reciprocal**
**verbs with**
**plural**
**subject**

**3.70** One of the structures in which you use reciprocal verbs is where the two groups are put together in a plural subject and the verb is then used intransitively.

*Their faces touched.*
*Their children are always fighting.*
*They kissed.*

**emphasizing**
**equal**
**involvement**

**3.71** When you want to emphasize that both participants are equally involved in the action, you put 'each other' or 'one another' after the verb group.

*We embraced each other.*
*They kissed each other in greeting.*
*They fought each other desperately for it.*
*The two boys started hitting one another.*

Here is a list of reciprocal verbs which are used transitively with the pronouns 'each other' and 'one another':

| | | | |
|---|---|---|---|
| consult | engage | kiss | meet |
| cuddle | fight | marry | touch |
| embrace | hug | match | |

With some verbs you need to use a preposition, usually 'with', in front of 'each other' or 'one another'.

*You've got to be able to communicate with each other.*
*Third World countries are competing with each other for a restricted market.*
*The two actors began to engage with one another.*

Here is a list of reciprocal verbs which must be followed by 'with' before the pronouns 'each other' and 'one another':

| | | | | |
|---|---|---|---|---|
| agree | coincide | consult | disagree | mix |
| alternate | collide | contend | engage | quarrel |
| argue | combine | contrast | integrate | struggle |
| balance | communicate | converse | mate | |
| clash | conflict | co-operate | merge | |

Here is a list of verbs which are used with a preposition other than 'with':

| | | | |
|---|---|---|---|
| compete (against) | correspond (with) | part (from) | talk (to) |
| compete (with) | fight (against) | relate (to) | talk (with) |
| correspond (to) | fight (with) | separate (from) | |

Note that 'consult', 'engage', and 'fight' can be used either transitively or with a preposition.

**indicating**
**unequal**
**involvement**

**3.72** In the examples given above, the user of the language obviously believes that both people or groups are equally involved in the event, because both are the subject. However, the user may want to suggest that one person is responsible for the action or has started it. In this case, a noun group which refers to that person is put in subject position.

If the verb can be used transitively, a noun group referring to the other participant is used as the object of the verb.

*He embraced her.*
*She married a young engineer.*
*You could meet me at a restaurant.*
*He is responsible for killing many people.*

If the verb needs a preposition after it, the other noun group is used as the object of the preposition.

*Our return coincided with the arrival of bad weather.*
*Youths clashed with police in Belfast.*
*The distribution of aid corresponds to need.*

**3.73** People sometimes make one person or group the subject when the event is a violent or unpleasant one, in order to make them appear aggressive or responsible for the violence. For example, the headline 'Police clash with youths' might suggest that the police were responsible for the clash, even though the youths also clashed with the police.

*Paul collided with a large man in a sweat-stained shirt.*
*The role of worker conflicts with the role of mother.*
*She liked him even when she was quarrelling with him.*

# Verbs which can have two objects: ditransitive verbs

**3.74** Sometimes you may want to talk about an event which involves someone in addition to the people or things that are the subject and object of the clause. This third participant is someone who benefits from the action or receives something as a result. They become the **indirect object** of the clause. The **direct object**, as usual, is the person or thing that something is done to. For example, in 'I gave John a book', 'John' is the indirect object and 'the book' is the direct object.

Verbs which can take both a direct object and an indirect object are called **ditransitive verbs.**

The indirect object is put immediately after the verb group, in front of the direct object.

*Dad gave me a car.*
*Can you pass me the sugar please?*
*She brought me a boiled egg and toast.*
*He had lent Tim the money.*
*A man promised him a job.*

**indirect objects in prepositional phrases**

**3.75** Instead of putting the indirect object in front of the direct object, it is possible to put it in a prepositional phrase that comes after the direct object.

*He handed his room key to the receptionist.*
*Ralph passed a message to Jack.*
*He gave it to me.*

This structure is used particularly in cases where you want to focus on the indirect object. You can use it, for example, when the indirect object is significantly longer than the direct object.

*He had taught English to all the youth of Ceylon and India.*
*He copied the e-mail to every single one of his staff.*

**pronouns as objects**

**3.76** It is normal to use this prepositional structure when the direct objec is a pronoun such as 'it' or 'them'.

*I took the bottle and offered it to Oakley.*
*Woodward finished the second page and passed it to the editor.*
*It was the only pound he had and he gave it to the little boy.*
*God has sent you to me.*

This is because pronouns usually refer to things that have already been mentioned, that is, to information that is known to your hearer or reader. In English, new information usually comes at the end of the clause. So, when the indirect object is new information and the direct object is not, the indirect object is put at the end of the clause.

Note that in informal spoken English, some people put the indirect object in front of the direct object when both objects are pronouns. For example, some people say 'He gave me it' rather than 'He gave it to me'. Both pronouns are unstressed and both refer to information that is already known, and so it does not matter what order they come in.

**indirect objects with 'to'**

**3.77** If you want to put the indirect object in a prepositional phrase, you use the preposition 'to' with some verbs, especially ones where the direct object is something which is transferred from one person to another.

*Mr Schell wrote a letter the other day to the New York Times.*
*I had lent my apartment to a friend for the weekend.*
*I took out the black box and handed it to her.*

Here is a list of verbs which can have an indirect object introduced by 'to':

| | | | | |
|---|---|---|---|---|
| accord | give | mail | quote | show |
| advance | grant | offer | read | sing |
| award | hand | owe | rent | take |
| bring | lease | pass | repay | teach |
| deal | leave | pay | sell | tell |
| feed | lend | play | send | write |
| forward | loan | post | serve | |

**indirect objects with 'for'**

**3.78** If the action you are describing involves one person doing somethin which will benefit another person, you can use the preposition 'for' to introduce the indirect object.

*He left a note for her on the table.*
*He poured more champagne for the three of them.*
*She brought presents for the children.*

Here is a list of verbs which can have an indirect object introduced by 'for'

| | | | | |
|---|---|---|---|---|
| book | design | leave | pour | spare |
| bring | fetch | make | prepare | take |
| build | find | mix | reserve | win |
| buy | fix | order | save | write |
| cash | get | paint | secure | |
| cook | guarantee | pick | set | |
| cut | keep | play | sing | |

**3.79** Note that the verbs 'bring', 'leave', 'play', 'sing', 'take', and 'write' are in both of the lists (3.77 and 3.78). That is because there are a few verbs which can take either 'to' or 'for' in front of the indirect object, depending on the meaning you want to express. For example, 'Karen wrote a letter to her boyfriend' means that the letter was addressed to her boyfriend and was for him to read. 'Karen wrote a letter for her boyfriend' means that her boyfriend wanted to send someone else a letter and Karen was the person who actually wrote it.

**3.80** There are some ditransitive verbs where the indirect object almost always comes in front of the direct object rather than being introduced by 'to' or 'for'. For example, you say 'He begrudged his daughter the bread she ate' and 'She allowed her son only two pounds a week'. It would be very unusual indeed to say 'She allowed two pounds a week to her son'.

Here is a list of verbs which do not usually have their indirect object introduced by 'to' or 'for':

| allow | bet | cost | envy | promise |
|---|---|---|---|---|
| ask | cause | deny | forgive | refuse |
| begrudge | charge | draw | grudge | |

Note that 'wish' can be used as this sort of ditransitive verb when its direct object is a word or phrase like 'luck', 'good luck', or 'happy birthday'.

**3.81** When you use a passive form of a ditransitive verb, either the direct object or the indirect object can become the subject. See 10.20 for full information.

**3.82** When the subject and the indirect object refer to the same person, you can use a **reflexive pronoun** as the indirect object.

*I'm going to buy myself some new clothes.*
*He had got himself a car.*
*He cooked himself an omelette.*

**Reflexive pronouns** are explained in paragraphs 1.115 to 1.122.

**transitive** **3.83** Most of the verbs listed above as ditransitive verbs can be used with
**uses** the same meaning with just a direct object.

*He left a note.*
*She fetched a jug from the kitchen.*

However, the following verbs always or usually have both a direct object and an indirect object:

| accord | deny | hand | save | write |
|---|---|---|---|---|
| advance | feed | lend | show | |
| allow | give | loan | tell | |

A few verbs can be used with the person who benefits from the action, or receives something, as the direct object.

*I fed the baby when she woke.*

*I forgive you.*

Here is a list of these verbs:

| | | |
|------|---------|-------|
| ask | feed | pay |
| envy | forgive | teach |

# Extending or changing the meaning of a verb: phrasal verbs

**3.84** There is a special group of verbs which consist of two or three words. These are called **phrasal verbs**. They consist of

● a verb followed by an adverb:

*He sat down.*
*The noise gradually died away.*
*The cold weather set in.*

● a verb followed by a preposition:

*She looked after her invalid mother.*
*She sailed through her exams.*
*She fell down the steps and broke her ankle.*

● or a verb followed by an adverb and a preposition.

*You may come up against unexpected difficulties.*
*I look forward to reading it.*
*Fame has crept up on her almost by accident.*

By combining a verb and an adverb or preposition in this way, we can extend the usual meaning of the verb or create a new meaning, different from any that the verb has on its own. You cannot, therefore, always guess the meaning of a phrasal verb from the usual meanings of the verb and the adverb or preposition.

In the case of a few phrasal verbs, the first part is not found independently as a verb. For example, there are phrasal verbs 'sum up', 'tamper with', and 'zero in on', but no verbs 'sum', 'tamper', or 'zero'.

Note that phrasal verbs are never written as a single word or with a hyphen.

**3.85** Most phrasal verbs consist of two words. These are explained below in paragraphs 3.86 to 3.111. Three-word phrasal verbs are explained in paragraphs 3.112 to 3.114.

**intransitive phrasal verbs with adverbs**

**3.86** Some phrasal verbs are used in intransitive clauses. Many of these are verb plus adverb combinations.

*Rosamund went away for a few days.*
*The boys were fooling around.*

*She must have dozed off.*

**3.87** Here is a list of phrasal verbs which consist of an intransitive verb and an adverb:

| | | | | |
|---|---|---|---|---|
| back away | come up | get along | opt out | spring up |
| back down | cool off | get by | own up | stand back |
| back off | creep in | get up | pass away | stand down |
| balance out | crop up | give in | pay up | stand in |
| barge in | cry off | glaze over | pine away | stand out |
| bear up | cuddle up | go ahead | play around | start out |
| boil over | curl up | go along | pop up | stay in |
| bounce back | cut in | go around | press ahead | stay on |
| bow down | die away | go away | press on | stay up |
| bow out | die down | go back | push ahead | steam up |
| branch out | die out | go down | push on | step aside |
| break away | dine out | go on | rear up | step back |
| break out | double back | go out | ride up | step down |
| butt in | doze off | go under | ring off | step in |
| camp out | drag on | go up | rise up | stick around |
| cast about | drop back | grow up | roll about | stock up |
| catch on | drop by | hang back | roll in | stop by |
| change down | drop out | hang together | roll over | stop off |
| change up | ease up | hit out | rot away | stop over |
| check up | ebb away | hold on | run away | tag along |
| chip in | end up | land up | run out | tail away |
| climb down | fade away | lash out | rush in | tail off |
| close in | fade out | let up | seize up | taper off |
| cloud over | fall apart | lie back | sell up | tick over |
| club together | fall away | lie down | set in | touch down |
| come about | fall back | live in | settle down | tune in |
| come along | fall behind | look ahead | settle in | wade in |
| come apart | fall out | look back | settle up | wait about |
| come away | fall over | look in | shop around | wait up |
| come back | fall through | loom up | simmer down | walk out |
| come down | fight back | make off | sink in | waste away |
| come forward | fizzle out | meet up | sit around | watch out |
| come in | flare up | melt away | sit back | wear off |
| come on | fool around | mount up | sit down | weigh in |
| come out | forge ahead | move off | slip up | |
| come round | get about | move over | speak up | |
| come to | get ahead | nod off | splash out | |

**intransitive phrasal verbs with prepositions**

**3.88** Other phrasal verbs used in intransitive clauses are verb plus preposition combinations.

*Ski trips now account for nearly half of all school visits.*
*I'm just asking for information.*
*...the arguments that stem from gossip.*

Note that the noun groups at the end of the above examples ('nearly half of all school visits', 'information', and 'gossip') are objects of the prepositions and not directly objects of the verbs.

**3.89** Here is a list of phrasal verbs which consist of an intransitive verb and a preposition:

| | | | |
|---|---|---|---|
| abide by | draw on | leap at | romp through |
| account for | drink to | level with | run across |
| allow for | dwell on | lie behind | run into |
| answer for | eat into | live for | run to |
| ask after | embark on | live off | sail through |
| ask for | enter into | live with | see to |
| bank on | expand on | look after | seize on |
| bargain for | fall for | look into | set about |
| break into | fall into | look to | settle for |
| break with | fall on | make for | settle on |
| brood on | feel for | meet with | skate over |
| bump into | flick through | part with | smile on |
| burst into | frown upon | pick at | stand for |
| call for | get at | pick on | stem from |
| call on | get into | pitch into | stick at |
| care for | get over | plan for | stick by |
| come across | go about | plan on | stumble across |
| come between | go against | play at | stumble on |
| come by | go for | play on | take after |
| come for | grow on | poke at | take against |
| come from | hang onto | pore over | tamper with |
| come into | head for | provide for | tangle with |
| come under | hit on | puzzle over | trifle with |
| come upon | hold with | rattle through | tumble to |
| count on | jump at | reason with | wade through |
| cut across | keep to | reckon on | wait on |
| dawn on | laugh at | reckon with | walk into |
| deal with | launch into | reckon without | watch for |
| dispose of | lay into | rise above | worry at |

**preposition** **3.90** In the case of some intransitive phrasal verbs, the second word can
**or adverb** be a preposition if the second thing involved needs to be mentioned, or
can be an adverb if the second thing involved is clear from the context.
*I could hang around your office.*
*We'll have to hang around for a while.*
*They all crowded around the table.*
*Everyone crowded around to see him jump into the water.*

**3.91** Here is a list of intransitive phrasal verbs whose second word can b
a preposition or an adverb:

| | | | |
|---|---|---|---|
| ask around | crowd around | go up | push through |
| bend over | do without | go without | rally round |
| break through | fall behind | hang around | run around |
| bustle about | fall down | join in | run down |
| come across | fall off | knock about | run up |
| come after | gather around | lag behind | scrape through |
| come along | get in | lean over | see round |
| come by | get off | lie about | shine through |
| come down | get on | look round | show through |
| come in | get round | look through | sit around |
| come off | go about | lounge about | spill over |
| come on | go along | move about | stand around |
| come over | go down | pass by | stop by |
| come through | go in | pass over | trip over |
| come up | go round | push by | |
| cross over | go through | push past | |

**3.92** Another group of phrasal verbs are nearly always used in transitive clauses, because the verb takes a direct object.

*We put our drinks down on the bar.*
*I finished my meal off as quickly as I could.*
*She read the poem out quietly.*

**3.93** Here is a list of phrasal verbs which consist of a transitive verb and an adverb:

| | | | |
|---|---|---|---|
| add on | fill in | pass down | screen off |
| beat up | fill up | pass over | seal off |
| blot out | filter out | pass round | see off |
| board up | find out | patch up | seek out |
| bring about | fix up | pay back | sell off |
| bring along | follow up | pay out | send up |
| bring back | frighten away | phase in | set apart |
| bring down | gather up | phase out | set aside |
| bring forward | give away | pick off | set back |
| bring in | give back | pick out | set down |
| bring off | give off | piece together | shake off |
| bring out | hammer out | pin down | shake up |
| bring round | hand down | pin up | shoot down |
| bring up | hand in | play back | shrug off |
| buy out | hand on | play down | shut away |
| buy up | hand out | plug in | shut in |
| call off | hand over | point out | shut off |
| call up | hand round | print out | shut out |
| carry off | have on | pull apart | size up |
| carry out | hire out | pull down | smooth over |
| cast aside | hold down | push about | snap up |
| catch out | hold up | push around | soak up |
| chase up | hunt down | push over | sort out |
| chat up | hush up | put about | sound out |
| clean out | keep back | put across | spell out |
| conjure up | kick out | put around | spin out |
| count out | knock down | put away | stamp out |
| cross off | knock out | put down | step up |
| cross out | knock over | put forward | stick down |
| cut back | lap up | put off | summon up |
| cut down | lay down | put on | switch on |
| cut off | lay on | put out | take apart |
| cut up | lay out | put through | take away |
| deal out | leave behind | put together | take back |
| dig up | leave out | put up | take down |
| do down | let down | read out | take in |
| do up | let in | reason out | take on |
| drag in | let off | reel off | take up |
| drag out | let out | rinse out | talk over |
| drag up | lift up | rip off | talk round |
| dream up | live down | rip up | tear apart |
| drink in | melt down | rope in | tear down |
| drive out | mess up | rope off | tear up |
| drum up | mix up | rub in | tell apart |
| eat away | nail down | rub out | tell off |
| eat up | note down | rule out | think over |
| explain away | order about | rush through | think through |
| fight off | pack off | scale down | think up |

| | | | |
|---|---|---|---|
| thrash out | tip off | try out | weigh up |
| throw away | tip up | turn down | whip up |
| throw off | tire out | turn on | win back |
| throw on | tone down | use up | win over |
| throw out | top up | warn off | wipe away |
| tidy away | track down | wash away | wipe out |
| tie down | trade in | weed out | wipe up |
| tie up | try on | weigh out | |

Phrasal verbs which consist of a transitive verb and a preposition are explained in paragraphs 3.108 to 3.111.

**phrasal verbs used transitively and intransitively**

**3.94** A large group of phrasal verbs can be used in intransitive as well as transitive structures.

Often this is because a phrasal verb has more than one meaning. For example, 'break in' is usually intransitive when it is used in the sense of 'get into a place by force'. But 'break in' is transitive when it is used in the sense of 'get someone used to a new situation'.

*If the door is locked, I will try to break in.*
*He believes in breaking in his staff gradually.*

*A plane took off.*
*Gretchen took off her coat.*

*The engine cut out.*
*She cut out some coloured photographs from a magazine.*

**3.95** Here is a list of phrasal verbs which can be used in intransitive as well as transitive clauses, depending on which meaning is being used:

| | | | | |
|---|---|---|---|---|
| add up | get down | kick off | put in | sum up |
| bail out | get in | knock about | roll up | switch off |
| black out | get out | knock off | run down | take off |
| break in | get together | lay off | run off | tear off |
| call in | give up | leave off | run over | throw up |
| carry on | hang out | look out | set forth | tuck in |
| clear out | hold off | look up | set off | turn away |
| cut out | hold out | make out | set out | turn back |
| draw on | join up | make up | show off | turn in |
| draw out | keep away | mess about | show up | turn out |
| draw up | keep down | miss out | split up | turn round |
| dress up | keep in | pass off | stick out | turn up |
| drop off | keep off | pass on | stick up | wind down |
| drop round | keep on | pay off | stow away | wind up |
| fight back | keep out | pick up | strike out | work out |
| finish up | keep up | pull in | string along | wrap up |

**3.96** There are a few phrasal verbs which only have one meaning, but which can be either transitive or intransitive. It is possible to use them intransitively because the object is either obvious or can be guessed in a particular context.

*It won't take me a moment to clear away.*
*I'll help you clear away the dishes.*

**3.97** Here is a list of phrasal verbs which have only one meaning but which can be used transitively or intransitively:

| | | | | |
|---|---|---|---|---|
| answer back | call back | cover up | open up | wash up |
| breathe in | clear away | drink up | take over | |
| breathe out | clear up | help out | tidy away | |

**ergative phrasal verbs**

**3.98** Just as with ordinary verbs, some phrasal verbs are **ergative verbs**; that is, you can use the object of the transitive verb as the subject of the intransitive verb.

*The guerrillas blew up the restaurant.*
*The gasworks blew up.*

*I won't wake him up just yet.*
*He woke up in the middle of the night.*

See paragraphs 3.60 to 3.68 for information about ergative verbs.

**3.99** Here is a list of ergative phrasal verbs:

| | | | | |
|---|---|---|---|---|
| back up | build up | get off | pull through | thaw out |
| block up | burn up | heat up | rub off | wake up |
| blow up | check in | hurry up | shut up | warm up |
| book in | check out | line up | sign up | wear down |
| break off | cheer up | move on | slow down | wear out |
| break up | close down | open up | spread out | |
| buck up | dry up | peel off | start off | |

**3.100** In the case of some ergative phrasal verbs, the second word can be a preposition if the other thing involved needs to be mentioned, or can be an adverb if the other thing involved is clear from the context.

*...leaves that had been blown off the trees.*
*My hat blew off.*

**3.101** Here is a list of ergative phrasal verbs whose second word can be a preposition or an adverb:

| | | | |
|---|---|---|---|
| blow off | get through | move up | stick in |
| chip off | get up | peel off | stick on |
| get down | move down | poke through | |

**object position**

**3.102** When you are using a phrasal verb in a transitive clause and the object is a short noun group, you usually have a choice as to where you put the object. It can be placed either after the second word of the phrasal verb or after the first word and before the second word.

*He filled up his car with petrol.*
*She filled my glass up.*

*He handed over the box.*
*Mrs Kaul handed the flowers over to Judy.*

**3.103** However, when the object consists of a long noun group, it is more likely to come after the second word of the phrasal verb, so that the two parts of the phrasal verb are not separated too widely. In this way, attention is focused on the information contained in the noun group, rather than on the second word of the phrasal verb.

*Police have been told to turn back all refugees who try to cross the border.*

**pronoun object** **3.104** When the object is a pronoun such as 'me', 'her', or 'it', it usually comes before the second word of the phrasal verb. This is because it is not new information, and so it is not put in a position of prominence at the end of the clause.

*I waited until he had <u>filled</u> it <u>up</u>.*
*He <u>tied</u> her <u>up</u> and bundled her into the car.*

**abstract nouns as object** **3.105** If the object of a phrasal verb is an abstract noun such as 'hope', 'confidence', or 'support', it usually comes after the second word of the phrasal verb. So, although you can say, 'He built his business up', you usually say, 'We are trying to build up trust with the residents'. Similarly, although you can say 'He put my parents up for the night', you normally say, 'The peasants are putting up a lot of resistance'.

*The newspapers <u>whipped up</u> sympathy for them.*
*They attempted to <u>drum up</u> support from the students.*
*He didn't <u>hold out</u> much hope for them.*

**object after first word of verb** **3.106** With a small number of phrasal verbs, the object is always placed between the first and the second words of the verb. For example, you can say 'I can't tell your brothers apart' but not 'I can't tell apart your brothers'.

*Captain Dean <u>was</u> still <u>ordering</u> everybody <u>about</u>.*
*I <u>answered</u> him <u>back</u> and took my chances.*

Note that most of these verbs take a human object.

Here is a list of phrasal verbs which always belong in this group when they are used transitively:

| | | | | |
|---|---|---|---|---|
| answer back | churn up | invite over | pull to | slap around |
| ask in | count in | jolly along | push about | stand up |
| bash about | drag down | keep under | push around | stare out |
| bind over | dress down | knock about | push to | string along |
| book in | drop round | mess about | run through | talk round |
| bring round | feel out | move about | see through | tear apart |
| bring to | get away | muck about | send ahead | tell apart |
| brush off | hear out | order about | send away | tip off |
| call back | help along | play along | send up | truss up |
| carry back | invite in | play through | shut up | turf out |
| catch out | invite out | pull about | sit down | |

Some phrasal verbs have more than one transitive sense but belong in this group when they are used with one particular meaning. For example, 'take back' belongs in this group when it means 'remind someone of something' but not when it means 'regain something'.

*The smell of chalk <u>takes</u> me <u>back</u> to my schooldays.*
*...his ambition of <u>taking back</u> disputed territory.*

Here is a list of phrasal verbs which belong in this group when used with a particular meaning:

| | | | | |
|---|---|---|---|---|
| bowl over | get out | nail down | set up | take off |
| bring down | give up | pass on | shake up | throw about |
| bring out | have on | pin down | show around | toss about |
| buoy up | hurry up | pull apart | show up | trip up |
| cut off | keep up | push around | start off | turn on |
| do over | kick around | put down | straighten out | ward off |
| draw out | knock out | put out | take back | wind up |
| get back | knock up | see out | take in | |

**prepositional objects**

**3.107** Remember that when a phrasal verb consists of an intransitive verb followed by a preposition, the noun group always comes after the preposition, even when it is a pronoun.

*A number of reasons can account for this change.*
*They had dealt with the problem intelligently.*
*If I went away and left you in the flat, would you look after it?*

There is a list of phrasal verbs which consist of an intransitive verb and a preposition in paragraph 3.89.

**transitive phrasal verbs with prepositions**

**3.108** Some phrasal verbs consist of a transitive verb and a preposition. They have one noun group after the first word, as the object of the verb, and a second noun group after the second word, as the object of the preposition.

*They agreed to let him into their secret.*
*The farmer threatened to set his dogs on them.*
*They'll hold that against you when you apply next time.*

**3.109** Here is a list of phrasal verbs which consist of a transitive verb and a preposition:

| | | | | |
|---|---|---|---|---|
| build into | hold against | lumber with | read into | thrust upon |
| build on | keep to | make of | set against | write into |
| draw into | lay before | put on | set back | |
| drum into | leave off | put onto | set on | |
| frighten into | let into | put through | talk into | |

**preposition or adverb**

**3.110** In the case of some transitive phrasal verbs, the second word can be a preposition if the third thing involved needs to be mentioned, or can be an adverb if the third thing involved is clear from the context.

*Rudolph showed them around the theatre.*
*Come on. I'll show you around.*

**3.111** Here is a list of transitive phrasal verbs whose second word can be a preposition or an adverb:

| | | | |
|---|---|---|---|
| cross off | hurl about | lop off | show around |
| dab on | keep off | push around | shut in |
| hawk around | knock off | scrub off | sink in |

**intransitive three-word phrasal verbs**

**3.112** Most phrasal verbs consist of two words: a verb and an adverb, or a verb and a preposition. However, there are a number of phrasal verbs which consist of three words: a verb, an adverb, and a preposition.

Most three-word phrasal verbs are intransitive. The preposition at the end is followed by its own object.

*His girlfriend walked out on him.*
*You're not going to get away with this!*
*She sometimes finds it hard to keep up with her classmates.*
*The local people have to put up with a lot of tourists.*

*Terry Holbrook caught up with me.*

**3.113** Here is a list of intransitive three-word phrasal verbs:

| | | | |
|---|---|---|---|
| be in for | come up with | go down with | play around with |
| be on to | crack down on | go in for | put up with |
| bear down on | creep up on | go off with | read up on |
| boil down to | crowd in on | go over to | run away with |
| break out of | cry out against | go through with | run off with |
| brush up on | cry out for | grow out of | run up against |
| bump up against | cut back on | keep in with | shy away from |
| burst in on | date back to | keep on at | sit in on |
| call out for | do away with | keep up with | snap out of |
| catch up with | double back on | kick out against | stick out for |
| chime in with | face up to | lead up to | stick up for |
| clamp down on | fall back on | live up to | suck up to |
| clean up after | fall in with | look down on | take up with |
| come across as | get away with | look forward to | talk down to |
| come down on | get down to | look out for | tie in with |
| come down to | get in on | look up to | walk away from |
| come down with | get off with | make away with | walk away with |
| come in for | get on to | make off with | walk off with |
| come on to | get on with | make up to | walk out on |
| come out in | get round to | match up to | wriggle out of |
| come out of | get up to | measure up to | zero in on |
| come out with | give up on | miss out on | |
| come up against | go along with | monkey about with | |
| come up to | go back on | play along with | |

**transitive three-word phrasal verbs**

**3.114** A few three-word phrasal verbs are transitive. The direct object of the verb comes immediately after the verb. A second noun group is put after the preposition, as normal.

*I'll let you in on a secret.*
*Kroop tried to talk her out of it.*
*They put their success down to hard work.*

Here is a list of transitive three-word phrasal verbs:

| | | | |
|---|---|---|---|
| do out of | let in on | put down to | take up on |
| frighten out of | play off against | put up to | talk out of |
| let in for | put down as | take out on | |

**WARNING**

**3.115** It is not possible to have indirect objects with phrasal verbs. The only objects you can have are direct objects of the verb and objects of prepositions.

**phrasal verbs in questions and relative clauses**

**3.116** There is one way in which a preposition that is part of a phrasal verb behaves differently from an ordinary preposition.

Normally, when the object of a preposition is put at the beginning of a question or a relative clause, it can be preceded by the preposition, especially in formal speech or writing. For example, you can say 'From which student did you get the book?' and 'the document on which he put his signature'.

However, if the preposition is part of a phrasal verb, it cannot be put before its object in such structures. You have to say 'What are you getting at?' not 'At what are you getting?', and 'the difficulties which he ran up against' not 'the difficulties against which he ran up'.

*Who were they laughing at?*
*This was one complication he had not bargained for.*

**3.117** Most phrasal verbs which contain a transitive verb can be used in the passive. So can a few phrasal verbs which contain an intransitive verb and a preposition. See paragraphs 10.17 and 10.23.

# Verbs which consist of two words: compound verbs

**3.118** There are a number of verbs such as 'cross-examine' and 'test-drive' which consist of two words. They are sometimes called **compound verbs**.

*He would have been cross-examined on any evidence he gave.*
*He asked to test-drive a top of the range vehicle.*
*It is not wise to hitch-hike on your own.*

**WARNING** **3.119** It is important to realize that you cannot always guess the meaning of a compound verb if you are not already familiar with it. For example, to 'soft-soap' does not mean to use soap which is soft; it means to flatter someone in order to persuade them to do something for you.

**written forms of compound verbs** **3.120** Compound verbs are usually written with a hyphen.

*No one had cross-referenced the forms before.*
*Children ice-skated on the sidewalks.*

However, some compound verbs may be written with a space between the words and some may be written as single words. For example, both 'roller-skate' and 'roller skate' are used, as are 'baby-sit' and 'babysit'.

**form of compound verbs** **3.121** Many compound verbs consist of a noun plus a verb.

*It may soon become economically attractive to mass-produce hepatitis vaccines.*

Others consist of an adjective plus a verb.

*Somebody had short-changed him.*

**3.122** A few compound verbs consist of words which seem strange because we do not normally use them as single words on their own, for example 'pooh-pooh' and 'shilly-shally'.

*Sally had pooh-poohed the idea of three good meals a day.*
*Come on, don't shilly-shally. I want an answer.*

Other compound verbs look strange because they have been borrowed from foreign languages, for example 'ad-lib' and 'kow-tow'.

*They ad-libbed so much that the writers despaired of them.*
*He resents having to kow-tow to anyone or anything.*

**intransitive compound verbs** **3.123** One group of compound verbs are typically used in intransitive clauses.

*Many people window-shopped in the glass of the great store.*

*If you keep to the rules, you may <u>roller-skate</u>.*
*He has learned to <u>lip-read</u>.*
*I'm learning to <u>water-ski</u>.*

Here is a list of intransitive compound verbs:

| | | | | |
|---|---|---|---|---|
| baby-sit | hitch-hike | kow-tow | roller-skate | water-ski |
| back-pedal | ice-skate | lip-read | shilly-shally | window-shop |
| goose-step | jack-knife | play-act | touch-type | wolf-whistle |

**transitive compound verbs**

**3.124** Another group of compound verbs are typically used in transitive clauses:

*You can <u>spin-dry</u> it and it will still retain its shape.*
*I didn't have time to <u>blow-dry</u> my hair.*
*At first we <u>cold-shouldered</u> him.*
*They <u>ill-treated</u> our ancestors.*

Here is a list of transitive compound verbs:

| | | | |
|---|---|---|---|
| back-comb | cross-reference | ghost-write | soft-soap |
| blow-dry | double-cross | ill-treat | spin-dry |
| cold-shoulder | double-glaze | pooh-pooh | spoon-feed |
| court-martial | dry-clean | proof-read | stage-manage |
| cross-check | field-test | rubber-stamp | tape-record |
| cross-examine | force-feed | short-change | toilet-train |
| cross-question | frog-march | short-weight | wrong-foot |

**transitive or intransitive**

**3.125** A third group of compound verbs may be used in intransitive as well as transitive clauses.

*He <u>chain-smoked</u> cheap cigars.*
*The husband is left to <u>chain-smoke</u> in the waiting-room.*

*I tried to <u>ad-lib</u> a joke.*
*The commentator decided to <u>ad-lib</u>.*

Here is a list of compound verbs which can be transitive or intransitive:

| | | | |
|---|---|---|---|
| ad-lib | chain-smoke | double-park | spring-clean |
| bottle-feed | criss-cross | mass-produce | stir-fry |
| breast-feed | deep-fry | short-circuit | tie-dye |
| bulk-buy | double-check | sight-read | |

**inflecting compound verbs**

**3.126** Only the second part of a compound verb inflects. If the second part is used on its own as a verb, the compound verb usually inflects in the same way as the verb on its own.

See the Reference Section for an explanation of how to inflect verbs.

# Describing and identifying things: complementation

**3.127** If you want to describe someone or something, for example to say who or what they are or what qualities they have, you use one of a special set of verbs. These verbs are called **link verbs** or **copulas**.

*Cigarette smoking is dangerous to your health.*
*The station seemed a very small one.*
*He looked English.*
*I became enormously fond of her.*

The most common link verbs are 'be', 'become', 'look', 'remain', and 'seem'.

**complements**  **3.128** A link verb links a subject and a **complement**. The subject, as usual, comes first and the complement comes after the verb. The complement describes or identifies the subject; it is a structure built around either an adjective or a noun.

*Her general knowledge is amazing.*
*The children seemed frightened.*
*That's a very difficult question.*
*She's the head of a large primary school.*
*Suleiman Salle became the first President of Eritrea.*

The use of link verbs with complements is explained in paragraphs 3.133 to 3.155.

Some other intransitive verbs are sometimes used with complements. See paragraphs 3.156 to 3.161.

**verbs with**  **3.129** Some verbs, such as 'make' and 'find', are used with both an object
**object**  and a complement. The complement describes the object and is called the
**complements**  **object complement**.

*The lights made me sleepy.*
*I found the forest quite frightening.*

These verbs are explained in paragraphs 3.162 to 3.172.

**prepositional**  **3.130** Instead of a complement, you can often use a prepositional phrase
**phrases**  or another kind of adjunct.

*The first-aid box is on the top shelf.*
*I began to get in a panic.*

These structures can also be used instead of object complements.

*An attack of malaria can keep a man off work for three days.*

For more information about adjuncts that can be used after link verbs, see paragraphs 3.173 to 3.182.

**'it' with 'be'**  **3.131** 'Be' is often used with 'it' as an impersonal subject. This structure is used to comment on places, situations, actions, experiences, and facts.

*It was very quiet in the hut.*
*It was awkward keeping my news from Ted.*
*It's strange you should come today.*

Some other link verbs are occasionally used in a similar way.

The use of 'it' as an impersonal subject is explained in paragraphs 10.31 to 10.45.

**'there' with**  **3.132** 'Be' is often used with 'there' as its subject to indicate the
**'be'**  existence of something.

*There is another explanation.*
*There is a rear bathroom with a panelled bath.*

This use of 'there' is explained in paragraphs 10.46 to 10.55.

# Describing things: adjectives as complements of link verbs

**3.133** Many **adjectives** can be used as complements.

*I am proud of these people.*
*They seemed happy.*
*You don't want them to become suspicious.*
*They have remained loyal to the Government.*

They can be modified in various ways or have various structures after them.

*We were very happy.*
*Your suspicions are entirely correct.*
*Their hall was larger than his whole flat.*
*He was capable of extraordinary kindness.*

Adjectives used after link verbs, and the structures used with them, are explained in paragraphs 2.45 to 2.57.

**3.134** Here is a list of verbs which can be used as link verbs with an adjective as the complement:

| be | prove | ~ | go | turn |
|---|---|---|---|---|
| ~ | seem | become | grow | |
| appear | smell | come | keep | |
| feel | sound | fall | remain | |
| look | taste | get | stay | |

Note that the third group of verbs refer to changing or to staying the same.

USAGE NOTE **3.135** Some verbs in the second group listed above have special features.

'Appear', 'prove', and 'seem' are often followed by 'to be' and a complement, instead of directly by a complement.

*Mary was breathing quietly and seemed to be asleep.*
*Some people appeared to be immune to the HIV virus.*

See paragraph 3.193 for information on using a 'to'-infinitive clause after these verbs.

**3.136** With some verbs in the second group, especially 'feel', 'look', and 'seem', you can use the **past participle** of a transitive verb as a complement.

*The other child looked neglected.*
*The quarrel of the night before seemed forgotten.*

**3.137** When you are using the second group of verbs to say what qualities someone or something seems to have, you may want to mention the person whose viewpoint you are giving. You can do this by using a prepositional phrase beginning with 'to'. It usually comes after the complement.

*They looked all right to me.*
*It sounds unnatural to you, I expect.*

**WARNING** **3.138** You cannot use all adjectives with all link verbs. Some verbs, such as 'be' and 'look', are used with a wide range of adjectives and some are used with a restricted range. For example, 'taste' is used only with adjectives which describe the taste of something; 'go' is used primarily with adjectives which indicate colour or madness; and 'fall' is used mainly with 'asleep', 'ill', and 'silent'.

*Sea water tastes nasty.*
*It tasted sweet like fruit juice.*

*Jack went red.*
*The world has gone crazy.*

*He fell asleep at the table.*
*The courtroom fell silent.*

## Saying that one thing is another thing: noun groups as complements of link verbs

**3.139** **Noun groups** can be used as complements after the following link verbs:

| | | | |
|---|---|---|---|
| be | feel | sound | represent |
| become | look | ~ | ~ |
| remain | prove | constitute | comprise |
| ~ | seem | make | form |

**qualities**

**3.140** You can use descriptive nouns or noun groups after 'be', 'become', 'remain', 'feel', 'look', 'prove', 'seem', 'sound', 'constitute', and 'represent' to indicate what qualities someone or something has.

*Their policy on higher education is an unmitigated disaster.*
*He always seemed a controlled sort of man.*
*I feel a bit of a fraud.*
*The results of these experiments remain a secret.*
*Any change would represent a turnaround.*

'Make' is only used as a link verb with a complement which indicates whether someone is good at a particular job.

*He'll make a good president.*

**using 'one'**

**3.141** With 'be', 'become', 'remain', 'feel', 'look', 'prove', 'seem', and 'sound', you can use a noun group based on 'one' instead of using an adjective on its own as a complement.

The noun group consists of 'a' or 'an' followed by the adjective and 'one', if your subject is singular. For example, instead of saying 'The school is large', you can say 'The school is a large one'.

*The sound is a familiar one.*
*The impression the region gives is still a rural one.*

If your subject is plural, you can use the adjective followed by 'ones'.

*My memories of a London childhood are happy ones.*

Another kind of complement consists of 'one' followed by a **prepositional phrase** or a **relative clause**.

*Their story was indeed one of passion.*
*The problem is one that always faces a society when it finds itself threatened.*

**size, age, colour, shape**

**3.142** If you want to make a statement about the size, age, colour, or shape of something, you can use a noun group based on 'size', 'age', 'colour', or 'shape' after the link verbs mentioned in the previous paragraph. The noun group begins with a determiner and has an adjective in front of the noun or the preposition 'of' after it.

*It's just the right size.*
*The opposing force would be about the same size.*
*The walls are a delicate pale cream colour.*
*His body was the colour of bronze.*
*It is only the size of a mouse.*

**types of people and things**

**3.143** You can use noun groups beginning with 'a' or 'an', or plural noun groups without a determiner, after 'be', 'become', 'remain', 'comprise', and 'form', to say what type of person or thing someone or something is.

*He is a geologist.*
*I'm not an unreasonable person.*
*He is now a teenager.*
*The air moved a little faster and became a light wind.*
*They became farmers.*
*Promises by MPs remained just promises.*
*These arches formed a barrier to the tide.*

**indicating identity**

**3.144** You can use names or noun groups referring to a particular person or thing after 'be', 'become', 'remain', 'constitute', 'represent', 'comprise', and 'form' to indicate exactly who or what someone or something is.

*This is Desiree, my father's second wife.*
*He's now the Director of the Office of Management and Budget.*
*The winner of the competition was Will Young.*
*The downstairs television room became my room for receiving visitors.*
*...the four young men who comprised the TV crew.*

**USAGE NOTE**

**3.145** When you use a noun group indicating a unique job or position within an organization, you do not have to put a determiner in front of the noun.

*At one time you wanted to be President.*
*He went on to become head of one of the company's largest divisions.*

**pronouns as complements**

**3.146** **Personal pronouns** are sometimes used as complements to indicate identity. Note that the object pronouns are used, except in very formal speech or writing.

*It's me again.*

**Possessive pronouns** are also used as complements, to indicate identity or to describe something.

*This one is yours.*
*This place is mine.*

**Indefinite pronouns** are sometimes used to describe something, usually with a qualifying structure after them.

*It's nothing serious.*
*You're someone who does what she wants.*

Pronouns are usually used as complements after 'be'.

**other complements**

**3.147** The use of noun groups containing **measurement nouns** after 'be' and other verbs is explained in paragraphs 2.269 to 2.271.

The use of **non-finite clauses** as complements is explained in paragraphs 10.27 and 10.97.

**combinations of verbs and prepositions**

**3.148** Some verbs function as link verbs when they are followed by a particular preposition.

The object of the preposition describes or classifies the subject of the verb.

*His fear turned into unreasoning panic.*
*Taylor's fascination with bees developed into an obsession.*
*An autobiography really amounts to a whole explanation of yourself.*

Here is a list of verb and preposition combinations which function as link verbs:

| | | | |
|---|---|---|---|
| amount to | change to | grow into | turn to |
| change into | develop into | turn into | |

These all have the same basic meaning as 'become', except for 'amount to', which has a similar meaning to 'constitute'.

The phrasal verb 'make up' also functions as a link verb.

*Wood made up 65% of the Congo's exports.*

# Commenting: 'to'-infinitive clauses after complements

**3.149** There are several ways in which a **'to'-infinitive clause** can be used after a complement to comment on someone or something in relation to an action.

**commenting on behaviour**

**3.150** If you want to say that someone shows a particular quality when they do something, you can use a 'to'-infinitive after a descriptive complement.

*Most people think I am brave to do this.*
*I think my father was a brave man to do what he did.*

The complement can be an adjective, or it can be a noun group consisting of 'a' or 'an' followed by an adjective and a noun.

**commenting on suitability**

**3.151** You can say that someone or something would do a particular task better than anyone or anything else by using a 'to'-infinitive clause after a complement.

*He was absolutely the right man to go to Paris and negotiate.*
*She may be an ideal person to look after the children.*
*He is just the man to cool their reforming zeal.*

The complement must be a noun group containing an adjective such as 'right', 'ideal', or 'best', or 'just the' followed by the noun 'person', 'man', or 'woman'. You cannot use adjectives as complements in constructions of this kind. For example, you can say, 'He was the ideal person to lead the expedition', but you cannot say, 'He was ideal to lead the expedition'.

Instead of a 'to'-infinitive clause, you can sometimes use a prepositional phrase beginning with 'for'. In this structure, an adjective can be used as the complement.

*He's not the right man for it.*
*They are ideal for this job.*

**commenting on an event**

**3.152** If you want to express your feeling about an event, you can use a 'to'-infinitive clause after a complement.

*It seemed such a terrible thing to happen.*

The 'to'-infinitive consists of 'to' and an intransitive verb, usually 'happen'.

The complement must be a noun group consisting of 'a' or 'an', an adjective, and a noun. You cannot use an adjective alone in constructions of this kind. For example, you can say 'It was a wonderful thing to happen' but you cannot say 'It was wonderful to happen'.

**commenting on willingness**

**3.153** If you want to say that someone is willing or unwilling to do something, you can use a 'to'-infinitive clause after a complement.

*They were willing to risk losing their jobs.*
*I am anxious to meet Mrs Burton-Cox.*
*She is eager to succeed.*
*He is unwilling to answer questions.*
*I was reluctant to involve myself in this private fight.*

The complement must be an adjective such as 'willing' or 'unwilling'. You cannot use noun groups as complements in constructions of this kind. For example, you can say 'He was willing to come', but you cannot say 'He was a willing person to come'.

**commenting on something**

**3.154** If you want to show your opinion of something by indicating what the experience of doing something to it is like, you can use a 'to'-infinitive clause after a complement.

*Silk is comfortable to wear.*
*It's a nice thing to have.*
*Telling someone they smell is a hard thing to do.*
*She was easy to talk to.*

The complement can be an adjective, or it can be a noun group consisting of 'a' or 'an' followed by an adjective and a noun.

Note that the 'to'-infinitive must be the 'to'-infinitive of a transitive verb or of an intransitive verb followed by a preposition.

**commenting on an action**

**3.155** If you want to show your opinion of an action, you can use a transitive 'to'-infinitive clause after a complement.

*They thought this was a sensible thing to do.*
*This is a very foolish attitude to take.*

The 'to'-infinitive is usually 'to do', 'to make', or 'to take'.

The complement must be a noun group consisting of 'a' or 'an', an adjective, and a noun. You cannot use an adjective alone in constructions of this kind. For example, you can say 'It was a silly thing to do', but you cannot say 'It was silly to do'.

# Describing as well as talking about an action: other verbs with complements

**3.156** Some intransitive verbs can be used with adjectives after them in the same way as link verbs.

*George stood motionless for at least a minute.*

*Pugin died insane at the early age of forty.*

However, it is clear that these verbs are not just link verbs. 'George stood motionless' does not mean the same as 'George was motionless'. In the sentence 'George stood motionless', the verb 'stand' is performing two functions: it is telling us that George was standing, and it is also acting as a link verb between 'George' and the complement 'motionless'.

Here is a list of verbs which can be used in this way:

| hang | gaze | go | flame | be born |
|------|------|------|------|------|
| lie | stare | pass | gleam | die |
| sit | ~ | survive | glow | return |
| stand | emerge | ~ | run | |
| ~ | escape | blush | ~ | |

Ways in which these verbs can be used with complements are discussed in the following paragraphs.

Adjectives are sometimes used in combination with other verbs, but are separated from the main clause by a comma. This use is dealt with in paragraph 8.135.

**USAGE NOTE**   **3.157** You can use adjectives describing states after 'hang', 'lie', 'sit', and 'stand'.

*I used to lie awake watching the rain seep through the roof.*
*A sparrow lies dead in the snow.*
*Francis Marroux sat ashen-faced behind the wheel.*
*She stood quite still, facing him.*

'Gaze' and 'stare' can be used in a similar way with a limited set of adjectives.

*She stared at him wide-eyed.*

**3.158** You can use some combinations of verbs and adjectives to say that something does not happen to someone or something, or that someone does not have something.

'Go', 'pass', 'emerge', 'escape', and 'survive' are often used in combinations like these. The adjectives they combine with are often formed by adding 'un-' to past participles.

*Your efforts won't go unnoticed.*
*I think that on this occasion the guilty should go unpunished.*
*Somehow, his reputation emerged unblemished.*
*Fortunately we all escaped unscathed.*
*Mostly, they go unarmed.*
*The children always went naked.*

**3.159** Verbs such as 'blush', 'flame', 'gleam', 'glow', and 'run' can be used with colour adjectives after them to say what colour something is or what colour it becomes.

*They blew into the charcoal until it glowed red.*
*The trees flamed scarlet against the grass.*

**3.160** 'Die', 'return', and the passive verb 'be born' can have either adjectives or noun groups as complements.

*She died young.*
*He died a disappointed man.*

*If he had fought in the First World War, he might have* returned a slightly different man.
*These girls have to work hard because they* were born poor.
*He* was born a slave.

**fixed phrases**   **3.161** Some combinations of verb and adjective are fixed phrases. You cannot use the verb in front of any other adjective.

*I wanted to* travel light.
*The children* ran wild.
*The response 'Oh don't'* was wearing thin *with use.*

## Describing the object of a verb: object complements

**3.162** Some transitive verbs can have a **complement** after their object. This complement describes the object, and is often called the **object complement.**

*Willie's jokes made her* uneasy.
*I find the British legal system* extremely complicated.

Some of these verbs are used to say that someone or something is changed or given a new job. Others are used to indicate a person's opinion of someone or something.

For information on how to use these verbs in the passive, see paragraph 10.21.

**verbs of causing**   **3.163** If you want to say that someone or something causes a person or thing to have a particular quality, you can use one of a group of transitive verbs, with an adjective as the complement.

*He said waltzes* made him dizzy.
*They're* driving me crazy.
*Then his captor had* knocked him unconscious.
*She* painted her eyelids deep blue.
*He* wiped the bottle dry *with a dishcloth.*

Here is a list of verbs which can be used in this way:

| | | | |
|---|---|---|---|
| cut | make | plane | shoot |
| drive | paint | render | sweep |
| get | pat | rub | turn |
| knock | pick | send | wipe |

Most of these verbs can have only one adjective or a very small range of adjectives as their complement. However 'make' and 'render' can be used with a wide range of adjectives.

**'keep', 'hold', 'leave'**   **3.164** You can also use 'keep', 'hold', and 'leave' transitively with an adjective as complement, to say that someone or something is caused to remain in a particular state.

*The light through the thin curtains* had kept her awake.
Leave the door open.
Hold it straight.

**verbs of appointing**   **3.165** If you want to say that someone is given an important job, you can use 'make', 'appoint', 'crown', or 'elect' with a noun group referring to the job as complement.

*In 1910 Asquith made him a junior minister.*

The noun used as the complement does not usually have a determiner when it refers to a unique job.

*Ramsay MacDonald appointed him Secretary of State for India.*

**verbs of opinion**

**3.166** Some transitive verbs with the general meaning 'consider' can be used with an adjective or noun group as complement to say what someone's opinion of a person or thing is.

*They consider him an embarrassment.*
*Do you find his view of America interesting?*

Here is a list of these verbs:

| | | |
|---|---|---|
| account | find | presume |
| believe | hold | reckon |
| consider | judge | think |

'Prove' can also have an adjective or a noun group as a complement, although it means 'show' not 'consider'.

*He had proved them all wrong.*

**3.167** These verbs are often used in the passive. 'Believe', 'presume', 'reckon', and 'think' are nearly always used in the passive in these structures.

*Her body was never found and she was presumed dead.*
*30 bombers were believed shot down.*

**3.168** All the verbs listed in paragraph 3.166 except 'account' can also be used with a 'to'-infinitive clause after their object indicating what someone thinks a person or thing is like or does.

*We believed him to be innocent.*

See paragraph 3.207 for information about using a 'to'-infinitive clause after the object of these verbs.

**3.169** You can use the verbs listed in 3.166 with 'it' as their object followed by a complement and a 'to'-infinitive clause to show someone's opinion of an action. For example, instead of saying 'She found breathing difficult', you can say 'She found it difficult to breathe'.

*Gretchen found it difficult to speak.*
*He thought it right to resign.*
*He considered it his duty to go.*

These are examples of 'it' being used in an impersonal way. For more information about the impersonal use of 'it', see paragraphs 10.31 to 10.45.

**describing and naming**

**3.170** If you want to say that people use a particular word, word group, or name to describe or refer to someone or something, you can use the word, word group, or name as the complement of one of a group of transitive verbs.

*People who did not like him called him dull.*
*They called him an idiot.*
*Everyone called her Molly.*

*He got his trial and was declared innocent.*
*They named the place 'Tumbo Kutu'.*

Here is a list of verbs which can be used in this way. The first group can have an adjective as their complement; the second group can have a noun group as their complement; and the third group can have a name as their complement.

| | | | | |
|---|---|---|---|---|
| call | pronounce | call | proclaim | christen |
| certify | term | declare | term | dub |
| declare | ~ | designate | ~ | name |
| label | brand | label | call | nickname |

**titles** **3.171** The passive verbs 'be entitled', 'be headed', and 'be inscribed' are used with a title or inscription as their complement.

*The draft document was entitled 'A way forward.'*

**describing** **3.172** A few transitive verbs can be used with an adjective as their
**states** complement to say that someone or something is in a particular state when something happens to them, or is preferred to be in that state.

*More than forty people were burned alive.*
*...a soup which can be served cold.*
*They found it dead.*
*Do you want it white or black?*

Here is a list of verbs which can be used in this way:

| | | |
|---|---|---|
| burn | leave | serve |
| eat | like | show |
| find | prefer | want |

Sometimes a past participle or a present participle describing a state is used as the complement.

*She found herself caught in a vicious tidal current.*
*Maureen came in and found Kate sitting on a straight chair staring at the window.*

This participle structure is like a **phase** structure. See paragraphs 3.205 and 3.213.

# Describing something in other ways: adjuncts instead of complements

**3.173** When you want to give information about someone or something by describing their circumstances, you can sometimes use a **prepositional phrase** after a link verb, rather than a complement.

**use after 'be'** **3.174** You can use many kinds of prepositional phrase after 'be'.

*He was still in a state of shock.*
*I walked home with Bill, who was in a very good mood.*
*She had an older brother who was in the army.*
*I'm from Dortmund originally.*
*...people who are under pressure.*
*Your comments are of great interest to me.*

This book is for any woman who has ever said 'If only I knew where to find help.'

**use after other verbs**

**3.175** Some other link verbs can be used with a more restricted range of prepositional phrases.

He seemed in excellent health.
We do ask people to keep in touch with us.
These methods have gradually fallen into disuse.
He got into trouble with the police.

Here is a list of other link verbs that are used with prepositional phrases:

| | | | |
|---|---|---|---|
| appear | feel | keep | seem |
| fall | get | remain | stay |

**adjuncts of place**

**3.176** Some verbs which are used with complements can also be used with **adjuncts of place** after them.

She's in California.
I'll stay here with the children.
The cat was now lying on the sofa.

Here is a list of these verbs:

| | | |
|---|---|---|
| be | stay | lie |
| keep | ~ | sit |
| remain | hang | stand |

For more information about adjuncts of place, see paragraphs 6.53 to 6.72 and 6.82 to 6.93.

**adjuncts of time**

**3.177** 'Be' can be used with **adjuncts of time** to say when something took place or will take place.

That final meeting was on 3 November.

For more information about adjuncts of time, see paragraphs 5.84 to 5.110.

**use in transitive structures**

**3.178** Prepositional phrases can also be used in transitive structures to say that someone or something is caused to be in a particular state.

They'll get me out of trouble.
The fear of being discovered kept me on the alert.

# Indicating what role something has or how it is perceived: the preposition 'as'

**3.179** Prepositional phrases beginning with 'as' can.be used after some intransitive and transitive verbs. The noun groups following 'as' have a similar meaning to **complements**.

**use in intransitive structures**

**3.180** Prepositional phrases beginning with 'as' can be used after certain intransitive verbs to indicate what role or function the subject has, or what identity they pretend to have.

Bleach removes colour and acts as an antiseptic and deodoriser.

*He served as Kennedy's ambassador to India.*
*The sitting room doubles as her office.*

Here is a list of verbs which can be followed by 'as' in this way:

| | | | |
|---|---|---|---|
| act | double | pass | serve |
| come | function | pose | |

'Work' can also be used in this way, when it has a human subject.

*She works as a counsellor with an AIDS charity.*

**use in transitive structures**  **3.181** A number of transitive verbs can be used with 'as' after their object.

With some, a noun group is used after 'as'. The 'as' phrase describes the role of the object or what it is thought to be.

*I wanted to use him as an agent.*
*I treated business as a game.*

Here is a list of transitive verbs which can be used with 'as' and a noun group:

| | | | | |
|---|---|---|---|---|
| brand | condemn | elect | label | suggest |
| cast | consider | establish | name | take |
| categorize | define | give | perceive | treat |
| certify | denounce | hail | recognize | use |
| characterize | depict | identify | regard | view |
| choose | describe | intend | scorn | |
| class | diagnose | interpret | see | |

With others, an adjective is used after 'as'. The adjective indicates what quality or characteristic the object is thought to have.

*Party members and officials described him as brilliant.*
*They regarded manual work as degrading.*

Here is a list of transitive verbs which can be used with 'as' and an adjective:

| | | | | |
|---|---|---|---|---|
| brand | class | depict | label | see |
| categorize | condemn | describe | perceive | view |
| certify | define | diagnose | regard | |
| characterize | denounce | establish | scorn | |

**3.182** 'Look upon', 'refer to', and 'think of' can also be used with 'as' in this way. 'As' must be followed by a noun group when used with 'refer to'.

*In some households the man was referred to as 'the master'.*

# Talking about closely linked actions: using two verbs together in phase

**3.183** This section describes the ways in which you use two verbs in a clause in order to talk about two actions or states which are closely linked. This structure is called **phase**.

These two actions may be performed by the same person. See paragraphs 3.190 to 3.202.

*She stopped speaking.*
*Davis likes to talk about horses.*

Alternatively, the actions may be performed by different people. If they are, the performer of the second action is the object of the first verb. See paragraphs 3.203 to 3.213.

*I don't want them to feel I've slighted them.*
*One of the group began pumping her chest to help her breathe.*

**3.184** Note that the first verb needs the second verb after it because it does not give enough information on its own. For example, 'I want' does not give enough information to be a useful statement, but 'I want to talk to you' does.

Some of the verbs dealt with below, for example 'want' and 'like', can also be ordinary transitive verbs, with a noun group after them. Transitive verbs are explained in paragraphs 3.15 to 3.26.

**3.185** If you want to talk about two actions that are less closely linked, you refer to each action in a separate clause. Ways of combining clauses are explained in Chapter 8.

**verb forms**    **3.186** The first verb involved in a phase structure is the main verb of the structure. It is usually **finite;** that is, it inflects for tense and agrees in number with the subject of the clause.

*I wanted to come home.*
*Lonnie wants to say 'sorry'.*
*More and more people are coming to appreciate the contribution which Muslims make to our society.*

However, it can be a **non-finite** form.

*There is a need to react to new opportunities with speed.*

**3.187** The second verb in the combination is always **non-finite,** which means that it does not inflect for tense or change its form at all.

*She tried to read.*
*They had been trying to read.*

Information about finite and non-finite forms can be found in the Reference Section.

**3.188** There are four non-finite verb forms that are used for the second verb in phase:

- the present participle
- the 'to'-infinitive form
- the infinitive without 'to'
- the past participle

Note that the infinitive without 'to' and the past participle form of the verb are used in only a few combinations.

Other kinds of '-ing' form and infinitive are also sometimes used. They are combinations of non-finite forms.

*Those very close to the blast risk being burnt.*
*Neither Rita nor I recalled ever having seen her.*

*She wanted to be reassured.*
*They claimed to have shot down 22 planes.*

**3.189** The position of 'not' in negative phase structures is explained in paragraphs 4.53 and 4.54.

## Talking about two actions done by the same person: phase verbs together

**3.190** When you are talking about two actions that are done by the same person, you use the second, non-finite, verb directly after the first verb.

*Children enjoy playing alongside each other.*
*You deserve to know the truth.*

**verbs followed by a present participle**    **3.191** Some verbs are always followed by a present participle clause in phase structures of this kind.

*She admitted lying to him.*
*Have you finished reading the paper?*
*He missed having someone to dislike.*
*I recall being very impressed with the official anthems.*

Here is a list of verbs which are used with a present participle, but not a 'to'-infinitive:

| | | | | |
|---|---|---|---|---|
| admit | defer | endure | loathe | resent |
| adore | delay | enjoy | mention | resist |
| appreciate | deny | fancy | mind | risk |
| avoid | describe | finish | miss | sit |
| celebrate | detest | go | postpone | stand |
| commence | discontinue | imagine | practise | stop |
| consider | dislike | keep | recall | suggest |
| contemplate | dread | lie | report | |

These verbs are also sometimes used with a passive '-ing' form.

*They enjoy being praised.*

'Admit', 'celebrate', 'deny', 'mention', and 'recall' are quite often used with a perfect '-ing' form.

*Carmichael had denied having seen him.*

**USAGE NOTE**    **3.192** Note that 'need' can be used with a present participle after it, but the present participle then has the same meaning as a passive 'to'-infinitive. For example, 'The house needs cleaning' means the same as 'The house needs to be cleaned'.

'Require' and 'want' are also occasionally used in the same way, although some people do not like this use of 'want'.

**verbs followed by a 'to'-infinitive**    **3.193** Other verbs are used with a 'to'-infinitive clause.

*Mrs Babcock had always longed to go to Ireland.*
*She forgot to bring a suitcase.*
*She wishes to ask a favour of you.*

Here is a list of verbs which are used with a 'to'-infinitive, but not a present participle:

| | | | | |
|---|---|---|---|---|
| ache | decide | hesitate | plan | swear |
| afford | demand | hope | pledge | tend |
| agree | deserve | intend | prepare | threaten |
| aim | desire | learn | pretend | venture |
| appear | disdain | live | promise | volunteer |
| arrange | endeavour | long | prove | vote |
| ask | expect | manage | reckon | vow |
| attempt | fail | mean | refuse | wait |
| care | fight | need | resolve | want |
| choose | forget | neglect | scorn | wish |
| claim | grow | offer | seek | |
| consent | happen | opt | seem | |
| dare | help | pay | survive | |

Most of these verbs can be used with a passive infinitive.

*She refused to be photographed.*
*He deserves to be shot.*

The following verbs from the above list are not usually used with a passive infinitive, because of their meanings:

| | | | |
|---|---|---|---|
| claim | intend | mean | threaten |
| dare | learn | neglect | trouble |
| forget | manage | pretend | venture |

'Appear', 'claim', 'happen', 'pretend', 'prove', 'seem', and 'tend' are quite often used with a perfect infinitive.

*They seemed to have disappeared.*

Note that 'help' is also followed by the infinitive without 'to'.

*Coffee helped keep him alert.*

**USAGE NOTE** **3.194** Note that 'afford' is always preceded by a modal, and that 'care' is normally used with a negative.

*Can we afford to ignore this source of power as other sources of energy are diminishing?*
*...a kitchen for someone who doesn't care to cook.*

**3.195** The use of 'have' followed by a 'to'-infinitive clause is explained in paragraph 4.248.

**verbs used with either form** **3.196** A few verbs can be used with either a present participle clause or a 'to'-infinitive clause without altering the meaning of the verb.

*It started raining.*
*A very cold wind had started to blow.*

*Maureen began dancing.*
*Anne began to cry.*

*I prefer wearing comfortable clothes.*
*Russians prefer to give gifts at New Year.*

*We both love dancing.*
*He loves to talk about metalwork.*

Here is a list of verbs which can be followed either by a present participle or a 'to'-infinitive without greatly altering the meaning:

| attempt | cease | fear | love | try |
|---------|-------|------|------|-----|
| begin | continue | hate | prefer | |
| bother | deserve | like | start | |

Note that 'bother' is often used with a negative or a broad negative.

*He didn't bother complaining about it.*
*We hardly even bother to clean it.*

**USAGE NOTE**    **3.197** With a few verbs, the meaning is altered depending on whether you use a present participle clause or a 'to'-infinitive clause. These verbs are 'come', 'go on', 'remember', and 'regret'.

If someone 'comes running, flying, or hurtling' somewhere, they move in that way. If you 'come to do something', you gradually start doing it.

*When they heard I was leaving, they both came running out.*
*People came to believe that all things were possible.*

With the other verbs, the difference in meaning relates to the timing of the action.

If you 'go on doing something', you continue to do it, but if you 'go on to do something', you subsequently start doing it.

*They went on arguing into the night.*
*She went on to talk about the political consequences.*

If you 'remember doing something', you did it in the past, but if you 'remember to do something', you do it at the present time.

*I remember promising that I would try.*
*We must remember to say thank-you.*

Likewise, if you 'regret doing something', you have already done it, but if you 'regret to do something', you have to do it at the present time.

*She did not regret accepting his offer.*
*I regret to say rents went up.*

'Regret' is only used with the 'to'-infinitive of a small number of verbs which share the meaning of giving or receiving information. These verbs are:

| announce | learn | see |
|----------|-------|-----|
| inform | say | tell |

**WARNING**    **3.198** When you have a choice between a present participle and a 'to'-infinitive, you do not use the present participle if the first verb is in a continuous tense.

*The Third World is beginning to export to the West.*
*The big clouds were starting to cover the sun.*
*Educational budgets are continuing to increase.*

With verbs that cannot be followed by a 'to'-infinitive, you normally use a noun group instead of the present participle.

*I knew Miss Head would just be finishing her cello practice.*

**3.199** Note that a few verbs, principally 'need', 'want', 'have', 'buy', and 'choose', are used with an object and a 'to'-infinitive when talking about two actions performed by the same person. The 'to'-infinitive must be transitive. It is understood as qualifying the noun, rather than being closely connected with the first verb.

*I need a car to drive to work.*
*She chose the correct one to put in her bag.*

**'to'-infinitive showing purpose**

3.200 Note that verbs which indicate a deliberate action are sometimes followed by a 'to'-infinitive clause which expresses purpose.

*Several women moved to help her.*
*The captain stopped to reload the machine-gun.*

This is not a phase structure because the first verb has a complete meaning of its own; the second verb is giving a reason for the first action, not completing the information about it.

Note that in this structure, 'to' can be extended to the phrase 'in order to'. See paragraphs 8.43 to 8.46 for more details.

**USAGE NOTE**

3.201 When the base form of 'try' is used, for example as an **imperative** or with a **modal**, it is sometimes used with 'and' followed by the base form of the second verb, rather than with a 'to'-infinitive. The two actions seem to be separate, because of the 'and', but are in fact very closely linked.

*Try and get a torch or a light, it's terribly dark down here.*
*I'll try and answer the question.*

Some speakers consider this to be informal or incorrect.

'Come' and 'go' are often used in a similar way with 'and', in simple tenses as well as in the base form. The verb after 'and' can also inflect.

*Come and see me whenever you feel depressed.*
*I went and fetched another glass.*

**'get' with a past participle**

3.202 In informal English, 'get' is sometimes used with a past participle directly after it, in a structure with a passive meaning.

*Then he got killed in a plane crash.*

# Talking about two actions done by different people: phase verbs separated by an object

3.203 If you want to talk about two closely linked actions which are performed by different people, you follow the first verb with an object. This object then functions as the subject of the second verb. For example, in 'She asked Ginny to collect the book', 'Ginny' is the person who is asked, and she is also the person who performs the action of collecting the book.

*I saw him looking at my name on the door.*
*You can't stop me seeing him!*
*They left her to lie on the wooden floor.*
*The committee's lawyers had advised certain people to stay away.*

**use of possessive determiner**

3.204 Note that when the second verb is a present participle, a possessive determiner is sometimes used in front of it, instead of a pronoun. This is rather formal.

...a set of professional ethics to prevent their discussing their clients with the public.
She did not like my living in London.

Note that a possessive determiner is only used in this way when the second verb can have a human subject.

**transitive verbs with a present participle**

3.205 Some verbs are used with an object and a present participle clause.

He caught Hooper looking at him.
I felt the rope tightening.
I heard him gasping and shrieking.

Here is a list of verbs which are used with an object and a present participle:

| | | | | |
|---|---|---|---|---|
| catch | hear | like | prevent | spot |
| describe | imagine | notice | save | stop |
| feel | keep | observe | see | want |
| find | leave | picture | send | watch |

'Listen to' also belongs in this group. The object after it is the object of the preposition 'to'.

I listened to Kaspar talking.

These verbs are sometimes used with a passive '-ing' form, but not usually with a perfect '-ing' form.

She felt herself being spun around.

**verbs with an infinitive without 'to'**

3.206 Some of the verbs in the above paragraph can also be used with an infinitive without 'to'.

She felt her hair rise on the back of her neck.
Dr Hochstadt heard her gasp.

There is a slight change of meaning depending on which form is used. If you choose the present participle, you emphasize that the action continued happening for a period of time.

But I lay on, listening to her singing.
I looked over and saw Joe staring at me.

If you choose the infinitive without 'to', you emphasize that the action was completed.

We listened to Jenny finish the Sonnet.
It was the first time she had heard him speak of his life.

Here is a list of verbs which can be used with a present participle or an infinitive without 'to', with the change of meaning described above:

| | | | |
|---|---|---|---|
| feel | listen to | observe | watch |
| hear | notice | see | |

Note that these verbs can only be used in the active when they are followed by an infinitive without 'to'. See also paragraph 3.209.

**transitive verbs with a 'to'-infinitive**

**3.207** Other verbs are used with an object and a 'to'-infinitive clause.

*His sister had taught him to sew.*
*I encourage students to do these exercises at home.*

Here is a list of verbs which are used with an object and a 'to'-infinitive:

| | | | | |
|---|---|---|---|---|
| advise | defy | instruct | pay | tell |
| allow | enable | intend | permit | train |
| ask | encourage | invite | persuade | trust |
| beg | expect | lead | prefer | urge |
| cause | forbid | leave | press | use |
| challenge | force | like | programme | want |
| choose | get | mean | prompt | warn |
| command | help | move | recruit | |
| compel | induce | oblige | remind | |
| dare | inspire | order | teach | |

Note that some of the verbs in the above list are used for reporting orders, requests and advice. For more information on this use, see paragraph 7.36.

Here is a list of verbs which are always or usually used in the passive when followed by a 'to'-infinitive:

| | | | | |
|---|---|---|---|---|
| allege | deem | know | require | understand |
| assume | discover | learn | rumour | |
| believe | estimate | prove | say | |
| claim | feel | reckon | see | |
| consider | find | report | think | |

They refer to saying, thinking, or discovering. The 'to'-infinitive that follows them is most commonly 'be' or 'have', or a perfect infinitive.

*The house was believed to be haunted.*
*After a series of tests, he was found to have meningitis.*
*...the primitive molecules which are believed to have given rise to life on Earth.*
*He was proved to be wrong.*

**using the passive**

**3.208** If you do not know who the subject of the second verb is, or you do not want to mention them, you can use a passive construction.

*A gardener was immediately sacked if he was caught smoking.*
*I was asked to come for a few days to help them.*
*Their children are left to play among the rubble.*

The following verbs are not usually used in the passive when followed by a present participle:

| | | | |
|---|---|---|---|
| feel | like | prevent | stop |
| imagine | listen to | save | want |

The following verbs are not usually used in the passive when followed by a 'to'-infinitive:

| | | |
|---|---|---|
| defy | like | want |
| get | prefer | |

**USAGE NOTE**  **3.209** 'Hear', 'observe', and 'see' are not used with a 'to'-infinitive when they are active but they can be used with either a present participle or a 'to'-infinitive when they are passive.

You use them with a present participle when you want to show that the action described by the second verb took place over a period of time.

*A terrorist was seen standing in the middle of the road.*
*Her companions could be heard playing games.*

If a 'to'-infinitive is used, you are implying that the action was completed.

*She could distinctly be seen to hesitate.*
*The baby was seldom heard to cry.*

See also paragraph 3.206.

**verbs followed by 'for' and a 'to'-infinitive**  **3.210** There is a group of verbs used in phase structures with a 'to'-infinitive which are followed by the preposition 'for' and its object, rather than by a direct object. The object of 'for' is the performer of the second action.

*He arranged for Waddell to have the services of another solicitor.*
*They called for action to be taken against the unions.*
*I waited for him to speak.*

Note that the 'to'-infinitive is often a passive one.

Here is a list of verbs which can be used in this way:

| | | | | |
|---|---|---|---|---|
| appeal | ask | long | plead | wait |
| apply | call | opt | press | wish |
| arrange | clamour | pay | vote | yearn |

**transitive verbs with an infinitive without 'to'**  **3.211** A few verbs are followed by an object and an infinitive without 'to', not a present participle or a 'to'-infinitive. They are 'let', 'make', and 'have' in the sense of 'cause to happen' or 'experience'.

*Jenny let him talk.*
*My father made me go for the interview.*
*...so that he could lie in a darkened room and have her bring him meals o trays.*

Verbs which can be used either with an infinitive without 'to' or with a present participle are explained in paragraph 3.206.

**causative use of 'have' and 'get'**  **3.212** A special use of 'have' in phase structures is to say that the subjec causes something to be dealt with by someone else. In this case, 'have' i followed by an object referring to the thing dealt with, and then by the pas participle of a transitive verb or of an intransitive verb followed by a preposition.

*I have my hair cut every six weeks.*

This structure is also used to say that something belonging to the subject of 'have' is affected in some way.

*She'd just lost her job and had some money stolen.*

If you want to mention the performer of the second action, you use 'by' followed by a noun group.

*He had to have his leg massaged by his trainer.*

'Get' can also be used with an object and a past participle to talk about causing something to be dealt with or affected in some way.

*We must get the car repaired.*
*You'll get yourself arrested if you carry on like that!*

**'want' and 'need' with past participle**

**3.213** 'Want' is also used with an object and a past participle, to indicate that you would like something to be done.

*I want the whole approach changed.*
*I don't want you hurt.*

'Need' is used in a similar way, usually when the object is something that belongs to the subject.

*You need your eyesight tested.*

# Contents of Chapter 4

# 4 Varying the message

**4.1** This chapter deals with three different ways in which the meaning of a sentence can be varied, by altering the order of words or by adding other words to the verb group.

Paragraphs 4.2 to 4.42 explain how **mood** is used to distinguish between the main types of sentence, for example how it is used to distinguish statements and questions.

Paragraphs 4.43 to 4.94 explain how **negative words** are used to indicate the opposite of something or the absence of something.

Paragraphs 4.95 to 4.262 explain how **modals** are used to talk about possibility, or to indicate the attitude of the speaker to the hearer or to what is being said.

## Statements, questions, orders, and suggestions

**4.2** Sentences can be used to do many different things.

The most common use is to give information.

*I went to Glasgow University.*
*Carol was one of my sister's best friends.*

Sometimes you use a sentence to obtain information, rather than to give it.

*Where is my father?*
*What did you say to Myra?*
*How long have you been out of this country?*

At other times you want to express an opinion, give an order, make a suggestion, or make a promise.

*That's an excellent idea.*
*Go away, all of you.*
*Shall we listen to the news?*
*If you have any questions, I'll do my best to answer them.*

When someone says or writes a sentence, they need to indicate what they are trying to do with it, so that it will be clear, for example, that they are asking a question and not making a statement.

**mood** **4.3** Often it is the order of words which indicates which way a sentence is being used. For example, if you say 'He is Norwegian', the word order makes it clear that you are making a statement. If you say 'Is he Norwegian?', the word order indicates that you are asking a question.

Another way of indicating which way a sentence is being used is to begin it with a verb, rather than with the subject. For example, if you say 'Give this

195

book to Michael', it is clear that you are giving an order or instruction, rather than making a statement or asking a question.

These ways of distinguishing between uses of language are examples of **mood.** The main clause of every sentence is in a particular **mood.**

**types of mood**

**4.4** There are three main moods in English. They are the **declarative mood,** the **interrogative mood,** and the **imperative mood.**

The **declarative mood** is the mood used in most main clauses. Statements are almost always made using the declarative mood. When a clause is in this mood, the subject is placed in front of the verb.

The declarative mood is sometimes called the **indicative mood.**

*I want to talk to Mr Castle.*
*Gertrude looked at Anne.*
*We'll give you fifteen pounds now.*

The **interrogative mood** is the mood usually used in questions. In clauses in this mood, the subject is often placed after the main verb or after an auxiliary verb.

*Is she very upset?*
*Where is my father?*
*Have you met Halliday?*
*Did you give him my letter?*

The **imperative mood** is the mood used to tell someone to do something. In clauses in the imperative mood, the subject is usually omitted and the **base form** of the verb is used.

*Come back this minute.*
*Show me the complete manuscript.*

There is a fourth mood called the **subjunctive mood.** This is a feature of English verbs which sometimes occurs in subordinate clauses. The subjunctive mood is not used to distinguish between different uses of language, and is therefore not dealt with in this chapter. Clauses in which the subjunctive mood occurs are explained in paragraphs 7.40, 8.41, and 8.48.

**4.5** The ways in which mood is used are explained in the following paragraphs.

Paragraphs 4.6 to 4.9 explain how the declarative mood is used to make statements. Paragraphs 4.10 to 4.30 explain how the interrogative mood is used to ask questions. Paragraphs 4.31 to 4.35 explain how the imperative mood is used to tell someone to do something. Other uses of the declarative, interrogative, and imperative moods are explained in paragraphs 4.36 to 4.42.

# Making statements: the declarative mood

**giving information**

**4.6** When you are giving information, you use the **declarative mood.**

*We ate dinner at six.*
*I like reading poetry.*
*Officials have refused to comment.*

**expressing opinions**

**4.7** When you are expressing an opinion, you usually use the declarative mood.

*I think she is a brilliant writer.*

*It's a good thing Father is deaf.*
*He ought to have let me know he was going out.*

**making**
**promises** **4.8** When you make a promise, you use the declarative mood.

*I shall do everything I can to help you.*
*I'll have it sent down by special delivery.*

**emphasis** **4.9** You can emphasize a statement by putting 'do', 'does', or 'did' in front of the **base form** of the verb.

*I do feel sorry for Roger.*
*A little knowledge does seem to be a dangerous thing.*
*He had no time or energy to play with his children or talk with his wife, but he did bring home a regular salary.*

## Asking questions: the interrogative mood

**4.10** When you ask a question, you usually use the **interrogative mood**.

**types of** **4.11** There are two main types of question.
**question**
Questions which can be answered by 'yes' or 'no' are called **'yes/no'-questions**.

*'Is he your only child?'—'Yes.'*
*'Are you planning to marry soon?'—'No.'*
*'Can I help you?'—'Yes, I'd like to book a single room, please.'*
*'Are you interested in racing?'—'Yes, I love it.'*
*'Are you a singer as well as an actress?'—'No, I'm not a singer at all.'*
*'Do you like it?' – 'Yes, I really like it.'*

The actual answer to a 'yes/no'-question is not always 'yes' or 'no'. For example, if you ask someone 'Do you read in bed?', they might say 'Sometimes' or 'Never'. If you say to someone 'Do you like Michael Jackson?', they might say 'I think he's wonderful'. But the questions 'Do you read in bed?' and 'Do you like Michael Jackson?' are still 'yes/no'-questions, because 'yes' and 'no' are the kind of answers the questioner expects. 'Sometimes' will be interpreted as a weak 'yes' answer, 'never' as a strong 'no' answer, and 'I think he's wonderful' as a strong 'yes' answer.

'Yes/no'-questions are fully explained in paragraphs 4.12 to 4.16.

The other main type of question begins with a **'wh'-word** such as 'what', 'where', or 'when'. When you ask a question of this type, the answer cannot be 'yes' or 'no'.

*'Who gave you my number?' – 'Your mother did.'*
*'Why didn't you ask me?'—'I was afraid to.'*
*'Where is he now?'—'He's at university.'*

This type of question is called a **'wh'-question**. When 'wh'-words are used as pronouns or adverbs at the beginning of a 'wh'-question, they are called **interrogative pronouns** or **interrogative adverbs**.

'Wh'-questions are explained in paragraphs 4.17 to 4.30.

## 'Yes/no'-questions

**position of** **4.12** In a 'yes/no'-question, if there is an auxiliary verb, the auxiliary verb
**auxiliary** comes first, followed by the subject, then the main verb.
**verbs**
*Are you staying here, by any chance?*

*Will they win again?*
*Will they like my garden?*
*Can he read yet?*

If there is more than one auxiliary verb, the first auxiliary verb comes at the beginning of the clause, followed by the subject, followed by the other verbs.

*Had he been murdered?*
*Has it been thrown away, perhaps?*

For information about auxiliaries, see the Reference Section.

**4.13** If there is no auxiliary verb, you put 'do', 'does', or 'did' at the beginning of the clause, in front of the subject, followed by the base form of the main verb.

*Do you understand what I'm saying?*
*Does it hurt much?*
*Did you meet George in France?*

Note that if the main verb is 'do', you still put 'do', 'does', or 'did' at the beginning of the clause, in front of the subject.

*Do they do the work themselves?*
*Does David do this sort of thing often?*

**'be' and 'have' as main verbs**

**4.14** If the verb is 'be', you do not use 'do'. You simply put the verb at the beginning of the clause, followed by the subject.

*Are you okay?*
*Is she Ricky's sister?*
*Am I right?*
*Was it lonely without us?*

If the verb is 'have', you usually put 'do', 'does', or 'did' at the beginning of the clause, in front of the subject.

*Do passengers have rights?*
*Does anyone have a question?*
*Did you have a good flight?*

However, when you use 'have' in the sense of 'own' or 'possess', you do not need to use 'do', 'does', or 'did'. You can simply put 'have', 'has', or 'had' at the beginning of the clause. This is a slightly formal use.

*Have we anything else we ought to talk about first?*
*Has he any idea what it's like?*

If you use 'have got' or 'has got' in a 'yes/no'-question, you put 'have' or 'has' at the beginning of the clause, followed by the subject, followed by 'got'.

*Have you got any brochures on Holland?*
*Has she got a car?*

'Have got' and 'has got' are explained in paragraph 3.17.

**tag questions**

**4.15** You can ask for confirmation that something is true by making a statement in the declarative mood, then adding an expression such as 'isn't it?' or 'was she?'. Constructions like these are called **tag questions.**

You add a negative expression such as 'isn't it?' to a positive statement, and a positive expression such as 'was she?' to a negative statement.

When you add a negative expression to a positive statement, you expect the answer 'yes'. When you add a positive expression to a negative statement, you expect the answer 'no'.

*'David's is quite a nice school, isn't it?'*—'Yes, *it is.'*
*'You don't always remember them, do you?'*—'No.'
*'You are going to do this, aren't you?'*—'Yes.'
*'We don't want these tables here like this, do we?'*—'No, *Dr Kirk.'*

Tag questions are explained in detail in paragraphs 10.110 to 10.114.

Positive expressions such as 'are you?' can also be added to positive statements. This use is explained in paragraph 4.40.

**'either/or'**
**questions**
**4.16** You sometimes ask a question in which you mention two or more possible answers. You link the possible answers with 'or'. For example, you might say 'Is he awake or asleep?' or 'Do you like your coffee white or black?'. You expect the actual answer to your question to be one of the answers you have mentioned.

Words, word groups, and clauses can all be linked in this way.

Questions like these are sometimes called **'either/or'-questions.**

*'Is it a boy or a girl?'*—'A beautiful *boy.'*
*'Was it healthy or diseased?'*—'Diseased, *I'm afraid.'*
*'Shall we take the bus or do you want to walk?'* – *'Let's walk, shall we?'*

# 'Wh'-questions

**4.17** When you ask someone a **'wh'-question,** you want them to specify a particular person, thing, place, reason, method, or amount. You do not expect them to answer 'yes' or 'no'.

**'wh'-words**
**4.18** 'Wh'-questions begin with a **'wh'-word.**

'Wh'-words are a set of pronouns, adverbs, and determiners which all, with the exception of 'how', begin with 'wh-'. Here is a list of the main 'wh'-words:

| | | |
|---|---|---|
| how | where | whom |
| what | which | whose |
| when | who | why |

**'wh'-word**
**as subject**
**4.19** When a 'wh'-word is the subject of a verb, or when it forms part of the subject, the word order of the clause is the same as that of a clause in the declarative mood, i.e. the subject is put first, followed by the verb.

*Who invited you?*
*And then what happened?*
*Which mattress is best?*

**'wh'-word**
**as object**
**or adverb**
**4.20** When a 'wh'-word is the object of a verb or preposition, or when it forms part of the object, or when it is an adverb, the position of the subject is the usual one in the interrogative mood; that is it comes after the first verb in the clause.

*What am I going to do without you?*
*Which graph are you going to use?*
*Why would Stephen lie to me?*
*When would you be coming down?*

If you are using the **simple present tense** or the **simple past tense** of any verb except 'be', you put 'do', 'does', or 'did' in front of the subject.

199

*What do you really think?*
*Which department do you want?*
*Where does she live?*
*How do you know what it's like?*
*When did you last see John Cartwright?*

If you are using the simple present tense or the simple past tense of 'be', the main verb goes in front of the subject. You do not use 'do', 'does', or 'did'.

*Where is the station?*
*How was your meeting?*
*When was the last time you cleaned the garage?*

**questions without a verb**

**4.21** In conversation, a 'wh'-question sometimes consists of a 'wh'-word on its own. For example, if you say to someone 'I'm learning to type', they might say 'Why?', meaning 'Why are you learning to type?'.

*'He saw a snake.'—'Where?'*
*'I have to go to Germany.'—'When?'*
*'I knew you were landing today.'—'How?'*

A 'wh'-question can also consist of a noun group containing a 'wh'-word. For example, if you say to someone 'I gave your book to that girl', they might say 'Which girl?', meaning 'Which girl did you give my book to?'.

*'He knew my cousin.'—'Which cousin?'*
*'Who was your friend?'—'What friend?'*

**'who' and 'whom'**

**4.22** The pronoun 'who' is used to ask questions about a person's identity. 'Who' can be the subject or object of a verb.

*Who discovered this?*
*Who were her friends?*
*Who is Michael Howard?*
*Who did he marry?*

In more formal English, 'whom' is sometimes used instead of 'who' as the object of a verb.

*Whom shall we call?*
*Whom did you see?*

'Who' and 'whom' can also be the object of a preposition. When 'who' is the object of a preposition, the preposition is put at the end of the clause

*Who did you dance with?*
*Who do I pay this to?*

When 'whom' is the object of a preposition, the preposition is put at the beginning of the clause, in front of 'whom'.

*For whom was he working while in Baghdad?*
*To whom is a broadcaster responsible?*

**'whose'**

**4.23** 'Whose' is used as a determiner or pronoun to ask which person something belongs to or is associated with.

*Whose babies did you think they were?*
*Whose body was it?*
*Whose is that?*

**'which'**

**4.24** 'Which' is used as a pronoun or determiner to ask someone to identify a specific person or thing out of a number of people or things.

*Which is the best restaurant?*
*Which is her room?*

*Which do you like best?*
*Which doctor do you want to see?*

When 'which' is a determiner, it can be part of the object of a preposition. The preposition is usually put at the end of the question.

*Which station did you come from?*
*Which character did you identify with?*

**'when' and 'where'**

**4.25** 'When' is used to ask questions about the time something happened, happens, or will happen.

*When did you find her?*
*When do we have supper?*
*Ginny, when are you coming home?*

'Where' is used to ask questions about place, position, or direction.

*Where does she live?*
*Where are you going?*
*Where do you go to complain?*

**'why'**

**4.26** 'Why' is used to ask a question about the reason for something.

*Why are you here?*
*Why does Amy want to go and see his grave?*
*Why does she treat me like that when we're such old friends?*

'Why' is sometimes used without a subject and with the base form of a verb, usually to ask why an action is or was necessary.

*Why wake me up?*
*Why bother about me?*
*Why make a point of it?*

'Why not' can be used with the base form of a verb, in order to make a suggestion or to ask why a particular action has not been taken.

*Why not end it now?*
*Why not read a book?*
*If you have money in the bank, why not use it?*

**'how'**

**4.27** 'How' is usually used to ask about the method used for doing something, or about the way in which something can be achieved.

*How do we open it?*
*How are you going to get that?*
*How could he explain it to her?*
*How did he know when you were coming?*

'How' is also used to ask questions about the way a person feels, about the way someone or something looks, or about the way something sounds, feels, or tastes.

*How are you feeling today?*
*'How do I look?'—'Very nice.'*
*How did you feel when you stood up in front of the class?*

**'how' with other words**

**4.28** 'How' can be combined with other words at the beginning of questions.

'How many' and 'how much' are used to ask what number of things there are or what amount of something there is.

'How many' is followed by a plural count noun.

*How many people are there?*
*How many languages can you speak?*
*How many times have you been?*

'How much' is followed by an uncount noun.

*How much money have we got in the bank?*
*Just how much time have you been devoting to this?*

'How many' and 'how much' can be used without a following noun when you do not need to make it clear what sort of thing you are talking about.

*How many did you find?*
*How much did he tell you?*
*How much does it cost?*
*How much do they really understand?*

'How long' is used to ask about the length of a period of time.

*How long have you lived here?*
*How long will it take?*
*How long can she live like this?*
*How long ago was that?*

'How long' is also used to ask questions about distance, although this use is less common.

*How long is this road?*

'How far' is used in questions about distance and extent.

*How far can we see?*
*How far is it to Montreal from here?*
*How far have you got with your homework?*

You can combine 'how' with an adjective when you are asking to what extent something has a particular quality or feature.

*How big's your overdraft at the moment?*
*How old are your children?*

**'what'**    **4.29**  'What' can be a pronoun or determiner, or it can be used in combination with 'if' or 'for'.

'What' is used as a pronoun to find out various kinds of specific information, for example details of an event, the meaning of a word or expression, or the reason for something.

*What's wrong with his mother?*
*What has happened to him?*
*What is obesity?*
*What keeps you hanging around here?*

'What' can be used to ask someone's opinion of something.

*What do you think about the present political situation?*

'What' is often used as the object of a preposition. The preposition usually goes at the end of the question.

*What are you interested in?*
*What did he die of?*
*What do you want to talk about?*

'What' is used as a determiner to find out the identity of something or to ask what kind of thing it is.

*What books does she read?*

*What church did you say you attend?*

'What if' goes in front of a clause in the declarative mood. It is used to ask what should be done if a particular difficulty occurs.

*What if it's really bad weather?*
*What if they didn't want to part with it, what would you do then?*

You put 'what' at the beginning of a question and 'for' at the end of it when you want to know the reason for something or the purpose of something. 'What are you staring for?' means the same as 'Why are you staring?'. 'What is this handle for?' means 'What is the purpose of this handle?'.

*What are you going for?*
*What are those lights for?*

'What' can also be used in combination with 'about' or 'of'. This use is explained in paragraph 4.41.

**'whatever',**
**'wherever',**
**and**
**'whoever'**

**4.30** If you want a question to sound more emphatic, you can use 'whatever' instead of 'what', 'wherever' instead of 'where', or 'whoever' instead of 'who'.

*Whatever is the matter?*
*Wherever did you get this?*
*Whoever heard of a bishop resigning?*

# Telling someone to do something: the imperative mood

**orders and**
**instructions**

**4.31** When someone gives a very clear order or instruction, they usually use the **imperative mood**.

*Discard any clothes you have not worn for more than a year.*
*Put that gun down.*
*Tell your mother as soon as possible.*

Written instructions are given in the imperative mood.

*Boil up a little water with washing up liquid in it.*
*Fry the chopped onion and pepper in the oil.*

An order can be made more forceful by putting 'you' in front of the verb.

*You get in the car.*
*You shut up!*

**advice and**
**warnings**

**4.32** You can use the imperative mood when you are giving advice or a warning.

*Be sensible.*
*You be careful.*

Often advice or a warning is expressed in a negative form. You form a negative imperative by putting 'don't' or 'do not' in front of the base form of the verb.

*Don't be afraid of them.*
*Don't be discouraged.*
*Do not approach this man under any circumstances.*

You can also form a negative imperative by putting 'never' in front of the base form of a verb.

*Never open the front door without looking through the peephole.*

Another way of giving advice or a warning is to use one of the modals 'should' or 'ought to' in a declarative sentence.

*You should get to know him better.*
*You shouldn't keep eggs in the refrigerator.*

This use is explained in detail in paragraph 4.219.

**appeals**   **4.33** You use the imperative mood when you are appealing to someone to do something.

*Come quickly... Come quickly... Hurry!*

You can make an appeal more forceful by putting 'do' in front of the verb.

*Oh do stop whining!*
*Do come and stay with us in Barbados for the winter.*

**explanations**   **4.34** You can use the imperative mood with some verbs when you are explaining something and you want the listener or reader to think about a particular thing or possibility, or to compare two things.

*Take, for instance, the new proposals for student loans.*
*Imagine, for example, an assembly line worker in a factory making children's blocks.*
*But suppose for a moment that the automobile industry had developed at the same rate as computers.*
*For example, compare a typical poor country like Indonesia with a rich one like Canada.*
*Consider, for example, the contrast between the way schools today treat space and time.*

Here is a list of verbs which are used in this way:

| compare | contrast | look at | suppose |
|---------|----------|---------|---------|
| consider | imagine | picture | take |

**'let'**   **4.35** 'Let' is used in imperative sentences in four different ways:

● it is used to give an order or instruction

*Let Phillip have a look at it.*

● you use it followed by 'us' when you are making a suggestion about what you and someone else should do. 'Let us' is almost always shortened to 'Let's'

*Let's go outside.*
*Let's creep forward on hands and knees.*

● you use it followed by 'me' when you are offering to do something

*Let me take your coat.*

● in very formal English, it is used to express a wish.

*Let the joy be universal.*
*Let confusion live!*
*Let the best man or woman win.*

## Other uses of moods

**confirming**   **4.36** You can confirm that something is true by asking a question using the **declarative mood.**

*So you admit something is wrong?*
*Then you think we can keep it?*

When you ask a question using the declarative mood, you expect the answer 'yes', unless you use a negative construction, in which case you expect the answer 'no'.

*'You mean it's still here?'—'Of course.'*
*'Your parents don't mind you being out so late?' – 'No, they don't'.*

Questions expressed in the declarative mood often begin with a conjunction.

*So you're satisfied?*
*And you think that's a good idea?*

**instructing**  **4.37** You can give an instruction in a fairly informal way by using a declarative sentence with 'you' as the subject.

*You put the month and the temperature on the top line.*
*You take the bus up to the landing stage at twelve-thirty.*
*You just bung it in the oven.*

**offers and**  **4.38** When you are making an offer or an invitation, you usually use a
**invitations**  **'yes/no'-question** beginning with a modal such as 'can' or 'would'. This use is explained in detail in paragraphs 4.177 to 4.182.

*Can I help you?*
*Can I give you a lift?*
*Would you like me to get something for you?*
*Would you like some coffee?*
*Would you like to go to Ernie's for dinner?*

You can make an offer or invitation in a more informal way by using the **imperative mood.** Note that you can only do this when it is clear that you are not giving an order.

*Have a cigar.*
*Come to my place.*
*Come in, Mrs Kintner.*

You can add emphasis by putting 'do' in front of the verb.

*Do have a chocolate biscuit.*
*Do help yourselves.*

**requests,**  **4.39** When you are making a request, you usually use a 'yes/no'-question
**orders, and**  beginning with one of the modals 'could', 'can', or 'would'.
**instructions**  *Could I ask you a few questions?*
*Can I have my hat back, please?*
*Would you mind having a word with my husband?*

You can also give an order or instruction using a 'yes/no'-question beginning with a modal.

*Will you tell Watson I shall be in a little late?*

These uses are explained in detail in paragraphs 4.160 to 4.170.

**rhetorical**  **4.40** When you use a 'yes/no'-question to offer help or to make a request,
**questions**  you still expect the answer 'yes' or 'no'. However, people sometimes say things which seem like 'yes/no'-questions, although they do not expect an answer at all. They are using the 'yes/no'-question form to express a strong feeling, opinion, or impression.

For example, instead of saying 'That's an ugly building', someone might say 'Isn't that an ugly building?'. Or instead of saying 'You never seem to get upset', someone might say 'Don't you ever get upset?'.

Questions like these are called **rhetorical questions.**

*Is there nothing she won't do?*
*Can't you see that I'm busy?*
*Hasn't anyone round here got any sense?*
*Does nothing ever worry you?*

Another kind of rhetorical question consists of a statement followed by an expression such as 'are you?' or 'is it?'. For example, someone might say 'So you are the new assistant, are you?' or 'So they're coming to tea, are they?'.

*So you want to be an actress, do you?*
*So they're moving house again, are they?*

Rhetorical questions can also begin with 'how'. They usually express a feeling of shock or indignation. For example, instead of saying 'You are very cruel', someone might say 'How can you be so cruel?'.

*How can you say such things?*
*How dare you speak to me like that?*

**Rhetorical questions** are dealt with fully in paragraph 10.109

**questions without a verb**

**4.41** You can ask a question consisting of 'what about' or 'what of' in front of a noun group, without a verb. You ask a question like this to remind someone of something, or to draw their attention to something. With this kind of question, you often expect an action, rather than a reply.

*What about the others on the list?*
*What about your breakfast?*
*But what of the growing disadvantages of having too many children?*

**suggestions**

**4.42** There are several ways in which you can make a suggestion:

● you can use the modal 'could' in a declarative sentence (see paragraph 4.187)

*We could have tea.*
*You could get someone to dress up as a pirate.*

● you can use a negative 'wh'-question beginning with 'why'

*Why don't we just give them what they want?*
*Why don't you write to her yourself?*

● you can use a question consisting of 'what about' or 'how about' in front of a non-finite clause

*What about becoming an actor?*
*How about using makeup to dramatize your features?*

● you can use the imperative mood.

*'Give them a reward each,' I suggested.*

You can also make a suggestion about what you and someone else might do by using 'let's'. This use is explained in paragraph 4.35.

# Negation

## Forming negative statements

**4.43** When you want to say that something is not true, is not happening, or is not the case, you normally use a **negative statement.** Negative statements contain words like 'not', 'never', or 'nowhere'. These are called **negative words**.

Here is the list of negative words in English:

| | | | |
|---|---|---|---|
| neither | nobody | nor | nowhere |
| never | none | not | |
| no | no one | nothing | |

Negative words indicate the opposite of something or an absence of something.

**4.44** There are some other words such as 'unhappy' or 'meaningless' which give a negative meaning to a statement because they contain a negative affix such as 'un-' or '-less'. These words are explained in paragraphs 4.76 to 4.82.

Another group of words such as 'scarcely' and 'seldom' can be used to make a statement almost negative. These words are called **broad negatives**. They are explained in paragraphs 4.83 to 4.90.

**4.45** If a statement about the existence of something has a negative word in it, you use 'any' (not 'no') as a determiner in front of the following noun group. You can also use a word beginning with 'any-' such as 'anyone' or 'anywhere'.

*We hadn't any money.*
*He writes poetry and never shows it to anyone.*
*It is impossible to park the car anywhere.*

For another use of 'any' see paragraph 2.168.

**WARNING** **4.46** It is almost always unacceptable to use two negative words in the same clause. For example, you do not say, 'I don't never go there', or 'I don't know nothing'.

**4.47** The use of negatives in **report structures** is explained in paragraph 7.13. The use of negatives with **modals** is explained in paragraph 4.105.

**'not'** **4.48** The most commonly used negative word is 'not'. Its use with different verbs corresponds to the way these verbs are used in **'yes/no'-questions** (see paragraphs 4.12 to 4.14).

**position in verb groups** **4.49** When 'not' is used with a verb group which contains an auxiliary verb, it comes after the first verb in the group.

*They could not exist in their present form.*
*They might not even notice.*
*The White House has not commented on the report.*
*He had not attended many meetings.*
*I was not smiling.*
*Her teachers were not impressed with her excuses.*

**adding 'do'** **4.50** If there is no auxiliary verb, you put 'do', 'does', or 'did' after the subject, followed by 'not' or '-n't', followed by the base form of the main verb.

*They do not need to talk.*
*He does not speak English very well.*
*I didn't know that.*

'Be' and 'have' are exceptions to this; this is explained in the following paragraphs 4.51 and 4.52. The shortening of 'not' to '-n't' is explained in paragraphs 4.55 and 4.56.

**'not' with 'be'**    **4.51** If the verb is 'be', you do not use 'do'. You simply put 'not' or '-n't' after the verb.

*It is not difficult to see why they were unsuccessful.*
*There is not much point in heading south.*
*This isn't my first choice of restaurant.*

**'not' with 'have' and 'have got'.**    **4.52** If the verb is 'have', you usually put 'do', 'does', or 'did' after the subject, followed by 'not' or '-n't', followed by the base form 'have'.

*The organization does not have a good track record.*
*He didn't have a very grand salary.*

You can simply put 'not' or '-n't' after the verb, but this use is less common.

*He hadn't enough money.*
*I haven't any papers to say that I have been trained.*

If you use 'have got', you put 'not' or '-n't' after 'have', followed by 'got'.

*I haven't got the latest figures.*
*He hasn't got a daughter.*

'Have got' is explained in paragraph 3.17.

**position with non-finite verbs**    **4.53** When 'not' is used with an '-ing' form or a 'to'-infinitive clause, it is placed in front of the '-ing' form or 'to'-infinitive.

*We stood there, not knowing what was expected of us.*
*He lost out by not taking a degree at another university.*
*Try not to worry.*
*It took a vast amount of patience not to strangle him.*

**with finite and non-finite verbs**    **4.54** When a clause contains a finite verb group and a non-finite verb group, you put 'not' either with the finite or non-finite group, depending on the meaning you want to express.

For example, you can say either 'Mary tried not to smile' or 'Mary did not try to smile', but they express different meanings. The first means that Mary tried to avoid smiling. The second means that Mary did not even try to smile.

However, with some verbs which are used with 'to'-infinitive clauses, the meaning is the same whether 'not' is placed with the main verb or with the 'to'-infinitive.

*She did not appear to have done anything.*
*Henry appears not to appreciate my explanation.*
*It didn't seem to bother them at all.*
*They seemed not to notice me.*

Here is a list of verbs which are used with 'to'-infinitives. With all of these, the meaning of the clause is the same, whether 'not' is put in front of the verb or in front of the 'to'-infinitive:

| | | |
|---|---|---|
| appear | intend | tend |
| expect | plan | want |
| happen | seem | wish |

The use of two verbs in a clause to talk about two actions or states is called **phase**. **Phase** is dealt with in paragraphs 3.183 to 3.213.

Note that with some **reporting verbs** the meaning is the same whether you put 'not' in front of the reporting verb or in front of the main verb. This is explained in paragraph 7.13.

**contractions of 'not'**

**4.55** In spoken English and in informal written English, 'not' is often shortened to '-n't' after 'be' or 'have' or after an auxiliary. '-n't' is attached to the end of the verb.

*Marigold isn't really my aunt at all.*
*He doesn't believe in anything.*
*I haven't heard from her recently.*

Note that 'cannot' is shortened to 'can't', 'shall not' is shortened to 'shan't', and 'will not' is shortened to 'won't'.

Here is a complete list of the shortened forms you can use:

| | | | | |
|---|---|---|---|---|
| aren't | didn't | hasn't | mightn't | shouldn't |
| isn't | doesn't | haven't | mustn't | won't |
| wasn't | don't | can't | oughtn't | wouldn't |
| weren't | hadn't | couldn't | shan't | |

**USAGE NOTE**

**4.56** Note that if the verb is already shortened and added to its subject, you cannot shorten 'not' to '-n't'. This means, for example, that you can shorten 'she is not' to 'she isn't' or 'she's not', but not to 'she'sn't'.

*It isn't easy.*
*It's not easy.*
*I haven't had time.*
*I've not had time.*

Note that you cannot add '-n't' to 'am'. You can only use 'I'm not' as the shortened form.

*I'm not excited.*

The form 'aren't I' is used in questions. For more information, see paragraph 10.125.

In questions, 'not' is usually shortened to '-n't' and added to the first verb in the verb group.

*Didn't she win at the Olympics?*
*Hasn't he put on weight?*
*Aren't you bored?*

However, in formal English, it is also possible to put 'not' after the subject.

*Did he not have brothers?*
*Was it not rather absurd?*

**other uses of 'not'**

**4.57** You can also use 'not' with almost any word or word group in a clause. For example, you can use it with noun groups, adjectives, adverbs, prepositional phrases, and quantifiers. You usually do this in order to be more forceful, careful, polite, hesitant, and so on. The following paragraphs 4.58 and 4.59 describe some of these uses.

**4.58** 'Very' is often used after 'not' to soften the negative meaning of a clause. You can put 'very' in front of an adjective complement, in front of a complement that contains an adjective, or in front of an adverb. This sounds more polite or hesitant than using 'not' without 'very'.

*His attitude is not very logical.*

*It's not very strong tea, it won't stain.*
*He wasn't a very good actor.*
*She shook her head, but not very convincingly.*

You can use 'not' with 'absolutely', 'altogether', 'entirely', or 'necessarily' in a similar way. You do this in order to sound more polite or less critical.

*Previous experience isn't absolutely necessary, but it helps.*
*I was not altogether sure.*
*They are not entirely reliable.*
*Science is not necessarily hostile to human values.*

You can use 'not' in front of a complement which has a negative meaning to indicate that the thing you are describing has in fact some good qualities, although you do not want to make them sound better than they really are. This structure is often used with words which have a negative affix such as 'un-' or '-less'.

*She's not an unattractive woman.*
*It's not a bad start.*
*It's a small point, but not an unimportant one.*
*America is very well developed, but not limitless.*

Words with negative affixes are discussed in paragraphs 4.76 to 4.82.

**'not' used for contrast** 4.59 'Not' can be used to contrast one part of a clause with another. Using 'not' in this way emphasizes the positive part of a statement.

*He held her arm in his hand, not hard, but firmly.*
*We move steadily, not fast, not slow.*
*'Were they still interested?'—'Not just interested. Overjoyed.'*
*I will move eventually, but not from Suffolk.*
*It's not a huge hotel, but it's very nice.*

**'never'** 4.60 'Never' is used to say that something was not or will not ever be the case.

When it is used with a verb group which contains an auxiliary verb, 'never' is put after the first verb in the verb group and in front of the main verb.

*I would never trust my judgement again.*
*...a type of glass which is rare and is never used.*
*The number of people who died will never be known.*
*Thirty years ago, the man was never expected to wash the dishes or help with the children.*
*I had never been to this big town before.*
*I've never done so much work in all my life.*

However, you can put 'never' in front of the first word in the verb group in order to emphasize the negative aspect of a statement.

*I never would have guessed if he hadn't told me.*
*There was no such person—there never had been.*

**with simple forms of 'be'** 4.61 If the main verb is the simple present or simple past of 'be', 'never' usually comes after the verb.

*She was never too proud to learn.*
*I'm never very keen on keeping a car for more than a year.*
*There were never any people in the house.*

However, you can put 'never' in front of a simple form of 'be' for emphasis.

*There never was enough hot water at home.*
*It never was very clear.*
*There never is any great change.*

**with simple forms of other verbs**
**4.62** If the main verb is the simple present or simple past of any verb except 'be', 'never' comes in front of the verb.

*I never want to see you in my classes again.*
*She never goes abroad.*
*He never went to university.*
*He never did any homework.*

**emphasis**
**4.63** You can make a negative statement more emphatic by using 'never' followed by 'do', 'does', or 'did' in front of the base form of the verb. For example, instead of saying 'I never met him', you can say 'I never did meet him'.

*I never do see her now.*
*They never did get their money back.*
*She never did find her real mother.*
*Some people never do adjust adequately.*

**'never' in imperatives**
**4.64** 'Never' can be used at the beginning of imperative structures.

*Never change a wheel near a drain.*
*Never dry clothes in front of an open fire.*

Imperative structures are explained in paragraph 4.4 and in paragraphs 4.31 to 4.35.

**'no'**
**4.65** 'No' is a general determiner which is used in front of singular and plural noun groups to say that something does not exist or is not available.

*There was no money for an operation.*
*We had no union, nobody to look after us.*
*He has no ambition.*
*I could see no tracks.*

General determiners are explained in paragraphs 1.208 to 1.235.

**4.66** In spoken English, '-n't' is often used with 'any' instead of 'no'. For example, instead of saying 'I had no money', you can say 'I hadn't any money'.

*They hadn't meant any harm to her.*
*I can't see any hope in it.*

**'none'**
**4.67** The pronoun 'none' is used to say that there is not a single thing or person, or not even a small amount of a particular thing.

*I waited for comments but none came.*
*The entire area is covered with shallow lakes, none more than a few yards in depth.*
*We have been seeing difficulties where none exist.*

For another use of 'none' see paragraph 1.154.

**'none of'**
**4.68** 'None of' is a quantifier.

*None of the townspeople had ever seen such weather.*
*None of this has happened without our consent.*

For an explanation of 'none of' see paragraphs 2.195 to 2.197 and paragraph 2.202.

**words beginning with 'no'**
**4.69** There are four words beginning with 'no-' which are used in negative statements. 'Nothing', 'no one', and 'nobody' are **indefinite pronouns**. 'Nowhere' is an **indefinite place adverb**.

*There's nothing you can do.*
*Nobody in her house knows any English.*
*There's almost nowhere left to go.*

**Indefinite pronouns** are explained in paragraphs 1.127 to 1.140.
**Indefinite place adverbs** are explained in paragraphs 6.90 and 6.100.

**followed by 'but'**   **4.70** 'Nothing', 'no one', 'nobody', and 'nowhere' can be followed by 'but' to mean 'only'. For example, 'There was nothing but cheese' means that there was only cheese.

*I look back on this period with nothing but pleasure.*
*He heard no one but his uncles.*

Indefinite pronouns and adverbs which begin with 'any' can be used in similar structures. However, in these structures 'but' means 'except', rather than 'only'.

*I could never speak about anything but business to Ivan.*
*It's been years since he has taken her to visit anyone but the children.*

**'neither' and 'nor'**   **4.71** 'Neither' and 'nor' are used together to say that two alternatives are not possible, likely, or true. 'Neither' goes in front of the first alternative and 'nor' goes in front of the second one.

*Neither Margaret nor John was there.*
*They had neither food nor money until the end of the week.*

**'neither' in replies**   **4.72** 'Neither' can be used on its own as a reply, to refer to two alternatives which have already been mentioned.

*'Does that mean Yes or No?'—'Neither'.*

**4.73** If a clause contains a negative word, particularly 'not', you can use 'neither' or 'nor' to negate a second clause. In the second clause, you put 'neither' or 'nor' first, followed by the verb, followed by the subject.

*This isn't a dazzling achievement, but neither is it a negligible one.*
*These people are not insane, nor are they fools.*

If there is an auxiliary, it is placed in front of the subject in the second clause.

*The organization had broken no rules, but neither had it acted responsibly.*
*I don't feel any shame. Neither do I think I should.*

**'neither' with singular nouns**   **4.74** 'Neither' can be used on its own in front of a singular noun referring to each of two things when you are making a negative statement about both of them. For example, 'Neither partner benefited from the agreement' means that there were two partners and the negative statement applies to both of them.

*Neither report mentioned the Americans.*
*Neither film was particularly good.*
*Neither sex has a monopoly on thought or emotion.*
*Neither parent is the good one or the bad one.*

Note that in this structure 'neither' is used with a singular verb.

**'neither of'**   **4.75** When 'neither' is followed by 'of', it is used as a quantifier to negate a set of two things. 'Neither of' is followed by a plural noun group.

*Neither of us was having any luck.*
*Neither of the boys screamed.*

*Neither of them was making any sound.*

'Neither of' is normally used with a singular verb.

*Neither of these extremes is desirable.*
*Neither of these opinions proves anything.*

However, it is also possible to use a plural verb.

*Neither of the children were there.*

**Quantifiers** are explained in paragraphs 2.193 to 2.210.

# Forming negative statements: negative affixes

**4.76** A prefix such as 'un-' or 'dis-' can be added to the beginning of some words to give them the opposite meaning. Words with prefixes can be looked up in any good dictionary. The suffix '-less' is added to the end of words to give them a negative meaning.

*She asked us to her house which was very small and untidy.*
*At last Janet sat down, as she was breathless.*

Here is a list of common negative prefixes:

| | | | | |
|---|---|---|---|---|
| a- | de- | il- | ir- | non- |
| anti- | dis- | im- | mal- | un- |
| counter- | ex- | in- | mis- | |

**'un-'**    **4.77** The most common of these prefixes is 'un-'. It can be added to many adjectives, adverbs, and verbs.

*They were unhappy with the way things were going.*
*He was treated rather unsympathetically.*
*She unpacked straightaway.*

'Un-' can also be added to some nouns.

*She wanted to save her sister from unhappiness.*

**'in-', 'il-', 'ir-'**    **4.78** Another common prefix is 'in-'. It is added to some adjectives, adverbs, and nouns instead of 'un-'.

*The footpath was invisible.*
*Some radiation continues almost indefinitely.*
*There's enormous inefficiency in the system.*

'Il-' is added to some adjectives, adverbs, and nouns beginning with 'l'. 'Im-' is added to others which begin with 'b', 'm', or 'p', and 'ir-' is added to some which begin with 'r'.

*He has reached an illogical conclusion.*
*The windows will be almost impossible to open.*
*How could you be so irresponsible!*

**'dis-'**    **4.79** 'Dis-' is added to some verbs, adjectives, nouns, and adverbs.

*I disliked change of any kind.*
*I was becoming discontented.*
*He gave a look of disapproval.*
*She just gets disagreeably rebellious.*

**'non-'**  **4.80** 'Non-' is added to some adjectives and nouns.

*...a peaceful, non-violent protest.*
*Traffic signals were inadequate or non-existent.*
*The match was a non-event.*
*The oil companies stubbornly pursued a course of non-cooperation.*

**'-less'**  **4.81** The suffix '-less' can be added to many nouns in order to form negative adjectives.

*They were completely helpless.*
*Many people were in tears and almost speechless.*
*That was very thoughtless of you.*
*...a cold, heartless smile.*

Here is a list of common words which have the suffix '-less':

| | | | | |
|---|---|---|---|---|
| breathless | harmless | lifeless | nameless | senseless |
| careless | heartless | limitless | needless | shapeless |
| childless | helpless | meaningless | pointless | speechless |
| countless | homeless | merciless | powerless | thoughtless |
| doubtless | hopeless | mindless | relentless | useless |
| endless | landless | motionless | restless | worthless |

**PRODUCTIVE FEATURE**  **4.82** You can add '-less' to many other nouns when it is clear from the context that you are talking about a lack of something. This is an example of a productive feature.

Productive features are explained in the Introduction.

## Forming negative statements: broad negatives

**4.83** Another way in which you can make a statement negative is by using a **broad negative**. **Broad negatives** are adverbs like 'rarely' and 'seldom' which are used to make a statement almost totally negative.

*The estimated sales will hardly cover the cost of making the film.*
*We were scarcely able to move.*
*Kuwait lies barely 30 miles from the Iranian coast.*

Here is a list of the most common broad negatives:

| | | | | |
|---|---|---|---|---|
| barely | hardly | rarely | scarcely | seldom |

**position in clause**  **4.84** The position of a broad negative within a clause is similar to that of 'never' (see paragraphs 4.60 to 4.62).

**4.85** When you use a broad negative with a verb group which contains an auxiliary verb, you put it after the first word in the verb group and in front of the main verb.

*I could scarcely believe my eyes.*
*Religion was rarely discussed in our house.*
*His eyes had hardly closed.*

**with simple form of 'be'**  **4.86** If the verb is the simple present or simple past of 'be', the broad negative usually comes after the verb.

*Change is seldom easy.*

*The new pressure group is barely six months old.*
*The office was hardly ever empty.*
*The lagoons are rarely deep.*
*The results were scarcely encouraging.*

**with other**
**verbs**

**4.87** If the verb is the simple present or simple past of any verb except 'be', the broad negative usually comes in front of the verb.

*He seldom bathed.*
*Marsha rarely felt hungry.*
*John hardly ever spoke to the Press.*

It is also possible to put a broad negative after the verb, but this is less common.

*Such moments happen rarely in life.*
*They met so seldom.*

**as first word**
**in the clause**

**4.88** In formal or literary English, a broad negative is sometimes placed at the beginning of a clause for emphasis. If you are using a verb group with an auxiliary, the first word in the verb group is placed after the broad negative, followed by the subject and then the remainder of the verb group.

*Seldom has society offered so wide a range of leisure time activities.*
*Hardly had he settled into his seat when Adam charged in.*

If there is no auxiliary, you put the simple present or simple past of 'do' after the broad negative, followed by the subject, followed by the base form of the main verb.

*Seldom did a week pass without a request for assessment.*
*Rarely do local matches live up to expectations.*

Note that 'barely' and 'scarcely' are not often used in this way.

**USAGE NOTE**

**4.89** If you make a **tag question** out of a statement that contains a broad negative, the tag on the end of the statement is normally positive, as it is with other negatives. Tag questions are explained in paragraphs **10.122** to **10.130**.

*She's hardly the right person for the job, is she?*
*You seldom see that sort of thing these days, do you?*

You can modify 'rarely' and 'seldom' by putting 'so', 'very', 'too', or 'pretty' in front of them. You can also modify 'rarely' by using 'only'.

*It happens so rarely.*
*Women were very seldom convicted.*
*He too seldom makes the first greeting.*
*Most people go to church only rarely.*

If you want to say there is very little of something, you can use a broad negative with 'any' or with a word which begins with 'any-'.

*The bonds show barely any interest.*
*Hardly anybody came.*
*In fact, it is seldom any of these.*
*With scarcely any warning, the soldiers charged.*
*Sometimes two or three relatives are admitted, but rarely any friends.*

**'almost'**

**4.90** Instead of using a broad negative, you can use 'almost' followed by a negative word such as 'no' or 'never'. For example, 'There was almost no food left' means the same as 'There was hardly any food left'.

*They've almost no money for anything.*

*The cars thinned out to <u>almost none</u>.*
*They were very private people, with <u>almost no</u> friends.*
*Men <u>almost never</u> began conversations.*

# Emphasizing the negative aspect of a statement

**'at all'**  **4.91** You can add 'at all' to a negative statement in order to make it more emphatic. You use 'at all' with any negative word, with 'without', or with a broad negative.

*She had <u>no</u> writing ability <u>at all</u>.*
*'There's <u>no</u> need' said Jimmie.—'None <u>at all</u>'.*
*He did it <u>without</u> any help <u>at all</u>.*
*He <u>hardly</u> read anything <u>at all</u>.*

**Broad negatives** are explained in paragraphs 4.83 to 4.90.

**'whatsoever'**  **4.92** You can put 'whatsoever' after 'none' and 'nothing' in order to emphasize the negative aspect of a statement.

*'You don't think he has any chance of winning?'—'None <u>whatsoever</u>.'*
*There is absolutely no enjoyment in that, <u>none whatsoever</u>.*
*You'll find yourself thinking about <u>nothing whatsoever</u>.*

If 'no' is used as a determiner in a noun group, you can put 'whatsoever' after the noun group.

*There is <u>no</u> need <u>whatsoever</u> to teach children how to behave.*
*There was <u>no</u> debate <u>whatsoever</u>, not even in Parliament.*

You can also use 'whatsoever' in negative statements which contain 'any' or a word which begins with 'any-'.

*You are not entitled to <u>any</u> aid <u>whatsoever</u>.*
*He was devoid of <u>any</u> talent <u>whatsoever</u>.*
*I knew I wasn't learning <u>anything whatsoever</u>.*

**'ever'**  **4.93** You can put 'ever' after negative words in order to emphasize the negative aspect of a statement.

*I can't say I <u>ever</u> had much interest in fishing.*
*Nobody <u>ever</u> leaves the airport.*
*I never <u>ever</u> believed we would have such success.*

**other**  **4.94** There are several expressions which can be used to emphasize a
**expressions**  negative statement which contains 'not'. These include 'in the least', 'the least bit', 'in the slightest', and 'a bit'.

*I don't mind <u>in the least</u>, I really don't.*
*Neither of the managers was <u>the least bit</u> repentant afterwards.*
*I don't really envy you <u>in the slightest</u>.*
*They're not <u>a bit</u> interested.*

If 'in the least' and 'in the slightest' are used with verbs, they are placed either immediately after the verb or after the object, if there is one.

*I wouldn't have objected <u>in the least</u>.*
*She did not worry Billy <u>in the least</u>.*
*The weather hadn't improved <u>in the slightest</u>.*

If 'in the least' is used with an adjective, it is put in front of it. 'In the slightest' usually comes after an adjective.

*I wasn't in the least surprised.*
*She wasn't worried in the slightest.*

'The least bit' and 'a bit' are only used with adjectives and are placed in front of the adjective.

*I'm not the least bit worried.*
*They're not a bit interested.*

# Using modals

**4.95** Language is not always used just to exchange information by making simple statements and asking questions. Sometimes we want to make requests, offers, or suggestions, or to express our wishes or intentions. We may want to be polite or tactful, or to indicate our feelings about what we are saying.

We can do all these things by using a set of verbs called **modals**. Modals are always used with other verbs. They are a special kind of **auxiliary verb**.

Here is a list of the modals used in English:

| | | | |
|---|---|---|---|
| can | might | shall | would |
| could | must | should | |
| may | ought to | will | |

In some grammars, 'dare', 'need', and 'used to' are also referred to as modals. In this grammar, we call these words **semi-modals**. They are dealt with separately in paragraphs 4.252 to 4.262.

'Ought' is sometimes regarded as a modal, rather than 'ought to'. For a further note about this, see paragraph 4.102.

Modals are sometimes called **modal verbs** or **modal auxiliaries**.

**4.96** The main uses of modals are explained in paragraphs 4.97 to 4.101. Special features of modals are described in paragraphs 4.102 to 4.109.

Ways of referring to time when using modals are explained in paragraphs 4.110 to 4.117. Ways of using modals to say whether something is possible are explained in paragraphs 4.118 to 4.157. Ways of using modals when interacting with other people are explained in paragraphs 4.158 to 4.226.

Expressions which can be used instead of modals are described in paragraphs 4.227 to 4.251. **Semi-modals** are explained in paragraphs 4.252 to 4.262.

## The main uses of modals

**4.97** Modals are mainly used when you want to indicate your attitude towards what you are saying, or when you are concerned about the effect of what you are saying on the person you are speaking or writing to.

**attitude to information** 4.98 When you are giving information, you sometimes use modals to indicate how certain you are that what you are saying is true or correct.

For example, if you say 'Mr Wilkins is the oldest person in the village', you are giving a definite statement of fact. If you say 'Mr Wilkins must be the oldest person in the village', the modal 'must' indicates that you think Mr Wilkins is the oldest person, because you cannot think of anyone in the village who is older than Mr Wilkins. If you say 'Mr Wilkins might be the oldest person in the village', the modal 'might' indicates that you think it is possible that Mr Wilkins is the oldest person, because he is very old.

**attitude to intentions** 4.99 You can use modals to indicate your attitude towards the things you intend to do, or intend not to do. For example, if you say 'I won't go without Simon', you are expressing strong unwillingness to do something. If you say 'I can't go without Simon', you are expressing unwillingness, but at the same time you are indicating that there is a special reason for your unwillingness. If you say 'I couldn't go without Simon', you are indicating that you are unwilling to go without Simon, because to do so would be unfair or morally wrong.

**attitude to people** 4.100 When you use language, you are affecting and responding to a particular person or audience. Modals are often used to produce a particular effect, and the modal you choose depends on several factors, such as the relationship you have with your listener, the formality or informality of the situation, and the importance of what you are saying.

For example, it would normally be rude to say to a stranger 'Open the door', although you might say it in an emergency, or you might say it to a close friend or a child. Normally, you would say to a stranger 'Will you open the door?', 'Would you open the door?', or 'Could you open the door?', depending on how polite you want to be.

**use in complex sentences** 4.101 Modals have special uses in three kinds of **complex sentence:**

• they are used in **reported clauses**

*Wilson dropped a hint that he might come.*
*I felt that I would like to wake her up.*

For more information about reported clauses see Chapter 7.

• they are used in **conditional structures**

*If he had died when he was 50, he would have died healthy.*
*If only things had been different, she would have been far happier with George.*

For more information about these structures see paragraphs 8.25 to 8.42.

• they are used in **purpose clauses.**

*He stole under the very noses of the store detectives in order that he might be arrested and punished.*
*He resigned so that he could spend more time with his family.*

For more information about these structures see paragraphs 8.47 and 8.48.

## Special features of modals

**form of following verb** 4.102 Modals are followed by the **base form** of a verb.

*I must leave fairly soon.*
*I think it will be rather nice.*

*They ought to <u>give</u> you your money back.*

Note that 'ought' is sometimes regarded as a modal, rather than 'ought to'. 'Ought' is then said to be followed by a 'to'-infinitive.

**4.103** Sometimes a modal is followed by the base form of one of the auxiliary verbs 'have' or 'be', followed by a participle.

When a modal is followed by 'be' and a present participle, this indicates that you are talking about the present or the future.

*People <u>may be watching.</u>*
*You <u>ought to be doing</u> this.*
*The play <u>will be starting</u> soon.*

When a modal is followed by 'have' and a past participle, this indicates that you are talking about the past.

*You <u>must have heard</u> of him.*
*She <u>may have gone</u> already.*
*I <u>ought to have sent</u> the money.*

In passive structures, a modal is followed by 'be' or 'have been' and a past participle.

*The name of the winner <u>will be announced.</u>*
*They <u>ought to be treated</u> fairly.*
*Such charges <u>may have been justified.</u>*

A modal is never followed by the auxiliary verb 'do', or by another modal.

**no inflections**  **4.104** Modals do not inflect. This means there is no '-s' form in the third person singular, and there are no '-ing' or '-ed' forms.

*There's nothing I <u>can</u> do about it.*
*I am sure he <u>can</u> do it.*

*I <u>must</u> leave fairly soon.*
*She insisted that Jim <u>must</u> leave.*

'Could' is sometimes thought to be the past tense of 'can'. This is discussed in paragraphs 4.113 and 4.114.

**negatives**  **4.105** Negatives are formed by putting a **negative word** such as 'not' immediately after the modal. In the case of 'ought to', you put the negative word after 'ought'. 'Can not' is usually written as one word, 'cannot'.

*You <u>must not</u> worry.*
*He <u>ought not to</u> have done so.*
*I <u>cannot</u> go back.*

After 'could', 'might', 'must', 'ought', 'should', and 'would', 'not' is often shortened to '-n't' and is added to the modal.

*You <u>mustn't</u> talk about Ron like this.*
*Perhaps I <u>oughtn't to</u> confess this.*

'Shall not', 'will not', and 'cannot' are shortened to 'shan't', 'won't', and 'can't'. 'May not' is not shortened at all.

*I <u>shan't</u> get much work done tonight.*
*He <u>won't</u> be finished for at least another half an hour.*
*I <u>can't</u> go with you.*

**questions**  **4.106** Questions are formed by putting the modal in front of the subject. In the case of 'ought to', you put 'ought' in front of the subject and 'to' after it.

*<u>Could you</u> give me an example?*

*Ought you to make some notes about it?*
*Mightn't it surprise people?*
*Why could they not leave her alone?*
*There are many questions we cannot answer, but must we not at least ask them?*

**question tags**

**4.107** Modals are used in **question** tags.

*They can't all be right, can they?*
*You won't tell anyone, will you?*

With a negative tag, the shortened form of the negative is used.

*It would be handy, wouldn't it?*
*It'll give you time to think about it, won't it?*

Question tags are explained in paragraphs 10.110 to 10.114.

**contractions**

**4.108** In spoken English, when 'will' and 'would' are used after a pronoun, they are often shortened to '-'ll' and '-'d' and added to the pronoun.

*I hope you'll agree.*
*She'll be all right.*
*They'd both call each other horrible names.*
*If I went back on the train, it'd be better.*

'Will' and 'would' cannot be shortened like this when they are used on their own, without a following verb. For example, you can say 'Paul said he would come, and I hope he will', but you cannot say 'Paul said he would come, and I hope he'll'.

**USAGE NOTE**

**4.109** You sometimes use a modal on its own, without a following verb. You do this when you are repeating a modal. For example, if someone says 'I expect Margaret will come tonight', you can say 'I hope she will', meaning 'I hope she will come'.

*'I must go.'—'I suppose you must.'*
*'You should have become an archaeologist.'—'You're dead right, I should.'*
*If you can't do it, we'll find someone who can.*

You can also omit the verb following a modal when this verb has just been used without a modal, or with a different modal. For example, if someone says 'George has failed his exam', you can say 'I thought he would', meaning 'I thought he would fail his exam'.

*I love him and I always will.*
*They had come to believe that it not only must go on for ever but that it should.*

However you cannot omit the verb 'be' after a modal when you have just used it without a modal. For example, if someone says 'Is he a teacher?', you cannot say 'I think he might'. You must say 'I think he might be'.

*Weather forecasts aren't very reliable and never will be.*
*The Board's methods are not as stringent as they could be.*
*Relations between the two countries have not been as smooth as they might have been.*

The feature of language in which you omit certain words to avoid repeating them is called **ellipsis**. For more information about ellipsis in verb groups see paragraphs 9.49 to 9.69.

## Referring to time

**4.110** Modals do not usually indicate whether you are talking about the past, the present, or the future. Usually you indicate this in other ways, for example by putting an auxiliary verb and a participle after the modal. Sometimes the general context makes it clear whether you are talking about a past, present, or future event or situation.

**the future: 'shall' and 'will'**    **4.111** 'Shall' and 'will' are exceptions to this.

'Shall' always indicates that you are talking about a future event or situation.

*I shall do what you suggested.*
*Eventually we shall find a solution.*

'Will' usually indicates that you are talking about a future event or situation.

*The farmer will feel more responsible towards his workers.*
*He will not return for many hours.*

However 'will' is sometimes used to talk about present situations.

*You will not feel much love for him at the moment.*

This use of 'will' is described in paragraph 4.124.

**4.112** 'Could' and 'would' are sometimes described as past tense forms of 'can' and 'will'. However this is true in only a few minor ways. These are explained in the following paragraphs.

**ability in the past: 'could'**    **4.113** 'Could' can be regarded as the past tense of 'can' if you are simply talking about the ability of a person or thing to do something.

For example, if you are talking about a living person, you can say 'He can speak Russian and Finnish'. If you are talking about a dead person, you can say 'He could speak Russian and Finnish'.

For a fuller explanation of these uses see paragraphs 4.119 to 4.121.

**reported speech**    **4.114** 'Could' and 'would' are sometimes used in place of 'can' and 'will' when you are reporting what someone has said.

For example, if a man has said 'I can come', you might report this as 'He said that he could come'. Similarly, if he has said, 'I will come', you might report this as 'He said that he would come'.

For a full explanation of reported speech see Chapter 7.

**regularity in the past: 'would'**    **4.115** 'Would' is used to talk about something that happened regularly in the past, but no longer happens.

*The other children would tease me and call me names.*
*A man with a list would come round and say you could go off duty.*

When you use 'would' like this, you often add an **adjunct of time.**

*She would often hear him grumbling.*
*Once in a while she'd give me some lilac to take home.*
*Every day I'd ring up home and asked if they'd changed their minds.*

You can use 'used to' instead of 'would'. 'Used to' is explained in paragraphs 4.258 to 4.262.

**thinking about the future: 'would'**    **4.116** 'Would' is also used in stories to talk about the thoughts that someone is having about the future. For example, if the hero of a story is thinking that he will see a girl called Jane the next day, the author might simply say 'He would see Jane the next day'.

*He would recognize it when he heard it again.*
*They would reach the castle some time.*

**unwillingness: 'would not'**   **4.117** When 'would' is used with 'not' to talk about something that happened in the past, it has a special meaning. It is used to say that someone was unwilling to do something, or refused to do something.

*They just would not believe what we told them.*
*After all this, I wouldn't come back to the farm.*

The use of modals to express unwillingness or a refusal is explained in paragraphs 4.200 to 4.205.

# Indicating possibility

**4.118** The following four sections explain the different ways in which modals are used to talk about the possibility of something happening or being done.

Paragraphs 4.119 to 4.122 explain how 'can' and 'could' are used to talk about the ability of a person or thing to do something.

Paragraphs 4.123 to 4.145 explain how modals are used to express degrees of certainty about past, present, and future situations and events

Paragraphs 4.146 to 4.149 explain how modals are used to say that something is permissible.

Paragraphs 4.150 to 4.157 explain how modals are used to say that something is forbidden or unacceptable.

# Indicating ability

**skills and abilities: 'can' and 'could'**   **4.119** 'Can' is used to say that someone has a particular skill or ability.

*You can all read and write.*
*Some people can ski better than others.*
*He cannot dance.*
*...the girl who can't act.*

'Could' is used to say that someone had a skill or ability in the past.

*When I arrived, I could speak no English.*
*I could barely walk.*
*He could kick penalty goals from anywhere.*

**awareness: 'can' and 'could'**   **4.120** 'Can' is also used to say that someone is aware of something through one of their senses.

*I can see you.*
*I can smell it. Can't you?*

'Could' is used to say that someone was aware of something through one of their senses on a particular occasion in the past.

*I could see a few faint stars in a clear patch of sky.*
*I could feel my heart bumping.*
*Police said they could smell alcohol on his breath.*

**capability: 'can' and 'could'**   **4.121** 'Can' and 'could' are also used to say that something or someone capable of having a particular effect, or of behaving in a particular way.

*It can be very unpleasant.*

*Art can be used to communicate.*
*Throwing parties can be hard work.*
*He could be very stiff, could Haggerty.*
*He could really frighten me, and yet at the same time he could be the most gentle and courteous of men.*

**WARNING**

**4.122** You cannot use 'can' or 'could' to say that someone or something will have a particular ability in the future. Instead you use 'be able to' or 'be possible to'.

'Be able to' and 'be possible to' can also be used to talk about someone's ability to do something in the present or the past.

'Be able to' and 'be possible to' are dealt with in paragraphs 4.228 to 4.235.

# Indicating likelihood

**4.123** The following paragraphs explain how modals are used to express different degrees of certainty about past, present, and future situations and events.

Paragraphs 4.124 to 4.131 explain the main ways in which modals are used to express degrees of certainty.

Paragraphs 4.132 to 4.138 explain special uses of modals when talking about possible future situations.

Paragraphs 4.139 to 4.145 explain special uses of modals when talking about possible situations in the past.

assumption: 'will' and 'would'

**4.124** You use 'will' when you are assuming that something is the case, and you do not think there is any reason to doubt it.

*Those of you who are familiar with the game will know this.*
*He will be a little out of touch, although he's a rapid learner.*
*She will have forgotten all about it by now.*

Similarly, you use 'will not' or 'won't' when you are assuming that something is not the case.

*The audience will not be aware of such exact details.*
*You won't know Gordon. He's our new doctor.*

After 'you', you can use 'would' instead of 'will', if you want to be more polite.

*You would agree that the United States should be involved in assisting these countries.*

certainty: 'would' and 'should'

**4.125** You also use 'would' to say that something is certain to happen in particular circumstances.

*Even an illiterate person would understand that.*
*Few people would agree with this as a general principle.*
*A picnic wouldn't be any fun without you.*

After 'I', you can use 'should' instead of 'would'.

*The very first thing I should do would be to teach you how to cook.*
*I should be very unhappy on the continent.*

belief: 'must' and 'cannot'

**4.126** You use 'must' to indicate that you believe something is the case, because of particular facts or circumstances.

*Oh, you must be Sylvia's husband.*

*Fashion must account for a small percentage of sales.*
*This article must have been written by a woman.*

When you are indicating that something is not the case, you use 'cannot'. You do not use 'must not'. (See paragraph 4.130.)

*The two conflicting messages cannot possibly both be true.*
*You can't have forgotten me.*
*He can't have said that. He just can't.*

| possibility: 'could', 'might', 'may' | **4.127** You use 'could', 'might', or 'may' to say that there is a possibility of something happening or being the case. 'May' is slightly more formal than 'could' or 'might'; otherwise there is very little difference in meaning between these modals. |
|---|---|

*Don't eat it. It could be a toadstool.*
*His route from the bus stop might be the same as yours.*
*In rare cases the jaw may be broken during extraction.*

| strong possibility: adding 'well' | **4.128** If you put 'well' after 'could', 'might', or 'may', you are indicating that it is fairly likely that something is the case. |
|---|---|

*It could well be that the economic situation is getting better.*
*His predictions could well have come true.*
*You might well be right.*
*I think that may well have been the intention.*

| negative possibility: 'might not' and 'may not' | **4.129** You use 'might not' or 'may not' to say that it is possible that something is not the case. |
|---|---|

*He might not be in England at all.*
*That mightn't be true.*
*That may not sound very imposing.*

| impossibility: 'could not' and 'cannot' | **4.130** You use 'could not' or 'cannot' to say that it is impossible that something is the case. |
|---|---|

*...knowledge which could not have been gained in any other way.*
*It couldn't possibly be poison.*
*He cannot know everything that is going on.*
*You can't talk to the dead.*

| strong assertion: 'could not' with comparatives | **4.131** 'Could' is sometimes used in negative constructions with the comparative form of an adjective. You use 'could' like this to say that it is not possible for someone or something to have more of a particular quality. |
|---|---|

*I couldn't be happier.*
*You couldn't be more wrong.*
*The setting couldn't have been lovelier.*
*He could hardly have felt more ashamed of himself.*

| talking about the future | **4.132** The following paragraphs explain how modals are used when you are talking about possible future situations. The uses of 'must', 'cannot', 'could', 'might', and 'may' are similar to their uses when you are talking about possible situations in the present. |
|---|---|

| certainty: 'will' | **4.133** You use 'will' to say that something is certain to happen or be the case in the future. |
|---|---|

*They will see everything.*
*The price of food will go up.*

*The service will have been running for a year in May.*

'Be going to' can also be used to say that something is certain to happen in the future. This use of 'be going to' is dealt with in paragraph 4.237.

**certainty: 'shall'**    **4.134** 'Shall' is also used to say that something is certain to happen. You usually use 'shall' when you are talking about events and situations over which you have some control. For example, you can use 'shall' when you are making a resolution or a promise.

*I shall be leaving as soon as I am ready.*
*Very well, my dear. You shall have the coat.*
*Of course he shall have water.*
*'You'll make a lot of money.'—'I shall one day.'*

**certainty: 'must' and 'cannot'**    **4.135** You use 'must' to say that something is certain to happen because of particular facts or circumstances.

*Computer interviewing and rudimentary computer diagnosis must eventually lead to computer decision-making.*

You use 'cannot' to say that something is certain not to happen because of particular facts or circumstances. You do not use 'must not'.

*A team cannot hope to win consistently without a good coach.*
*The repression can't last.*

**expectation: 'should' and 'ought to'**    **4.136** You use 'should' or 'ought to' to say that you expect something to happen.

*She should be back any time now.*
*This course should be quite interesting for you.*
*The Court of Appeal ought to be able to help you.*
*It ought to get better as it goes along.*

'Should' and 'ought to' are also used when you are talking about the importance of doing something. This use is explained in paragraph 4.219.

**possibility: 'could', 'might', and 'may'**    **4.137** You use 'could', 'might', or 'may' to say that it is possible that a particular thing will happen.

*England's next fixture in Salzburg could be the decisive match.*
*The river could easily overflow.*
*They might be able to remember what he said.*
*Clerical work may be available for two students who want to learn about publishing.*

**4.138** If you put 'well' after 'could', 'might', or 'may', you are indicating that it is fairly likely that something will happen or be the case.

*When it is finished it may well be the largest cathedral in the world.*
*We might well get injured.*

If you put 'possibly' or 'conceivably' after 'could', 'might', or 'may', you are indicating that it is possible, but fairly unlikely, that something will happen or be the case.

*These conditions could possibly be accepted.*
*Rates could conceivably rise by as much as a whole percentage point.*

**talking about the past**    **4.139** The following paragraphs explain how you use modals when you are talking about possible situations in the past.

| | |
|---|---|
| **expectation:** 'should have', 'ought to have' | **4.140** You use 'should' or 'ought to' with 'have' to say that you expect something to have happened already. |

*Dear Mom, you should have heard by now that I'm O.K.*

You also use 'should' or 'ought to' with 'have' to say that something was expected to happen, although it has not in fact happened.

*Muskie should have won by a huge margin.*
*She ought to have been home by now.*

| | |
|---|---|
| **possibility:** 'would have' | **4.141** You use 'would' with 'have' to talk about actions and events that were possible in the past, although they did not in fact happen. |

*Denial would have been useless.*
*I would have said yes, but Julie talked us into staying at home.*
*You wouldn't have pushed him, would you?*

| | |
|---|---|
| **possibility:** 'could have', 'might have' | **4.142** You use 'could' or 'might' with 'have' to say that there was a possibility of something happening in the past, although it did not in fact happen. |

*It could have been awful.*
*I could easily have spent the whole year on it.*
*You could have got a job last year.*
*A lot of men died who might have been saved.*
*You might have found it very difficult.*

| | |
|---|---|
| **uncertainty:** 'could have', 'might have', 'may have' | **4.143** You also use 'could', 'might', or 'may' with 'have' to say that it is possible that something was the case, but you do not know whether it was the case or not. |

*It is just possible that such a small creature could have preyed on dinosaur eggs.*
*They might have moved house by now.*
*I may have seemed to be overreacting.*

| | |
|---|---|
| **negative possibility:** 'might not have', 'may not have' | **4.144** You use 'might not' or 'may not' with 'have' to say that it is possible that something did not happen or was not the case. |

*They might not have considered me as their friend.*
*My father mightn't have been to blame.*
*The parents may not have been ready for this pregnancy.*

| | |
|---|---|
| **impossibility:** 'could have' with negative | **4.145** You use 'could' with a negative and 'have' to say that it is impossible that something happened or was the case. |

*It couldn't have been wrong.*
*The money was not, and never could have been, the property of the Workers Party.*

## Indicating permission

| | |
|---|---|
| **permission:** 'can' | **4.146** 'Can' is used to say that someone is allowed to do something. |

*You can drive a van up to 3-ton capacity using an ordinary driving licence.*

If you are giving permission for something, you use 'can'.

*You can borrow that pen if you want to.*
*You can go off duty now.*
*She can go with you.*

| | |
|---|---|
| **formal permission: 'may'** | **4.147** In more formal situations, 'may' is used to give permission. |

*You may speak.*
*They may do exactly as they like.*

**permission in the past: 'could'** **4.148** 'Could' is used to say that someone was allowed to do something in the past.

*We could go to any part of the island we wanted to.*

**WARNING** **4.149** You cannot use 'can' or 'could' to say that someone will be allowed to do something in the future. Instead you use 'be able to'.

'Be able to' is dealt with in paragraphs 4.228 to 4.235.

## Indicating unacceptability

**4.150** Modals are often used in negative structures to say that an action is forbidden or unacceptable.

**prohibition: 'cannot'** **4.151** 'Cannot' is used to say that something is forbidden, for example because of a rule or law.

*Children cannot bathe except in the presence of two lifesavers.*
*We're awfully sorry we can't let you stay here.*

**prohibition: 'may not'** **4.152** 'May not' is used in a similar way to 'cannot', but is more formal.

*You may not make amendments to your application once we have received it.*
*This material may not be published, broadcast, or redistributed in any manner.*

**prohibition: 'will not'** **4.153** 'Will not' is used to tell someone very firmly that they are not allowed to do a particular thing. Usually, the speaker has the power to prevent the hearer from doing this thing.

*'I'll just go upstairs.'—'You will not.'*
*Until we have cured you, you won't be leaving here.*

**prohibition: 'shall not'** **4.154** 'Shall not' is used to say formally that a particular thing is not allowed. 'Shall not' is often used in written rules, laws, and agreements.

*Persons under 18 shall not be employed in nightwork.*
*Equality of rights under the law shall not be denied or abridged by the United States or by any State.*

'Shan't' is used in a similar way to 'will not' and 'won't'.

*You shan't leave without my permission.*

**prohibition: imperatives** **4.155** You can also say that something is not allowed by using an imperative sentence. Imperative sentences are explained in paragraph 4.4 and in paragraphs 4.31 to 4.35.

**undesirable actions: 'should not'** **4.156** 'Should not' is used to tell someone that an action is unacceptable or undesirable.

*You should not take her help for granted.*
*You shouldn't do that.*
*You shouldn't be so unfriendly.*

<table>
<tr><td>

**undesirable**
**actions:**
**'must not'**

</td><td>

**4.157** 'Must not' is used to say much more firmly that something is unacceptable or undesirable.

*You must not accept it.*
*You mustn't do that.*
*You mustn't breathe a word of this to anyone.*

</td></tr>
</table>

## Interacting with other people

**4.158** You often say things in order to get someone to behave in a particular way. For example, you may want someone to take a particular action, to accept an offer, or to give their permission for something to be done.

In these situations, modals are often used. The modal you choose depends on several factors. The main ones are:

● the formality or informality of the situation
● the relationship between yourself and the person you are speaking to
● the degree of politeness you want to show.

In particular situations, other factors can be important. For example, if you are making an offer or suggestion, the modal you choose may depend on how persuasive you want to be.

**4.159** The following sections explain how to use modals in different situations.

Paragraphs 4.160 to 4.176 explain how to give instructions and make requests.

Paragraphs 4.177 to 4.185 explain how to make an offer or an invitation.

Paragraphs 4.186 to 4.193 explain how to make suggestions.

Paragraphs 4.194 to 4.199 explain how to state an intention.

Paragraphs 4.200 to 4.205 explain how to express unwillingness or a refusal to do something.

Paragraphs 4.206 to 4.214 explain how to express a wish.

Paragraphs 4.215 to 4.219 explain how to indicate the importance of doing something.

Paragraphs 4.220 to 4.226 explain various ways of introducing what you are going to say.

## Giving instructions and making requests

**4.160** When you give an instruction or make a request, you usually use a modal in an interrogative sentence.

You use 'will', 'would', 'can', or 'could' with 'you' to tell someone to do something, or to ask someone to do something.

You use 'can', 'could', 'may', or 'might' with 'I' or 'we' or with other personal pronouns or noun groups to ask someone's permission to do something.

Instructions and requests are always made more polite by adding 'please'. 'Please' and other markers of politeness are explained in paragraph 4.176.

**instructions and appeals** **4.161** 'Will', 'would', and 'could' are used with 'you' in two ways:

• you use them to give an instruction or an order
• you use them to ask for help or assistance.

**instructions and appeals: 'will'** **4.162** 'Will' is used to give an instruction or order in a fairly direct way. It is slightly less forceful than using the imperative.

*Will you pick those toys up please?*
*Will you please, at once, pack up and leave.*

'Will' is used to ask for help in fairly informal situations.

*Mummy, will you help me?*

**instructions and appeals: 'would'** **4.163** When 'would' is used to give an instruction or order, it is more polite than 'will'.

*Would you tell her that Adrian phoned?*
*Would you ask them to leave, please?*

When 'would' is used to ask for help, it is less informal and more polite than 'will'.

*Would you do me a favour?*

**instructions and appeals: 'could'** **4.164** When 'could' is used to give an instruction or order, it is more polite than 'would'.

*Could you follow me please?*
*Could you just switch the projector on behind you?*

When 'could' is used to ask for help, it is more polite than 'would'.

*Could you show me how to do this?*

**appeals: 'can'** **4.165** 'Can' can be used with 'you' to ask for help. You usually use 'can' when you are not sure whether someone will be able to help you or not.

*Oh hello. Can you help me? I've been trying to get a London number for ten minutes and I can't get through.*

**requests** **4.166** 'Can', 'could', 'may', and 'might' are used with 'I' or 'we' when you are asking for something, or are asking permission to do something.

These modals can also be used with 'he', 'she', or 'they', or with other noun groups, when you are asking for something on behalf of someone else. For example, you can say 'Can she borrow your car?' or 'Could my mother use your telephone?'

**requests: 'can'** **4.167** 'Can' is used to make a request in a simple and direct way.

*Can I ask a question?*
*'Can I change this?' I asked the box office lady, offering her my ticket.*

**requests: 'could'** **4.168** 'Could' is more polite than 'can'.

*Could I have a bottle of Vermouth, please?*
*Could I just interrupt a minute?*

**requests: 'can't' and 'couldn't'** **4.169** You can make a request sound more persuasive by using 'can't' or 'couldn't' instead of 'can' or 'could'. For example, you can say 'Can't I come with you?' instead of 'Can I come with you?'.

*Can't we have some music?*
*Couldn't we stay here?*

| requests: 'may' and 'might' | **4.170** 'May' and 'might' are more formal than 'can' and 'could'. People used to be taught that, when asking for something, it was correct to say 'may' rather than 'can', and 'might' rather than 'could'. However 'can' and 'could' are now generally used. Requests beginning with 'might' are unusual, and are considered by most people to be old-fashioned. |
|---|---|

*May I have a cigarette?*
*May we have something to eat?*
*May I ask what your name is?*
*Might I inquire if you are the owner?*

| instructions: 'would like' | **4.171** 'Would like' can be used with 'I' or 'we' in a declarative sentence to give an instruction or order. It is followed by 'you' and a 'to'-infinitive clause. |
|---|---|

*Penelope, I would like you to get us the files.*

'Want' can be used in a similar way to 'would like'. This use of 'want' is dealt with in paragraph 4.240.

| firm instructions: 'will' | **4.172** An instruction or order can also be given using 'will' in a declarative sentence. This form is used when the speaker is angry or impatient. |
|---|---|

*You will go and get one of your parents immediately.*
*You will give me those now.*

| formal instructions: 'shall' | **4.173** 'Shall' is sometimes used in a declarative sentence to give an instruction or order. This is a very formal use. |
|---|---|

*There shall be no further communication between you.*

| imperatives | **4.174** The **imperative mood** can also be used to give an instruction or order. This use is explained in paragraph 4.31. |
|---|---|

| requests: 'would like', 'should like' | **4.175** You can use 'would like' or 'should like' in a declarative sentence to make a request. 'Would like' and 'should like' are followed by a 'to'-infinitive clause or a noun group. |
|---|---|

*I would like to ask you one question.*
*I'd like to have a little talk with you.*
*I should like a list of your customers over the past year.*

| polite additions to requests | **4.176** All the ways of giving instructions or making requests described above can be made more polite by using 'please'. |
|---|---|

*Can I speak to Nicola please?*
*Could you tell me please what time the flight arrives?*
*Please may I have the key?*

You can also make a request more polite by adding the name of the person you are addressing at the beginning or end of your question.

*Martin, could you make us a drink?*
*Can I talk to you, Howard?*

Another way of making a request more polite is to add an adverb such as 'perhaps' or 'possibly' after the subject of the verb.

*Could I perhaps bring a friend with me?*
*May I possibly have a word with you, please?*

## Making an offer or an invitation

**4.177** Modals are often used to make an offer or an invitation.

You use 'will' or 'would' with 'you' to ask someone to accept something, or to make an invitation.

You use 'can', 'may', 'shall', or 'should' with 'I' or 'we' when you are offering to help someone.

Some of these structures are similar to those described in the previous section.

**offers and invitations: 'will'**

**4.178** 'Will' is used with 'you' in an interrogative sentence to offer something to someone, or to make an invitation in a fairly informal way. You use 'will' when you know the person you are talking to quite well.

_Will you have a whisky, Doctor?_
_Will you stay for lunch?_

**offers and invitations: 'would' and 'wouldn't'**

**4.179** A more polite way of offering something or making an invitation is to use 'would' with a verb which means 'to like'.

_Would you like a drink?_
_Would you care to stay with us?_

If you want to sound more persuasive without seeming impolite or insistent, you can use 'wouldn't' instead of 'would'.

_Wouldn't you like to come with me?_
_Wouldn't you care for some more coffee?_

**offers of help: 'can'**

**4.180** When you are offering to do something for someone, you usually use 'can' followed by 'I' or 'we'.

_Can I help you with the dishes?_
_Can we give you a lift into town?_

**offers of help: 'may'**

**4.181** 'May' is also used when you are offering to do something for someone. It is less common than 'can', and is rather formal and old-fashioned.

_May I help you?_
_May I take your coat?_

**offers of help: 'shall' and 'should'**

**4.182** You can also use 'shall' or 'should' when you are offering to do something.

If you are fairly confident that your offer will be accepted, you use 'shall'.

_Shall I shut the door?_
_Shall I spell that for you?_

If you are uncertain whether your offer will be accepted, you use 'should'.

_Should I give her a ring?_

**emphasizing ability: 'can'**

**4.183** If you want to emphasize your ability to help, you can make an offer using 'can' in a declarative sentence.

_I have a car. I can drop Daisy off on my way home._
_I can pop in at the shop tomorrow._

**persuasive invitations: 'must'**

**4.184** If you want to make an invitation in a very persuasive way, you can use a declarative sentence beginning with 'you' and 'must'.

_You must join us for drinks this evening._
_You must come and visit me._

You only use 'must' like this with people who you know well.

**4.185** Other ways of making an offer or invitation are dealt with in paragraph 4.38.

# Making suggestions

**4.186** Suggestions can be made by using a modal in a declarative or interrogative sentence. The subject of the sentence is usually 'we' or 'you'.

**suggesting: 'could'**

**4.187** You can make a suggestion by using 'could' in a declarative sentence or 'couldn't' in an interrogative sentence.

*If the business doesn't work out we could sell it.*
*You could have a nursery there.*
*Couldn't you just build more factories?*
*Couldn't some international agreement be concluded to ban these weapons?*

**suggesting: 'should' and 'ought to'**

**4.188** If you are making a suggestion and you want to indicate that you feel strongly that it is a good idea, you can use 'should' or 'ought to'.

*You should ask Norry about this.*
*I think you should get in touch with your solicitor.*
*We ought to celebrate. Let's get a bottle of champagne.*
*I think you ought to try a different approach.*

A more polite way of making a suggestion that you feel strongly about is to use 'shouldn't' or 'oughtn't to' in an interrogative sentence.

*Shouldn't we at least give her a chance?*
*Oughtn't we to phone the police?*

**persuading: 'must'**

**4.189** If you are suggesting an action and you are trying to persuade someone that it should be done, you use 'must'. You only use 'must' like this when you are talking to someone you know well.

*You must say hello to your daughter.*
*We must go to the place, perhaps have a weekend there.*

**polite suggestions: 'might'**

**4.190** If you want to make a suggestion in a very polite way, you can use 'might' with 'you' in a declarative sentence. 'Might' is followed by a verb meaning 'to like' or 'to want'.

*You might like to comment on his latest proposal.*
*I thought perhaps you might like to come along with me.*

You can also make a polite suggestion by using a sentence beginning with 'It might be', followed by a noun group or adjective and a 'to'-infinitive clause.

*I think it might be a good idea to stop the recording now.*
*It might be better to wait a while.*

**suggesting: 'might as well', 'may as well'**

**4.191** You can also make suggestions using the expressions 'might as well' and 'may as well'.

You use 'might as well' when what you are suggesting seems to be the only sensible course of action, although you are not enthusiastic about it.

*He might as well take the car.*
*We might as well call the whole thing off.*

You use 'may as well' to show that it is not important to you whether your suggestion is accepted or not.

*You may as well open them all.*
*We may as well give her a copy.*

| | |
|---|---|
| suggesting: 'shall' | **4.192** You can make a suggestion about what you and someone else could do by using an interrogative sentence beginning with 'shall' and 'we'. |

_Shall we go and see a film?_
_Shall we go on to question number six?_
_Shall we talk about something different now?_

**4.193** Other ways of making suggestions are described in paragraph 4.42.

## Stating an intention

**4.194** Intentions are usually stated by using 'will', 'shall', or 'must' in a declarative sentence. The subject is 'I' or 'we'.

| | |
|---|---|
| intentions: 'will' | **4.195** The usual way to state an intention is to use 'I' or 'we' with 'will'. The shortened forms 'I'll' and 'we'll' are very common. |

_I will call you when I am ready._
_We will stay here._
_I'll write again some time._
_We'll discuss that later._

You state your intention not to do something using 'will not' or 'won't'.

_I will not follow her._
_I won't keep you any longer._
_We won't let them through the gate._

**4.196** You can indicate that you are very determined to do something by using the full form 'I will' or 'we will' and stressing 'will'.

You can indicate that you are very determined not to do something either by using 'I won't' or 'we won't' and stressing 'won't', or by using 'I will not' or 'we will not' and stressing 'not'.

| | |
|---|---|
| intentions: 'shall' | **4.197** Another way of stating an intention is to use 'I' or 'we' with 'shall'. This use is slightly old-fashioned and rather formal. |

_I shall be leaving soon._
_I shall make some enquiries and call you back._
_We shall continue to monitor his progress._

You can indicate that you are very determined not to do something by using 'shall not' or 'shan't'. This is more emphatic than using 'will not' or 'won't'.

_I shall not disclose his name._
_I shan't go back there._

| | |
|---|---|
| intentions: 'must' | **4.198** If you want to indicate that it is important that you do something, you can use 'must' with 'I'. |

_I must leave fairly soon._
_I must ask her about that._
_I haven't seen her for ages. I must phone her up._

**4.199** Ways of stating an intention without using a modal are explained in paragraphs 4.241 to 4.244.

## Indicating unwillingness or refusal

**4.200** Unwillingness or a refusal can be expressed by using a modal in a negative declarative sentence. The subject is usually 'I' or 'we', but other personal pronouns or noun groups can be used.

| | |
|---|---|
| unwillingness: 'will not' and 'won't' | **4.201** If you want to say firmly that you are unwilling to do something, you use 'will not' or 'won't'. |

*I will not hear a word said against the National Health Service.*
*I won't let this happen.*

If you are refusing to do something, you can just say 'I won't'.

*'Tell me your secret.'—'I won't. It wouldn't be a secret if I told you.'*
*It isn't that I won't. I can't.*

You can use 'won't' to say that someone else is unwilling to do something.

*He won't give her a divorce.*

| | |
|---|---|
| unwillingness: 'would not' | **4.202** If you want to say that you were unwilling to do something in the past, you use 'would not' or 'wouldn't'. |

*He thought I was a freak because I wouldn't carry a weapon.*

| | |
|---|---|
| unwillingness: 'cannot' | **4.203** If you want to indicate that you have strong feelings which prevent you from doing something, you use 'cannot' or 'can't'. |

*I cannot leave everything for him.*
*I can't give you up.*

| | |
|---|---|
| unwillingness: 'couldn't' | **4.204** 'Couldn't' is used in two ways to express unwillingness to do something. |

You use it to indicate that you are unwilling to do something because you are afraid, embarrassed, or disgusted.

*I couldn't possibly go out now.*
*I couldn't let him touch me.*

You use it to indicate that you are unwilling to do something because you think it would be unfair or morally wrong.

*I couldn't leave Hilary behind to cope on her own.*
*I couldn't take your last cigarette.*

**4.205** Other ways of expressing unwillingness are described in paragraphs 4.245 to 4.247.

## Expressing a wish

**4.206** Wishes can be expressed by using a modal in a declarative sentence.

| | |
|---|---|
| wishes: 'would' | **4.207** You can say what someone wants by using 'would' followed by a verb meaning 'to like'. After the verb meaning 'to like' you put a 'to'-infinitive clause or a noun group. |

*I would like to know the date.*
*I would prefer to say nothing about this problem.*
*We'd like to keep you here.*
*Oh, I hope it will be twins. I'd love twins.*

**4.208** You can say what someone does not want by using 'would not'.

*I would not like to see it.*
*We wouldn't like to lose you.*

Normally, when you are using 'would' with 'like' to say what someone does not want, you put 'not' after 'would'. If you put 'not' after 'like', you change the meaning slightly.

For example, if you say 'I would not like to be a student', you mean you are not a student and do not want to be one. But if you say 'I would like not to be a student', you mean you are a student and do not want to be one.

*They would like not to have to go through all that.*

You can also say what someone does not want by using 'would' with a verb meaning 'to dislike'.

*I would hate to move to another house now.*
*Personally, I would loathe to be dragged into this dispute.*

**wishes:**
**'should'**
4.209 You can also say what someone wants or does not want by using 'should'. 'Should' is less common than 'would', and is slightly more formal.

*I should like to live in the country.*
*I should hate to see them disappear.*

**preference:**
**'would**
**rather',**
**'would**
**sooner'**
4.210 You can say that someone prefers one situation to another by using 'would rather' or 'would sooner'.

*He would rather have left it.*
*She'd rather be left alone.*
*I'd sooner walk than do any of these things.*

**wishes:**
**'would have'**
4.211 If you want to say that someone wanted something to happen, although it did not happen, you use 'would have' and a past participle.

*I would have liked to hear more from the patient.*
*She would have liked to remain just where she was.*

**USAGE NOTE**
4.212 Another way of saying that you want something is to use 'wouldn't' with a verb or expression such as 'mind' or 'object to' which is normally used to refuse something.

*I wouldn't mind being a manager of a store.*
*'Drink, Ted?'—'I wouldn't say no, Bryan.'*

**regret:**
**'would that'**
4.213 In very old-fashioned English, 'would' is used without a subject to express a wish that a situation might be different, or to express regret that something did not happen in the past. 'Would' is followed by a 'that'-clause.

*'Are they better off now than they were two years ago?'—'Would that they were.'*
*Would that the developments had been so easy.*

When 'I', 'he', 'she', or 'it' is the subject of the 'that'-clause, the verb is usually 'were', not 'was'.

*Would that you were here tonight.*
*Two years ago we were told that they would be much better off by now. Would that they were.*

**hopes and**
**wishes:**
**'may'**
4.214 In very formal English, 'may' is used in interrogative sentences to express a hope or wish.

*Long may they continue to do it.*
*May he justify our hopes and rise to the top.*

# Indicating importance

**4.215** Modals can be used in declarative sentences to say that it is important that something is done. Different modals indicate different degrees of importance.

importance: 'must'

**4.216** 'Must' is used in three common ways to talk about the importance of doing something.

You use 'must' with 'you' or 'we' to urge someone to do something, because you feel it is important. 'Must not' is used to urge someone not to do something.

*You must come at once.*
*We must accept the truth about ourselves.*
*You must not worry.*
*You mustn't let her suffer for it.*

You use 'must' to say that something is required by a rule or law.

*People who qualify must apply within six months.*
*European Community standards must be met.*

You use 'must' to say that it is necessary that something happens or is done, in order that something else can happen.

*Meadows must have rain.*
*To travel properly, you must have a valid ticket.*

'Have to', 'have got to', and 'need to' can be used instead of 'must' to talk about the importance of doing something. This is explained in paragraphs 4.248 and 4.249.

necessity: 'will have to', 'will need to'

**4.217** If you want to say that an action will be necessary in the future, you use 'will have to' or 'will need to'.

*They will have to pay for the repairs.*
*Mr Smith will have to make the funeral arrangements.*
*You will need to cover it with some kind of sheeting.*
*Electric clocks will need to be reset.*

necessity: 'shall have to'

**4.218** 'Shall have to' is sometimes used instead of 'will have to' after 'I' or 'we'. This is a slightly formal use.

*I shall have to speak about that to Peter.*
*We shall have to assume that you are right.*

importance: 'should' and 'ought to'

**4.219** 'Should' and 'ought to' are used in three different ways when you are talking about the importance of doing something.

You use 'should' or 'ought to' when you are trying to help someone by advising them to do something.

*Carbon steel knives should be wiped clean after use.*
*You should claim your pension 3-4 months before you retire.*
*You ought to try a different approach.*

You use 'should' or 'ought to' when you are saying that something is the right or correct thing to do.

*We should send her a postcard from Eastbourne.*
*The judges should offer constructive criticism.*
*We ought to stay with him.*

*You ought not to do that.*

You use 'should' or 'ought to' with 'have' and a past participle to say that something was desirable in the past, although it did not in fact happen.

*One sailor should have been asleep and one on watch.*
*We ought to have stayed in tonight.*
*A more junior member of staff ought to have done the work.*

You also use 'should' and 'ought to' to say that you expect something to happen. This use is explained in paragraph 4.136.

# Introducing what you are going to say

**4.220** Sometimes you introduce what you are going to say by using a modal followed by a verb such as 'say' or 'ask' which refers to the act of saying something. You can also combine a modal with a verb such as 'think' or 'believe' which refers to the holding of an opinion.

You use a modal in order to sound more polite, or to indicate your feelings about what you are going to say.

In structures like these, the subject is usually 'I'. Sometimes you use an impersonal structure beginning with 'it' or 'you'. For example, instead of saying 'I ought to mention that he had never been there', you can say 'It ought to be mentioned that he had never been there'.

**importance: 'must'**

**4.221** If you feel strongly that what you are saying is important, you use 'must'.

*I must apologise to you.*
*I must object.*
*It must be said that he has a point.*

**importance: 'should' and 'ought to'**

**4.222** If you feel that it is important or appropriate that something is said, you indicate that you are going to say it by using 'should' or 'ought to'.

*I should explain at this point that there are two different sorts of microscope.*
*It should also be said that I learned a great deal from the experience.*
*I ought to stress that this was not a trial.*
*Perhaps I ought to conclude with a slightly more light-hearted question.*

**politeness: 'can' and 'could'**

**4.223** If you want to say something during a discussion, you can indicate politely that you are going to say it by using 'can'.

*Perhaps I can mention another possibility.*
*If I can just intervene for one moment...*

If you want to be even more polite, you use 'could'.

*Perhaps I could just illustrate this by mentioning two cases that I know of personally.*
*Perhaps I could just ask you this...*

**4.224** You also use 'can' and 'could' when you are mentioning an opinion or a way of describing something.

'Can' suggests that you approve of the opinion or description.

*Such behaviour can be a cover-up for deep emotional upset.*

'Could' is more neutral.

*You could argue that this is irrelevant.*
*You could call it a political offence.*

**approval: 'may' and 'might'**

**4.225** 'May' and 'might' can also be used to mention an opinion or a way of describing something.

'May' suggests that you approve of the opinion or description. It is more formal than 'can'.

*This, it may be added, greatly strengthened him in his resolve.*

'Might' also suggests that you approve of the opinion or description. You use 'might' when you think there is a possibility that the person you are talking to will disagree with you.

*You might say she's entitled to get angry.*
*That, one might argue, is not too terrible.*

**politeness: 'should' and 'would'**

**4.226** If you are stating an opinion of your own, you can indicate politely that you are going to state it by using 'should'.

*I should think it would last quite a long time.*

'Would' is used in a similar way, but is less common.

*I would guess it may well come down to cost.*

# Expressions used instead of modals

**4.227** Several ordinary verbs and fixed expressions are used to express the same attitudes and ideas as modals. These verbs and expressions are explained in the following paragraphs. Each group of paragraphs corresponds to an earlier section in the chapter dealing with the use of modals in a particular type of situation.

**saying whether something is possible**

**4.228** 'Be able to' and 'be possible to' can be used instead of 'can' and 'could' to say whether or not something is possible.

The subject of 'be able to' and 'be unable to' usually refers to a person or group of people, but it can refer to any living thing. It can also refer to something organized or operated by people, such as a company, a country, or a machine.

The subject of 'be possible to' is always the impersonal pronoun 'it'.

**4.229** If you want to say that it is possible for someone or something to do something, you can use 'be able to'.

*All members are able to claim travelling expenses.*
*The college is able to offer a wide choice of subjects.*

You use 'be able to' with a negative to say that it is not possible for someone or something to do something.

*They are not able to run fast or throw a ball.*

**4.230** You can also use 'be unable to' to say that it is not possible for someone or something to do something.

*I am having medical treatment and I'm unable to work.*
*We are unable to comment on this.*

**4.231** You can also use 'be possible to' with 'it' as the subject to say that something is possible. You usually use this expression to say that something is possible for people in general, rather than for an individual person.

*It is possible to insure against loss of earnings.*
*Is it possible to programme a computer to speak?*

If you use 'be possible to' to say that something is possible for a particular person or group, you put 'for' and a noun group after 'possible'.

*It is possible for us to measure his progress.*
*It's possible for each department to support new members.*

You use 'be possible to' with a negative to say that something is not possible.

*It is not possible to quantify the effect.*

**4.232** You can also use 'be impossible to' to say that something is not possible.

*It is impossible to fix the exact moment in time when it happened.*
*It is impossible for most males to watch TV and talk.*

**4.233** To change the tense of 'be able to', 'be unable to', 'be possible to', or 'be impossible to', you simply change the form of 'be' to an appropriate simple tense.

*The doctor will be able to spend more time with the patient.*
*Their parents were unable to send them any money.*
*It was not possible to dismiss crowd behaviour as a contributing factor.*
*It was impossible for the husband to obey this order.*

**4.234** All modals except 'can' and 'could' can be used with these expressions.

*A machine ought to be able to do this.*
*The United States would be unable to produce any wood.*
*It may be impossible to predict which way things will develop.*

**4.235** 'Used to' can be used with 'be able to' and 'be possible to'.

*You used to be able to go to the doctor for that.*
*It used to be possible to buy second-hand wigs.*

For more information about 'used to', see paragraphs 4.258 to 4.262.

**saying**
**how likely**
**something is**

**4.236** You can use 'have to' or 'have got to' instead of 'must' to indicate that you think something is the case, because of particular facts or circumstances.

*'That looks about right.'—'It has to be.'*
*Money has got to be the reason.*

**4.237** You can use 'be going to' instead of 'will' to say that something is certain to happen or be the case in the future.

*The children are going to be fishermen or farmers.*
*Life is going to be a bit easier from now on.*

**4.238** You can use 'be bound to' to say emphatically that something is certain to happen in the future.

*Marion's bound to be back soon.*

*It was bound to happen sooner or later.*
*They'd be bound to know if it was all right.*

**giving instructions and making requests**

**4.239** Instead of beginning a question with 'can' or 'could' when you are making a request, you can begin it with 'is' and the impersonal pronoun 'it'. After 'it', you put an expression such as 'all right' and either a 'to'-infinitive clause or an 'if'-clause.

*Is it all right for him to come in and sit and read his paper?*
*Is it okay if we have lunch here?*

**4.240** You can use 'want' instead of 'would like' to give an instruction or make a request. 'Want' is more direct and less polite than 'would like'.

*I want you to turn to the front of the atlas.*

*I want to know what you think about this.*
*I want to speak to the manager.*

'Wanted' is also sometimes used. It is more polite than 'want'.

*I wanted to ask if you could give us any advice.*
*Good morning, I wanted to book a holiday in the South of France.*

**stating an intention**

**4.241** You can use 'be going to' instead of 'will' to state an intention.

*I am going to talk to Boris.*
*I'm going to show you our little school.*

**4.242** You use 'intend to' to state a fairly strong intention.

*I intend to go to Cannes for a month in August.*
*I don't intend to stay too long.*

**4.243** You use 'be determined to' or 'be resolved to' to indicate a very strong intention to do something. 'Be resolved to' is rather formal.

*I'm determined to try.*
*She was resolved to marry a rich American.*

**4.244** You can use 'have to' or 'have got to' instead of 'must' to indicate that it is important that you do something.

*I have to get home now.*
*It's something I have got to overcome.*

**expressing unwillingness**

**4.245** You can use 'I am not' instead of 'I will not' to say firmly that you are unwilling to do or accept something. 'I am not' is followed by a present participle.

*I am not staying in this hospital.*
*I'm not having dirty rugs.*

**4.246** You can use 'refuse' instead of 'will not' when you are refusing to do something. 'Refuse' is followed by a 'to'-infinitive clause.

*I refuse to list possible reasons.*
*I refuse to pay.*

**4.247** You can use 'unwilling' or 'reluctant' with a 'to'-infinitive clause to say that someone is not willing to do or accept something.

*He is unwilling to answer the questions.*

*They seemed reluctant to talk about what had happened.*

You can use several adjectives with 'not' to say that someone is unwilling to do or accept something.

*Exporters are not willing to supply goods on credit.*
*I'm not prepared to teach him anything.*
*Thompson is not keen to see history repeat itself too exactly.*

**indicating**  **4.248** You can use 'have to' or 'have got to' instead of 'must' to say that
**importance**  something is necessary or extremely important.

*The pine tree has to produce pollen in gigantic quantities.*
*We have to look more closely at the record of their work together.*
*This has got to be put right.*
*You've got to be able to communicate.*

**4.249** 'Need to' can also be used instead of 'must'.

*We need to change the balance of power.*

*You do not need to worry.*

**4.250** You can also say that something is important or necessary by using a sentence beginning with the impersonal pronoun 'it', followed by 'is', an adjective such as 'important' or 'necessary', and a 'that'-clause.

*It is important that you should know precisely what is going on.*
*It is essential that immediate action should be taken.*
*It is vital that a mother takes time to get to know her baby.*

'Important' and 'necessary' can also be followed by a 'to'-infinitive clause.

*It's important to recognise what industry needs at this moment.*
*It is necessary to examine this claim before we proceed any further.*

**4.251** You can use 'had better' instead of 'should' or 'ought to' to say that something is the right or correct thing to do. You use 'had better' with 'I' or 'we' to indicate an intention. You use it with 'you' when you are giving advice or a warning.

*I think I had better show this to my brother.*
*He decided that we had better meet.*
*You'd better go.*

# Semi-modals

**4.252** 'Dare', 'need', and 'used to' can be used as modals, or they can be used in other ways. When they are used as modals, they have some characteristics which other modals do not have. For these reasons, they are sometimes called **semi-modals**.

The use of 'dare' and 'need' as modals is explained in the following paragraphs 4.253 to 4.257.

The use of 'used to' as a modal is explained in paragraphs 4.258 to 4.262.

**'dare' and**  **4.253** When 'dare' and 'need' are used as modals, they have the same
**'need'**  meaning as when they are followed by a 'to'-infinitive clause. However, they are normally used as modals only in negative sentences and in questions.

*Nobody dare disturb him.*
*No parent dare let their child roam free.*
*With his father, he need not fear.*
*How dare you speak to me like that?*
*Need you go so soon?*

'Dare not' and 'need not' are often shortened to 'daren't' and 'needn't'.

*I daren't ring Jeremy again.*
*We needn't worry about that.*

**inflected forms** 4.254 Unlike other modals, 'dare' has some inflected forms which are occasionally used.

In the simple present tense, the third person singular form can be either 'dare' or 'dares'.

*He dare not admit he had forgotten her name.*
*What nobody dares suggest is that women be told to stay at home.*

In the simple past tense, either 'dare' or 'dared' can be used. 'Dare' is more formal than 'dared'.

*He dare not take his eyes off his assailant.*
*He dared not show he was pleased.*

'Need' is not inflected when it is used as a modal.

**use with other modals** 4.255 Normally, modals cannot be used with other modals. However 'dare' can be used with 'will', 'would', 'should', and 'might'.

*No one will dare override what the towns decide.*
*I wouldn't dare go to Europe.*
*I should not dare dogmatize about a matter such as this.*

**use with 'do'** 4.256 Unlike other modals, 'dare' can be used with the auxiliary verb 'do'.

*We do not dare examine it.*
*Don't you ever dare come here again!*

In ordinary speech, 'did not dare' and 'didn't dare' are much more common than 'dared not' or 'dare not'.

*She did not dare leave the path.*
*I didn't dare speak or move.*
*We didn't dare say that many of us would prefer to go home.*

**other uses of 'dare' and 'need'** 4.257 Besides being used as modals, 'dare' and 'need' are used in other ways in which they are not followed by the base form of another verb. Both verbs can be followed by a 'to'-infinitive clause, and 'need' is a common transitive verb.

**'used to'** 4.258 'Used to' has no inflected forms, and cannot be used with other modals.

*She used to get quite cross with Lally.*
*...these Westerns that used to do so well in Hollywood.*
*What did we used to call it?*

However, 'used to' can be used with the auxiliary verb 'do'. This is explained in paragraphs 4.261 and 4.262.

'Used' is sometimes regarded as a modal, rather than 'used to'. 'Used' is then said to be followed by a 'to'-infinitive.

4.259 'Used to' is used to say that something happened regularly or existed in the past, although it no longer happens or exists.

'Used to' is similar to 'would' when it is used to describe repeated actions in the past. However, unlike 'would', 'used to' can also describe past states and situations.

*I'm not quite as mad as I used to be.*
*You used to bring me flowers all the time.*

The use of 'would' to talk about things which happened regularly in the past is dealt with in paragraph 4.115.

**omitting the following verb group**

4.260 'Used to' can be used on its own without a following verb group when it is clear from the context what the subject matter is.

*People don't work as hard as they used to.*
*I don't feel British anymore. Not as much as I used to.*

**negatives**

4.261 'Used to' is not common in negative structures.

In informal speech, people sometimes make negative statements by putting 'didn't' in front of 'used to'.

*They didn't used to mind what we did.*

However, many people consider this use to be incorrect.

Another way to form the negative is to put 'never' in front of 'used to'.

*Where I was before, we never used to have posters on the walls.*

Sometimes 'not' is put between 'used' and 'to'. This is a fairly formal use.

*It used not to be taxable.*

Some grammar books give a contracted form for the negative, 'usedn't to' or 'usen't to'. This is now rarely used, and is thought to be very old-fashioned.

**questions**

4.262 You normally form questions with 'used to' by putting 'did' in front of the subject, followed by 'used to'. 'Wh'-questions are formed by putting the 'wh'-word at the beginning, followed by 'used to'.

*Did she used to be nice?*
*What used to annoy you most about him?*

You can form negative questions by putting 'didn't' in front of the subject, followed by the subject and 'used to'.

*Didn't they used to mind?*

In more formal English, 'did' is put in front of the subject and 'not' after it, followed by 'used to'.

*Did she not used to smile?*

# Contents of Chapter 5

# 5 Expressing time

## Introduction

**5.1** When you are making a statement, you usually need to indicate whether you are referring to a situation which exists now, existed in the past, or is likely to exist in the future. The point in time that a statement relates to is usually indicated in part by the **verb group** used in the clause.

A set of verb forms that indicate a particular point in time or period of time in the past, present, or future is called a **tense**.

The set of forms belonging to a particular tense is usually obtained by the addition of **inflections** to the base form of the verb, or by the inclusion of **auxiliaries** or **modals** in the verb group.

*smile...smiled*
*was smiling...has been smiling...had smiled*
*will smile...may smile*

Some verbs have irregular forms for past tenses.

*fight...fighting...fought*
*go...going...went*

For information about all these forms and which tenses they refer to, see the Reference Section.

**5.2** Sometimes the point in time that the clause relates to is sufficiently indicated by the tense of the verb group, and no other time reference is required. However, if you want to draw attention to the time of the action, you use an **adjunct** of time.

*She's moving tomorrow.*
*Record profits were announced last week.*
*He was better after undergoing surgery on Saturday.*

An adjunct of time can be an **adverb**, a **noun group**, or a **prepositional phrase**.

For more general information about adjuncts, see the beginning of Chapter 6.

**position of adjuncts**
**5.3** Adjuncts of time normally come at the end of a clause, after the verb or after its object if there is one. You can put more focus on the time by placing the adjunct at the beginning of the clause.

*We're getting married next year.*
*Next year, the museum is expecting even more visitors.*
*I was playing golf yesterday.*
*Yesterday the atmosphere at the factory was tense.*

If the adjunct is an adverb, it can also come immediately after 'be' or after the first auxiliary in a verb group.

*She is now pretty well-known in this country.*
*Cooper had originally been due to retire last week.*
*Public advertisements for the post will soon appear in the national press.*

adjuncts of
duration and
frequency

**5.4** Some verb forms are used to say that an event takes place
continuously over a period of time, or is repeated several times. You may
also want to say how long something lasts, or how often it happens. To do
this, **adjuncts of duration** and **adjuncts of frequency** are used.

*America has <u>always</u> been highly influential.*
*People are <u>sometimes</u> scared to say what they really think.*
*Hundreds of people are killed <u>every year</u> in fires.*
*They would go on talking <u>for hours</u>.*

Adverbs of frequency are explained and listed in paragraphs 5.114 to
5.122. Adverbs of duration are explained and listed in paragraphs 5.123
to 5.144.

**5.5** The following paragraphs describe the ways in which you can refer to
the present, the past, and the future. After each of these, there is a
section on the ways in which you use adjuncts with each tense.

There are some adjuncts which are used mainly with the past tenses.
These are explained in paragraph 5.41. Adjuncts which are used with
future tenses can be found in paragraphs 5.60 to 5.62.

subordinate
clauses

**5.6** This chapter deals only with the choice of tense in **main clauses.**
Sometimes, the point in time that a clause relates to is not indicated by
an adjunct, but by a **subordinate clause.** Subordinate clauses of time are
introduced by conjunctions which refer to time, such as 'since', 'until',
'before' and 'after'.

For information about the tense of the verb in the subordinate clause, see
paragraph 8.9.

# The present

**5.7** In situations where you are discussing an existing state of affairs, you
use a verb which is in the present tense. Usually, the verb tense is
sufficient to indicate that you are referring to the present. You normally
only use an adjunct of time for emphasis, or to refer to something which is
unrelated to the present moment.

## The present in general: the simple present

the present
moment

**5.8** If you want to talk about your thoughts and feelings at the present
moment, or about your immediate reactions to something, you use the
**simple present.**

*I'm awfully busy.*
*They both <u>taste</u> the same.*
*God, he <u>looks</u> awful.*
*I <u>want</u> a breath of fresh air.*

You can also use the simple present to talk about a physical feeling that is
affecting you or someone else.

*I <u>feel</u> heavy. I do. I <u>feel</u> drowsy.*
*My stomach <u>hurts</u>.*

Note, however, that if you are talking about physical perceptions such as seeing and hearing, you normally use the modal 'can', although the simple present is occasionally used.

*I can see the fishing boats coming in.*
*I can smell it. Can't you?*
*I see a flat stretch of ground.*
*I hear approaching feet.*

**general present including present moment**

**5.9** If you want to talk about a settled state of affairs which includes the present moment but where the particular time reference is not important, you use the simple present.

*My dad works in Saudi Arabia.*
*He lives in the French Alps near the Swiss border.*
*He is a very good brother. We love him.*
*She's a doctor's daughter.*
*Meanwhile, Atlantic City faces another dilemma.*

**general truths**

**5.10** If you want to say that something is always or generally true, you use the simple present.

*Near the equator, the sun evaporates greater quantities of water.*
*A molecule of water has two atoms of hydrogen and one of oxygen.*
*A chemical reaction occurs in the fuel cell.*
*Windmills intended for electricity generation rotate rapidly and have a small number of vanes.*

**regular or habitual actions**

**5.11** If you want to talk about something that a particular person or thing does regularly or habitually, you use the simple present.

*Do you smoke?*
*I get up early and eat my breakfast listening to the radio.*

**used in reviews**

**5.12** You usually use the simple present when you are discussing what happens in a book, play, or film.

*In the film he plays the central character of Charles Smithson.*
*In those early chapters, he does keep himself very much in the background.*

**USAGE NOTE**

**5.13** You can use the simple present of the verb 'say' when you are describing something you have read in a book.

*The criminal justice system, the author says, has failed to keep pace with the drug problem.*
*The Bible says love of money is the root of all evil.*

**used in commentaries**

**5.14** On radio and television, commentators often use the simple present when describing an event such as a sports match or a ceremony at the time that it is happening.

*He swivels, he shoots, he scores!*

**used in reporting**

**5.15** When you are reporting what someone said to you at some point in the recent past, you can use the simple present of a **reporting verb** such as 'hear' or 'tell'.

*I've never been greyhound-racing myself, but they tell me it's a fascinating sport.*
*Tamsin's a good cook, I hear.*

*Grace says you told her to come over here.*

For more detailed information about reporting verbs, see Chapter 7.

**used in commenting** **5.16** When commenting on what you are saying or doing, you use the simple present of a **performative verb** such as 'admit', 'promise', 'reject', or 'enclose'. For more information on performative verbs, see paragraphs 10.102 to 10.105.

*This, I admit, was my favourite activity.*
*I enclose a small cheque which may come in handy.*
*I leave it for you to decide.*

## Accent on the present: the present continuous

**the moment of speaking** **5.17** If you want to talk about something that is happening at the moment you are speaking, you use the **present continuous**.

*We're having a meeting. Come and join in.*
*What am I doing? I'm looking out of the window.*
*My head is aching.*
*I'm already feeling tense.*

**emphasizing the present moment** **5.18** If you want to emphasize the present moment or to indicate that a situation is temporary, you use the present continuous.

*Only one hospital, at Angal, is functioning.*
*We're trying to create a more democratic society.*
*She's spending the summer in Europe.*
*I'm working as a British Council Officer.*

**progressive change** **5.19** You also use the present continuous to indicate changes, trends, development, and progress.

*The village is changing but it is still undisturbed.*
*His handwriting is improving.*
*World energy demand is increasing at a rate of about 3% per year.*

**habitual actions** **5.20** If you want to talk about a habitual action that takes place regularly, especially one which is new or temporary, you use the present continuous.

*'You're drinking too much.'—'Only at home. No one sees me but you.'*
*Do you know if she's still playing these days?*
*She's seeing a lot more of them.*

## Emphasizing time in the present: using adjuncts

**5.21** You do not normally need to use an adjunct of time or other time expression with present tenses, but you can add them in order to emphasize the immediate present or general present, or to contrast the present with the past or future.

*They're getting on quite well at the moment.*
*We're safe now.*
*What's the matter with you today, Marnie?*
*I haven't got a grant this year.*

**general truths** **5.22** If you are using the simple present to talk about something that is always or generally true, you can reinforce or weaken your statement by using an adverb.

*Babies normally lose weight in the beginning.*
*The official attitude is usually one of ridicule.*
*Traditionally, the Japanese prefer good quality clothes.*

Here is a list of common adverbs that can be used to modify your statement in this way:

| | | | |
|---|---|---|---|
| always | mainly | often | usually |
| generally | normally | traditionally | |

The use of the simple present to talk about general truths is explained in paragraph 5.10.

**regular actions** **5.23** When you use the simple present to say that an action takes place regularly, you can use an **adjunct of frequency** to be more specific about how often it happens.

*Several groups meet weekly.*
*I visit her about once every six months.*
*It seldom rains there.*
*I never drink alone.*

The use of the simple present to talk about regular activities is explained in paragraph 5.11.

More information about adjuncts of frequency, including a list of the most common ones, can be found in paragraphs 5.114 to 5.122.

**frequent actions** **5.24** The present continuous is also used with adjuncts of frequency when you want to emphasize how often the action takes place. This is often done to express disapproval or annoyance. The adjunct of frequency is placed after the auxiliary verb.

*You're always looking for faults.*
*It's always raining.*
*And she's always talking to him on the telephone.*
*They are forever being knocked down by cars.*

The use of the present continuous to talk about frequent, habitual actions is explained in paragraph 5.20.

**adjuncts with present tenses** **5.25** Note that many adjuncts of time such as 'now' and 'today' which refer to the present time are also sometimes used with other tenses. However, there are a few adjuncts which are almost always used with present tenses.

*I'm not planning on having children at present.*

*...the camping craze that is currently sweeping America.*
*Nowadays fitness is becoming a generally accepted principle of life.*

The following is a list of adjuncts which are normally only used with the present tense:

| | | |
|---|---|---|
| at present | in this day and age | presently |
| currently | nowadays | these days |

Note that in this list the word 'presently' means 'now'.

# The past

**5.26** When talking about the past, an adjunct of time or other time expression is necessary to specify the particular time in the past you are referring to. The time reference can be established in a previous clause, and the verbs in the following clauses are therefore put in the past tense.

*It was very cold that night. Over my head was a gap in the reed matting of the roof.*
*The house was damaged by fire yesterday. No-one was injured.*

## Stating a definite time in the past: the simple past

**5.27** If you want to say that an event occurred or that something was the case at a particular time in the past, you use the **simple past**.

*The Israeli Prime Minister flew into New York yesterday to start his visit to the US.*
*Our regular window cleaner went off to Canada last year.*
*On 1 February 1968 he introduced the Industrial Expansion Bill.*
*They gave me medication to help me relax.*

**past situations** **5.28** If you want to say that a situation existed over a period of time in the past, you also use the simple past.

*He lived in Paris during his last years.*
*Throughout his life he suffered from epilepsy.*

**5.29** If you are talking about something that happened in the past, and you mention a situation that existed at that time, you use the simple past. You can do this whether or not the situation still exists.

*All the streets in this part of Watford looked alike.*
*About fifty miles from the university there was one of India's most famous and ancient Hindu temples.*

**habitual and regular actions** **5.30** If you want to talk about an activity that took place regularly or repeatedly in the past, but which no longer occurs, you use the simple past.

*We walked a great deal in my boyhood.*
*Each week we trekked to the big house.*

'Would' and 'used to' can also be used to say that something happened regularly in the past but no longer does so. See paragraphs 4.115 and 4.259 for more information.

## Accent on the past: the past continuous

**repeated actions** **5.31** If you want to talk about continued states or repeated actions which occurred in the past, you use the **past continuous**.

*Her tooth was aching, her burnt finger was hurting.*

*He was looking ill.*
*Everyone was begging the captain to surrender.*
*I was meeting thousands of people and getting to know no one.*

**contrasting events** **5.32** If you want to contrast a situation with an event which happened just after that situation existed, you use the past continuous to describe the first situation. You then use the simple past to describe and draw attention to the event which occurred after it.

*We were all sitting round the fire waiting for my soldier brother to come home. He arrived about six in the evening.*
*I was waiting angrily on Monday morning when I saw Mrs. Miller.*

# The past in relation to the present: the present perfect

**5.33** If you want to mention something that happened in the past but you do not want to state a specific time, you use the **present perfect** tense.

*They have raised £180 for a swimming pool.*
*I have noticed this trait in many photographers.*

**WARNING** **5.34** You cannot use adjuncts which place the action at a definite time in the past with the present perfect. You cannot say 'I have done it yesterday'.

You can, however, use an **adjunct of duration.**

*The settlers have left the bay forever.*
*I ate brown rice, which I have always hated, and vegetables from my garden.*

Adjuncts of duration are explained and listed in paragraphs 5.123 to 5.142.

You can also use 'since' and 'for' with the present perfect because when they are used in this way they refer to a definite time.

*They have been back every year since then.*
*She has worked for him for ten years.*

For more information on 'since' see paragraph 5.137. Other uses of 'for' are explained in paragraphs 5.125 to 5.128.

**situations that still exist** **5.35** If you want to talk about an activity or situation that started at some time in the past, continued, and is still happening now, you use the present perfect or the **present perfect continuous.**

*All my adult life I have waited for the emergence of a strong centre party.*
*She's always felt that films should be entertaining.*
*National productivity has been declining.*
*I have been dancing since I was a child.*

**emphasizing duration of event** **5.36** If you want to emphasize the duration of a recent event, you use the present perfect continuous.

*She's been crying.*
*It will no doubt be argued by some that what I have been describing is not a crisis of industry.*

*The Department of Aboriginal Affairs has recently been conducting a survey of Australian Aborigines.*

## Events before a particular time in the past: the past perfect

**5.37** If you want to talk about a past event or situation that occurred before a particular time in the past, you use the **past perfect**.

*One day he noticed that a culture plate had become contaminated by a mould.*
*Before the war, he had worked as a bank manager.*
*She had lost her job as a real estate agent and was working as a waitress.*
*I detested any form of games and had always managed to avoid children's parties.*

**emphasizing time and duration**
**5.38** If you want to emphasize the recentness and the duration of a continuous activity which took place before a particular time in the past, you use the **past perfect continuous**.

*Until now the rumours that had been circulating were exaggerated versions of the truth.*
*The doctor had been working alone.*
*He died in hospital where he had been receiving treatment for cancer.*
*They had been hitting our trucks regularly.*

**expectations and wishes**
**5.39** If you want to say that something was expected, wished for, or intended before a particular time in the past, you use the past perfect or the past perfect continuous.

*She had naturally assumed that once there was a theatre everybody would want to go.*
*It was the remains of a ten-rupee note which she had hoped would last till the end of the week.*
*It was not as nice on the terrace as Clarissa had expected.*
*I had been expecting some miraculous obvious change.*

## Emphasizing time in the past: using adjuncts

**5.40** When you are using past tenses, you normally use an adjunct of time at some point to indicate that you are talking about the past.

*At one time the arts of reading and writing were classed among the great mysteries of life for the majority of people.*
*I've made some poor decisions lately, but I'm feeling much better now.*
*It was very splendid once, but it's only a ruin now.*
*It's Mark who lost his wife. A year last January.*
*It was terribly hot yesterday.*

**types of adjuncts**
**5.41** Adjuncts of time can refer either to a specific time, or to a more general indefinite period of time.

The lists below give the most common adjuncts of indefinite time which are used mainly with past tenses. With the exception of 'since' and 'ever since' which come at the end of a clause, you put them after the auxiliary or modal in a verb group which has more than one word. If you use them with the simple past, you put them in front of the verb.

The words in the following list can be used with all past tenses:

| | | | |
|---|---|---|---|
| again | ever since | in the past | previously |
| already | finally | just | recently |
| earlier | first | last | since |

The words in the following list can be used with all past tenses except the present perfect:

| | | |
|---|---|---|
| afterwards | formerly | once |
| at one time | immediately | originally |
| eventually | next | subsequently |

Note that 'once' here means 'at some time in the past'. For its uses as an adverb of frequency, see paragraph 5.115.

For the uses of 'since' as a preposition in adjuncts of time, see paragraph 5.137.

Some adjuncts used with past tenses are more specific. If you want to be more exact about the time reference, you use adjuncts which include the word 'yesterday', and those involving time expressions such as 'ago', 'other' and 'last'. Note that 'ago' is placed after the noun group.

I saw him *yesterday evening*.
We bought the house from her *the day before yesterday*.
*Three weeks ago* I was staying in San Francisco.
I saw my goddaughter *the other day*.
It all happened *a long time ago*.

**WARNING**

5.42 You say 'last night', not 'yesterday night'.

**used for emphasis**

5.43 There are some cases where adjuncts have to be used to specify the time reference. In other cases, you may simply want to make the timing of the action clear, or emphatic. These uses are described below.

**used with the simple past**

5.44 When you use the simple past to describe habitual or regular activities, you can use an **adjunct of frequency** to indicate the regularity or repetition of the activity.

He *often agreed* to work quite cheaply.
*Sometimes* he *read* so much that he *became* confused.
Etta *phoned* Guppy *every day*.

The use of the simple past to describe habitual actions is explained in paragraph 5.30.

**used with the past continuous**

5.45 If you are using the past continuous to talk about repeated actions, you can add an adjunct of frequency such as 'always' or 'forever' after the auxiliary to emphasize the frequency of the action or to express your annoyance about it.

In the immense shed where we worked, something *was always going wrong*.
She *was always knitting* – making sweaters or baby clothes.
Our builder *was forever going* on skiing holidays.

The use of the past continuous to describe repeated actions is explained in paragraph 5.31.

**used with the present perfect**

**5.46** When you use the present perfect to mention something that is still relevant to the present, you can add an adjunct of frequency to indicate that the action was repeated.

*I've often wondered why we didn't move years ago.*
*Political tensions have frequently spilled over into violence.*

The use of the present perfect to talk about situations which are still relevant is explained in paragraph 5.33.

**5.47** Note that if you are talking about a quality, attitude, or possession that still exists or is still relevant, you need to use the present perfect with an adjunct of duration.

*We've had it for fifteen years.*
*He's always liked you, you know.*
*I have known him for years.*
*My people have been at war since 1917.*

**5.48** If you use the present perfect and the present perfect continuous to mention a continuing activity that began in the past, you can add an adjunct of duration to indicate how long it has been going on.

*For about a week he had been complaining of a bad headache.*
*They have been meeting together weekly now for two years.*
*He has looked after me well since his mother died.*

The use of the present perfect and the present perfect continuous to talk about activities that began in the past is explained in paragraph 5.35.

**used with the past perfect**

**5.49** When you use the past perfect to describe a repeated event that took place before a particular time in the past, you use an adjunct of frequency to indicate how often it was repeated.

*Posy had always sought her out even then.*
*The house keeper mentioned that the dog had attacked its mistress more than once.*

The use of the past perfect to describe events that occurred before a particular time in the past are explained in paragraph 5.37.

**5.50** If you are using the past perfect to talk about a situation which did not change in the past, you use an adjunct of duration to emphasize the length of time during which it existed.

*They weren't really our aunt and uncle, but we had always known them.*
*All through those many years he had never ever lost track of my father.*
*His parents had been married for twelve years when he was born.*

**5.51** If you are using the past perfect continuous to mention a recent, continuous activity, you can specify when it began by using an adjunct.

*The Home Office had until now been insisting on giving the officers only ten days to reach a settlement.*
*Since then, the mother had been living with her daughter.*

Adjuncts of frequency or duration can also be added for emphasis.

*The drive increased the fatigue she had been feeling for hours.*
*The rain had been pouring all night.*

The use of the past perfect continuous to talk about a recent, continuous activity is explained in paragraph 5.38.

# The future

**5.52** It is not possible to talk with as much certainty about the future as it is about the present or the past. Any reference you make to future events is therefore usually an expression of what you think might happen or what you intend to happen.

## Indicating the future using 'will'

**5.53** If you want to say that something is planned to happen, or that you think it is likely to happen in the future, you use the **modal** 'will' in front of the base form of the verb. This is called the **future tense**.

*Nancy will arrange it.*
*These will be dealt with in chapter 7.*
*'I will check,' said Brody.*
*When will I see them?*
*What do you think Sally will do?*
*You will come back, won't you?*

If the subject is 'I' or 'we' the modal 'shall' is sometimes used instead of 'will' to talk about future events.

*I shall do everything I can to help you.*
*You will stay at home and I shall go to your office.*
*'We shall give him some tea,' Naomi said.*

'Will' and 'shall' are also used in several ways as modals. For more information, see Chapter 4.

**general truths**
**5.54** If you want to talk about general truths and to say what can be expected to happen if a particular situation arises, you use the future tense.

*When peace is available, people will go for it.*
*An attack of malaria can keep a man off work for three days. He will earn nothing and his family will go hungry.*

**indicating certainty**
**5.55** If you are sure that something will happen because arrangements have been made, you can use the **future continuous** tense.

*I'll be seeing them when I've finished with you.*
*She'll be appearing tomorrow and Sunday at the Royal Festival Hall.*
*I'll be waiting for you outside.*
*I understand you'll be moving into our area soon.*
*They'll spoil our picnic. I'll be wondering all the time what's happening.*
*Our people will be going to their country more.*

Note that an adjunct of time or an adjunct of frequency is normally required with the future continuous tense.

**5.56** If you are referring to something that has not happened yet but will happen before a particular time in the future, you can use the **future perfect** tense.

*By the time you get to the school, the concert will have finished.*
*Maybe by the time we get to the dock he'll already have started.*

*Maybe when you come up, you'll have heard from your sister.*

Note that you must indicate the future time referred to by using an adjunc or another clause.

**indicating**    **5.57** If you want to indicate the duration of an event at a specific time in
**duration**    the future, you can use the **future perfect continuous**.

*By then, a date for a trial will have been made.*
*The register will have been running for a year in May.*

Note that you need to use an adjunct of time to indicate the future time and an adjunct of duration to state the duration of the event.

## Other ways of indicating the future

**'be going to'**    **5.58** If you think the event you are referring to will happen quite soon or i
you are stating your intention that it will happen, you can use 'be going to
followed by an **infinitive**.

*I'm going to explore the neighbourhood.*
*Evans knows lots of people. He's going to help me. He's going to take me there.*
*You're going to have a heart attack if you're not careful.*
*We're going to see a change in the law next year.*

**planned**    **5.59** You can also use 'be due to' and 'be about to' to refer to planned
**events**    future events that you expect to happen soon. They are followed by
infinitive clauses.

*He is due to start as a courier shortly.*
*The work is due to be started in the summer.*
*Another 385 people are about to lose their jobs.*
*Are we about to be taken over by the machine?*

## Adjuncts with future tenses

**vague**    **5.60** When you want to make a general or vague reference to future time
**time**    you use an adjunct which refers to indefinite time.
**reference**

*I'll drop by sometime.*
*Sooner or later he'll ask you to join him there.*
*In future she'll have to take sedentary work of some sort.*

Here is a list of adjuncts of indefinite time which are used mainly with future tenses:

| | | |
|---|---|---|
| in future | one of these days | sometime |
| in the future | some day | sooner or later |

**'tomorrow'**    **5.61** Adjuncts which include the word 'tomorrow' are mainly used with
future tenses.

*We'll try somewhere else tomorrow.*
*Shall I come tomorrow night?*

He'll be here *the day after tomorrow.*
*This time tomorrow* I'll be in New York.

**'next'** **5.62** Some adjuncts mainly used with future tenses involve time
expressions with 'next'. If you are using a specific day or month such as
'Saturday' or 'October', you can put 'next' either before or after the day or
month. Otherwise, 'next' is placed in front of the time reference.

*Next week* Michael Hall will be talking about music.
*Next summer* your crops will be very much better.
I think we'll definitely be going *next year.*
Will your accommodation be available *next October?*
The boots will be ready by *Wednesday next.*
A post mortem examination will be held on *Monday next.*
She won't be able to do it *the week after next.*

# Other uses of tenses

**5.63** So far in this chapter, we have dealt with the commonest and
simplest uses of the various tenses. However, there are also some less
common uses of tenses.

## Vivid narrative

**present** **5.64** Stories are normally told using past tenses. However, if you want to
**tenses** make a story seem vivid, as if it were happening now, you can use present
tenses, the **simple present** for actions and states and the **present
continuous** for situations.

*There's* a loud explosion behind us. Then I *hear* Chris giggling. Sylvia *is*
*upset.*
The helicopter *climbs over* the frozen wasteland.
Chris *is crying* hard and others *look* over from the other tables.
He *sits down* at his desk chair, *reaches* for the telephone and *dials* a
number.

## Firm plans for the future

**present** **5.65** Both the **simple present** and the **present continuous** can be used to
**tenses** state firm plans that you have for the future. An adjunct is necessary
unless you are sure that the hearer or reader knows that you are talking
about the future.

My last train *leaves* Euston *at 11.30.*
The UN General Assembly *opens* in New York *later this month.*
*Tomorrow night* we *exchange* packages.
*I'm leaving* at the end of this week.
My mum *is coming* to help look after the new baby.

## Forward planning from a time in the past

**5.66** There are several ways of talking about an event which was in the
future at a particular time in the past, or which was thought to be going to
occur. These are described in the following paragraphs.

<table>
<tr><td>

**events<br>planned<br>in the past**

</td><td>

**5.67** The **past continuous** can be used to refer to events planned in the past, especially with some common verbs such as 'come' and 'go'.

*Four of them <u>were coming</u> for Sunday lunch.*
*Her daughter <u>was going</u> to a summer camp tomorrow.*
*My wife <u>was joining</u> me later with the two children.*

</td></tr>
</table>

**5.68** The **simple past** of 'be' can be used in structures used to express future events, such as 'be going to', 'be about to', and 'be due to'. The implication is usually that the expected event has not happened or will not happen. For more information on 'be going to', see paragraph 4.237.

*I thought for a moment that she <u>was going to cry</u>.*
*He <u>was about to raise</u> his voice at me but stopped himself.*
*The ship <u>was due to sail</u> the following morning.*

# Timing by adjuncts

**5.69** In many statements, it is the adjunct rather than the tense of the verb which carries the time reference. For this reason, many adjuncts can be used with more than one set of tenses, because they refer to time and not to tense.

For example, a common use is to put adjuncts which normally refer to future time with the present tense when it is used to refer to future actions, including habitual actions. They can also be used with references to the future that are made in the past.

*The company <u>celebrates</u> its 50th anniversary <u>this year</u>.*
*After all, you're <u>coming</u> back <u>next week</u>.*
*The farmer just laughed and rode away. So <u>the next week I tried</u> my luck at another farm.*
*We <u>arranged</u> to meet <u>in three week's time</u>.*

The adjuncts 'now', 'today', 'tonight' and those involving 'this' refer to a period of time which includes the present moment. They are used fairly commonly with all tenses. This is because an event can be located before, during, or after the time specified by the tense of the verb.

*I was <u>now</u> in a Scottish regiment.*
*Your boss will <u>now</u> have no alternative but to go to his superiors and explain the situation.*
*One of my children wrote to me <u>today</u>.*
*I will ski no more <u>today</u>.*
*It's dark <u>today</u>.*
*'I went to the doctor <u>this morning</u>,' she said.*
*He won't be able to fight <u>this Friday</u>.*
*I'm doing my ironing <u>this afternoon</u>.*

<table>
<tr><td>

**relative time**

</td><td>

**5.70** If you want to refer to a period of time in relation to another period of time, or in relation to an event, you use an adjunct. For example, you can use an adverb such as 'soon' or 'later' to refer to time which follows a particular event or period of time, and you can use an adverb such as 'beforehand' or 'earlier' to refer to time which preceded a particular period of time or an event.

*Sita was delighted with the house and <u>soon</u> began to look upon it as home.*

</td></tr>
</table>

*It'll have to be replaced <u>soon.</u>*
*He <u>later</u> settled in Peddie, a small town near Grahamstown.*
*I'll explain <u>later.</u>*
*I was very nervous <u>beforehand.</u>*
*You'll be having a bath and going to the hairdresser's <u>beforehand.</u>*
*She had seen him only <u>five hours earlier.</u>*

This type of time reference is common with past and future tenses. It is sometimes used with present tenses when they are used to refer to past, future, or habitual actions.

*Sometimes I <u>know beforehand</u> what I'm going to talk about.*
*I <u>remember the next day</u> at school going round asking the boys if they'd ever seen a ghost.*
*But <u>afterwards,</u> as you <u>read</u> on, you <u>relate</u> back to it.*

Here is a list of adjuncts which are used to refer to time in a relative way:

| | | |
|---|---|---|
| afterwards | suddenly | the week after |
| at once | within minutes | the month after |
| before long | within the hour | the year after |
| eventually | ~ | ~ |
| finally | the next day | beforehand |
| immediately | the next week | early |
| in a moment | the next month | earlier |
| instantly | the next year | earlier on |
| later | the following day | in advance |
| later on | the following week | late |
| presently | the following month | one day |
| shortly | the following year | on time |
| soon | the day after | punctually |

Note that in this list 'presently' means 'soon'.

You can use 'early' to indicate that something happens before the expected or planned time, and 'late' to indicate that it happens after that time. 'On time', and 'punctually' are used to indicate that something happens at the planned time.

These adverbs come after the verb and at the end of the clause.

*Tired out, he had gone to bed <u>early.</u>*
*If you get to work <u>early,</u> you can get a lot done.*
*He had come to the political arena <u>late,</u> at the age of 62.*
*We went quite <u>late</u> in the afternoon.*
*If Atkinson phoned <u>on time,</u> he'd be out of the house in well under an hour.*
*He arrived <u>punctually.</u>*

With 'early' and 'late' you can also use the comparative forms 'earlier' and 'later'.

*I woke <u>earlier</u> than usual.*
*<u>Later,</u> the dealer saw that it had been sold.*

Note that 'early', 'late', and 'on time' are also used as complements.

*The door bell rang. Barbara was appalled. 'They're <u>early.</u>'*
*The Paris train was slightly <u>late.</u>*
*What time is it now? This bus is usually <u>on time.</u>*

For more information on complements, see paragraph 3.128.

**5.71** You can also specify a time by relating it to an event, using a qualifying expression or a relative clause after the time expression.

*I didn't sleep well the night before the prosecution.*
*I called him the day I got back.*

**5.72** You can also use some prepositions to relate events to each other, or to particular periods of time. These prepositions are listed in paragraph 5.99, and there is a full explanation in paragraphs 5.102 to 5.107.

*After the war, he returned to teaching.*
*Joseph had been married prior to his marriage to Mary.*
*Wages have fallen during the last two months.*

**necessary time**

**5.73** If you want to refer to a 'necessary time', beyond which an event will no longer be relevant, useful, or successful, you can use 'in time' as an adjunct or a complement.

*I would have to do some fast hiking over the hills to reach the rendezvous in time.*
*He leapt back, in time to dodge the lashing hooves.*

If something happens before the necessary time, you can use 'too early', and if it happens after the necessary time, you can use 'too late'. 'Too early' and 'too late' may be used as adjuncts or as complements.

*Today they hear too much about sex too early.*
*It's much too early to assess the community service scheme.*
*They arrived too late for the information to be any good.*
*It's too late to change that now.*

**previously mentioned time**

**5.74** If the time you are referring to in the past or future has already been mentioned, you can use the adverb 'then'.

*We kept three monkeys then.*
*We were all so patriotic then.*
*It'll be too late then.*

To be more specific, you can use 'that' with the name of a day, month, season, and so on, or with a general time word.

*William didn't come in that Tuesday.*
*So many people will be pursuing other activities that night.*

# Emphasizing the unexpected: continuing, stopping, or not happening

**5.75** If you want to comment on the existence of the relationship between past, present, and future situations, you can use one of the following adjuncts:

| | | | |
|---|---|---|---|
| already | as yet | still | yet |
| any longer | no longer | up till now | |
| any more | so far | up to now | |

**'still' for existing situations**

**5.76** If you want to say that a situation exists up to the present time, you use 'still'. If you are using 'be' as a main verb or an auxiliary verb, you put 'still' after 'be' or the auxiliary. If you are using any simple verb except 'be', you put 'still' in front of the verb. 'Still' often suggests that the continuation of the situation is surprising or undesirable.

*It's a marvel that I'm still alive to tell the tale.*

*Male prejudice still exists in certain quarters.*
*Years had passed and they were still paying them off.*

In negative statements which use the 'n't' contraction, 'still' is placed in front of 'be' or the auxiliary.

*We've been working on it for over two years now. And it still isn't finished.*
*We still don't know where we're going.*

**'still'
for expected
situations**

**5.77** You can also use 'still' in front of a 'to'-infinitive to say that something has not happened yet, although it is expected to, or you feel that it should.

*The Government had still to agree on the provisions of the bill.*
*The problems were still to come.*
*There are many other questions still to be answered.*

'Still' is not used in negative statements in this way; see paragraph 5.78 for a similar use of 'yet'.

**'yet'
for expected
situations**

**5.78** If you want to indicate that something has not happened up to the present time, but is likely to happen in the future, you use 'yet' with a negative. 'Yet' usually comes at the end of a sentence.

*We don't know the terms yet.*
*I haven't set any work yet. I suppose I shall some day.*
*They haven't heard yet.*

If you want to sound more emphatic, you can put 'yet' before a simple verb or after the auxiliary and negative word.

*No one yet knows exactly what it means.*
*Her style had not yet matured.*

'Yet' can also be used in questions, where it is usually put at the end of the clause.

*Has she had the baby yet?*
*Has Mr. Harris not come yet?*

**5.79** You can also use 'yet' in affirmative statements to say that something that is expected has not happened up to the present time. In this case, 'yet' is followed by a 'to'-infinitive clause.

*The true history of art in post-war America is yet to be written.*
*He had yet to attempt to put principles into practice.*

**5.80** 'Yet' is also used in affirmative statements with superlatives to indicate that the statement applies up to the present, but may not apply in the future. 'Yet' normally comes at the end of the clause.

*This is the best museum we've visited yet.*
*Mr. Fowler said that February had produced the best results yet.*
*This would be the biggest and best version yet.*

**likely change**

**5.81** If you want to say that a situation which has existed up to the present time may change in the future, you can use 'as yet', 'so far', 'up to now', or 'up till now'. They are normally placed either at the beginning or the end of the clause. They are also occasionally placed after an auxiliary verb.

*As yet, no group has claimed responsibility for the attack.*
*Only Mother knows as yet.*
*So far, the terms of the treaty have been carried out according to schedule.*

*You've done well so far, Mrs Rutland.*
*Up till now, the most extraordinary remark I remember was made by you.*
*...something he had up to now been reluctant to provide.*
*It's been quiet so far.*
*You haven't once up till now come into real contact with our authorities.*

Note that these expressions can be used in affirmative and negative statements.

**past not present**

**5.82** If you want to say that a past situation does not exist in the present, you can use 'no longer', or a negative with 'any longer' or 'any more'.

*She was no longer content with a handful of coins.*
*They didn't know any longer what was funny and what was entertaining.*
*They don't live together any more.*

**'already' for emphasizing occurrence**

**5.83** If you want to emphasize that a situation exists, rather than not yet having occurred, you use 'already'. It is usually put in front of any simple verb except 'be', or after 'be' as a main verb, or following an auxiliary verb.

*The energy already exists in the ground.*
*Senegal already has a well established film industry.*
*He was just a year younger than Rudolph, but was already as tall and much stockier.*
*My watch says nine o'clock. And it's already too hot to sleep.*
*We have already advertised your post in the papers.*
*Britain is already exporting a little coal.*

You can put 'already' at the beginning or the end of the clause for emphasis.

*Already, robberies and lootings have increased.*
*I was happy for her; she looked better already.*

'Already' is not often used with the simple past tense, except with the verbs 'be', 'have', and 'know'.

Note that 'already' cannot normally be used in negative statements, but can be used in negative 'if'-clauses, negative questions, and relative clauses.

*Refer certain types of death to the coroner if this has not already been done.*
*Those who have not already left are being advised to do so.*
*What does it show us that we haven't already felt?*

# Time expressions and prepositional phrases

## Specific times

**5.84** Specific time expressions are used as complements when you want to state the current time, day, or year.

*'Well what time is it now?'—'It's one o'clock'.*
*It was a perfect May morning.*

*Six weeks isn't all that long ago, it's January.*

They are also often used in prepositional phrases to say when something happened, or when it is expected to happen.

*I got there at about 8 o'clock.*
*The submarine caught fire on Friday morning.*
*That train gets in at 1800 hours.*

**clock times**   **5.85** Clock times are usually expressed in terms of hours and parts of an hour or minutes, for example 'one o'clock', 'five minutes past one', 'one twenty', 'half past one'. The day is usually divided into two sets of twelve hours, so it is sometimes necessary to specify which set you mean by adding 'a.m.', 'p.m.', or a prepositional phrase such as 'in the morning' or 'in the evening'.

In many official contexts, a twenty-four hour system is used.

If the hour is known, only the minutes are specified: 'five past, ten to, quarter to, half past' and so on. 'Midday' and 'noon' are occasionally used.

**times of**   **5.86** The most frequently used words for periods of the day are 'morning',
**the day**   'afternoon', 'evening', and 'night'. There are also some words which refer to the rising and setting of the sun, such as 'dusk' and 'sunset', and others which refer to mealtimes.

*On a warm, cloudy evening, Colin went down to the river.*
*They seem to be working from dawn to dusk.*
*Most of the trouble comes outside the classroom, at break-time and dinner-time.*

Here is a list of words that are used to talk about periods of the day:

| morning | daybreak | ~ | teatime |
|---|---|---|---|
| afternoon | first light | daytime | dinnertime |
| evening | sunrise | night-time | suppertime |
| night | dusk | breakfast-time | bedtime |
| ~ | sunset | break-time | |
| dawn | nightfall | lunchtime | |

**naming days**   **5.87** The seven days of the week are **proper nouns**:

| Monday | Thursday |
|---|---|
| Tuesday | Friday |
| Wednesday | Saturday |
| | Sunday |

Saturday and Sunday are often referred to as 'the weekend', and the other days as 'weekdays'.

A few days in the year have special names, for example:

| New Year's Day | Easter Monday | Christmas Day |
|---|---|---|
| St Valentine's Day | Halloween | Boxing Day |
| Good Friday | Christmas Eve | New Year's Eve |

You can also name a day by giving its date using an **ordinal** number.

*'When does your term end?'—'First of July'.*
*The Grand Prix is to be held here on the 18th July.*

*Her season of films continues until <u>October the ninth</u>.*

You can omit the month if it is clear from the context which month you are referring to.

*So Monday will be the <u>seventeenth</u>.*
*St Valentine's Day is on the <u>fourteenth</u>.*

There is more information about ordinals in the Reference Section.

**months, seasons, and dates**

**5.88** The twelve months of the year are also **proper nouns**:

| | | |
|---|---|---|
| January | May | September |
| February | June | October |
| March | July | November |
| April | August | December |

There are four seasons: 'spring', 'summer', 'autumn' ('fall' in American English) and 'winter'. 'Springtime', 'summertime' and 'wintertime' are also used.

Some periods of the year have special names; for example, 'Christmas', 'Easter', and 'the New Year'.

**years, decades, and centuries**

**5.89** Years are referred to in English by numbers.

*...the eleventh of January, <u>1967</u>.*
*A second conference was held in February <u>1988</u>.*
*My mother died in <u>1945</u>.*

To refer to periods longer than a year, decades (ten years) and centuries (a hundred years) are used. Decades start with a year ending in zero and finish with a year ending in nine: 'the 1960s' (1960 to 1969), 'the 1820's (1820 to 1829). If the century is already known, it can be omitted: 'the 20s', 'the twenties', 'the Twenties'.

To be more specific, for example in historical dates, 'AD' is added before or after the numbers for years or centuries after Christ is believed to have been born: '1650 AD', 'AD 1650', 'AD 1650-53', '1650-53 AD'. 'BC' is added after the numbers for years or centuries before Christ is believed to have been born: '1500 BC', '12-1500 BC'.

Centuries start with a year ending in two zeroes and finish with a year ending in two nines. Ordinals are used to refer to them. The 'first century' was from '0 AD' to '99 AD', the 'second century' was '100-199 AD', and so on, so the period '1800-1899 AD' was the 'nineteenth century' and we are currently in the 'twentieth century' (1900-1999 AD). Centuries can also be written using numbers: 'the 20th century'.

**'at' for specific times**

**5.90** If you want to say when something happens, you use 'at' with clock times, periods of the year, and periods of the day except for 'morning', 'evening', 'afternoon', and 'daytime'.

*Our train went <u>at 2.25</u>.*
*I got up <u>at eight o'clock</u>.*
*The train should arrive <u>at a quarter to one</u>.*
*You should go to church <u>at Easter</u> and <u>Christmas</u>.*
*I went down and fetched her back <u>at the weekend</u>.*
*On Tuesday evening, just <u>at dusk</u>, Brody had received an anonymous phone call.*
*He regarded it as his duty to come and read to me <u>at bedtime</u>.*
*<u>At night</u> we kept them shut up in a wire enclosure.*
*Let the fire burn out now. Who would see smoke <u>at night-time</u> anyway?*

You can also use 'at' with 'time' and similar words such as 'moment' and 'juncture' and with units of clock time such as 'hour' and 'minute'.

*General de Gaulle duly attended the military ceremony <u>at the appointed time</u>.*
*It was <u>at this juncture</u> that his luck temporarily deserted him.*
*If I could have done it <u>at that minute</u> I would have killed him.*
*There were no lights <u>at this hour,</u> and roads, bungalows and gardens lay quiet.*

**'at' for relating events**

**5.91** You can also use 'at' when you want to relate the time of one event to another event such as a party, journey, election, and so on.

*I had first met Kruger <u>at a party</u> at the British Embassy.*
*She represented the Association <u>at the annual meeting of the American Medical Association</u> in Chicago.*
*It is to be reopened <u>at the annual conference</u> in three weeks' time.*

**5.92** 'At' is also used with ages, stages of development, and points within a larger period of time:

*<u>At the age of twenty,</u> she married another Spanish dancer.*
*He left school <u>at seventeen</u>.*
*<u>At an early stage of the war</u> the British Government began recruiting a team of top mathematicians and electronics experts.*
*We were due to return to the United Kingdom <u>at the beginning of March.</u>*

**'in' for periods of time**

**5.93** If you want to mention the period of time in which something happens, you use 'in' with centuries, years, seasons, months, and the periods of the day 'morning', 'afternoon' and 'evening'. You also use 'in' with 'daytime' and 'night-time'.

*<u>In the sixteenth century</u> there were three tennis courts.*
*It's true that we expected a great deal <u>in the sixties.</u>*
*Americans visiting Sweden <u>in the early 1950's</u> were astounded by its cleanliness.*
*If you were to go on holiday on the continent <u>in wintertime</u> what sport could you take part in?*
*To be in Cornwall at any time is a pleasure, to be here <u>in summer</u> is a bonus.*
*It's a lot cooler <u>in the autumn.</u>*
*She will preside over the annual meeting of the Court <u>in December.</u>*
*<u>In September</u> I travelled to California to see the finished film.*
*I'll ring the agent <u>in the morning.</u>*
*Well, she does come in to clean the rooms <u>in the day-time.</u>*

Note that if 'morning', 'afternoon', and 'evening' are used with a modifier or a qualifier, you use 'on'. See paragraph 5.95 for details.

**'in' for specific time**

**5.94** 'In' is also used when you want to specify a period of time, minutes, hours, days, and so on, using an **ordinal**.

*Vehicle sales <u>in the first eight months</u> of the year have plunged by 24.4 per cent.*
*...<u>in the early hours</u> of the morning.*

'In' is also used with some other nouns referring to events and periods of time.

*My father was killed <u>in the war.</u>*
*Everyone does unusual jobs <u>in wartime.</u>*
*<u>In the holidays,</u> we tend to get up later.*

*Two people came to check my cabin in my absence.*
Ordinals are explained in paragraphs 2.249 to 2.256.

**'on' for short periods of time**

**5.95** If you want to mention the day when something happens, you use 'on'. You can do this with named days, with days referred to by ordinals, and with days referred to by a special term such as 'birthday' or 'anniversary'.

*I'll send the cheque round on Monday.*
*Everybody went to church on Christmas Day.*
*I hear you have bingo on Wednesday.*
*Pentonville Prison was set up on Boxing Day, 1842.*
*He was born on 3 April 1925 at 40 Grosvenor Road.*
*...the grey suit Elsa had bought for him on his birthday.*
*Many of Eisenhower's most cautious commanders were even prepared to risk attack on the eighth or ninth.*
*...addressing Parliament on the 36th anniversary of his country's independence.*

You can use 'the' with named days for emphasis or contrast, and 'a' to indicate any day of that name.

*He died on the Friday and was buried on the Sunday.*
*We get a lot of calls on a Friday.*

You also use 'on' with 'morning', 'afternoon', 'evening', and 'night' when they are modified or qualified.

*...at 2.30 p.m. on a calm afternoon.*
*There was another important opening on the same evening.*
*Tickets will be available on the morning of the performance.*
*It's terribly good of you to turn out on a night like this.*

**'on' for longer periods of time**

**5.96** 'On' is also used with words indicating travel such as 'journey', 'trip', 'voyage', 'flight' and 'way' to say when something happened.

*But on that journey, for the first time, Luce's faith in the eventual outcome was shaken.*
*Eileen was accompanying her father to visit friends made on a camping trip the year before.*

**'on' for subsequent events**

**5.97** 'On' can be used in a slightly formal way with nouns and 'ing'-forms referring to actions or activities to indicate that one event occurs after another.

*I shall bring the remaining seven hundred pounds on my return in eleven days.*
*On being called 'young lady', she laughed.*

**ordering of time expressions**

**5.98** On the few occasions when people have to specify a time and date exactly, for example in legal English or formal documents, the usual order is: clock time, followed by period of day, day of the week, and date.

*...at eight o'clock on the morning of 29 October 1618.*
*...on the night of Thursday July 16.*

# Non-specific times

**approximate times**

**5.99** If you want to be less precise about when something happened, you can use an approximating adverb or approximating expression. It is also possible to use prepositions to relate events to less specific points or periods of time, for example when the exact time of an event is not known, or when events happen gradually, continuously, or several times.

*At about four o'clock in the morning, we were ambushed.*
*The device that exploded at around midnight on Wednesday severely damaged the fourth-floor bar.*
*The supply of servants continued until about 1950, then abruptly dried up.*
*He developed central chest pain during the night.*
*For, also over the summer, his book had come out.*
*The attack began shortly before dawn.*

Here is a list of approximating adverbs and expressions:

| | | | |
|---|---|---|---|
| about | just after | round about | soon after |
| almost | just before | shortly after | thereabouts |
| around | nearly | shortly before | |

'About', 'almost', 'around', 'nearly', and 'round about', are usually used with clock times or years. With 'about', 'around', and 'round about', the preposition 'at' can often be omitted in informal English.

*Then quite suddenly, round about midday, my mood began to change.*
*About nine o'clock he went out to the kitchen.*

Here is a list of prepositions which are used to relate events to a non-specific time:

| | | | |
|---|---|---|---|
| after | by | following | prior to |
| before | during | over | |

**WARNING**

**5.100** 'Almost' or 'nearly' can only be used after the verb 'be'.

**5.101** You can also use 'or thereabouts' after the time expression.

*Back in 1975 or thereabouts someone lent me an article about education.*
*...at four o'clock or thereabouts.*

**'during' for periods of time**

**5.102** 'During' can be used instead of 'in' with periods of the day, months, seasons, years, decades, and centuries.

*We try to keep people informed by post during September.*
*She heated the place during the winter with a huge wood furnace.*
*During 1973 an Anti-Imperialist Alliance was formed.*
*During the Sixties various levies were imposed.*
*During the seventh century incendiary weapons were invented.*
*They used to spend the whole Sunday at chapel but most of them behaved shockingly during the week.*

**5.103** 'During' can be used with most event nouns to indicate that one event takes place while another is occurring:

*During his stay in prison, he has written many essays and poems.*
*...trying to boost police morale during a heated battle with rioters.*
*The young princes were protected from press intrusion during their education.*
*Some families live in the kitchen during a power cut.*
*During the journey I came to like and respect them.*

**WARNING**

**5.104** 'During the week' means on weekdays, in contrast to the weekend.

**'over' for events**

**5.105** 'Over' can be used with 'winter', 'summer', and special periods of the year to indicate that an event occurred throughout the period or at an unspecified time during it.

*...to help keep their families going <u>over the winter</u>.*
*My friends had a marvellous time <u>over the New Year</u>.*

'Over' is also used when referring to a period of time immediately before or after the time of speaking or the time being talked about.

*The number will increase considerably <u>over the next decade</u>.*
*They have been doing all they can <u>over the past twenty-four hours</u>.*
*We packed up the things I had accumulated <u>over the last four years</u>.*

'Over' can be used with meals and items of food or drink to indicate that something happens while people are eating or drinking.

*Davis said he wanted to read it <u>over lunch</u>.*
*Can we discuss it <u>over a cup of coffee</u>?*

**relating**
**events**
**and times**

**5.106** You can also be more general by stating the relationship between an event and a period of time or specific point in time.

'Before', 'prior to', and 'after' can be used to relate events to a time.

*She gets up <u>before six</u>.*
*If you're stuck come back and see me <u>before Thursday</u>.*
*...the construction of warships by the major powers <u>prior to 1914</u>.*
*City Music Hall is going to close down <u>after Easter</u>.*
*He will announce his plans <u>after the holidays</u>.*

They can also be used to relate one event to another.

*I was in a bank for a while <u>before the war</u>.*
*She gave me much helpful advice <u>prior to my visit to Turkey</u>.*
*Jack left <u>after breakfast</u>.*
*He was killed in a car accident <u>four years after their marriage</u>.*
*<u>After much discussion</u>, they had decided to take the coin to a jeweller.*

'Following', 'previous to' and 'subsequent to' can also be used with events.

*He has regained consciousness <u>following a stroke</u>.*
*He suggests that Ross was prompted <u>previous to the parade</u>.*
*The testimony and description of one witness would be supplied prior to the interview; those of the other two <u>subsequent to it</u>.*

**order of**
**events**

**5.107** 'Before' and 'after' can also be used to indicate the order of events when the same person does two actions or two people do the same action.

*I should have talked about that <u>before anything else</u>.*
*He knew Nell would probably be home <u>before him</u>.*
*I do the floor <u>after the washing-up</u>.*

You can also sometimes use 'earlier than' or 'later than'.

*Smiling develops <u>earlier than laughing</u>.*

**simultaneous**
**events**

**5.108** To indicate that two or more events happen at the same time, the adverbs 'together' and 'simultaneously', or the adjuncts 'at the same time' and 'at once' can be used:

*Everything had happened <u>together</u>.*
*His fear and his hate grew <u>simultaneously</u>.*
*Can you love two women <u>at the same time</u>?*
*I can't be everywhere <u>at once</u>.*

**linking**
**adverbs**

**5.109** You can also indicate what order things happen in using adverbs such as 'first', 'next', and 'finally'. 'Simultaneously', and 'at the same time' are used in a similar way to link clauses. This is dealt with in paragraph 10.78.

**5.110** 'By' is used to emphasize that an event occurs at some time before a specific time, but not later. 'By' is also used to indicate that a process is completed or reaches a particular stage not later than a specific time.

*By eleven o'clock, Brody was back in his office.*
*The theory was that by Monday their tempers would have cooled.*
*By next week, there will be no supplies left.*
*Do you think we'll get to the top of this canyon by tomorrow?*
*By now the moon was up.*
*But by then he was bored with the project.*

# Subordinate time clauses

**5.111** Subordinate time clauses can often be used instead of prepositional phrases to indicate when an event occurs.

For example, instead of saying 'He was killed in a car accident four years after their marriage', you could say 'He was killed in a car accident four years after they were married'.

Or, instead of saying 'During his stay in prison, he has written many essays and poems', you could say 'While he has been in prison, he has written many essays and poems'.

It is often possible or preferable to use a subordinate clause introduced by 'before' or 'after' to indicate the order or simultaneity of a number of events.

Subordinate time clauses are explained in paragraphs 8.8 to 8.24.

# Extended uses of time expressions

**5.112** Time expressions and prepositional phrases can be used as qualifiers to specify events or periods of time.

*I'm afraid the meeting this afternoon tired me badly.*
*The sudden death of his father on 17 November 1960 did not find him unprepared.*
*...until I started to recall the years after the Second World War.*
*No admissions are permitted in the hour before closing time.*

Clock times, periods of the day, days of the week, months, dates, seasons, special periods of the year, years, decades, and centuries can be used as modifiers to specify things.

*Every morning he would set off right after the eight o'clock news.*
*Castle was usually able to catch the six thirty-five train from Euston.*
*But now the sun was already shredding away the morning mists.*
*He learned that he had missed the Monday flight.*
*I had summer clothes and winter clothes.*
*Ash had spent the Christmas holidays at Pelham Abbas.*

Possessive forms can also be used.

*...a discussion of the day's events.*
*It was Jim Griffiths, who knew nothing of the morning's happenings.*
*The story will appear in tomorrow's paper.*
*This week's batch of government statistics added to the general confusion over the state of the economy.*

For more information on modifiers and qualifiers, see Chapter 2.

# Frequency and duration

**5.113** When indicating how often something happens, or how long it last or takes, units of time are often used:

| | | | |
|---|---|---|---|
| moment | hour | week | year |
| second | day | fortnight | decade |
| minute | night | month | century |

'Fortnight' is used only in the singular. 'Moment' is not used with numbers because it does not refer to a precise period of time, so you cannot say for example 'It took five moments'.

Words for periods of the day, days of the week, months of the year, and seasons are also used, such as 'morning', 'Friday', 'July', and 'winter'.

Clock times may also be used.

## Adjuncts of frequency

**5.114** Some adverbs and adverbial expressions indicate approximately how many times something happens:

| | | | |
|---|---|---|---|
| again and again | ever | never | repeatedly |
| a lot | frequently | normally | seldom |
| all the time | from time to time | occasionally | sometimes |
| always | hardly ever | often | sporadically |
| constantly | infrequently | periodically | usually |
| continually | intermittently | rarely | |
| continuously | much | regularly | |

*I never did my homework on time.*
*Sometimes I wish I was back in Africa.*
*We were always being sent home.*
*He blinked a lot.*

'Never' is a negative adverb.

*She never goes abroad.*

'Ever' is only used in questions, negative clauses, and 'if'-clauses.

*Have you ever been to a concert?*

'Much' is usually used with 'not'.

*The men didn't talk much to each other.*

Some adverbs of frequency such as 'often' and 'frequently' can also be used in the comparative and superlative.

*Disasters can be prevented more often than in the past.*
*I preached much more often than that.*
*They cried for their mothers less often than might have been expected.*
*...the mistakes which women make most frequently.*

**USAGE NOTE**   **5.115** To indicate how many times something happens, you can use a specific number, 'several', or 'many' followed by 'times'.

*We had to ask three times.*

*It's an experience I've repeated many times since.*
*He carefully aimed his rifle and fired several times.*

If the number you are using is 'one' you use 'once' (not 'one time') in this structure. If it is 'two' you can use 'twice'.

*I've been out with him once, that's all.*
*The car broke down twice.*

If something happens regularly, you can say how many times it happens within a period of time by adding 'a' and a word referring to a period of time.

*The group met once a week.*
*You only have a meal three times a day.*
*The committee meets twice a year.*

You can also use a frequency expression such as 'once' with a unit of time preceded by 'every' to say that something happens a specified number of times and on a regular basis within that unit of time.

*The average Briton moves house once every seven and a half years.*
*We meet twice every Sunday.*
*Three times every day, he would come to the kiosk to see we were all right.*

If an event happens regularly during a specific period of the day, you can use the period of day instead of 'times':

*I used to go in three mornings a week.*
*He was going out four and sometimes five nights a week.*

A regular rate or quantity can also be expressed by adding 'a' and a general time word. 'Per' can be used instead of 'a', especially in technical contexts.

*He earns about £1000 a week.*
*I was only getting three hours of sleep a night.*
*...rising upwards at the rate of 300 feet per second.*
*He hurtles through the air at 600 miles per hour.*

**estimating**
**frequency**

**5.116** If you want to be less precise about how frequently something happens, you can use one of the following approximating adverbs or approximating expressions: 'almost', 'about', 'nearly', 'or so', 'or less', and 'or more'.

You can use 'almost' and 'about' in front of 'every'.

*In the last month of her pregnancy, we took to going out almost every evening.*

You can also use 'almost' in front of '-ly' time adverbs derived from general time words:

*Small scale confrontations occur almost daily in many states.*

'Or so', 'or less', and 'or more' are used after frequency expressions, but not after adverbs of frequency.

*Every hour or so, my shoulders would tighten.*
*If the delay is two hours or more, the whole cost of the journey should be refunded.*

**regular**
**intervals**

**5.117** If you want to say that something happens at regular intervals, you can use 'every' followed by either a general or a specific unit of time. 'Each' is sometimes used instead of 'every'.

*We'll go hunting every day.*

*You get a lump sum and you get a pension <u>each week.</u>*
*Some people write out a new address book <u>every January.</u>*

'Every' can also be used with a number and the plural of the unit of time.

*<u>Every five minutes</u> the phone would ring.*

The regular or average rate or quantity of something can also be expressed using 'every' and 'each'.

*One fighter jet was shot down <u>every hour.</u>*
*...the 300,000 garments the factory produces <u>each year.</u>*

**USAGE NOTE**   **5.118** If something happens during one period of time but not during the next period, then happens again during the next, and so on, you can use 'every other' followed by a unit of time or a specific time word. 'Every second' is sometimes used instead of 'every other'.

*We wrote <u>every other day.</u>*
*Their local committees are usually held <u>every other month.</u>*
*He used to come and take them out <u>every other Sunday.</u>*
*It seemed easier to shave only <u>every second day.</u>*

Prepositional phrases with 'alternate' and a plural time word can also be used.

*<u>On alternate Sunday nights,</u> I tell the younger children a story.*
*Just do some exercises <u>on alternate days</u> at first.*

**particular**   **5.119** The adverbs 'first', 'next', and 'last' are used to indicate the stage
**occurrences**   at which an event takes place.
**of an event**
The adverb 'first', the noun group 'the first time', and the prepositional phrase 'for the first time' can indicate the first occurrence of an event.

*He was, I think, in his early sixties when I <u>first</u> encountered him.*
*They had seen each other <u>first</u> a week before, outside this hotel.*
*...the tactical war games which were <u>first</u> fought in Ancient Greece.*
*It rained heavily twice while I was out. <u>The first time</u> I sheltered in a copse,*
*but the second time I galloped through it.*
*<u>For the first time</u> Anne Marie felt frightened.*

The repetition of an event or situation that has not happened for a long time can be indicated by using 'for the first time' with 'in' and the plural form of a general time word.

*He was happy and relaxed for the <u>first time in years.</u>*

A future occurrence is indicated by 'next time' or 'the next time'.

*Don't do it again. I mightn't forgive you <u>next time.</u>*
*<u>The next time</u> I come here, I'm going to be better.*

The use of 'next' with statements referring to the future is described in paragraph 5.62.

The most recent occurrence of an event can be indicated by using 'last' as an adverb or the noun groups 'last time' or 'the last time'.

*He seemed to have grown a lot since he <u>last</u> wore it.*
*He could not remember when he had <u>last</u> eaten.*
*When did you <u>last</u> see him?*
*You did so well <u>last time.</u>*

The final occurrence can be indicated by 'for the last time'.

*<u>For the last time</u> he waved to the three friends who watched from above.*

The use of 'last' in statements about the past is described in paragraph 5.41.

You can also use 'before', 'again', and noun groups with an **ordinal** and 'time' to say whether an event is a first occurrence, or one that has happened before.

You can use 'before' with a perfect tense to indicate whether something is happening for the first time or is a repeated occurrence.

*I've never been in a policeman's house before.*
*He's done it before.*

The adverb 'again' can be used to indicate a second or subsequent occurrence of an event. Ordinals can be used with 'time', in noun groups or in more formal prepositional phrases with 'for', to specify a particular occurrence of a repeated event.

*Someone rang the front door bell. He stood and listened and heard it ring again and then a third time.*
*'We have no reliable information about that yet,' he found himself saying for the third time.*

**'-ly' time adverbs**

**5.120** Some general time words can be changed into adverbs by adding '-ly' and used to indicate the frequency of an event.

| | | | |
|---|---|---|---|
| hourly | weekly | monthly | yearly |
| daily | fortnightly | quarterly | |

Note the spelling of 'daily'. The adverb 'annually' and the adjective 'annual' have the same meaning as 'yearly'.

*It was suggested that we give each child an allowance yearly or monthly to cover all he or she spends.*
*She phones me up hourly.*

The same words can be used as adjectives.

*To this, we add a yearly allowance of £65.00 towards repairs.*
*The media gave us hourly updates.*
*They had a long-standing commitment to making a weekly cash payment to mothers.*

**Prepositional phrases**

**5.121** Prepositional phrases with plural forms of specific time words can also be used to indicate frequency. For example, 'on' can be used with days of the week, 'during' and 'at' with 'weekends'.

*We've had teaching practice on Tuesdays and lectures on Thursdays.*
*She does not need help with the children during week-ends.*
*We see each other at week-ends.*

'In' is used with periods of the day, except 'night'.

*I can't work full time. I only work in the afternoons, I have lectures in the mornings.*
*Harry Truman loved to sit in an old rocking chair in the evenings and face the lawns behind the White House.*

**Development and regular occurrence**

**5.122** To indicate that something develops gradually, or happens at regular intervals, you can use a general time word with 'by' followed by the same general time word.

*She was getting older year by year, and lonelier, and more ridiculous.*
*Millions of citizens follow, day by day, the unfolding of the drama.*

Gradual development can also be indicated by the adverbs 'increasingly' and 'progressively'.

*...the computers and information banks upon which our world will increasingly depend.*
*His conduct became increasingly eccentric.*
*As disposable income rises, people become progressively less concerned with price.*

# Adjuncts of duration

**5.123** The following section explains ways of indicating how long something lasts or takes.

Some adverbs and adverbial expressions can be used to indicate the duration of an event or state. Here is a list of adverbs which are used to indicate duration:

| | | | |
|---|---|---|---|
| always | for ever | long | permanently |
| briefly | indefinitely | overnight | temporarily |

*She glanced briefly at Lucas Simmonds.*
*You won't live for ever.*
*The gates are kept permanently closed.*

'Briefly' and 'permanently' can be used in the comparative.

*This new revelation had much the same outward effect, though more briefly.*
*This is something I would like to do more permanently.*

The form 'long' is only used as an adverb in negative clauses, and questions.

*I haven't been in England long.*
*How long does it take on the train?*

In positive clauses, it is used in expressions such as 'a long time' and prepositional phrases such as 'for a long time'. However, the comparative and superlative forms 'longer' and 'longest' can be used in positive and negative clauses.

*Then of course you'll go with Parry. She's been your friend longer.*
*I've been thinking about it a lot longer than you.*
*She remained the longest.*

In affirmative and negative 'if'-clauses, you can use 'for long'.

*If she's away for long we won't be able to wait.*

**prepositional phrases**  **5.124** However, prepositional phrases are more commonly used. The following prepositions are used in adjuncts of duration:

| | | |
|---|---|---|
| after | from | throughout |
| before | in | to |
| for | since | until |

The prepositional object can be a noun group referring to a specific period of time. This can be in the singular after the determiner 'a' (or 'one' for emphasis), or in the plural after a number or quantifier.

The noun group can also refer to an indefinite period, for example expressions such as 'a long time', 'a short while', 'a while', or 'ages', or plural time words such as 'hours'.

**'for' for length of time**

**5.125** The preposition 'for' indicates how long something continues to happen.

*Is he still thinking of going away to Italy for a month?*
*The initial battle continued for an hour.*
*This precious happy time lasted for a month or two.*
*For the next week, she did not contact him.*
*We were married for fifteen years.*
*I didn't speak for a long time.*
*She would have liked to sit for a while and think.*

You use 'the' instead of 'a' when the period of time is already known, with seasons, periods of the day, and 'weekend', or when you modify the time word with words like 'past', 'coming', 'following', 'next', 'last', or an **ordinal**.

*Tell Aunt Elizabeth you're off for the day.*
*We've been living together for the past year.*
*For the first month or two I was bullied constantly.*
*For the next few days he remained prone on his bed in his quarters.*
*Put them in cold storage for the winter.*
*I said I'm off to Brighton for the weekend.*

Remember that you do not use a determiner with special periods of the year.

*At least come for Christmas.*

**5.126** 'For' can also be used with specific time expressions to indicate the time when something is to be used, not how long it takes or lasts.

*Everything was placed exactly where I wanted it for the morning.*

**5.127** 'For' can also be used in negative statements when you want to say that something need not or will not happen until a certain period of time has passed. 'Yet' is often added.

*It won't be ready to sail for another three weeks.*
*I don't have to decide for a month yet.*

**'for' for emphasis**

**5.128** 'For' is used with a plural noun group to emphasize how long something lasts.

*Settlers have been coming here for centuries.*
*I don't think he's practised much for years.*
*I've been asking you about these doors for months.*

**USAGE NOTE**

**5.129** You can also use a general time word with 'after' followed by the same general time word to emphasize that a state continues for a long time or that an action is repeated continuously for a long time.

*I wondered what kept her in Paris decade after decade.*
*They can go on making losses, year after year, without fearing that they will go bust.*

**'in' and 'within' for end of a period**

**5.130** 'In' is used to indicate that something happens or will happen before the end of a certain period of time. In more formal English 'within' is used.

*Can we get to the airport in an hour?*

*That coat must have cost you more than I make <u>in a year</u>.*
*The face of a city can change completely <u>in a year</u>.*
*They should get the job finished <u>within a few days</u>.*

**5.131** 'In' and 'within' are also used to indicate that something only took or takes a short time.

*The clouds evaporated <u>in seconds</u>.*
*What an expert can do <u>in minutes</u> may take you hours to accomplish.*
*<u>Within a few months,</u> the barnyard had been abandoned.*

**'for' and 'in'**
**with general**
**or**
**specific time**

**5.132** 'For' and 'in' can be used in negative statements to say that something does not happen during a period of time. You can use them in this way with specific units of time, and with more general time references.

*He hadn't had a proper night's sleep <u>for a month</u>.*
*I haven't seen a chart <u>for forty years</u>!*
*The team had not heard from Stabler <u>in a month</u>.*
*He hasn't slept <u>in a month</u>.*
*I haven't seen him <u>for years</u>.*
*Let's have a dinner party. We haven't had one <u>in years</u>.*
*I haven't fired a gun <u>in years</u>.*

**noun group**
**adjuncts**

**5.133** Note that with the verbs 'last', 'wait', and 'stay', which have duration as part of their meaning, the adjunct of duration can be a noun group instead of a prepositional phrase with 'for'.

*The campaign <u>lasts four weeks</u> at most.*
*His speech <u>lasted for exactly 14 and a half minutes</u>.*
*'Wait a minute,' the voice said.*
*He <u>stayed a month, five weeks, six weeks</u>.*

The verbs 'take' and 'spend' can also indicate duration but the adjunct of duration can only be a noun group.

*It <u>took me a month</u> to lose that feeling of being a spectator.*
*What once <u>took a century</u> now <u>took only ten months</u>.*
*He <u>spent five minutes</u> washing and shaving.*

**approximate**
**duration**

**5.134** If you want to be less precise about how long something lasts, you can use one of the following approximating adverbs or approximating expressions: 'about', 'almost', 'nearly', 'around', 'more than', 'less than', and so on.

*They've lived there for <u>more than</u> thirty years.*
*They have not been allowed to form unions for <u>almost</u> a decade.*
*The three of us travelled around together for <u>about</u> a month that summer.*
*In <u>less than</u> a year, I learned enough Latin to pass the entrance exam.*
*He had been in command of HMS Churchill for <u>nearly</u> a year.*

When making a general statement about the duration of something, you can indicate the maximum period of time that it will last or take by using 'up to'.

*Refresher training for <u>up to</u> one month each year was the rule for all.*

You can also use expressions such as 'or so', 'or more', 'or less', 'or thereabouts' to make the duration less specific.

*He has been writing about tennis and golf for forty years <u>or so</u>.*
*Our species probably practised it for a million years <u>or more</u>.*
*...hopes which have prevailed so strongly for a century <u>or more</u>.*

'Almost', 'about', 'nearly', and 'thereabouts' are also used when talking about when an event takes place; see paragraph 5.99 for details of this.

# Indicating the whole of a period

**5.135** If you want to emphasize that something lasts for the whole of a period of time, you can use 'all' as a determiner with many general time words.

*'I've been wanting to do this all day,' she said.*
*I've been here all night.*
*They said you were out all afternoon.*
*We've not seen them all summer.*

You can also use 'whole' as a modifier in front of a general time word.

*It took me the whole of my first year to adjust.*
*...scientists who are monitoring food safety the whole time.*
*...women who have stopped menstruating for a whole year*

You can also use 'all through', 'right through', and 'throughout' with 'the' and many general time words, or with a specific decade, year, month, or special period.

*Discussions and arguments continued all through the day.*
*Right through the summer months they are rarely out of sight.*
*Throughout the Sixties, man's first voyage to other worlds came closer.*

Words referring to events can be used instead of the time words, to emphasize that something happened for the entire duration of the event.

*He wore an expression of angry contempt throughout the interrogation.*
*A patient reported a dream that had recurred throughout her life.*
*All through the cruelly long journey home, he lay utterly motionless.*

**5.136** If you want to emphasize that something happens all the time, you can list periods of the day or seasons of the year, or mention contrasting ones.

*...people coming in morning, noon, and night.*
*I've worn the same suit summer, winter, autumn and spring, for five years.*
*Thousands of slave labourers worked night and day to build the fortifications.*
*Ten gardeners used to work this land, winter and summer.*

# Indicating the start or end of a period

start time   **5.137** You can also indicate how long a situation lasts by using prepositional phrases to give the time when it begins or the time when it ends, or both.

If you want to talk about a situation that began in the past and is continuing now, or to consider a period of it from a time in the past to the present, you use the preposition 'since' with a time expression or an event to indicate when the situation began. The verb is in the present perfect tense.

*I've been here since twelve o'clock.*
*I haven't had a new customer in here since Sunday.*
*Since January, there hasn't been any more trouble.*

*I haven't been out since Christmas.*
*The situation has not changed since 2001.*
*There has been no word of my friend since the revolution.*

'Since' is also used to indicate the beginning of situations that ended in the past. The verb is in the past perfect tense.

*I'd been working in London since January at a firm called Kendalls.*
*He hadn't prayed once since the morning.*
*I'd only had two sandwiches since breakfast.*

'Since' can also be used with other prepositional phrases that indicate a point in time.

*I haven't seen you since before the summer.*

The noun group after 'since' can sometimes refer to a person or thing rather than a time or event, especially when used with a superlative, 'first' or 'only', or with a negative.

*They hadn't seen each other since Majorca.*
*I have never had another dog since Jonnie.*
*Ever since London, I've been working towards this.*

**5.138** The time when a situation began can also be indicated by using the preposition 'from' and adding the adverb 'on' or 'onwards'. The noun group can be a date, an event, or a period. The verb can be in the simple past tense or in a perfect tense.

*...the history of British industry from the mid sixties on.*
*From the eighteenth century on, great private palaces went up.*
*But from the mid-1960s onwards the rate of public welfare spending has tended to accelerate.*
*The family size starts to influence development from birth.*
*They never perceived that they themselves had forced women into this role from childhood.*
*...the guide who had been with us from the beginning.*

**5.139** You can also use the preposition 'after' to give the time when a situation began.

*They don't let anybody in after six o'clock.*
*After 1929 I concentrated on canvas work.*
*He'd have a number of boys to help him through the summer-time but after October he'd just have the one.*

**end time** **5.140** Similarly, if you want to say that a situation continues for some time and then stops, you can indicate the time when it stops by using the preposition 'until' with a time expression or an event.

*The school was kept open until ten o'clock five nights a week.*
*They danced and laughed and talked until dawn.*
*She walked back again and sat in her room until dinner.*
*I've just discovered she's only here until Sunday.*
*He had been willing to wait until the following summer.*
*Until the end of the 18<sup>th</sup> century little had been known about Persia.*
*Until that meeting, most of us knew very little about him.*

'Until' can also be used in negative clauses to say that something did not or will not happen before a particular time.

*We won't get them until September.*
*My plane does not leave until tomorrow morning.*
*No one I knew had cars until the twenties.*

*It won't happen for many good months to come—probably <u>not</u> <u>until the spring</u>.*

'Until' can also be used with other prepositional phrases that indicate a point in time.

*I decided to wait <u>until after Easter</u> to visit John.*

Some people use 'till' instead of 'until', especially in informal English.

*Sometimes I lie in bed <u>till nine o'clock</u>.*

'Up to' and 'up till' are also sometimes used, mainly before 'now' and 'then'.

*<u>Up to now</u>, I have been happy with his work.*
*It was something he had never even considered <u>up till now</u>.*
*I had a three-wheel bike <u>up to a few years ago</u> but it got harder and harder to push it along.*
*<u>Up to 1989</u>, growth averaged 1 per cent.*

**5.141** You can also use the preposition 'before' to indicate when a situation ends.

*<u>Before 1716</u> Cheltenham had been a small market town.*
*<u>Before ten</u> and after six the area is empty.*

**start and end times** **5.142** The duration of a situation or event can be indicated by saying when it begins and when it ends. You can use 'from' to indicate when it begins and 'to', 'till', or 'until' to indicate when it ends.

*The Blitz on London began with nightly bombings <u>from 7 September to 2 November</u>.*
*They are active in the line <u>from about January until October</u>.*
*...<u>from four</u> in the morning <u>until ten</u> at night.*
*They seem to be working <u>from dawn till dusk</u>.*

You can also use 'between' and 'and' instead of 'from' and 'to'.

*<u>Between 1966 and 1970</u> Mintech invested 8m in advanced machinery.*
*It's usually in the garage <u>between Sunday and Thursday</u> in winter.*
*...illuminated advertising <u>between midnight and dawn</u>.*

In American English, 'through' is often placed between the two times:

*The chat shows goes out <u>midnight through six a.m.</u>*

If you are using figures to refer to two times or years, you can separate them with a dash, instead of using 'from' and 'to'.

*...open <u>10-5</u> weekdays, <u>10-6</u> Saturdays and <u>2-6</u> Sundays.*

# Duration expressions as modifiers

**5.143** You can also use time expressions involving a cardinal number and a general time word to modify nouns. Note that an apostrophe is added to the time word.

*Four of those were sentenced to <u>15 days' detention</u>.*
*They want to take on staff with <u>two years' experience</u>.*

This use of cardinal numbers is described in paragraph 2.248.

**5.144** Time expressions are also used as **compound adjectives** to modify count nouns.

*They all have to start off with a <u>six month course</u> in German.*
*I arrived at the University for a <u>three month stint</u> as a visiting lecturer.*

Compound adjectives are explained in paragraphs 2.98 to 2.107.

# Contents of Chapter 6

# 6 Expressing manner and place

## Introduction to adjuncts

**6.1** When you are talking about an event or situation, you sometimes want to say something about it which has not been indicated by the subject, verb, object, or complement. You can do this by using an **adjunct**.

An adjunct is a word or group of words which you add to a clause when you want to say something about the circumstances of an event or situation, for example when it occurs, how it occurs, how much it occurs, or where it occurs.

*I was soon lost.*
*She laughed quietly.*
*She was tremendously impressed.*
*He fumbled in his pocket.*

In other grammars, adjuncts are sometimes called **adverbials, adverb phrases**, or **adverbial phrases**.

**adverbial groups** **6.2** The two main types of adjuncts are **adverbial groups** and **prepositional phrases**. Adverbial groups usually consist of **adverbs**.

*He acted very clumsily.*
*I cannot speak too highly of their courage and skill.*
*He takes his job very seriously indeed.*
*He did not play well enough throughout the week to deserve to win.*

However, adverbs very often occur on their own.

*I shook her gently.*
*He greatly admired Cezanne.*
*He scarcely knew his aunt.*
*The number will probably be higher than we expected.*

For more information about adverbs, see the section beginning at paragraph 6.16.

**prepositional phrases** **6.3** Adjuncts consisting of a **preposition** and a **noun group**, such as 'in a box' and 'to the station', are called **prepositional phrases**. The most basic use of prepositional phrases is to indicate position and direction, so they are dealt with in detail at the section on **place** beginning at paragraph 6.53.

*Large cushions lay on the floor.*
*The voice was coming from my apartment.*

**noun groups** **6.4** Occasionally, **noun groups** can also be used as adjuncts.

*He was looking really ill this time yesterday.*
*'There's a massive market that side of the water,' he says, gesturing out of his window.*
*I'm going to handle this my way.*

When noun groups are used as adjuncts, they are most often adjuncts of time, which are dealt with in Chapter 5. Noun groups as adjuncts of place are dealt with at paragraph 6.101, as adjuncts of manner at paragraph 6.44, and as adjuncts of degree at paragraph 6.52.

For more information on noun groups in general, see Chapters 1 and 2.

**adding meaning to verb groups**

**6.5** The most common way in which adverbial groups give additional information is by adding something to the meaning of a verb group within a clause.

*He nodded and smiled warmly.*
*The report says that hospitals and rescue services coped extremely well.*
*I could find that out fairly easily.*

Prepositional phrases have a wider range of meanings.

*It was estimated that at least 2,000 people were on the two trains.*
*Kenny Stuart came second, knocking two minutes off his previous best time.*
*For the first time since I'd been pregnant I felt well.*

Many **intransitive verbs** normally require an adjunct. See paragraph 3.11 for more information about these.

*Ashton had behaved abominably.*
*She turned and rushed out of the room.*

Some **transitive verbs** normally require an adjunct after the object of the verb. For more information about these, see paragraph 3.20.

*I put my hand on the door.*

**adding meaning to clauses**

**6.6** Adjuncts can also add meaning to a whole clause, for example by giving the writer's or speaker's comment on it. For more information, see the section on **sentence adjuncts** beginning at paragraph 10.56.

*Obviously crime is going to be squeezed in a variety of ways.*
*Fortunately, the damage had been slight.*
*Ideally the dairy should have a concrete or tiled floor.*
*No doubt she loves Gertrude too.*

They can also indicate the way in which one clause is linked to another clause. For more information, see the section on **linking adjuncts** beginning at paragraph 10.73.

*Manufacturers are developing engines which use less fuel and therefore pump out less toxic gas.*

# Position of adjuncts

**normal position: end of clause**

**6.7** The position of adjuncts within clauses is flexible, allowing many changes of emphasis and focus.

Adjuncts are normally placed at the end of the clause after the verb group or after an object or complement if there is one.

*She packed carefully.*
*They would go on talking for hours.*
*I enjoyed the course immensely.*
*These employers were famous for their meanness.*

**beginning of clause for emphasis**

**6.8** You can emphasize the adjunct by placing it at the beginning of the clause, in front of the subject.

*Gently Fanny leaned forward and wiped the old lady's tears away.*

*In his excitement Billy had forgotten the letter.*

The adjunct is often separated by a comma from the rest of the clause.

*After much discussion, they had decided to take the coin to the jeweller.*

This position is often used in written stories to draw attention to the adjunct. For more information, see paragraph 10.93.

Note that adverbs of degree are rarely used at the beginning of a clause: see paragraph 6.45.

**between subject and verb**

**6.9** Adjuncts can also be placed between the subject and the main verb. This focuses on the adjunct more than when it is at the end of the clause, but not as much as putting it at the beginning of the clause. However, this position is much more common with adverbs than with prepositional phrases.

*I quickly became aware that she was looking at me.*
*We often swam in the surf.*
*He carefully wrapped each component in several layers of foam rubber.*
*He noisily opened the fridge and took out a carton of milk.*

Note that in verb groups containing auxiliaries, the adjunct is still placed in front of the main verb.

*I had almost forgotten about the trip.*
*We will never have enough money to provide all the services that people want.*
*It would not in any case be for him.*

Long adjuncts in this position are usually separated by commas from the rest of the clause.

*Fred, in his own way, was a great actor.*

Adjuncts of place rarely occur in this position. For more information about adjuncts of place, see the section beginning at paragraph 6.53.

**6.10** Some adjuncts are often placed in front of the main verb:

most adverbs of indefinite frequency (see paragraph 5.114)

| | | | | |
|---|---|---|---|---|
| always | ever | normally | regularly | usually |
| constantly | frequently | occasionally | repeatedly | |
| continually | hardly ever | often | seldom | |
| continuously | never | rarely | sometimes | |

some adverbs of indefinite time (see paragraph 5.41)

| | | | |
|---|---|---|---|
| again | finally | last | since |
| already | first | previously | |
| earlier | just | recently | |

some adverbs of degree (see paragraph 6.45), especially emphasizing adverbs (see paragraph 6.49)

| | | | | |
|---|---|---|---|---|
| absolutely | completely | greatly | quite | utterly |
| almost | deeply | largely | rather | virtually |
| altogether | entirely | nearly | really | well |
| badly | fairly | perfectly | somewhat | |

focusing adverbs, when modifying a verb: see paragraph 10.90.

| | | |
|---|---|---|
| even | merely | really |
| just | only | simply |

Note that some adjuncts have a different reference when placed in front c the main verb rather than at the end of the clause:

*The Trade Unions have acted <u>foolishly</u>.*
*Baldwin had <u>foolishly</u> opened the door.*

The first example means that the Unions acted in a foolish way. The second example means that opening the door was a foolish action, and not that the door was opened in a foolish way.

*Americans always tip <u>generously</u>.*
*He <u>generously</u> offered to drive me home.*

The first example tells us how well the drivers are paid, the second example indicates that Cram's admission was a generous action.

**WARNING**  6.11 If the verb is a 'to'-infinitive, you usually put adjuncts after it, or afte the object or complement if there is one.

*He tried to leave <u>quietly</u>.*
*Thomas made an appointment to see him <u>immediately</u>.*

Some people do put adverbs between the 'to' and the infinitive, but this use is not considered correct by some speakers of English.

*'My wife told me <u>to probably expect</u> you,' he said.*
*Vauxhall are attempting <u>to really break</u> into the market.*

**minor**  6.12 If a clause has two adjuncts, and one is an adverb and the other is ɛ
**positional**  prepositional phrase, you can usually place either of them first.
**points**  *Miss Burns looked <u>calmly</u> at Marianne.*
*They were sitting <u>happily</u> in the car.*
*The women shouted <u>at me</u> <u>savagely</u>.*
*He got <u>into the car</u> <u>quickly</u> and drove off.*

However, if the prepositional phrase is rather long, it is more common to place the adverb first, immediately after the verb.

*He listened <u>calmly</u> to the report of his aides.*
*She would sit <u>crosslegged</u> in her red robes.*

Similarly, if the verb group is followed by a long object, the adverb comes after the verb and before the object.

*He could picture <u>easily</u> the consequences of being found by the owners.*
*She sang <u>beautifully</u> a school song the children had taught her when they were little.*

**manner,**  6.13 In clauses with more than one adjunct, the meaning of the adjuncts
**place,**  can also affect their order. The usual order is adjunct of manner, then
**then time**  adjunct of place, then adjunct of time.

*They knelt <u>quietly</u> <u>in the shadow of the rock</u>.*
*I tried to reach you <u>at home</u> <u>several times</u>.*
*He was imprisoned <u>in Cairo</u> <u>in January 1945</u>.*
*Parents may complain that their child eats <u>badly</u> <u>at meals</u>.*
*The youngsters repeat this <u>in unison</u> <u>at the beginning of each session</u>.*

However, if a clause contains an adverb of manner and an adverb of direction such as 'down', 'out', or 'home', the adverb of direction is usuallyꞏ put in front of the adverb of manner.

*Lomax drove <u>home</u> <u>fast</u>.*
*I reached <u>down</u> <u>slowly</u>.*

**adjuncts of**  6.14 Adjuncts of different types can be placed together, sometimes
**the same**  separated by a comma, buꞇ adjuncts of the same type, for example two
**type**  adjuncts of manner, are usually linked by conjunctions such as 'and' and

'but', or structures such as 'rather than'. For more information about linking adjuncts with conjunctions, see paragraphs 8.176 and 8.180.

*She sang clearly and beautifully.*
*They help to combat the problem at source, rather than superficially.*

**inversion after adjuncts** 6.15 When clauses begin with an adjunct, the normal order of subject and verb group can sometimes be inverted. For example, after adjuncts of place the verb group usually comes before the subject. For more information about adjuncts of place, see the section beginning at paragraph 6.53.

*Next to it stood a pile of paper cups.*
*Beyond them lay the fields.*

This also happens when **broad negative** adverbs and some other **negative words** are placed at the beginning of the clause. For more information about these, see paragraphs 4.43 to 4.94.

*Never in history had technology made such spectacular advances.*
*Seldom can there have been such a happy meeting.*

Both these cases of inversion are particularly common in written stories. Inversion can occur after other adjuncts, but only in poetry or old-fashioned English. The following example is from a Christmas carol written in 1853:

*Brightly shone the moon that night, though the frost was cruel.*

# Giving information about manner: adverbs

**types of adverbs** 6.16 There are several types of adverbs:

● **adverbs of time, frequency,** and **duration,** for example 'soon', 'often', and 'always'. Because these are all related to time, they are dealt with fully in Chapter 5.

● **adverbs of place,** for example 'around', 'downstairs', and 'underneath'. These are dealt with in the section on **place** beginning at paragraph 6.82.

● **adverbs of manner,** for example 'beautifully', 'carefully', and 'silently'. See the section beginning at paragraph 6.36 for more information about these.

● **adverbs of degree,** for example 'almost', 'badly', 'terribly', and 'well'. See the section beginning at paragraph 6.45 for more information about these.

● **linking adverbs,** for example 'consequently', 'furthermore', and 'however'. These are dealt with in paragraphs 10.73 to 10.81.

● **sentence adverbs,** for example 'alas', 'apparently', 'chiefly', and 'interestingly'. See the section beginning at paragraph 10.56 for more information on these.

● **broad negative adverbs,** for example 'barely', 'hardly', 'rarely', 'scarcely', and 'seldom'. These are dealt with at paragraphs 4.83 to 4.90.

● **focusing adverbs,** for example 'especially' and 'only'. These are dealt with in the section beginning at paragraph 10.87.

# Adverb forms and meanings related to adjectives

'-ly' adverbs **6.17** Many adverbs are related to adjectives. The main relationships and rules of formation are explained below.

Many adverbs are formed by adding '-ly' to an adjective. For example, the adverbs 'quietly' and 'badly' are formed by adding '-ly' to the adjectives 'quiet' and 'bad'.

Most of the adverbs formed in this way are **adverbs of manner,** so some people refer to adverbs of manner as '**-ly' adverbs.**

*Sit there quietly, and listen to this music.*
*I didn't play badly.*
*He reported accurately what they said.*
*He nodded and smiled warmly.*

For more information about adjectives, see Chapter 2.

spelling **6.18** Some '-ly' adverbs have slightly different spellings from the adjectives they are related to, for example 'nastily', 'gently', 'terribly', 'academically', 'truly', and 'fully'. For information about these adverbs, see the Reference Section.

**6.19** Not all adverbs ending in '-ly' are adverbs of manner. Some are adverbs of degree, such as 'extremely' and 'slightly': see the list at paragraph 6.45.

*I enjoyed the course immensely.*
*Sales fell slightly last month.*

A few are adverbs of time, duration, or frequency, such as 'presently', 'briefly', and 'weekly': see the lists of these in Chapter 5.

*At 10.15 a.m. soldiers briefly opened fire again.*
*...allegations which are presently being investigated by my legal team.*

Others are adverbs of place, such as 'locally' and 'internationally', linking adverbs such as 'consequently', or sentence adverbs such as 'actually'. For lists of adverbs of place, see the section beginning at paragraph 6.82. For lists of sentence adverbs, see Chapter 10.

*The lady replied: 'Well, you live locally and have never caused any bother.*
*These efforts have received little credit internationally.*
*They did not preach. Consequently, they reached a vastly wider audience.*
*There still remains something to say. Several things, actually.*

adverb meaning **6.20** Most adverbs formed by adding '-ly' to an adjective have a similar meaning to the adjective, for example 'quietly' and 'beautifully' have similar meanings to 'quiet' and 'beautiful'.

*She is thoughtful, quiet and controlled.*
*'I'm going to do it', I said quietly.*
*His costumes are beautiful, a big improvement on the previous ones.*
*The girls had dressed more beautifully than ever, for him.*

**6.21** Some '-ly' adverbs have a different meaning from the meanings of their related adjectives. For example, 'hardly' means 'not very much' or 'almost not at all' and is not used with any of the meanings of the adjective 'hard'.

*This has been a long hard day.*
*Her bedroom was so small she could hardly move in it.*

| | | |
|---|---|---|
| barely | lately | scarcely |
| hardly | presently | shortly |

**6.22** Some '-ly' adverbs are not related to adjectives, for example 'accordingly'. Some are related to nouns, for example 'bodily', 'purposely', 'daily' and 'weekly'. For lists of these, see the Reference Section.

**6.23** Adverbs ending in '-ly' are very rarely formed from some types of adjectives:

● most classifying adjectives, for example 'racist', 'eastern', 'female', 'urban', 'foreign', and 'available'. See Chapter 2 for lists of classifying adjectives.

● most colour adjectives, although '-ly' adverbs from these are occasionally found in works of literature.

*The hills rise greenly to the deep-blue sky.*
*He lay still, staring blackly up at the ceiling.*

● some very common qualitative adjectives which refer to basic qualities:

| | | | |
|---|---|---|---|
| big | old | tall | wet |
| fat | small | tiny | young |

● adjectives which already end in '-ly', for example 'friendly', 'lively', 'cowardly', 'ugly', and 'silly'.

● most adjectives that end in '-ed', such as 'frightened' and 'surprised'. See the Reference Section for a list of the common ones which do form '-ly' adverbs, such as 'excitedly' and 'hurriedly'.

**same form as adjective**

**6.24** In some cases, an adverb has the same form as an adjective and is similar in meaning. For example, 'fast' is an adverb in the sentence 'News travels fast' and an adjective in the sentence 'She likes fast cars'.

*...a fast rail link from London to the Channel Tunnel.*
*The driver was driving too fast for the conditions.*

In these cases, the adverb is usually placed immediately after the verb or object, and rarely in front of the verb.

| | | | | |
|---|---|---|---|---|
| alike | far | long | overseas | through |
| downtown | fast | next | past | |
| extra | inside | outside | straight | |

There are also a number of words ending in '-ly' which are both adverbs and adjectives, for example 'daily', 'monthly', and 'yearly'. These relate to frequency and are explained in paragraph 5.120.

**6.25** Several postdeterminers, including 'further', 'next', 'only', 'opposite', and 'same', have the same form as adverbs but no direct relation in meaning. Note that 'well' is an adverb and adjective, but usually means 'not ill' as an adjective, and 'with skill or success' as an adverb.

*He has done well.*

**two forms**

**6.26** Sometimes, two adverbs are related to the same adjective. One adverb has the same form as the adjective, and the other is formed by adding '-ly'.

*He closed his eyes tight.*

*He closed his eyes <u>tightly</u>.*
*Failure may yet cost his country <u>dear</u>.*
*Holes in the road are a menace which costs this country <u>dearly</u> in lost man hours every year.*
*The German manufacturer was urging me to cut out the middle man and deal with him <u>direct</u>.*
*The trend in recent years has been to deal <u>directly</u> with the supplier.*

Here is a list of common adverbs that have both these forms:

| | | | | |
|---|---|---|---|---|
| clear | deep | fine | high | thick |
| clearly | deeply | finely | highly | thickly |
| close | direct | first | last | thin |
| closely | directly | firstly | lastly | thinly |
| dear | easy | hard | late | tight |
| dearly | easily | hardly | lately | tightly |

Note that the '-ly' adverb often has a different meaning from the adverb with the same form as the adjective,

*The river was running <u>high</u> and swiftly.*
*I thought <u>highly</u> of the idea.*

*He has worked <u>hard</u>.*
*Border could <u>hardly</u> make himself heard above the din.*

*When the snake strikes, its mouth opens <u>wide</u>.*
*Closing dates for applications vary <u>widely</u>.*

Note that, with some words that are adverbs and adjectives, the addition of '-ly' forms a new adverb and a new adjective, for example 'dead' and 'deadly', 'low' and 'lowly'.

**no adverb from adjective**

**6.27** Some adjectives do not form adverbs at all. These include the common qualitative adjectives listed in paragraph 6.23, such as 'big' and 'old'.

Here is a list of some more adjectives that do not form adverbs:

| | | | |
|---|---|---|---|
| afraid | awake | foreign | little |
| alive | content | good | long |
| alone | difficult | hurt | sorry |
| asleep | drunk | ill | standard |

Note that the adverbs relating to 'content' and 'drunk' are formed by adding '-ly' to the forms 'contented' and 'drunken', thus giving 'contentedly' and 'drunkenly'.

**USAGE NOTE**

**6.28** If there is no adverb related to an adjective, and you want to give additional information about an event or situation, you can often use a prepositional phrase.

In some cases, the prepositional phrase involves a noun that is related to the adjective. For example, there is no adverb related to the adjective 'difficult', but you can use the related noun 'difficulty' in the prepositional phrase 'with difficulty' instead.

*He stood up slowly and <u>with difficulty</u>.*

In other cases, for example with adjectives that end in '-ly', a general noun such as 'way', 'manner', or 'fashion' is used.

*He walks <u>in a funny way</u>.*
*He greeted us <u>in his usual friendly fashion</u>.*

Prepositional phrases may be used even if an adverb does exist, for example when you want to add more detailed information or to add emphasis.

*She comforted the bereaved relatives in a dignified, compassionate and personalized manner.*
*At these extreme velocities, materials behave in a totally different manner from normal.*

**adverbs not related to adjectives**

6.29 Some adverbs are not related to adjectives at all. This is especially true of adverbs of time and place. See Chapter 5 for adverbs of time, and the section beginning at paragraph 6.82 for adverbs of place.

*It will soon be Christmas.*

There are also some other adverbs that are not related to adjectives.

For a list of the common adverbs that are not related to adjectives, see the Reference Section.

# Comparative and superlative adverbs

6.30 You may want to say how something happens or is done in relation to how it happens on a different occasion, or how it was done by someone or something else. You can do this by using adverbs in the **comparative** or **superlative**.

*He began to speak more quickly.*
*Chemotherapy is most commonly used in younger patients.*

Most **adverbs of manner** (see paragraph 6.36) have comparatives and superlatives.

A few other adverbs also have comparatives and superlatives: some adverbs of **time** ('early' and 'late', see paragraph 5.70), **frequency** ('often' and 'frequently', see paragraph 5.114), **duration** ('briefly', 'permanently', and 'long', see paragraph 5.123), and **place** ('near', 'close', 'deep', 'high', 'far', and 'low', see paragraphs 6.68 and 6.89).

6.31 The forms and uses of comparative and superlative adverbs are generally similar to those of adjectives. For more information about comparatives and superlatives of adjectives, see paragraphs 2.108 to 2.117.

However, unlike adjectives, the comparative of an adverb is usually formed with 'more' and the superlative with 'most', and not by adding '-er' and '-est'.

*The people needed business skills so that they could manage themselves more effectively.*
*First she might have some useful information. More importantly, a damaging precedent could be set.*
*...the text which Professor Williams's volume most closely resembles.*
*Valium is most often prescribed as an anti-anxiety drug.*

**irregular forms**

6.32 Some very common adverbs have comparatives and superlatives that are single words and not formed using 'more' and 'most'. Note that adverbs that have irregular comparatives also have irregular superlatives.

'Well' has the comparative 'better' and the superlative 'best'.

*She would ask him later, when she knew him better.*
*I have to find out what I can do best.*

'Badly' has the comparative 'worse' and the superlative 'worst'.

*'I don't think the crowd helped her,' Gordon admitted. 'She played worse.'*
*The expedition from Mozambique fared worst.*

Note that 'worse' and 'worst' are also the comparative and superlative of
'ill' when it is an adverb or adjective.

**6.33** Adverbs which have the same form as adjectives also have the same
comparatives and superlatives as the adjectives. For example, 'fast' has
'faster' and 'fastest', and 'hard' has 'harder' and 'hardest'. For a list of
common adverbs which have the same form as adjectives, see paragraph
6.24.

*This would enable claims to be dealt with faster.*
*They worked harder, they were more honest.*
*The winning blow is the one that strikes hardest.*
*The sugar should be preserving sugar as this dissolves fastest.*
*The tax burden increased fastest for the poor and for those with children.*

**6.34** Some adverbs have comparatives and superlatives with 'more' and
'most', but also have single word comparatives and superlatives.

*They can be built more quickly.*
*You probably learn quicker by having lessons.*
*Those women treated quickest were those most likely to die.*
*The American computer firm will be relying more heavily on its new
Scottish plant.*
*It seems that the rights of soldiers weigh heavier than the rights of
those killed.*
*The burden fell most heavily on Kanhai.*
*Illiteracy, like other forms of educational disadvantage, weighs heaviest
on the groups who are already disadvantaged in other ways.*

**USAGE NOTE** **6.35** The structures involving comparatives and superlatives are generally
the same for adverbs as for adjectives:

● the use of 'no' and 'any' with comparatives: see paragraph 2.168

*He began to behave more and more erratically.*
*Omoro didn't want to express it any more strongly.*

● the optional use of 'the' with superlatives: see paragraph 2.122

*His shoulders hurt the worst.*
*Old people work hardest.*

● the use of submodifiers with comparatives and superlatives: see the
section beginning at paragraph 2.162

*The situation resolved itself much more easily than I had expected.*
*There the process progresses even more rapidly.*

● the use of 'than' after comparatives: see paragraph 2.111

*This class continues to grow more rapidly than any other group.*
*Prices have been rising faster than incomes.*
*You might know this better than me.*
*They managed to keep his circulation going more successfully than we
did.*

● repeating comparatives to indicate changes in extent: see paragraph 2.166.

*He began to behave more and more erratically.*

# Adverbs of manner

**adverbs of manner** **6.36** You often want to say something about the manner or circumstances of an event or situation. The most common way of doing this is by using **adverbs of manner**. Adverbs of manner give more information about the way in which an event or action takes place.

*He nodded and smiled warmly.*
*She accidentally shot herself in the foot.*

**manner** **6.37** Many adverbs of manner are used to describe the way in which something is done. For example, in the sentence 'He did it carefully', 'carefully' means 'in a careful way'.

*They think, dress and live differently.*
*He acted very clumsily.*
*You must be able to speak fluently and correctly.*

**6.38** Here is a list of common '-ly' adverbs which describe the way in which something is done :

| | | | |
|---|---|---|---|
| abruptly | economically | peacefully | steadily |
| accurately | effectively | peculiarly | steeply |
| awkwardly | efficiently | perfectly | stiffly |
| badly | evenly | plainly | strangely |
| beautifully | explicitly | pleasantly | subtly |
| brightly | faintly | politely | superbly |
| brilliantly | faithfully | poorly | swiftly |
| briskly | fiercely | professionally | systematically |
| carefully | finely | properly | tenderly |
| carelessly | firmly | quietly | thickly |
| casually | fluently | rapidly | thinly |
| cheaply | formally | readily | thoroughly |
| clearly | frankly | richly | thoughtfully |
| closely | freely | rigidly | tightly |
| clumsily | gently | roughly | truthfully |
| comfortably | gracefully | ruthlessly | uncomfortably |
| consistently | hastily | securely | urgently |
| conveniently | heavily | sensibly | vaguely |
| correctly | honestly | sharply | vigorously |
| dangerously | hurriedly | silently | violently |
| delicately | intently | simply | vividly |
| differently | meticulously | smoothly | voluntarily |
| discreetly | neatly | softly | warmly |
| distinctly | nicely | solidly | widely |
| dramatically | oddly | specifically | willingly |
| easily | patiently | splendidly | wonderfully |

**feelings and manner** **6.39** Adverbs formed from adjectives which describe people's feelings, for example 'happily' or 'nervously', indicate both the way in which something is done and the feelings of the person who does it.

For example, the sentence 'She laughed happily' means both that she laughed in a happy way and that she was feeling happy.

*We laughed and chatted <u>happily</u> together.*
*Gaskell got up <u>wearily</u> and headed for the stairs.*
*They looked <u>anxiously</u> at each other.*
*The children waited <u>eagerly</u> for their presents.*
*The children smiled <u>shyly</u>.*

**6.40** Here is a list of adverbs which describe the feelings of the person who does something as well as the way in which it is done:

| | | | |
|---|---|---|---|
| angrily | eagerly | hopefully | sadly |
| anxiously | excitedly | hopelessly | shyly |
| bitterly | furiously | impatiently | sincerely |
| boldly | gladly | miserably | uncomfortably |
| calmly | gloomily | nervously | uneasily |
| cheerfully | gratefully | passionately | unhappily |
| confidently | happily | proudly | wearily |
| desperately | helplessly | reluctantly | |

**circumstances**   **6.41** Adverbs of manner can also indicate the circumstances in which something is done, rather than how it is done. For example, in the sentence 'He spoke to me privately' 'privately' means 'when no one else was present' rather than 'in a private way'.

*I need to speak to you <u>privately</u>.*
*He had <u>publicly</u> called for an investigation of the entire school system.*
*Britain and France <u>jointly</u> suggested a plan in 1954.*
*Since then I have undertaken all the enquiries <u>personally</u>.*

**6.42** Here is a list of adverbs which are used to indicate the circumstances in which an action takes place:

| | | | |
|---|---|---|---|
| accidentally | first-class | legally | privately |
| alone | full-time | logically | publicly |
| artificially | illegally | mechanically | regardless |
| automatically | independently | naturally | retail |
| bodily | indirectly | officially | scientifically |
| collectively | individually | openly | secretly |
| commercially | innocently | overtly | solo |
| deliberately | instinctively | part-time | specially |
| directly | involuntarily | personally | symbolically |
| duly | jointly | politically | wholesale |

**forms**   **6.43** Most adverbs of manner are formed from qualitative adjectives, for example 'stupidly' from 'stupid', and 'angrily' from 'angry'. For more information about the forms of adverbs, see paragraph 6.17.

**USAGE NOTE**   **6.44** Instead of using an adverb of manner, you can sometimes use prepositional phrases or noun groups to give more information about the manner or circumstances of an action.

*'Come here,' he said <u>in a low voice</u>.*
*I know I have to do it <u>this way</u>.*

In some cases you may have to do this, because there is no adverb. See paragraph 6.23.

# Adverbs of degree

**6.45** When you want to give more information about the extent of an action or the degree to which an action is performed, you often use an **adverb of degree**.

*I enjoyed the course immensely.*
*I had almost forgotten about the trip.*
*A change of one word can radically alter the meaning of a statement.*

**6.46** Here is a list of adverbs of degree:

| | | | |
|---|---|---|---|
| absolutely | extraordinarily | partly | somewhat |
| adequately | extremely | perfectly | soundly |
| almost | fairly | poorly | strongly |
| altogether | fantastically | positively | sufficiently |
| amazingly | fully | powerfully | supremely |
| awfully | greatly | practically | surprisingly |
| badly | half | pretty | suspiciously |
| completely | hard | profoundly | terribly |
| considerably | hugely | purely | totally |
| dearly | immensely | quite | tremendously |
| deeply | incredibly | radically | truly |
| drastically | intensely | rather | unbelievably |
| dreadfully | just | really | utterly |
| enormously | largely | reasonably | very |
| entirely | moderately | remarkably | virtually |
| exceedingly | nearly | significantly | well |
| excessively | noticeably | simply | wonderfully |
| extensively | outright | slightly | |

**from adjectives**

**6.47** Adverbs of degree are often formed from adjectives by adding '-ly'. Some are formed from qualitative adjectives, for example 'deeply', 'hugely', and 'strongly', and some from classifying adjectives, for example 'absolutely', 'perfectly', and 'utterly'.

A few adverbs of degree are formed from postdeterminers, such as 'entirely'.

See Chapter 2 for more information about types of adjectives.

**position in clause**

**6.48** You can use adverbs of degree in the usual positions for adjuncts.

*I admired him greatly.*
*I greatly enjoyed working with them.*
*Yoga can greatly diminish stress levels.*

However, you rarely use an adverb of degree at the beginning of a clause. For example, you do not usually say 'Greatly I admired him'. For more information about placing adverbs at the beginning of a clause, see paragraph 10.93.

A few adverbs of degree are nearly always used in front of the main verb:

| | | | | |
|---|---|---|---|---|
| almost | largely | nearly | really | virtually |

For example, you usually say 'He almost got there', not 'He got there almost'.

*This type of institution has largely disappeared now.*

*He really enjoyed talking about flying.*
*The result virtually ensures Scotland's place in the finals.*

Some adverbs of degree are almost always used after the main verb:

| | | | |
|---|---|---|---|
| altogether | hard | somewhat | well |
| enormously | outright | tremendously | |

*This was a different level of communication altogether.*
*The proposal was rejected outright.*
*I enjoyed the book enormously.*

**emphasizing adverbs**

**6.49** A group of adverbs of degree are called **emphasizing adverbs**. Thes are formed from emphasizing adjectives (see paragraph 2.40).

| | | | | |
|---|---|---|---|---|
| absolutely | just | positively | really | truly |
| completely | outright | purely | simply | utterly |
| entirely | perfectly | quite | totally | |

Note that the emphasizing adverb 'outright' has the same form as an adjective, an adverb of manner, and an adverb of degree.

**6.50** You use an emphasizing adverb such as 'absolutely', 'just', 'quite', 'simply' to add emphasis to the action described by a verb. Emphasizing adverbs usually come in front of verbs.

*I quite agree.*
*I absolutely agree.*
*I just know I'm going to be late.*
*I simply adore this flat.*

In a verb group, the emphasizing adverb comes after the auxiliary or mod and in front of the verb.

*Someone had simply appeared.*
*I was absolutely amazed.*

However, 'absolutely' can occasionally be used after verbs as well.

*I agree absolutely with what Geoffrey has said.*

For other uses of emphasizing adverbs, see paragraphs 10.85 to 10.86.

**submodifiers**

**6.51** You can use some adverbs of degree in front of other adverbs. Whe adverbs of degree are used like this they are called **submodifiers.**

They can also be used as submodifiers in front of adjectives; this use is explained in paragraphs 2.145 to 2.173, where lists of submodifiers and their meanings are also given.

*He prepared his speech very carefully.*
*He was having to work awfully hard.*
*Things changed really dramatically.*
*We get on extremely well with our neighbours.*
*We were able to hear everything pretty clearly.*
*The paper disintegrated fairly easily.*
*He dressed rather formally.*
*Every child reacts somewhat differently.*

Note that 'moderately' and 'reasonably' are mainly used in front of adver which do not end in '-ly'.

*He works reasonably hard.*

A few adverbs of degree can be used as submodifiers with comparatives: see the section beginning at paragraph 2.162.

*This could all be done very much more quickly.*
*I thanked him again, even more profusely than before.*
*I hope you can see slightly more clearly what is going on.*

Note that 'still' can also be placed after the comparative.

*They're doing better in some respects now. Of course they've got to do better still.*

**other adverbs of degree**    6.52 There are some special adverbs of degree. These include 'much', which can be used as an adverb of degree in negative clauses, and in reported questions after 'how'.

*She was difficult as a child and hasn't changed much.*
*These definitions do not help much.*
*Have you told him how much you love him?*

'Very much' is also used in a similar way.

*She is charming. We like her very much.*

The comparative adverbs 'better' and 'worse' and the superlative adverbs 'best' and 'worst' can also be adverbs of degree.

*You know him better than anyone else.*
*It is the land itself which suffers worst.*

'More' and 'less' can be used as comparative adverbs of degree.

*Her tears frightened him more than anything that had ever happened to him before.*
*The ground heats up less there.*

'Most' and 'least' can be used as superlative adverbs of degree.

*She gave me the opportunity to do what I wanted to do most.*
*They staged some of his least known operas.*

Comparative adverbs and superlative adverbs are explained in the section beginning at paragraph 6.30.

The noun groups 'a bit', 'a great deal', 'a little', and 'a lot' are also used as adverbs of degree.

*I don't like this a bit.*
*The situation's changed a great deal since then.*

# Giving information about place: prepositions

6.53 This section explains how to indicate the place where an action occurs, the place where someone or something is, the place they are going to or coming from, or the direction they are moving in.

This usually involves using a **prepositional phrase** as an **adjunct**. For general information on adjuncts, see paragraphs 6.1 to 6.15.

A **prepositional phrase** consists of a **preposition** and its **object**, which is nearly always a noun group.

The most basic use of most prepositions is to indicate position and direction.

*He fumbled in his pocket.*
*On your left is the river.*
*Why did he not drive to Valence?*
*The voice was coming from my apartment.*
*I ran inside and bounded up the stairs.*

**6.54** A **preposition** is a word which opens up the possibilities of saying more about a thing or an action, because you can choose any appropriate noun group after it as its object. Most prepositions are single words, although there are some that consist of more than one word, such as 'out of' and 'in between'.

Here is a list of common one-word prepositions which are used to talk about place or destination:

| | | | | |
|---|---|---|---|---|
| about | before | down | opposite | towards |
| above | behind | from | outside | under |
| across | below | in | over | underneath |
| along | beneath | inside | past | up |
| alongside | beside | into | round | within |
| among | between | near | through | |
| around | beyond | off | throughout | |
| at | by | on | to | |

Here is a list of prepositions which consist of more than one word and which are used to talk about place or destination:

| | | | |
|---|---|---|---|
| ahead of | close by | in front of | on top of |
| all over | close to | near to | out of |
| away from | in between | next to | |

**6.55** Many prepositions can also be adverbs, that is, they can be used without an object. See paragraph 6.83 for a list of these.

**WARNING** **6.56** Because English has a large number of prepositions, some of them, such as 'beside', 'by', 'near' and 'next to', are very close in meaning. Other prepositions, for example 'at' and 'in', can be used for several different meanings. The meaning and usage of prepositions should be checked where possible in a dictionary.

**6.57** Prepositions have an **object**, which comes after the preposition.

*The switch is by the door.*
*Look behind you, Willie!*

Note that if a personal pronoun is used as the object of a preposition, it must be the object pronoun: 'me', 'you', 'him', 'her', 'it', 'us', 'them'.

Prepositions can also combine with complex noun groups to describe places in some detail. See paragraph 2.297 for information on the use of 'of' in noun groups.

*I stood alone in the middle of the yard.*
*He was sitting towards the rear end of the room.*
*He went to the back of the store.*

# Position of prepositional phrases

**after verbs indicating position**

**6.58** Prepositional phrases are most commonly used after verbs. They are used after verbs which indicate position in order to specify where something is.

*She lives in Newcastle.*
*An old piano stood in the corner of the room.*
*You ought to stay out of the sun.*

The following verbs are often used to indicate position:

| | | | |
|---|---|---|---|
| be | lie | sit | stay |
| belong | live | be situated | |
| hang | remain | stand | |

**after verbs indicating movement**

**6.59** Prepositional phrases are used after verbs indicating movement to specify the direction of movement.

*I went into the kitchen and began to make the dinner.*
*Mrs Kaul was leading him to his seat.*
*The others burst from their tents.*
*The storm had uprooted trees from the ground.*
*He took her to Edinburgh.*

**after verbs indicating activities**

**6.60** Prepositional phrases are used after verbs indicating activities to specify where an activity takes place.

*...children playing in the street.*
*The meeting was being held at a community centre in Logan Heights.*
*He was practising high jumps in the garden.*

**6.61** Prepositional phrases usually come at the end of the clause, after the verb or after the object of the verb if there is one.

*We landed at a small airport.*
*We put the children's toys in a big box.*

**at beginning of clause: for emphasis or contrast**

**6.62** If you want to focus on the prepositional phrase for emphasis or contrast, it can be placed at the beginning of the clause. This ordering is mainly used in descriptive writing or reports.

*In the garden everything was peaceful.*
*Under some brown paper was the body of a woman.*

**at beginning of clause: inversion of subject and verb**

**6.63** If you put a prepositional phrase which refers to the position of something at the beginning of the clause when you are using a verb **intransitively**, the normal word order after it is often changed, and the verb is placed before the subject.

*On the ceiling hung dustpans and brushes.*
*Inside the box lie the group's US mining assets.*
*Beyond them lay the fields.*

If you are using 'be' as a main verb, the verb always comes before the subject; so, for example, you cannot say 'Under her chin a colossal brooch was'.

*Under her chin was a colossal brooch.*
*Next to it is a different sign which says simply 'Beware'.*
*Alongside him on the rostrum will be Mr Mitchell Fromstein.*

# Indicating position

**6.64** The prepositional phrases in the following examples indicate the place where an action occurs, or the place where someone or something is.

*The children shouted, waving leafy branches above their heads.*
*The whole play takes place at a beach club.*
*Two minutes later we were safely inside the taxi.*
*He stood near the door.*
*She kept his picture on her bedside table.*

**prepositions** **6.65** The following prepositions are used to specify position:
**indicating**
**position**

| | | | | |
|---|---|---|---|---|
| aboard | among | between | near | through |
| about | around | beyond | near to | under |
| above | astride | by | next to | underneath |
| across | at | close by | off | up |
| against | away from | close to | on | upon |
| ahead of | before | down | on top of | with |
| all over | behind | in | opposite | within |
| along | below | in between | out of | |
| alongside | beneath | in front of | outside | |
| amidst | beside | inside | past | |

**USAGE NOTE** **6.66** Some prepositions can only be used with a restricted group of nouns.

For example, 'aboard' is used with a noun referring to a form of transport, such as 'ship', 'plane', 'train', or 'bus', or with the name of a particular ship, the flight number for a particular plane journey, and so on.

*There's something terribly wrong aboard this ship, Dr Marlowe.*
*More than 1500 people died aboard the Titanic.*
*...getting aboard that flight to Rome.*
*He climbed aboard a truck.*

Here is a list of nouns which you can use with 'aboard' to indicate position

| | | | |
|---|---|---|---|
| aircraft carrier | coach | rocket | train |
| bike | ferry | ship | trawler |
| boat | jet | sledge | truck |
| bus | plane | space shuttle | yacht |

'Astride' is mainly used to indicate that a person has one leg on each side of something, usually sitting on it or riding it.

*He whipped out a chair and sat astride it.*
*He spotted a man sitting astride a horse.*

When 'before' is used to indicate position, the object is usually a person ( group of people.

*Leading representatives were put firmly in their place before a live television audience.*
*He appeared before a disciplinary committee.*

'All over' usually has a large or indefinite area as its object.

*Hundreds of Jews all over the world are finding their way back to their ancestral traditions.*
*There were pieces of ship all over the place.*

**USAGE NOTE**

**6.67** Some prepositions have several meanings. For example, 'on' can be used to indicate that someone or something is resting on a horizontal surface or is attached to something, or that someone's place of work is an area such as a farm or a building site.

*The phone was on the floor in the hallway.*
*I lowered myself into the ravine on a rope tied to the trunk of a tree.*
*My father worked on a farm.*

**prepositions with comparative forms**

**6.68** 'Near', 'near to', and 'close to' have comparative forms that can also be used as prepositions.

*We're moving nearer my parents.*
*Venus is much nearer to the Sun than the Earth.*
*The judge's bench was closer to me than Ruchell's chair.*

**more specific position**

**6.69** If you want to say more exactly which part of the other thing an object is nearest to, or exactly which part of an area or room it is in, you can use one of the following prepositions: 'at', 'by', 'in', 'near', 'on', 'round'. 'To' and 'towards', usually used to indicate direction, are used to express position in a more approximate way.

The objects of the prepositions are nouns referring to parts of an object or place, such as 'top', 'bottom', and 'edge'. Here is a list of words which are used to refer to parts of an object or place:

| | | | | |
|---|---|---|---|---|
| back | side | south | graveside | roadside |
| bottom | top | south-east | hillside | seaside |
| edge | ~ | south-west | kerbside | waterside |
| end | east | west | lakeside | |
| front | east-west | ~ | mountainside | |
| left | north | bankside | poolside | |
| middle | north-east | bedside | quayside | |
| right | north-west | dockside | ringside | |

When the place that you are referring to is obvious or has been stated earlier, you use the nouns in the singular with the determiner 'the'.

*I ran inside and bounded up the stairs. Wendy was standing at the top.*
*He was sitting towards the rear.*
*To the north are the main gardens.*
*We found him sitting by the fireside.*

Other determiners, for example 'this' and 'each', can be used with nouns such as 'side', 'end', and 'edge', because an object or place may have several sides, ends, or edges.

*Loosen the two screws at each end of the fuse.*
*Standing on either side of him were two younger men.*

If the person or thing has been mentioned or is obvious, a possessive determiner can be used.

*...a doll that turns brown in the sun, except for under its swimsuit.*
*There was a gate on our left.*

**6.70** Note that two or three word prepositions which include the word 'of' are more specific because 'of' can be followed by any nominal group.

*She turned and rushed out of the room.*
*There was a man standing in front of me.*
*My sister started piling the books on top of each other.*

**specific**
**distances**

6.71 The place where an action occurs, or where someone or something is, can also be indicated by stating its distance from another object or place.

You can mention the actual distance before a prepositional phrase with 'from' or 'away from'.

*Here he sat on the terrace a few feet from the roaring traffic.*
*The ball swerved two feet away from her to lodge in the net.*

Distance can also be expressed in terms of the time taken to travel it.

*My house is only 20 minutes from where I work.*
*They lived only two or three days away from Juffure.*

The method of travelling can be stated to be even more precise.

*It is less than an hour's drive from here.*
*It's about five minutes' walk from the bus stop.*

**indicating**
**position**
**and distance**

6.72 To indicate both where something is and how far from another object or place it is, the distance can be stated before the following prepositions:

| | | | |
|---|---|---|---|
| above | below | down | past |
| along | beneath | inside | under |
| behind | beyond | outside | up |

*The volcano is only a few hundred metres below sea level.*

The distance can also be stated before prepositional phrases including 'left' and 'right' or points of the compass such as 'north' and 'south-east'.

*We lived forty miles to the east of Ottawa.*

## Indicating direction

6.73 The prepositional phrases in the following examples indicate the place that someone or something is going to, or the place that they are moving towards.

*I'm going with her to Australia.*
*They dived into the water.*
*He saw his mother running towards him.*
*He screwed the lid tightly onto the top of the jar.*
*She stuck her knitting needles into a ball of wool.*

**prepositions**
**used**

6.74 The following prepositions are used to indicate destinations and targets:

| | | | | |
|---|---|---|---|---|
| aboard | at | inside | out of | up |
| all over | away from | into | round | |
| along | beside | near | to | |
| alongside | down | off | toward | |
| around | from | onto | towards | |

Note that 'onto' is sometimes written as two words:

*The bird hopped up on to a higher branch.*

In American English and some varieties of British English, 'out' is used as a preposition without 'of' to indicate direction.

*He walked <u>out the door</u> for the last time.*
*The children were jumping <u>around the room</u> laughing and shouting.*

The prepositional phrases 'to the left' and 'to the right' are also used to indicate direction, from your own viewpoint or that of someone else. See paragraph 6.76.

**6.75** There are some restrictions in the choice of preposition.

'At' is not usually used to indicate the place that the subject of the verb is moving to or towards. It is used to indicate what someone is looking at, or what they cause an object to move towards.

*They were staring <u>at a garage roof.</u>*
*Supporters threw petals <u>at his car.</u>*

'After' is used to indicate that someone or something is following another moving person or thing, or is moving in the same direction but behind them.

*He hurried <u>after his men.</u>*
*...dragging the sacks <u>after us</u> along the ground.*

**direction**
**relative**
**to the front**
**6.76** You can use the prepositional phrases 'to the left' and 'to the right' to say which direction someone or something is moving in relation to the direction they are facing.

*When the light changed they turned <u>to the left</u> and drove away.*

**several**
**directions**
**6.77** The prepositions 'about', 'round', 'around', and 'all over' are used to indicate movement in several directions within a place.

*I wandered <u>round the orchard.</u>*
*The old woman jumped <u>around the clearing</u> in front of the children as she acted out her story.*
*The Rangers began climbing <u>all over the ship.</u>*

**starting point** **6.78** Prepositional phrases can indicate the place or object that is the starting point of a movement.

The following prepositions are used: 'away from', 'from', 'off', and 'out of'.

*The coffee was sent up by the caterer <u>from the kitchens</u> below.*
*She turned and rushed <u>out of the room.</u>*
*He took his hand <u>off her arm.</u>*

**'from' before**
**prepositions**
**and adverbs**
**6.79** 'From' can also be used before another preposition or before some adverbs to indicate the starting point of a movement.

*I had taken his drinking bowl <u>from beneath the kitchen table.</u>*
*...goods imported <u>from abroad.</u>*
*Thomas had stopped bringing his lunch <u>from home.</u>*

'From' can be used before the following adverbs:

| | | | | |
|---|---|---|---|---|
| above | below | everywhere | next door | somewhere |
| abroad | beneath | here | nowhere | there |
| anywhere | downstairs | home | outside | underneath |
| behind | elsewhere | inside | overseas | upstairs |

# Prepositional phrases as qualifiers

**6.80** As well as being used as adjuncts after verbs, prepositional phrases can be used after nouns as qualifiers to give information about place.

*The muscles below Peter's knees were beginning to ache a little.*
*The chestnut trees in the back garden were a blazing orange.*
*They stood and watched the boats on the river.*
*...the clock in her bedroom.*
*...the low wall round the garden.*
*...the black shapeless masses to the left and right of the road.*

**6.81** Prepositional phrases can be added after roads, routes, and so on, to specify them by indicating their destination or direction.

*...the main road from Paris to Marseilles.*
*...the road between the camp and the hospital.*
*...the road through the canyon.*

Similarly, doors, entrances, and so on can be specified by adding prepositional phrases indicating where you can get to through them.

*He opened the door to his room.*
*...at the entrance to the library.*

Prepositional phrases can also be used after nouns to indicate where someone or something comes from.

*...a veterinary officer from Singapore.*
*...an engineer from Hertfordshire.*

# Other ways of giving information about place

**adverbs**  **6.82** As well as a prepositional phrase, an **adverb** can be used as an adjunct to give information about place. For more general information about **adverbs** see the section beginning at paragraph 6.16.

*No birds or animals came near.*
*Seagulls were circling overhead.*

In many cases the same word can be used as a preposition and as an adverb.

*The limb was severed below the elbow.*
*This information is summarized below.*

**adverbs indicating position**  **6.83** Here is a list of words which are used as adverbs to indicate position. Note that some adverbs consist of more than one word, for example, 'out of doors'.

| | | | | |
|---|---|---|---|---|
| abroad | downstream | inland | out of doors | underwater |
| ahead | downtown | midway | overhead | upstairs |
| aloft | downwind | nearby | overseas | upstream |
| ashore | eastward | next door | southward | uptown |
| away | halfway | northward | there | upwind |
| close to | here | offshore | underfoot | westward |
| downstairs | indoors | outdoors | underground | |

The common adverbs of place, such as 'in' and 'up', which are used as adverbs and as prepositions are sometimes called **adverb particles** or **adverbial particles**. The following words are used as adverbs to indicate position, and can also be used as prepositions:

| | | | | |
|---|---|---|---|---|
| aboard | below | down | off | throughout |
| about | beneath | in | opposite | underneath |
| above | beside | in between | outside | up |
| alongside | beyond | inside | over | |
| behind | close by | near | round | |

**6.84** An adverb can be used as an adjunct of place or direction if the adverb itself makes it clear what place or direction you mean.

*The young men hated working <u>underground</u>.*
*The engine droned on as we flew <u>northward</u>.*

You can also use an adverb as an adjunct when it is clear from the context what place or direction you are referring to. For example, you may have mentioned the place earlier, or the adverb may refer to your own location, or to the location of the person or thing being talked about.

*He moved to Portugal, and it was <u>there</u> where he learnt to do the samba.*
*She walked <u>away</u> and my mother stood in the middle of the road, watching.*
*They had spent the autumn of 1855 in the Seeoni hills. And it was <u>here</u> that Hilary had written a report on the events that followed the annexation.*

**USAGE NOTE** **6.85** A small group of adverbs of position are used to indicate the area in which a situation exists:

| | | | |
|---|---|---|---|
| globally | locally | universally | worldwide |
| internationally | nationally | widely | |

*Everything we used was bought <u>locally</u>.*

Unlike most other adverbs of position, they cannot be used after 'be' to state the position of something.

**USAGE NOTE** **6.86** Another small group of adverbs are used to indicate where two or more people or things are in relation to each other: 'together', 'apart', 'side by side' and 'abreast'.

*All the villagers and visitors would sit <u>together</u> round the fire.*
*...a little kneeling figure revealed by two angels holding the curtains <u>apart</u>.*

**adverbs of position with a following adjunct** **6.87** Some adverbs of position are normally followed by another adjunct of position. This is particularly common when the verb 'be' is used as a main verb.

*Barbara's <u>down at the cottage</u>.*
*Adam was <u>halfway up the stairs</u>.*
*Out <u>on the quiet surface of the river</u>, something moved.*
*She is <u>up in her own bedroom</u>.*

**adverbs of position with adjunct, modifier, or qualifier** **6.88** The adverbs 'deep', 'far', 'high', and 'low', which indicate distance as well as position, are also usually followed by another adjunct of position or are modified or qualified in some other way.

*Many of the eggs remain buried <u>deep among the sand grains</u>.*
*One plane, flying <u>very low</u>, swept back and forth.*

'Deep down', 'far away', 'high up', and 'low down' are often used instead of the adverbs on their own.

*The window was <u>high up</u>, miles above the rocks.*
*Sita scraped a shallow cavity <u>low down</u> in the wall.*

'Far' and 'far away' are often qualified by a prepositional phrase beginning with 'from'.

*I was standing <u>far away from the ball</u>.*
*We lived <u>far from the nearest village</u>.*

adverbs
of position:
comparatives
and
superlatives **6.89** Some adverbs have comparative and superlative forms. The superlative form is not used to indicate position, but to specify which of several things you are talking about.

'Deeper', 'further' (or 'farther'), 'higher', and 'lower' are usually followed by another adjunct of position.

*Further along the beach, a thin trickle of smoke was climbing into the sky.*
*The beans are a bit higher on the stalk this year.*

'Nearer' can be used as an adverb as well as a preposition (see paragraph 6.68 above). 'Closer' can only be used as an adverb.

*The hills were nearer now.*
*Thousands of tourists stood watching or milled around trying to get closer*

**indefinite place adverbs** **6.90** There are four indefinite adverbs of position: 'anywhere', 'everywhere', 'nowhere', and 'somewhere'. They are used to indicate a position which is not definite or is very general.

*I dropped my cigar somewhere round here.*
*I thought I'd seen you somewhere.*
*There were bicycles everywhere.*
*No-one can find Howard or Barbara anywhere.*

'Nowhere' makes a clause negative.

*There was nowhere to hide.*

If 'nowhere' is at the beginning of a clause, the subject of the verb must be placed after an auxiliary or a form of 'be' or 'have'.

*Nowhere have I seen any serious mention of this.*
*Nowhere are they overwhelmingly numerous.*

**adding information** **6.91** There are several structures you can use with indefinite place adverbs in order to give more information. You can use:

● an adverb of place:

*I would like to work somewhere abroad.*
*We're certainly nowhere near.*

● an adjective:

*We could go to Majorca if you want somewhere lively.*
*Are you going somewhere special?*

● a prepositional phrase:

*The waiter wasn't anywhere in sight.*
*In 1917, Kollontai was the only woman in any government anywhere in the world.*

● or a 'to'-infinitive clause:

*We mentioned that we were looking for somewhere to live.*
*I wanted to have somewhere to put it.*

You can also use a relative clause. Note that the relative pronoun is usually omitted.

*Was there anywhere you wanted to go?*
*Everywhere I went, people were angry or suspicious.*

**different or additional places** **6.92** 'Else' is used after the indefinite place adverb to indicate a different or additional place.

*We could hold the meeting somewhere else.*

*More people die in bed than anywhere else.*

'Elsewhere' can be used instead of 'somewhere else'.

*Gwen pulled down a folding seat and strapped herself in. The other girls had found seats elsewhere.*
*Elsewhere in the tropics, rainfall is notoriously variable and unreliable.*

**6.93** 'Everywhere' and 'anywhere' can also be used as the subjects of verbs, especially 'be'.

*Sometimes I feel that anywhere, just anywhere, would be better than this.*
*I looked around for a shop where I could buy chocolate, but everywhere was closed.*

# Destinations and directions

**adverbs indicating destinations and targets**

**6.94** Adverbs can be used to indicate destinations and targets.

*'I have expected you,' she said, inviting him inside.*
*No birds or animals came near.*

The following adverbs are used to indicate destinations or targets:

| | | | | |
|---|---|---|---|---|
| aboard | heavenward | inside | out of doors | upstairs |
| abroad | home | inward | outside | uptown |
| ashore | homeward | inwards | overseas | |
| close | in | near | skyward | |
| downstairs | indoors | next door | there | |
| downtown | inland | outdoors | underground | |

The comparative forms 'nearer' and 'closer' are more commonly used than 'near' or 'close'.

*Come nearer.*

'Deep', 'far', 'high', and 'low' are also used as adverbs indicating a destination or target but only when followed by another adjunct or modified in some other way.

*The dancers sprang high into the air brandishing their spears.*

The comparative forms 'deeper', 'further' (or 'farther'), 'higher', and 'lower' are also used, and so is the superlative form 'furthest' (or 'farthest'). These do not have to be followed by another adjunct or modified in another way.

*We left the waterfall and climbed higher.*
*People have to trek further and further from the villages.*

**relative direction**

**6.95** Adverbs can be used to indicate direction in relation to the particular position of the person or thing you are talking about.

*Go north from Leicester Square up Wardour Street.*
*Don't look down.*
*...the part of the engine that was spinning around.*
*Mrs James gave a little cry and hurried on.*
*They grabbed him and pulled him backwards.*
*He turned left and began strolling slowly down the street.*

They can also indicate the direction in which someone or something is facing in relation to the front of the place they are in.

*The seats face forward.*

The following adverbs are used to indicate direction of this sort:

| | | | |
|---|---|---|---|
| ahead | right | eastward | south-east |
| along | sideways | eastwards | south-west |
| back | ~ | north | round |
| backward | anti-clockwise | northward | up |
| backwards | around | northwards | upward |
| forward | clockwise | north-east | upwards |
| forwards | down | north-west | west |
| left | downward | south | westward |
| on | downwards | southward | westwards |
| onward | east | southwards | |

**movement in several directions**

**6.96** The adverbs 'round', 'about', and 'around' can indicate movement in several directions within a place.

*Stop rushing about!*
*They won't want anyone else trampling around.*

The following adverbial expressions indicate repeated movement in different directions:

| | | |
|---|---|---|
| back and forth | hither and thither | to and fro |
| backwards and forwards | in and out | up and down |
| from side to side | round and round | |

*At other times she would pace up and down outside the trailer.*
*Burke was walking back and forth as he spoke.*
*The Princess ran hither and thither in the orchard.*

**movement away**

**6.97** The following adverbs can be used to indicate movement away from someone or something:

| | | | | |
|---|---|---|---|---|
| aside | away | off | out | outward |

*The farmer just laughed and rode away.*
*It took just one tug to pull them out.*

The adverb 'apart' indicates that two or more things move away from each other.

*I rushed in and tried to pull the dogs apart.*

**movement along a path**

**6.98** The following adverbs can be used to indicate movement along a road, path, or line:

| | | |
|---|---|---|
| alongside | downhill | uphill |
| beside | downstream | upstream |

*Going downhill was easy.*
*It wasn't the moving that kept me warm; it was the effort of pushing Daisy uphill.*

**movement across or past something**

**6.99** The following adverbs can be used to indicate movement across or past something:

| | | | |
|---|---|---|---|
| across | over | past | through |
| by | overhead | round | |

*There's an aircraft coming over.*
*'Where are you going?' demanded Miss Craig as Florrie rushed by.*

**indefinite**
**direction**

**6.100** The indefinite place adverbs are used to indicate a destination or direction when you want to be more general or vague.

*He went off somewhere for a shooting weekend.*
*Dust blew everywhere, swirling over dry caked mountains.*
*There was hardly anywhere to go.*
*Can't you play elsewhere?*

'Nowhere' is mainly used metaphorically, to indicate lack of progress.

*They were getting nowhere and had other things to do.*

See paragraph 6.90 for more information on these indefinite adverbs.

**adverbs as**
**qualifiers**

**6.101** Like prepositional phrases, adverbs can also be used as qualifiers after nouns rather than as adjuncts after verbs.

*...the man who watched him from the terrace above.*
*The man opposite rises, and lifts down her case.*
*People everywhere are becoming more conscious of inequality.*
*...the road south.*

# Noun groups referring to place: place names

**6.102** There are a number of verbs of position and movement which are followed by noun groups referring to places instead of by adjuncts. These are described in paragraph 3.22.

*Peel approached the building.*

**6.103** Instead of using a noun group to refer to a place, you can use the name of the place.

*This great block of land became Antarctica.*
*...a Baltic island roughly the size of the Isle of Man.*
*Outstanding examples of her work are included in an exhibition at the National Museum of Film and Photography in Bradford.*

**verbs after**
**place names**

**6.104** Most place names are singular nouns, although some look like plural nouns, for example 'The Netherlands'. Some place names, for example those referring to groups of islands or mountains, are plural nouns. Verbs used with place names follow the normal rules, so a singular verb form is used with a singular noun and a plural verb form with a plural noun.

*Milan is a very interesting city.*
*The Andes split the country down the middle.*

**place names**
**referring to**
**people**

**6.105** The name of a place can be used to refer to the people who live there. If the place name is a singular noun, a singular verb form is still used, even though the noun is being used to refer to a plural concept.

*Europe was sick of war.*

The name of a country or its capital city is often used to refer to the government of that country.

*Britain* and *France* jointly suggested a plan.
*Washington* had put a great deal of pressure on *Tokyo*.

**place names referring to events**   **6.106** Place names can also be used to refer to a well-known historical o recent event that occurred there, such as a battle, a disaster, an international sports competition, or an important political meeting.

*After Waterloo, trade and industry surged again.*
*...the effect of Chernobyl on British agriculture.*

**place names used as modifiers**   **6.107** Many place names can be used as modifiers, to indicate where things come from or are characteristic of as well as where things are. If a place name begins with 'the', you omit it when you use the name as a modifier.

*...a London hotel.*
*...Arctic explorers.*
*She has a Midlands accent.*
*...the New Zealand rugby team.*

Note that the names of continents and of many countries cannot be used as modifiers. Instead, you use classifying adjectives such as 'African' and 'Italian'.

## Other uses of prepositional phrases

**6.108** Prepositions are commonly used to indicate things other than place as well, for example to indicate a time, a means, or an attribute. The following paragraphs from 6.109 to 6.116 describe these uses briefly, and give cross references to fuller explanations elsewhere. The following prepositions are only or mainly used to indicate things other than place:

| | | | |
|---|---|---|---|
| after | during | like | until |
| as | except | of | |
| despite | for | since | |

**referring to time**   **6.109** Although the main use of prepositional phrases is to talk about position or direction, they are also used to refer to time.

*I'll see you on Monday.*
*They are expecting to announce the sale within the next few days.*

The use of prepositions to talk about time is explained in paragraphs 5.99 and 5.102 to 5.107.

**referring to manner**   **6.110** Prepositional phrases are also used to say something more about the manner in which an action was performed, or the way in which it should be done.

*'Oh yes,' Etta sneered in an offensive way.*
*A bird can change direction by dipping one wing and lifting the other.*
*He brushed back his hair with his hand.*

Prepositional phrases such as 'on foot' or 'by bus' can be used to indicate a method of travelling.

*I usually go to work on foot.*
*I travelled home by bus.*

The use of adverbs to talk about manner is explained in the section beginning at paragraph 6.36.

**6.111** You can also use prepositional phrases to give more information about the feelings of the person performing the action.

*Fanny saw <u>with amazement</u> that the letter was addressed to herself.*

**'like' and 'as' in comparison**

**6.112** You can use the preposition 'like' to indicate that someone or something behaves in a similar way to someone or something else.

*She treated me <u>like a servant.</u>*
*She shuffled <u>like an old lady.</u>*

There is more information about comparison in general in the section beginning at paragraph 2.108.

**6.113** You can also use 'like' and 'as' to say that someone or something is treated in a similar way to someone or something else. The noun group after 'like' or 'as' describes the person or thing affected by the action, not the person or thing doing the action.

*My parents dressed me <u>like a little doll.</u>*
*Their parents continue to treat them <u>as children.</u>*
*She treated her <u>more like a daughter than a companion.</u>*

You can also use expressions such as 'like this' or 'like that' to refer to a particular manner of doing something.

*If you're going to behave <u>like this,</u> the best thing you can do is to go back to bed.*
*How dare you speak to me <u>like that?</u>*

The use of 'like' and 'as' in subordinate clauses is explained in paragraphs 8.78 to 8.80.

**6.114** You can say that one way of doing something has as much of a quality as another way of doing something, by using 'as' followed by an adverb followed by another 'as'. The second 'as' is followed by a noun group, a pronoun, an adjunct, or a clause.

*The company has not grown <u>as quickly as many of its rivals.</u>*
*She wanted someone to talk to <u>as badly as I did.</u>*

**circumstances of an action**

**6.115** You can use prepositional phrases to indicate something about the circumstances accompanying an action.

*'No,' she said <u>with a defiant look.</u>*
*...struggling to establish democracy <u>under adverse conditions.</u>*

**reason, cause or purpose**

**6.116** Prepositional phrases can also be used to say something about the reason for an action, or the cause or purpose of it.

*In 1923, the Prime Minister resigned <u>because of ill health.</u>*
*He was dying <u>of pneumonia.</u>*

'As' is used to indicate the function or purpose of something.

*He worked <u>as a truck driver.</u>*
*During the war they used the theatre <u>as a warehouse.</u>*

# Prepositions used with verbs

**in phrasal verbs**

**6.117** Some verbs always have a prepositional phrase after them in particular meanings. They are called **phrasal verbs,** and information about them can be found in paragraphs 3.84 to 3.117.

*She sailed through her exams.*
*What are you getting at?*

**verbs with optional prepositional phrases**

**6.118** Some verbs can have a prepositional phrase instead of a direct object. For more information on these verbs, see paragraph 3.11.

*The Polish Army fought the Germans for nearly five weeks.*
*She was fighting against history.*
*We climbed the mountain.*
*I climbed up the tree.*

**indirect objects of ditransitive verbs**

**6.119** A prepositional phrase is used as the indirect object of a **ditransitive verb** when the indirect object comes after the direct object.

For information on ditransitive verbs see paragraphs 3.74 to 3.83.

If the action described by the verb involves the transfer of something from one person or thing to another, the preposition 'to' is used.

*I passed the letter to my husband.*
*The recovered animals will be given to zoos.*

If the action involves a person doing something for the benefit of another person, the preposition 'for' is used.

*She left a note for her on the table.*

**with reciprocal verbs**

**6.120** Some **reciprocal verbs** require a prepositional phrase when a second noun group is mentioned.

For information on reciprocal verbs, see paragraphs 3.69 to 3.73.

*Our return coincided with the arrival of bad weather.*
*She has refused to cooperate with investigators.*

**with passive verbs**

**6.121** Prepositional phrases are used after verbs in the **passive.**

*90 men found themselves cut off by storms.*
*Moisture must be drawn out first with salt.*

The use of prepositional phrases after passive verbs is explained in paragraphs 10.14 to 10.16.

**position of prepositional phrases and adverbs after verbs**

**6.122** When verbs are followed by prepositional phrases and adverbs, a long prepositional phrase is usually placed after the adverb.

*He listened calmly to the report of his aides.*

A short prepositional phrase can come before or after the adverb.

*The women shouted at me savagely.*
*Miss Burns looked calmly at Marianne.*

# Prepositional phrases after nouns and adjectives

**6.123** Prepositional phrases are sometimes used as qualifiers to describe the subject or object of a clause rather than the manner of an action or situation. See the section beginning at paragraph 2.292 for more information.

*...a girl in a dark grey dress.*
*...a man with a quick temper.*

**particular prepositions after nouns and adjectives**

**6.124** Particular prepositions are used after some nouns and adjectives when adding information. See paragraphs 2.49 to 2.54 and 2.304 to 2.307.

*My respect for her is absolutely enormous.*
*Women's tennis puts an emphasis on technique, not strength.*
*...the solicitor responsible for pursuing the claim.*

**comparisons with 'than' and 'like'**

**6.125** A prepositional phrase with 'than' often indicates the person or thing that is the basis of a comparison.

*He was smarter than you.*
*She was more refined than her husband.*

For more information on **comparisons,** see the section beginning at paragraph 2.108.

The preposition 'like' is used to indicate that someone or something is similar to someone or something else, without comparing any specific quality.

*The British forces are like permanent tourists.*
*We need many more people like these.*

**'of'**

**6.126** 'Of' can be used in prepositional phrases after any noun to indicate various relationships between one noun group and another, especially belonging, possession, and connection. It can be used to state what something is, what it contains, what it is made from, or how much of it there is.

*He was a member of the golf club.*
*She's a friend of Stephen's.*
*...the Mayor of Moscow.*

# Extended meanings of prepositions

**6.127** The uses of prepositional phrases as adjuncts of time and manner are really extended or metaphorical uses that cover a wide range of prepositions and are part of a metaphor that affects many other aspects of language as well. For example, when we talk about 'approaching a point in time', 'a short stretch of time', and so on, we are using words that refer to space to talk about time.

However, there are also extended meanings that apply only to small groups of prepositions, or sometimes only to individual prepositions.

For example, 'in' basically indicates position inside a container.

*What's that in your bag?*
*It will end up in the dustbin.*

However, it is often used with reference to areas rather than containers.

*Emma sat in an armchair with her legs crossed.*
*Then we were told what had happened in Sheffield.*

'In' is also used to indicate relative position.

*We had to do something in the centre of the town to attract visitors.*

However, 'in' is also used in ways that extend its meaning further away from physical position. For example, it can be used to say that someone is involved in a particular situation, group, or activity.

*They were in no danger.*
*The child was in trouble with the police.*
*This government won't be in power for ever.*
*Mr Emile Gumbs has remained in office but the island has no Parliament.*

It can indicate inclusion in a more abstract way.

*Some of her early Hollywood experiences were used in her 1923 film, Ma of the Movies.*
*In any book, you have a moral purpose.*

It can also indicate that something has reached a particular stage, or appears in a particular way.

*The first primroses are in flower.*
*Her hair was in pigtails over either shoulder.*

A few other prepositions with a basic meaning relating to containers can be used in similar ways: for example 'within', 'into', 'out of'.

*Anything within reason should be considered.*
*Those men, when we get them into the police force, are going to be real heroes.*
*Heroines considered attractive by earlier generations now seem hopelessly out of touch.*

# Contents of Chapter 7

# 7 Reporting what people say or think

**7.1** This chapter of the grammar explains the different ways of reporting what people say or think.

**7.2** One way of reporting what someone has said is to repeat their actual words.

*'I don't know much about music,' Judy said.*

A sentence like this is called a **quote structure**.

Instead of repeating Judy's words, the writer could have said, 'Judy said that she didn't know much about music'. This is called a **report structure**.

Quote structures and report structures both consist of two clauses. The main clause is called a **reporting clause**. The other clause indicates what someone said or thought.

In a **quote structure**, this other clause is called the **quote**.

*'Have you met him?' I asked.*
*'I'll see you tomorrow,' said Tom.*

In a **report structure**, the other clause is called the **reported clause**.

*He mentioned that he had a brother living in London.*
*He asked if you would be able to call and see him.*
*He promised to give me the money.*

Note that the reported clause can be a non-finite clause beginning with a 'to'-infinitive.

**7.3** In ordinary conversation, we use **report structures** much more often than **quote structures**. This is because we usually do not know, or cannot remember, the exact words that someone has said. **Quote structures** are mainly used in written stories.

When we report people's thoughts, we almost always use **report structures**, because thoughts do not usually exist in the form of words, so we cannot quote them exactly. **Report structures** can be used to report almost any kind of thought.

**7.4** Paragraphs 7.5 to 7.13 explain verbs used in **reporting clauses**. Paragraphs 7.14 to 7.23 explain **quote structures**. Paragraphs 7.24 to 7.67 explain **report structures**. Paragraphs 7.68 to 7.77 explain how to refer to the speaker and hearer in a quote structure or report structure. Paragraphs 7.78 to 7.81 explain other ways of indicating what someone says or talks about. Paragraphs 7.82 to 7.94 explain other ways of using reported clauses.

## Indicating that you are reporting: reporting verbs

**7.5** You indicate that you are quoting or reporting what someone has said or thought by using a **reporting verb**. Every reporting clause contains a reporting verb.

*'I don't see what you are getting at,'* Jeremy <u>said</u>.
*He looked old, Harold <u>thought,</u> and sick.*
*They <u>were complaining</u> that Canton was hot and noisy.*

**basic**
**reporting**
**verbs**

**7.6** You use 'say' when you are simply reporting what someone said and do not want to add any more information about what you are reporting.

*She <u>said</u> that she didn't want to know.*

You use 'ask' when you are reporting a question.

*'How's it all going?'* Derek <u>asked</u>.

**showing**
**the purpose**
**of speaking**

**7.7** Some reporting verbs such as 'answer', 'complain', and 'explain' tell you what purpose an utterance was intended to serve. For example, 'answer' tells you that a statement was intended as an answer, and 'complain' tells you that a statement was intended as a complaint.

*He <u>answered</u> that the price would be three pounds.*
*'He never told me, sir,'* Watson <u>complained</u>.
*'Please don't,'* I <u>begged</u>.
*I <u>suggested</u> that it was time to leave.*

Some reporting verbs used in quote structures show the manner of speaking. See paragraph 7.17.

Here is a list of reporting verbs which can be used to report what people say:

| | | | | |
|---|---|---|---|---|
| acknowledge | concede | imply | predict | say |
| add | confess | inform | proclaim | scream |
| admit | confirm | inquire | promise | shout |
| advise | contend | insist | prophesy | shriek |
| agree | continue | instruct | propose | state |
| allege | convince | invite | reassure | stipulate |
| announce | cry | maintain | recall | storm |
| answer | declare | mention | recite | suggest |
| argue | decree | mumble | recommend | swear |
| ask | demand | murmur | record | teach |
| assert | deny | muse | refuse | tell |
| assure | describe | mutter | remark | threaten |
| beg | direct | note | remind | thunder |
| begin | discuss | notify | repeat | urge |
| boast | dispute | object | reply | vow |
| call | enquire | observe | report | wail |
| chorus | explain | order | request | warn |
| claim | forbid | persuade | respond | whisper |
| command | grumble | plead | reveal | write |
| comment | guarantee | pledge | rule | yell |
| complain | hint | pray | be rumoured | |

**WARNING**

**7.8** Note that the verbs 'address', 'converse', 'lecture', 'speak', and 'talk', although they mean 'to say something', cannot be used as reporting verbs.

**verbs**
**of thinking**
**and knowing**

**7.9** Many reporting verbs are used to refer to people's thoughts, rather than to what they say. Reporting verbs can be used to refer to many different kinds of thought, including beliefs, wishes, hopes, intentions, and decisions. They can also be used to refer to acts of remembering and forgetting.

*We both <u>knew</u> that the town was cut off.*

*'I'll go to him in a minute,' she <u>thought</u>.*
*I <u>had</u> always <u>believed</u> that one day I would see him again.*

Here is a list of reporting verbs which can be used to report people's thoughts:

| | | | | |
|---|---|---|---|---|
| accept | expect | intend | prefer | think |
| agree | fear | judge | propose | understand |
| assume | feel | know | reason | vow |
| believe | figure | long | recall | want |
| consider | foresee | mean | reckon | wish |
| decide | forget | muse | reflect | wonder |
| determine | guess | note | regret | worry |
| doubt | hold | plan | remember | |
| dream | hope | ponder | resolve | |
| estimate | imagine | pray | suppose | |

**verbs of learning and perceiving**

**7.10** A third group of reporting verbs refer to learning and perceiving facts.

*I have since <u>learned</u> that the writer of the letter is now dead.*
*Then she <u>saw</u> that he was sleeping.*

Here is a list of reporting verbs which refer to learning and perceiving facts:

| | | | |
|---|---|---|---|
| conclude | gather | note | read |
| discover | hear | notice | realize |
| elicit | infer | observe | see |
| find | learn | perceive | sense |

**7.11** Some of the verbs in the above lists, such as 'tell' and 'promise', must be or can be followed by an object indicating who the hearer is. See paragraphs 7.71 to 7.72.

Note that some verbs appear in more than one list, because they have more than one meaning.

**indicating the way that something is said**

**7.12** When you use a quote structure or a report structure, you can give more information about the way that something is said by putting an adverb or a prepositional phrase after the reporting verb.

*'I've got the key!' he announced <u>triumphantly</u>.*
*His secretary explained <u>patiently</u> that this was the only time he could spare from his busy schedule.*
*'I know what you mean,' Carrie replied <u>with feeling</u>.*

You can indicate how the thing that is said fits into the conversation by using a prepositional phrase.

*'A gift from my mother,' he added <u>in explanation</u>.*

**negatives in reporting clauses**

**7.13** With a small number of reporting verbs, the negative is often expressed in the reporting clause rather than in the reported clause. 'I don't think Mary is at home' means the same as 'I think Mary is not at home', and 'She doesn't want to see him' means 'She wants not to see him'.

*I <u>do not think</u> she suspects me.*
*She <u>didn't believe</u> she would ever see him again.*
*He <u>didn't want</u> to go.*

We *don't intend* to put him on trial.

Here is a list of reporting verbs which are often used with a negative in this way:

| | | | |
|---|---|---|---|
| believe | imagine | propose | think |
| expect | intend | reckon | want |
| feel | plan | suppose | wish |

# Reporting someone's actual words: quote structures

**7.14** When you want to say that a person used particular words, you use a **quote structure.** You can do this even if you do not know, or do not remember, the exact words that were spoken. When you use a quote structure, you report what someone said as if you were using their own words.

Quote structures are sometimes called **direct speech.** A quote structure consists of two clauses. One clause is the **reporting clause,** which contains the reporting verb.

*'I knew I'd seen you,' I said.*
*'Yes please,' replied John.*

The other part is the **quote,** which represents what someone says or has said.

*'Let's go and have a look at the swimming-pool,' she suggested.*
*'Leave me alone,' I snarled.*

You can quote anything that someone says—statements, questions, orders, suggestions, and exclamations. In writing, you use inverted commas (' ') or (" ") at the beginning and end of a quote.

*'Thank you,' I said.*
*After a long silence he asked: 'What is your name?'*

Note that, in written stories, quotes can be used without reporting clauses if the speakers have been established, and if you do not wish to indicate what kind of utterances the quotes are.

*'When do you leave?'—'I should be gone now.'—'Well, good-bye, Hamo.'*

**7.15** Thinking is sometimes represented as speaking to oneself. You can therefore use some verbs which refer to thinking as reporting verbs in **quote structures.**

*I must go and see Lynn, Marsha thought.*

When you are using a quote structure to say what someone thought, you usually omit the inverted commas at the beginning and end of the quote.

*How much should he tell her? Not much, he decided.*
*Perhaps that's no accident, he reasoned.*
*Why, she wondered, was the flag at half mast?*

**7.16** Here is a list of reporting verbs which are often used with quote structures:

| | | | | |
|---|---|---|---|---|
| add | begin | demand | proclaim | state |
| admit | boast | explain | promise | suggest |
| advise | claim | grumble | read | tell |
| agree | command | inquire | reason | think |
| announce | comment | insist | recite | urge |
| answer | complain | muse | reflect | vow |
| argue | conclude | observe | remark | warn |
| ask | confess | order | reply | wonder |
| assert | continue | plead | report | write |
| assure | decide | ponder | respond | |
| beg | declare | pray | say | |

A few of these verbs can or must be used with an object referring to the hearer. See paragraphs 7.71 to 7.72.

**verbs which describe the manner of speaking**

**7.17** If you want to indicate the way in which something was said, you can use a reporting verb such as 'shout', 'wail', or 'scream'. Verbs like these usually occur only in written stories.

*'Jump!' shouted the oldest woman.*
*'Oh, poor little thing,' she wailed.*
*'Get out of there,' I screamed.*

Here is a list of verbs indicating the way in which something is said:

| | | | | |
|---|---|---|---|---|
| call | mumble | scream | storm | whisper |
| chorus | murmur | shout | thunder | yell |
| cry | mutter | shriek | wail | |

**PRODUCTIVE FEATURE**

**7.18** Another way of indicating the manner of speaking is to use a verb which is usually used to describe the sound made by a particular kind of animal.

*'Excuse me!' Susannah barked.*

You can use a verb such as 'smile', 'grin', or 'frown' to indicate the expression on someone's face while they are speaking.

*'I'm awfully sorry.'—'Not at all,' I smiled.*
*'Hardly worth turning up for,' he grinned.*

You use verbs like 'bark' and 'smile' in quote structures when you want to create a particular effect, especially in writing. This is a productive feature of English. For more information about productive features see the Introduction.

**position of reporting verb**

**7.19** There are several positions in which you can put the reporting clause in relation to a quote. The usual position is after the quote, but it can also go in front of the quote or in the middle of the quote.

*'You have to keep trying, Mabel,' he said.*
*He stepped back and said, 'Now look at that.'*
*'You see,' he said, 'my father was a clergyman.'*

**7.20** If you put the reporting clause in the middle of a quote, it must go in one of the following positions:

● after a **noun group**

*'That man,'* I said, *'never opened a window in his life.'*

● after a **vocative**

*'Darling,'* Max said to her, *'don't say it's not possible.'*

● after a **sentence adverb**

*'Maybe,'* he said hesitantly, *'maybe there is a beast.'*

● after a **clause,** if the quote contains more than one clause.

*'Your father,'* said James, *'was a kind and generous man'.*

**7.21** You can use most reporting verbs in front of a quote.

*She replied, 'My first thought was to protect him.'*
*One student commented: 'He seems to know his material very well.'*

However, the reporting verbs 'agree', 'command', 'promise', and 'wonder' are hardly ever used in front of a quote.

**inversion of subject and reporting verb**

**7.22** When a reporting verb comes after a quote, the subject is often put after the verb.

*'Perhaps he isn't a bad sort of chap after all,'* <u>remarked Dave.</u>
*'I see,'* <u>said John.</u>
*'I am aware of that,'* <u>replied the Englishman.</u>

Note that this is not done when the subject is a pronoun.

**punctuation of quotes**

**7.23** The following examples show how you punctuate quotes. You can use either single inverted commas (' ') or double inverted commas (" "). The ones used to begin a quote are called **opening** inverted commas, and the ones used to end a quote are called **closing** inverted commas.

*'Let's go,'* I whispered.
*"We have to go home,"* she told him.
*Mona's mother answered: 'Oh yes, she's in.'*
*'He nodded and said, 'Yes, he's my son.'*
*'Margaret,'* I said to her, *'I'm so glad you came.'*
*'What are you doing?'* Sarah asked.
*'Of course it's awful!'* shouted Clarissa.
*'What do they mean,'* she demanded, *'by a "population problem"?'*

If you are quoting more than one paragraph, you put opening inverted commas at the beginning of each paragraph, but you put closing inverted commas only at the end of the last paragraph.

# Reporting in your own words: report structures

**7.24** When you report what people have said using your own words rather than the words they actually used, you use a **report structure**.

*The woman said she had seen nothing.*
*I replied that I had not read it yet.*

You usually use a report structure when you report what someone thinks.

*He thought she was worried.*

Report structures are sometimes called **indirect speech.** A report structure consists of two parts. One part is the **reporting clause,** which contains the reporting verb.

*I told him that nothing was going to happen to me.*
*I have agreed that he should do it.*
*I wanted to be alone.*

The other part is the **reported clause.**

*He answered that he thought the story was extremely clever.*
*He felt that he had to do something.*
*He wondered where they could have come from.*

You usually put the reporting clause first, in order to make it clear that you are reporting rather than speaking directly yourself.

*Henry said that he wanted to go home.*

The exact words that Henry used are unlikely to have been 'I want to go home', although they might have been. It is more likely that he said something like 'I think I should be going now'. You are more likely to report what he meant rather than what he actually said.

There are many reasons why you do not quote a person's exact words. Often you cannot remember exactly what was said. At other times, the exact words are not important or not appropriate in the situation in which you are reporting.

**types of reported clause**

**7.25** There are several types of **reported clause.** The type you use depends on whether you are reporting a statement, a question, an order, or a suggestion.

Most reported clauses either are **'that'-clauses** or begin with a **'to'-infinitive.** When a question is being reported, the reported clause begins with 'if', 'whether', or a **'wh'-word.** The use of **'that'-clauses** as reported clauses is discussed in paragraphs 7.26 to 7.28. **Reported questions** are discussed in paragraphs 7.29 to 7.35. The use of **'to'-infinitive clauses** in report structures is discussed in paragraphs 7.36 to 7.45.

# Reporting statements and thoughts

**7.26** If you want to report a statement or someone's thoughts, you use a reported clause beginning with the conjunction 'that'.

*He said that the police had directed him to the wrong room.*
*He wrote me a letter saying that he understood what I was doing.*
*Mrs Kaul announced that the lecture would now begin.*

In informal speech and writing, the conjunction 'that' is commonly omitted.

*They said I had to see a doctor first.*
*She says she wants to see you this afternoon.*
*He knew the attempt was hopeless.*
*I think there's something wrong.*

In each of these sentences, 'that' could have been used. For example, you can say either 'They said I had to see a doctor first' or 'They said that I had to see a doctor first'.

'That' is often omitted when the reporting verb refers simply to the act of saying or thinking. You usually include 'that' after a verb which gives more information, such as 'complain' or 'explain'.

*The FBI <u>confirmed that</u> the substance was an explosive.*
*I <u>explained that</u> she would have to stay in bed.*

This kind of reported clause is often called a **'that'-clause,** even though many occur without 'that'.

Note that some relative clauses also begin with 'that'. In these clauses, 'that' is a relative pronoun, not a conjunction. Relative clauses are explained in paragraphs 8.83 to 8.116.

**verbs used with hat'-clauses**

**7.27** Here is a list of verbs which are often used as reporting verbs with 'that'-clauses:

| | | | | |
|---|---|---|---|---|
| accept | contend | guess | pledge | say |
| acknowledge | convince | hear | pray | see |
| add | decide | hold | predict | sense |
| admit | deny | hope | promise | state |
| agree | determine | imagine | prophesy | suggest |
| allege | discover | imply | read | suppose |
| announce | dispute | inform | realize | swear |
| answer | doubt | insist | reason | teach |
| argue | dream | judge | reassure | tell |
| assert | elicit | know | recall | think |
| assume | estimate | learn | reckon | threaten |
| assure | expect | maintain | record | understand |
| believe | explain | mean | reflect | vow |
| boast | fear | mention | remark | warn |
| claim | feel | mention | remember | wish |
| comment | figure | note | repeat | worry |
| complain | find | notice | reply | write |
| concede | foresee | notify | report | |
| conclude | forget | object | resolve | |
| confirm | gather | observe | reveal | |
| consider | guarantee | perceive | be rumoured | |

Note that some of these verbs are only used in report structures in some of their senses. For example, if you say 'He accepted a present' you are using 'accept' as an ordinary transitive verb.

A few of these verbs can or must be used with an object referring to the hearer. See paragraphs 7.71 to 7.72.

Some of these verbs, such as 'decide' and 'promise', can also be used with a 'to'-infinitive clause. See paragraphs 7.36 and 7.42.

Some other verbs, such as 'advise' and 'order', can be used as reporting verbs with 'that'-clauses only if the 'that'-clause contains a **modal** or a **subjunctive.** 'That'-clauses of this kind are discussed in paragraph 7.40.

**position of reported clauses**

**7.28** You usually put the reporting clause before the 'that'-clause, in order to make it clear that you are reporting rather than speaking directly yourself.

*I said that I would rather work in the forest.*
*Georgina said she was going to bed.*

However, if you want to emphasize the statement contained in the reported clause, you can alter the order and put the reported clause first, with a comma after it. You do not use 'that' to introduce the clause.

*All these things were trivial, he said.*
*She was worried, he thought.*

If the reported clause is long, you can put the reporting clause in the middle.

*Ten years ago, Moumoni explained, some government people had come t inspect the village.*

# Reporting questions

**7.29** As well as reporting what someone says or thinks, you can also report a question that they ask or wonder about.

Questions in report structures are sometimes called **reported questions o indirect questions.**

**the reporting verb**    **7.30** The reporting verb most often used for reporting questions is 'ask'. Questions can be reported in a more formal way using 'enquire' or 'inquire'.

*I asked if I could stay with them.*
*He asked me where I was going.*
*She inquired how Ibrahim was getting on.*

**WARNING**    **7.31** When you report a question:

● you do not treat it as a question by using interrogative word order
● you do not use a question mark.

So the question 'Did you enjoy it?' could be reported: 'I asked her if she had enjoyed it'.

Questions are explained in paragraphs 4.10 to 4.30.

**'yes/no' questions**    **7.32** There are two main types of question, and so two main types of report structure for questions.

One type of question is called a **'yes/no' question.** These are questions which can be answered simply with 'yes' or 'no'.

When you report a 'yes/no' question, you use an **'if'-clause** beginning with the conjunction 'if', or a **'whether'-clause** beginning with the conjunction 'whether'.

You use 'if' when the speaker has suggested one possibility that may be true. 'Do you know my name?' could be reported as 'A woman asked if I knew her name'.

*She asked him if his parents spoke French.*
*Someone asked me if the work was going well.*
*He inquired if her hair had always been that colour.*

You use 'whether' when the speaker has suggested one possibility but ha left open the question of other possibilities. After 'whether', you can suggest another possibility, or you can leave it unstated.

*I was asked whether I wanted to stay at a hotel or at his home.*
*She asked whether the servants were still there.*
*I asked Professor Fred Bailey whether he agreed.*
*A policeman asked me whether he could be of help.*

Sometimes the alternative possibility is represented by 'or not'.

*The barman didn't ask whether or not they were over eighteen.*
*They asked whether Britain was or was not a Christian country.*

For more information about 'yes/no' questions, see paragraphs 4.12 to 4.16.

**7.33** There are a few other verbs which can be used before 'if'-clauses or 'whether'-clauses, because they refer to being unsure of facts or to discovering facts.

*I didn't know <u>whether to believe him or not.</u>*
*Simon wondered <u>if he should make conversation.</u>*
*She didn't say <u>whether he was still alive.</u>*

Here is a list of other verbs which can be used before 'if'-clauses and 'whether'-clauses:

| | | |
|---|---|---|
| discover | remember | see |
| know | say | wonder |

Note that 'know', 'remember', 'say', and 'see' are usually used in a negative or interrogative clause, or a clause with a modal.

All the verbs in the list, except 'wonder', can also be used with 'that'-clauses: see paragraph 7.27. They can all also be used with clauses beginning with 'wh'-words: see paragraph 7.35.

**'wh'-questions**

**7.34** The other type of question is called a **'wh'-question**. These are questions in which someone asks for information about an event or situation. 'Wh'-questions cannot be answered with 'yes' or 'no'.

When you report a 'wh'-question, you use a **'wh'-word** at the beginning of the reported clause.

*He asked <u>where I was going.</u>*
*She enquired <u>why I was so late.</u>*
*She started to ask <u>what had happened,</u> then decided against it.*
*I asked <u>how they liked the film.</u>*
*It never occurred to me to ask <u>who put it there.</u>*

When the details of the question are clear from the context, you can sometimes leave out everything except the 'wh'-word. This happens mostly in spoken English, especially with 'why'.

*I asked <u>why.</u>*
*They enquired <u>how.</u>*

For more information about 'wh'-questions see paragraphs 4.17 to 4.30.

**7.35** Other verbs can be used before clauses beginning with 'wh'-words, because they refer to knowing, learning, or mentioning one of the circumstances of an event or situation.

*She doesn't know <u>what we were talking about.</u>*
*They couldn't see <u>how they would manage without her.</u>*
*I wonder <u>what's happened.</u>*

Here is a list of other verbs which can be used before clauses beginning with 'wh'-words:

| | | | | |
|---|---|---|---|---|
| decide | forget | realize | suggest | wonder |
| describe | guess | remember | teach | |
| discover | imagine | reveal | tell | |
| discuss | know | say | think | |
| explain | learn | see | understand | |

Note that 'imagine', 'say', 'see', 'suggest', and 'think' are usually used in a negative or interrogative clause, or a clause with a modal.

All the verbs in the list, except 'describe', 'discuss', and 'wonder', can als
be used with 'that'-clauses: see paragraph 7.27.

# Reporting orders, requests, advice, and intentions

**reporting
requests
made to
the hearer**

**7.36** If someone orders, requests, or advises someone else to do
something, this can be reported by using a 'to'-infinitive clause after a
reporting verb such as 'tell'. The person being addressed, who is to
perform the action, is mentioned as the object of the reporting verb.

*He told her to wait there for him.*
*He commanded his men to retreat.*
*He ordered me to fetch the books.*
*My doctor advised me to see a neurologist.*

This is a type of **phase** structure (see paragraphs 3.203 and 3.207).

Here is a list of reporting verbs which can be used with a person as objec'
followed by a 'to'-infinitive clause:

| | | | | |
|---|---|---|---|---|
| advise | command | invite | remind | urge |
| ask | forbid | order | teach | warn |
| beg | instruct | persuade | tell | |

**USAGE NOTE**

**7.37** A few verbs can be used with a 'to'-infinitive clause to report
requests when the hearer is mentioned in a prepositional phrase.

*An officer shouted to us to stop all the noise.*
*I pleaded with him to tell me.*

Here is a list of these verbs and the prepositions used with them:

| | | |
|---|---|---|
| appeal to | shout at | whisper to |
| plead with | shout to | yell at |

**7.38** In ordinary conversation, requests are often put in the form of a
question. For example, you might say 'Will you help me?' instead of 'Help
me'. Similarly, reported requests often look like reported questions.

*People ask me if I can lend them fifty dollars.*

When you report a request like this, you can mention both the person
receiving it and the person making it.

*He asked me whether I would help him.*

Alternatively, you can just mention the person making it.

*He asked if I would answer some questions.*

**7.39** You can report a request in which someone asks if they can do
something by using a 'to'-infinitive clause after 'ask' or 'demand'.

*I asked to see the manager.*

**reporting
suggestions**

**7.40** When someone makes a suggestion about what someone else, no'
their hearer, should do, you report it by using a 'that'-clause. This clause
often contains a **modal**, usually 'should'.

*He proposes that the Government should hold an inquiry.*
*Most travel agents advise that people should change their money*
*before they travel.*

Note that this structure can also be used to report a suggestion about
what the hearer should do. Consider the example: 'Her father had
suggested that she ought to see a doctor'; her father might have
suggested it directly to her.

If you do not use a modal, the result is more formal.

*Someone suggested that they break into small groups.*

Note that when you leave out the modal, the verb in the reported clause
still has the form it would have if the modal were present. This use of the
base form is sometimes called the **subjunctive.**

*It was his doctor who advised that he change his job.*
*I suggested that he bring them all up to the house.*
*He urges that the restrictions be lifted.*

Here is a list of reporting verbs which can be followed by a 'that'-clause
containing a modal or a subjunctive:

| | | | | |
|---|---|---|---|---|
| advise | decree | order | recommend | urge |
| agree | demand | plead | request | |
| ask | direct | pray | rule | |
| beg | insist | prefer | stipulate | |
| command | intend | propose | suggest | |

Note that 'advise', 'ask', 'beg', 'command', 'order', and 'urge' can also be
used with an object and a 'to'-infinitive, and 'agree', 'pray', and 'suggest'
can also be used with 'that'-clauses without a modal.

**7.41** When someone makes a suggestion about what someone else
should do, or about what they themselves and someone else should do,
you can report this using one of the reporting verbs 'suggest', 'advise',
'propose', or 'recommend' with a non-finite clause beginning with a
present participle.

*Barbara suggested going to another coffee-house.*
*Deirdre proposed moving to New York.*

**reporting**
**intentions**
**and hopes**
**7.42** When you are reporting an action that the speaker (the subject of
the reporting verb) intends to perform, you can report it in two ways. You
can either report it simply as an action, using a 'to'-infinitive clause, or you
can report it as a statement or fact, using a 'that'-clause.

For example, promises relate to actions (eg 'He promised to phone her')
but they can also be seen as relating to facts (eg 'He promised that he
would phone her').

The verb group in the 'that'-clause always contains a **modal.**

*I promised to come back.*
*She promised that she would not leave hospital until she was better.*

*I decided to withhold the information till later.*
*She decided that she would leave her money to him.*

*I had vowed to fight for their freedom.*
*She vowed that she would not leave her home.*

Here is a list of verbs which can be used either with a 'to'-infinitive clause or with a 'that'-clause containing a modal:

| | | | |
|---|---|---|---|
| decide | hope | propose | threaten |
| expect | pledge | resolve | vow |
| guarantee | promise | swear | |

**USAGE NOTE**   **7.43** 'Claim' and 'pretend' can also be used with these two structures, when you are saying that someone is claiming or pretending something about himself or herself. For example, 'He claimed to be a genius' has the same meaning as 'He claimed that he was a genius'.

*He claimed to have witnessed the accident.*
*He claimed that he had found the money in the forest.*

Note that the infinitive in the 'to'-infinitive clause can be a perfect infinitive, referring to a past event or situation.

**7.44**  Note that a few verbs which indicate personal intentions can only be used with a 'to'-infinitive clause.

*I intend to say nothing for the present.*
*They are planning to move to the country.*
*I don't want to die yet.*

Here is a list of these verbs:

| | | |
|---|---|---|
| intend | mean | refuse |
| long | plan | want |

**reporting**   **7.45**  When you are reporting an action that someone is wondering about
**uncertain**   doing themselves, you can use a 'to'-infinitive clause beginning with
**things**   'whether'.

*I've been wondering whether to retire.*
*He didn't know whether to feel glad or sorry at his dismissal.*

Here is a list of verbs that can be used with 'to'-infinitive clauses of this kind:

| | | | | |
|---|---|---|---|---|
| choose | debate | decide | know | wonder |

Note that 'choose', 'decide', and 'know' are usually used in a negative or interrogative clause, or a clause with a modal.

When you are mentioning information about something involved in an action, you can use a 'to'-infinitive clause after a 'wh'-word as the reported clause.

*I asked him what to do.*
*I shall teach you how to cook.*

Here is a list of verbs which can be used with 'to'-infinitive clauses of this kind:

| | | | | |
|---|---|---|---|---|
| describe | forget | learn | say | tell |
| discover | guess | realize | see | think |
| discuss | imagine | remember | suggest | understand |
| explain | know | reveal | teach | wonder |

As an alternative to both kinds of 'to'-infinitive clause, you can use a clause containing 'should'.

*I wondered whether I should call for help.*
*He began to wonder what he should do now.*

All the verbs in the above lists, except 'choose' and 'debate', can also be used with ordinary clauses beginning with 'whether' or 'wh'-words. See paragraphs 7.32 to 7.35.

# Time reference in report structures

**7.46** This section explains how to show time reference in report structures.

**past tense for both verbs**

**7.47** When you use a report structure, you are usually reporting something that was said or believed in the past. Both the reporting verb and the verb in the reported clause are therefore usually in a past tense.

*She said you threw away her sweets.*
*Brody asked what happened.*
*In the Middle Ages, people thought the world was flat.*

**reporting verb in other tenses**

**7.48** If you are reporting something that someone says or believes at the time that you are speaking, you use a present tense of the reporting verb.

*A third of adults say that work is bad for your health.*
*I think it's going to rain.*

However, you can also use a present tense of the reporting verb when you are reporting something said in the past, especially if you are reporting something that someone often says or that is still true.

*She says she wants to see you this afternoon.*
*My doctor says it's nothing to worry about.*

If you are predicting what people will say or think, you use a future tense of the reporting verb.

*No doubt he will claim that his car broke down.*
*They will think we are making a fuss.*

**tense of verb in reported clause**

**7.49** Whatever the tense of your reporting verb, you put the verb in the reported clause into a tense that is appropriate at the time that you are speaking.

If the event or situation described in the reported clause is in the past at the time that you are speaking, you use the simple past tense, the past continuous, or the present perfect: 'She said she enjoyed the course', 'She said she was enjoying the course' or 'She said she has enjoyed the course'. See Chapter 5 for information on when to use these tenses.

*Dad explained that he had no money.*
*She added that she was smoking too much.*
*He says he has never seen a live shark in his life.*

However, when the reporting verb is in a past tense, a past tense is also usually used for the verb in the reported clause even if the reported situation still exists. For example, you could say 'I told him I was eighteen' even if you are still eighteen. You are concentrating on the situation at the past time that you are talking about.

*He said he was English.*

A present tense is sometimes used instead, to emphasize that the situation still exists.

*I told him that I don't drink more than anyone else.*

If the event or situation was in the past at the time that the reported statement was made, or had existed up to that time, you use the past perfect tense: 'She said she had enjoyed the course.'

*He knew he had behaved badly.*
*Mr Benn said that he had been in hospital at the time.*

If the event or situation is still going on, you use a present tense if you are using a present tense of the reporting verb: 'She says she's enjoying the course.'

*Don't assume I'm a complete fool.*
*He knows he's being watched.*

If the event or situation was in the future at the time of the statement or is still in the future, you use a modal. See paragraphs 7.50 to 7.53, below.

**modals in reported clauses**

**7.50** The basic rules for using modals in reported clauses are as follows.

If the verb in the reporting clause is in a past tense or has 'could' or 'would' as an auxiliary, you usually use 'could', 'might', or 'would' in the reported clause.

If, as is less common, the verb in the reporting clause is in a present tense or has 'can' or 'will' as an auxiliary, you usually use 'can', 'may', or 'will' in the reported clause.

**USAGE NOTE**

**7.51** When you want to report a statement or question about someone's ability to do something, you normally use 'could'.

*They believed that war could be avoided.*
*Nell would not admit that she could not cope.*

If you want to report a statement about possibility, you normally use 'might'.

*They told me it might flood here.*
*He said you might need money.*

If the possibility is a strong one, you use 'must'.

*I told her she must be out of her mind.*

When you want to report a statement giving permission or a request for permission, you normally use 'could'. 'Might' is used in more formal English.

*I told him he couldn't have it.*
*Madeleine asked if she might borrow a pen and some paper.*

When you want to report a prediction, promise, or expectation, or a question about the future, you normally use 'would'.

*She said they would all miss us.*
*He insisted that reforms would save the system, not destroy it.*

**7.52** If the reported event or situation still exists or is still in the future, and you are using a present tense of the reporting verb, you use 'can' instead of 'could', 'may' instead of 'might', and 'will' or 'shall' instead of 'would'.

*Helen says I can share her flat.*
*I think the weather may change soon.*
*I don't believe he will come.*

Note that you cannot use 'can have' instead of 'could have', or 'will have' instead of 'would have'. You cannot use 'may have' instead of 'might have' if you are using it like 'could have' to talk about something that did not happen.

You can also use 'can', 'may', 'will', and 'shall' when you are using a past tense of the reporting verb, if you want to emphasize that the situation still exists or is still in the future.

*He claimed that a child's early experiences of being separated from his mother <u>may</u> cause psychological distress in later life.*

If you are using a present reporting verb and want to indicate that the reported event or situation is hypothetical or very unlikely, you can use the modals 'could', 'might', or 'would'.

*I believe that I <u>could</u> live very comfortably here.*

**7.53** When you want to report a statement about obligation, it is possible to use 'must', but the expression 'had to' (see paragraph 4.248) is more common.

*He said he really <u>had to</u> go back inside.*
*Sita told him that he <u>must</u> be especially kind to the little girl.*

You use 'have to', 'has to', or 'must' if the reported situation still exists or is in the future.

When you want to report a statement prohibiting something, you normally use 'mustn't'.

*He said they <u>mustn't</u> get us into trouble.*

When you want to report a strong recommendation, you can use 'ought to'. You can also use 'should'.

*He knew he <u>ought to</u> be helping Harold.*
*I felt I <u>should</u> consult my family.*

**7.54** When you want to report a habitual past action or a past situation, you can use the semi-modal 'used to'.

*I wish I knew what his favourite dishes <u>used to</u> be.*

**7.55** The use of modals in reported clauses can be compared with the ordinary use of modals (see paragraphs 4.95 to 4.262). Many of the functions are similar, but some are rarely or never found in reported clauses.

**reporting conditional statements**    **7.56** When you are reporting a conditional statement, the tenses of the verbs are, in most cases, the same as they would be normally. However, they are different if you are using the simple past tense of a reporting verb, and reporting a conditional statement such as 'If there is no water in the radiator, the engine will overheat'. In this case, you can use the simple past instead of the simple present and 'would' instead of 'will' in the reported conditional statement: 'She said that if there was no water in the radiator, the engine would overheat'.

For information about conditional statements, see paragraphs 8.25 to 8.42.

# Making your reference appropriate

**7.57** People, things, times, and places can be referred to in different ways, depending on who is speaking or on when or where they are speaking. For example, the same person can be referred to as 'I', 'you', or 'she', and the same place can be referred to as 'over there' or 'just here'.

If you use a **report structure** to report what someone has said, the words you use to refer to things must be appropriate in relation to yourself, the time when you are speaking, and the place in which you are speaking. The words you use may well be different from the words originally spoken, which were appropriate from the point of view of the speaker at the time.

**referring to people and things**

7.58 For example, if a man is talking to someone about a woman called Jenny, and he says, 'I saw her in the High Street', there are a number of ways in which this statement can be reported. If the original speaker repeats what he said, he could say, 'I said I saw her in the High Street.' 'I' and 'her' do not change, because they still refer to the same people.

If the original listener reports what was said, he or she could say, 'He said he saw her in the High Street.' 'I' becomes 'he', because the statement is reported from the point of view of a third person, not from the point of view of the original speaker.

If the original listener reports the statement to Jenny, 'her' becomes 'you': 'He said he saw you in the High Street'.

The original listener might report the statement to the original speaker. This time, 'I' has to change to 'you': 'You said you saw her in the High Street'.

*You're crazy.*
*I told him he was crazy.*

Possessive determiners and pronouns change in the same way as personal pronouns in order to keep the same reference. So the following sentences could all report the same question: 'She asked if he was my brother', 'She asked if you were my brother', 'I asked if he was her brother.' The original question might have been expressed as 'Is he your brother?'

**referring to time**

7.59 When reporting, you may need to change **adjuncts of time** such as 'today', 'yesterday', or 'next week'.

For example, if someone called Jill says 'I will come tomorrow', you could report this statement the following day as 'Jill said she would come today'. At a later time, you could report the same statement as 'Jill said she would come the next day' or 'Jill said she would come the following day'.

*We decided to leave the city the next day.*
*I was afraid people might think I'd been asleep during the previous twenty-four hours.*

**referring to places**

7.60 You may need to change words which relate to position or place.

For example, if you are talking to a man about a restaurant, he might say 'I go there every day'. If you report his statement while you are actually in the restaurant, you could say 'He said he comes here every day'.

## Using reporting verbs for politeness

7.61 Reporting verbs are often used to say something in a polite way.

7.62 If you want to contradict someone or to say something which might be unwelcome to them, you can avoid sounding rude by using a reporting verb such as 'think' or 'believe'.

*I think it's time we stopped.*
*I don't think that will be necessary.*
*I believe you've said enough now.*

Alternatively, you can make the reporting clause into a negative question.

*Don't you think we'd better wait and see?*
*Don't you think you'd better slow down?*

For more information on the use of reporting verbs to decrease the strength of a statement, see the section on **performative verbs** in Chapter 10 (10.102 to 10.105).

'suppose'
and 'wonder'

**7.63** You can use 'suppose' and 'wonder' to introduce polite requests. When you use 'suppose' like this, you can make either the reporting clause or the reported clause negative.

*I wonder if you've got any books on linguistics?*
*I suppose you couldn't just stay an hour or two longer?*
*I don't suppose you'd be prepared to stay in Edinburgh?*

# Avoiding mention of the person speaking or thinking

**7.64** There are a number of report structures which you can use if you want to avoid saying whose opinion or statement you are giving.

use of
passives
to express
general
beliefs

**7.65** If you want to indicate or imply that something is an opinion which is held by an unspecified group of people, you can use a passive form of a reporting verb with 'it' as the **impersonal** subject.

*It is assumed that the government will remain in power.*
*In former times it was believed that all enlarged tonsils should be removed.*
*It is now believed that foreign languages are most easily taught to young children.*
*It was said that half a million dollars had been spent on the search.*

Here is a list of reporting verbs which are used in the passive with 'it' as their subject:

| | | | | |
|---|---|---|---|---|
| accept | concede | find | observe | rule |
| acknowledge | conclude | foresee | predict | rumour |
| admit | confirm | forget | propose | say |
| agree | consider | guarantee | realize | state |
| allege | decide | hold | recall | stipulate |
| announce | decree | hope | reckon | suggest |
| argue | discover | imply | recommend | suppose |
| assert | estimate | know | record | think |
| assume | expect | mention | remember | understand |
| believe | explain | note | report | |
| claim | fear | notice | request | |
| comment | feel | object | reveal | |

This structure has much in common with a phase structure using a passive reporting verb and a 'to'-infinitive clause. In the phase structure, the main person or thing involved in the reported opinion is put as the subject of the reporting verb.

*Intelligence is assumed to be important.*
*He is said to have died a natural death.*
*He is believed to have fled to France.*

Note that the 'to'-infinitive is most commonly 'be' or 'have', or a perfect infinitive.

Here is a list of reporting verbs, from the list above, which are also used in the phase structure:

| | | | | |
|---|---|---|---|---|
| agree | consider | find | predict | think |
| allege | discover | guarantee | reckon | understand |
| assume | estimate | hold | report | |
| believe | expect | know | rumour | |
| claim | feel | observe | say | |

**'seem' and 'appear'**

**7.66** If you want to say that something appears to be the case, you can use either of the verbs 'seem' and 'appear'. These verbs can be used as reporting verbs followed by a 'that'-clause or they can be used with a 'to'-infinitive clause. You can be giving your own opinion or that of someone else.

If you want to mention an apparent fact, you can use 'seem' or 'appear', followed by a 'that'-clause. The subject of 'seem' or 'appear' is 'it', used impersonally.

*It seemed that she had not been careful enough.*
*It seemed that he had lost his chance to win.*
*It appears that he followed my advice.*

Alternatively, you can use a phase structure involving 'seem' or 'appear' and a 'to'-infinitive clause. The main person or thing involved in the fact that appears to be true is put as the subject of the reporting verb.

*She seemed to like me.*
*He appears to have been an interesting man.*
*The system appears to work impartially.*

If you want to mention the person whose viewpoint you are giving, you can add a prepositional phrase beginning with 'to' after 'seem' or 'appear'.

*It seemed to Jane that everyone was against her.*
*It seems to me to be a remarkable pronouncement.*

**USAGE NOTE**

**7.67** There are a few expressions containing impersonal 'it' which are used as reporting clauses before 'that'-clauses to indicate that someone suddenly thought of something: 'It occurred to me', 'It struck me', and 'It crossed my mind'.

*It occurred to her that someone was missing.*
*It crossed my mind that somebody must have been keeping things secret.*

## Referring to the speaker and hearer

**referring to the speaker**

**7.68** You usually use a reporting verb to report what one person has said or thought, so the subject of a reporting verb is usually a singular noun.

*Henry said that he wanted to go home.*

*He claimed his health had been checked several times at a clinic.*

When you report the statements, opinions, orders, or questions of a group of people, you can use a plural noun or a collective noun as the subject of the reporting verb.

*The judges demanded that the race be run again.*
*The committee also noted that this was not the first case of its kind.*

When you report what was said on television or radio, or what is printed or written in a newspaper or other document, you can mention the source or means of communication as the subject of a reporting verb.

*The newspaper said he was hiding somewhere near Kabul.*
*His contract stated that his salary would be £50,000 a year.*

Note that you can also use 'say' with nouns such as 'sign', 'notice', 'clock', and 'map' as the subject.

*...a notice saying that on no account should the attendants be tipped.*
*A sign over the door said 'Dreamland Cafe'.*
*The road map said it was 210 kilometres to the French frontier.*

**use of the passive**

7.69 As explained in paragraph 7.65, when you want to avoid mentioning the person who said something, you can use a reporting verb in the passive.

*It was said that some of them had become insane.*
*He was said to be the oldest man in the firm.*

If you want to avoid mentioning the person giving an order or giving advice, you use a passive reporting verb with the person who receives the order or advice as the subject of the clause.

*Harriet was ordered to keep away from my room.*

**USAGE NOTE**

7.70 If you want to distance yourself from a statement you are making, you can indicate that you are reporting what someone else has said by using a phrase beginning with 'according to', rather than using a report structure.

*According to Dime, he had strangled Jed in the course of a struggle.*

**referring to the hearer**

7.71 After some reporting verbs that refer to speech, you have to mention the hearer as a direct object. 'Tell' is the most common of these verbs.

*I told them you were at the dentist.*
*I informed her that I was unwell and could not come.*
*Smith persuaded them that they must support the strike.*

You can use these verbs in the passive, with the hearer as the subject.

*She had been told she could leave hospital.*
*Members had been informed that the purpose of the meeting was to elect a new chairman.*
*She was persuaded to look again.*

Here is a list of reporting verbs which must have the hearer as the direct object when they are used with a 'that'-clause:

| | | | |
|---|---|---|---|
| assure | inform | persuade | remind |
| convince | notify | reassure | tell |

Here is a list of reporting verbs which must have the hearer as the direct object when they are used with a 'to'-infinitive clause:

| | | | | |
|---|---|---|---|---|
| advise | forbid | order | teach | warn |
| beg | instruct | persuade | tell | |
| command | invite | remind | urge | |

**verbs with or without the hearer as object**

**7.72** After a few reporting verbs that refer to speech, you can choose whether or not to mention the hearer.

*I promised that I would try to phone her.*
*I promised Myra I'd be home at seven.*

*The physicians warned that, without the operation, the child would die.*
*Thomas warned her that his mother was slightly deaf.*

Here is a list of reporting verbs which can be used with or without the hearer as object when used with a 'that'-clause:

| | | | |
|---|---|---|---|
| ask | promise | teach | warn |

'Promise' can also be used with or without an object when it is used with a 'to'-infinitive clause. 'Ask' has to be used with an object when it is used with a 'to'-infinitive clause to report a request for the hearer to do something, but it is used without an object when the request is for permission to do something (see paragraphs 7.36 and 7.39).

**the hearer in prepositional phrases**

**7.73** With many other reporting verbs, if you want to mention the hearer, you do so in a prepositional phrase beginning with 'to'.

*I explained to her that I had to go home.*
*'Margaret,' I said to her, 'I'm so glad you came.'*

Here is a list of reporting verbs which are used with 'that'-clauses or quotes and which need the preposition 'to' if you mention the hearer:

| | | | | |
|---|---|---|---|---|
| admit | confess | insist | report | suggest |
| announce | declare | mention | reveal | swear |
| boast | explain | murmur | say | whisper |
| complain | hint | propose | shout | |

'Propose' and 'swear' can also be used with a 'to'-infinitive clause, but not if you mention the hearer.

*I propose to mention this at the next meeting.*

**7.74** When you are describing a situation in which a speaker is speaking forcefully to a hearer, you can mention the hearer in a prepositional phrase beginning with 'at'.

*The tall boy shouted at them. 'Choir! Stand still!'*
*'Shut up!' he bellowed at me.*

Here is a list of reporting verbs which are used to describe forceful speech. If you want to mention the hearer, you use a prepositional phrase beginning with 'at':

| | | | | |
|---|---|---|---|---|
| bark | grumble | scream | snap | wail |
| bellow | howl | shout | storm | yell |
| growl | roar | shriek | thunder | |

**7.75** With verbs which describe situations where both the speaker and th hearer are involved in the speech activity, you can mention the hearer in a prepositional phrase beginning with 'with'.

*He agreed with us that it would be better to have no break.*
*Can you confirm with Ray that this date is ok?*

Here is a list of reporting verbs which take the preposition 'with' if you mention the hearer:

| agree | argue | confirm | plead | reason |
|-------|-------|---------|-------|--------|

**7.76** With verbs which describe situations where someone is getting information from someone or something, you use a prepositional phrase beginning with 'from' to mention the source of the information.

*I discovered from her that a woman prisoner had killed herself.*

Here is a list of reporting verbs where the source of the information is mentioned using 'from':

| discover | gather | infer | see |
|----------|--------|-------|-----|
| elicit | hear | learn | |

**reflexive pronouns**

**7.77** A reflexive pronoun can be used as the object of a reporting verb or preposition in order to say what someone is thinking. For example, 'to say something to yourself' means to think it rather than to say it aloud.

*I told myself that he was crazy.*
*It will soon be over, I kept saying to myself.*

# Other ways of indicating what is said

**objects with reporting verbs**

**7.78** Sometimes you use a noun such as 'question', 'story', or 'apology' to refer to what someone has said or written. You can use a reporting verb with one of these nouns as its object instead of a reported clause.

*He asked a number of questions.*
*Simon whispered his answer.*
*He told funny stories and made everyone laugh.*
*Philip repeated his invitation.*

Here is a list of reporting verbs which are often used with nouns that refer to something spoken or written:

| accept | deny | know | refuse | tell |
|--------|------|------|--------|------|
| acknowledge | expect | learn | remember | understand |
| ask | explain | mention | repeat | whisper |
| begin | forget | mutter | report | write |
| believe | guess | note | shout | |
| continue | hear | notice | state | |
| demand | imagine | promise | suggest | |

**7.79** Some reporting verbs can have as their objects nouns that refer to events or facts. These nouns are often closely related to verbs. For example, 'loss' is closely related to 'lose', and instead of saying 'He admitted that he had lost his passport', you can say 'He admitted the loss of his passport'.

*British Airways announce the <u>arrival</u> of flight BA 5531 from Glasgow.*
*The company reported a 45 per cent <u>drop</u> in profits.*

Here is a list of reporting verbs which are often used with nouns that refer
to events or facts:

| | | | | |
|---|---|---|---|---|
| accept | discuss | imagine | prefer | sense |
| acknowledge | doubt | mean | promise | suggest |
| admit | expect | mention | recommend | urge |
| announce | explain | note | record | |
| demand | fear | notice | remember | |
| describe | foresee | observe | report | |
| discover | forget | predict | see | |

**USAGE NOTE**

**7.80** Note that 'say' is usually only used with an object if the object is a
very general word such as 'something', 'anything', or 'nothing'.

*I must have said something wrong.*
*The man nodded but said nothing.*

**prepositional**
**phrases**
**with**
**reporting**
**verbs**

**7.81** A few verbs referring to speech and thought can be used with a
prepositional phrase rather than a reported clause, to indicate the general
subject matter of a statement or thought.

*Thomas explained <u>about the request from Paris.</u>*

Here are three lists of verbs which can be used with a prepositional phrase
referring to a fact or subject. The first group of verbs in each list are used
without an object, and the second group are used with an object referring
to the hearer. Note that 'ask' and 'warn' can be used with or without an
object.

The following verbs are used with 'about':

| | | | | |
|---|---|---|---|---|
| agree | dream | inquire | wonder | teach |
| ask | explain | know | worry | tell |
| boast | forget | learn | write | warn |
| complain | grumble | mutter | ~ | |
| decide | hear | read | ask | |

*No one knew <u>about my interest in mathematics.</u>*
*I asked him <u>about the horses.</u>*

The following verbs are used with 'of':

| | | | | |
|---|---|---|---|---|
| complain | learn | write | inform | remind |
| dream | read | ~ | notify | warn |
| hear | think | assure | persuade | |
| know | warn | convince | reassure | |

*They never complained <u>of the incessant rain.</u>*
*No-one had warned us <u>of the dangers.</u>*

The following verbs are used with 'on'. None of them take an object
referring to the hearer.

| | | | |
|---|---|---|---|
| agree | decide | insist | report |
| comment | determine | remark | write |

*He had already decided <u>on his story.</u>*

*They are insisting on the release of all political prisoners.*

Note that 'speak' and 'talk' are used with 'about' and 'of' but not with reported clauses.

## Other ways of using reported clauses

**other verbs used with reported clauses**

**7.82** There are a few verbs which do not refer to saying, thinking, or learning but which are followed by 'that'-clauses because they refer to actions which relate to facts: for example, checking facts or proving facts.

*He checked that both rear doors were safely shut.*
*Research with animals shows that males will mother an infant as well as any female.*

Here is a list of verbs which are not verbs of speech or thought but can be followed by a 'that'-clause:

| | | | |
|---|---|---|---|
| arrange | determine | pretend | reveal |
| check | ensure | prove | show |
| demonstrate | indicate | require | |

Note that 'determine' can also be a verb of thought and 'reveal' can also be a verb of speech. See paragraphs 7.27, 7.35, and 7.45.

'Arrange' and 'require' are used with a 'that'-clause containing a modal or a subjunctive. 'Arrange' can also be used with a 'to'-infinitive clause.

*They had arranged that I would spend Christmas with them.*
*They'd arranged to leave at four o'clock.*

'Demonstrate', 'prove', 'reveal', and 'show' can also be followed by a clause beginning with a 'wh'-word which refers to a circumstance involved in a fact.

*The woman took the gun and showed how the cylinder slotted into the barrel.*

'Prove', 'require', and 'show' can also be used in the passive followed by a 'to'-infinitive clause.

*No place on earth can be shown to be safe.*

If you want to mention another person involved in these actions, you can put an object after 'show', use 'to' after 'demonstrate', 'indicate', 'prove', and 'reveal', and use 'with' after 'arrange' and 'check'.

*This attitude of the children showed me that watching violence can lower a child's standards of behaviour.*
*This incident proved to me that Ian is not to be trusted.*
*She arranged with the principal of her school to take the necessary time off.*

**7.83** If you want to say that something happens, that something is the case, or that something becomes known, you can use a 'that'-clause after 'happen', 'transpire', or 'emerge'. The subject of the reporting clause is **impersonal** 'it'.

*It often happens that a mother asks for advice and does not get it.*
*It just happened that he had a client who rather liked that sort of thing.*
*It transpired that there was not a word of truth in the letter.*

*It emerged that, during the afternoon, she had gone home unwell.*

Note that the 'that'-clause must be introduced by 'that'.

**nouns used with reported clauses**

**7.84** There are many nouns, such as 'statement', 'advice', and 'opinion', which refer to what someone says or thinks. Many of the nouns used in this way are related to reporting verbs. For example, 'information' is related to 'inform', and 'decision' is related to 'decide'. These nouns can be used in report structures in a similar way to reporting verbs. They are usually followed by a reported clause beginning with 'that'.

*He referred to Copernicus' statement that the earth moves around the sun.*
*They expressed the opinion that I must be mentally retarded.*
*There was little hope that he would survive.*

Here is a list of nouns which have related reporting verbs and which can be used with 'that'-clauses:

| | | | |
|---|---|---|---|
| admission | claim | information | sense |
| advice | conclusion | knowledge | statement |
| agreement | decision | promise | thought |
| announcement | dream | reply | threat |
| answer | expectation | report | understanding |
| argument | explanation | response | warning |
| assertion | feeling | rule | wish |
| assumption | guess | rumour | |
| belief | hope | saying | |

Some of these nouns can also be followed by a 'to'-infinitive clause:

| | | | |
|---|---|---|---|
| agreement | decision | promise | warning |
| claim | hope | threat | wish |

*The decision to go had not been an easy one to make.*
*Barnaby's father had fulfilled his promise to buy his son a horse.*

Note that some nouns that are not related to reporting verbs can be followed by 'that'-clauses, because they refer or relate to facts or beliefs. Here is a list of some of these nouns:

| | | | | |
|---|---|---|---|---|
| advantage | effect | idea | principle | view |
| benefit | evidence | impression | risk | vision |
| confidence | experience | news | sign | word |
| danger | fact | opinion | story | |
| disadvantage | faith | possibility | tradition | |

*He didn't want her to get the idea that he was rich.*
*She can't accept the fact that he's gone.*
*Eventually, a distraught McCoo turned up with the news that his house had just burned down.*

**adjectives with reported clauses**

**7.85** There are many adjectives that can be followed by reported clauses when they are the complement of a link verb, usually 'be'.

**mentioning the cause of a feeling**

**7.86** If you want to say what causes someone to have a particular feeling, you can mention the cause of the feeling in a 'that'-clause after an adjective describing the feeling.

*Everybody was sad that she had to return to America.*

*I am confident that I shall be able to persuade them to go.*
*I was worried that she'd say no.*

Here is a list of adjectives describing feelings:

| | | | | |
|---|---|---|---|---|
| afraid | confident | happy | sad | upset |
| angry | frightened | pleased | sorry | worried |
| anxious | glad | proud | surprised | |

**saying what someone knows**

**7.87** If you want to say that someone knows something, you can say what they know in a 'that'-clause after an adjective such as 'aware' or 'conscious'.

*He was aware that he had drunk too much whisky.*
*She is conscious that some people might be offended by her views.*

Here is a list of adjectives indicating knowledge:

| | | | |
|---|---|---|---|
| aware | conscious | positive | unaware |
| certain | convinced | sure | |

'Aware' is occasionally used with a reported clause beginning with a 'wh'-word.

*None of our staff were aware what was going on.*

**commenting on a fact**

**7.88** If you want to comment on a fact, you can use an adjective describing the fact followed by a 'that'-clause. The link verb has **impersonal** 'it' as its subject.

*It was sad that people had reacted in the way they did.*
*It is true that the authority of parliament has declined.*
*It is extraordinary that we should ever have met!*
*It seems probable that the world can go on producing enough food for everyone.*

Here is a list of adjectives used to comment on facts:

| | | | | |
|---|---|---|---|---|
| apparent | essential | good | lucky | probable |
| appropriate | evident | important | natural | sad |
| awful | extraordinary | inevitable | obvious | true |
| bad | fair | interesting | plain | unlikely |
| clear | funny | likely | possible | |

After a few adjectives, a clause beginning with a 'wh'-word can be used.

*It's funny how they don't get on.*
*It was never clear why she worked all her life as a domestic servant.*

For more information, see paragraph 10.43.

**nominal use of 'that'-clauses**

**7.89** 'That'-clauses can be used as complements after 'be' to refer to a fact or idea. The subject is usually one of the nouns listed in paragraph 7.84.

*The fact is that a happy person makes a better worker.*
*The answer is simply that they are interested in doing it.*
*The most favoured explanation was that he was finally getting tired.*
*Our hope is that this time all parties will cooperate.*

**7.90** In formal English, 'that'-clauses are sometimes used as the subject of a verb, when people want to comment on a fact.

*That she is not stupid is self-evident.*
*That he is a tortured soul is obvious.*

In less formal English, 'the fact' plus a 'that'-clause is often used as a subject instead of a simple 'that'-clause.

*The fact that what they are doing is illegal is a trivial irrelevance.*
*The fact that your boss is actually offering to do your job for you should certainly prompt you to question his motives.*

The normal way of commenting on a fact is to use an impersonal 'it' structure. See paragraph 7.88.

**7.91** People also use 'the fact' plus a 'that'-clause as the object of prepositions and of verbs which cannot be followed by a simple 'that'-clause.

*He is proud of the fact that all his children went to university.*
*We overlooked the fact that the children's emotional development had been retarded.*

**nominal use of 'wh'-clauses**

**7.92** When you want to refer to matters which are not certain or definite, or about which a choice has to be made, you can use clauses beginning with a 'wh'-word or 'whether', like the clauses used for **reported questions**. They can be used after prepositions, and as the subject of verbs such as 'be', 'depend', and 'matter'.

*...the question of who should be President of the Board of Trade.*
*The State is desperately uncertain about what it wants artists to do.*
*What you get depends on how badly you were injured.*
*Whether I went twice or not doesn't matter.*
*Whether you think they are any good or not is irrelevant.*

**7.93** Structures consisting of a 'wh'-word plus a 'to'-infinitive clause, which refer to a possible course of action, are used after prepositions but not usually as subjects.

*...the problem of what to tell the adopted child.*
*...a book on how to avoid having a heart attack.*
*People are very worried about how to fill their increased leisure time.*

**WARNING**

**7.94** Note that 'if'-clauses, which are used for reported questions, cannot be used after prepositions or as the subject of a verb.

# Contents of Chapter 8

# 8 Combining messages

**8.1** Sometimes we want to make a statement which is too complex or detailed to be expressed in a single clause. We make statements of this kind by putting two or more clauses together in one sentence.

There are two ways in which we do this. One way is to use one clause as a main clause and to add other clauses which express subordinate meanings.

*I came because I want you to help me.*
*I didn't like the man who did the gardening for them.*
*You have no right to keep people off your land unless they are doing damage.*
*When he had gone, Valentina sighed.*

The other way is simply to link clauses together.

*I'm an old man and I'm sick.*
*I like films but I don't go to the cinema very often.*

Questions and orders can also consist of more than one clause.

*What will I do if he doesn't come?*
*If she is ambitious, don't try to hold her back.*

Clauses are explained in Chapters 3 and 4.

**conjunctions**  **8.2** When you put two clauses into one sentence, you use a **conjunction** t link them and to indicate the relationship between them.

*When he stopped, no one said anything.*
*They were going by car because it was more comfortable.*
*The telephone rang and Judy picked it up.*
*The food looked good, but I was too full to eat.*

**8.3** There are two kinds of conjunction. They indicate the different kinds of relationship between clauses in a sentence.

**subordinating conjunctions**  **8.4** When you are adding a clause in order to develop some aspect of what you are saying, you use a **subordinating conjunction**.

*The cat jumped onto my father's lap while he was reading his letters.*
*He had cancer although it was detected at an early stage.*
*When the jar was full, he turned the water off.*

A clause which begins with a subordinating conjunction is called a **subordinate clause**.

*When an atom is split, it releases neutrons.*
*If he had had a gun, he would have killed the man.*
*The house was called Elm View, although there were no elms anywhere in sight.*

Subordinate clauses can also be added to questions and imperative clauses.

*How long is it since you've actually taught?*

*Know what fibre you are dyeing before you start.*

Sentences containing a main clause and one or more subordinate clauses are often called **complex sentences.**

There are three main kinds of subordinate clause:

**Adverbial clauses** are dealt with in paragraphs 8.6 to 8.82.

**Relative clauses** are dealt with in paragraphs 8.83 to 8.116.

**Reported clauses** are dealt with in Chapter 7.

**coordinating**
**conjunctions**
**8.5** If you are simply linking clauses, you use a **coordinating conjunction.**

*Her son lives at home and has a steady job.*
*He's a shy man, but he's not scared of anything or anyone.*

Coordinating conjunctions can also be put between questions and between imperative clauses.

*Did you buy those curtains or do you make your own?*
*Visit your local dealer or phone for a brochure.*

Clauses joined by a coordinating conjunction are called **coordinate clauses.**

*She turned and left the room.*

Sentences which contain coordinate clauses are sometimes called **compound sentences.**

A full explanation of coordinate clauses is given in paragraphs 8.137 to 8.151. Other uses of coordinating conjunctions are explained in paragraphs 8.152 to 8.189.

# Adverbial clauses

**8.6** There are eight types of adverbial clause:

| kind of clause | usual conjunction | paragraphs |
|---|---|---|
| time clauses | when, before, after, since, while, as, until | paragraphs 8.8 to 8.24 |
| conditional clauses | if, unless | paragraphs 8.25 to 8.42 |
| purpose clauses | in order to, so that | paragraphs 8.43 to 8.48 |
| reason clauses | because, since, as | paragraphs 8.49 to 8.53 |
| result clauses | so that | paragraphs 8.54 to 8.64 |
| concessive clauses | although, though, while | paragraphs 8.65 to 8.72 |
| place clauses | where, wherever | paragraphs 8.73 to 8.77 |
| clauses of manner | as, like, the way | paragraphs 8.78 to 8.82 |

**Non-finite clauses,** when they begin with a subordinating conjunction, are dealt with in the sections dealing with adverbial clauses. Non-finite clauses which do not begin with a subordinating conjunction are dealt wit separately in paragraphs 8.117 to 8.133. Other structures which functior like non-finite clauses are described in paragraphs 8.134 to 8.136.

**position of**
**adverbial**
**clause**

**8.7** The usual position for an adverbial clause is just after the main clause.

*I couldn't think of a single thing to say after he'd replied like that.*
*The performances were cancelled because the leading man was ill.*

However most types of adverbial clause can be put in front of a main clause.

*When the city is dark, we can move around easily.*
*Although crocodiles are inactive for long periods, on occasion they can ru very fast indeed.*

Occasionally, you can put an adverbial clause in the middle of another clause, although this is unusual.

*They make allegations which, when you analyse them, do not have too many facts behind them.*

There are a few types of adverbial clause which always go after a main clause; other types always go in front of one. This is explained in the sections dealing with the different types of clause.

# Time clauses

**8.8 Time clauses** are used to say when something happens by referring t a period of time or to another event.

*Her father died when she was young.*
*Stocks of food cannot be brought in before the rains start.*
*He was detained last Monday after he returned from a business trip overseas.*
*When I first saw the wreckage I just didn't expect there to be so many survivors.*

Time clauses can be used after **adjuncts of time.**

*We'll give him his presents tomorrow, before he goes to school.*
*I want to see you for a few minutes at twelve o'clock, when you go to lunch.*

**Adjuncts of time** are explained in Chapter 5.

**tenses in**
**time clauses**

**8.9** When you are talking about the past or the present, the verb in a time clause has the same tense that it would have in a main clause or in a simple sentence.

*I was standing by the window when I heard her speak.*
*I haven't given him a thing to eat since he arrived.*
*I look after the children while she goes to London.*

However, if the time clause refers to something that will happen or exist ir the future, you use the **simple present tense**, not a future tense.

For example, you say 'When he comes, I will show him the book', not 'When he will come, I will show him the book'.

*As soon as we get the tickets, we'll send them to you.*
*He wants to see you before he dies.*
*Let me stay here till Jeannie comes to bed.*

If you mention an event in a time clause which will happen before an event referred to in the main clause, you use the **present perfect tense** in the time clause, not the future perfect tense.

For example, you say 'When you have had your supper, come and see me', not 'When you will have had your supper, come and see me'.

*We won't be getting married until we've saved enough money.*
*Come and tell me when you have finished.*

**8.10** The most common conjunction in time clauses is 'when'. 'When' is used to say that something happened, happens, or will happen on a particular occasion.

*When the telegram came and I read of his death, I couldn't believe it.*
*He didn't know how to behave when they next met.*

**8.11** You can mention the circumstances in which something happens or happened by using 'when', 'while', or 'as'.

*The train has automatic doors that only open when the train is stationary.*
*While he was still in the stable, there was a loud knock at the front door.*
*He would swim beside me as I rowed in the little dinghy.*

'Whilst' is a more formal form of 'while'.

*We chatted whilst the children played in the crèche.*

**USAGE NOTE** **8.12** If you want to emphasize that something happened at a particular time, you can use 'It was' followed by an expression such as 'six o'clock' or 'three hours later', followed by a 'when'-clause.

For example, instead of saying 'I left at six o'clock', you say 'It was six o'clock when I left'.

*It was about half past eight when he arrived at Sutwick.*
*It was late when he returned.*

This is an example of a **cleft structure**. Cleft structures are explained in paragraphs 10.25 to 10.30.

**repeated** **8.13** If you want to say that something always happened or happens in
**events** particular circumstances, you use 'when', 'whenever', 'every time', or 'each time'.

*When he talks about the Church, he does sound like an outsider.*
*Whenever she had a cold, she ate only fruit.*
*Every time I go to that class I panic.*
*He flinched each time she spoke to him.*

**8.14** You use an expression such as 'the first time', 'the next time', or 'the third time' to say that something happened during one occurrence of an event.

*The last time we talked he said he needed another two days.*
*The next time I come here, I'm going to be better.*

**events** **8.15** You can also use 'when', 'after', or 'once' to talk about one event
**in sequence** happening immediately after another.

*When his wife left him he started drinking heavily.*

*Stop me when you've had enough.*
*The turtle returns to the sea after it has laid its eggs.*
*Once environmental damage is done, it takes many years for the system to recover.*

If you want to say how long one event happened after another, you put a noun group such as 'two days' or 'three years' in front of 'after'.

*Exactly six weeks after she had arrived, she sent a cable to her husband and caught the plane back to New York.*

'As soon as', 'directly', 'immediately', 'the moment', 'the minute', and 'the instant' are all used to talk about one event happening a very short time after another.

*They heard voices as soon as they pushed open the door.*
*The minute someone left the room, the others started talking about them.*
*Immediately the meal was over, it was time for prayer.*

**8.16** When you want to say that something happened, happens, or will happen at an earlier time than something else, you use 'before'.

*It was necessary for them to find a roof to live under before the cold weather set in.*
*They had not even bothered to bury their comrades before they fled.*
*Before they moved to the city, she had never seen a car.*

If you want to say how long one event happened before another, you put a noun group such as 'three weeks' or 'a short time' in front of 'before'.

*He had a review with the second organiser, about a month before the report was written.*
*Long before you return she will have forgotten you.*

**8.17** When you are telling a story, you sometimes want to say what was happening when a particular event occurred. You first say what was happening, then add a clause beginning with 'when' in which you mention the event.

*I had just started back for the house to change my clothes when I heard voices.*
*He was having his Christmas dinner when the telephone rang.*

If you want to say that one event happened a very short time after another, you use a clause in the past perfect tense, followed by a time clause in the simple past tense. After 'had' in the first clause, you put 'no sooner' or 'hardly'.

When you use 'no sooner', the time clause begins with 'than'.

*I had no sooner checked into the hotel than he arrived with the appropriate documents.*

When you use 'hardly', the time clause begins with 'when' or 'before'.

*He had hardly got his eyes open before she told him that they were leaving.*

'No sooner' or 'hardly' is often put at the beginning of the first clause, followed by 'had' and the subject.

*No sooner had he asked the question than the answer came to him.*
*Hardly had he settled into his seat when Alan came bursting in.*

*Hardly had he got on his horse before people started firing at him.*

**8.18** When something is the case because of a new situation, you can say what is the case and then add a subordinate clause saying what the new situation is. The subordinate clause begins with 'now' or 'now that'.

*I feel better now I've talked to you.*
*He soon discovered how much faster he could travel now that he was alone.*

**saying when a situation began**

**8.19** If you want to say that a situation started to exist at a particular time and still exists, you use 'since' or 'ever since'. In the time clause, you use the **simple past tense**.

*I've been in politics since I was at university.*
*It's been making money ever since it opened.*

You also use 'since' or 'ever since' to say that a situation started to exist at a particular time, and still existed at a later time. In the time clause, you use the **simple past tense** or the **past perfect tense**.

*He slept alone, as he had done ever since he left Didcot.*
*Back in Caen, Janine had been busy ever since she had heard the news.*

If you are mentioning someone's age at the time when a situation started, you always use the **simple past tense**.

*I was seven years older than Wendy and had known her since she was twelve.*

'Since' is also used in **reason clauses**. This is explained in paragraph 8.50.

**saying when a situation ends**

**8.20** If you want to say that a situation stopped when something happened, you use 'until' or 'till'.

*I stayed there talking to them until I saw Sam Ward leave the building.*
*He grabbed me and shook me till my teeth rattled.*

You also use 'until' or 'till' to say that a situation will stop when something happens in the future. In the time clause you use the **simple present tense** or the **present perfect tense**.

*Stay with me until I go.*
*We'll support them till they find work.*
*Tell him I won't discuss anything until I've spoken to my wife.*

**8.21** 'By which time', 'at which point', 'after which', 'whereupon', and 'upon which' are also used at the beginning of time clauses.

You use 'by which time' to say that something had already happened or will already have happened before the event you have just mentioned.

*He was diagnosed in 1999, by which time he was already very ill.*

You use 'at which point' to say that something happened immediately after the event you have just mentioned.

*Later, service trades such as toolmaking and blacksmithing appeared, at which point the simple swapping of produce was no longer feasible.*

You use 'after which' to say that a situation started to exist or will start to exist after the event you have just mentioned.

*The clothes were sent away for chemical analysis, after which they were never seen again.*

You use 'whereupon' or 'upon which' to say that something happened immediately after the event you have just mentioned and was a result of

*His department was shut down, whereupon he returned to Calcutta.*
*I told Dr Johnson of this, upon which he called for Joseph.*

USAGE
NOTE
**8.22** You can use a clause beginning with 'when' after a question beginning with 'why'. For example, you can say 'Why should I help her when she never helps me?' However this clause is not a time clause. In your question, you are expressing surprise or disagreement at something that has been said, and the 'when'-clause indicates the reason for your surprise or disagreement.

*Why should he do me an injury when he has already saved my life?*
*Why worry her when it's all over?*

**using non-finite clauses**

**8.23** Instead of using a finite time clause, you can often use a **non-finite clause**.

For example, you can say 'I often read a book when travelling by train', meaning 'I often read a book when I am travelling by train', and you can say 'When finished, the building will be opened by the Prince of Wales', meaning 'When it is finished, the building will be opened by the Prince of Wales'.

*Adults sometimes do not realize their own strength when dealing with children.*
*Mark watched us while pretending not to.*
*I deliberately didn't read the book before going to see the film.*
*After evicting the inhabitants, he declared the houses derelict.*
*They had not spoken a word since leaving the party.*
*Michael used to look hurt and surprised when scolded.*
*Once convinced about an idea, he pursued it relentlessly.*

Note that you can only use a non-finite clause when it does not need to have a new subject, that is, when it is about the same thing as the main clause.

**using prepositional phrases and adjectives**

**8.24** For some statements about time, you can use a phrase consisting of 'when', 'while', 'once', 'until', or 'till', followed by a prepositional phrase or an adjective.

For example, you can say, 'When in Paris, you should visit the Louvre', meaning 'When you are in Paris, you should visit the Louvre'.

*He had read of her elopement while at Oxford.*
*Man acquires great technological mastery of this world but, when under threat, reverts with terrifying ease to his primitive past.*
*Steam or boil them until just tender.*

You can use a phrase consisting of 'when', 'whenever', 'where', or 'wherever' and an adjective such as 'necessary' or 'possible'.

For example, you can say 'You should take exercise whenever possible', meaning 'You should take exercise whenever it is possible'.

*She had previously spoken seldom and then only when necessary.*
*It paid to speak the truth whenever possible.*
*Help must be given where necessary.*
*All experts agree that, wherever possible, children should learn to read in their own way.*

# Conditional clauses

**8.25** When you want to talk about a possible situation and its consequences, you use a **conditional clause.**

Conditional clauses are used:

- to talk about a situation which sometimes exists or existed

*If they lose weight during an illness, they soon regain it afterwards.*
*Government cannot operate effectively unless it is free from such interference.*
*If I saw him in the street, he'd just say 'Good morning.'*

- to talk about a situation which you know does not exist

*If England had a hot climate, the attitude would be different.*
*If I could afford it I would buy a boat.*

- to talk about a situation when you do not know whether it exists or not

*If he is right it would be possible once more to manage the economy in the old way.*
*The interval seemed unnecessary, unless it was to give them a break.*

- to talk about a situation which may exist in the future.

*If I leave my job I'll have no money to live on.*
*If I went back on the train it'd be cheaper.*
*Don't bring her unless she's sober.*

Sentences containing conditional clauses are sometimes called **conditional sentences.**

**8.26** Conditional clauses usually begin with 'if' or 'unless'.

You use 'if' to say that a consequence of something happening or being the case would be that something else would happen or be the case.

*If you do that I shall be very pleased.*
*If I asked for something I got it.*
*They will even clean your car if they're in the mood.*

When an 'if'-clause is put first, 'then' is sometimes put at the beginning of the main clause.

*If this is what was happening in the Sixties, then I'm glad I wasn't around then.*

'Unless' means 'if...not'. For example, 'You will fail your exams unless you work harder' means 'If you do not work harder, you will fail your exams'.

*There can be no new growth unless the ground is cleared.*
*Nobody gets anything unless they ask for it.*

Clauses beginning with 'unless' usually go after a main clause.

**modals and imperatives**   **8.27** When you are using a conditional clause, you often use a **modal** in the main clause.

You always use a modal in the main clause when you are talking about a situation which does not exist.

*If you weren't here, she would get rid of me in no time.*
*If anybody had asked me, I could have told them what happened.*

Modals are explained in paragraphs 4.95 to 4.262.

Conditional clauses are often used with **imperative** structures.

*If you dry your washing outdoors, wipe the line first.*
*If it's four o'clock in the morning, don't expect them to be pleased to see you.*

Imperative structures are explained in paragraphs 4.4 and 4.31 to 4.35.

**tenses in conditional clauses**

**8.28** There are special rules about which tense to use in conditional sentences.

Foreign learners are often taught that there are three kinds of conditional sentence:

● the **first conditional**, in which the verb in the main clause is 'will' or 'shall' and the verb in the conditional clause is in the **simple present tense**.

● the **second conditional**, in which the verb in the main clause is 'would' or 'should' and the verb in the conditional clause is in the **simple past tense**.

● the **third conditional**, in which the verb in the main clause is 'would have' or 'should have' and the verb in the conditional clause is in the **past perfect tense.**

This is largely correct, but does not fully describe the normal patterns of tense in conditional clauses which are set out in the following paragraphs.

**common occurrences**

**8.29** When you are talking about a common occurrence, you use the **simple present tense** or the **present continuous tense** in the conditional clause and in the main clause.

*If a man looks at me, I am flattered.*
*He never rings me up unless he wants something.*
*If the baby's crying, she probably needs feeding.*
*If an advertisement conveys information which is false or misleading, the advertiser is committing an offence.*

**occurrences in the past**

**8.30** When you are talking about a common occurrence in the past, you use the **simple past tense** or the **past continuous tense** in the conditional clause. In the main clause, you use the **simple past tense** or a **modal.**

*They sat on the grass if it was fine.*
*If it was raining, we usually stayed indoors.*
*If anyone came, they'd say 'How are you?'*
*If they wanted to go out, they could always count on me to stay with the baby.*
*Often I could not fall asleep unless I exercised to the point of exhaustion.*

**possible situations**

**8.31** When you are talking about a possible situation in the present, you usually use the **simple present tense** or the **present perfect tense** in the conditional clause. In the main clause you usually use a **modal.**

*If anyone doubts the truth of this, they should look at the two most successful post-war economies, Germany and Japan.*
*Unless you've tried it, you can't imagine how pleasant it is.*

'If'-clauses of this kind can be used when you are offering to do something, or giving permission for something to be done. You use a modal in the main clause, and the subordinate clause consists of 'if', a pronoun, and 'want', 'like', or 'wish'.

*I'll teach you, if you want.*
*You can leave if you like.*

**possible future occurrences**

**8.32** When you are talking about a possible future occurrence, you use the **simple present tense** in the conditional clause, and the **simple future tense** in the main clause.

*If I ever <u>get</u> out of this alive, I'll never <u>leave</u> you again.*
*If nuclear weapons <u>are employed</u> in a world war, the world <u>will be</u>*
*destroyed.*
*Willie <u>will be</u> a failure in life unless he <u>is pushed</u>.*

**USAGE NOTE**  8.33 A more formal way of talking about a possible future situation is to use 'should' in the conditional clause. For example, instead of saying 'If anything happens, I will return immediately', you can say 'If anything should happen, I will return immediately'. In the main clause you use a modal, usually 'will' or 'would'.

*If that <u>should</u> happen, you <u>will</u> be blamed.*

Another way of talking about a possible future situation is to use 'were' and a 'to'-infinitive in a conditional clause. For example, instead of saying 'If he goes, I will go too', you can say 'If he were to go, I would go too'. In the main clause you use 'would', 'should', or 'might'.

*If we <u>were to move</u> north, we <u>would</u> be able to buy a bigger house.*

**unlikely**  8.34 When you are talking about an unlikely situation, you use the **simple**
**situations**  **past tense** in the conditional clause, and 'would', 'should', or 'might' in the main clause.

*The older men <u>would</u> find it difficult to get a job if they <u>left</u> the farm.*
*I <u>should</u> be surprised if it <u>was</u> less than five pounds.*
*If I <u>frightened</u> them, they <u>might</u> take off and I <u>would</u> never see them again.*

In the conditional clause, 'were' is sometimes used instead of 'was', especially after 'I'.

*If I <u>were</u> a guy, I <u>would</u> fancy Sophie.*
*If I <u>were asked</u> to define my condition, I'<u>d</u> say 'bored'.*

**what might**  8.35 When you are talking about something that might have happened in
**have been**  the past but did not happen, you use the **past perfect tense** in the conditional clause. In the main clause, you use 'would have', 'could have', 'should have', or 'might have'.

*Perhaps if he <u>had realized</u> that, he <u>would have</u> run away while there was still time.*
*If she <u>had not married</u>, she <u>would</u> probably <u>have</u> become something special in her field.*

**putting the**  8.36 In formal or literary English, if the first verb in an 'if'-clause is
**verb first**  'should', 'were', or 'had', this verb is sometimes put at the beginning of the clause and 'if' is omitted. For example, instead of saying 'If any visitors should come, I will say you are not here', someone might say 'Should any visitors come, I will say you are not here'.

*<u>Should</u> ministers decide to instigate an inquiry, we would welcome it.*
*<u>Were</u> it all true, it would still not excuse their actions.*
*<u>Were</u> they to cease advertising, prices would be significantly reduced.*
*<u>Had</u> I known that there was never to be another opportunity, I would have filmed the occasion.*

**USAGE NOTE**  8.37 Instead of using a conditional clause containing the word 'be', you can sometimes use a phrase consisting of 'if' followed by an adjective or a prepositional phrase. For example, instead of saying 'We will sell the car, if it is necessary', you can say 'We will sell the car, if necessary'.

*This unfortunate situation is to be avoided <u>if possible</u>.*
*If I were innocent, I'd rather be tried here; <u>if guilty</u>, in America.*
*<u>If in doubt</u>, ask at your local library.*

**necessary conditions**

**8.38** If you want to say that one situation is necessary for another, you use 'provided', 'providing', 'as long as', 'so long as', or 'only if'. 'Provided' and 'providing' are often followed by 'that'.

*Ordering is quick and easy provided you have access to the internet.*
*Provided that it's not too much money, I'd love to come to Spain.*

*The oven bakes magnificent bread providing there is a hot enough fire in the furnace.*
*They are content for the world to stay as it is, poverty, pain and everything as long as they are comfortable.*
*These activities can flourish only if agriculture and rural industry are flourishing.*

When you are using 'only if', you can put the 'only' in the main clause, separated from the 'if'. For example, instead of saying 'I will come only if he wants me', you can say 'I will only come if he wants me'.

*He told them that disarmament was only possible if Britain changed her foreign policy.*

Another way of saying that one situation is necessary for another is to use a conditional clause consisting of 'if' followed by the subject, a form of 'be', and a 'to'-infinitive clause. In the main clause, you say what is necessary using 'must'.

*It's late, and if I am to get any sleep I must go.*
*If you are to escape, you must leave me and go on alone.*

**8.39** If you want to say that one situation would not affect another, you can use 'even if'.

*I would have married her even if she had been penniless.*
*Even if you've never been taught to mend a fuse, you don't have to sit in the dark.*
*Even if we do not resort to such dramatic measures, it seems likely that there will be many exciting opportunities in the future.*

'Even if' is also used in **concessive clauses**. This is explained in paragraph 8.67.

**8.40** If you want to say that a situation would not be affected by any of two or more things, you use 'whether'. You put 'or' between the different possibilities.

*If the lawyer made a long, oratorical speech, the client was happy whether he won or lost.*
*Catching a frog can be a difficult business, whether you're a human or a bird or a reptile.*
*Whether you go to a launderette or do your washing at home, the routine the same.*

If you want to say that what happens would not be affected by either of tw opposite situations, you use a clause beginning with 'whether or not'.

*Whether or not people have religious faith, they can believe in the power of love.*
*I get an electrician to check all my electrical appliances every autumn, whether or not they are giving trouble.*

'Or not' can be put at the end of the clause.

*Whether I agreed or not, the search would take place.*

**8.41** When the verb in a 'whether'-clause is 'be', the **subjunctive mood** is sometimes used. When you use the subjunctive mood, you use the **base form** of a verb rather than the third person singular. This is rather formal.

*Always immediately report such behaviour to the nearest person in authority, whether it be a school teacher or a policeman or anyone else.*

When the verb in a 'whether'-clause is 'be' and the subject is a personal pronoun such as 'they' or 'it', you can omit 'be' and the pronoun. For example, instead of saying 'All the villagers, whether they are young or old, help with the harvest', you can say 'All the villagers, whether young or old, help with the harvest'.

*A fresh pepper, whether red or green, lasts about three weeks.*
*They help people, whether chance visitors or students of medieval history, to learn more of our past.*

**8.42** When you want to say that something is the case and that it does not matter which person, place, cause, method, or thing is involved, you use 'whoever', 'wherever', 'however', 'whatever', or 'whichever'.

*Whoever wins this civil war there will be little rejoicing at the victory.*
*Wherever it is, you aren't going.*
*However it began, the battle was bound to develop into a large-scale conflict.*

'Whatever' and 'whichever' are used either as determiners or pronouns.

*Whatever car you drive, keep fixing it and keep it forever.*
*That is why the deficit remains of key importance this year, whatever the Chancellor might say.*
*Whichever way you do it, it's hard work.*
*Whatever you decide, I'm sure it will be just fine.*

Another way of saying that it does not matter who or what is involved is to use 'no matter' followed by 'who', 'where', 'how', 'what', or 'which'.

*Most people, no matter who they are, seem to have at least one.*
*Our aim is to recruit the best person for the job, no matter where they are from.*
*No matter how I'm playing, I always get that special feeling.*

# Purpose clauses

**8.43** When you want to indicate the purpose of an action, you use a **purpose clause**.

Here is a list of the most common conjunctions used in purpose clauses:

| in order that | so | so that |
| in order to | so as to | to |

**types of purpose clause** **8.44** There are two kinds of purpose clause.

**Non-finite purpose clauses** are the most common kind. They contain a 'to'-infinitive.

*They had to take some of his land in order to extend the churchyard.*
*Farmers have put up barricades to prevent hippies moving on to their land.*

The subject of a non-finite purpose clause is always the same as the subject of the main clause.

Non-finite purpose clauses are explained in paragraphs 8.45 to 8.46.

**Finite purpose clauses** usually contain a **'that'-clause.**

*Be as clear and factual as possible in order that there may be no misunderstanding.*

Finite purpose clauses are explained in paragraphs 8.47 to 8.48.

**non-finite clauses**

**8.45 Non-finite purpose clauses** usually begin with 'in order to' or 'so as to'.

*They were shoving each other out of the way in order to get to the front.*
*We had to borrow money in order to buy the house.*
*The best thing to do is to fix up a screen so as to let in the fresh air and keep out the flies.*

If you want to make one of these clauses negative, you put 'not' in front of the 'to'.

*Rose trod with care in order not to spread the dirt.*
*When removing a stain, work from the edge inwards so as not to enlarge the area affected.*

**8.46** Non-finite purpose clauses can simply be 'to'-infinitive clauses.

*People would stroll down the path to admire the garden.*
*The children sleep together to keep warm.*
*To understand what is happening now, we need to reflect on what has been achieved in the last decade.*

However, you cannot use a negative with one of these structures. You cannot say, for example, 'We keep the window shut not to let the flies in'. You would have to say, 'We keep the window shut in order not to let the flies in'.

**finite clauses**

**8.47 Finite purpose clauses** usually begin with 'in order that', 'so that', or 'so'. They usually contain a **modal.**

If the verb in the main clause is in a **present tense** or in the **present perfect tense,** you usually use one of the modals 'can', 'may', 'will', or 'shall' in the purpose clause.

*...drugs used to stupefy a victim in order that they may be raped.*
*...people who are learning English in order that they can study a particular subject.*

If the verb in the main clause is in a **past tense,** you usually use 'could', 'might', 'should', or 'would' in the purpose clause.

*A stranger in the crowd had hoisted Philip up on his shoulder so that he might see the procession depart.*
*I bought six cows so that we should have some milk to sell.*
*She said she wanted tea ready at six so she could be out by eight.*

Ordinary verbs are occasionally used instead of modals, especially in negative purpose clauses.

*Make sure you get plenty of rest, so that you don't fall asleep at work.*

'So that' is also used in **result clauses**. This use is explained in paragraphs 8.55 and 8.56.

**8.48** In formal or old-fashioned English, 'lest' is sometimes used at the beginning of a finite purpose clause to say what an action is intended to prevent.

For example, 'They built a statue of him lest people should forget what he had done' means the same as 'They built a statue of him so that people would not forget what he had done'.

*He was put in a cell with no clothes and shoes lest he injure himself.*
*He spoke in whispers lest the servants should hear him.*

In clauses beginning with 'lest', you use either the **subjunctive mood** or a **modal**.

# Reason clauses

**8.49** When you want to indicate the reason for something, you use a **reason clause**.

Here is a list of the main conjunctions used in reason clauses:

| as | because | in case | just in case | since |
|----|---------|---------|--------------|-------|

**8.50** If you are simply indicating the reason for something, you use 'because', 'since', or 'as'.

*I couldn't feel anger against him because I liked him too much.*
*I didn't know that she had been married, since she seldom talked about herself.*
*As we had plenty of time, we decided to go for a coffee.*

**8.51** You use 'in case' or 'just in case' when you are mentioning a possible future situation which is someone's reason for doing something. In the reason clause, you use the **simple present tense.**

*Mr Woods, I am here just in case anything out of the ordinary happens.*

When you are talking about someone's reason for doing something in the past, you use the **simple past tense** in the reason clause.

*He did not sit down in case his trousers got creased.*

**8.52** 'In that', 'inasmuch as', 'insofar as', and 'to the extent that' are used to say why a statement you have just made is true. These are formal expressions.

*I'm in a difficult situation in that I have been offered two jobs and they both sound interesting.*
*Censorship is feeble inasmuch as it does not protect anyone.*
*We are traditional insofar as we do traditional sketches, but we try and do them about original ideas.*
*He feels himself to be dependent to the extent that he is not free to question decisions affecting his daily life.*

**8.53** People sometimes use reason clauses beginning with 'for' or 'seeing that'. 'For' means the same as 'because'. Its use in reason clauses is now considered to be old-fashioned.

*I hesitate, <u>for</u> I am not quite sure of my facts.*

'Seeing that' means the same as 'since'. It is used only in informal speec[

*<u>Seeing that</u> you're the guest on this little trip, I won't tell you what I think
of your behaviour last night.*

'Now' and 'now that' are used to say that a new situation is the reason fo
something. Clauses beginning with 'now' or 'now that' are dealt with as
**time clauses.** They are explained in paragraph 8.18.

# Result clauses

**8.54** When you want to indicate the result of something, you use a **resul
clause.**

Result clauses always come after the main clause.

**8.55** Result clauses usually begin with 'so that'.

You can use 'so that' simply to say what the result of an event or situatio
was.

*My suitcase had become damaged on the journey home, <u>so that</u> the lid
would not stay closed.*
*A great storm had brought the sea right into the house, <u>so that</u> they had
been forced to make their escape by a window at the back.*
*There's a window above the bath <u>so that</u> when I'm relaxing here I can
watch the sky.*

'So', 'and so', and 'and' can also be used.

*The young do not have the money to save and the old are consuming the
savings, <u>so</u> it is mainly the middle-aged who are saving.*
*She was having great difficulty getting her car out, <u>and so</u> I had to move
my car to let her out.*
*Her boy friend was shot in the chest <u>and</u> died.*

With these result clauses, you usually put a comma after the main claus

**8.56** You can also use 'so that' to say that something is or was done in a
particular way to achieve a desired result.

For example, 'He fixed the bell so that it would ring when anyone came in'
means 'He fixed the bell in such a way that it would ring when anyone
came in'.

*Explain it <u>so that</u> a 10-year-old could understand it.*
*They arranged things <u>so that</u> they never met.*

With these result clauses, you do not put a comma after the main clause

**8.57** 'So that' is also used in **finite purpose clauses.** This use is explaine
in paragraph 8.47.

**USAGE**  **8.58** 'So' and 'that' are also used in a special kind of structure to say tha
**NOTE**  a result happens because something has a quality to a particular extent.
or because something is done in an extreme way.

In these structures. 'so' is used as a **modifier** in front of an adjective or
adverb. A 'that'-clause is then added as a **qualifier. Modifiers** and

qualifiers are explained in Chapter 2. See paragraph 2.309 for similar structures to the one described in this paragraph.

*The crowd was so large that it overflowed the auditorium.*
*They were so surprised they didn't try to stop him.*
*He dressed so quickly that he put his boots on the wrong feet.*
*She had fallen down so often that she was covered in mud.*

Sometimes 'as' is used instead of 'that'. 'As' is followed by a 'to'-infinitive clause.

*...small beaches of sand so white as to dazzle the eye.*
*I hope that nobody was so stupid as to go around saying those things.*

**8.59** 'So' and 'that' can also be used in this way with 'many', 'few', 'much', and 'little'.

*We found so much to talk about that it was late at night when we remembered the time.*
*There were so many children you could hardly squeeze in the room.*

USAGE NOTE **8.60** When the verb in the main clause is 'be' or when an auxiliary is used, the normal order of words is often changed for greater emphasis. 'So' is put at the beginning of the sentence, followed by the adjective, adverb, or noun group. 'Be' or the auxiliary is placed in front of the subject.

For example, instead of saying 'The room was so tiny that you could not get a bed into it', you can say 'So tiny was the room that you could not get a bed into it'.

*So successful have they been that they are moving to Bond Street.*
*So rapid is the rate of progress that advance seems to be following advance on almost a monthly basis.*

**8.61** 'Such' and 'that' are also used to say that a result happens because something has a quality to a particular extent. You put 'such' in front of a noun group, and then add a 'that'-clause.

If the noun in the noun group is a singular count noun, you put 'a' or 'an' in front of it.

*I slapped her hand and she got such a shock that she dropped the bag.*
*He says his country's political system is such a mess a coup may be necessary.*
*She was in such pain that she almost collapsed.*
*These birds have such small wings that they cannot get into the air even if they try.*

**8.62** 'Such' can be used in a similar structure as an adjective with the meaning 'so great'. The 'that'-clause goes immediately after it.

*The extent of the disaster was such that the local authorities were quite unable to cope.*

Sometimes 'such' is put at the beginning of a sentence, followed by 'be', a noun group, and the 'that'-clause. For example, instead of saying 'Her beauty was such that they could only stare', you can say 'Such was her beauty that they could only stare'.

*Such is the power of suggestion that within a very few minutes she fell asleep.*

**8.63** You can also use 'such' as an adjective to say that a result is obtained by something being of a particular kind. 'Such' is followed by a 'that'-clause or by 'as' and a 'to'-infinitive clause.

*The dangers are such that an organized tour is a more sensible option.*
*Conditions in prison should be such as to lessen the chances of prisoners reoffending.*

You can use the expression 'in such a way' to say that a result is obtained by something being done in a particular way. It is followed by a 'that'-clause or by 'as' and a 'to'-infinitive clause.

*She had been taught to behave in such a way that her parents would have as quiet a life as possible.*
*Is it right that this high tax should be spent in such a way as to give bene mainly to the motorist?*

**8.64** You use 'otherwise', 'else', or 'or else' to say that a result of something not happening or not being the case would be that something else would happen or be the case.

For example, 'Give me back my money, otherwise I'll ring the police' mea 'If you don't give me back my money, I'll ring the police'.

*I'm not used to living on my own so I want a house I'll like, otherwise I'll get depressed.*
*I must have done something wrong, or else they wouldn't have kept me here.*

# Concessive clauses

**8.65** Sometimes you want to make two statements, one of which contrasts with the other or makes it seem surprising. You can put both statements into one sentence by using a **concessive clause**.

Here is a list of conjunctions used in concessive clauses:

| | | | |
|---|---|---|---|
| although | even though | much as | whereas |
| despite | except that | not that | while |
| even if | in spite of | though | whilst |

contrast **8.66** If you simply want to contrast two statements, you use 'although', 'though', 'even though', or 'while'.

*I used to read a lot although I don't get much time for books now.*
*Though he has lived for years in London, he writes in German.*
*I used to love listening to her, even though I could only understand about half of what she said.*
*While I did well in class, I was a poor performer at games.*

'Whilst' and 'whereas' can also be used. They are fairly formal words.

*Raspberries have a matt, spongy surface whilst blackberries have a taut, shiny skin.*
*To every child adult approval means love, whereas disapproval means hate.*

**8.67** If you want to say that something which is probably true does not affect the truth of something else, you use 'even if'.

*All this is part of modern commercial life (even if it is not as essential an activity as most participants care to believe).*

*From the minute he does these things he begins to be a different person, even if he doesn't realize it.*

'Even if' is also used in **conditional clauses**. This use is explained in paragraph 8.39.

**8.68** You can use 'not that' instead of using 'although' and a negative. For example, instead of saying 'I have decided to leave, although no one will miss me', you can say 'I have decided to leave—not that anyone will miss me'.

Clauses beginning with 'not that' always go after a main clause.

*He's got a new girlfriend – not that I care.*
*I think I looked very chic for the party. Not that anyone noticed.*

**exceptions**   **8.69** If you want to mention an exception to a statement that you have just made, you use 'except that'.

*She treats her daughter the same as her younger boy except that she takes her several times a week to a special clinic.*
*Nobody said a thing except that one or two asked me if I was better.*

This kind of clause is sometimes called an **exception clause**.

**USAGE NOTE**   **8.70** When a clause beginning with 'though' ends with a complement, the complement can be brought forward to the beginning of the clause. For example, instead of saying 'Though he was tired, he insisted on coming to the meeting', you can say 'Tired though he was, he insisted on coming to the meeting'.

*Tempting though it may be to follow this point through, it is not really relevant and we had better move on.*
*I had to accept the fact, improbable though it was.*
*Astute business man though he was, Philip was capable at times of extreme recklessness.*

When the complement is an adjective, you can use 'as' instead of 'though'.

*Stupid as it sounds, I was so in love with her that I believed her.*

When a clause beginning with 'though' ends with an adverb, you can often put the adverb at the beginning of the clause.

*Some members of the staff couldn't handle Murray's condition, hard though they tried.*

When you are talking about a strong feeling or desire, you can use 'much as' instead of 'although' and an adjunct. For example, instead of saying 'Although I like Venice very much, I couldn't live there' you can say 'Much as I like Venice, I couldn't live there'.

*Much as they admired her looks and her manners, they had no wish to marry her.*

**non-finite clauses**   **8.71** 'Although', 'though', 'while', and 'whilst' are sometimes used in **non-finite** concessive clauses. For example, instead of saying 'Whilst he liked cats, he never let them come into his house', you can say 'Whilst liking cats, he never let them come into his house'.

*While conceding the importance of freedom of speech, I believe it must be exercised with sensitivity and responsibility.*

'Despite' and 'in spite of' can also be used at the beginning of non-finite concessive clauses. 'Despite working hard, I failed my exams' means 'Although I worked hard, I failed my exams'.

*Sensible, interested mothers still play a big part in their children's lives, despite working and having a full-time nanny.*
*We had two more years of profit in spite of paying higher wages than the previous owner.*

**8.72** 'Although', 'though', 'while', and 'whilst' are also used in front of noun groups, adjective groups, and adjuncts. For example, instead of saying 'Although she was fond of Gregory, she did not love him', you can say 'Although fond of Gregory, she did not love him'. Similarly, instead of saying 'They agreed to his proposal, though they had many reservations', you can say 'They agreed to his proposal, though with many reservations'.

*It was an unequal marriage, although a stable and long-lasting one.*
*Though not very attractive physically, she possessed a sense of humour.*
*They had followed her suggestion, though without much enthusiasm.*

'Even if', 'if', and 'albeit' can also be used in this way. 'Albeit' is a formal word.

*Other species have cognitive abilities, even if not as intricate as our own.*
*...some pleasant, if unexciting, tunes.*
*Like mercury, lead affects the brain, albeit in different ways.*

# Place clauses

**8.73** Sometimes, when you want to talk about the location or position of something, you need to use a clause rather than a simple adjunct. The kind of clause you use is called a **place clause.**

**8.74** Place clauses usually begin with 'where'.

*He said he was happy where he was.*
*He left it where it lay.*
*Stay where you are.*

'Where' is also used in **relative clauses.** This use is explained in paragraphs 8.104 to 8.106.

**8.75** In formal or literary English, 'where'-clauses are sometimes put in front of a main clause.

*Where Kate had stood last night, Maureen now stood.*
*Where the pink cliffs rose out of the ground there were often narrow tracks winding upwards.*

**8.76** When you want to say that something happens or will happen in every place where something else happens, you use 'wherever'.

*Soft-stemmed herbs and ferns spread across the ground wherever there was enough light.*
*In Bali, wherever you go, you come across ceremonies.*
*Wherever I looked, I found patterns.*

'Everywhere' can be used instead of 'wherever'.

*Everywhere I went, people were angry or suspicious.*

**8.77** 'Where' and 'wherever' are sometimes used in front of adjectives such as 'possible' and 'necessary'. When they are used like this, they mean 'when' or 'whenever', rather than 'where'. For a full explanation of this use, see paragraph 8.24.

# Clauses of manner

**8.78** When you want to talk about someone's behaviour or the way something is done, you use a **clause of manner**.

Here is a list of conjunctions used in clauses of manner:

| | | |
|---|---|---|
| as | as though | like |
| as if | just as | much as |

'The way', 'in a way', and 'in the way' are also used in clauses of manner in a similar way to conjunctions. These expressions are often followed by 'that'.

**saying how something is done**

**8.79** If you simply want to talk about someone's behaviour or the way something is done, you use 'like', 'as', 'the way', 'in a way', or 'in the way'.

*Is she often rude and cross like she's been this last month?*
*I don't understand why he behaves as he does.*
*I was never allowed to do things the way I wanted to do them.*
*He was looking at her in a way she did not recognise.*
*We have to make it work in the way that we want it to.*

**making comparisons**

**8.80** You can also use these expressions to compare the way something is done with the way someone or something else does it.

*Surely you don't intend to live by yourself like she does?*
*Joyce looked at her the way a lot of girls did.*

If you want to make a strong comparison, you use 'just as'.

*You can think of him and feel proud, just as I do.*

If you want to make a fairly weak comparison, you use 'much as'.

*These tanks speed across the desert, much as they did in World War II.*

**8.81** You sometimes want to say that something is done in the way that it would be done if something were the case. You do this by using 'as if' or 'as though'. You use a **past tense** in the clause of manner.

*He holds his head forward as if he has hit it too often on low doorways.*
*Presidents can't dispose of companies as if people didn't exist.*
*I put some water on my clothes to make it look as though I had been sweating.*
*He behaved as though it was nothing to be ashamed of.*

You also use 'as if' or 'as though' after link verbs such as 'feel' or 'look'. You do this when you are comparing someone's feelings or appearance to the feelings or appearance they would have if something were the case.

*She felt as if she had a fever.*
*His hair looked as if it had been combed with his fingers.*
*Her pink dress and her frilly umbrella made her look as though she had come to a garden party.*

In formal English, 'were' can be used instead of 'was' in clauses beginning with 'as if' or 'as though'.

*She shook as if she were crying, but she made no sound.*
*I felt as if I were the centre of the universe.*
*You talk as though he were already condemned.*

You can use 'just' in front of 'as if' or 'as though' for emphasis.

*He had no right to run off and leave her alone, just as if she was someone of no importance at all.*

**8.82** You can also use 'as if' and 'as though' in **non-finite** clauses. The clause begins with a 'to'-infinitive or a participle.

*For a few moments, he sat as if stunned.*
*He ran off to the house as if escaping.*
*He shook his head as though dazzled by his own vision.*

You can also use 'as if' and 'as though' in front of adjectives and prepositional phrases.

*One must row steadily onwards as if intent on one's own business.*
*He shivered as though with cold.*

# Relative clauses

**8.83** When you mention someone or something in a sentence, you often want to give further information about them. One way to do this is to use a **relative clause.**

You put a relative clause immediately after the noun which refers to the person, thing, or group you are talking about.

*The man who came into the room was small and slender.*
*Opposite is St. Paul's Church, where you can hear some lovely music.*

Relative clauses have a similar function to adjectives, and they are sometimes called **adjectival clauses.**

**Nominal relative clauses**, which have a similar function to noun groups, are explained in paragraphs 8.112 to 8.116.

**relative pronouns**

**8.84** Many relative clauses begin with a **relative pronoun**. The relative pronoun usually acts as the subject or object of the verb in the relative clause.

*He is the only person who might be able to help.*
*Most of the mothers have a job, which they take both for the money and the company.*

Here is a list of the most common relative pronouns:

| that | which | who | whom | whose |
|------|-------|-----|------|-------|

Relative pronouns do not have masculine, feminine, or plural forms. The same pronoun can be used to refer to a man, a woman, or a group of people.

*She didn't recognize the man who had spoken.*

*I met a girl who knew Mrs Townsend.*
*There are many people who find this intolerable.*

Some relative clauses do not have a relative pronoun.

*Nearly all the people I used to know have gone.*

This is explained in paragraphs 8.90, 8.91, and 8.96.

**kinds of relative clause**

**8.85** There are two kinds of relative clause.

**Defining relative clauses** explain which person or thing you are talking about. For example, if you say 'I met the woman', it might not be clear who you mean, so you might say, 'I met the woman who lives next door'. In this sentence, 'who lives next door' is a **defining relative clause.**

*Shortly after the shooting, the man who had done it was arrested.*
*Mooresville is the town that John Dillinger came from.*

Defining relative clauses are a kind of **qualifier**. Qualifiers are explained in paragraphs 2.289 to 2.320.

**Non-defining relative clauses** give further information which is not needed to identify the person, thing, or group you are talking about. For example, if you say 'I saw Kylie Minogue', it is clear who you mean. But you might want to add more information about Kylie Minogue, so you might say, for example, 'I saw Kylie Minogue, who was staying at the hotel opposite'. In this sentence, 'who was staying at the hotel opposite' is a **non-defining relative clause.**

*He was waving to the girl, who was running along the platform.*
*He walked down to Broadway, the main street of the town, which ran parallel to the river.*

Non-defining relative clauses are used mainly in writing rather than speech.

**punctuation**

**8.86** A non-defining relative clause usually has a comma in front of it and a comma after it, unless it is at the end of a sentence, in which case you just put a full stop. Dashes are sometimes used instead of commas.

*My son, who is four, loves Spiderman.*

You never put a comma or a dash in front of a defining relative clause.

*The woman who owns this cabin will come back in the autumn.*

**use after pronouns**

**8.87** Defining relative clauses can be used after some pronouns.

They are used after **indefinite pronouns** such as 'someone', 'anyone', and 'everything'.

*This is something I'm very proud of.*
*In theory anyone who lives or works in the area may be at risk.*
*We want to thank everyone who supported us through this.*

They are sometimes used after 'some', 'many', 'much', 'several', 'all', or 'those'.

*Like many who met him in those days I was soon charmed.*
*...the feelings of those who have suffered from the effects of crime.*

They can also be used after **personal pronouns**, but only in formal or old-fashioned English.

*He who is not for reform is against it.*

*...we who are supposed to be so good at talking and writing.*

Non-defining relative clauses are never used after pronouns.

**non-finite clauses**

**8.88** Relative clauses can sometimes be reduced to **non-finite clauses**.

For example, instead of saying 'Give it to the man who is wearing the bowler hat', you can say 'Give it to the man wearing the bowler hat'. Similarly, instead of saying 'The bride, who was smiling happily, chatted to the guests', you can say 'The bride, smiling happily, chatted to the guests'.

These uses are explained in paragraphs 8.117 to 8.133. See also paragraphs 2.317 and 2.318 in the section on **qualifiers**.

## Using relative pronouns in defining clauses

**8.89** The following paragraphs explain which pronouns you use in **defining relative clauses**.

**referring to people**

**8.90** When you are referring to a person or group of people, you use 'who' or 'that' as the **subject** of a defining clause. 'Who' is more common than 'that'.

*The man who employed me would transport anything anywhere.*
*...the people who live in the cottage.*
*...somebody who is really ill.*
*...the man that made it.*

You use 'who', 'that', or 'whom' as the **object** of a defining clause, or you do not use a pronoun at all.

*...someone who I haven't seen for a long time.*
*...a woman that I dislike.*
*...distant relatives whom he had never seen.*
*...a man I know.*

You use 'that' as the **complement** of a defining clause, or you do not use a pronoun.

*...the distinguished actress that she later became.*
*That was the kind of person she was.*

After a **superlative**, you do not usually use a pronoun.

*He was the cleverest man I ever knew.*
*...the best thing I ever did.*

For more information about **superlatives** see paragraphs 2.117 to 2.127.

**referring to things**

**8.91** When you are referring to a thing or group of things, you use 'which' or 'that' as the **subject** of a defining clause.

*...pasta which came from Milan.*
*We need to understand the things which are important to people.*
*There are a lot of things that are wrong.*

You use 'which' or 'that' as the **object** of a defining clause, or you do not use a pronoun.

*...shells which my sister had collected.*
*...the oxygen that it needs.*
*...one of the things I'll never forget.*

After 'much' or 'all', you use 'that'. You do not use 'which'.

*There was not much that the military men could do.*
*Happiness is all that matters.*

# Using relative pronouns in non-defining clauses

**8.92** The following paragraphs explain which pronouns you use in **non-defining relative clauses.**

Unlike defining clauses, these clauses cannot be used without a relative pronoun.

**referring to people**   **8.93** When you are referring to a person or group of people, you use 'who' as the **subject** of a non-defining clause.

*Heath Robinson, who died in 1944, was a graphic artist and cartoonist.*
*The horse's rider, who has not been named, was too distressed to talk to police.*

You use 'who' or 'whom' as the **object** of a non-defining clause.

*That's one of the things which Heath, who I do not like, had a clear idea about.*
*He then became involved in a row with the party chairman, whom he accused of lying.*

**referring to things**   **8.94** When you are referring to a thing or group of things, you use 'which' as the subject or object of a non-defining clause.

*The treatment, which is being tried by researchers at four hospitals, has helped patients who have failed to respond to other remedies.*
*The company, which has about 160 shops, is in financial trouble.*
*He was a man of considerable inherited wealth, which he ultimately spent on his experiments.*
*...this offer, which few can resist.*

# Using relative pronouns with prepositions

**8.95** A relative pronoun can be the object of a preposition. Usually the preposition goes towards the end of the clause, and not in front of the pronoun.

*...the job which I'd been training for.*
*...the universe that we live in.*
*...the woman who Muller left his money to.*

**no pronoun**   **8.96** Often, in ordinary speech, no pronoun is used.

*Angela was the only person I could talk to.*
*...that place I used to go to last term.*
*That's all we have time for this week.*

**indirect objects**   **8.97** When a relative pronoun is the indirect object of a verb, you use 'to' or 'for'. For example, you say 'the man that she wrote the letter to', not 'the man that she wrote the letter'.

*...pieces of work that we give a mark to.*

You also use 'to' or 'for' when there is no relative pronoun.

*...the girl I sang the song for.*

**formal use**    **8.98** In formal English, the preposition can go at the beginning of a clause in front of 'whom' or 'which'.

*These are the people to whom Catherine was referring.*
*...a woman friend with whom Rose used to go for walks.*
*...questions to which there were no answers.*

Note however that you cannot put the preposition at the beginning of a clause in front of 'who' or 'that'.

**phrasal verbs**    **8.99** If the verb in a relative clause is a **phrasal verb** ending with a preposition, you cannot move the preposition to the beginning of the clause.

*...all the things I've had to put up with.*
*...the kind of life he was looking forward to.*
*There are other problems, which I don't propose to go into at the moment.*

**USAGE NOTE**    **8.100** Words such as 'some', 'many', and 'most' can be put in front of 'of whom' or 'of which' at the beginning of a non-defining relative clause.

*At the school we were greeted by the teachers, most of whom were middle aged.*
*It is a language shared by several quite diverse cultures, each of which uses it differently.*

Numbers can be put before or after 'of whom'.

*They act mostly on suggestions from present members (four of whom are women).*
*Altogether 1,888 people were prosecuted, of whom 1,628 were convicted.*

# Using 'whose'

**8.101** If you want to talk about something relating to the person, thing, or group you are talking about, you use a relative clause beginning with 'whose' and a noun group.

For example, instead of saying 'I am writing a letter to Nigel. His father is ill', you can say 'I am writing a letter to Nigel, whose father is ill'.

'Whose' can be used in defining or non-defining clauses.

*...workers whose bargaining power is weak.*
*...anyone whose credit card is stolen.*
*She asked friends whose opinion she respected.*
*...a country whose population was growing.*
*The man, whose identity was not released, was attacked at 10pm last night.*

The noun after 'whose' can be the subject or object of the verb in the clause, or it can be the object of a preposition. If it is the object of a preposition, the preposition can come at the beginning or end of the clause.

*...the governments in whose territories they operate.*
*...writers whose company he did not care for.*

**8.102** In written English, 'of which' and 'of whom' are sometimes used instead of 'whose'. You put these expressions after a noun group beginning with 'the'.

For example, instead of writing 'a town whose inhabitants speak French', you can write 'a town the inhabitants of which speak French'.

*...a competition the results of which will be announced today.*
*I travelled in a lorry the back of which the owner had loaded with yams.*

# Using other relative pronouns

**8.103** Some other words and expressions can be used as relative pronouns.

**non-defining clauses**

**8.104** 'When' and 'where' are used in **non-defining clauses.**

*I want to see you at 12 o'clock, when you go to your lunch.*
*My favourite holiday was in 1999, when I went to Jamaica.*
*He came from Herne Bay, where Lally had once spent a holiday.*
*She carried them up the stairs to the art room, where the brushes and paints had been set out.*

**defining clauses**

**8.105** 'When' and 'where' can also be used in **defining clauses**, but only when the clause is preceded by a particular kind of noun.

'When'-clauses must be preceded by the word 'time' or by the name of a period of time such as 'day' or 'year'.

*There had been a time when she thought they were wonderful.*
*This is the year when the profits should start.*

'Where'-clauses must be preceded by the word 'place' or by the name of a kind of place such as 'room' or 'street'.

*...the place where they work.*
*...the room where I did my homework.*
*...the street where my grandmother had lived.*

Note that place names such as 'London' are **proper nouns** and so do not have defining relative clauses after them.

**8.106** 'Where' can also be used in defining clauses after words such as 'situation' and 'stage'.

*Increasing poverty has led to a situation where the poorest openly admit that they cannot afford to have children.*
*In time we reached a stage where we had more black readers than white ones.*

**8.107** 'Why' is used in defining clauses after the word 'reason'.

*That is a major reason why they were such poor countries.*

'Whereby' is used in defining clauses after words such as 'arrangement' and 'system'.

*...the new system whereby everyone pays a fixed amount.*
*Counselling is a process whereby the person concerned can learn to manage the emotional realities that face them.*

**USAGE NOTE**  **8.108** Other expressions can be used in defining clauses in place of 'when', 'where', 'why', and 'whereby'.

After 'time' you can use 'at which' instead of 'when'.

*…the time at which the original mineral was formed.*

After 'place' and words such as 'room', 'street', 'year', and 'month', you can use 'in which' instead of 'where' or 'when'.

*…the place in which they found themselves.*
*…the room in which the meeting would be held.*
*…the year in which Lloyd George lost power.*

After 'day' you can use 'on which' instead of 'when'.

*Sunday was the day on which we were expected to spend some time with my father.*

After 'reason' you can use 'that' or no pronoun instead of 'why'.

*…the reason that non-violence is considered to be a virtue.*
*That's the reason I'm checking it now.*

After words such as 'situation', 'stage', 'arrangement' or 'system' you can use 'in which' instead of 'where' or 'whereby'.

*…a situation in which there's a real political vacuum.*

## Additional points about non-defining relative clauses

**8.109** In written English, you can use a non-defining clause to say that one event happened after another.

For example, instead of saying 'I gave the book to George. George then gave it to Mary', you can say 'I gave the book to George, who gave it to Mary'.

*I sold my car to a garage, who sold it to a customer at twice the price.*
*The molten metal ran out on to the flagstones, which promptly exploded.*
*Later he went to New Zealand, where he did all sorts of jobs.*

**commenting on a fact**  **8.110** You can use a non-defining clause beginning with 'which' to say something about the whole situation described in a main clause, rather than about someone or something mentioned in it.

*Minute computers need only minute amounts of power, which means that they will run on small batteries.*
*I never met Brando again, which was a pity.*
*Prior to speaking she was a little tense, which was understandable.*

**commenting on a time or situation**  **8.111** When you want to add something to what you have said, you sometimes use a non-defining clause beginning with a preposition, 'which', and a noun. The noun is often a word like 'time' or 'point', or a very general word for a situation like 'case' or 'event'.

*They remain in the pouch for some seven weeks, by which time they are about 10cm long.*
*I was told my work was unsatisfactory, at which point I submitted my resignation.*

*Sometimes you may feel too frail to cope with things, in which case do
them as soon as it is convenient.*

# Nominal relative clauses

**8.112** When it is difficult to refer to something by using a noun group, you
can sometimes use a special kind of relative clause called a **nominal
relative clause.**

*What he really needs is a nice cup of tea.*
*Whatever she does will determine the future of her administration.*

**8.113** Nominal relative clauses beginning with 'what' can be used as
subjects, objects, or complements. 'What' can mean either 'the thing
which' or 'the things which'.

*What he said was perfectly true.*
*They did not like what he wrote.*
*I believe that is a very good account of what happened.*
*I'm what's generally called a traitor.*

People often use a 'what'-clause in front of 'is' or 'was' to say what kind of
thing they are about to mention.

*What I need is a lawyer.*
*What you have to do is to choose five companies to invest in.*

These structures are explained in paragraphs 10.28 to 10.30.

For another use of 'what' in nominal relative clauses see paragraph 8.116.

**8.114** Nominal relative clauses beginning with 'where' are usually used
after a preposition or after the verb 'be'. 'Where' means 'the place where'.

*I threw down my book and crossed the room to where she was sitting.*
*He lives two streets down from where Mr Stobie died.*
*This is where I crashed the car.*

**8.115** Nominal relative clauses beginning with 'whatever', 'whoever', or
'whichever' are used to refer to something or someone that is unknown or
indefinite.

'Whatever' is used only to refer to things. 'Whoever' is used to refer to
people. 'Whichever' is used to refer to either things or people.

'Whatever', 'whoever', and 'whichever' can be used as pronouns.
'Whichever' is often followed by 'of'.

*I'll do whatever you want.*
*These wild flowers are so rare I want to do whatever I can to save them.*
*...a person with written authority from whoever is dealing with the will.*
*People will choose whichever of these regimes they find suits them best.*

'Whatever' and 'whichever' can also be used as determiners.

*She had had to rely on whatever books were lying around there.*
*Choose whichever one of the three methods you fancy.*

For more information about 'whatever', 'whoever', and 'whichever' see
paragraph 8.42.

**8.116** 'What' can be used with the same meaning as 'whatever', both as a
pronoun and a determiner.

*Do what you like.*
*We give what help we can.*

The main use of 'what' in nominal relative clauses is explained in paragraph 8.113.

# Non-finite clauses

**8.117** A **non-finite clause** is a subordinate clause which contains a participle or an infinitive, but which does not contain a **finite verb.**

There are two kinds of non-finite clause. One kind begins with a **subordinating conjunction.**

*She fainted while giving evidence in court.*
*You've got to do something in depth in order to understand it.*

This kind of clause is dealt with in the sections on **adverbial clauses** (paragraphs 8.8 to 8.82).

The other kind of non-finite clause does not begin with a subordinating conjunction.

*He pranced about, feeling very important indeed.*
*I wanted to talk to her.*

This kind of clause sometimes consists of a participle and nothing else.

*Ellen shook her head, smiling.*
*Bet, grumbling, had departed to her harp lesson.*

Clauses which contain a participle and do not begin with a subordinating conjunction are explained in the following paragraphs.

**kinds of non-finite clause**

**8.118** The non-finite clauses discussed in this section function in a similar way to **relative clauses,** and, like relative clauses, they can have a defining or non-defining function.

**Non-defining clauses** are dealt with in paragraphs 8.120 to 8.131. These clauses are often used in writing, but are not usually used in spoken English.

**Defining clauses** are dealt with in paragraphs 8.132 and 8.133. These clauses are occasionally used in both written and spoken English.

**position of non-finite clauses**

**8.119** Non-defining clauses can go in front of a main clause, after a main clause, or in the middle of one. A non-defining clause is usually separated by a comma from the words in front of it and after it.

Defining clauses always go after a noun group. You never put a comma in front of a defining clause.

## Using non-defining clauses

**8.120** Non-defining clauses give further information which is not needed to identify the person, thing, or group you are talking about.

The following paragraphs 8.121 to 8.126 explain how these clauses are used when they relate to the **subject** of the verb in a main clause. The subject is not mentioned in the non-defining clause.

**present participle: simultaneous events**

**8.121** If you want to say that someone is doing or experiencing two things at the same time, you mention one of them in the main clause and the other in a clause containing a **present participle.**

*Laughing and shrieking, the crowd rushed under the nearest trees.*
*Jane watched, weeping, from the doorway.*
*Feeling a little foolish, Pluskat hung up.*
*Walking about, you notice something is different.*
*People stared at her. Seeing herself in a shop window, she could understand why.*

**present participle: one action after another**

**8.122** If you want to say that someone did one thing immediately after another, you mention the first action in a clause containing a present participle and the second one in the main clause.

*Leaping out of bed, he dressed so quickly that he put his boots on the wrong feet.*

**present participle: reasons**

**8.123** If you want to explain why someone does something or why something happens, you say what happens in the main clause and give the reason in a clause containing a present participle.

*At one point I made up my mind to go and talk to Uncle Sam. Then I changed my mind, realising that he could do nothing to help.*
*The baby would probably not live to grow up, being a scrawny little thing, unlikely to survive the normal ailments of childhood.*

**8.124** You can also use a present participle directly after a verb in a sentence such as 'I stood shivering at the roadside'. This use is explained in paragraphs 3.190 to 3.203.

**'having' and past participle: results**

**8.125** If you want to say that someone did or experienced one thing before another, you mention the first thing in a clause containing 'having' and a **past participle.** Often this kind of construction indicates that the second event was a result of the first one.

*I did not feel terribly shocked, having expected him to take the easiest way out.*
*Having admitted he was wrong, my husband suddenly fell silent.*

**past participle: earlier events**

**8.126** If you want to say what happened to someone or something before a situation or event described in the main clause, you say what happened in a clause containing a past participle on its own.

*The novels of Mary Webb, praised by Stanley Baldwin and so popular in the 30s, were great favourites of mine.*
*Angered by the policies of the union, she wrote a letter to the General Secretary.*

**mentioning the subject**

**8.127** Sometimes you want to use a non-defining clause which has a different subject from the subject of the main clause. These clauses are explained in the following paragraphs 8.128 to 8.131.

**8.128** In this kind of non-defining clause, you usually have to mention the subject.

*Jack being gone, Stephen opened his second letter.*

However, if the non-defining clause comes after the main clause, and it is clear from the context that it relates to the object of the main clause, you do not need to mention the object again.

*They picked me up, <u>kicking and bawling,</u> and carried me up to the road.*

**present participle** 8.129 You use a non-defining clause containing a subject and a **present participle**:

● when you want to mention something that is happening at the same time as the event or situation described in the main clause

*The embarrassed young man stared at me, <u>his face reddening.</u>*

● when you want to mention a fact that is relevant to the fact stated in the main clause.

*Bats are surprisingly long-lived creatures, <u>some having a life-expectancy of around twenty years.</u>*

'With' is sometimes added at the beginning of the non-finite clause.

*The old man stood up <u>with tears running down his face.</u>*

**past participle** 8.130 You use 'having' and a **past participle** to mention something which happened before the thing described in the main clause.

*<u>The argument having finished,</u> Mr Lush was about to leave and revved his engine.*
*<u>The Border having become more settled,</u> they had selected a site near the Kalpani River.*
*<u>George having been carried to his cabin,</u> Ash had gone up to the deserted deck.*
*<u>The subject having been opened,</u> he had to go on with it.*

You use a past participle on its own to say that something was done or completed before the event or situation described in the main clause.

*He proceeded to light his pipe. <u>That done,</u> he put on his woollen scarf and went out.*

**USAGE NOTE** 8.131 In a negative non-defining clause, you put 'not' in front of the participle, or in front of 'having'.

*He paused, <u>not wishing to boast.</u>*
*He failed to recognize her at first, <u>not having seen her for fifteen years or so.</u>*
*He began hitting them with his stick, <u>their reply not having come as quickly as he wanted.</u>*

## Using defining clauses

8.132 **Defining non-finite clauses** explain which person or thing you are talking about. They are always placed after the noun in a noun group.

*The old lady <u>driving the horse</u> was all in black.*
*The bus <u>carrying the freedom riders</u> arrived just before noon.*

**use after pronouns** 8.133 Defining clauses can be used after indefinite pronouns such as 'anyone'.

*Anyone <u>following this advice</u> could find himself in trouble.*
*Ask anybody <u>nearing the age of retirement</u> what they think.*

## Other structures used like non-finite clauses

**8.134** Phrases which do not contain a verb are sometimes used in writing in a similar way to non-finite clauses.

**8.135** In writing, you can add a phrase containing one or more adjectives to a sentence. This is another way of making two statements in one sentence.

For example, instead of writing 'We were tired and hungry. We reached the farm', you could write 'Tired and hungry, we reached the farm'.

*Surprised at my reaction, she tried to console me.*
*Much discouraged, I moved on to Philadelphia.*
*The boy nodded, pale and scared.*
*He knocked at the door, sick with fear and embarrassment.*
*'Of course,' said Ash, astonished.*

**8.136** In a similar way, you can use a phrase to describe something which is connected with the subject of a sentence. The phrase consists of a noun group, followed by an adjective, an adjunct, or another noun group.

For example, instead of writing 'He came into the room. His hat was in his hand', you could write 'He came into the room, his hat in his hand'.

*'What do you mean by that?' said Hugh, his face pale.*
*She stood very erect, her body absolutely stiff with fury.*
*He was waiting, drumming with his fingers, his eyes on his napkin.*

'With' is sometimes added at the beginning of a phrase.

*She walked on, with her eyes straight ahead.*
*It was a hot, calm day, with every object at the sea's surface visible for miles.*

# Coordination

**8.137** When you say or write something, you often want to put together two or more clauses of equal importance. You do this by using a **coordinating conjunction.**

*Anna had to go into town and she wanted to go to Bride Street.*
*I asked if I could borrow her bicycle but she refused.*
*He was a great player, yet he never played for Ireland.*

Here is a list of the most common coordinating conjunctions:

| | | |
|---|---|---|
| and | nor | then |
| but | or | yet |

Coordinating conjunctions are also used to link words and word groups.

*The boys shouted and rushed forward.*
*...domestic animals such as dogs and cats.*
*Her manner was hurried yet painstakingly courteous.*
*She spoke slowly but firmly.*

Sometimes coordinating conjunctions can be used together.

*The software is quite sophisticated and yet easy to use.*
*Eric moaned something and then lay still.*

The linking of clauses, words, or word groups using coordinating conjunctions is called **coordination**. Coordinating conjunctions are sometimes called **coordinators**.

**8.138** The different uses of coordinating conjunctions are explained in the following paragraphs:

| clauses | paragraphs 8.139 to 8.151 |
|---|---|
| verbs | paragraphs 8.152 to 8.158 |
| noun groups | paragraphs 8.159 to 8.167 |
| adjectives and adverbs | paragraphs 8.168 to 8.177 |
| other word groups | paragraphs 8.178 to 8.181 |

Ways of emphasizing coordinating conjunctions are described in paragraphs 8.182 to 8.187.

The linking of more than two clauses, words, or word groups is explained in paragraphs 8.188 and 8.189.

## Linking clauses

**8.139** You can use a coordinating conjunction to link clauses which have the same subject, or clauses which have different subjects.

**omitting words in the second clause**

**8.140** When you link clauses which have the same subject, you do not always need to repeat the subject in the second clause.

If the conjunction is 'and', 'or', or 'then', you do not usually repeat the subject.

*I picked up the glass and raised it to my lips.*
*It's a long time since you've bought them a drink or talked to them.*
*When she recognized Morris she went pale, then blushed.*

If the conjunction is 'but', 'so', or 'yet', it is usual to repeat the subject.

*I try and see it their way, but I can't.*
*I had no car, so I hired one for the journey.*
*He lost the fight, yet somehow he emerged with his dignity enhanced.*

When you link clauses which have different subjects but which have some common elements, you do not need to repeat all the elements in the second clause.

For example, instead of saying 'Some of them went to one pub and some of them went to the other pub', you can say 'Some of them went to one pub and some to the other'.

*One soldier was killed and another wounded.*
*One of its sides was painted black and the other white.*

**functions of coordinating conjunctions**

**8.141** A coordinating conjunction can be used simply to link clauses, or it can be used in addition to indicate a relationship between them. These uses are explained in the following paragraphs.

**related facts**

**8.142** If you simply want to mention two related facts, you use 'and'.

*He has been successful in Hollywood and has worked with such directors as Norman Jewison and Richard Attenborough.*
*The company will not be split up and will continue to operate from Belfast.*

*He gained a B in English and now plans to study Spanish.*

You also use 'and' to indicate that two things happened or are happening at the same time.

*I sat and watched him.*

Other uses of 'and' are explained in the following paragraphs.

**sequence** **8.143** If you use 'and' between two clauses which describe events, you are indicating that the event described in the first clause happens or happened before the event described in the second one.

*She was born in Budapest and raised in Manhattan.*
*He opened the car door and got out.*

'Then' can be used in the same way, but it is less common.

*We finished our drinks then left.*

**vo negative facts** **8.144** When you want to link two negative clauses, you usually use 'and'.

*When his appointment ceased he did not return to his home country and he has not been there since 1979.*

However, you can use 'or' when the clauses have the same subject and the same auxiliaries. In the second clause, you omit the subject, the auxiliaries, and 'not'.

For example, instead of saying 'She doesn't drink and she doesn't smoke', you can say 'She doesn't drink or smoke'.

*We will not damage or destroy the samples.*
*He didn't yell or scream.*

You can also link negative clauses by using 'and neither', 'and nor', or 'nor'. You put 'be' or the auxiliary at the beginning of the second clause, in front of the subject.

For example, instead of saying 'My sister doesn't like him, and I don't like him', you can say 'My sister doesn't like him, and neither do I'.

*I was not happy and neither were they.*
*I could not afford to eat in restaurants and nor could anyone else I knew.*
*Clearly these people are not insane, nor are they fools.*

'But neither' and 'but nor' can also be used.

*This isn't a dazzling record, but neither is it rubbish.*
*Institutions of learning are not taxed but nor are they much respected.*

When you use 'and' to link two negative statements, you can put 'either' after the second statement.

*I hadn't been to a pop festival before and Mike hadn't either.*
*Electricity didn't come into Blackhall Farm until recently and they hadn't any water either.*

For emphasis, you can join two negative clauses by using 'neither' and 'nor'. This use is explained in paragraph 8.186.

**contrast** **8.145** When you are adding a contrasting fact, you usually use 'but'.

*I'm only 63, but I feel a hundred.*
*It costs quite a lot but it's worth it.*
*I've had a very pleasant two years, but I can't wait to get back to the City.*

*Yes, we will be using motor racing to promote our products, but we will also be using it to promote good, safe and sober driving.*

If you want to add a fact which contrasts strongly with what you have just said, you use 'yet' or 'and yet'.

*Everything around him was blown to pieces, yet the minister escaped without a scratch.*
*I want to leave, and yet I feel obliged to stay.*

You usually put a comma in front of 'but', 'yet', or 'and yet'.

**alternatives**    **8.146** When you want to mention two alternatives, you use 'or'.

*I could kill a rabbit with my bare hands or shoot a bullock without the least bother.*
*We can try to increase the intelligence of our domestic animals or evolve wholly new ones with much higher intelligence.*
*Did he jump, or was he pushed?*

**USAGE NOTE**    **8.147** When you are giving advice, you sometimes want to tell someone what will happen if they do a particular thing. You do this by using an imperative clause, followed by 'and' and a clause containing a verb in a future tense.

For example, instead of saying 'If you go by train, you'll get there quicker' you can say 'Go by train and you'll get there quicker'.

*Do as you are told and you'll be alright.*
*You speak to me again like that and you'll be in serious trouble.*

When you are giving advice, a warning, or an order, you sometimes want to tell someone what will happen if they do not do what you say. You do this by using an imperative clause, followed by 'or' and a clause containing a verb in a future tense.

For example, instead of saying 'Go away! If you don't go away, I'll scream' you can say 'Go away, or I'll scream'.

*Hurry up, or you'll be late for school.*
*So don't go prying into my affairs or you'll get hurt.*

**USAGE NOTE**    **8.148** In writing, you can sometimes begin a sentence with a coordinating conjunction. You do this to make the sentence seem more dramatic or forceful. Some people think this use is incorrect.

*The villagers had become accustomed to minor earth tremors. But everyone knew that something unusual had woken them on Monday.*
*Do you think there is something wrong with her? Or do you just not like her?*
*Send him ahead to warn Eric. And close that door.*

**USAGE NOTE**    **8.149** Sometimes, in writing, two clauses can be made into one sentence without a coordinating conjunction being used. Instead, a semicolon or a dash is put between the clauses. This is a way of expressing two statements in one sentence when no particular coordinating conjunction seems appropriate.

*The neighbours drove by; they couldn't bear to look.*
*When we embraced I couldn't say thank you—those words were far too small for someone who had risked her life to save mine.*

**non-finite**    **8.150** Coordinating conjunctions can be used to link **non-finite clauses**.
**clauses**    'To'-infinitive clauses can be linked by 'and' or 'or'.

*We need to persuade more drivers to leave their cars at home and to use the train instead.*

*She may decide to remarry or to live with one of her sisters.*

Sometimes the second 'to' is omitted.

*Soldiers tried to clear road obstructions and remove flags and graffiti.*

When the second clause is negative, you can use 'not' instead of 'and not'.

*I am paid to treat people, not to interrogate them.*

Clauses beginning with a participle can be linked by 'and' or 'or'.

*The mother lay on the bed gazing at the child and smiling at him.*
*You may be more comfortable wearing a cotton dress or shirt or sleeping under a cotton blanket.*

However, if the first clause begins with 'standing', 'sitting', or 'lying', you do not usually put 'and' between the clauses.

*Inside were two lines of old people sitting facing each other.*

**8.151** For information on how to coordinate more than two clauses, see paragraph 8.188.


## Linking verbs

**8.152** When you are talking about two actions performed by the same person, thing, or group, you can use a coordinating conjunction to link two verbs.

**intransitive verbs**   **8.153** Coordinating conjunctions can be used to link **intransitive** verbs.

*Mostly, they just sat and chatted.*
*We both shrugged and laughed.*

**transitive verbs**   **8.154** When you are describing actions involving the same subject and object, you can link two **transitive** verbs. You put the object after the second verb only.

For example, instead of saying 'He swept the floor and polished the floor', you say 'He swept and polished the floor'.

*Wash and trim the leeks.*

Similarly, instead of saying 'They walk to work or cycle to work', you can say 'They walk or cycle to work'.

*I shouted and hooted at them.*

**omitting the auxiliary**   **8.155** When you are linking verb groups which contain the same auxiliary, you do not need to repeat the auxiliary in the second clause.

*Someone may be killed or seriously injured.*
*Now he is praised rather than criticized.*
*He knew a lot about horses, having lived and worked with them all his life.*

**emphasizing repetition or duration**   **8.156** If you want to say that someone does something repeatedly or for a long time, you can use 'and' to link two identical verbs.

*They laughed and laughed.*
*Isaacs didn't give up. He tried and tried, but he kept getting unhelpful replies.*

USAGE NOTE **8.157** In informal speech, 'and' is often used between 'try' and another verb. For example, someone might say 'I'll try and get a newspaper'. However, this means the same as 'I'll try to get a newspaper', and it refers to one action, not two.

For more information about this use see paragraph 3.201.

**8.158** For information on how to coordinate more than two verbs, see paragraph 8.188.

## Linking noun groups

**8.159** When you are talking about two people or things, you can use a coordinating conjunction to link two noun groups.

**8.160** In simple statements about two people or things, you use 'and'.

*There were men and women working in the fields.*
*I'll give you a nice cup of tea and a ginger biscuit.*
*...a friendship between a boy and a girl.*

Instead of 'and not', you use 'not' with a comma in front of it.

*I prefer romantic comedies, not action movies.*

If both people or things are the object of the verb in a negative sentence, you use 'or'.

*We didn't play cricket or football.*

**alternatives** **8.161** When you are giving alternatives, you use 'or'.

*Serve fruit or cheese afterwards.*
*Do you have any brothers or sisters?*

**omitting** **8.162** When you refer to two people or things using 'and' or 'or', you
**determiners** usually repeat the determiner.

*He was holding a suitcase and a birdcage.*

However, if the people or things are closely associated in some way, you do not need to repeat the determiner.

*My mother and father worked hard.*
*The jacket and skirt were skilfully designed.*
*...a boy in a jacket and tie.*

Sometimes both determiners are omitted.

*Mother and daughter stared at each other.*
*All this had of course been discussed between husband and wife.*
*The legal position for both worker and employer is now as fair as the law can make it.*

**referring to** **8.163** You can sometimes use noun groups linked by 'and' to refer to just
**one person** one person or thing.
**or thing**
*He's a racist and a sexist.*
*...the novelist and playwright, Somerset Maugham.*

**omitting** **8.164** When you are linking two nouns, an adjective in front of the first
**adjectives** noun is normally interpreted as applying to both nouns.

*...the young men and women of England.*
*...a house crammed with beautiful furniture and china.*

**verb agreement**

**8.165** When the subject of a clause consists of two or more nouns linked by 'and', you use a plural verb.

*My mother and father are ill.*
*Time, money and effort were needed.*

However, you do not use a plural verb if the nouns refer to the same person or thing.

*The writer and filmmaker Masanori Hata disagrees.*

You also do not use a plural verb with uncount nouns preceded by 'all', or with singular count nouns preceded by 'each' or 'every'.

*All this effort and sacrifice has not helped to alleviate poverty.*
*It became necessary to involve every man, woman and child who was willing to help.*

When you link two or more nouns with 'or', you use a plural verb after plural nouns, and a singular verb after singular nouns or uncount nouns.

*One generation's problems or successes are passed to the next.*
*Can you say 'No' to a friend or relative who wants to insist?*

**linking pronouns**

**8.166** You can put 'and', 'or', or 'not' between a pronoun and a noun group, or between two pronouns.

*Howard and I are planning a party.*
*She and I have a very good relationship.*
*Do you or your partner smoke?*
*I'm talking to you, not her.*

When you say something about yourself and someone else, you usually put the pronoun or noun group referring to the other person first, and the pronoun referring to yourself second.

*My sister and I lived totally different kinds of lives.*
*You and I must have a talk together.*
*...a difference of opinion between John and me.*
*The first people to hear were the Foreign Secretary and myself.*

**8.167** For information on how to coordinate more than two noun groups, see paragraph 8.188.

# Linking adjectives and adverbs

**8.168** When you use two adjectives to describe someone or something, you sometimes put a conjunction between them. This is explained in the following paragraphs 8.169 to 8.175. Conjunctions are also sometimes placed between adverbs. This is explained in paragraph 8.176.

**qualitative adjectives**

**8.169** When you put two **qualitative adjectives** in front of a noun, you put 'and' or a comma between the adjectives.

*...an intelligent and ambitious woman.*
*...an intelligent, generous man.*

**colour adjectives**

**8.170** When you put two **colour adjectives** in front of a noun, you put 'and' between them.

*...a black and white swimming suit.*

| **classifying adjectives** | **8.171** When you put two **classifying adjectives** in front of a noun, you have to decide whether the adjectives relate to the same system of classification or to different systems. |
|---|---|

For example, 'geographical' and 'geological' relate to the same system; 'British' and 'industrial' relate to different systems.

When you put two classifying adjectives in front of a noun, and the adjectives relate to the same classifying system, you put 'and' between them.

*...a social and educational dilemma.*

When the adjectives relate to different classifying systems, you do not put 'and' between them, or use a comma.

*...the French classical pianists Katia and Marielle Labeque.*
*...medieval Muslim philosophers.*
*...a square wooden table.*
*...American agricultural exports.*

| **different kinds of adjectives** | **8.172** When you put two adjectives of different kinds in front of a noun, for example a qualitative adjective and a classifying adjective, you do not put 'and' between them or use a comma. |
|---|---|

*...a large circular pool of water.*
*...a beautiful pink suit.*
*...rapid technological advance.*

| **adjectives with plural nouns** | **8.173** When you put two adjectives in front of a plural noun in order to talk about two groups of things which have different or opposite qualities, you put 'and' between the adjectives. |
|---|---|

*...business people from large and small companies.*
*...European and American traditions.*

| **adjectives after verbs** | **8.174** When you use two adjectives after a **link verb**, you put 'and' between them. |
|---|---|

*Mrs Scott's house was large and imposing.*
*The room was large and square.*
*On this point we can be clear and categorical.*

| **using other conjunctions** | **8.175** You can also put 'but', 'yet', or 'or' between adjectives. |
|---|---|

When you link contrasting adjectives, you put 'but' or 'yet' between them.

*...a small but comfortable hotel.*
*We are poor but happy.*
*...a firm yet gentle hand.*

When you want to say that either of two adjectives could apply, or to ask which adjective applies, you use 'or'.

*You can use red or black paint.*
*Call me if you feel lonely or depressed.*
*Is this good or bad?*

If you want to say that neither of two adjectives applies, you use 'or' in a negative sentence.

*He was not exciting or good-looking.*

Another way of saying that neither of two adjectives applies is to put 'neither' in front of the first one and 'nor' in front of the second one.

*He is neither young nor handsome.*
*The older men were careful to be neither too soft nor too loud in their reciting.*

**linking adverbs**

**8.176** You can put 'and' between **adverbs**.

*Mary was breathing quietly and evenly.*
*We have to keep airports running smoothly and efficiently.*
*They walk up and down, smiling.*

When you link contrasting adverbs, you put 'but' or 'yet' between them.

*Quickly but silently she darted out of the cell.*

If you want to say that neither of two adverbs applies, you use a negative sentence with 'or' between the adverbs, or you put 'neither' in front of the first adverb and 'nor' in front of the second one.

*Giving birth does not happen easily or painlessly.*
*The story ends neither happily nor unhappily.*

**8.177** For information on how to coordinate more than two adjectives, see paragraph 8.189.

## Linking other word groups

**8.178** Coordinating conjunctions can also be used to link **prepositions, prepositional phrases, modifiers**, and **determiners**.

**linking prepositions**

**8.179** You can use 'and' to link **prepositions** which apply to the same noun group.

*We see them on their way to and from school.*
*The group has called on the Government to investigate whether human rights were violated during and after the riots.*

**linking prepositional phrases**

**8.180** You can use 'and' to link **prepositional phrases** when you are describing similar actions, situations, or things.

*They walked across the gravel and down the drive.*
*They had crumbs around their mouths and under their chins.*

However, if the phrases describe the same action, situation, or thing, you do not put 'and' between them.

*Her husband was hit over the head with a mallet.*
*They walked down the drive between the chestnut trees.*
*...a man of about forty with glaring defiant eyes.*

**linking modifiers and determiners**

**8.181** You can use 'and' or 'or' to link **modifiers**.

*...the largest electrical equipment and electronics manufacturer in Germany.*
*This would not apply to a coal or oil supplier.*

You can use 'or' to link the **determiners** 'his' and 'her'.

*Your child's school will play an important part in shaping the rest of his or her life.*

## Emphasizing coordinating conjunctions

**8.182** When you are using coordinating conjunctions, you sometimes want to emphasize that what you are saying applies to both the word groups linked by the conjunction. You usually do this by putting a word such as 'both' or 'neither' in front of the first word group.

**8.183** When you are using 'and', the most common way of emphasizing that what you are saying applies to two word groups is to put 'both' in front of the first word group.

*By that time both Robin and Drew were overseas.*
*They feel both anxiety and joy.*
*These headlines both mystified and infuriated him.*
*Investment continues both at home and abroad.*
*Because the medicine is both expensive and in great demand, huge profits can be made.*

Another way is to use 'and also' instead of 'and'.

*Wilkins drove racing cars himself and also raced powerboats.*
*The job of the library is to get books to people and also to get information to them.*

**8.184** For stronger emphasis, you can put 'not only' or 'not just' in front of the first word group, and 'but' or 'but also' between the two groups.

*The team is playing really well, not only in England but now in Europe.*
*Employers have got to think more seriously not only of attracting staff, but of keeping them.*
*Professor Kleber suggests that law enforcement activities should be directed not just at drug importers and main suppliers, but also at local dealers.*

**8.185** When you are using 'or', the most common way of emphasizing that what you are saying applies to two word groups is to put 'either' in front of the first word group.

*Sentences can be either true or false.*
*You can either buy a special insecticide or get help from an expert.*
*Either Margaret or John should certainly have come to see me by now.*
*Either we raise money from outside or we face unpalatable options such as closing part of the museum.*

When you are linking clauses in this way, you can use 'or else', instead of 'or'.

*They should either formally charge the men or else let them go.*

**8.186** If you want to emphasize that a negative statement applies to two word groups, you put 'neither' in front of the first group and 'nor' in front of the second group.

For example, instead of saying 'The girl did not speak or look up', you say 'The girl neither spoke nor looked up'.

*The thought neither distressed nor delighted her.*
*She had neither received nor read the letter.*
*Neither Margaret nor John was there.*

Note that you use a singular verb after singular noun groups and a plural verb after plural noun groups.

*Neither Binta nor anyone else was going to speak.*
*Neither city councils nor wealthy manufacturers have much need of painters or sculptors.*

**8.187** Sometimes you want to draw attention to a clause or word group by contrasting it with something different. One way to do this is to link the two elements by putting 'but' between them. You put 'not' in front of the first element.

*I wasn't smiling, not because I was cross but because it was painful to move my face.*
*I felt not jubilation but sadness.*
*The upright chairs were not polished but painted.*

# Linking more than two clauses or word groups

**8.188** You can link more than two clauses, words, or word groups using 'and' or 'or'. Usually you use the conjunction only once, putting it between the last two clauses, words, or word groups. After each of the others you put a comma.

*Haggarty marched him to the door, literally threw him out and returned.*
*...courses in accountancy, science, maths or engineering.*

Some people also put a comma in front of the conjunction. We do this in this grammar, for the sake of clarity.

*Mrs Roberts cooked, cleaned, mended, and went to meetings of the sewing club.*

In informal speech, people sometimes put 'and' or 'or' between each pair of clauses, words, or word groups. Occasionally, you do this in writing when you want to emphasize that all the statements you are making are true.

*Mrs Barnett has a gate and it's not locked and that's how they get out.*

**linking adjectives**

**8.189** There are special rules for linking more than two adjectives.

When you put more than two **qualitative adjectives** in front of a noun, you put commas between the adjectives and do not use a conjunction.

*...a large, airy, comfortable room.*

When you put more than two **classifying adjectives** in front of a noun, you have to decide whether the adjectives relate to the same system of classification or to different systems. (This is explained in paragraph 8.171.)

If the classifying adjectives relate to the same system, you put 'and' between the last two adjectives and a comma after each of the others.

*...the country's social, economic and political crisis.*

If the classifying adjectives relate to different systems of classification, you do not put anything between any of the adjectives.

*...an unknown medieval French poet.*

When you put both qualitative and classifying adjectives in front of a noun, you do not put anything between them.

*...a little white wooden house.*

When you put more than two adjectives after a **link verb,** you put 'and' between the last two adjectives and a comma after each of the others.

*He was big, dark and morose.*
*We felt hot, tired and thirsty.*

# Contents of Chapter 9

# 9 Making texts

**9.1** When you speak or write, you very often want to make some connection with other things that you are saying or writing. There are several ways of doing this and they provide **cohesion** in your use of language.

The most common way of providing cohesion is by referring back to something that has already been mentioned. The different ways of referring back are explained in paragraphs 9.2 to 9.40.

There are also a few ways of referring forward to what you are about to say. These are explained in paragraphs 9.41 to 9.48.

People often avoid repeating words when they are referring back. This is called **ellipsis**. Ellipsis is explained in paragraphs 9.49 to 9.69.

Another way of providing cohesion is by using various cohesive words and phrases such as 'firstly' and 'in conclusion' that show the connection between things. These are explained in Chapter 10 (10.73 to 10.81), with other **sentence adjuncts.**

## Referring back

**9.2** When you speak or write, you very often refer back to something that has already been mentioned or make a connection with it.

pronouns  **9.3** One common way of referring back to something is to use a **personal pronoun** such as 'she', 'it', or 'them', or a **possessive pronoun** such as 'mine' or 'hers'.

*Avery came across a discarded camera in a rubbish bin. He cleaned <u>it</u> up and used <u>it</u> to win several photography awards.*
*Tom and Jo are still together. In fact I saw <u>them</u> in town the other day. <u>They</u> were buying clothes.*
*I held <u>her</u> very close. My cheek was against <u>hers</u>.*

Personal pronouns are explained in paragraphs 1.96 to 1.109. Possessive pronouns are explained in paragraphs 1.110 to 1.114.

There are also other pronouns which can be used to refer back. These include pronouns such as 'another' and 'many' which have the same form as general determiners. These are explained in paragraph 1.153.

*...programmes which tell the computer to do one thing rather than <u>another.</u>*

You can also use a **quantifier** or a **cardinal number.**

*The women were asked to leave. <u>Some</u> of them refused.*
*These soldiers had no doubt that the invasion was upon them. <u>Many of them</u> had already been involved in fighting.*
*...the Guatemalan earthquake which killed 24,000 people and injured 77,000.*

Quantifiers are explained in paragraphs 2.193 to 2.210. Numbers are explained in paragraphs 2.230 to 2.248.

**determiners** **9.4** Another common way of referring back to something is to use a **specific determiner** such as 'the' or 'its' in front of a noun.

*A man and a woman were struggling up the dune. The man wore shorts, a T-shirt, and basketball sneakers. The woman wore a print dress.*
*'Thanks,' said Brody. He hung up, turned out the light in his office, and walked out to his car.*

Specific determiners are explained in paragraphs 1.162 to 1.207.

Some **general determiners** can also be used to refer back to something.

*A dog was running around in the yard. Soon another dog appeared.*

Here is a list of general determiners used to refer back to something:

| | | | |
|---|---|---|---|
| another | each | every | other |
| both | either | neither | |

These are explained fully in paragraphs 1.221 to 1.235.

**9.5** As indicated above, pronouns and determiners used to refer back are explained in Chapter 1, where other pronouns and determiners are explained. The **demonstratives** 'this' and 'that' are used to refer back to whole sentences and sections of text as well as to things, so all their cohesive uses are set out in the following section (paragraphs 9.7 to 9.17), which also explains other words which are used to refer back in a specific way.

**other ways of** **9.6** There are also several other ways of referring back to something that
**referring** has already been mentioned. These involve
**back**
• the use of various nouns to refer back to sections of text

These are explained in paragraphs 9.18 to 9.23.

• the use of 'so' and 'not' as substitutes for several types of word or structure which you want to avoid repeating

This use of 'so' and 'not' is explained in paragraphs 9.24 to 9.27.

• the use of 'such', adjectives, and adjuncts to make comparisons with things that have already been mentioned.

This is explained in paragraphs 9.28 to 9.40.

# Referring back in a specific way

**demonstratives** **9.7** 'This' and 'that', and the plural forms 'these' and 'those', are used to
**referring** refer back clearly to a thing or fact that has just been mentioned.
**to things**
They can be used both as pronouns and as determiners.

*More and more money is being pumped into the educational system, and it is reasonable to assume this will continue.*
*My mother died a few months ago. This event was a lot more frightening than I had anticipated.*

Note that 'this' and 'that' are not very often used as pronouns to refer to people. When they are used like this, they are only used in front of the verb 'be'.

*'Some kind young man helped me to my seat.'* – *'That was John'.*

**9.8** When you use 'this' or 'these', you are linking yourself with the thing you are referring to.

*The concert began with his Second Piano Sonata. This is a work that has usually been considered as fundamentally negative.*
*After you've set your goals, remember them by using a list. Anything that is worth doing should go on this list.*
*Only small pines are left. Many of these have twisted and stunted shapes.*
*They had destroyed over 2 million animals. The vast majority of these animals did not need to die.*

In contrast, when you use 'that' or 'those', you are distancing yourself slightly from the thing you are referring to.

*There's a lot of material there. You can use some of that.*
*There's one boss and that boss is in France.*
*There were only strangers around to observe him, and not many of those.*
*The rooms are inhabited by boys from twelve to sixteen years of age. The majority of those boys have reached the stage of caring for comfort and decorations.*

**9.9** Although 'this' and 'that' are singular pronouns, you can use them to refer back to a number of things or facts that have just been mentioned, instead of using a plural pronoun.

*He's got lank hair, thick glasses and the remains of a childhood stutter, but despite all this he's destined for the top.*
*He had played rugby at school, had been in the army and had briefly been a professional footballer. That was thought to be to his favour when the job came up later.*

**demonstratives** **9.10** Demonstratives can also be pronouns or determiners which refer
**referring** back to an entire sentence or a number of sentences.
**to sentences**
*'You're the new doctor, aren't you?'—'That's right.'*
*'Were you worried about the disrespect for the law exhibited by your two heroes?'—'That's a hard question to answer.'*
*'I'll think about it, Mother.' That statement was the end of most of their discussions.*
*I accept neither of these arguments.*

Note that when 'these' and 'those' are pronouns referring back to an entire statement they are only used in front of the verb 'be'.

*It was hard for me to believe these were his real reasons for wanting to get rid of me.*
*I put my arms around her. 'Thanks, Ollie.' Those were her last words.*

**'previous'** **9.11** You can also use the adjective 'previous' attributively to refer back to a section of text.

*As explained in the previous chapter, the bottle needs only to be washed in cold water.*
*I think we can now answer the question posed at the end of the previous chapter.*

**'above'** **9.12** In written English you can also refer to what you have just mentioned by using 'above' as a modifier.

*I have not been able to validate the above statement.*

You can also use 'the above' without a noun group after it.

*Keep supplies of rice and spaghetti. Also, to go with <u>the above,</u> Parmesan cheese and tins of tomatoes.*

**'former'**
**and 'latter'**

**9.13** When you have just referred separately to two things or groups of things, you can refer to the first one as 'the former' and the second one as 'the latter'. These expressions are used mainly in formal English.

*It used to be said that the oil exporting countries depended on the oil importing countries just as much as <u>the latter</u> depended on <u>the former.</u>*
*I could do one of two things—obey him or get my own protection. I chose <u>the latter.</u>*

'Former' and 'latter' can also be attributive adjectives.

*You have the option of one or two bedrooms. The <u>former</u> choice allows room for a small bathroom.*
*Guy had studied classics and philosophy at Oxford and always felt a sort of lingering interest in the <u>latter</u> subject.*

**USAGE NOTE**

**9.14** When you want to refer generally to a whole class of things like the one that has been mentioned, you can say 'things of this kind' or 'things of that kind'. Alternatively you can say 'this kind of thing' or 'that kind of thing'.

*We'll need a special new terminal to incorporate customs facilities, immigration facilities, and things <u>of that kind.</u>*
*Most of us would attach a great deal of importance to considerations <u>of this kind.</u>*
*I don't see many advantages in <u>that kind of</u> education.*
*All arts theatres have <u>that type of</u> problem.*

If you are referring to things of two or more kinds, you use 'these' and 'those' in front of 'kinds', 'sorts', or 'types', followed by 'of' and a noun.

*Both these countries want to reduce the production of <u>these kinds of</u> weapons.*
*There are specific regulations governing <u>these types of machines.</u>*
*Outsiders aren't supposed to make <u>those kinds of jokes.</u>*

You can also use 'such' to refer back to things of a type that has just been mentioned. This is explained in paragraphs 9.28 to 9.32.

**time**

**9.15** The adverb 'then' is used to refer back to the time that has just been mentioned or discussed.

*In ancient times poetry was a real force in the world. Of course the world was different <u>then.</u>*

**place**

**9.16** The adverb 'there' is used to refer back to the place that has just been mentioned.

*I decided to try Newmarket. I soon found a job <u>there.</u>*
*I hurried back into the kitchen. There was nothing <u>there.</u>*

**manner**

**9.17** After describing a way of doing something or a way in which something happens, you can refer back to it using the adverb 'thus'. 'Thus' is a formal word.

*Joanna was pouring the drink. While she was <u>thus</u> engaged, Charles sat on one of the bar-stools.*
*It not only pleased him to work with them, but the few pence <u>thus</u> earned gave him an enormous sense of importance.*

Note that 'in this way' or 'in that way' are commonly used instead.

*Last week I received the 'Entrepreneur of the Year' award. It's a privilege to be honoured <u>in this way</u>.*

# Referring back in a general way

**9.18** There are various groups of nouns which are used to refer back in a general way to what has already been said. They refer to whole sections of spoken or written text.

**referring to spoken or written texts**

**9.19** You can often refer back to what has already been said in a text by using a noun which classes it as a type of verbal action, for example an admission, suggestion, or question.

*'Martin, what are you going to do?'—'That's a good <u>question</u>, Larry.'*
*'You claim to know this man's identity?'—'I do.'—'You can substantiate this <u>claim</u>?'*

The noun that you use to refer back like this not only refers to the text but also shows your feelings about it. For example, if you refer back to someone's reply to something using the noun 'response', this shows that your feelings about it are quite neutral, whereas if you use the noun 'retort', this shows that your feelings about the reply are much stronger.

Here is a list of nouns which refer back to texts, classing them as types of verbal action:

| | | |
|---|---|---|
| account | defence | prophecy |
| accusation | definition | proposal |
| acknowledgement | demand | proposition |
| admission | denial | protest |
| advice | denunciation | question |
| allegation | description | reference |
| announcement | digression | refusal |
| answer | disclosure | remark |
| apology | discussion | reminder |
| appeal | endorsement | reply |
| argument | excuse | report |
| assertion | explanation | request |
| assurance | exposition | response |
| boast | gossip | retort |
| charge | information | revelation |
| claim | judgement | rumour |
| comment | lie | statement |
| complaint | message | stipulation |
| compliment | narrative | story |
| concession | objection | suggestion |
| condemnation | observation | summary |
| confession | plea | tale |
| contention | point | threat |
| correction | prediction | verdict |
| criticism | promise | warning |
| declaration | pronouncement | |

Note that many of these nouns are related to reporting verbs. Reporting verbs are explained in Chapter 7.

*People will feel the need to be <u>informed</u> and they will go wherever they can to get this <u>information</u>.*
*'I don't know what we should do about that.' This <u>remark</u> had the effect of totally dumbfounding the audience.*

*She remarked that she preferred funerals to weddings.*

**referring to ideas**

**9.20** In the same way, you can also refer back to ideas that you know or think someone has by using a noun which also indicates your feelings about the ideas. For example, if you refer to someone's idea using the noun 'view', this shows that your feelings about it are quite neutral, whereas if you use the noun 'delusion', this shows that your feelings are stronger.

*His view of marriage is that it can destroy a relationship. Even previous, unmarried people can hold this view if they experienced the break-up of their parents' marriage.*
*'There is nothing to cry for. They cannot keep me there against my will.' Secure in this belief, he hugged her reassuringly and followed the servants out.*

Here is a list of nouns which refer to ideas and show your feelings about the ideas:

| | | | |
|---|---|---|---|
| analysis | diagnosis | illusion | reasoning |
| assessment | doctrine | inference | supposition |
| assumption | doubt | insight | theory |
| attitude | estimate | interpretation | thinking |
| belief | evaluation | misinterpretation | view |
| conclusion | fear | notion | viewpoint |
| conjecture | finding | opinion | vision |
| concept | guess | picture | wish |
| deduction | hope | plan | |
| delusion | idea | position | |

**referring to what is mentioned**

**9.21** You can also refer back to actions and events using nouns which show your feelings about the action or event. For example, if you use the noun 'incident' to refer to an accident at a nuclear power station, this appears to simply describe the event, whereas if you use the noun 'disaster', this shows your reaction to the event.

*There might be an uncomfortable moment or two when Gwen learned of his intention, but she was not the kind to make a fuss. In any event, he could handle the situation, which would not be a new one.*
*I believed the press would cooperate on this issue.*
*Parents may complain that their child eats badly at meals but is always begging for food between meals. This problem doesn't arise because th parents have been lenient about food between meals.*
*He entered his name for the Boxing Day race, which to Belinda's delight subsequently won. She seemed for some reason to regard the exploit as reflecting credit on herself.*

Here is a list of nouns which refer to events and are neutral:

| | | | |
|---|---|---|---|
| act | episode | method | result |
| action | event | move | situation |
| affair | experience | phenomenon | state |
| aspect | fact | position | state of affairs |
| case | factor | possibility | subject |
| circumstances | feature | practice | system |
| context | incident | process | thing |
| development | issue | reason | topic |
| effect | matter | respect | way |

Here is a list of nouns which refer to events and show your feelings about them:

| | | | | |
|---|---|---|---|---|
| achievement | crisis | disaster | nightmare | problem |
| advantage | difficulty | exploit | plight | solution |
| answer | disadvantage | feat | predicament | tragedy |

**PRODUCTIVE FEATURE**

**9.22** When you are referring back to something that has been said or mentioned, you can use almost any noun which refers to texts, ideas, events, and sometimes even to people. The noun you use allows you to express your exact reaction to the thing which is being referred to. For example, you can refer to a football defeat using nouns such as 'tragedy' or 'farce', and you can refer to an argument using nouns such as 'wrangle' and 'battle'. This is a productive feature of English. Productive features are explained in the Introduction.

**referring to pieces of writing**

**9.23** You can refer in a neutral way to a previous piece of writing.

*As explained in the previous paragraph, the bottle needs only to be washed clean.*
*We have seen in this chapter how the tax burden has increased fastest for households with children.*

Here is a list of nouns used to refer to a piece of writing:

| | | | | |
|---|---|---|---|---|
| chapter | instalment | passage | sentence | text |
| example | item | phrase | statement | words |
| excerpt | letter | quotation | summary | |
| extract | paragraph | section | table | |

# Substituting for something already mentioned: using 'so' and 'not'

**'so' as substitute complement**

**9.24** 'So' is sometimes used in formal English as a substitute for a complement that has already been mentioned or implied.

*They are wildly inefficient and will remain so for some time to come.*
*The Court was criticized, but unfairly so.*
*They are just as isolated, if not more so, than before.*

**'so' and 'not' after 'if'**

**9.25** 'So' is used to substitute for a clause after 'if', when the action or situation you are talking about has already been mentioned.

*Will that be enough? If so, do not ask for more.*

'Not' is used to substitute for a negative clause, to imply the opposite situation to the one already mentioned.

*You will probably have one of the two documents mentioned below. If not, you will have to buy one.*

**'so' and 'not' with reporting verbs**

**9.26** 'So' and 'not' are also used to substitute for clauses after some common reporting verbs. They are also used after the expression 'I'm afraid', which is used to report an unwelcome fact.

*'Are you all right?'—'I think so.'*
*You're a sensible woman—I've always said so.*
*'You think he's dead, don't you?'—'I'm afraid so, Sally.'*
*'It doesn't often happen.'—'No, I suppose not.'*
*'You haven't lost the ticket, have you?'—'I hope not.'*

Here is a list of reporting verbs which can be followed by 'so' and 'not':

| | | | |
|---|---|---|---|
| believe | hope | suppose | think |
| expect | say | tell | |

Note that the use of 'not' as a substitute with 'think', 'expect', and 'believe' is rare or formal. Also, 'not' is not used with 'tell', and when it is occasionally used with 'say', there is a modal in front of 'say'.

Occasionally 'so' is put at the beginning of the clause. This often has the effect of casting doubt on the truth of the fact involved.

*Everybody in the world, so they say, has a double.*

'So' can also be used at the beginning of a clause for emphasis. This is explained in paragraph 10.85.

**'do so'** 9.27 'Do so' is used to mean 'perform the action just mentioned'. The various forms of the verb 'do' can be used. This structure is rather formal.

*A signal which should have turned to red failed to do so.*
*Most of those who signed the letter did so because of her involvement.*
*She asked him to wait while she considered. He did so.*
*Individuals are free to choose private insurance and 10% of the population have done so.*

## Comparing with something already mentioned

9.28 The word 'such' can be used in several ways to provide cohesion. You use it when you want to indicate that something is of the same sort as something that has already been mentioned. The grammatical patterns of 'such' are unique. It can behave as a **determiner**, a **predeterminer**, and an **adjective**.

**'such' as a determiner** 9.29 'Such' can be a determiner referring back to something that has already been mentioned.

*Some 60% of the state's electricity comes from burning imported oil, the highest use of such fuel in the country.*
*New business on a small scale has been found to provide the great majority of new jobs. By their nature such businesses take risks.*

**'such' as a predeterminer** 9.30 'Such' can be a predeterminer (see paragraph 1.236) referring back to something that has already been mentioned. It comes in front of the determiner 'a' or 'an'.

*They lasted for hundreds of years. On a human time scale, such a period seems an eternity.*
*On one occasion the school parliament discussed the dismissal of a teacher. But such an event is rare.*

**'such' as an adjective** 9.31 'Such' can be an adjective referring back to something that has already been mentioned.

*He can be very moralistic. This was one such occasion.*

*'Did you call me a liar?' – 'I never said any such thing!'*
*Mr Bell's clubs were privately owned. Like most such clubs everywhere, they were organizations of congenial people who shared a certain interest.*
*I hated the big formal dances and felt very awkward and out of place at the one or two such events I attended.*

**9.32** 'Such' is also sometimes used as a headword after 'one' and 'many' in formal usage.

*Some shows are successful before they even open, and this musical is one such.*
*It is not surprising that people are prepared to envisage radical alternatives. Many such have been proposed in the last few years.*

**adjectives** **9.33** There are a number of adjectives which are used to indicate a comparison, contrast, or connection with something that has already been mentioned.

**'same'** **9.34** The adjective 'same' is used attributively to indicate emphatically that you are referring back to something that has just been mentioned.

*We accept that thought is a common property of the human race. But we cannot make the same assumption about machines.*
*The door opened and a man popped his head into the room and said 'Next please'. About ten minutes later, the same man returned.*
*He watched her climb into a compartment of the train and he chose the same one so as to watch her more closely.*

Note that when 'same' is used attributively, it nearly always follows 'the', but it can occasionally follow other specific determiners.

*These same smells may produce depression in others.*

**9.35** 'Same' can also be the complement of a link verb when you want to indicate that something is similar in every way to something that has just been mentioned. When 'same' is used after a link verb it always follows 'the'.

*The Queen treated us very well. The Princess Royal was just the same.*
*My brothers and myself were very poor, but so happy. I think other families were the same.*

**9.36** You can also use 'the same' without a following noun as the subject or object of a clause, to refer back to something that has just been mentioned.

*The conversion process is inefficient and about two-thirds of the energy is wasted. The same is true of nuclear power stations.*
*'I've never heard of him.'—'I wish I could say the same.'*

'The same thing' can be used exactly like 'the same', as a subject or object.

*He was stopped and sent back to get a ticket. On the return journey the same thing happened.*
*I learnt how to kill people with my bare hands. And I'm not proud of the fact that I taught a number of other people to do the same thing.*

**'opposite' and 'reverse'**

**9.37** The adjectives 'opposite' and 'reverse' are used to indicate that something is as different as possible from the thing that has already been mentioned. They usually follow 'the'.

> *It was designed to impress, but probably had the opposite effect.*
> *I don't do a lot of reading but my brother is just the opposite.*
> *In the past ten years I think we've seen the reverse process.*
> *This time the position is the reverse.*

When 'opposite' is used attributively, it occasionally follows 'an'.

> *Other studies draw an opposite conclusion.*

You can sometimes use 'the opposite' and 'the reverse' without a following noun to refer back to something.

> *I once heard a police commissioner say that we would have to learn to live with crime. The opposite is true; we have to learn not to live with crime.*
> *He has an excellent record of saying one thing and doing the opposite.*
> *Older males are desirable to women but the reverse is not true.*
> *It hasn't happened. The reverse has happened.*

**other adjectives**

**9.38** You can also use a variety of other adjectives to indicate that something is similar to, different from, or connected with something that has already been mentioned. Some of these adjectives are only used attributively and others can also be complements of a link verb.

> *It's really fabulous. Do you think that there are any other comparable tombs left at all?*
> *She wore a red dress with a red matching straw hat.*
> *West Germany, Denmark and Italy face declines in young people. Ireland is confronted with a contrasting problem.*
> *That's what I would say. But his attitude was different altogether.*

Here is a list of adjectives which can only be used attributively to refer back:

| | | | |
|---|---|---|---|
| adjacent | contrary | equal | opposing |
| conflicting | contrasting | equivalent | parallel |
| contradictory | corresponding | matching | |

Here is a list of adjectives which can be used both attributively and as complements to refer back:

| | | |
|---|---|---|
| analogous | different | separate |
| comparable | identical | similar |
| compatible | related | unrelated |

**adjuncts**

**9.39** To indicate that an action or a way of doing something is similar to the one just mentioned, you can use the adjuncts 'in the same way', 'in a similar way', 'similarly', or 'likewise'.

> *She spoke of Jim and Karl tolerantly but with frowns and sighs. And presumably she spoke to them of me in the same way.*
> *As the children surged silently around them, the soldiers glanced along the line to see their colleagues similarly surrounded.*

**9.40** To indicate that an action or a way of doing something is different from the one just described, you can use the adjuncts 'otherwise' and 'differently'.

*I thought life was simply splendid. I had no reason to think <u>otherwise</u>.*
*She had been ashamed of her actions but she had been totally incapable*
*of doing <u>otherwise</u>.*
*My parents <u>hit me</u>, but I'm going to do things <u>differently</u> with my kids.*

# Referring forward

**9.41** There are various ways of referring forward to things that are about
to be mentioned. These ways often involve the nouns listed in paragraphs
9.18 to 9.23 which are more commonly used when you are referring back
to something.

'this'
and 'these'

**9.42** The use of 'this' to refer back to something was explained in
paragraphs 9.7 to 9.10. You can also use 'this' or 'these' to refer forward
to what you are about to say. They can be both pronouns and determiners.
Note that 'these' can only be a pronoun when it is the subject.

*Well, you might not believe <u>this</u> but I don't drink very much.*
*Perhaps I shouldn't confess <u>this</u>, but I did on one occasion break the law.*
*<u>This</u> chapter will follow the same pattern as the previous one.*
*<u>These</u> were the facts: on a warm February afternoon, Gregory Clark and a*
*friend were cruising down Washington Boulevard in a Mustang.*
*On the blackboard <u>these</u> words were written: Reading. Writing. Arithmetic.*

**9.43** When 'this' and 'these' are used as determiners to refer forward to
something, they are most commonly used with nouns which refer to a
piece of writing (see paragraph 9.23). Sometimes they are used with
nouns which refer to what is said (see paragraph 9.19) and with nouns
which refer to ideas (see paragraph 9.20). They occasionally occur with
nouns which refer to actions or events (see paragraph 9.21).

'following'

**9.44** You can also refer to what you are about to mention using the
adjective 'following' attributively. When 'following' is used like this, it is
used with nouns which refer to texts, ideas, and pieces of writing (see
paragraphs 9.19, 9.20, and 9.23.). Very occasionally, it is used with
nouns which refer to actions and events (see paragraph 9.21.).

*After a while he received the <u>following</u> letter: 'Dear Sir, The Undersecretary*
*of State regrets that he is unable to reconsider your case.'*
*The <u>following</u> account is based on notes and jottings from that period.*
*They arrived at the <u>following</u> conclusion: children with disabilities are*
*better off in normal classes.*

You can also used 'the following' without a noun group after it.

*...a box containing <u>the following</u>: a packet of tissues, two small sponges,*
*two old handkerchiefs, and a clothes brush.*

'next'

**9.45** The adjective 'next' can be used to refer forward with nouns which
refer to pieces of writing.

*In the <u>next</u> chapter, we will examine this theory in detail.*

'below'

**9.46** You can also use 'below' to refer forward to something you are about
to mention. You use 'below' like this after nouns which refer to texts and
pieces of writing (see paragraphs 9.19 and 9.23).

*... the coming together of the Japanese and Chinese economic miracles*
*(see the Ex-secretary's report <u>below</u>).*

*The overlap can be seen in the table <u>below</u>.*

'Below' can occasionally be used to refer forward with nouns which refer to actions and things. When it is used with them, it is used in past participle clauses.

*The report <u>given below</u> appeared in the Daily Mail on 8 August 1985.*

**'such'**    **9.47** 'Such' can be used as a predeterminer to refer to a kind of thing that is specified immediately afterwards in a phrase or clause beginning with 'as'.

*I thought he had invited you for just <u>such</u> a purpose <u>as this</u>.*

'Such' is also sometimes used to qualify a noun, followed by a specifying phrase or clause beginning with 'as'.

*...a general prolonged rise in prices <u>such as occurred in the late 1960s</u>.*
*Then try redistributing the items under headings <u>such as I've suggested</u>.*

**other ways**    **9.48** There are also other ways of referring forward to things which also involve focusing on the thing referred to. These involve **cleft clauses,** which are explained in paragraphs 10.28 to 10.30 and sentences beginning with 'there', which are explained in paragraphs 10.46 to 10.55.

# Leaving out words: ellipsis

**9.49** In English people often omit words rather than repeating them. This is called **ellipsis.** Some kinds of ellipsis only occur in **coordinate clauses** and coordinated groups of words. These are explained in paragraphs 8.140 to 8.164.

This section deals with ellipsis that occurs in subordinate clauses and separate sentences as well as in coordinate clauses. The second clause or sentence could be said or written by the same person, or it could be part of a reply or comment by someone else. The use of ellipsis in conversation is explained in paragraphs 9.63 to 9.69.

**contrasting**    **9.50** If you have just described an action or state and you want to
**subjects**    introduce a new subject only, you do not need to repeat the rest of the sentence. Instead, you can just use an **auxiliary.**

*There were nineteen- and twenty-year-olds on the paper who were earning more than I <u>was</u>.*
*They can distinguish finer detail than we <u>can</u>.*

**contrasting**    **9.51** If you only want to change the verb tense or modality, you use a new
**tense**    auxiliary, with a subject referring to the same person or thing.
**or modality**
*They would stop it if they <u>could</u>.*
*How does the Department of the Environment ensure, as it says it <u>must</u>, that the quality of the operation remains high?*
*Very few of us have that tremendous enthusiasm, although we know we <u>ought to</u>.*
*I never did go to Stratford, although I probably <u>should have</u>.*
*...a topic which should have attracted far more attention from philosophers than it <u>has</u>.*

**'do'**    **9.52** If you choose no other auxiliary verb, you must usually use 'do', 'does', or 'did'.

*You look just as bad as he <u>does</u>.*
*I think we want it more than they <u>do</u>.*

| | |
|---|---|
| **'be' as a main verb** | **9.53** However, the link verb 'be' is repeated, in an appropriate form. For example, 'I was scared and the children were too'. |

*'I think you're right.'—'I'm sure I am.'*

If the second verb group contains a modal, you usually put 'be' after the modal.

*'Bit of an unfair question to ask me, because I'm biased.'—'Thought you might be.'*
*'He thought that it was hereditary in his case.'—'Well, it might be.'*

However, this is not necessary if the first verb group also contains a modal.

*I'll be back as soon as I can.*

'Be' is sometimes used after a modal in the second clause to contrast with another link verb such as 'seem', 'look', or 'sound'.

*'It looks like tea to me.'—'Yes, it could be.'*

**'have' as a main verb**  **9.54** If the first verb is the main verb 'have', a form of 'have' is sometimes used instead of a form of 'do'.

*She probably has a temperature—she certainly looks as if she has.*

**ellipsis with 'not'**  **9.55** You can make the second verb group negative by adding 'not' to the auxiliary. These combinations are contracted in informal speech and writing to 'don't', 'hasn't', 'isn't', 'mustn't', and so on (see paragraph 4.55 for a list of these contractions). You use the same forms for a negative response to a question.

*Some managed to vote but most of them didn't.*
*'You're staying here!'—'But Gertrude, I can't, I mustn't!'*
*'And did it work?'—'No, I'm afraid it didn't.'*
*Widows receive state benefit; widowers do not.*
*He could have listened to the radio. He did not.*

**USAGE NOTE**  **9.56** With passives, 'be' is often, but not always, kept after a modal.

*He argued that if tissues could be marketed, then anything could be.*

However, with perfect passives, you can just use the auxiliary 'have' or 'has'. For example, you could say, 'Have you been interviewed yet? I have'.

Note that when a modal with 'have' is used for a passive or continuous verb group, 'been' cannot be omitted.

*I'm sure it was repeated in the media. It must have been.*
*She was not doing her homework as she should have been.*

**9.57** If the second verb group contains the auxiliary 'have' in any form, you can add 'done' to the group. For example, instead of saying 'He says he didn't see it but he must have', you can say 'He says he didn't see it but he must have done'.

*He hadn't kept a backup, but he should have done.*
*It would have been nice to have won, and I might have done if my concentration hadn't lapsed.*

Similarly, you can use 'do' after modals.

*It makes a click like the lid of a tin may do.*

Note that when the verb used in the first mention of an action or state is the main verb 'have', instead of using 'do' after a modal in the second mention, you often use 'have' instead.

*'Do you think that academics have an appreciation of the administrative difficulties of running a University?'—'No, and I don't think they should have.'*

**9.58** Usually ellipsis occurs in a clause which comes after a clause in which the action or state has been mentioned with a main verb. Occasionally, however, for a deliberate effect, the clause containing the ellipsis comes before the clause explicitly mentioning the action or state

*If, as they should be, directors are themselves scholars, they will appreciate the language that scholars use.*

**repeating the main verb**

**9.59** If you want to be emphatic, you repeat the main verb, instead of using ellipsis.

*It was the largest swarm of locusts that had ever been seen or that ever would be seen.*

**contrasting objects and adjuncts**

**9.60** Note that if you want to contrast two different things affected by an action, or two different factors or circumstances, you can put a new object or adjunct in the second clause, with an auxiliary or form of 'be'.

*Cook nettles exactly as you would spinach.*
*You don't get as much bickering on a farm as you do in most jobs.*
*Survival rates for cancer are twice as high in America as they are in Britain.*
*No one liked being young then as they do now.*

However, the main verb is sometimes repeated.

*Can't you at least treat me the way you treat regular clients?*

**USAGE NOTE**

**9.61** You can omit a verb after the semi-modals 'dare' and 'need', but only when they are used in the negative.

*'I don't mind telling you what I know.'—'You needn't. I'm not asking you for it.'*
*'You must tell her the truth.'—'But, Neill, I daren't.'*

Similarly, the verb is only omitted after the modal expressions 'had rather' and 'would rather' when they are used in the negative. However, the verb is sometimes omitted after 'had better' even when it is used affirmatively.

*'Will she be happy there?'—'She'd better.'*
*It's just that I'd rather not.*

**9.62** Ellipsis also occurs with 'to'-infinitive clauses. Instead of using a full 'to'-infinitive clause after a verb, you can just use 'to', if the action or state has already been mentioned.

*Don't tell me if you don't want to.*
*At last he agreed to do what I asked him to.*

You can also do this in conversation.

*'Do you ever visit a doctor?' I asked her.—'No. We can't afford to.'*

Note that there are some verbs, such as 'try' and 'ask', which are also often used on their own, without 'to'.

*They couldn't help each other, and it was ridiculous to try.*
*I'm sure she'll help you, if you ask.*

# Ellipsis in conversation

**9.63** Ellipsis often occurs in conversation in replies and questions. When ellipsis occurs like this, it can involve ellipsis of the main verb in the ways that have been explained above (see paragraphs 9.49 to 9.62). This is common with questions which show that you find what someone has said interesting or surprising, or that you do not agree with them. These questions always have a pronoun as their subject.

*'He gets free meals.'—'Does he?'*
*'They're starting up a new arts centre there.'—'Are they?'*
*'I've checked everyone.'—'Have you now?'*

**ellipsis in questions**

**9.64** You can often use ellipsis in questions when the context makes it clear what is meant. The question can consist of just a **'wh'-word.**

*Someone's in the house' – 'Who?'.' – 'I think it might be Gary.'*
*'But I'm afraid there's more.'—'What?'*
*'Can I speak to you?' I asked, undaunted.—'Why?'—'It's important.'*
*'We're going on holiday tomorrow.' – 'Where?' – 'To Majorca.'*

Note that you can also use 'why not'.

*'Maria! We won't discuss that here.'—'Why not?'*

Note also that you can use a 'wh'-word after a reporting verb, especially 'why'.

*I asked why.*
*They enquired how.*

**9.65** Other questions can also consist of only a very few words when the context makes it clear what is meant. Short questions of this kind are often used to express surprise or to offer something to someone.

*'Could you please come to Ira's right away and help me out?'—'Now? Tonight?'—'It's incredibly important.'*
*'Does she drink? Heavily, I mean.'—'Drink? No, she never touches the stuff.'*
*'He's going to die, you see.'—'Die?'*
*'Cup of coffee?' Lionel asked, kindly.*
*He drank the water and handed me the glass. 'More?' 'No, that's just fine, thank you.'*

**ellipsis in replies**

**9.66** When you reply to **'wh'-questions,** you can often use one word or a group of words rather than a full sentence. You do this to avoid repeating words used in the question. For example, if someone asks 'What is your favourite colour?', the normal reply is a single word, for example 'Blue', rather than a sentence such as 'My favourite colour is blue'.

*'What's your name?'—'Pete.'*
*'How do you feel?'—'Strange.'*
*'Where do you come from?'—'Cardiff.'*
*'Where are we going?—'Up the coast.'*
*'How long have you been out of this country?'—'About three months.'*
*'How much money is there in that case?'—'Six hundred pounds.'*
*'Why should they want me to know?'—'To scare you, perhaps. Who can tell?'*

'Wh'-questions are explained in paragraphs 4.17 to 4.30.

**9.67** You can often use a **sentence adjunct** or an **adverb of degree** rather than a sentence in answer to a **'yes/no'-question.**

*'Do you think you could keep your mouth shut if I was to tell you something?'—'Definitely.'*
*'Do you think they're very important?'—'Maybe.'*
*'Do you enjoy life at the university?'—'Oh yes, very much.'*
*'Are you interested?'—'Very.'*
*'Are you ready, Matthew?'—'Not quite.'*
*'Is she sick?'—'Not exactly.'*

'Yes/no'-questions are explained in paragraphs 4.12 to 4.16. Sentence adjuncts are listed in Chapter 10 (10.57 to 10.72). Adverbs of degree are listed in Chapter 2 (2.145 to 2.173) and Chapter 6 (6.45 to 6.52).

**ellipsis in agreement**

**9.68** You often use ellipsis when you want to show that you agree with something that has just been said, or to say that it also applies to someone or something else. One way of doing this is by using 'too' after an auxiliary or form of 'be'.

*'I like baked beans.'—'Yes, I do too.'*
*'I failed the exam.' – 'I did too.'*

The other way of doing this is to use 'so' followed by the auxiliary or form of 'be', followed by the subject.

*'I find that amazing.'—'So do I.'*

Note that you can also use ellipsis like this within a sentence to indicate that someone or something is the same.

*He does half the cooking and so do I.*

**9.69** You can also use ellipsis when you want to show that you agree with something negative that has just been said, or to say that it also applies to someone or something else. One way of doing this is by using an auxiliary or form of 'be' followed by 'not' and 'either'.

*'I don't know.'—'I don't either.'*
*'I can't see how she thinks it's to be done.'—'I can't either.'*

The other way is to use 'nor' or 'neither' followed by an auxiliary or form of 'be', followed by the subject.

*'I don't like him.'—'Nor do I.'*
*'I'm not going to change my mind.' – 'Nor should you.'*
*'I'm not joking, Philip.'—'Neither am I.'*

Note that you can also use ellipsis in these ways within a sentence.

*I don't know what you're talking about, Miss Haynes, and I'm pretty sure you don't either.*
*I will never know all that was in his head at the time, nor will anyone else.*
*I can't do anything about this and neither can you.*

# Contents of Chapter 10

# 10 The structure of information

## Introduction

**10.1** The position of the elements of clause structure in a statement usually follows the sequence 'subject, verb, object, complement, adjunct'. The subject, which is what you are going to talk about, comes first. If you want to express yourself normally and not draw special attention to any part of the clause, then you follow this sequence.

*Donald was lying on the bed.*
*She has brought the tape with her.*
*He wiped the glass dry with a tea-towel.*

The examples above are in the **declarative mood.** Chapter 4 explains the mood system in English and shows how other meanings can be expressed using the **interrogative** and **imperative** moods. These other moods involve regular changes in the sequence of elements in the clause.

*Is he ill?*
*Put it on the table.*

**10.2** However, there are other ways of putting the elements of clause structure in a different sequence, in order to give special emphasis or meaning to the clause or a part of it.

*In his enthusiasm, he overlooked a few big problems.*
*The third sheet he folded and placed in his pocket.*

This applies mainly to **main clauses.** This Chapter shows how you can vary the order of the clause elements in a main clause when you want to give special force to the whole clause or to one of its elements.

In most **subordinate clauses,** you have no choice about the order of the clause elements (see Chapter 8).

**passive voice**   **10.3** One way of varying the sequence of elements in the clause is to use the **passive voice.** The passive voice allows you to talk about an event from the point of view of the thing or person affected, and even to avoid mentioning who or what was responsible for the action.

*A girl from my class was chosen to do the reading.*

The passive is explained in paragraphs 10.8 to 10.24.

**cleft structures**   **10.4** Another way of varying the sequence of elements in the clause is to use a **cleft structure.** There are three different types.

One type allows you to focus on the person or thing you are talking about, as in 'It was Jason who told them'.

The second type allows you to focus on an action, as in 'What they did was break a window and get in that way' or 'All I could do was cry'.

The third type allows you to focus on the circumstances of an action, for example the time or the place, as in 'It was one o'clock when they left', or 'It was in Paris that they met for the first time'.

Cleft structures are dealt with in the section beginning at paragraph 10.25.

**impersonal** **10.5** When you want to say something about a fact, an action, or a
**'it'** particular state, you can use a structure beginning with 'it', for example 'It's strange that he didn't call', 'It's easy to laugh', and 'It's no fun being stupid'.

You also use an 'it' structure to talk about the weather or the time, for example 'It's raining', 'It's a nice day', and 'It's two o'clock'.

'It' structures are dealt with in the section beginning at paragraph 10.31.

**'there'** **10.6** 'There' is used followed by 'be' and a noun group to introduce the
**with 'be'** idea of the existence or presence of something. This makes the noun group, which is new information, the focus of the clause. For more information, see paragraphs 10.46 to 10.55.

*There is someone in the bushes.*

**adjuncts** **10.7** There are also several types of adjunct which you can use to focus on a clause as a whole, or on different elements of the clause. These include sentence adjuncts (see the section beginning at paragraph 10.56), linking adjuncts (see paragraphs 10.73 to 10.81), and focusing adverbs (see paragraphs 10.87 to 10.91).

*He never writes, of course.*
*This can be done reasonably easily. Still, it's not a nice idea.*
*As a child she was particularly close to her elder sister.*

# Focusing on the thing affected: the passive voice

**10.8** Many actions involve two people or things—one that performs the action and one that is affected by the action. These actions are typically referred to using **transitive verbs**. Transitive verbs are explained fully in Chapter 3.

In English the person or thing you want to talk about is usually put first as the subject of the clause. So, when you want to talk about someone or something that is the performer of an action (the **agent**), you make them the subject of the verb and you use an **active** form of the verb. The other person or thing is made the **object** of the verb.

However, you may want to focus on the person or thing affected by an action, which would be the object of an active form of the verb. In that case, you make that person or thing the subject of a **passive** form of the verb.

For example, you could report the same event by using an active form of a verb, as in 'The dog's eaten our dinner' or by using a passive form of a verb, as in 'Our dinner's been eaten by the dog', depending on whether you wanted to talk about the dog or your dinner.

Clauses which contain an active form of a verb are in the **active voice** and clauses with a passive form of a verb are in the **passive voice**.

**formation of passive tenses**

**10.9** Passive forms consist of an appropriate tense of 'be' followed by the past participle of the verb. For example, the passive form of the simple present of 'eat' is the simple present of 'be' followed by 'eaten': 'It is eaten'.

*She escaped uninjured but her boyfriend was shot in the chest and died.*
*He was being treated for a stomach ulcer.*
*He thinks such events could have been avoided.*

For details of passive forms of verbs, see the Reference Section.

**not mentioning the agent**

**10.10** Using a passive form of a verb gives you the option of not mentioning the person or thing responsible for the action, often called the agent of the action.

You may want to do this for one of these reasons:

● because you do not know who or what the agent is

*He's almost certainly been murdered.*
*The fence between the two properties had been removed.*

● because it is not important who or what the agent is

*I had been told that it would be perfectly quiet.*
*Such items should be carefully packed in tea chests.*

● because it is obvious who or what the agent is

*She found that she wasn't being paid the same wage as him.*
*...the number of children who have been vaccinated against measles.*

● because the agent has already been mentioned

*His pictures of dogs were executed with tremendous humour.*
*The government responded quickly, and new measures were passed which strengthened their powers.*

● because people in general are the agents

*Both of these books can be obtained from the public library.*
*It is very strange and has never been adequately explained.*

● because you wish to conceal the agent's identity or to distance yourself from your own action

*The original has been destroyed.*
*I've been told you wished to see me.*
*The government was forced to say that the report would be implemented.*

**10.11** In accounts of processes and scientific experiments, the passive is used and no agent is mentioned because the focus is on what happens and not on who or what makes it happen.

*The principle of bottling is very simple. Food is put in jars, the jars and their contents are heated to a temperature which is maintained long enough to ensure that all bacteria, moulds and viruses are destroyed.*

**10.12** The passive form of reporting verbs is often used in an impersonal 'it' structure, when it is clear whose words or thoughts you are giving or when you are giving the words or thoughts of people in general. See 10.45 in the section on impersonal 'it' structures.

*It was agreed that he would come and see us again the next day.*

*It was rumoured that he had been sentenced to life imprisonment, but had escaped.*

**10.13** When people in general are the agents, an **active** form of the verb is sometimes used instead, with 'you' or 'they' as the subject. 'One' is used as the subject in this kind of clause in formal speech and writing.

*You can't buy iron now, only steel.*
*They say she's very bright.*
*If one decides to live in the country then one should be prepared to put up with the unexpected.*

For more information, see the section on personal pronouns beginning at paragraph 1.96.

You can also use the **indefinite pronouns** 'someone' or 'something'. This allows you to mention an agent, without specifying who or what they are. For more information about indefinite pronouns, see paragraphs 1.127 to 1.140.

*I think someone's calling you.*
*Something has upset him.*

**Ergative verbs** can also enable you to avoid mentioning the performer of an action. For example, instead of saying 'She opened the door', you can say 'The door opened'. See the section on ergative verbs in paragraphs 3.60 to 3.68.

**mentioning the agent with 'by'** **10.14** When you use the passive, you can of course mention the agent at the end of the clause by using 'by'. But this puts emphasis on the agent, because the end of the clause is an important position, and so you often do this when you want to refer back to the agent in the next clause.

*His best friend was killed by a grenade, which exploded under his car.*
*Some of the children were adopted by British couples.*
*This view has been challenged by a number of workers.*

**mentioning things or methods used** **10.15** As with active forms of verbs, you can mention something that the agent used to perform the action after the preposition 'with'.

*A circle was drawn in the dirt with a stick.*
*Moisture must be drawn out first with salt.*

You can mention the method using an '-ing' form after 'by'.

*Much of their strong taste can be removed by changing the cooking water.*

**passive of verbs referring to states** **10.16** A few transitive verbs refer to states rather than actions. When some of these verbs are used in the passive, the agent is put after the preposition 'with'.

*The room was filled with pleasant furniture.*
*The railings were decorated with thousands of bouquets.*

Here is a list of transitive verbs referring to states which are used with 'with' in the passive:

| | | |
|---|---|---|
| cram | decorate | ornament |
| crowd | fill | throng |

However, 'by' is used with some verbs which describe a state.

*The building was illuminated by thousands of lights.*

Here is a list of transitive verbs referring to states which are used with 'by' in the passive:

| | | |
|---|---|---|
| conceal | illuminate | occupy |
| exceed | inhabit | overshadow |

Some verbs, such as 'adorn' and 'surround' can be used with 'with' or 'by' after them.

*Her right hand was covered with blood.*
*One entire wall was covered by a gigantic chart of the English Channel.*
*The house was surrounded with tanks and policemen with dogs.*
*The building was surrounded by a deep green lawn.*

Here is a list of transitive verbs which can be used with either 'with' or 'by' in the passive:

| | | |
|---|---|---|
| adorn | cover | overrun |
| besiege | encircle | surround |

There are also several verbs which are used with 'in'.

*She claimed the drug was contained in a cold cure given to her by the team doctor.*
*Free transport was not included in the contract.*
*The walls of her flat are covered in dirt.*

Here is a list of transitive verbs which can be used with 'in' in the passive:

| | | |
|---|---|---|
| contain | embody | involve |
| cover | include | subsume |

Note that 'cover' can be used with 'in', 'by' or 'with'.

**phrasal verbs** **10.17 Phrasal verbs** which consist of a transitive verb followed by an adverb or preposition, or by an adverb and a preposition, can be used in the passive. Lists of phrasal verbs are given in paragraphs 3.84 to 3.117.

*Two totally opposing views have been put forward to explain this phenomenon.*
*Millions of tons of good earth are being washed away each year.*
*I was talked into meeting Norman Granz at a posh London restaurant.*
*Such expectations are drummed into every growing child.*

**verbs usually used in the passive** **10.18** Because of their meaning, some transitive verbs are usually used in the passive. The agent of the action is usually thought to be not worth mentioning or is not known.

*He was deemed to be the guardian of the child.*
*The meeting is scheduled for February 14.*

*Drunken airmen <u>were alleged</u> to have rampaged through the hotel.*

The following transitive verbs are usually used in the passive:

| | | | |
|---|---|---|---|
| be acclaimed | be disconcerted | be misdirected | be scheduled |
| be alleged | be dubbed | be overcome | be shipped |
| be annihilated | be dwarfed | be paralysed | be shipwrecked |
| be baffled | be earmarked | be penalized | be short-listed |
| be born | be empowered | be perpetrated | be shrouded |
| be compressed | be fined | be pilloried | be staffed |
| be conditioned | be gutted | be populated | be stranded |
| be construed | be headed | be prized | be strewn |
| be couched | be horrified | be punctuated | be subsumed |
| be cremated | be hospitalized | be rationed | be suspended |
| be dazed | be indicted | be reconciled | be swamped |
| be deafened | be inundated | be reprieved | be wounded |
| be debased | be jailed | be reunited | |
| be deemed | be mesmerized | be rumoured | |

The following phrasal verbs are usually used in the passive:

| | | | |
|---|---|---|---|
| be bowled over | be pensioned off | be scaled down | be taken aback |
| be caught up | be ploughed up | be struck off | be written into |
| be handed down | be rained off | be sworn in | |

*They <u>were bowled over</u> by the number of visitors who came to the show.*
*The journalists <u>were taken aback</u> by the ferocity of the language.*

**verbs rarely used in the passive**

10.19 A few transitive verbs are rarely used in the passive because the thing affected by the action they describe is rarely the thing you are interested in.

The following transitive verbs are rarely used in the passive:

| | | | |
|---|---|---|---|
| elude | get | like | suit |
| escape | have | race | survive |
| flee | let | resemble | |

The following phrasal verbs containing a transitive verb are rarely used in the passive:

| | | | | |
|---|---|---|---|---|
| band together | cry out | have on | let through | stand off |
| bite back | ease off | have out | pace out | tide over |
| boom out | eke out | heave up | phone back | wait out |
| brush up | flick over | hunt up | ring back | walk off |
| call down on | get back | jab at | ring out | while away |
| cast back | get down | jack in | sit out | |
| chuck in | give over | jerk out | sob out | |

**ditransitive verbs**

10.20 In the case of **ditransitive verbs** such as 'give', 'teach', and 'show', which can have an indirect object as well as a direct object in an active clause, either object can be the subject of a passive clause.

For example, instead of 'He gave the receptionist the key', you can say 'The receptionist was given the key', where the indirect object of the active clause is the subject of the passive clause. Note that the direct object is still mentioned after the verb.

*They <u>were given a pint of water</u> every day.*
*He <u>had been offered drugs</u> by an older student.*

But you can also say 'The key was given to the receptionist', where the direct object of the active clause is the subject of the passive clause. The indirect object can be mentioned after 'to' or 'for'.

*The building had been given to the town in the late 1920s by an investment banker.*
*Shelter had been found for most of those still wandering the streets.*

Sometimes it is unnecessary to mention the indirect object at all.

*The vaccine can be given at the same time as injections against diphtheria and tetanus.*
*Interest is charged at 2 per cent a month.*

For lists of ditransitive verbs, see paragraphs 3.74 to 3.83.

**transitive verbs with object complement**
**10.21** There is a group of transitive verbs which can have a complement after their object. They are listed and described in paragraphs 3.162 to 3.172. When these verbs are used in the passive, the complement is put directly after the verb.

*He was shot dead in San Francisco.*
*If a person today talks about ghosts, he is considered ignorant or nutty.*

**reflexive verbs**
**10.22 Reflexive verbs,** whose object is a reflexive pronoun referring to the subject of the verb, are not used in the passive. For more information on reflexive verbs, see the section beginning at paragraph 3.27.

**intransitive phrasal verbs**
**10.23** Many intransitive phrasal verbs can be used in the passive. The verbs are followed by a preposition and a noun group referring to the thing affected by the action the verb describes. The object of the preposition can be made the subject of the passive form of the verb. The preposition remains after the verb, with no object after it.

*In some households, the man was referred to as 'the master'.*
*Two people at the head of the line were being dealt with by a couple of clerks.*
*The performance had been paid for by a local cultural society.*
*The children were being looked after by family friends.*

The following is a list of intransitive phrasal verbs which are quite often used in the passive:

| | | | | |
|---|---|---|---|---|
| accede to | deal with | jump on | pick on | see to |
| account for | decide on | keep to | plan for | seize on |
| act on | despair of | laugh at | plan on | send for |
| adhere to | dictate to | lean on | play with | set on |
| aim at | dispense with | leap on | plot against | settle on |
| allow for | dispose of | light upon | point to | shoot at |
| allude to | enter into | listen to | pore over | skate over |
| approve of | frown upon | long for | pounce on | stamp on |
| ask for | fuss over | look after | preside over | stare at |
| aspire to | get at | look at | prevail on | subscribe to |
| attend to | get round | look into | prey on | talk about |
| bargain for | gloss over | look through | provide for | talk to |
| bite into | guess at | look to | put upon | tamper with |
| break into | hear of | meddle with | puzzle over | tinker with |
| budget for | hint at | minister to | reason with | touch on |
| build on | hope for | mourn for | refer to | trample on |
| call for | impose on | object to | rely on | trifle with |
| call on | improve on | operate on | remark on | wait on |
| care for | indulge in | pander to | resort to | watch over |
| cater for | inquire into | paper over | rush into | wonder at |
| count on | insist on | pay for | see through | work on |

A few phrasal verbs which consist of an intransitive verb, an adverb, and a preposition are used in the passive.

*He longs to be looked up to.*
*I was afraid of being done away with.*

The following list contains three-word phrasal verbs used in the passive:

| | | | |
|---|---|---|---|
| do away with | look down on | look out for | play around with |
| live up to | look forward to | look up to | talk down to |

**USAGE NOTE**   **10.24** Note that in informal English, 'get' is sometimes used instead of 'be' to form the passive. The agent is not usually mentioned.

*Our car gets cleaned about once every two months.*
*I got stopped by the police.*

# Selecting focus: cleft sentences

**10.25** One way of focusing on a particular part of a sentence is to use a **cleft structure**. This involves using the verb 'be', either with 'it' as an impersonal subject or with a clause such as a relative clause or a 'to'-infinitive clause as the subject or complement. Sentences containing this structure are called **cleft sentences.**

**'it' as the subject**   **10.26** If you want to emphasize one noun group and make the whole clause say something about it, you can make the noun group the complement of an impersonal 'it' structure, and follow it with a relative clause containing the rest of your message. The complement can refer to the subject or object of the relative clause.

For example, instead of saying 'George found the right answer', you may want to stress the fact that George did it by saying 'It was George who found the right answer'.

*It was Ted who broke the news to me.*
*It is usually the other vehicle that suffers most.*

Similarly, instead of saying 'Henry makes clocks', you can say 'It's clocks that Henry makes'.

*It's money that they want.*
*It was me Dookie wanted.*

**other kinds of focus**   **10.27** In a cleft sentence, you usually focus on a noun group. However, you can focus on other clause elements or even on a whole clause. You then use a relative clause beginning with 'that'.

You can make an **adjunct** the focus of a cleft sentence. For example, you can focus on a prepositional phrase or an adverb of time or place in order to stress the circumstances of an event.

*It was from Francis that she first heard the news.*
*It was then that I recalled that I had left my wristwatch up in the saloon.*
*It was in Elliotdale that I first saw these films.*

You can also focus on a **non-finite clause,** if you are stressing an action.

*It was meeting Peter that really started me off on this new line of work.*

You can focus on a clause beginning with 'because' to stress the reason for something.

*Perhaps it's <u>because he's a misfit</u> that I get along with him.*

**'what' or 'all' to focus on an action**

**10.28** If you want to focus on an action performed by someone, you can use a cleft sentence consisting of 'what' followed by the subject, the verb 'do', the verb 'be', and an **infinitive** clause with or without 'to'.

For example, instead of saying 'I wrote to George immediately', you can say 'What I did was to write to George immediately'.

*What I did was to create a diversion.*
*What you have to do is to choose five companies to invest in.*
*What it does is draw out all the vitamins from the body.*
*What he did was get Christopher followed by a private detective.*

You can use 'all' instead of 'what' if you want to emphasize that just one thing is done and nothing else.

*All he did was shake hands and wish me good luck.*
*All she ever does is make jam.*

**focusing on the topic**

**10.29** Clauses with 'what' as their subject can be used to focus on the thing you are talking about. They can be put after the verb 'be' as well as in front of it. For example, you can say 'Its originality was what appealed to me', as well as 'What appealed to me was its originality'.

*What impressed me most was their sincerity.*
*These six factors are what constitutes intelligence.*

**focusing on what someone wants or needs**

**10.30** If you want to focus on the thing that someone wants, needs, or likes, you can use a cleft sentence beginning with a clause consisting of 'what' followed by the subject and a verb such as 'want' or 'need'. After this clause, you use the verb 'be' and a noun group referring to the thing wanted, needed, or liked.

Here is a list of verbs which can be used with 'what' in this structure:

| | | | |
|---|---|---|---|
| adore | hate | love | want |
| dislike | like | need | |
| enjoy | loathe | prefer | |

For example, instead of saying 'We need a bigger garden', you can say 'What we need is a bigger garden'.

*What we as a nation want is not words but deeds.*
*What you need is a doctor.*
*What he needed was an excuse to talk.*

You can use 'all' instead of 'what' with the verbs 'want' or 'need' if you want to emphasize that someone wants or needs a particular thing and nothing else.

*All they want is a holiday.*
*All a prisoner needed was a pass.*

If you do not want to mention the agent in the above structures, you can use a passive form of the verb, after 'what' or 'all that'.

*What was needed was an organized struggle.*
*All that was needed was to copy everyone else.*

# Taking the focus off the subject: using impersonal 'it'

**10.31** You often only want to mention one thing or fact in a clause. For example, you often want to focus on the type of information that is normally expressed by an adjective. But an adjective cannot stand alone as the subject of a clause. A common way of presenting information of this kind is to make the adjective the complement of 'be', with 'it' as the subject.

If you do not want to choose any of the clause elements as the thing you are going to talk about, you can use several structures with 'it' as subject.

'It' can be used:

● to describe a place or situation

*It's lonely here.*

● to talk about the weather or to say what the time is.

*It had been raining all day.*
*It is seven o'clock.*

These uses are often called the **impersonal** uses of 'it'.

**10.32** In these uses, 'it' does not refer back to anything earlier in the speech or writing, and so it is different from the **personal pronoun,** which usually refers back to a particular noun group:

*The ending, when it arrives, is completely unexpected.*
*Paris is special, isn't it?*

For more information about personal pronouns, see the section beginning at paragraph 1.96.

Note that the pronoun 'it' can also be used to refer to a whole situation or fact which has been described or implied.

*He's never come to see his son. It's most peculiar, isn't it?*
*It doesn't matter.*
*It's my fault.*

**10.33** 'It' can also be used to introduce a comment on an action, activity, or experience. The subject 'it' refers forward to a 'to'-infinitive clause or a finite subordinate clause.

*It costs so much to get there.*
*It was amazing that audiences came to the theatre at all.*

This structure with 'it' allows you to avoid having a long subject, and to put what you are talking about in a more prominent position at the end of the sentence.

## Describing a place or situation

**10.34** If you want to describe the experience of being in a particular place, you can use 'it' followed by a **link verb** such as 'be', an adjective, and an **adjunct of place**.

*It was very hard in Germany after the war.*

*It was terribly cold in the trucks.*
*It's nice down there.*

For more information about adjuncts of place, see the section beginning at paragraph 6.53.

Similarly, you can indicate your opinion of a situation using 'it', 'be', an adjective, and a clause beginning with 'when' or 'if'.

*It's so nice when it's hot, isn't it?*
*Won't it seem odd if I have no luggage?*

**using 'it' as an object**

10.35 You can also use 'it' as the object of verbs such as 'like' and 'hate' to describe your feelings about a place or situation.

*I like it here.*
*He knew that he would hate it if they said no.*

Here is a list of common verbs that are used in this way:

| | | | |
|---|---|---|---|
| adore | enjoy | like | love |
| dislike | hate | loathe | prefer |

# Talking about the weather and the time

**describing the weather**

10.36 You can describe the weather by using 'it' as the subject of a verb.

*It's still raining.*
*It was pouring with rain.*
*It snowed steadily throughout the night.*

The following verbs are used after 'it' to talk about the weather:

| | | | |
|---|---|---|---|
| drizzle | pour | sleet | thunder |
| hail | rain | snow | |

You can also describe the weather by using 'it' followed by 'be' and a **complement**. The complement can either be an adjective by itself, or an adjective followed by a noun referring to a period of time.

*'Can I go swimming?'—'No, it's too cold.'*
*It was very windy.*
*It was a warm, sunny evening.*
*It's a lovely day, isn't it?*

Here is a list of common adjectives that are used to describe the weather

| | | | | |
|---|---|---|---|---|
| bitter | cold | freezing | misty | warm |
| blowy | cool | frosty | muggy | wet |
| blustery | damp | hot | rainy | windy |
| boiling | dark | humid | showery | |
| breezy | dry | icy | stormy | |
| chilly | fine | light | sunny | |
| cloudy | foggy | lovely | thundery | |

Note that you can describe a change in the weather or light by using 'it' followed by 'get' and an adjective complement.

*It's getting cold. Shall we go inside?*
*It's getting dark.*

| | |
|---|---|
| **giving times and dates** | **10.37** You can say what the time, day, or date is by using 'it' followed by 'be' and a complement. |

*It's eight o'clock.*
*It's Saturday afternoon and all my friends are out.*
*It was July, but freezing cold.*

| | |
|---|---|
| **emphasizing time** | **10.38** You can form many useful time expressions using a structure with 'it' followed by 'be' and a noun group referring to time. The use of this structure puts emphasis on the time of the event. |

You can say when something happened using 'when'.

*It was 11 o'clock at night <u>when</u> 16 armed men came to my house.*
*It was nearly midnight <u>when</u> Kunta finally slept.*

You can say how long ago something happened using 'since'.

*It's two weeks now <u>since</u> I wrote to you.*
*It was forty years <u>since</u> the war.*

You can say how long the interval was between one event and another using 'before'.

*It was ninety days <u>before</u> Rodin's search was over.*
*It was four minutes <u>before</u> half-time.*

You can say how soon something will happen using 'to'.

*It was only two days <u>to</u> the wedding.*

## Commenting on an action, activity, or experience

| | |
|---|---|
| **using link verbs** | **10.39** A common way of commenting on what you are doing or experiencing is to use 'it' followed by a **link verb** and a **complement**. After the complement you use a **present participle** or a **'to'-infinitive** clause. |

*It's fun working for him.*
*It was difficult trying to talk to her.*
*It's nice to see you with your books for a change.*
*It will be a stimulating experience to see Mrs Oliver.*

If you want to mention the person who performs the action or has the experience, you use a **prepositional phrase** beginning with 'for' and a 'to'-infinitive clause after the complement.

*It becomes hard for a child to develop a sense of identity.*

You can also use the structure with a 'to'-infinitive clause when you are recommending a course of action or saying that something is necessary.

*It's important to know your own limitations.*
*It's a good idea to have a little notebook handy.*
*It is necessary to examine this claim before we proceed any further.*

| | |
|---|---|
| **using other verbs** | **10.40** Similar structures can be used with verbs other than link verbs. |

If you want to say what effect an experience has on someone, you can use 'it' with a verb such as 'please', 'surprise', or 'shock', followed by a noun group and a 'to'-infinitive clause. For a list of these verbs, see paragraph 10.44.

*It always pleased him to think of his father.*
*It shocked me to see how much weight he'd lost.*

*It interests him to hear what you've been buying.*

You can use 'it' with 'take' and a 'to'-infinitive clause to indicate what is used in a particular action or activity, or is needed for it, for example the amount of time or the type of person that is needed.

*It takes an hour to get to Idlewild.*
*It takes an exceptional parent to cope with a child like that.*
*It took a lot of work to put it together.*

If there is also an **indirect object,** this can be placed immediately after the verb.

*It took me a year to save up for a new hat.*

If the indirect object is expressed by a prepositional phrase, usually beginning with 'for', it is placed after the direct object.

*It took some time for him to realize what was required.*
*It takes a lot more guts for a woman to resign than for a man.*

'Cost' can be used in similar structures when talking about the amount of something, usually money, that is used in an activity.

*It costs about £150 a week to keep someone in prison.*

With 'find' and 'think', you can use 'it' as the object, followed by an **object complement** and either a 'to'-infinitive clause or a 'that'-clause.

*He found it hard to make friends.*
*He thought it right to resign immediately.*

**other ways** **10.41** If you want to focus on a non-finite clause, you can use this clause
**of talking** as the subject of the main clause, instead of 'it'. For example, instead of
**about** saying 'It's fun working for him' you can say 'Working for him is fun'.
**actions** *Measuring the water correctly is most important.*

In formal English, 'to'-infinitive clauses are sometimes used.

*To sell your story to the papers is a risky strategy.*

## Commenting on a fact that you are about to mention

**10.42** When you want to comment on a fact, event, or situation, you can use 'it' followed by a **link verb,** a **complement,** and a 'that'-clause giving the fact.

*It is strange that it hasn't been noticed before.*
*It's a shame he didn't come.*
*From the photographs it seems clear my mother was no beauty.*

Here is a list of adjectives used in complements in this structure:

| | | | | |
|---|---|---|---|---|
| amazing | essential | inevitable | plain | true |
| apparent | evident | interesting | possible | unlikely |
| appropriate | extraordinary | likely | probable | wonderful |
| awful | fair | lucky | queer | |
| bad | funny | natural | sad | |
| clear | good | obvious | strange | |
| doubtful | important | odd | surprising | |

Here is a list of nouns used in complements in this structure:

| | | | |
|---|---|---|---|
| disgrace | nuisance | shame | wonder |
| marvel | pity | surprise | |

**USAGE NOTE**   **10.43** After adjectives like 'funny', 'odd', and 'strange', a clause beginning with 'how' is sometimes used instead of a 'that'-clause, with the same meaning.

*It's funny how they don't get on.*
*It's strange how life turns out.*
*It is astonishing how he has changed.*

'What'-clauses can be used after similar adjectives when you want to comment on something that is the object of an action.

*It's surprising what you can dig up.*
*It's amazing what some of them would do for a little publicity.*

'Why'-clauses can be used after adjectives such as 'obvious' and 'clear' when you want to comment on how clear the reason for something is.

*Looking back on these cases, it is clear why the unions distrust the law.*

'Whether'-clauses can be used after adjectives such as 'doubtful' and 'irrelevant' when you want to comment on something that may or may not be true.

*It is doubtful whether supply could ever have kept up with consumption.*

**other verbs**   **10.44** If you want to say what someone thinks about a fact, you can use 'it' followed by a verb such as 'please' or 'surprise'. The verb is followed by a noun group and a 'that'-clause.

*It won't surprise you that I stuck it in my pocket.*
*It grieved her that Ashok could not sleep there.*

Here is a list of verbs that can be used in this way:

| | | | | |
|---|---|---|---|---|
| amaze | astonish | delight | horrify | surprise |
| amuse | astound | disgust | interest | upset |
| annoy | bewilder | distress | please | worry |
| appal | bother | grieve | shock | |

**passives of reporting verbs**   **10.45** If you want to say what is said, thought, or discovered by a group of people, you can use 'it' as the subject of the passive form of a **reporting verb**, followed by a 'that'-clause.

*It was agreed that the transaction should be kept secret.*
*It was felt that there had been some duplication of effort.*
*It was found that no cases of hypothermia had been recorded.*

For a list of verbs that can be used in this way, see paragraph 7.65.

# Introducing something new: 'there' as subject

**saying that something exists**   **10.46** When you want to say that something exists, or when you want to mention the presence of something, you can use 'there' followed by 'be' and a noun group.

This structure is used in English because finite verbs must have a subject.

But something new cannot be talked about until it has been introduced. ? 'there' is used as the subject of the sentence and the new information is introduced after 'be'.

This use is different from the **adverb of place** 'there' and does not refer to a place. In spoken English, the difference is often clearer, because this use of 'there' is often pronounced without stress as /ðə/ whereas the adverb of place is almost always pronounced fully as /ðɛə/.

'There' has very little meaning in the structures that are being explained here. For example, the sentence 'There is a good reason for this' just means 'A good reason for this exists'.

**10.47** The noun group is usually followed by an **adjunct,** a 'wh'-clause, o one of the adjectives 'available', 'present', or 'free'.

*There were thirty boys in the class.*
*There are three reasons why we should support this action.*
*There were no other jobs available.*

**Adjuncts of place** can be put either in front of 'there' or after the noun group.

*On a marble-topped table there was a big white china mug.*
*There was a long table in the middle of the room.*

**saying that**
**something**
**happened**

**10.48** You can also use 'there' followed by 'be' and a noun group referrir to an event to say that something happened or will happen.

*There was a knock at his door.*
*There were two general elections that year.*
*There will be bloodshed tonight.*

**describing**
**something**
**that is**
**happening**

**10.49** When you are describing a scene or situation, you can use a structure consisting of 'there' followed by 'be', a noun group, and a **prese participle.**

For example, instead of saying 'Flames were coming out of it', you can sa 'There were flames coming out of it'.

*There was a monsoon raging outside.*
*There were men and women working in the fields with horses.*
*There was a revolver lying there.*

**verb**
**agreement**

**10.50** Usually a plural form of 'be' is used if the noun group after it is plural.

*There were two men in the room.*

You use a singular form of 'be' when you are giving a list of items and the first noun in the list is singular or uncountable.

*There was a sofa and two chairs.*
*There is a spirit and a will to win in the team.*

Note that you use a plural form of 'be' in front of plural **quantifiers** beginning with 'a', such as 'a number of', 'a lot of', and 'a few of'.

*There were a lot of people camped there.*

You also use a plural form of 'be' in front of numbers beginning with 'a', such as 'a hundred', 'a thousand', and 'a dozen'.

*There were a dozen reasons why a man might hurry from a bar.*

**contractions**
**with 'there'**

**10.51** In spoken and informal written English, 'there is' and 'there has' are often contracted to 'there's', 'there had' and 'there would' to 'there'd', and 'there will' to 'there'll'.

*There's no danger.*
*I didn't even know there'd been a murder.*

**'there' with adjectives**

**10.52** 'There' is also used with adjectives such as 'likely', 'unlikely', 'sure', and 'certain' to indicate the likelihood of something occurring.

*There are unlikely to be any problems with the timetable.*

**'there' with other verbs**

**10.53** A few other verbs can be used after 'there' in a similar way to 'be'. If you want to say that something seems to be the case or that something seems to have happened, you can use 'there' with 'seem' or 'appear' followed by 'to be' or 'to have been'.

*There seems to have been some carelessness recently.*
*There appears to be a vast amount of confusion on this point.*

'To be' is sometimes omitted, especially in front of an uncount noun.

*There seems little doubt that he was insane.*

'There' is sometimes used followed by a passive form of a **reporting verb** and the infinitive 'to be' to indicate that people say or think that something exists. For more information on reporting verbs, see the section beginning at paragraph 7.5.

*There is expected to be an announcement about the proposed building next month.*
*Behind the scenes, there is said to be intense conflict.*

'Happen' is used in the same kind of structure to indicate that a situation exists by chance.

*There happened to be a roll of nylon tubing lying on the desk.*

You can also use 'tend' in this kind of structure to say that something generally happens or exists.

*There tend to be overlapping networks of Mums who have each other's children round to play.*

**formal and literary uses**

**10.54** 'Exist', 'remain', 'arise', 'follow', and 'come' can be used after 'there' to say that something exists or happens. These structures only occur in formal English or literary writing.

*There remained a risk of war.*
*There followed a great flood of indignation in the newspapers.*
*There comes a time when you have to make a choice.*

**10.55** Another construction commonly used in literary writing is to begin a sentence with an **adjunct of place** followed by 'there' and a verb of position or motion.

For example, instead of saying 'The old church stands at the top of the hill', a writer might say 'At the top of the hill there stands the old church'.

*From his hands there dangles a shiny new briefcase.*
*Beside them there curls up a twist of blue smoke.*

# Focusing on clauses or clause elements using adjuncts

## Commenting on your statement: sentence adjuncts

**10.56** There are many adjuncts that are used to indicate your attitude to what you are saying or to make your hearer have a particular attitude to what you are saying. These are dealt with in paragraphs 10.57 to 10.72.

Others are used to show a particular link between sentences. These are dealt with in paragraphs 10.73 to 10.81.

There are also some that are used to make a statement narrower or to focus attention on a particular thing that it applies to. These are dealt wi in paragraphs 10.87 to 10.91.

All these adjuncts are called **sentence adjuncts** because they apply to the whole sentence they are in. They are sometimes called **sentence adverbials** or **disjuncts** in other grammars.

Sentence adjuncts are often placed at the beginning of a sentence. Som are also used in other positions, as shown in the examples given below, but they are usually separated from the words around them by intonation or by commas, to show that they apply to the whole sentence.

For more general information about adjuncts, see Chapter 6.

## Indicating your attitude to what you are saying

**indicating your opinion**

**10.57** One group of sentence adjuncts is used to indicate your reaction to, or your opinion of, the fact or event you are talking about.

*Surprisingly, I found myself enjoying the play.*
*Luckily, I had seen the play before so I knew what it was about.*
*It is fortunately not a bad bump, and Henry is only slightly hurt.*
*Interestingly, the solution adopted in these two countries was the same.*

The following adjuncts are commonly used in this way:

| | | | |
|---|---|---|---|
| absurdly | fortunately | oddly | true |
| admittedly | happily | of course | typically |
| alas | incredibly | paradoxically | unbelievably |
| anyway | interestingly | please | understandably |
| astonishingly | ironically | predictably | unexpectedly |
| at least | luckily | remarkably | unfortunately |
| characteristically | mercifully | sadly | unhappily |
| coincidentally | miraculously | significantly | unnecessarily |
| conveniently | mysteriously | strangely | |
| curiously | naturally | surprisingly | |

One of the uses of 'at least' and 'anyway' is to indicate that you are pleased about the fact you are giving, although there may be other less desirable facts.

*At least we're agreed on something.*
*I like a challenge anyway, so that's not a problem.*

**USAGE NOTE**
**10.58** There are a small number of adverbs which are often followed by 'enough' when used to indicate your opinion of what you are talking about:

| | | | | |
|---|---|---|---|---|
| curiously | funnily | interestingly | oddly | strangely |

*Oddly enough*, she'd never been abroad.
*Funnily enough*, old people seem to love bingo.
I find myself *strangely enough* in agreement with John for a change.

**distancing and qualifying**
**10.59** There are a number of sentence adjuncts which have the effect of showing that you are not completely committed to the truth of your statement.

Rats eat *practically* anything.
It was *almost* a relief when the race was over.
They are, *in effect*, still trapped in a history which they do not understand.
*In a way* I liked her better than Mark.

The following adjuncts are used in this way:

| | |
|---|---|
| almost | so to speak |
| in a manner of speaking | to all intents and purposes |
| in a way | to some extent |
| in effect | up to a point |
| more or less | virtually |
| practically | |

Note that 'almost', 'practically', and 'virtually' are not used at the beginning of a clause.

Expressions such as 'I think', 'I believe', and 'I suppose' are also used to indicate your lack of commitment to the truth of what you are saying.

**indicating viewpoint**
**10.60** With adverbs such as 'luckily', 'fortunately', 'happily', and 'unfortunately', you can indicate whose viewpoint you are giving by adding 'for' and a noun group referring to the person.

'Does he do his fair share of the household chores?'—'Oh yes, *fortunately for me*.'
*Luckily for me and them*, love did eventually grow and flourish.

**indicating quality of the agent**
**10.61** Another group of sentence adjuncts is used to indicate the quality you think someone showed by doing an action. They are formed from adjectives which can be used to describe people, and are often placed after the subject of the sentence and in front of the verb.

The League of Friends *generously* provided about five thousand pounds.
The doctor had *wisely* sent her straight to hospital.
She *very kindly* arranged a beautiful lunch.
*Foolishly*, we had said we would do the decorating.

The following adverbs are used in this way:

| | | | |
|---|---|---|---|
| bravely | correctly | kindly | wrongly |
| carelessly | foolishly | rightly | |
| cleverly | generously | wisely | |

**indicating your justification for a statement**
**10.62** If you are basing your statement on something that you have seen, heard, or read, you can use a sentence adverb to indicate this. For example, if you can see that an object has been made by hand, you might say 'It is obviously made by hand.'

*His friend was <u>obviously</u> impressed.*
*Higgins <u>evidently</u> knew nothing about their efforts.*
*<u>Apparently</u> they had a row.*

These are some common adverbs used in this way:

| | | | |
|---|---|---|---|
| apparently | evidently | obviously | unmistakably |
| clearly | manifestly | plainly | visibly |

**assuming hearer's agreement**

**10.63** People often use sentence adjuncts to persuade someone to agree with them. By using the adjunct, they indicate that they are assuming that what they are saying is obvious.

*<u>Obviously</u> I can't do the whole lot myself.*
*Price, <u>of course,</u> is a critical factor.*

The following adjuncts are often used in this way:

| | | | | |
|---|---|---|---|---|
| clearly | naturally | obviously | of course | plainly |

**indicating reality or possibility**

**10.64** A number of adjuncts are used to indicate whether a situation actually exists or whether it merely seems to exist, or might exist.

*She comes across as confident but <u>actually</u> she's quite shy.*
*Germs were <u>allegedly</u> scattered from airplanes.*
*Extra cash is <u>probably</u> the best present.*

The following adjuncts are used like this:

| | | | | |
|---|---|---|---|---|
| actually | in fact | officially | unofficially | potentially |
| certainly | in practice | perhaps | ~ | seemingly |
| conceivably | in reality | possibly | allegedly | supposedly |
| definitely | in theory | presumably | apparently | theoretically |
| doubtless | maybe | probably | nominally | undoubtedly |
| hopefully | no doubt | really | ostensibly | |

The adverbs in the second group are often used in front of adjectives.

*We drove along <u>apparently empty</u> streets.*
*They pointed out that it would be <u>theoretically possible</u> to lay a cable from a satellite to earth.*

**indicating your attitude**

**10.65** If you want to make it clear what your attitude is to what you are saying, you can use a sentence adjunct.

*<u>Frankly</u>, the more I hear about him, the less I like him.*
*<u>In my opinion</u> it was probably a mistake.*
*<u>In fairness</u>, she is not a bad mother.*

Here is a list of some of the common adjuncts used in this way:

| | | | |
|---|---|---|---|
| frankly | in fairness | in retrospect | seriously |
| honestly | in my opinion | on reflection | to my mind |
| in all honesty | in my view | personally | |

**using infinitive clauses**

**10.66** Another way of indicating the sort of statement you are making is to use 'to be' followed by an adjective, or 'to put it' followed by an adverb.

*I don't really know, <u>to be honest</u>.*

*To put it bluntly,* someone is lying.

**politeness**   **10.67** When someone who is making a request wants to be polite, they use the sentence adverb 'please'.

*May I have a word with you, please?*
*Would you please remove your glasses?*
*Please be careful.*

# Stating your field of reference

**specification**   **10.68** When you are making it clear what aspect of something you are talking about, you use sentence adverbs formed from classifying adjectives. For example, if you want to say that something is important in the field of politics or from a political point of view, you can say that it is 'politically important'. These adverbs often come in front of an adjective, or at the beginning or end of a clause.

*It would have been politically damaging for him to retreat.*
*Biologically, we are not designed for eight hours sleep in one block.*
*We had a very bad year last year financially.*

The following is a list of adverbs that can refer to a particular aspect of something:

| | | | |
|---|---|---|---|
| aesthetically | ethically | numerically | spiritually |
| biologically | financially | outwardly | statistically |
| chemically | geographically | physically | superficially |
| commercially | ideologically | politically | technically |
| culturally | intellectually | psychologically | technologically |
| ecologically | logically | racially | visually |
| economically | mechanically | scientifically | |
| emotionally | mentally | sexually | |
| environmentally | morally | socially | |

**PRODUCTIVE FEATURE**   **10.69** 'Speaking' is sometimes added to these adverbs. For example, 'technically speaking' can be used to mean 'from a technical point of view'.

*He's not a doctor technically speaking.*
*He and Malcolm decided that, racially speaking, anyway, they were in complete agreement.*

This is a productive feature of English. Productive features are explained in the Introduction.

**generalization**   **10.70** You often want to avoid making a firm, forceful statement, because you are aware of facts that do not quite fit in with what you are saying.

One way of doing this is to use a sentence adjunct which indicates that you are making a general, basic, or approximate statement.

*Basically, the more craters a surface has, the older it is.*
*By and large the broadcasters were free to treat this material very much as they wished.*

*I think <u>on the whole</u> we don't do too badly.*

The following adjuncts are used like this:

| | | |
|---|---|---|
| all in all | by and large | on average |
| all things considered | essentially | on balance |
| altogether | for the most part | on the whole |
| as a rule | fundamentally | overall |
| at a rough estimate | generally | ultimately |
| basically | in essence | |
| broadly | in general | |

Note that you can also use the expressions 'broadly speaking', 'generally speaking', and 'roughly speaking'.

*We are all, <u>broadly speaking,</u> middle class.*
*<u>Roughly speaking,</u> the problem appears to be confined to the tropics.*

**PRODUCTIVE FEATURE** 10.71 You can also use prepositional phrases formed with classifying adjectives, such as 'in financial terms' or 'from a political point of view'. Similar prepositional phrases can be formed using the nouns related to these adjectives, for example using 'money' instead of 'financial': 'in money terms', 'in terms of money', 'with regard to money', or 'from the money point of view'.

*Life is going to be a little easier <u>in economic terms.</u>*
*That is the beginning of a very big step forward <u>in educational terms.</u>*
*This state was a late developer <u>in terms of commerce.</u>*

This is a productive feature of English. Productive features are explained in the Introduction.

**PRODUCTIVE FEATURE** 10.72 Another way of saying something like 'with regard to money' is 'money-wise'. You add the suffix '-wise' to a noun referring to the aspect you mean. This is generally used to avoid the creation of long phrases.

*What do you want to do <u>job-wise</u> when the time comes?*
*We are mostly Socialists <u>vote-wise.</u>*

This is a productive feature in American English, but is not so common in British English. Productive features are explained in the Introduction.

## Showing connections: linking adjuncts

10.73 The following section explains the functions of different groups of **linking adjuncts**. Linking adjuncts are used to show what sort of connection there is between one sentence and another.

**indicating an addition** 10.74 In the course of speaking or writing, you can introduce a related comment or an extra reinforcing piece of information using one of the following adjuncts:

| | | | |
|---|---|---|---|
| also | at the same time | furthermore | on top of that |
| as well | besides | moreover | too |

*I cannot apologize for his comments. <u>Besides,</u> I agree with them.*
*<u>Moreover,</u> new reserves continue to be discovered.*

*His first book was published in 1932, and it was followed by a series of novels. He also wrote a book on British pubs.*
*The demands of work can cause gaps in regular attendance. On top of that, many students are offered no extra lessons during the vacations.*

Note that 'too' is not usually placed at the beginning of a sentence.

*They had arrived in style, carnations in their buttonholes; they went out in style too.*

**indicating**
**a parallel**

**10.75** You can emphasize that you are adding a fact that illustrates the same point as the one you have just made, or a suggestion that has the same basis, by using one of the following adjuncts:

| | | |
|---|---|---|
| again | equally | likewise |
| by the same token | in the same way | similarly |

*Every baby's face is different from every other's. In the same way, every baby's pattern of development is different.*
*Being a good player doesn't guarantee you will be a good manager, but, by the same token, neither does having all the coaching badges.*
*Never feed your rabbit raw potatoes that have gone green—they contain a poison. Similarly, never feed it rhubarb leaves.*

**contrasts**
**and**
**alternatives**

**10.76** When you want to add a sentence that contrasts with the previous one or gives another point of view, you can use one of the following adjuncts:

| | | | |
|---|---|---|---|
| all the same | even so | nonetheless | still |
| alternatively | however | on the contrary | then again |
| by contrast | instead | on the other hand | though |
| conversely | nevertheless | rather | yet |

*He had forgotten that there was a rainy season in the winter months. It was, however, a fine, soft rain and the air was warm.*
*Her aim is to punish the criminal. Nevertheless, she is not convinced that imprisonment is always the answer.*
*Her children are hard work. She never loses her temper with them though.*

If you are mentioning an alternative, you can use 'instead', 'alternatively', or 'conversely'.

*People who normally consulted her began to ask other people's advice instead.*
*The company is now considering an appeal. Alternatively, they may submit a new application.*

**causes**

**10.77** When you want to indicate that the fact you are mentioning exists because of the fact or facts previously given, you link your statements using one of the following adjuncts:

| | | | |
|---|---|---|---|
| accordingly | consequently | so | therefore |
| as a result | hence | thereby | thus |

*Oxford and Cambridge have a large income of their own. So they are not in quite the same position as other universities.*
*It isn't giving any detailed information. Therefore it isn't necessary.*
*We want a diverse press and we haven't got it. I think as a result a lot of options are denied us.*

**indicating sequence in time**

**10.78** There are a number of **adjuncts of time** which are used to indicate that something takes place after or before an event that you have already mentioned or at the same time as that event:

| | | | |
|---|---|---|---|
| afterwards | first | presently | subsequently |
| at the same time | in the meantime | previously | suddenly |
| beforehand | last | simultaneously | then |
| earlier | later | since | throughout |
| ever since | meanwhile | soon | |
| finally | next | soon after | |

*Go and see Terry Brown about it. Come back to me <u>afterwards</u>.*
*Published in 1983, the book has <u>since</u> gone through six reprints.*
*Never set out on a journey without telling someone <u>beforehand</u>.*
*We look forward to the Commission studying this agreement. <u>In the meantime</u> we are pressing ahead with our plans.*

**ordering points**

**10.79** In formal writing and speech, people often want to indicate what stage they have reached in writing or speaking. They do this using the following adjuncts:

| | | | |
|---|---|---|---|
| first | secondly | finally | then |
| firstly | third | in conclusion | to sum up |
| second | thirdly | lastly | |

*What are the advantages of geo-thermal energy? <u>Firstly</u>, there's no fuel required, the energy already exists. <u>Secondly</u>, there's plenty of it. <u>Finally</u>, I want to say something about the heat pump.*

**conjunctions**

**10.80** When people are speaking or writing informally, they often add an extra piece of information using one of the conjunctions 'and', 'but', 'yet', 'or', and 'nor' to begin a new sentence.

*He's a very good teacher. <u>And</u> he's good-looking.*
*I think it's motor cycling. <u>But</u> I'm not sure.*
*It's not improving their character. <u>Nor</u> their home life.*

**linking adjuncts after conjunctions**

**10.81** Linking adjuncts are often put after the conjunctions 'and' or 'but' at the beginning of a clause or sentence.

*That will take a long time <u>and besides</u> you'd get it wrong.*
*They were familiar <u>and therefore</u> all right.*
*Her accent is not perfect. <u>But still</u>, it's a marvellous performance.*

If you are linking two negative sentences or clauses, you can put 'either' the end of the second one.

*I can't use it, but I can't bear not to use it <u>either</u>.*

## Indicating a change in a conversation

**10.82** Sometimes people want to avoid abruptness when changing the topic of conversation, or when starting to talk about a different aspect of it. They do this by using a particular group of sentence adjuncts. These adjuncts are mostly used when you are continuing a conversation, and rarely to begin one.

The following adjuncts are commonly used in this way:

| | | | |
|---|---|---|---|
| actually | incidentally | okay | well |
| anyhow | look | right | well now |
| anyway | now | so | well then |
| by the way | now then | then | you know |

They usually occur at the beginning of a clause. However, a few of them can be used in other places in the clause, when you want to pause or want to draw attention to the fact that you are introducing a new topic.

'Actually', 'anyhow', 'anyway', 'by the way', 'incidentally', and 'you know' can be used at the end of a clause. 'By the way', 'incidentally', and 'you know' can be used after the subject or after the first word in a verb group.

Here are some examples showing adjuncts used to change the topic of a conversation:

*Actually, Dan, before I forget, she asked me to tell you about my new job.*
*Well now, we've got a very big task ahead of us.*

Here are some examples showing adjuncts used to start talking about a different aspect of the same topic:

*What do you sell there anyway?*
*This approach, incidentally, also has the advantage of being cheap.*

Unlike the other adjuncts, 'then' by itself is not used at the beginning of a clause, only at the end.

*That's all right then.*
*Are you fond of her, then?*

**10.83** Some adjuncts are used at the beginning of a clause to introduce a fact, often one that corrects the statement just made. They can also be used at the end of a clause, and elsewhere, to emphasize the fact.

| | | |
|---|---|---|
| actually | as it happens | indeed |
| as a matter of fact | I mean | in fact |

Note that 'actually' is used here to add information on the same topic, whereas in the previous paragraph it indicated a change of topic.

*Actually, I do know why he made the solicitors write that letter.*
*He rather envies you actually.*
*I'm sure you're right. In fact, I know you're right.*
*There's no reason to be disappointed. As a matter of fact, this could be rather amusing.*
*They cannot hop or jump. Indeed, they can barely manage even to run.*

'You see' is used to preface or point to an explanation.

*'You don't want to come with me, then?'—'No. You see, it's not often that I get the chance to be absolutely free.'*
*He didn't have anyone to talk to, you see.*

'After all' is used to preface or point to a reason or justification of what you have just said.

*She did not regret accepting his offer. He was, after all, about the right age.*

**USAGE NOTE**  **10.84** Prepositional phrases can sometimes be used to introduce a new topic or a different aspect of the same topic. 'As to' or 'as for' can be used at the beginning of a sentence to introduce a slightly different topic.

*As to what actually transpired at the headquarters, there are many differing accounts.*
*We will continue to expand our economy. As for the US, we will ask that they take steps to reduce their budget deficit.*

'With' and 'in the case of' can be used to mention another thing that is involved in a type of situation that was previously mentioned.

*With children, you have to plan a bit more carefully.*
*When the death was expected, the period of grief is usually shorter than in the case of an unexpected death.*

## Emphasizing

**10.85** You may want to emphasize the truth of your statement or to stress the seriousness of the situation you are describing. You can do this using the following sentence adjuncts:

| | | | |
|---|---|---|---|
| above all | even | simply | truly |
| actually | for heaven's sake | so | without exception |
| at all | indeed | surely | |
| believe me | positively | to put it mildly | |
| by all means | really | to say the least | |

*Sometimes we actually dared to penetrate their territory.*
*Above all, do not be too proud to ask for advice.*
*Eight years was indeed a short span of time.*
*I really am sorry.*
*Believe me, if you get robbed, the best thing to do is forget about it.*

Note that 'indeed' is often used after complements containing 'very'.

*I think she is a very stupid person indeed.*

'At all' is used for emphasis in negative clauses, usually at the end.

*I didn't like it at all.*
*I would not be at all surprised if they turned out to be the same person.*

'Surely' is used when you are appealing for agreement.

*Surely it is better to know the truth than to be deluded.*
*Here, surely, is a case for treating people as individuals.*

'Even' is placed in front of a word or group to draw attention to a surprising part of what you are saying.

*Even at mid-day the air was sharp and chilly.*
*Some men were even singing.*
*There was no one in the cafe, not even a waiter.*

'So' is used as an emphatic introduction when agreeing or commenting.

*'Derek! It's raining!'—'So it is.'*
*'He's very grateful!'—'So he ought to be.'*

'By all means' is used for emphasis when giving permission.

*If your baby likes water, by all means give it to him.*

'For heaven's sake' is used when making a request or asking a question.

*For heaven's sake, don't pull, Chris.*
*What are you staring at, for heaven's sake?*

**emphasizing exactness** 10.86 You may want to emphasize that your statement is not only generally true, but that it is true in all its details. The adverbs 'exactly', 'just', and 'precisely' are used for this.

*They'd always treated her exactly as if she were their own daughter.*
*Their decor was exactly right.*
*I know just how you feel.*
*The peasants are weak precisely because they are poor.*

## Indicating the most relevant thing: focusing adverbs

10.87 If you want to indicate the most relevant thing involved in what you are saying, for example the main reason for something or the main quality of something, you can use a **focusing adverb**.

*I'm particularly interested in classical music.*
*They have been used in certain countries, notably in South America.*
*We want especially to thank the numerous friends who encouraged us.*

The following adverbs can be used like this:

| | | | |
|---|---|---|---|
| chiefly | mostly | predominantly | specially |
| especially | notably | primarily | specifically |
| mainly | particularly | principally | |

**restricting** 10.88 Some focusing adverbs can be used to emphasize that only one particular thing is involved in what you are saying.

*The drug is given only to seriously ill patients.*
*This is solely a matter of money.*
*It's a large canvas covered with just one colour.*

The following adverbs can be used like this:

| | | | |
|---|---|---|---|
| alone | just | purely | solely |
| exclusively | only | simply | |

**selecting** 10.89 Focusing adverbs can be used to add a further piece of information which selects a particular group of people or things from a larger set. They can be used in this way with noun groups, prepositional phrases, adjectives, and subordinate clauses.

*I enjoy the company of young people, especially my grandchildren.*
*In some communities, notably the inner cities, the treatment has backfired.*
*They were mostly professional people.*
*You'll enjoy it down in London, especially if you get a job.*

**position of focusing adverbs** 10.90 In careful writing, focusing adverbs are usually put immediately in front of the word or clause element they apply to, in order to avoid ambiguity. In speech, it is usually clear from the intonation of the speaker what they apply to.

However, in many cases the focusing adverb does not necessarily focus on the word or element immediately after it. For example, in the sentence 'He mainly reads articles about mechanical things' the word 'mainly' almost certainly applies to 'about mechanical things', not to 'reads'.

Focusing adverbs are not normally used at the beginning of a sentence. However, you can use 'only' to begin a sentence when it focuses on the thing that follows it.

*Only thirty-five per cent of four-year-olds get nursery education.*
*Only in science fiction is the topic touched on.*

You can use 'just' and 'simply' at the beginning of sentences giving instructions.

*Just add boiling water.*
*Simply remove one cube at a time.*

'Alone' is always used after the element that it focuses on. 'Only' is sometimes used in this position.

*People don't work for money alone.*
*They were identified by their first names only.*

In informal speech and writing, other focusing adverbs are sometimes used after the element they focus on. For example, you can say 'We talked about me mostly' instead of 'We talked mostly about me'.

*We have talked about France mainly.*
*Chocolate, particularly, is suspected of causing decay of the teeth.*
*In the early years, especially, a child may be afraid of many things.*

This position can also be used when adding a piece of information.

*He liked America, New York particularly.*
*She was busy writing, poetry mostly.*

**USAGE NOTE**   **10.91** Some other adjuncts can be used to focus on additional information. The adverbs of degree 'largely', 'partly', and 'entirely', and adverbs of frequency such as 'usually' and 'often', can be used.

*The situation had been created largely by lurid newspaper tales.*
*The house was cheap partly because it was falling down and partly because Seyer Street was a slum.*
*The females care for their young entirely by themselves.*
*They often fought each other, usually as a result of arguments over money.*
*Some witnesses refuse to give evidence, often because they feel intimidated.*

The adjunct 'in particular', which has a similar meaning to 'particularly', can be used in the positions shown in the examples below.

*Wednesday in particular is very busy.*
*Next week we shall be taking a look at education and in particular comprehensive schools.*
*He swore at life in general and Otto in particular.*
*In particular, I'm going to concentrate on hydro-electricity.*

# Other information structures

## Putting something first: fronting

**10.92** In English, the first element in a declarative clause is usually the subject of the verb. However, if you want to emphasize another element, you can put that first instead.

Putting a word at the front of a clause for emphasis is called **fronting**. Sometimes when fronting takes place the normal order of subject and verb is changed. This is called **inversion**.

**adjuncts**     **10.93 Adjuncts** can often be put first. This is the normal position for sentence adjuncts (see paragraph 10.56), so they are not particularly emphatic in this position. Other adjuncts are sometimes placed first, usually for extra vividness in stories and accounts.

*At eight o'clock I went down for my breakfast.*
*For years I'd had to hide what I was thinking.*

Inversion often occurs after adjuncts of place and negative adjuncts.
*When they emptied his pockets, out fell a bag of cocaine.*
*On no account must they be let in.*

However, inversion does not occur after an adjunct of place when the subject is a pronoun.

*The door opened and in she came.*

For general information on adjuncts, see Chapter 6. Negative adjuncts are dealt with in Chapter 4.

**reported**     **10.94** When you are saying that you do not know something, you can put
**questions**    the **reported question** first.

*What I'm going to do next I don't quite know.*
*How he escaped a fractured skull I can't imagine.*

For more information on reported questions, see paragraphs 7.29 to 7.35.

**other clause**   **10.95** A complement can occasionally be put first, but this is not
**elements**      common.

*Noreen, she was called. She came from the village.*
*Rare indeed is the individual who does not belong to one of these groups.*

The object of a verb is sometimes put first, usually in formal or literary uses. Note that the subject still has to be mentioned.

*The money I gave to the agent.*
*When they scented my fear, they would attack. This I knew.*

# Introducing your statement: prefacing structures

**10.96** People often use structures which point forward to what they are going to say and classify or label it in some way. These are called **prefacing structures** or **prefaces**.

A preface usually introduces the second part of the same sentence, usually a 'that'-clause or a 'wh'-clause, but occasionally a non-finite clause or a noun group. However, you can also use a whole sentence as the preface to another sentence (see paragraph 10.101).

**prefaces to**   **10.97** A common prefacing structure is 'the' and a noun, followed by 'is'.
**second part**   The noun is sometimes modified or qualified. The nouns most commonly
**of sentence**   used in this structure are:

| answer | point | rule | tragedy | wonder |
| conclusion | problem | solution | trouble | |
| fact | question | thing | truth | |

'The fact is', 'the point is', and 'the thing is' are used to indicate that what you are about to say is important.

*The simple fact is that if you get ill, you may be unable to take the examination.*
*The point is to find out who was responsible.*
*The thing is, how are we to get her out?*

**classifying** 10.98 Some of these nouns are used in prefaces to indicate what sort of thing you are about to say.

*The rule is: if in doubt, dry clean.*
*Is medicine an art or a science? The answer is that it is both.*
*The inevitable conclusion is that man is not responsible for what he does.*

**labelling** 10.99 Some of these nouns are used in prefaces to label what you are about to talk about.

*The problem is that the demand for health care is unlimited.*
*The only solution is to approach each culture with an open mind.*
*The answer is planning, timing, and, above all, practical experience.*

**other ways of labelling** 10.100 Cleft structures (see paragraphs 10.25 to 10.30) can be used in labelling.

*What we need is law and order.*

Impersonal 'it' structures with adjectives followed by a 'that'-clause are a less emphatic way of prefacing (see paragraph 10.42).

*It is interesting that the new products sell better on the web than in shops.*

You can use the sentence adjuncts 'at any rate', 'at least', and 'rather' as prefaces when you are slightly correcting a previous statement, often after 'or'.

*This had saved her life; or at any rate her sanity.*

'Anyway' can also be used, usually after the correction.

*It is, for most of its length anyway, a painful romantic comedy.*

**using sentences as prefaces** 10.101 A whole sentence can be used as a preface to the sentence or sentences that follow it. For example, a sentence containing an adjective like 'interesting', 'remarkable', or 'funny', or a general abstract word such as 'reason' or 'factor' (see paragraphs 9.19 to 9.23), is often used as a preface.

*It was a bit strange. Nobody was talking to each other.*
*This has had very interesting effects on different people.*
*There were other factors, of course: I too was tired of London.*
*But there were problems. How could the eggs be prevented from drying o*
*and how could tadpoles develop out of water?*

# Doing by saying: performative verbs

10.102 People sometimes explicitly say what function their statement is performing. They do this using 'I' and the simple present of a **reporting verb** such as 'admit' or 'promise' which refers to something that is done with words. For example, instead of saying 'I'll be there' you could say 'I promise I'll be there', which makes the statement stronger.

*I suggest we draw up a document.*
*I'll be back at one, I promise.*
*I was somewhat shocked, I admit, by these events.*

The following verbs can be used in this way:

| | | | | |
|---|---|---|---|---|
| acknowledge | contend | pledge | say | vow |
| admit | demand | predict | submit | warn |
| assure | deny | promise | suggest | |
| claim | guarantee | prophesy | swear | |
| concede | maintain | propose | tell | |

For more detailed information about reporting verbs, see Chapter 7.

**10.103** Some other verbs which refer to doing something with words are used without a 'that'-clause after them. When used without a 'that'-clause, the use of the simple present with 'I' performs the function of a statement in itself, rather than commenting on another statement.

*I apologize for any delay.*
*I congratulate you with all my heart.*
*I forgive you.*

The following verbs are commonly used in this way:

| | | | | |
|---|---|---|---|---|
| absolve | authorize | declare | nominate | renounce |
| accept | baptize | dedicate | object | resign |
| accuse | challenge | defy | order | second |
| advise | confess | forbid | pronounce | sentence |
| agree | congratulate | forgive | protest | |
| apologize | consent | name | refuse | |

**10.104** The verbs in the above lists are sometimes called **performative verbs** or **performatives,** because they perform the action they refer to.

**USAGE NOTE** **10.105** Some of these verbs are used with modals when people want to be emphatic, polite, or tentative.

*I must apologize for Mayfield.*
*I would agree with a lot of their points.*
*She was very thoroughly checked, I can assure you.*
*May I congratulate you again on your excellent performance.*

# Exclamations

**10.106** **Exclamations** are words and structures that express something emphatically. You usually show this in speech by your intonation and in writing by the use of an **exclamation mark** at the end of the sentence, although full stops are often used instead. If the exclamation is only a part of a sentence, it is separated from the rest of the sentence by a comma.

**showing your reactions** **10.107** There are various ways of showing your reaction to something that you are experiencing or looking at, or that you have just been told. One way is to use an exclamation such as 'bother'. 'good heavens'. 'oh dear'. or 'ouch'.

*Ow! That hurt.*
'*Margaret Ravenscroft may have been responsible for her sister's death.*'—'*Good heavens!*' *said Dr Willoughby.*
'*She died last autumn.*'—'*Oh dear, I'm so sorry.*'

Some exclamations are only used to show reactions. Here is a list of some common ones:

| | | | | |
|---|---|---|---|---|
| aha | damn | gosh | oops | what |
| blast | good gracious | honestly | ouch | whoops |
| blimey | good grief | hurray | ow | wow |
| bother | good heavens | oh | really | yippee |
| bravo | good lord | oh dear | ugh | you're joking |
| crikey | goodness me | ooh | well I never | yuk |

**other clause elements**

**10.108** Other clause elements or clauses can be used in exclamations.

Noun groups can be used to show your reaction to something. Some nouns, for example 'rubbish' and 'nonsense', can be used on their own to express strong disagreement.

'*No-one would want to go out with me*' – '*Nonsense. You're a very 'attractive man.*'

Predeterminers, especially 'what', are often used before the noun.

*What a pleasant surprise!*
*Such an intelligent family!*
*Quite a show!*

Qualitative adjectives can be used on their own, or with 'how' in front of them, usually to show a positive reaction to a statement.

'*I've arranged a surprise party for him.*' – '*Lovely.*'
*Oh! Look! How sweet!*

A prepositional phrase with 'of' can be used to specify a person, and a 'to' infinitive clause to refer to the action.

*How nice of you to come!*
*How nice to see you.*

Sentences with 'how' and an adjective or adverb, or 'what' and a noun group can also be used as exclamations. The adjective or noun group is the complement or object of the verb, even though it comes first.

*How nice you look!*
*How cleverly you hid your feelings!*
*What an idiot I am.*
*What morbid thoughts we're having.*

'How' can be placed at the beginning of an ordinary sentence to indicate the intensity of a feeling or action.

*How I hate posters.*
*How he talked!*

**rhetorical questions**

**10.109** People often use **questions** as a way of making a comment or exclamation. They do not expect an answer. Questions like this are called **rhetorical questions**.

You can use a negative 'yes/no'-question, if you want to encourage other people to agree with you.

*Oh Albert, isn't she lovely?*

*Wouldn't it be awful with no Christmas!*

In informal English, you can use a positive question.

*'How much?'—'A hundred million.'—'Are you crazy?'*
*Have you no shame!*

'Wh'-questions, especially ones containing modals, are also used.

*How the hell should I know?*
*Why must she be so nasty to me?*
*Why bother?*

See Chapter 4 for more information about questions.

# Making a statement into a question: question tags

**10.110** This section deals with **tags** or **question tags**. A **tag** is a short structure that is added to the end of a statement to turn it into a question. This is usually done when you expect the person you are addressing to agree with you or confirm your statement. Tags are most often used in spoken English. The whole sentence, consisting of the statement and the tag, is called a **tag question.**

**forming tags** **10.111** Tags are formed using an auxiliary or a form of 'be' or 'do', followed by a personal pronoun referring to the subject.

If the main clause is in the affirmative, you use a negative tag. Negative tags are always contracted, except in old-fashioned or very formal English.

*It is quite warm, isn't it?*

If the main clause is in the negative, you use an affirmative tag.

*You didn't know I was an artist, did you?*

If the main clause of your statement has an auxiliary in it, you use the same auxiliary in the tag.

*You will stay in touch, won't you?*

If the main clause has the simple past or present form of 'be' as the main verb, you use this in the tag.

*They are, aren't they?*

If the main clause does not have an auxiliary or the verb 'be', you use 'do', 'does', or 'did' in the tag.

*After a couple of years the heat gets too much, doesn't it?*
*He played for Ireland, didn't he?*

Note that the negative tag with 'I' is 'aren't I', when 'am' is the auxiliary or main verb in the main clause.

*I'm controlling it, aren't I?*

**checking** **10.112** If you have an opinion or belief about something and you want to
**statements** check that it is true or to find out if someone agrees with you, you can make a statement and add a tag after it to make it into a question.

If you are making an affirmative statement and you want to check that it is true, you use a negative tag.

*You like Ralph a lot, don't you?*
*They are beautiful places, aren't they?*

If you are making a negative statement and want to check that it is true, you use an affirmative tag.

*It doesn't work, does it?*
*You won't tell anyone else all this, will you?*

You can also use an affirmative tag if your statement contains a broad negative, a negative adverb, or a negative pronoun.

*That hardly counts, does it?*
*You've never been to Benidorm, have you?*
*Nothing had changed, had it?*

**replying**
**to tags**

**10.113** The person you are speaking to replies to the content of your statement rather than to the tag, and confirms an affirmative statement with 'yes' and a negative statement with 'no'.

*'It became stronger, didn't it?'*—*'Yes it did.'*
*'You didn't know that, did you?'*—*'No.'*

**other uses**
**of tags**

**10.114** If you are making a statement about yourself and you want to check if the person you are talking to has the same opinion or feeling, you can put a tag with 'you' after your statement.

*I think this is the best thing, don't you?*
*I love tea, don't you?*

Tags can also be used to show your reaction to something that someone has just said or implied, for example to show interest, surprise, or anger. Note that you use an affirmative tag after an affirmative statement.

*You fell on your back, did you?*
*You've been to North America before, have you?*
*Oh, he wants us to make films as well, does he?*

When using 'let's' to suggest doing something, you can add the tag 'shall we' to check that the people you are talking to agree with you.

*Let's forget it, shall we?*

If you are suggesting that you do something and you want to check that the person you are speaking to agrees, you can add the tag 'shall I?'

*I'll call the doctor, shall I?*

If you are telling someone to do something and you want to make your order sound less forceful, you can do so by adding a tag. The tag is usually 'will you', but 'won't you' and 'can't you' are also used.

*Come into the kitchen, will you?*
*Look at that, will you?*
*See that she gets safely back, won't you?*

When you are using a negative imperative, you can only use 'will you' as a tag.

*Don't tell Howard, will you?*

## Addressing people: vocatives

**10.115** When you are talking to people, you sometimes address them using their own name or title, or a word like 'darling' or 'idiot'. Words used like this are called **vocatives**.

Vocatives are not used in British English as commonly as in some other languages, or even in American English. Some are used only in formal contexts, some only in informal ones. Look in a Cobuild dictionary for more detailed information.

**position of vocatives**

**10.116** Vocatives are often used at the end of a sentence or clause. In writing, they are usually preceded by a comma.

*Where are you staying, Mr Swallow?*
*That's lovely, darling.*

You can put them at the beginning of a sentence in order to attract someone's attention before speaking to them.

*John, how long have you been at the university?*
*Dad, why have you got that suit on?*

**titles**

**10.117** When you address someone in a fairly formal way, you use their title and surname. Information about titles is given in 1.56 to 1.58.

*Goodbye, Dr Kirk.*
*Thank you, Mr Jones.*
*How old are you, Miss Flewin?*

Titles indicating a special qualification, rank, or job can be used on their own.

*What's wrong, Doctor?*
*Well, professor?*

**WARNING**

**10.118** The titles 'Mr', 'Mrs', 'Miss', and 'Ms' are used only with a surname. To address people formally without their surname, 'sir' and 'madam' are used, especially by employees to customers or clients.

*Yes, sir.*
*What is that, madam?*

**other vocatives**

**10.119** You can use noun groups to show your opinion of someone. Those which show dislike or contempt are often used with 'you' in front of them.

*No, you fool, the other way.*
*Shut your big mouth, you stupid idiot.*

Vocatives showing affection are usually used by themselves, but 'my' can be used in more old-fashioned or humorous contexts.

*Goodbye, darling.*
*We've got to go, my dear.*

Nouns that refer to family or social relationships can be used as vocatives.

*Someone's got to do it, mum.*
*Sorry, Grandma.*
*She'll be all right, mate.*
*Trust me, kid.*

Vocatives are occasionally used in the plural.

*Sit down, kids.*
*Stop her, you fools!*

Note that 'ladies', 'gentlemen', and 'children' are only used in the plural.

*Ladies and gentlemen, thank you for coming.*

# Contents of the
# Reference Section

# Reference Section

## Pronunciation guide

**R1** Here is a list of the phonetic symbols for English:

**vowel sounds**

| | |
|---|---|
| ɑː | heart, start, calm. |
| æ | act, mass, lap. |
| aɪ | dive, cry, mind. |
| aɪə | fire, tyre, buyer. |
| aʊ | out, down, loud. |
| aʊə | flour, tower, sour. |
| ɛ | met, lend, pen. |
| ɛɪ | say, main, weight. |
| ɛə | fair, care, wear. |
| ɪ | fit, win, list. |
| iː | feed, me, beat. |
| ɪə | near, beard, clear. |
| ɒ | lot, lost, spot. |
| əʊ | note, phone, coat. |
| ɔː | more, cord, claw. |
| ɔɪ | boy, coin, joint. |
| ʊ | could, stood, hood. |
| uː | you, use, choose. |
| ʊə | sure, poor, cure. |
| ɜː | turn, third, word. |
| ʌ | but, fund, must. |
| ə | the weak vowel in butter, about, forgotten. |

**consonant sounds**

| | | | |
|---|---|---|---|
| b | bed | t | talk |
| d | done | v | van |
| f | fit | w | win |
| g | good | x | loch |
| h | hat | z | zoo |
| j | yellow | ʃ | ship |
| k | king | ʒ | measure |
| l | lip | ŋ | sing |
| m | mat | tʃ | cheap |
| n | nine | θ | thin |
| p | pay | ð | then |
| r | run | dʒ | joy |
| s | soon | | |

Here is a list of the vowel letters:

a   e   i   o   u

Here is a list of the consonant letters:

b   c   d   f   g   h   j   k   l   m   n   p   q   r   s   t   v   w   x   y   z

## Forming plurals of count nouns

**R2** Information on which nouns have plurals is given in Chapter 1 (1.14 to 1.193).

**R3** In most cases, the plural is written 's'.

hat ⇨ hats
tree ⇨ trees

**R4** The plural is written 'es' after 'sh', 'ss', 'x', or 's', and it is pronounced /ɪz/.

bush ⇨ bushes
glass ⇨ glasses
box ⇨ boxes
bus ⇨ buses

The plural is also written 'es' and pronounced /ɪz/ after 'ch', when the 'ch' is pronounced /tʃ/.

church ⇨ churches
match ⇨ matches
speech ⇨ speeches

**R5** When the 's' follows one of the sounds /f/, /k/, /p/, /t/, or /θ/, it is pronounced /s/.

belief ⇨ beliefs
week ⇨ weeks
cap ⇨ caps
pet ⇨ pets
moth ⇨ moths

**R6** When the 's' follows one of the sounds /s/, /z/, or /dʒ/, it is pronounced /ɪz/.

service ⇨ services
prize ⇨ prizes
age ⇨ ages

**R7** Some nouns which end with the sound /θ/, for example 'mouth', have their plural forms pronounced as ending in /ðz/. With others, such as 'bath' and 'path', the pronunciation can be either /θs/ or /ðz/. You may need to check the pronunciations of words like these in a Cobuild dictionary.

**R8** In most other cases the 's' is pronounced /z/.

bottle ⇨ bottles
degree ⇨ degrees
doctor ⇨ doctors
idea ⇨ ideas
leg ⇨ legs
system ⇨ systems
tab ⇨ tabs

**R9** With nouns which end in a consonant letter followed by 'y', you substitute 'ies' for 'y' to form the plural.

country ⇨ countries
lady ⇨ ladies
opportunity ⇨ opportunities

With nouns which end in a vowel letter followed by 'y', you just add 's' to form the plural.

boy ⇨ boys
day ⇨ days
valley ⇨ valleys

**R10** There are a few nouns ending in 'f' or 'fe' where you form the plural by substituting 'ves' for 'f' or 'fe'.

| | | | |
|---|---|---|---|
| calf : calves | leaf : leaves | sheaf : sheaves | wife : wives |
| elf : elves | life : lives | shelf : shelves | wolf : wolves |
| half : halves | loaf : loaves | thief : thieves | |
| knife : knives | scarf : scarves | turf : turves | |

**R11** With many nouns which end in 'o', you just add 's' to form the plural.

photo ⇨ photos
radio ⇨ radios

However, the following nouns ending in 'o' have plurals ending in 'oes':

| | | | |
|---|---|---|---|
| domino | embargo | negro | tomato |
| echo | hero | potato | veto |

The following nouns ending in 'o' have plurals which can end in either 's' or 'es':

| | | | |
|---|---|---|---|
| buffalo | ghetto | memento | stiletto |
| cargo | innuendo | mosquito | tornado |
| flamingo | mango | motto | torpedo |
| fresco | manifesto | salvo | volcano |

**R12** The following nouns in English have special plural forms, usually with different vowel sounds from their singular forms:

| | | |
|---|---|---|
| child ⇨ children | louse ⇨ lice | ox ⇨ oxen |
| foot ⇨ feet | man ⇨ men | tooth ⇨ teeth |
| goose ⇨ geese | mouse ⇨ mice | woman ⇨ women |

**R13** Most nouns which refer to people and which end with 'man', 'woman', or 'child' have plural forms ending with 'men', 'women', or 'children'.

postman ⇨ postmen
Englishwoman ⇨ Englishwomen
grandchild ⇨ grandchildren

**R14** In addition to the nouns mentioned above, there are words which are borrowed from other languages, especially Latin, and which still form their plurals according to the rules of those languages. Many of them are technical or formal, and some are also used with a regular 's' or 'es' plural ending in non-technical or informal contexts. You may need to check these in a Cobuild dictionary.

**R15** Some nouns ending in 'us' have plurals ending in 'i'.

focus ⇨ foci
nucleus ⇨ nuclei
radius ⇨ radii
stimulus ⇨ stimuli

**R16** Some nouns ending in 'um' have plurals ending in 'a'.

aquarium ⇨ aquaria
memorandum ⇨ memoranda
referendum ⇨ referenda
spectrum ⇨ spectra
stratum ⇨ strata

**R17** Most nouns ending in 'is' have plurals in which the 'is' is replaced by 'es'.

| | |
|---|---|
| analysis ⇨ analyses | diagnosis ⇨ diagnoses |
| axis ⇨ axes | hypothesis ⇨ hypotheses |
| basis ⇨ bases | neurosis ⇨ neuroses |
| crisis ⇨ crises | parenthesis ⇨ parentheses |

**R18** With some nouns ending in 'a', the plurals are formed by adding 'e'.

larva ⇨ larvae
vertebra ⇨ vertebrae

Some, such as 'antenna', 'formula', 'amoeba', and 'nebula', also have less formal plurals ending in 's'.

**R19** Other nouns form their plurals in other ways. Some of these have two plural forms, one formed with 's' and one formed in a different way. Usually the form with 's' is used in less formal English.

appendix ⇨ appendices or appendixes
automaton ⇨ automata or automatons
corpus ⇨ corpora
criterion ⇨ criteria
genus ⇨ genera
index ⇨ indices or indexes

matrix ⇨ matrices
phenomenon ⇨ phenomena
tempo ⇨ tempi or tempos
virtuoso ⇨ virtuosi or virtuosos
vortex ⇨ vortices

# Forming comparative and superlative adjectives

**R20** Information on how to use the comparatives and superlatives of adjectives is given in Chapter 2 (2.108 to 2.127).

**R21** The comparative of an adjective is formed either by adding 'er' to the end of the normal form of the adjective, or by putting 'more' in front of it. The superlative is formed by adding 'est' to the end of the adjective, or by putting 'most' in front of it.

The choice between adding 'er' and 'est' or using 'more' and 'most' usually depends on the number of syllables in the adjective.

Superlatives are usually preceded by 'the'.

**R22** With one-syllable adjectives, you usually add 'er' and 'est' to the end of the normal form of the adjective.

tall ⇨ taller ⇨ the tallest
quick ⇨ quicker ⇨ the quickest

Here is a list of common one-syllable adjectives which form their comparatives and superlatives usually, or always, by adding 'er' and 'est':

| | | | | |
|---|---|---|---|---|
| big | dull | large | proud | strong |
| bright | fair | late | quick | sweet |
| broad | fast | light | rare | tall |
| cheap | fat | long | rich | thick |
| clean | fine | loose | rough | thin |
| clear | firm | loud | sad | tight |
| close | flat | low | safe | tough |
| cold | fresh | new | sharp | warm |
| cool | full | nice | short | weak |
| cross | great | old | sick | wet |
| dark | hard | pale | slow | wide |
| deep | high | plain | small | wild |
| dry | hot | poor | soft | young |

Note that when 'er' and 'est' are added to some adjectives, a spelling change needs to be made.

The patterns of spelling change in forming comparatives and superlatives from adjectives are explained in paragraph R27.

**R23** You also add 'er' and 'est' with two-syllable adjectives ending in 'y', such as 'angry', 'dirty', and 'silly'.

happy ⇨ happier ⇨ the happiest
easy ⇨ easier ⇨ the easiest

Note that there is a spelling change here, which is explained in paragraph R27.

Here is a list of common two-syllable adjectives ending in 'y' whose comparatives and superlatives are formed like this:

| angry | easy | happy | lovely | silly |
|-------|------|-------|--------|-------|
| busy | friendly | heavy | lucky | steady |
| dirty | funny | likely | pretty | tiny |

**R24** Other two-syllable adjectives usually have comparatives and superlatives formed with 'more' and 'most'.

careful ⇨ more careful ⇨ the most careful
famous ⇨ more famous ⇨ the most famous

Note, however, that 'clever' and 'quiet' have comparatives and superlatives formed by adding 'er' and 'est'.

**R25** Some two-syllable adjectives have comparatives and superlatives with either the endings 'er' and 'est', or 'more' and 'most'.

*I can think of many pleasanter subjects.*
*It was more pleasant here than in the lecture room.*
*Exposure to sunlight is one of the commonest causes of cancer.*
*…five hundred of the most common words.*

Here is a list of common adjectives which can have either kind of comparative and superlative:

| common | handsome | narrow | polite | simple |
|--------|----------|--------|--------|--------|
| cruel | likely | obscure | remote | stupid |
| gentle | mature | pleasant | shallow | subtle |

**R26** Adjectives which have three or more syllables usually have comparatives and superlatives with 'more' and 'most'.

dangerous ⇨ more dangerous ⇨ the most dangerous
ridiculous ⇨ more ridiculous ⇨ the most ridiculous

However, some three-syllable adjectives are formed by adding 'un' to the beginning of other adjectives. For example, 'unhappy' is related to 'happy' and 'unlucky' to 'lucky'. These three-syllable adjectives have comparatives and superlatives formed either by adding 'er' and 'est' or by using 'more' and 'most'.

*He felt crosser and unhappier than ever.*

**R27** When you add 'er' or 'est' to an adjective, you sometimes need to make another change to the end of the adjective as well.

If a one-syllable adjective ends in a single vowel letter followed by a single consonant letter, you double the consonant letter when adding 'er' or 'est'.

big ⇨ bigger ⇨ the biggest
hot ⇨ hotter ⇨ the hottest

However, you do not do this with two-syllable adjectives.

common ⇨ commoner ⇨ the commonest
stupid ⇨ stupider ⇨ the stupidest

If an adjective ends in 'e', you remove the 'e' when adding 'er' or 'est'.

wide ⇨ wider ⇨ the widest
simple ⇨ simpler ⇨ the simplest

Note that with adjectives ending in 'le', the comparative and superlative have two syllables, not three. For example, 'simpler' (from 'simple' /sɪmpəl/) is pronounced /sɪmplə/

If an adjective ends in a consonant letter followed by 'y', you replace the 'y' with 'i' when adding 'er' or 'est'.

dry ⇨ drier ⇨ the driest
angry ⇨ angrier ⇨ the angriest
unhappy ⇨ unhappier ⇨ the unhappiest

Note that with 'shy', 'sly', and 'spry', you add 'er' and 'est' in the ordinary way.

**R28** 'Good' and 'bad' have special comparatives and superlatives which are not formed by adding 'er' and 'est' or by using 'more' and 'most'.

'Good' has the comparative 'better' and the superlative 'the best'.

*There might be better ways of doing it.*
*This is the best museum we've visited yet.*

'Bad' has the comparative 'worse' and the superlative 'the worst'.

*Things are worse than they used to be.*
*The airstrip there was the worst place in the world.*

Note that 'ill' does not have a comparative form and so 'worse' is used instead.

*Each day Kunta felt a little worse.*

**R29** The adjective 'old' has regular comparative and superlative forms but, in addition, it has the forms 'elder' and 'the eldest'. These forms are used only to talk about people, usually relatives.

*…the death of his two elder sons in the First World War.*
*Bill's eldest boy is a doctor.*

Note that unlike 'older', 'elder' never has 'than' after it.

**R30** There is no comparative or superlative of 'little' in standard English, although children sometimes say 'littler' and 'the littlest'. When you want to make a comparison, you use 'smaller' and 'the smallest'.

**R31** The comparatives and superlatives of compound adjectives are usually formed by putting 'more' and 'most' in front of the adjective.

self-effacing ⇨ more self-effacing ⇨ the most self-effacing
nerve-racking ⇨ more nerve-racking ⇨ the most nerve-racking

Some compound adjectives have adjectives as their first part. Comparatives and superlatives of these compounds are sometimes formed using the comparative and superlative of the adjective.

good-looking ⇨ better-looking ⇨ the best-looking

Similarly, some compound adjectives have adverbs as their first part. Their comparatives and superlatives are sometimes formed using the comparative and superlative of the adverb.

well-paid ⇨ better-paid ⇨ the best-paid
badly-planned ⇨ worse-planned ⇨ the worst-planned

The comparatives and superlatives of adverbs are explained in paragraphs R150 to R154.

# The spelling and pronunciation of possessives

**R32** The use of the possessive form of names and other nouns is explained in Chapter 2 (2.180 to 2.192).

**R33** The possessive form of a name or other noun is usually formed by adding apostrophe s ('s) to the end.

*Ginny's mother didn't answer.*
*Howard came into the editor's office.*

**R34** If you are using a plural noun ending in 's' to refer to the possessor, you just add an apostrophe (').

*I heard the girls' steps on the stairs.*
*The Kirks go to publishers' parties in Bloomsbury.*

However, if you are using an irregular plural noun which does not end in 's', you add apostrophe s ('s) to the end of it.

*It would cost at least three policemen's salaries per year.*
*The Equal Pay Act has failed to bring women's earnings up to the same level.*
*...children's birthday parties.*

**R35** If something belongs to more than one person or thing whose names are linked by 'and', the apostrophe s ('s) is put after the second name.

*...Helen and Tim's apartment.*
*...Colin and Mary's relationship.*
*The crowd met outside father and mother's house.*

**R36** If you want to say that two people or things each possess part of a group of things, both their names have apostrophe s ('s).

*The puppy was a superb blend of his father's and mother's best qualities.*

**R37** When you are using a name which already ends in 's', you can simply add an apostrophe, for example 'St James' Palace', or you can add apostrophe s ('s), for example 'St James's Palace'. These spellings are pronounced differently. If you simply add an apostrophe, the pronunciation remains unaltered, whereas if you add apostrophe s ('s), the possessive is pronounced /ɪz/.

**R38** Apostrophe s ('s) is pronounced differently in different words. It is pronounced

- /s/ after the sound /f/, /k/, /p/, /t/, or /θ/.
- /ɪz/ after the sound /s/, /z/, /ʃ/, /ʒ/, /tʃ/, or /dʒ/.
- /z/ after all other sounds.

**R39** If you are using a compound noun, you add apostrophe s ('s) to the last item in the compound.

*He went to his mother-in-law's house.*
*The parade assembled in the Detective Constable's room.*

**R40** Apostrophe s ('s) can be added to abbreviations and acronyms in the same way as to other words.

*He will get a majority of MPs' votes in both rounds.*
*He found the BBC's output, on balance, superior to that of ITV.*
*The majority of NATO's members agreed.*

# Numbers

**R41** The uses of **cardinal numbers**, **ordinal numbers**, and **fractions** have been explained in Chapter 2 (2.225 to 2.266). The use of ordinals to express dates is explained in paragraph 5.87. Lists of numbers and details about how to say and write numbers and fractions are given below.

## Cardinal numbers

**R42** Here is a list of cardinal numbers. The list shows the patterns of forming numbers greater than 20.

| | | | |
|---|---|---|---|
| 0 | zero, nought, nothing, oh | 26 | twenty-six |
| 1 | one | 27 | twenty-seven |
| 2 | two | 28 | twenty-eight |
| 3 | three | 29 | twenty-nine |
| 4 | four | 30 | thirty |
| 5 | five | 40 | forty |
| 6 | six | 50 | fifty |
| 7 | seven | 60 | sixty |
| 8 | eight | 70 | seventy |
| 9 | nine | 80 | eighty |
| 10 | ten | 90 | ninety |
| 11 | eleven | 100 | a hundred |
| 12 | twelve | 101 | a hundred and one |
| 13 | thirteen | 110 | a hundred and ten |
| 14 | fourteen | 120 | a hundred and twenty |
| 15 | fifteen | 200 | two hundred |
| 16 | sixteen | 1000 | a thousand |
| 17 | seventeen | 1001 | a thousand and one |
| 18 | eighteen | 1010 | a thousand and ten |
| 19 | nineteen | 2000 | two thousand |
| 20 | twenty | 10,000 | ten thousand |
| 21 | twenty-one | 100,000 | a hundred thousand |
| 22 | twenty-two | 1,000,000 | a million |
| 23 | twenty-three | 2,000,000 | two million |
| 24 | twenty-four | 1,000,000,000 | a billion |
| 25 | twenty-five | | |

**R43** When you say or write in words a number over 100, you put 'and' before the number expressed by the last two figures. For example, 203 is said or written 'two hundred and three' and 2840 is said or written 'two thousand, eight hundred and forty'.

*Four hundred and eighteen men were killed and a hundred and seventeen wounded.*

'And' is often omitted in American English.

*...one hundred fifty dollars.*

**R44** If you want to say or write in words a number between 1000 and 1,000,000, there are various ways of doing it. For example, the number '1872' can be said or written in words as

- eighteen hundred and seventy two
- one thousand eight hundred and seventy-two
- one eight seven two
- eighteen seventy-two

Note that you cannot use 'a' instead of 'one' for the second way.

The third way is often used to identify something such as a room number. With telephone numbers, you always say each figure separately like this.

The last way is used if the number is a date.

**R45** Unlike some other languages, in English when numbers over 9999 are written in figures, a comma is usually put after the fourth figure from the end, the seventh figure from the end, and so on, dividing the figures into groups of three. For example, 15,500 or 1,982,000. With numbers between 1000 and 9999, a comma is sometimes put after the first figure. For example 1,526.

When a number contains a full stop, the number or numbers after the full stop indicate a fraction. For example, 2.5 is the same as two and a half.

# Ordinal numbers

**R46** Here is a list of ordinal numbers. The list shows the patterns of forming ordinal numbers greater than 20.

| | | | |
|---|---|---|---|
| 1st | first | 26th | twenty-sixth |
| 2nd | second | 27th | twenty-seventh |
| 3rd | third | 28th | twenty-eighth |
| 4th | fourth | 29th | twenty-ninth |
| 5th | fifth | 30th | thirtieth |
| 6th | sixth | 31st | thirty-first |
| 7th | seventh | 40th | fortieth |
| 8th | eighth | 41st | forty-first |
| 9th | ninth | 50th | fiftieth |
| 10th | tenth | 51st | fifty-first |
| 11th | eleventh | 60th | sixtieth |
| 12th | twelfth | 61st | sixty-first |
| 13th | thirteenth | 70th | seventieth |
| 14th | fourteenth | 71st | seventy-first |
| 15th | fifteenth | 80th | eightieth |
| 16th | sixteenth | 81st | eighty-first |
| 17th | seventeenth | 90th | ninetieth |
| 18th | eighteenth | 91st | ninety-first |
| 19th | nineteenth | 100th | hundredth |
| 20th | twentieth | 101st | hundred and first |
| 21st | twenty-first | 200th | two hundredth |
| 22nd | twenty-second | 1000th | thousandth |
| 23rd | twenty-third | 1,000,000th | millionth |
| 24th | twenty-fourth | 1,000,000,000th | billionth |
| 25th | twenty-fifth | | |

**R47** As shown in the above list, ordinals can be written in abbreviated form, for example in dates or headings or in very informal writing. You write the last two letters of the ordinal after the number expressed in figures. For example, 'first' can be written as '1st', 'twenty-second' as '22nd', 'hundred and third' as '103rd', and 'fourteenth' as '14th'.

...on August 2nd.
...the 1st Division of the Sovereign's Escort.

# Fractions and percentages

**R48** You can write a fraction in figures, for example $\frac{1}{2}$, $\frac{1}{4}$, $\frac{3}{4}$, and $\frac{2}{3}$. These correspond to 'a half', 'a quarter', 'three-quarters', and 'two-thirds' respectively.

**R49** Fractions are often given in a special form as a number of hundredths. This type of fraction is called a **percentage**. For example. 'three-hundredths', expressed as a percentage, is 'three per cent'. It can also be written as 'three percent' or '3%'. 'A half' can be expressed as 'fifty per cent', 'fifty percent', or '50%'.

About <u>20 per cent</u> of student accountants are women.
<u>90 percent</u> of most food is water.
Before 1960 <u>45%</u> of British trade was with the Commonwealth.

You can use percentages on their own as noun groups when it is clear what they refer to.

<u>Ninety per cent</u> were self employed.
...interest at <u>10%</u> per annum.

# Verb forms and the formation of verb groups

**R50** Verbs have several forms. These forms can be used on their own or combined with special verbs called **auxiliaries**. When a verb or a combination of a verb and an auxiliary is used in a clause, it is called a **verb group**. Verb groups can be **finite** or **non-finite**. If a verb group is finite, it has a **tense**.

Verb groups are used to refer to actions, states, and processes. The use of verb groups in clauses to make statements is explained in Chapter 3.

**R51** Verb groups can be **active** or **passive**. You use an active verb group if you are concentrating on the performer of an action, and you use a passive verb group if you are concentrating on someone or something that is affeced by an action. Further information on the use of passive verb groups is given in Chapter 10 (10.8 to 10.24).

**R52** Regular verbs have the following forms:

- a base form EG *walk*
- an 's' form EG *walks*
- a present participle EG *walking*
- a past form EG *walked*

The base form of a verb is the form that is used in the infinitive. It is the form that is given first in a dictionary where a verb is explained, and that is given in the lists in this grammar.

The 's' form of a verb consists of the base form with 's' on the end.

The present participle usually consists of the base form with 'ing' on the end. It is sometimes called the '-ing' form.

The past form of a verb usually consists of the base form with 'ed' on the end.

In the case of regular verbs. the past form is used for the past tense and is also used as the past participle.

However, with many irregular verbs (see paragraph R72) there are two past forms:

- a past tense form EG *stole*
- a past participle form EG *stolen*

There are rules about the spelling of the different forms of verbs. depending on their endings. These are explained in paragraphs R54 to R70.

Certain verbs. especially common ones. have irregular forms. These are listed in paragraphs R72 to R75.

The forms of the auxiliaries 'be'. 'have'. and 'do' are given in paragraph R80.

**R53** Each verb form has various uses.

The base form is used for the present tense, the imperative, and the infinitive, and is used after modals.

The 's' form is used for the third person singular of the present tense.

The present participle is used for continuous tenses, '-ing' adjectives, '-ing' nouns, and some non-finite clauses.

The past form is used for the simple past tense, and for the past participle of regular verbs.

The past participle is used for perfect tenses, passive tenses, '-ed' adjectives, and some non-finite clauses.

**R54** The basic verb forms have been described in paragraph R52. The following paragraphs explain how the various forms of verbs are spelled. They also give details of verbs which have irregular forms. The forms of the auxiliaries 'be', 'have', and 'do' are dealt with separately in paragraphs R80 to R88.

**R55** The 's' form of most verbs consists of the base form of the verb with 's' added to the end.

sing ⇨ sings
write ⇨ writes

When the 's' follows one of the sounds /f/, /k/, /p/, /t/, or /θ/, it is pronounced /s/.

break ⇨ breaks
keep ⇨ keeps

When the 's' follows one of the sounds /s/, /z/, or /dʒ/, it is pronounced /ɪz/.

dance ⇨ dances
manage ⇨ manages

In most other cases the 's' is pronounced /z/.

leave ⇨ leaves
refer ⇨ refers

**R56** With verbs whose base form ends in a consonant letter followed by 'y', you substitute 'ies' for 'y' to form the 's' form.

try ⇨ tries
cry ⇨ cries

**R57** With verbs which end in 'sh', 'ch', 'ss', 'x', 'zz', or 'o', 'es' rather than 's' is added to the base form of the verb. The 'es' is pronounced /iz/ when it is added to a consonant sound, and pronounced /z/ when it is added to a vowel sound.

diminish ⇨ diminishes       mix ⇨ mixes
reach ⇨ reaches             buzz ⇨ buzzes
pass ⇨ passes               echo ⇨ echoes

**R58** With one-syllable verbs which end in a single 's', you add 'ses'.

bus ⇨ busses
gas ⇨ gasses

**R59** Most verbs have present participles formed by adding 'ing' to the base form, and past forms formed by adding 'ed' to the base form.

paint ⇨ painting ⇨ painted
rest ⇨ resting ⇨ rested

With all present participles, the 'ing' is pronounced as a separate syllable: /ɪŋ/.

With verbs whose base form ends with one of the sounds /f/, /k/, /p/, /s/, /ʃ/, or /tʃ/, the 'ed' of the past form is pronounced /t/. For example, 'pressed' is pronounced /prɛst/ and 'watched' is pronounced /wɒtʃt/.

With verbs whose base forms ends with the sound /d/ or /t/, the 'ed' of the past form is pronounced /ɪd/. For example, 'patted' is pronounced /pætɪd/ and 'faded' is pronounced /feɪdɪd/.

With all other verbs, the 'ed' of the past form is pronounced /d/. For example, 'joined' is pronounced /dʒɔɪnd/ and 'lived' is pronounced /lɪvd/.

**R60** With most verbs which end in 'e', the present participle is formed by substituting 'ing' for the final 'e'. Similarly, you substitute 'ed' for the final 'e' to form the past form.

dance ⇨ dancing ⇨ danced
smile ⇨ smiling ⇨ smiled
fade ⇨ fading ⇨ faded

**R61** In the case of a few verbs ending in 'e', you just add 'ing' in the normal way to form the present participle. You still substitute 'ed' for 'e' to form the past form.

singe ⇨ singeing ⇨ singed
agree ⇨ agreeing ⇨ agreed

Here is a list of these verbs:

| | | |
|---|---|---|
| age | dye | referee |
| agree | free | singe |
| disagree | knee | tiptoe |

**R62** To form the present participle of a verb which ends in 'ie', you substitute 'ying' for 'ie'.

tie ⇨ tying

Note that the past form of such verbs is regular, following the pattern in R60.

**R63** To form the past form of a verb which ends in a consonant letter followed by 'y', you substitute 'ied' for 'y'.

cry ⇨ cried

Note that the present participle of such verbs is regular, following the pattern in R59.

**R64** If the base form of a verb has one syllable and ends with a single vowel letter followed by a consonant letter, you double the final consonant letter before adding 'ing' to form the present participle or 'ed' to form the past form.

dip ⇨ dipping ⇨ dipped
trot ⇨ trotting ⇨ trotted

Note that this does not apply if the final consonant letter is 'w', 'x', or 'y'.

row ⇨ rowing ⇨ rowed
box ⇨ boxing ⇨ boxed
play ⇨ playing ⇨ played

**R65** The final consonant letter of some two-syllable verbs is also doubled. This happens when the second syllable ends in a single vowel letter followed by a consonant letter, and is stressed.

refer ⇨ referring ⇨ referred
equip ⇨ equipping ⇨ equipped

**R66** In British English, when a two syllable verb ends in a single vowel letter followed by a single 'l', the 'l' is doubled before 'ing' or 'ed' is added to it, even if there is no stress on the last syllable.

travel ⇨ travelling ⇨ travelled
quarrel ⇨ quarrelling ⇨ quarrelled

A few other verbs also have their final consonant letter doubled.

program ⇨ programming ⇨ programmed
worship ⇨ worshipping ⇨ worshipped
hiccup ⇨ hiccupping ⇨ hiccupped
kidnap ⇨ kidnapping ⇨ kidnapped
handicap ⇨ handicapping ⇨ handicapped

**R67** All the verbs described in R66, except 'handicap', can have their present participle and past form spelled with a single consonant letter in American English.

travel ⇨ traveling ⇨ traveled
worship ⇨ worshiping ⇨ worshiped

**R68** Here is a list of the verbs whose final consonant letter is doubled before 'ing' and 'ed' in both British and American English:

| | | | | | |
|---|---|---|---|---|---|
| ban | fit | mar | shop | strut | defer |
| bar | flag | mob | shred | stun | deter |
| bat | flap | mop | shrug | sun | distil |
| beg | flip | mug | shun | swab | embed |
| blot | flop | nag | sin | swap | emit |
| blur | fog | net | sip | swat | enrol |
| bob | fret | nip | skid | swig | enthral |
| brag | gas | nod | skim | swot | equip |
| brim | gel | pad | skin | tag | excel |
| bug | glut | pat | skip | tan | expel |
| cap | grab | peg | slam | tap | incur |
| chat | grin | pen | slap | thin | instil |
| chip | grip | pet | slim | throb | occur |
| chop | grit | pin | slip | tip | omit |
| clap | grub | pit | slop | top | outwit |
| clog | gun | plan | slot | trap | patrol |
| clot | gut | plod | slum | trek | propel |
| cram | hem | plug | slur | trim | rebel |
| crib | hop | pop | snag | trip | rebut |
| crop | hug | prod | snap | trot | recap |
| cup | hum | prop | snip | vet | recur |
| dab | jam | rib | snub | wag | refer |
| dam | jet | rig | sob | wrap | regret |
| dim | jig | rip | spot | ~ | remit |
| din | jog | rob | squat | abet | repel |
| dip | jot | rot | stab | abhor | submit |
| dot | knit | rub | star | acquit | transfer |
| drag | knot | sag | stem | admit | transmit |
| drop | lag | scan | step | allot | ~ |
| drug | lap | scar | stir | commit | handicap |
| drum | log | scrap | stop | compel | |
| dub | lop | scrub | strap | confer | |
| fan | man | ship | strip | control | |

Note that verbs such as 're-equip' and 'unclog', which consist of a prefix and one of the above verbs, also have their final consonant letter doubled.

**R69** Here is a list of verbs whose final consonant letter is doubled before 'ing' and 'ed' in British English but not always in American English:

| | | | | |
|---|---|---|---|---|
| cancel | funnel | libel | quarrel | stencil |
| dial | gambol | marvel | refuel | swivel |
| duel | grovel | model | revel | total |
| enamel | hiccup | panel | rival | travel |
| enrol | initial | pedal | shovel | tunnel |
| enthral | kidnap | pencil | shrivel | unravel |
| equal | label | program | snivel | worship |
| fuel | level | pummel | spiral | |

**R70** With verbs ending in 'c', 'king' and 'ked' are usually added instead of 'ing' and 'ed'.

mimic ⇨ mimicking ⇨ mimicked
panic ⇨ panicking ⇨ panicked

**R71** A large number of verbs have irregular past forms and past participles, which are not formed by adding 'ed' to the base form.

With regular verbs, the past participle is the same as the past form. However, with some irregular verbs, the two forms are different.

**R72** The table opposite gives a list of irregular verbs and their forms.
Note that the past form and past participle of 'read' appear the same as the base form but are pronounced differently. The base form is pronounced /riːd/ and the past form and past participle /rɛd/. See a Cobuild dictionary for the pronunciation of irregular forms of verbs.

**R73** Some verbs have more than one past form or past participle form. For example, the past form and past participle of 'spell' can be either 'spelled' or 'spelt', and the past participle of 'prove' can be either 'proved' or 'proven'.

He _burned_ several letters.
He _burnt_ all his papers.
His bandaged foot had _swelled_ to three times normal size.
His wrist had _swollen_ up and become huge.

**R74** Some verbs have two forms which can be used as either the past form or the past participle. Here is a list of these verbs. The regular form is given first, although it may not be the more common one.

burn ⇨ burned, burnt
bust ⇨ busted, bust
dream ⇨ dreamed, dreamt
dwell ⇨ dwelled, dwelt
fit ⇨ fitted, fit
hang ⇨ hanged, hung

kneel ⇨ kneeled, knelt
lean ⇨ leaned, leant
leap ⇨ leaped, leapt
light ⇨ lighted, lit
relay ⇨ relayed, relaid
smell ⇨ smelled, smelt

speed ⇨ speeded, sped
spell ⇨ spelled, spelt
spill ⇨ spilled, spilt
spoil ⇨ spoiled, spoilt
wet ⇨ wetted, wet

**R75** Here is a list of verbs with two past forms:

bid ⇨ bid, bade
lie ⇨ lied, lay

wake ⇨ waked, woke
weave ⇨ weaved, wove

Here is a list of verbs with two past participle forms:

bid ⇨ bid, bidden
lie ⇨ lied, lain
mow ⇨ mowed, mown
prove ⇨ proved, proven

swell ⇨ swelled, swollen
wake ⇨ waked, woken
weave ⇨ weaved, woven

'Gotten' is often used instead of 'got' as the past participle of 'get' in American English.

Note that some verbs appear in both the above lists as they have a different past form and past participle form, each of which has more than one form.

REFERENCE SECTION

| base form | past form | past participle | base form | past form | past participle | base form | past form | past participle |
|---|---|---|---|---|---|---|---|---|
| arise | arose | arisen | freeze | froze | frozen | shut | shut | shut |
| awake | awoke | awoken | get | got | got | sing | sang | sung |
| bear | bore | borne | give | gave | given | sink | sank | sunk |
| beat | beat | beaten | go | went | gone | sit | sat | sat |
| become | became | become | grind | ground | ground | slay | slew | slain |
| begin | began | begun | grow | grew | grown | sleep | slept | slept |
| bend | bent | bent | hear | heard | heard | slide | slid | slid |
| bet | bet | bet | hide | hid | hidden | sling | slung | slung |
| bind | bound | bound | hit | hit | hit | slink | slunk | slunk |
| bite | bit | bitten | hold | held | held | sow | sowed | sown |
| bleed | bled | bled | hurt | hurt | hurt | speak | spoke | spoken |
| blow | blew | blown | keep | kept | kept | spend | spent | spent |
| break | broke | broken | know | knew | known | spin | spun | spun |
| breed | bred | bred | lay | laid | laid | spread | spread | spread |
| bring | brought | brought | lead | led | led | spring | sprang | sprung |
| build | built | built | leave | left | left | stand | stood | stood |
| burst | burst | burst | lend | lent | lent | steal | stole | stolen |
| buy | bought | bought | let | let | let | stick | stuck | stuck |
| cast | cast | cast | lose | lost | lost | sting | stung | stung |
| catch | caught | caught | make | made | made | stink | stank | stunk |
| choose | chose | chosen | mean | meant | meant | strew | strewed | strewn |
| cling | clung | clung | meet | met | met | stride | strode | stridden |
| come | came | come | pay | paid | paid | strike | struck | struck |
| cost | cost | cost | put | put | put | string | strung | strung |
| creep | crept | crept | quit | quit | quit | strive | strove | striven |
| cut | cut | cut | read | read | read | swear | swore | sworn |
| deal | dealt | dealt | rend | rent | rent | sweep | swept | swept |
| dig | dug | dug | ride | rode | ridden | swim | swam | swum |
| draw | drew | drawn | ring | rang | rung | swing | swung | swung |
| drink | drank | drunk | rise | rose | risen | take | took | taken |
| drive | drove | driven | run | ran | run | teach | taught | taught |
| eat | ate | eaten | saw | sawed | sawn | tear | tore | torn |
| fall | fell | fallen | say | said | said | tell | told | told |
| feed | fed | fed | see | saw | seen | think | thought | thought |
| feel | felt | felt | seek | sought | sought | throw | threw | thrown |
| fight | fought | fought | sell | sold | sold | thrust | thrust | thrust |
| find | found | found | send | sent | sent | tread | trod | trodden |
| flee | fled | fled | set | set | set | understand | understood | understood |
| fling | flung | flung | sew | sewed | sewn | wear | wore | worn |
| fly | flew | flown | shake | shook | shaken | weep | wept | wept |
| forbear | forbore | forborne | shed | shed | shed | win | won | won |
| forbid | forbade | forbidden | shine | shone | shone | wind | wound | wound |
| forget | forgot | forgotten | shoe | shod | shod | wring | wrung | wrung |
| forgive | forgave | forgiven | shoot | shot | shot | write | wrote | written |
| forsake | forsook | forsaken | show | showed | shown | | | |
| forswear | forswore | forsworn | shrink | shrank | shrunk | | | |

**R76** In some cases, different past forms or past participle forms relate to different meanings or uses of the verb. For example, the past form and the past participle of the verb 'hang' is normally 'hung'. However, 'hanged' can also be used but with a different meaning. Check the different meanings in a Cobuild dictionary.

*An Iron Cross hung from a ribbon around the man's neck.*
*He had been found guilty of murdering his child and hanged.*
*They had bid down the chemical company's stock.*
*He had bidden her to buy the best.*
*Everyone gathered as he relayed the tragic news.*
*They carefully relaid the pavements.*

**R77** Some verbs consist of more than one word, for example 'browbeat' and 'typeset', and some consist of a prefix plus a verb, for example 'undo' and 'disconnect'.

*His teachers underestimate his general ability.*
*Physical miracles of our time outdo their creators.*
*No-one knows better how you mismanage your time than those who live or work with you.*

**R78** Verbs which consist of more than one word or of a prefix plus a verb usually inflect in the same way as the verbs which form their final part. For example, the past form of 'foresee' is 'foresaw' and the past participle is 'foreseen', the past form and past participle of 'hamstring' is 'hamstrung', and the past form and past participle of 'misunderstand' is 'misunderstood'.

*I underestimated him.*
*He had outdone himself.*
*I had misunderstood and mismanaged everything.*
*She had disappeared into the kitchen and reappeared with a flashlight.*

**R79** With many verbs of this sort, the fact that they consist of two parts does not make any difference to their forms. They follow the normal spelling rules.

Here is a list of verbs whose second part is an irregular verb:

| | | | | |
|---|---|---|---|---|
| browbeat | overeat | mislead | beset | undertake |
| broadcast | befall | remake | reset | foretell |
| forecast | forego | repay | typeset | retell |
| miscast | undergo | misread | outshine | rethink |
| recast | outgrow | override | overshoot | overthrow |
| typecast | overheat | outrun | oversleep | misunderstand |
| overcome | mishear | overrun | misspell | rewind |
| undercut | behold | re-run | withstand | unwind |
| outdo | uphold | foresee | hamstring | rewrite |
| overdo | withhold | oversee | mistake | underwrite |
| undo | mislay | outsell | overtake | |
| withdraw | waylay | resell | retake | |

Note the past forms and past participles of the verbs shown below, whose second part is a verb with alternative past forms and past participles.

refit ⇨ refitted ⇨ refitted
overhang ⇨ overhung ⇨ overhung
floodlight ⇨ floodlit ⇨ floodlit

Here is a list of compound verbs whose second part is an irregular verb:

| | | |
|---|---|---|
| bottle-feed | spoon-feed | proof-read |
| breast-feed | baby-sit | sight-read |
| force-feed | lip-read | ghost-write |

**R80** The different forms of the auxiliaries 'be', 'have', and 'do' are summarized in the table below.

| | be | | have | | do |
|---|---|---|---|---|---|
| Simple present: | | | | | |
| with 'I' | am | 'm | | | |
| | | | have | 've | do |
| with 'you', 'we', 'they', & plural noun groups | are | 're | | | |
| with 'he', 'she', 'it' & singular noun groups | is | 's | has | 's | does |
| Simple past: | | | | | |
| with 'I', 'he', 'she', 'it' & singular noun groups | was | | | | |
| | | | had | 'd | did |
| with 'you', 'we', 'they' & plural noun groups | were | | | | |
| Participles: | | | | | |
| present participle | being | | having | | doing |
| past participle | been | | had | | done |

**R81** The present tense forms of 'be' can usually be contracted and added to the end of the subject of the verb, whether it is a noun or a pronoun. This is often done in spoken English or in informal written English.

_I'm interested in the role of women all over the world._
_You're late._
_We're making some progress._
_It's a delightful country._
_My car's just across the street._

The contracted forms of 'be' are shown in the table above.

**R82** Contracted forms of 'be' are not used at the end of affirmative statements. The full form must be used instead. For example, you say 'Richard's not very happy but Andrew is'. You can not say 'Richard's not very happy but Andrew's'.

However, you can use a contracted form of 'be' at the end of a negative statement if it is followed by 'not'. For example, 'Mary's quite happy, but her mother's not'.

**R83** When 'be' is used in negative clauses, either the verb or 'not' can be contracted. For more information on contractions in negative clauses, see paragraphs 4.55 to 4.56.

**R84** The present tense and past tense forms of 'have' can also be contracted. This is usually only done when 'have' is being used as an auxiliary.

_I've changed my mind._
_This is the first party we've been to in months._
_She's become a very interesting young woman._
_I do wish you'd met Guy._
_She's managed to keep it quiet._
_We'd done a good job._

The contracted forms of 'have' are shown in the table at paragraph R80.

**R85** 's can be short for either 'is' or 'has'. You can tell what 's represents by looking at the next word. If 's represents 'is', it is followed by a present participle, complement, or adjunct. If it represents 'has', it is usually followed by a past participle.

*She's going to be all right.*
*She's a lovely person.*
*She's gone to see some social work people.*

**R86** A noun ending in 's could also be a **possessive**. It is followed by another noun when this is the case. For more information on possessives see paragraphs 2.180 to 2.192.

**R87** 'Is' and 'has' are written in full after nouns ending in 'x', 'ch', 'sh', 's', or 'z', although in speech 'has' is sometimes pronounced as /əz/ after these nouns.

**R88** 'd can be short for either 'had' or 'would'. You can tell what 'd represents by looking at the next word. If 'd represents 'would', it is followed by the base form of a verb. If it represents 'had', it is usually followed by a past participle.

*We'd have to try to escape.*
*'It'd be cheaper to get married,' Alan said.*
*At least we'd had the courage to admit it.*
*She'd bought new sunglasses with deep-blue tinted lenses.*

# Finite verb groups and the formation of tenses

**R89** A **finite verb group** is the kind of verb group that goes with a subject in most clauses that have a subject. It contains a form of the verb that you are using to convey your meaning (the **main verb**), and often one or more **auxiliaries**.

A finite verb group has the following structure:
(modal)(have)(be)(be) main verb.

The elements in brackets are chosen according to factors relating to your message, for example, whether you are talking about the past or the present, or whether you are concentrating on the performer of an action or the thing affected by it. They are called **auxiliaries**.

If you want to indicate possibility, or indicate your attitude to your hearer or to what you are saying, you use a kind of auxiliary called a **modal**. Modals must be followed by a base form. The use of modals is explained in Chapter 4 (4.95 to 4.262).

*She might see us.*
*She could have seen us.*

If you want to use a perfect tense, you use a form of 'have'. This must be followed by a past participle.

*She has seen us.*
*She had been watching us for some time.*

If you want to use a continuous tense, you use a form of 'be'. This must be followed by a present participle.

*She was watching us.*
*We were being watched.*

If you want to use the passive, you use a form of 'be'. This must be followed by a past participle.

*We were seen.*
*We were being watched.*

If there is an auxiliary in front of the main verb, you use an appropriate form of the main verb, as indicated above. If there is no auxiliary, you use an appropriate simple tense form.

The verb 'do' is also used as an auxiliary, with simple tenses, but only in questions, negative statements, and negative imperative clauses, or when you want to be very emphatic. It is followed by the base form of the main verb. Detailed information on the uses of 'do' is given in Chapter 4.

*Do you want me to do something about it?*
*I do not remember her.*
*I do enjoy being with you.*

**R90** A finite verb group always has a **tense**, unless it begins with a modal. **Tense** is the relationship between the form of a verb and the time to which it refers.

This section deals with the ways in which main verbs and auxiliaries can be used to form different tenses. The way in which particular tenses are used to indicate particular times in relation to the time of speaking or to the time of an event is covered in paragraphs 5.7 to 5.68.

**R91** When a verb is being used in a **simple tense**, that is, the **simple present** or the **simple past**, it consists of just one word, a form of the main verb.

*I feel tired.*
*Mary lived there for five years.*

For other tenses, one or more auxiliaries are used in combination with the main verb.

*I am feeling reckless tonight.*
*I have lived here all my life.*

**R92** The first word of a finite verb group must agree with the subject of the clause. This affects the simple present tense, and all tenses which begin with the present or past tense of 'be' or the present tense of 'have'.

For example, if the tense is the present perfect and the subject is 'John', then the form of the auxiliary 'have' must be 'has'.

*John has seemed worried lately.*
*She likes me.*
*Your lunch is getting cold.*

**R93** In this section the examples given are declarative clauses. The order of words in questions is different from the order in declarative clauses. See paragraphs 4.10 to 4.30 for information about this.

**R94 Continuous tenses** are formed by using an appropriate tense of the auxiliary 'be' and the present participle. Detailed information on the formation of these tenses is included below. The uses of continuous tenses are explained in detail in paragraphs 5.7 to 5.68.

**R95** The formation of active tenses is explained below. The formation of passive tenses is explained in paragraphs R109 to R118.

**R96** The **simple present** tense of a verb is the same as the base form with all subjects except the third person singular.

*I want a breath of air.*
*We advise everyone to ring before they leave.*
*They give you a certificate and then tell you to get a job.*

The third person singular form is the 's' form.

*Nora puts her head back, and laughs again.*
*'Money decides everything,' she thought.*
*Mr Painting plays Phil Archer in the radio serial.*

**R97** The **present continuous** is formed by using the present tense of 'be' and the present participle of the main verb.

*People who have no faith in art are running the art schools.*
*The garden industry is booming.*
*Things are changing.*

**R98** The **simple past** tense of a verb is the past form.

*The moment he entered the classroom all eyes turned on him.*
*He walked out of the kitchen and climbed the stairs.*
*It was dark by the time I reached East London.*

**R99** The **past continuous** is formed by using the past tense of 'be' and the present participle of the main verb.

*The tourists were beginning to drive me crazy.*
*We believed we were fighting for a good cause.*
*At the time, I was dreading transfer.*

**R100** The **present perfect** tense is formed by using the present tense of 'have' and the past participle of the main verb.

*Advances have continued, though actual productivity has fallen.*
*Football has become international.*
*I have seen this before.*

The **present perfect** is sometimes called the **perfect tense** in other grammars.

**R101** The **present perfect continuous** is formed by using the present perfect of 'be' and the present participle of the main verb.

*Howard has been working hard over the recess.*
*What we have been describing is very simple.*
*Their shares have been going up.*

**R102** The **past perfect** tense is formed by using 'had' and the past participle of the main verb.

*The Indian summer had returned for a day.*
*Everyone had liked her.*
*Murray had resented the changes I had made.*

**R103** The **past perfect continuous** is formed by using 'had been' and the present participle of the main verb.

*She did not know how long she had been lying there.*
*For ten years of her life, teachers had been making up her mind for her.*
*I had been showing a woman around with her little boy.*

**R104** There are several ways of referring to the future in English. The one that is usually called the **future tense** involves using the modal 'will' or 'shall' and the base form of the verb.

*It is exactly the sort of scheme he will like.*
*My receptionist will help you choose the frames.*
*Don't go scattering seed about or we shall have mice.*

In spoken English, the contracted form 'll is usually used instead of 'will' or 'shall', unless you want to be emphatic.

*Send him into the Army, he'll learn a bit of discipline.*
*As soon as we get the tickets they'll be sent out to you.*
*Next week we'll be taking a look at mathematics.*

**R105** If the full forms are used, 'will' is generally used if the subject of the verb is not 'I' or 'we'. 'Shall' is sometimes used if the subject is 'I' or 'we', otherwise 'will' is used.

*Inflation is rising and will continue to rise.*
*I shall be away tomorrow.*

**R106** The **future continuous** is formed by using 'will' or 'shall', followed by 'be' and the present participle of the main verb.

*Indeed, we will be opposing that policy.*
*Ford manual workers will be claiming a ten per cent pay rise.*
*I shall be leaving soon.*

**R107** The **future perfect** is formed by using 'will' or 'shall', followed by 'have' and the past participle of the main verb.

*Long before you return, they will have forgotten you.*
*Before the end of this era, computer games will have reached such heights of realism.*
*By that time, I shall have retired.*

**R108** The **future perfect continuous** is formed by using 'will' or 'shall', followed by 'have been' and the present participle of the main verb.

*By March, I will have been doing this job for six years.*
*Saturday week, I will have been going out with Susan for three months.*

**R109** Passive tenses are formed by using an appropriate tense of 'be' and the past participle of the main verb. Detailed information on forming passive tenses is given below.

**R110** The **simple present passive** is formed by using the simple present of 'be' and the past participle of the main verb.

*The earth is baked by the sun into a hard, brittle layer.*
*If your course is full time you are treated as your parents' dependent.*
*Specific subjects are discussed.*

**R111** The **present continuous passive** is formed by using the present continuous of 'be' and the past participle of the main verb.

*The buffet counter is being arranged by the attendant.*
*It is something quite irrelevant to what is being discussed.*
*Jobs are still being lost.*

**R112** The **simple past passive** is formed by using the simple past of 'be' and the past participle of the main verb.

*No date was announced for the talks.*
*The walls of his tiny shop were plastered with pictures of actors and actresses.*
*A number of cottages were built, all with the most modern of conveniences.*

**R113** The **past continuous passive** is formed by using the past continuous of 'be' and the past participle of the main verb.

*The stage was being set for future profits.*
*Before long, machines were being used to create codes.*
*Strenuous efforts were being made last night to end the dispute.*

**R114** The **present perfect passive** is formed by using the present perfect of 'be' and the past participle of the main verb.

*The guest-room window has been mended.*
*Once real progress has been made, the gains are likely to be immense.*
*The dirty plates have been stacked in a pile on the kitchen cabinet.*

**R115** The **past perfect passive** is formed by using 'had been' and the past participle of the main verb.

*They had been taught to be critical.*
*They had been driven home in the station wagon.*

**R116** The **future passive** is formed by using 'will' or 'shall', followed by 'be' and the past participle of the main verb.

*His own authority will be undermined.*
*Congress will be asked to approve an increase of 47.5 per cent.*

**R117** The **future perfect passive** is formed by using 'will' or 'shall', followed by 'have been' and the past participle of the main verb.

*Another phase of the emancipation of man from the need to work for his living will have been achieved.*
*The figures will have been heavily distorted by the continuing effects of the civil servants' strike.*

**R118** The future continuous passive and the perfect continuous passive are rarely used.

**R119** The table below gives a summary of the active and passive tenses. The passive tenses marked with a star are very rarely used.

|  | active | passive |
|---|---|---|
| simple present | He eats it. | It is eaten. |
| present continuous | He is eating it. | It is being eaten. |
| present perfect | He has eaten it. | It has been eaten. |
| present perfect continuous | He has been eating it. | It has been being eaten.* |
| simple past | He ate it. | It was eaten. |
| past continuous | He was eating it. | It was being eaten. |
| past perfect | He had eaten it. | It had been eaten. |
| past perfect continuous | He had been eating it. | It had been being eaten.* |
| future | He will eat it. | It will be eaten. |
| future continuous | He will be eating it. | It will be being eaten.* |
| future perfect | He will have eaten it. | It will have been eaten. |
| future perfect continuous | He will have been eating it. | It will have been being eaten.* |

**R120** There are a number of verbs which are not usually used in continuous tenses, and some that are not used in continuous tenses in one or more of their main meanings.

Here is a list of verbs which are not usually used in continuous tenses:

| | | | | |
|---|---|---|---|---|
| admire | despise | imagine | owe | seem |
| adore | detest | impress | own | sound |
| appear | dislike | include | please | smell |
| astonish | doubt | involve | possess | stop |
| be | envy | keep | prefer | suppose |
| believe | exist | know | reach | surprise |
| belong | fit | lack | realize | survive |
| concern | forget | last | recognize | suspect |
| consist | guess | like | remember | understand |
| contain | hate | love | resemble | want |
| deserve | have | matter | satisfy | wish |
| desire | hear | mean | see | |

Verbs of this kind are sometimes called **stative verbs**. Verbs which are used in continuous tenses are sometimes called **dynamic verbs**.

**R121** 'Be' is not generally used as a main verb in continuous tenses with complements which indicate permanent characteristics, or with attributes which do not relate to behaviour. However, 'be' is used in continuous tenses to indicate someone's behaviour at a particular time.

*He is extremely nice.*
*He was an American.*
*You're being very silly.*

'Have' is not used as a main verb in continuous tenses when it indicates possession, but it is sometimes used in continuous tenses when it indicates that someone is doing something.

*I have two dinghies.*
*We were just having a philosophical discussion.*

**R122** Some verbs have very specific senses in which they are not used in continuous tenses. For example, 'smell' is often used in continuous tenses when it means 'to smell something', but seldom when it means 'to smell of something'. Compare the sentences 'I was just smelling your flowers', and 'Your flowers smell lovely'.

Here is a list of verbs which are not used in continuous tenses when they have the meanings indicated:

| | |
|---|---|
| depend (be related to) | taste (of something) |
| feel (have an opinion) | think (have an opinion) |
| measure (have length) | weigh (have weight) |
| smell (of something) | |

**R123** The **imperative** form of a verb is regarded as finite, because it can stand as the verb of a main clause. However, it does not show tense in the same way as other finite verb groups. It is always in the base form. See paragraphs 4.31 to 4.35 for the uses of the imperative.

*Stop being silly.*
*Come here.*

# Non-finite verb groups: infinitives and participles

**R124** A non-finite verb group is an infinitive, a participle, or a verb group beginning with a participle. It cannot be combined with a subject to form a sentence.

Non-finite verb groups are used after verbs in **phase structures** (see paragraphs 3.183 to 3.213) and are also used in **non-finite subordinate clauses** (see the section on subordination in Chapter 8). They are also used in some structures with **impersonal 'it'** (see paragraphs 10.39 to 10.41).

'To'-infinitives are also used after some nouns and adjectives (see paragraphs 2.310 to 2.316, and 2.55 to 2.66). Present participles are also used as the objects of prepositions.

Non-finite verb groups can have objects, complements, or adjuncts after them, just like finite verb groups. A clause beginning with a 'to'-infinitive is called a **'to'-infinitive clause**, a clause beginning with a present participle is called a **present participle clause**, and a clause beginning with a past participle is called a **past participle clause**.

**R125** The order of auxiliaries is the same for non-finite verb groups as for finite verb groups (see paragraph R89). Note that modals are never used in non-finite verb groups.

**R126** The active **'to'-infinitive** consists of 'to' and the base form of the verb. This is sometimes called the **present infinitive** or simply the **infinitive**.

*I want to escape from here.*
*I asked Don Card to go with me.*

**R127** The active **infinitive without 'to'** consists of the base form of the verb. It is sometimes called the **bare infinitive**.

*They helped me get settled here.*

**R128** Other active infinitive forms are occasionally used.

The **present continuous infinitive** consists of 'to be' or 'be', followed by the present participle.

*It is much better for young children to be living at home.*

The **perfect** or **past infinitive** consists of 'to have' or 'have', followed by the past participle.

*Only two are known to have defected.*

The **perfect** or **past continuous infinitive** consists of 'to have been' or 'have been', followed by the present participle.

*I seem to have been eating all evening.*

**R129** There are also passive infinitives. The ordinary **passive infinitive** consists of 'to be' or 'be', followed by the past participle.

*I didn't want to be caught off guard.*

The **perfect** or **past passive infinitive** consists of 'to have been' or 'have been', followed by the past participle.

*He seems to have been completely forgotten.*

**R130** The table below gives a summary of infinitives. The passive infinitives marked with a star are very rarely used.

|  | active | passive |
|---|---|---|
| present continuous<br>perfect<br>perfect continuous | (to) eat<br>(to) be eating<br>(to) have eaten<br>(to) have been eating | (to) be eaten<br>(to) be being eaten*<br>(to) have been eaten<br>(to) have been being eaten* |

**R131** The **present participle** is used as a non-finite verb group, usually with an active meaning.

*'You could play me a tune,' said Simon, sitting down.*
*He could keep in touch with me by writing letters.*

**R132** Combinations beginning with 'having' are occasionally used.

The **perfect** or **past '-ing' form** consists of 'having' and the past participle.

*Ash, having forgotten his fear, had become bored and restless.*

The **perfect** or **past continuous '-ing'** form consists of 'having been' and the present participle. It is rarely used.

*Having been supporting Tom and Mick on the climb for a week, they needed a rest.*

**R133** There are also combinations beginning with 'being' and 'having' which have a passive meaning.

The ordinary **passive 'ing' form** consists of 'being' and the past participle.

*...fears that patients would resent <u>being interviewed</u> by a medical computer.*

The **perfect** or **past 'ing' form** consists of 'having been' and the past participle.

*<u>Having been declared</u> insane, he was confined for four months in a prison hospital.*
*Some were shot full of arrows after <u>having been</u> mortally <u>wounded</u> by gunshot.*

**R134** The table below gives a summary of '-ing' forms. The '-ing' form marked with a star is very rarely used.

|  | active | passive |
|---|---|---|
|  | eating | being eaten |
| perfect | having eaten | having been eaten |
| perfect continuous | having been eating | having been being eaten* |

**R135** The **past participle** is also used as a non-finite verb group, with a passive meaning.

*<u>Stunned</u> by the swiftness of the assault, the enemy were overwhelmed.*
*When <u>challenged</u>, she started and seemed quite surprised.*

# Forming adverbs

**R136** The uses of adverbs are explained in Chapters 2, 5, 6, and 10.

**R137** Most adverbs are related to adjectives in form, and often in meaning. They are formed by adding 'ly' to the adjective. For information on which adjectives you can add 'ly' to, see paragraphs 6.17 to 6.27.

sad ⇨ sadly
cheerful ⇨ cheerfully
private ⇨ privately
accidental ⇨ accidentally
surprising ⇨ surprisingly

**R138** Sometimes the formation is slightly different.
With adjectives ending in 'le', you replace the 'le' with 'ly'.

suitable ⇨ suitably
terrible ⇨ terribly
gentle ⇨ gently

Note that 'whole' has the related adverb 'wholly'.

**R139** With adjectives ending in 'y', you replace the 'y' with 'ily'.

easy ⇨ easily
satisfactory ⇨ satisfactorily

Note that one-syllable adjectives ending in 'y' usually have 'ly' added, in the normal way.

wry ⇨ wryly
shy ⇨ shyly

Note that the adverb related to 'dry' can be spelled 'drily' or 'dryly'.

**R140** With adjectives ending in 'ic', you add 'ally'.

automatic ⇨ automatically
tragic ⇨ tragically

Note that 'public' has the related adverb 'publicly'.

**R141** With a few adjectives ending in 'e' (not 'le'), you replace the 'e' with 'ly'.

due ⇨ duly
true ⇨ truly
undue ⇨ unduly
eerie ⇨ eerily

**R142** With 'full' and 'dull', you just add 'y'.

full ⇨ fully
dull ⇨ dully

**R143** Note that 'ly' is not generally added to adjectives ending in 'ed' to form adverbs. However, here is a list of adverbs which are formed in this way:

| | | | |
|---|---|---|---|
| absent-mindedly | dejectedly | frenziedly | reportedly |
| admittedly | delightedly | guardedly | reputedly |
| allegedly | deservedly | half-heartedly | resignedly |
| assuredly | determinedly | heatedly | supposedly |
| belatedly | distractedly | hurriedly | undoubtedly |
| blessedly | doggedly | light-heartedly | unexpectedly |
| contentedly | exaggeratedly | markedly | unhurriedly |
| crookedly | excitedly | pointedly | wholeheartedly |
| decidedly | fixedly | repeatedly | wickedly |

**R144** A few adverbs which end in 'ly' are related to nouns.

These include some time adverbs.

day ⇨ daily
fortnight ⇨ fortnightly
hour ⇨ hourly
month ⇨ monthly
quarter ⇨ quarterly
week ⇨ weekly
year ⇨ yearly

Note the spelling of 'daily'. These words are also themselves used as adjectives. Other adverbs related to nouns are shown below.

name ⇨ namely
part ⇨ partly
purpose ⇨ purposely
body ⇨ bodily

**R145** A few adverbs ending in 'ly' are not related to any adjective or noun.

| | | | |
|---|---|---|---|
| accordingly | jokingly | manfully | presumably |
| exceedingly | longingly | mostly | |

**R146** Here is a list of adverbs which have the same form as adjectives:

| | | | | |
|---|---|---|---|---|
| alike | fine | just | off-hand | solo |
| all right | first | kindly | only | still |
| alone | free | last | outright | straight |
| clean | freelance | late | overall | tight |
| deep | full | little | part-time | well |
| direct | full-time | long | past | wide |
| even | further | loud | pretty | wrong |
| extra | hard | low | quick | |
| far | high | next | right | |
| fast | jolly | non-stop | slow | |

Note that the adverb is sometimes not related in meaning to the adjective whose form it shares. Check the meanings in a Cobuild dictionary.

With some of these words, there are also related forms ending in 'ly'.

| | | | | |
|---|---|---|---|---|
| cleanly | finely | hardly | lately | slowly |
| directly | firstly | highly | loudly | tightly |
| deeply | freely | justly | quickly | widely |
| evenly | fully | lastly | rightly | wrongly |

Note that these 'ly' forms sometimes have the same meaning as the other adverb form, and sometimes not.

The adverbs of time ending in 'ly' which are mentioned in paragraph R144 also have the same form as adjectives.

**R147** Note that **ordinal numbers** are used both as modifiers and as adverbs. They also have related adverbs ending in 'ly'.

**R148** Here is a list of adverbs which are not related to any adjective:

| | | | | |
|---|---|---|---|---|
| afresh | besides | indeed | otherwise | though |
| alas | doubtless | instead | perhaps | thus |
| alike | either | likewise | quite | together |
| almost | enough | maybe | rather | too |
| aloud | forthwith | meanwhile | regardless | very |
| also | furthermore | more | so | whatsoever |
| altogether | half | moreover | somehow | |
| anyhow | hence | much | somewhat | |
| anyway | hereby | nevertheless | therefore | |
| apart | however | nonetheless | thereupon | |

**R149** Adverbs of time and many adverbs of place are also not related to adjectives. See Chapters 5 and 6 for lists of these adverbs.

# Forming comparative and superlative adverbs

**R150** Information on how to use comparatives and superlatives of adverbs, and which adverbs have them, is given in Chapter 6 (6.30 to 6.35).

**R151** The comparative of an adverb usually consists of the normal form of the adverb preceded by 'more'.

freely ⇨ more freely
appropriately ⇨ more appropriately

**R152** The superlative of an adverb usually consists of the normal form of the adverb preceded by 'most'.

commonly ⇨ most commonly
eagerly ⇨ most eagerly

**R153** A few very common adverbs have comparatives and superlatives that are single words and not formed using 'more' and 'most'.

'Well' has the comparative 'better' and the superlative 'best'.

*She would ask him later, when she knew him <u>better</u>.*
*I have to find out what I can do <u>best</u>.*

'Badly' has the comparative 'worse' and the superlative 'worst'.

*She was treated far <u>worse</u> than any animal.*
*The expedition from Mozambique fared <u>worst</u>.*

Adverbs which have the same form as adjectives have the same comparatives and superlatives as the adjectives. For example, the comparative and superlative of the adverb 'fast' are 'faster' and 'fastest', and the comparative and superlative of the adverb 'hard' are 'harder' and 'hardest'.

*Prices have been rising <u>faster</u> than incomes.*
*You probably learn <u>quicker</u> by having lessons.*
*The old people work <u>the hardest</u>.*
*The ones with the shortest legs run <u>the slowest</u>.*

**R154** A few adverbs of time and place have irregular comparatives and superlatives. See Chapter 5 (5.69, 5.114, and 5.123) and Chapter 6 (6.89).

early ⇨ earlier ⇨ earliest
late ⇨ later (no superlative)
soon ⇨ sooner (no superlative)
long ⇨ longer ⇨ longest

deep ⇨ deeper ⇨ deepest
far ⇨ farther, further ⇨ farthest, furthest
near ⇨ nearer ⇨ nearest
close ⇨ closer ⇨ closest

# Index

*Note:* entries in **bold** are grammatical terms; entries in *italics* are lexical items; and an arrow ⇨ denotes a cross-reference within the index. A number preceded by R refers to a paragraph in the Reference Section.

# R

# U